THE RISE AND FALL OF
REVOLUTIONARY ENGLAND

The Rise and Fall of Revolutionary England

An Essay on the Fabrication of
Seventeenth-Century History

Alastair MacLachlan

St. Martin's Press
New York

St. Martin's Press, Scholarly and Reference Division,
175 Fifth Avenue, New York, N.Y. 10010

First published in the United States of America in 1996

Printed in Malaysia

ISBN 0–312–12841–X

Library of Congress Cataloging-in-Publication Data
MacLachlan, Alastair.
The rise and fall of revolutionary England : an essay on the
fabrication of seventeenth-century history / Alastair MacLachlan.
p. cm.
Includes bibliographical references (p.   ) and index.
ISBN 0–312–12841–X (cloth)
1. Great Britain—History—Puritan Revolution, 1642–1660–
–Historiography. 2. Great Britain—History—Stuarts, 1603–1714–
–Historiography. I. Title. II. Series.
DA403.M33   1996
941.06—dc20
                                                95–31667
                                                    CIP

Contents

Preface   vii

　Introduction   1

1　The Great Bourgeois Revolutions: A False Genealogy?   7

2　Reclaiming the Revolution   32

3　Marxist History in a Cold War Era   79

4　Saving Appearances   122

5　Levelling out the Revolution   169

6　Retreating from the Revolution   210

7　Revolution as Text and Discourse   252

　Conclusion: The End of the Line?   298

Notes   326

Index   420

England is a perpetual Theatre of revolutions . . . in an instant the calm is changed into the most furious tempest, and this tempest changes in a moment into calm.

Eustache Le Noble,
Lettres sur l'Angleterre, 1697

One would expect people to remember the past and imagine the future. But in fact, when discoursing or writing about history, they imagine it in terms of their own experience, and when trying to gauge the future they cite supposed analogies from the past: till, by a double process of repetition, they imagine the past and remember the future.

Sir Lewis Namier, 'Symmetry and Repetition',
in Conflicts (London, 1942)

Preface

During the writing of this book I have been aided by a number of institutions. My thanks to Sydney University and my colleagues in the History Department for an extended absence on an Overseas Study Programme and Long Service leave in 1992 and 1993, and to the directors and secretarial staff of The History of Ideas Unit and the Humanities Research Centre at the Australian National University for placing their resources at my disposal and for providing such an ideal ambience for writing during a significant portion of those years. Likewise, to the Communist Party Archive in North London, the Marx Memorial Library Archive, the Cambridge University Library and the British Library Manuscript Room for allowing access to materials in their possession. To the late Eugene Kamenka and to Alice Tay, and to Pat and Liz Collinson for their hospitality and encouragement in Canberra and Cambridge; to my dear friends, the late Nigel and Marjorie Edgerton, and to my sister and brother-in-law, Sheila and Alan Bracewell, for hospitality and support in London; to John Morrill for some particularly helpful criticism and advice; likewise to Nick Sadington, George Matthews, David Burchall, Jonathan Bordo, Iain MacCalman, Iain Wright, John Mee, John Reeve, Tony Cahill, Stuart MacIntyre, Tony Cousins, and Conal Condren. My thanks also to Meg Miller and to Antony Howe for reading and commenting on my typescript and for removing many errors. A special word of thanks to Vicki for the title; also, for the sharpness and perceptiveness of her criticism, and for goading an incorrigible procrastinator into finishing his work.

My greatest debt, however, is to my research students over the past decade: to Mark Gibson for his work on Anderson, to Alistair Waring for his on the New Left, and, above all, to Antony Howe for his writing and research on Hill (*Christopher Hill: A Study of a British Marxist Historian*, unpublished M.A. 'Long Essay', Sydney, 1988) and on The Historians' Group of the Communist Party. Chapters 2, 3 and 4 of this book have benefited greatly from his highly critical but not (in my view) unfair examination of Hill's early work in the light of discussions in Soviet historiography and the charting of a 'correct line' by the Communist Party of Great Britain.

In 1990 and 1992 Howe conducted extensive interviews and archival work in England for a PhD (in progress) on the Historians' Group of the Communist Party. As his supervisor over these years, I benefited enormously from discussions with him, and in particular from access to his draft chapters on Marx House, Dona Torr and the origins of the Historians' Group from the 1930s to 1946. He has also allowed me to use his files of research materials and provided me with photocopies from the CP Archive (Historians' Group and Dutt MSS), the Labour Archive at the University of Hull, the Marx Memorial Library Archive, the Morris MSS at University College London, and from Eric Hobsbawm's private papers (more Morris MSS) – my heart-felt thanks. He is, of course, in no way responsible for the judgements expressed in the text.

There is one other debt – to the historians themselves. In the pages that follow, I have often been critical of the work of Christopher Hill, Eric Hobsbawm, Lawrence Stone, the late Edward Thompson and Perry Anderson. But even though they might well profoundly disagree with much of the argument of this book, I would like to place on record my appreciation for the stimulus of their writing.

ALASTAIR MACLACHLAN

Introduction

This book is about the fabrication of a revolutionary model of English history. Its focus will be the 'discovery' of an epochal revolution in the England of Charles I and Oliver Cromwell. Its starting point will be the distinctive but contiguous concepts of 'bourgeois revolution' and 'modern society', and the attempt to relate both to seventeenth-century English religious and political conflicts – an endeavour which can be traced back to the writings of contemporary political theorists and to the subsequent 'speculative histories' of eighteenth-century Scottish sociologists, but which only achieved historiographical significance in the pedigrees sought by the French liberal historians of the nineteenth century for their own revolution, and in the overlapping but distinctive body of Marx's writings and subsequent Marxist theory. The first chapter will attempt to chart some of the problems of this interpretative hybrid, and to show how a distinctively non-revolutionary, 'constitutionalist' reading of England's seventeenth-century past became canonical in the hundred years from 1840 to 1940.

The second section of the book will examine the recovery of seventeenth-century English history for the radical Left in the 1930s and 1940s, and the invented tradition of an 'English Revolution', culminating in the native Marxism, often associated with the collective endeavour of 'The Historians' Group of the Communist Party', and with early work of Christopher Hill. It will explain how a particular reading of 'dialectical and historical materialism' taken from the teaching of Lenin and Stalin came to be applied to England's supposed bourgeois transformation. And it will attempt to place this militant and self-consciously Marxist reading of England's revolutionary past within the Communist Party's 'battle of ideas' in the contemporary political arena during the period from the 1930s to the mid 1950s. It will also, however, trace its coexistence with an earlier radical and democratic version of England's heritage, stretching back through the work of early twentieth-century socialist historians to the 'reformers' of the late eighteenth century and thence to the seventeenth-century Levellers

1

and Diggers themselves. And it will suggest that the bifocal model of Marxist theory and 'people's history' – fused by the radical patriotism pronounced at the end of the Second World War – accounted for much of its empirical richness, attractiveness of idiom, and long-term resilience; but, that it was also responsible for its inconsistencies as a coherent explanation of political, social and ideological change.

A third section will consider the partial fragmentation of this model in the twenty-year span from the mid 1950s to the 1970s, and the heroic endeavours of Christopher Hill, Lawrence Stone and others at 'saving appearances': through refining categories and stretching chronology; shifting the argument from causes and intentions to outcomes and unintended legacies, from political rupture and class struggle to ideological or psychic transforma-tion; conflating Marxism with other models of social change and collapsing it into Whiggism once more; or, at the very least, celebrat-ing the people's experiences when it could no longer salvage the triumph of the bourgeoisie. Particular attention will be given to the ambience of counter-cultural expectation in the late 1960s and 1970s: something which explained the attractions of 'a world turned upside down' during the 1640s and 1650s also, and helped to reorientate Marxist historiography in a manner that ensured its continuing radical appeal.

A further section will examine the attempt to rethink Marxist history in a post-Stalinist era, and the celebrated debate which this engendered between E. P. Thompson and Perry Anderson over the 'peculiarities' of England's past and the place of the seventeenth-century 'revolution' within it. In one sense, it will contend, this was a restatement of the argument between an exceptionalist version of England's radical heritage and the quest for a more theoretical Marxist explanation of its insufficiencies; in another, however, that it marked a retreat from the 'revol-utionary' reading of English history, and paralleled the 'new wave' of 'revisionist' writing during the late 1970s and 1980s: the attack both on Marxist or Marxisant theories of social change and on the traditional Whig story of constitutional struggle and liberal reform. Another chapter will examine the survival of the Marxist interpretation in a new form – as 'cultural materialism': a radicalized literary history or a celebration of an invisible church of cultural 'witness' in unpropitious times. A concluding chapter will assess these various survivals and challenges in the age of Mrs Thatcher,

Mr Major, Mr Mitterrand, Mr Gorbachev and President Yeltsin. The book will also attempt to address a number of questions pertinent to the application of Marxist theory to the sheer messiness of the English past. How did the 'English Revolution', so-called, come to occupy a decisive place in the genealogy of modernism; how did it come to be interpreted through the categories and the nomenclature of post-French-revolutionary discourse; and what was the relationship between the two dominant nineteenth-century metahistorical models of social change and political struggle, between the Whig and the Marxist interpretations of seventeenth-century England? How did a particular reading of revolutionary action and outcome borrowed from experiences and the theoretical justifications of the Russian Revolution come to be applied to the 1640s and 1650s; and how was it seen as a rebuttal rather than an extension of Whiggism? How, nevertheless, did it coexist with an older radical celebration of the vanguard that never was: the Levellers, the Baptists, Fifth Monarchy Men and the Ranters, the supposed victims of the emerging bourgeois state? Why did this historiographical mélange of bourgeois revolution and socialist prefiguration come to occupy so dominant a place in the teaching of British history in the 1960s and 1970s: how was it that Marxist historians in Britain were so successful in interpreting the world, when their Communist counterparts were so abysmally unsuccessful in changing it? And now in the 1990s, with the whole Marxist enterprise in seeming ruins, has its interpretation of modern history also crumbled under the weight of an autonomous and unpredictable present? More particularly, has the revolutionary model of the historical change lost credibility; and has the pivot of that interpretation in seventeenth-century England, as in eighteenth-century France, been buried under the accumulated rubble of 'revisionism'? Or were the 'great bourgeois revolutions' always products of a false or, at least, a misplaced genealogy?

An appreciation of historical writings which gives proper weight to the circumstances and intentions surrounding their production, to the rhetorical qualities of their composition, and to their 'value' or 'verisimilitude' from the standpoint of the present, is not easy to achieve. Literary theorists tell us nowadays that there is no external reality outside texts and that texts themselves are capable of unending deconstruction: that there is no privileged authorial voice, and that there are as many meanings as there are readers. Historians, on the other hand, are still inclined to invoke what J. H. Hexter called the 'reality' rule: to cultivate olympian authorial invisibility and write as though language and form are transparencies – the vehicles of conveying 'discoveries'. They are apt to think of their discipline as an expanding body of knowledge or a deepening field of comprehension, in which older works are 'superseded' by more up-to-date research or sophisticated analysis. At the same time, however, all but the most unreconstructed 'empiricists' are aware of the ways in which the personal and ideological assumptions of the author, the issues and presuppositions of the period of composition, the narrative shapes and strategies of the texts themselves, help to fashion their 'truths' also. They probably accept that there is no such thing as an atheoretical history: that there are no definitive answers, only provisional findings, that history is rewritten in every generation.

By and large, the writings examined in this book have either been treated as components of a self-contained tradition of radical and Marxist thought, or they have been considered solely as contributions to the current state of scholarly understanding and debate over a particular period of the English past. The former – for the most part studies by Left-wing political scientists, nostalgically attached to a heroic age when these writings appeared to have a doctrinal coherence, a political purposefulness and a self-assurance long since departed – are either expository in character or critical only so far as the work in question is deemed to correspond or depart from a Marxist orthodoxy or an approved strategy of revision and adaptation. Works of piety or polemic conceived within the Marxist church and addressed to fellow believers, they possess little reference to the historical content of the writings or to the ways in which they may have been challenged or modified by others.[1] Studies by non-Marxist professional historians, on the other hand, have little interest in the theoretical discussions surrounding these writings and are concerned to evaluate them exactly as they would other 'contributions to scholarship', solely in terms of their supposed proximity to a supposed historical reality.[2] Neither approach is particularly concerned with the milieus in which these works were conceived, the contemporary discussions which attended and influenced their composition, or the rhetorical qualities of the writing itself.

One approach to historical writing which registers their function as cultural artifacts is to read them off against the shifting intellectual and political currents of the time: to read them as documents in 'contemporary history'. This need not imply that they have no other worth: some features may have been incorporated into the common perception of the periods in question; others may have become part of the fabric of historical consciousness. Yet, even if it does not necessarily exclude these broader areas of significance, the purely contextual reading is apt to place the writings in a passive role as mere transparencies or reflections of their time – to ignore those elements which 'mediated' or worked against the grain, or have perpetuated older world-pictures or have anticipated later configurations. Marxist writings may not be a timeless body of 'scientific' truths, but they are more than a series of 'moments' in the life of Communist parties: there are continuities to be observed, stemming from the inspiration which men and women found what was deemed a continuum of Marxist exegesis and practice over more than a century. There are traditions of imagining as well as imagined traditions.

A text is never simply a product of circumstances and intentions, however compelling; it is also shaped by the nature and function of the work itself. With historical texts – lengthy and substantial pieces of research and writing occupying many years – there is often a hiatus between conception and performance, between their moment of composition and some unanticipated 'conclusions'. Perhaps this is particularly true with the work of historians who freely acknowledged the contemporary influences and purposes of their work, but who also believed that Marxist theory gave them access to a more 'scientific' understanding of the past and expected their history to be judged by the conventional standards of 'bourgeois' historical scholarship. There are, in other words, features of the historical artifact and of its production, which enforce a critical and evaluative obligation on the observer as well as a 'historicist' one of empathetic reconstruction within an intellectual or a cultural milieu.

In the pages that follow I shall attempt, therefore, to combine the functions of the expositor and the censor. Among the dwindling band of Marxist historians and the rather more numerous body of Marxisant sociologists, political scientists and 'cultural materialists', this may sometimes be deemed an exercise in 'revisionist' aspersion; amongst the ranks of non-Marxist professional historians, a misplaced resuscitation or superfluous flogging of dead horses. Historians sympathetic to the Marxist enterprise but not themselves

Marxist – for whom the Communist writings of the 1940s and early 1950s are an embarrassment – may consider the attention given to polemical juvenilia disproportionate to their empirical worth or importance. Others, for whom the Marxist leopard has never changed his spots, may find the chapters on the substantive historical texts of the 1960s and 1970s something of a weariness: the bare skeleton of the early writings has indicated sufficiently the physiognomy of the beast. Yet, Marxist historical writing in England did renew itself over time: old orthodoxies were modified and sometimes overthrown; new lines of inquiry were opened up; new interests developed. The English Marxist historians were unusually sensitive to the changing world around them, and to the criticisms and the substantive work of their bourgeois colleagues. To a remarkable extent, they operated within an 'empirical mode', common perhaps to all intellectuals of their generation; indeed, to a degree which is only now becoming clear, they and their opponents argued within a common nexus of ideas, values and assumptions. At the same time, they never surrendered their Marxist faith or the overall historical vision that went with it. And central to that vision was the idea of a seventeenth-century English Revolution.

1

The Great Bourgeois Revolutions: A False Genealogy?

A comparison of the English and French Revolutions, which examines first their congruence and then their divergence in nineteenth- and twentieth-century historiography.

1.1 MODELS OF BOURGEOIS REVOLUTION

Nearly thirty years ago, E. P. Thompson complained of the model of modern history 'which concentrates attention upon one dramatic episode – the Revolution – to which all that goes before and after must be related; and which insists on an ideal type of . . . Revolution against which all others must be judged'. 'Minds which thirst for tidy platonism', he added, 'soon become impatient with actual history'.[1] Thompson's complaint – more telling, coming as it did from a radical warrior whose own *Making of the English Working Class* leaned so heavily on a periodization outlined in *Capital* – encapsulates a peculiarly damaging criticism of orthodox Marxism: its frequent elision of evolution and revolution, of the long slow haul of social processes and concentrated bursts of political struggle; its conflation of continuity, with capitalism as the summation of world history, and of episodic discontinuities, involving moments of dramatic transformation. These elisions are to be found in the writings of Marx himself: in *The Communist Manifesto* or the Preface to *A Contribution to the Critique of Political Economy* with the emphasis on a single progressive evolutionary process of one humanity over time; and the Marx of the so called *Formen*,[2] the *Class Struggles* and *The Eighteenth Brumaire*, with the progressivist evolutionary schema split asunder by what Anthony Giddens has called 'time-space edges', as points of encounter between societies organized according to different structural principles, by the

7

antinomies and residues within historical societies, and by the sheer crookedness of actual history.[3]

Marx may have referred to revolutions as 'the locomotives of history', but in his deployment of the term to cover everything from the centuries-long capitalist accumulation in England to the events of February 1848 on the Boulevarde des Capucines, he was remarkably inexplicit about the means and speed of locomotion. Perhaps one should not be too squeamish about a terminology which fuses process and event: the 'English' and 'French Revolutions' have, after all, become so standardized in the currency of historiography that they need not pre-empt too many interpretative options. Amongst such options, however, should be the possibility that they were not revolutions in Marx's sense of the word at all: that a history conceived in terms of a *before* and an *after*, with a self-evident San Andreas fault – the term is Lawrence Stone's – lying athwart seventeenth-century England and late eighteenth-century France, is open to question.[4] Without the benefit of modern seismography, seventeenth-century Englishmen preferred to speak of the events of the 1640s as a 'Great Rebellion' or a further 'Reformation';[5] and even in 1789, Louis XVI was as close to contemporary idiom as was his interlocutor during the famous exchange with the Duc de Liancourt, in referring to the events of 14 July, as 'a revolt' rather than '*The* Revolution'.[6]

Unfortunately, the theoretical baggage attached to the notion of a 'bourgeois revolution' cannot allow for these meanings, however much sanctioned by seventeenth- or eighteenth-century usage. On the face of it, the use of 'bourgeois' as a descriptive label seems unexceptional, encompassing a whole range of a non-noble and non-plebeian activities characteristic of town dwellers; and the observation that the politics of 1789 and even 1641 revolved around these heterogeneously defined bourgeois, borders on the anodyne. When pressed, indeed, Marxist historians are apt to assert that this is all they have ever meant: that to attribute to them belief in a bourgeois Jack the Giantkiller slowly climbing the beanstalk of economic progress, decisively liquidating the old order in the English and the French Revolutions, and putting in its place something called capitalist society, is to accuse them of vulgar Marxist error, reductionism even, the better to refute their much more modest claims.[7]

But as the English case makes clear, the term does carry a range of immodest implications. The bourgeoisie in question were not any old townsfolk: they were those associated with burgeoning overseas trade or an internal market economy. And most of them, it soon transpires, were not townsfolk at all. For the dominant group in English politics and society were not townsmen but countrymen, 'gentry'. The age-old structure of national representation which provided for no institutionalized 'Burgertum', but distinguished between an Upper House composed of a small hereditary peerage and a Lower House effectively controlled by country gentlemen, who in a continental 'Ständesstaat' would have sat as nobles and have been separated from 'burgesses' or townsmen, 'has always made a bourgeois interpretation of English history linguistically difficult'; and any attempt to apply the terminology has had to convert the gentry of the House of Commons into a 'bourgeoisie of convenience'.[8]

To refer to their activities as 'bourgeois', therefore, is not designed to strain semantic patience, but to assert something about their status and significance other than their place of residence and their source of income. Under their rural trappings, the English gentry are 'the main representatives of a decisive historical trend modifying the structure of English rural society', destroying old 'feudal–aristocratic' relations, bringing in agricultural revolution, the expropriation of the peasantry, the triumph of market forces and capital accumulation; they are the agents of an epochal transformation which changed England 'from a backward economy to one on the threshold of industrial revolution'.[9] Similarly, to 'state the obvious', as did Soboul, 'that the French bourgeoisie led the Revolution', is to imply more than that publicists, small town officials, avocats and lawyers dominated the politics of 1789.[10] Though he admitted that 'sections of it were integrated into the social and economic structure of the ancien regime', Soboul's real concern was with 'the initiators of new production and exchange': 'a new class of big farmers', 'a rural' or even 'peasant bourgeoisie', 'impatient with the impediments of a semi-feudal society'; an 'already mature', 'commercial bourgeoisie' determined to smash a 'decadent' aristocratic order and to transform state and civil society.[11]

In both instances, the bourgeoisie are a bourgeoisie after the manner of *The Communist Manifesto*, that 'historically has played a most revolutionary part'; or, in the more domesticated vocabulary of professional history, our friend the 'rising middle class', having arrived at its appointed time and place, and done what it had to do before moving on to the next assignment.[12] As for its revolution, this is not so much a political or a religious struggle pure and simple, as a 'social revolution', 'a legal enactment' or 'recognition' of its economic power, a 'bursting asunder of feudal relations of production', 'the crown of a long evolution which made the bourgeoisie the mistress of the world'.[13]

In this sense, even Thompson would have us read the English Civil War as the critical episode in the making of modern society: the revolutionary moment may be dispersed, but the epochal process – the 'great arch' of bourgeois transformation – is further strengthened. For all his caveats about Marxist method – about the inadequacy of the meccano set of base and superstructure, the privileging of economics over culture, and the transgressions of terminology 'so epochal as to include William de la Pole, Oliver Cromwell and Mr Edward Heath' – for all his empirical qualifications – about the subsequent 'equilibrium of social forces', the 'silting up' of elites, and the 'tough fibres' of traditional patronage and 'parasitism' – Thompson, too, writes his English history along the lines of a *before* and *after* the seventeenth-century divide, with 'its main beneficiaries' a 'superbly successful and self confident' post-revolutionary class of 'agrarian capitalists', the class which set up the Bank of England, controlled the East India Company, dominated the slave trade, and battened on to the political cornucopia of 'Old Corruption'. The genealogy of modernism is still preserved: England is the 'first modern society', and the English and French Revolutions are decisive and comparable episodes in the evolution of a bourgeois world.[14]

For Marx, the English and French Revolutions were two renditions of the same drama: 'the proclamation of the political order for the new European society'.[15] There is only one history of Europe, and this history could be traced by turns in seventeenth-century England and eighteenth-century France. The years 1648 and 1789 are the two great moments in the making of modernity: 'they accomplished the same historical task . . . with the same strategic disposition of collective actors – the bourgeoisie and the people on the one hand, the monarchy, the nobility and the church on the other' – and under the banner of a similarly energizing ideology.[16] Once the task was complete, both shed their heroic illusions and articulated a self-interested and mundane set of practices and assumptions more appropriate to the new capitalist civil society.

Models are metaphors of the historical process, but the model borrowed from Marx's 'natural history' or genealogy of the capitalist mode of production, petrified into the axiom of a single bourgeois revolution, and made to fit both England and France, can easily stifle recognition of historical particularity. 'One can almost hear the stretching of historical textures,' commented Thompson in 1965, 'as the garment of English events is strained to cover the buxom model of "La Revolution Française".'[17] Nearly thirty years on, it is now apparent that the French fit isn't that much better: that the problem is not so much with Marianne's ample proportions, as with the constricting Marxist *soutien-gorge*.[18]

* * *

Instead of examining the constitutive problems of Marx's 'bourgeois revolution' through the conventional but somewhat abstract analysis of Marxist theory, however, this first chapter will attempt to show how French Liberal accounts of bourgeois political struggle and Scottish sociological trajectories of the growth of civilization and commerce came to inform both the revolutionary Marxism of the 1840s and the evolutionary Marxism of the Second International. It will contend that a central defect of the 'revolutionary' model subsequently deployed by Marxist historians in England and France is to be found precisely in this 'contamination' of Marxist and 'Liberal' categories: the incomplete fusion of dialectical conflict, political rupture and class struggle, and of long-term economic and social evolution, of event and process. And it will try to show how these unresolved tensions and a set of perceived differences between the English Civil War and the French Revolution, as well as the self-regarding complacencies of Victorian constitutionalism, helped to explain the dominance of a specifically non-revolutionary Whiggish reading of England's seventeenth-century past.

1.2 THE MARXIST/LIBERAL GENEALOGY

As the Marxist analysis of modern capitalist development came to be something of an embarrassment and the study of contemporary socialist regimes diplomatically off limits, English and French Marxists were to turn to history. It was, moreover, a history of a particular time and type: one which concerned itself pre-eminently

with the origin and growth of capitalist society, with the transition
from feudalism and the era of so-called bourgeois revolution, but
one which was nevertheless conceived as a contribution to the
debate on contemporary capitalism.[19]

A roll-call of British Marxist historians, for example, would
establish three features: a focus on pre-industrial or early industrial economies, an initial concentration on economic relations,
later transformed by a growing interest in culture and ideas, and
a conviction that their work as historians was part and parcel of
their political activity.[20] In France, for many generations, the writing
of Marxist history meant celebrating the Revolution: 'the only
empirical skeleton' on to which socialist intellectuals could graft
'their fleshy metaphysical corpus of thought'. Whereas English
Marxists had first to 'discover' their revolution and clothe it with
epochal significance, their French counterparts required no such
reclamation. The two great instances of bourgeois revolution,
indeed, presented its Marxist proponents with divergent problems:
in England, that of locating a revolutionary class struggle which
could be attached to the extensive Marxist analysis of capitalist
evolution; in France, that of demonstrating epochal capitalist transformation which could be dovetailed with the class struggles articulated within its democratic revolution. For all that, in different
ways, and in both cases, the chosen field of history was circum-
scribed by its function as genealogy – a genealogy, that is, of
capitalist formation and also of present thought and politics.[21]

But the genealogy was more complicated than they thought.
As a number of commentators recently have pointed out,[22] the
concept of bourgeois revolution and the coupling of the English
and French examples was a central theme in the work of French
Liberal historians of the 1820s. And either because he was
preoccupied with the workings of capitalist class relations, or
because the idea of a bourgeois revolution set in the recent past
provided him with the only historical precedent for the proletarian revolution which he believed to be ripening in the womb
of capitalist society, Karl Marx, the unmasker of bourgeois liberal
ideology, nevertheless, and to his cost, ingested this crucial item
of its intellectual baggage.[23]

The interpretation of seventeenth-century English conflicts as
the political and religious expression of the bourgeois transformation of society in fact went back even further, to eighteenth-
century Scottish sociology, and thence to some seventeenth-century

Republican political writers – social theorists by adoption. For David Hume, the English Revolution was a local and eccentric example of a general European phenomenon: the dislocation of 'Gothic' forms of government, caused by the spread of commerce and civilization, and what he called 'a universal fermentation', bringing about variously in Europe the rise of pure monarchy, and in England political liberty.[24] As a good genealogist, concerned only with 'the most curious, interesting and instructive part of the past', Hume wrote his history backwards, starting with 1603 and finishing with Julius Caesar; and he was explicitly concerned with the roots of what he called 'the present establishment', something that he believed was to be found in the 'revolutions' of the seventeenth century. The peculiarities of English government owed nothing, he argued, to the superior qualities of national customs or native 'genius', but much to the alienation of church and crown lands in the sixteenth and seventeenth centuries: to the displacement both of the barons and of small peasant proprietors by the 'middling rank of men'. In short, it was the product of 'a new plan of liberty' based on an alteration in the balance of wealth and landed property.

> Residing on their estates and thereby husbanding their resources and acquiring independence and formidable local influence, [the gentry] were insensibly changing and perhaps improving the spirit and genius of the ... constitution. For their spirit and judgement appeared not only in defence of their own privileges but in their endeavour to free trade from those shackles which ... prerogative had imposed upon it ... and likewise landed property, [from] the burden of wardship and the remains of feudal tenures [under which] they still laboured.[25]

Little of this was original; much was simply an illustration of the 'Harringtonian' commonplace that power follows property. Conceived within the framework of a historiographical revisionism – a riposte to antiquarian Whig fundamentalism which depicted 'The Great Rebellion' as a defence of ancient rights against the alien innovations of the Stuarts – it sought to elucidate English political particularity, not to expose fundamental class conflict or social transformation.[26] Hume was no proto-Marxist; and it was only in the nineteenth century, and in the light of the French Revolution, that what was a minor theme in the context of his history as a whole was extended and given wider significance: that the English Civil War was upgraded from 'a time of troubles'

to a revolution. So great was the desire of Restoration French
Liberals to find a pedigree for their own political and social struggles, that 1641 and 1789 were now aligned as parallel 'victories
in the same war and to the profit of the same cause', to wit the
triumph of 'progressive and general interests against stationary
and sectional ones'. The conflict of religious and political parties
in England, claimed Guizot, was 'a screen for the social question,
and the struggle of various classes for power and influence'.[27]
The Cromwellians were drawn into the long shadow of the Jacobins;
the parliamentary enactments and religious divisions of the 1640s
were retrospectively coated with French revolutionary terminology;
and the Civil War was lined up with the French Revolution as
'the latest skirmish in an age-old campaign' between the people
and its oppressors, part of a battle in every era between Frank
and Gaul, Norman and Saxon, seigneur and peasant, noble and
middle class. Or as Thierry put it:

> One could say that the rallying cry of the two armies were, on the
> one side, *idleness and power*, and on the other *industry and liberty*: because
> the idlers, those who wanted no other occupation in life than pleasure
> without pains, of whatever caste, enlisted with the royalist troops to
> defend interests conforming to their own: whereas those families from
> the caste of the former conquerors that had been won over to industry
> joined the party of the commons

– 'bourgeois revolution' as liberal ideology.[28]

This is, of course, also the schema of *The Communist Manifesto*:
the bourgoisie are the vehicles of civilization and progress; their
class interests temporarily encapsulate the general will of society
and its potential for further development; their adversary is a
tottering apparatus of parasitism and privilege which 'everywhere
hampers trade and industry'; their victory, a victory of free
competition over constrictions, 'brutal vigour' over 'slothful
indolence', a commercial 'means of production and exchange' over
a regime of guilds, monopolies, corporations and regulations
designed to perpetuate feudal property relations; their revolution,
yet another chapter in the age-old history of class struggles:
'Freeman and slave, patrician and plebeian, lord and serf, guild
master and journeyman, in a word, oppressor and oppressed in . . .
a fight that each time ended . . . in a revolutionary re-constitution
of society at large.'[29]

The coupling of this heroic 'bourgeois' class struggle with the supposed transition from a feudal 'mode of production' to a capitalist one, which also looms so large in Marxist accounts of the English and French Revolutions, likewise draws on liberal ideology. The 'invention' of feudalism by seventeenth-century English lawyers, as a denominator of 'feudal' law and tenure, and by the French *philosophes* as a term to describe a confused welter of seigneurial residues – all of the things 'for ever abolished' in the famous *auto da fé* of 4 August 1789 – was established 'tradition' long before Marx wrote of a 'feudal mode of production'.[30] But once again, it was the Scottish philosophers whose use of the term was probably crucial. Living in an environment where social polarity was particularly marked – where a Cameron of Lochiel could be juxtaposed with a James Watt – perhaps they found the contrast of feudal and commercial forms of subsistence and exchange glaringly obvious. For whatever reasons, it was the Scots who gave feudalism its modern meaning, as an economic stage in the development of humankind from ignoble savage to civilized consumer, a corresponding set of social relations and a concomitant scale of values or an ideology. Out of this configuration of feudal arrangements, they maintained, modern commercial society had emerged in the period from the eighth to the eighteenth-century, with the appearance of towns and long distance trade: catalysts of increased specialization and a monied economy which gradually percolated into the most backward recesses of rural life and reshaped the whole society.[31]

As an account of the growth of commerce and civility, the Scottish sociological model may have much to recommend it; as an explanation of revolutionary class struggle and violent structural transformation, however, it manifestly does not. A transition occurring over many centuries through mechanisms of exchange and competition already essentially bourgeois in character, leading ineluctably to the self-transcendence of traditional modes of subsistence, as feudal lords and their royal masters reveal that they too are economic calculators and have acquisitive 'middle-class' aspirations in the presence of commercial opportunities: there is little place in any of this for 'dialectical conflict' within the 'womb' of the old society or for the forcible substitution of one type of social organization and structure for another. A feudalism so porous and adaptive can never constitute much of a fetter to new productive forces. The bourgeoisie's rise to power is both assumed and assured: once the barbarian invasions are at an end and order is restored, towns and trade reappear, and commercial society resumes its natural progression; 'bourgeois revolution', if it occurs at all, does so in the early stages of the process, in the communal revolts of the early Middle Ages, in which town and crown ally themselves against the feudal barons to secure the loosening of feudal controls and the conditions for urban development. Scottish economics and French politics did not cohere; and the notion of a further instalment of bourgeois revolutions during the seventeenth and eighteenth-centuries was either utterly superfluous, or, at best, a small shove of the 'invisible hand' which speeded up the inevitable triumph of the James Watts over the Camerons of Lochiel: a 1745 not a 1789.[32]

But it was precisely this theory which Marx was to draw on in the 1840s and 1850s as the explanatory key to early modern bourgeois revolutions.[33] Adam Smith's categories of subsistence and exchange were poured into the Hegelian mould of 'becoming' and yoked to the trajectory of the divided spirit and its painful path to metaphysical wholeness, with the clash of new economic forms and old social arrangements standing in for the 'labour of the negative', and revolutionary transformations for existential ruptures and their periodic transcendence. Metaphysic was made flesh; poetic vision clothed in science; and the ceaseless activities of the dialectic transformed into the clash of historical forces and the underlying transition from one type of social organization to another. But the harnessing of Scottish economics to German philosophy proved every bit as artificial as it had to French politics; and when the composite explanatory model of world history which combined a Smithean sociological chassis and a Hegelian motor left the workshop of pure theory in the 1840s, it hit the road as the familiar double-decker Marxism of base and superstructure, with its 'techno-functionalist' explanation of class and property relations, its 'meccano-set' version of dialectical contradiction, and its clumsy and incompletely synchronized gearbox of political revolution and structural transformation: the ill-assorted mechanism of a model which combined evolutionary inevitabilism with revolutionary struggle – a mechanism given further rigidity by the naturalistic determinism and the scientism of second generation assembly workers like the later Engels, Kautsky and Plekhanov.[34]

Mature Marxist analysis of capitalist society was, of course, far less mechanistic, concerned more with the social relations of production than with modes of subsistence and exchange. 'Capital' is driven to its eventual destruction by the contradictions between surplus value and labour value, by the uncontrollable market forces unlocked by industrialization and blind competition, by commodity fetishism and internal class exploitation.[35] And in the *Formen* and Part I of *Capital*, Marx was also to modify his understanding of feudal property relations and their 'reproduction': to provide them with their own distinctive forms of economic functioning and their characteristic 'laws of motion', to explain how these precapitalist communal arrangements could coexist and perpetuate themselves alongside the individualist enterprise imperatives of trade and commerce, and consequently how structural transformation marking the passage from feudal to bourgeois society would need to occur within the envelope of the existing agrarian community, with the separation of 'the direct producers from possession of the means of production', the deprivation of rural proprietors of the capacity 'to reproduce themselves by extra-economic coercion', and the replacement of communities of peasant cultivators and feudal lords by the famous tripartite structure of capitalist agriculture constituted by landlord, tenant farmer and wage labourer.[36]

Such a model, if completed, would have allowed for the co-existence of different types of social formation and explained the otherwise unnatural and paradoxical persistence of feudalism in parts of Europe. But it would have totally undermined the historical and theoretical foundations of bourgeois revolution in a triple sense. Since it revolved around a mechanism of 'primitive accumulation' within the already existing rural structures, it made the *deus ex machina* of a new bourgeois class altogether unnecessary; since it explained the collapse of feudalism as the dissolution of the whole rural community and the transformation of all its members, it left no room for a significant feudal class fettering productive forces to be overthrown; and since it catered for alternative instrumentalities of the process of dissolution – either, as in England, the commercialization of landlordism or, in France, ever-increasing peasant ownership or, even, in parts of Eastern Europe, large-scale state agrarian enterprise – it cleared the way for different routes to capitalism and perhaps even for a pluralist typology of capitalist society also.[37] But the project of a distinctive model of feudal structure and the exploration of the various 'time-space edges' of its encounter with capitalist formation was never completed; and its partial torso simply added to the confusion of subsequent Marxist accounts of transition, by fostering belief in deeply rooted structural contradiction and painful ruptures within the envelope of feudal property relations which could never, in fact, be substantiated.[38]

As it was, a 'dialectically' updated one-track evolutionary model of capitalist formation brought about by the 'rise' of a commercialized middle class, dominated Marxist analysis of pre-industrial society – besetting Marxist historians with a range of problems. There were difficulties associated with a dissolution of 'feudalism' brought about by external forces – the *deus ex machina* of an internal market, the New World and burgeoning overseas commerce; the impact of a monied economy on self-sufficient feudal structures; even attitudinal differences between the spendthrift habits of the traditional feudal nobility and the accumulative, acquisitive 'spirit' of the bourgeoisie – rather than by the ineluctable workings of the dialectic deep within feudalism itself, by increasing social polarization and class conflict leading inevitably to the destruction of the old relations of production.[39] There were troubles with a 'transition', completed in some cases but 'failed' or 'arrested' in others, and everywhere elongated to cover three, four or five centuries, with some well-defined characteristics of their own, which appeared to 'belong' to none of the 'modes' listed in the Marxist inventory. And these problems of efficient cause, periodization and content were never really solved by the epicycles or semantics of twentieth-century Marxists: by 'bastardized feudalisms' and supposed 'feudal reactions'; 'government sponsored monopolies', restrictive trade regulations or 'Absolutist states', standing in as 're-deployed and recharged apparatus(es) of feudal domination'.[40]

Certainly, many of these 'answers', in turn, can also be traced back to nineteenth-century liberal theory. In his *History of the English Revolution*, Guizot explained how both English and French Revolutions were triggered by a similar combination of circumstances. Whereas the development of civilization in both countries had revolved around the tension between the monarchy, the aristocracy and the church,

> in seventeenth century England as in eighteenth century France, all struggle between the three . . . had ceased, and they lived together in sluggish peace. It may even be said that they had lost their historical character – the aristocracy no longer protected public liberty . . . royalty no longer laboured to abolish aristocratic privilege; . . . the clergy . . .

feared the human mind. Forsaken by their ancient leaders . . . the people began to think it had better transact its own affairs itself; and assuming in its own person all the functions its former leaders no longer fulfilled, claimed at once of the crown, liberty; of the aristocracy, equality; and of the clergy, the rights of human intellect. Then burst forth revolutions.[41]

The reading of the English Revolution through the French, 'the stretching of historical textures' which Thompson complained of, is flagrant; and indeed Guizot argued that one could only grasp the events of seventeenth-century England through the experiences of eighteenth- and nineteenth-century France.[42] But, equally, the argument used to dispose of the hiatus between process and conjuncture, and to explain a 'revolution' unnecessary to the evolution of bourgeois society, is a primitive formulation of the theme sketched by Marx and elaborated by Hill, Lefebvre and Soboul: of aristocratic and clerical reaction and a monarchy once the enemy but now the ally of a parasitic feudal nobility; of a state perverted into becoming the vehicle of a privileged and archaic civil society; and of a liberal revolt against a political and ideological apparatus which turned itself into a bourgeois social revolution.[43]

1.3 THE TRIUMPH OF GRADUALISM

Despite the soldering operation, the Marxist model of structural contradiction, class conflict and revolution, and the liberal historical scenario of institutional emancipation, political progress and commercial evolution, never properly fused. The emphasis in Guizot and Hume is on progress and social development, with the middle class as the vectors of political freedom and civilization. The theme is triumphalist and reconciliatory rather than critical and conflictual.[44] Revolution is an undesirable and avoidable appendage to semi-automatic commercial development, the outcome of impatience and misunderstanding, rather than the product of deep and irreconcilable social and economic fissures. There is no single San Andreas fault-line in these histories, no sense of a *before* and *after* '*the* Revolution', since most of the 'after' elements are either permanent features of human nature or assumed elements in the slow maturation of bourgeois society; and since political arrangements are often unpredictable and proceed along an independent, sometimes ironic, trajectory: an age-old conflict or a 'see-saw' scenario of expansion and contraction, optimism and pessimism, 'enthusiasm' and 'superstitition', rather than a product of slow-moving laws leading to socialism.[45]

For Hume, no general law of social progress could be derived from the English experience: the English Civil War was an aberration of European development, brought about by the peculiar 'mixed' form of government, the unpredictable enthusiasm of the Puritans and the 'great mixture of accident which commonly concurs with a small ingredient of wisdom and foresight in erecting the complicated fabric of the most perfect government'. Order rather than liberty was the *sine qua non* of trade; civilization and commerce were concurrently advanced elsewhere through the traditional alliance of absolute monarchy and *nouveaux riches*; and the precarious balance of plebeian and aristocratic elements in the English constitution was likely in time, through the ebb and flow of excessive liberty and authority, to produce its euthanasia in absolute monarchy once more.[46] For Guizot, 'the social movement' was continuous and cumulative, not disrupted or punctured by the substitution of one type of social formation by another: the middle class had risen, were rising and would continue to rise. As for political arrangements, the struggle for liberty had to be refought in every age; and liberty was to be found in compromise and reconciliation rather than in the conquest and suppression of one part of society by another – in durable representative institutions, as the concomitant of middle-class consensus or equilibrium, a French 1830 to set alongside England's 1688; not a 1792 or a 1648.

In the French case, admittedly, the disjunction of Marxist and Liberal scenarios of revolution was less marked. French historians had a greater experience of continuing political and social division and a more pressing need to relive or to celebrate a revolutionary past.[47] True, many Liberals were to revise their triumphalist social readings in the light of 1848; and for the next generation, even sympathizers had difficulty in coming to terms with the actual course of the Revolution. But after 1870 and under an embattled Third Republic, latter-day Liberalism shaded off into Republicanism and thence through various Socialisms to an apostolic Marxist succession. Since, on the one hand, for Republicans of all persuasions, the Revolution marked a fundamental break in French history, since it could be accorded almost ecumenical significance as the 'foundation stone' of a modern secular France, and since its history became increasingly after 1870 part of a discourse on contemporary 'civic identity';[48] since, on the other, Marxism itself was a product of the political agenda created by the Revolution, since – thanks to events in Russia and elsewhere – it could be regarded as central to any twentieth-century debate on the nature of modern society, and since, after all, its historiographical emphases were reasonably flattering to French sensibilities, the differences between them – though not without famous confrontations – focused on the precise meaning and significance of the revolutionary divide and the relative merits of its protagonists, not on its existence or their 'world historical' roles. In 'the ideologically tolerant years of the Second International', when the orthodox interpretation of the Revolution was established, the elision of Marxist and Liberal Republican categories of analysis and explanation was almost imperceptible; and Jaurès could claim without incongruity that his 'Histoire Socialiste' combined 'the materialism of Marx and the mysticism of Michelet'.[49]

But in the English case, the differences seemed acute. The Restoration French Liberals, who in the 1820s had first put the case for the convergence of the two revolutions and who after 1830 had confidently anticipated a native version of the arrangements of 1688, were forced to rethink their historiographical categories and assumptions after the events of February 1848 and December 1851. Once the former 'had sounded the death knell of Guizot's historical ambition' to terminate the revolutionary cycle by combining durable representative government with 'natural' social inequalities, he was to affirm the fundamental divergence of the English and French instances of bourgeois revolution, and attribute the superiority of the English to its fundamentally religious and constitutional character.[50] And in the light of the second Napoleonic *coup d'état*, Tocqueville was to emphasize, in addition, radically different class and state formations in the two countries stretching back to the late Middle Ages.[51] For chastened Liberals, as for Burke, indeed, these profoundly dissimilar religious and institutional characteristics – the traditional and restorative features of the English Revolution, the continuities of English self-government and an Anglo-American Protestant *esprit morale* – now became the standard counterpoint to what they saw as the overwhelmingly destructive social divisions and the centralizing imperatives of French history.[52]

Certainly, these conservative reassessments goaded Marx into some of his more furious exercises in polemic. The supposed polarity was simply a spuriously differentiated identity: the 'free thought' which Guizot and Tocqueville believed had distorted the nature of the French Revolution was an English import; and the French Revolution began just as conservatively as its English counterpart – with the revival of 'its ancient constitution' in the form of the long dormant Estates General. As Furet explains:

> All that Guizot nostalgically listed as English peculiarities . . . Marx felt it sufficient to cast as so many products of bourgeois society . . . If there is indeed a difference between the two revolutions, it is neither religious, nor political, nor institutional but social: the seventeenth-century English bourgeoisie contracted an alliance with the large landowners, who for their part were engaged in developing a capitalist agriculture, whereas the French Revolution, to the contrary, had to destroy the great 'feudal' landowners. The famous difference between the two histories thus comes down to two modalities of a single history: the history of capitalism.[53]

Even the temporary divergence effected by the fragile and provisional English social compromise was destined to be swept away by the industrial bourgeoisie; and an era of class struggle and political turmoil after the French model was about to unfold in England also. The march of capitalism and the coming of the proletarian revolution would retrospectively demonstrate their common revolutionary ancestry and allow 'the two histories to be reconciled and comprehended as one'.[54]

Native English observers, however, were by no means convinced that their country was about to return to the French revolutionary mainstream: that inexorable social forces were destined to carry them away from their indigenous constitutional and religious moorings. Here, the common genealogy was either denied or ignored. To counter Hume's 'revisionism', English historians had settled for a progressivist rather than a fundamentalist reading of the seventeenth century, had incorporated Scottish 'conjectural history' into their constitutional pieties, and substituted what Duncan Forbes has called a 'scientific' for a vulgar 'Whiggism'.[55] By the time of Macaulay, what mattered was constitutional evolution and adaptation, as the counterpart of a social development from rural desolation to nineteenth-century metropolitan amenity, from drunken boor to gentleman manufacturer, from

Torbay to Torquay: 'The history of England during the seventeenth century is the history of the transformation of a limited monarchy constituted after the fashion of the middle ages into a limited monarchy suited to a more advanced state of society.'[56] Burke, Locke and Adam Smith were happily united in the person of Lord John Somers and a celebration of English history which coupled political and legal conservatism with a view of social progress, commercial to the point of philistinism.[57] Since adaptation rather than political or religious conflict was the theme, the events of the 1640s and 1650s were now subsumed within a gradualist reading of the whole period.

But this was not the whole story. Since the late eighteenth century, the notion of seventeenth-century continuity and adaptation had been challenged by a more radical reading, as a small but vocal minority sought to resurrect the 1640s and 1650s from what they saw as a hundred years of Whig neglect and Tory revisionism. Indeed, the political struggles of the period from the 1780s to the 1830s sometimes assumed the form of a conflict of revolutionary pedigrees.[58] For the 'revolution families', unrevolutionary descendants of the victors of 1688, the 'heroes' of the 1640s – their political professions and Puritan 'enthusiasms' demythologized by David Hume – lived on solely in the attenuated tradition of an aristocratic 'Republicanism': a legacy wherein Sidney and Locke were transformed from latter day adherents of the 'Good Old Cause' into models of constitutional propriety, the architects of 1688. The year 1688 itself – Glorious or Bloodless according to the degree of peculiarly English forgetfulness required – purged of uncomfortable residues, translated from disturbing history into comforting 'myth-history' – was, of course, the Revolution: not a rebellion, as Anglican apologists insisted, not a usurpation but an abdication, and certainly not a 'fourth civil war' – a disaster miraculously avoided by James II's psychological collapse and by the spectacular crumbling of his support.[59] By the 1760s, 'constitutional anxieties about the example of 1688 were on the retreat'; and even Hume was at pains to emphasize the obloguy of the later Stuarts and the legitimacy of resistance to their breaches of convention. But for radicals, the very blandness and ecumenical nature of its celebration indicated the need for less ambiguous foundation deeds.[60]

Some rejected pedigree hunting altogether. For Paine, like his French counterpart, the Abbé Sieyes, historical appeals were irrelevant: freedom was not to be sought in Germanic forests or Stuart parchments but in transhistorical natural rights. Many of his fellow radicals, however, were to find inspiration in the events of the 1640s and in the example of its patriot heroes. Catherine Macaulay whose history 'breathed the spirit of Vane and Ludlow' had already written of the period from the execution of Charles I as 'the brightest age that ever adorned the page of history'; Cartwright was to find the name of Hampden worth a million signatures for parliamentary reform; and when the crisis of the ancien régime came, Wordsworth was to invoke the ghost of John Milton.[61] For it was the French Revolution which was to play the pivotal role in the radicals' shift from 1688 to 1641 or 1649: the spectre of regicide and social revolution which persuaded uneasy Whig oligarchs to bury 1688 and 'say nothing in favour of Hampden or Russell or Sidney for fear it might give spirits to Robespierre, Danton or Marat', turned more hardy souls away from the aristocratic coup to the Great Rebellion.

The range of responses was considerable: some barely went beyond the indiscriminate invocation of Milton, Marvell and Harrington – 'sages and patriots that being dead do speak to us'; others – drawing on the tradition of the eighteenth-century 'Commonwealthsman', most recently articulated in James Burgh's *Political Disquisitions* – recalled the Republic as 'a true government by representation', destroyed by 'the villainous Cromwell' and his 'standing army'; others, again, like the young Southey, provocatively celebrated the execution of Charles I or, like his fellow poet-radical, Coleridge, conjured up the utopian experiments of the Diggers for his attack on the tyranny of property and power. The 1640s and 1650s were, it is true, rarely more than an illustrative resource – though it is worth commenting on the millenarian expectation and saturation in the 'Revolutionary Bible', which people like Priestley, Coleridge, William Blake and Joanna Southcott shared with the 'prophets' of 150 years before. But their real subject was located in the 1790s and 1800s, and in the conjuncture of English politics and the French Revolution. To the Jacobin, John Thelwell, the appeal to seventeenth-century English history was simply diagnostic: a warning of the fragility of any revolution which was less than truly democratic and which substituted 'the active spirit of fanaticism' for 'the true spirit of liberty', a combination which, he believed, had led directly to Cromwell's usurpation and to the 'unfortunate Restoration' of the

Stuarts – a 'catastrophe' ruled out in France by the mobilization of 'public and almost universal opinion'. The radical engagement with the history and the texts of the 1640s and 1650s was concerned with resurrecting, but not repeating, the experiences of the English revolutionaries.[62]

After Bonaparte's coup and still more after Louis XVIII's return, repetition appeared more apposite: in retrospect, indeed, it was the total trajectory of French Revolution which now explained political and social change in England also. To many observers, it seemed like a speeded up version of the Civil War and the Interregnum: 'an immense collection of experiments on the nature and effects of the various parts of various governments'. In a few short years, the Revolution had 'described the whole cycle' of human history; the Fall of the Bastille, Constitutional Monarchy, the Republic, the egalitarian Jacobin Utopia, and the Napoleonic dictatorship charted the 'dissolution and the renovation of society'. But the new society was a radically different society: 'the Bastille was fallen', wrote the young Macaulay, 'and could never rise from the ruins'. The only period of the national past which had seen the same dissolution, renovation and transformation was, he thought, the Civil War and Commonwealth, not 1688: there were, therefore, only 'two portions of modern history pre-eminently important and interesting' – 1789 and 1641.[63]

The French Revolution changed the focus of political discussion in contemporary England also: the central issue in the reform debates of the 1820s and 1830s was no longer aristocratic resistance to royal tyranny but the social identity and the political influence of the middling ranks. And once again, the example of the 1640s seemed more in tune with the spirit of democratic reform than did that of 1688: the *Quarterly Review* was not alone in drawing attention on the eve of the Reform Bill of 1832 to the 'extraordinary resemblances between the reign of Charles I and our time: we have amongst us', it warned, 'all the moving principles of the Great Rebellion'.[64] The second and third decades of the nineteenth century had indeed witnessed another spurt of interest in the mid-seventeenth century. James Brodie and John Rutt had laid the foundation of modern Civil War studies; even more provocatively, William Godwin found in the period from 1647 to 1653 the principles of public virtue and social merit so conspicuously lacking in the rest of English history.[65] In the 1840s John Foster could pronounce it 'a grave reproach to English political biography that the attention rightly due to statesmen who opposed Charles I, in themselves the most remarkable men of any age or nation, should have been suffered to be borne away by the poorer imitators of their memorable deeds, the authors of the imperfect settlement of 1688'. He need not have worried. The mid-nineteenth century saw the high tide of Hampden, Vane and Milton worship; and before the decade was out, even Cromwell had been resuscitated and fitted out for Victorian approval in the heady pages of Thomas Carlyle's 'Letters and Speeches'.[66]

Yet recovery went hand in hand with domestication. After 1848 particularly, it was desirable to forget disconcerting Scottish models and sever unwelcome French connections. Scots history – triply suspect for 'speculative', philosophical features, at odds with what was now construed as the factual, if not fully Rankean, character of the historical enterprise; for scepticism of matters religious or spiritual, to many Victorians the driving force of political life; and for a comparative approach which belittled the self-regarding 'peculiarities' of the English – was now damned for a sociological interpretation of power relations which assumed a quite different significance now that capitalism was no longer emerging but consolidating its position in the face of a growing working class.[67] The supposed similarity of the English and French Revolutions was even more alarming. The older Macaulay – cured of political enthusiasm by the success of 1832 – now restated the 'old Whig' commonplace and returned 'The English Revolution' to 1688: a 'maintaining' revolution, complaisantly contrasted in 1849 with the violent upheavals in continental Europe, a revolution which spared England 'the barricades, the houses dinted with bullets, the gutters foaming with blood', a revolution without class struggles or ideological conflict.[68]

Others were still prepared to see the period leading to the Civil War as the decisive era of English history, but for nearly all of them it was now decisive for unrevolutionary reasons – for the step by step victory of constitutional rights and parliamentary government. The Gladstonian era witnessed a burgeoning of interest in the early Stuarts and especially in the person of Oliver Cromwell, and Gardiner produced the definitive whig narrative of the period. True, he affixed to it the influential label of 'The Puritan Revolution'. But Gardiner's 'Puritan Revolution' on analysis turns out to be a series of constitutional adjustments and victories for religious freedom rather than a fundamental social transformation. 'Puritanism' moves in a constitutional–ideological empyrean above classes; and Cromwell 'stands forth as the typical Englishman of the modern world', part of the English tradition, formalized by his statue at the entrance to the House of Commons, rather than a revolutionary fanatic, a military dictator or a bourgeois class warrior.[69] The genealogy is a genealogy of parliamentary democracy and religious pluralism not of capitalism or revolution – 'peculiarities' of an English 'liberal descent' which had few parallels in France. Even T. H. Green, whose thought transcended and sometimes even deconstructed the parliamentary pieties of his contemporaries, believed that the 'English Revolution' had merely saved England from the conventional 'transition of a feudal into an absolute monarchy' and 'prepare(d) the way for the plutocracy under feudal forms which has governed England ever since the death of William III'. In the larger scheme of things its 'cycle was limited'; it was the end point of the era ushered in by the Reformation: 'doubtless . . . its force has been felt throughout the subsequent series of political action and reaction, but the current along which European society is being carried has another and wider sweep'; unlike the French Revolution, it 'belonged essentially to another world than that in which we live'.[70]

For G. M. Trevelyan, writing in the heyday of progressive Edwardian Liberalism, the English Civil War was quite unlike the 'dark story' of the French Revolution. 'The French Revolution was a war of two societies . . . but the Great Rebellion was a war of two parties':

> The French Revolution appealed to the needs as well as to the aspirations of mankind. But in England the revolutionary passions were stirred by no class in its own material interest. Our patriots were prosperous men, enamoured of liberty, or of religion, or of loyalty, each for her own sake, not as the handmaid of class greed. This was the secret of the moral splendour of our Great rebellion and our Civil War.[71]

Even this self-regarding differentiation was too much for the mature Trevelyan; and by 1938, it was 1688 once more that was characterized as 'The English Revolution', 'the miracle' of common sense and constitutional adjustment which had preserved English liberties to his day.[72] In the sensible compromising virtues of the Whigs and Tories of the Convention Parliament, Trevelyan now descried 'the English way': the victory of moderation over 'fanaticism in religion and politics', toleration over 'enthusiasm';

the confirmation of 'respect for law' which over time 'stood up to the stress of the democratic movement, the French Revolution and the social problems of industrial change'; 'the beginnings of the great emollient of the common ills of life': the English humanitarian movement. From the Puritan Revolution to the origins of the SPCK, it was a bit of a come-down! In his *English Social History*, published in 1942, the middle decades of the seventeenth century were treated as an interlude, uncomfortably sandwiched between Shakespeare's England and Defoe's. Since 'the Cromwellian revolution was not social or economic in its causes and motives' but 'the result of political and religious thought and aspiration', it could only be briefly alluded to as one of a number of episodes which had eroded the power of the crown and shaped the rich fabric of English dissent.[73]

The writing of the 'Puritan Revolution' out of British history was certainly quite evident in the Whiggism of the 1930s. The liberal–radical reading which had taken pride in the revolutionary achievements of the seventeenth-century Puritans and parliamentarians was all very well in the placid atmosphere of 1880 or 1906, but in 1926 or 1929, it was another matter. 'The old Whig party was dead; its Liberal successor was in disarray.' Britain had been embroiled in a massive and destructive war. Europe was in turmoil. On the Indian subcontinent, the Empire was threatening to unravel. Capitalism was in crisis and the confidence of the British bourgeoisie was shaken. In such a context, Hampden and Cromwell were more likely to appeal to Indian Congress leaders than to their British rulers; and the slogans of the Stuarts' opponents to striking miners and hunger marchers than to frightened parliamentary and industrial elites.[74] The residual Whiggism of historians like H. A. L. Fisher and the later Trevelyan was marked by a 'profound distrust of democracy', an increased uncertainty about 'the rule of progress', a despairing denial of any 'plot', or 'rhythm' or 'predetermined pattern' to events, and by a nostalgia for lost causes and departed ways of life. And where Fisher equivocated and Trevelyan backtracked, others were now explicit about their conservatism.[75] Thus, Winston Churchill and Arthur Bryant, those two popular bell-wethers of a decadent nineteenth-century tradition, were quite clear about banishing the events of the 1640s and 1650s from the evolution of English and American freedoms.

We must not, [wrote Churchill], be led by Victorian writers into re-garding this triumph of the Ironsides and Cromwell, as a kind of victory for democracy and the parliamentary system over Divine Right and old world dreams. It was the triumph of some twenty thousand resolute, ruthless, disciplined military fanatics over all that England has ever willed or wished.[76]

The authentic voice of the historical establishment was not as robust as Churchill's. It was heard rather in Godfrey Davies's strangulated Oxford history of the 'Early Stuarts': Davies followed dutifully in Gardiner's footsteps, but without any of the religious passion or parliamentary faith of his exemplar; and his 'Great Rebellion' was a narrowly constructed political affair, 'consti-tutionally preordained' to be sure, but without epochal social or ideological significance.[77] Alternatively, it could be deduced from the selective memory of its literary counterpart. Thus, *The Shorter Oxford English Dictionary*, first published 1933, gave two exam-ples from English history, under the heading of 'Revolution', meaning 'a complete overthrow of the established government. . . .: (a) The overthrow of the Rump Parliament in 1660 which resulted in the restoration of the monarchy', and (b) 'The expulsion in 1688, of the Stuart monarchy under James II, and the transfer of sovereignty to William and Mary.' As one bemused Marxist com-mentator put it, 'a foreigner might find it strange that while their revolutions led to the suppression of monarchy, ours should only result in the restoration of a king or the substitution of one for another'.[78]

After the secular canonization of the parliamentary leaders during the heyday of Victorian Liberalism, the tide was now flowing strongly in the opposite direction. Probably it was most pronounced at the biographical level: in the rehabilitation of the King's ser-vants – Strafford as a great imperial proconsul, battling against grasping and unscrupulous settlers in Ireland; Laud, a heroic if somewhat misguided rescuer of the church from laxism and de-spoliation; Charles himself as King and Martyr, a victim of his upbringing and his shyness – and in the correspondingly critical reassessment of parliamentary worthies like Pym and Hampden.[79] But it could also be found in celebrations of the 'King's Peace' and the genteel oases of aristocratic life in the 1630s – 'a spring-time shattered by the Civil War' and beyond recall in the 'bruised world of the Restoration'; in the return of narrative, with the origins of 'The Great Rebellion' placed much where Clarendon had left them, no earlier than 1637; or in 'the attempt to recover history as experience' and to understand how people 'felt at the time and why in their own estimation they acted as they did' – an attempt in which most sympathy was reserved for the sensitive and the dispassionate: those who mourned the collapse of social harmony and saw faults on both sides.[80] Many writing in the 1930s and 1940s saw the events of 1641 and 1642 through the prism not of Victorian England but of the Nazi era – with Pym as the uncrowned king of London, employing the scare tactics, the rabble rousing, the calculated violence and the propaganda techniques of 'modern totalitarian regimes'.[81] And even setting aside the more extreme 'throne and altar' effusions of Hilaire Belloc and Esmé Wingfield-Stratford, what was striking in the conventional historiography of the Civil War and 'Interregnum' was the banishment of the progressive idioms of Victorian Liberalism. Admittedly, when the chips were down, Cromwell could be resurrected as a patriot hero and a symbol of bulldog courage once more, but the idiom was consensual and unrevolutionary.[82] It was, indeed, as Max Beloff suggested, significant that 'the Whig, Trevelyan, and the Tory, Feiling, were as one in their handling of men and events down to very recent times. . . . Happy is the country,' he smugly concluded, 'whose major historians find so little to quarrel about.'[83]

How happily different it was from the doctrinal battles and professorial wars which disfigured the writing of history in France![84] When Butterfield, the erstwhile scourge of complacent whig progressivism in the 1930s, reconverted to complacent whig antiquarianism in World War II, he could specifically contrast the Englishman's alliance with his history through compromise and continuity, with 'the French romantic hypostasization of Revolution as such'.[85] He was quite explicit about the difference between an English Whiggism, based on institutional elasticity, organic development and the alliance of past and present, and a 'Messianic' Marxism which insisted on the 'strategic place', the 'scientifically calculated role', and the 'necessity' of revolution. For whereas the Whig seeks through his 'genius for political adjustment, his aptitude for give-and-take . . . his disposition to co-operate with the trend of events themselves' to read 'the danger signals' and avoid the 'ultimate catastrophe', Marxists, as revolutionaries *avant la lettre*, 'determined to see that it happens and to hurry its coming'

– 'setting out to widen rather than to heal breaches, whipping up exasperations and manufacturing the ultimate hatreds', 'see in these labours and birth pangs of time, the prelude to a great delivery . . . a Millenium which will liquidate and wind up for ever the historical process as they themselves have formulated it'. English history had no room for the Marxist interpretation; and French history could have excluded it also, if only the French had been equally sensible and flexible, and avoided the 'long way round' to their Third Republic version of English Whiggism through the 'noise' and 'violence' of revolution, counter-revolution, democracy and dictatorship.[86] Or, as Trevelyan put it in a famous and priceless aside: 'if the French noblesse had been capable of playing cricket with their peasants, their chateaux would never have been burnt'.[87] From the inevitable triumph of the bourgeoisie and variant chapters in a single history of capitalist formation to cricket lessons and their absence: further from a Marxist reading it would be difficult to go.

2

Reclaiming the Revolution

On the reclamation of the seventeenth-century English Revolution by the Left in the 1930s and 1940s and the interplay of Marxist theory, radical tradition and patriotism.

2.1 MARXIST RENEWAL, RADICAL SURVIVAL

The reclamation of seventeenth-century England for the Marxists in the 1930s and 1940s was, in large measure, a reaction against the constitutional smugness of latter-day whiggism and its conservative ramifications. In 1982, Christopher Hill – the major protagonist of the story from this point on – recalled how the combination of 'slump, dreadful unemployment, apparent successes of USSR and the bottom falling out of our middle class universe' rubbed up against 'the insular complacency' of English and especially Oxford history – 'Anglo-centred, all about liberty and the constitution', and the English Revolution 'as something which never really happened'. 'Marxism,' he said, 'seemed to make better sense of the world situation and of seventeenth century English history: I wanted to show that England's peaceful gradualist evolution [there]after . . . was the consequence of what happened then.'[1]

In the 1930s and 1940s, Hill's concern was less academic than this would suggest: 'if there [was] any point in studying history at all', it was 'by understanding the past, to control the present';[2] and by controlling the present, to influence the future. To change bourgeois society, one had to realize its contingency; and to understand its contingency, one had to study its revolutionary birthpangs. Like other invented traditions, the 'English Revolution' of the 1640s served as a legitimator of social action and an indicator of group cohesion: so much so, indeed, that in the face of sectarian confusion over the nature of true socialism, one might almost define British Marxists in the latter half of the twentieth century by a set of shared beliefs about the historic activities and attitudes of the bourgeoisie.[3]

Although committed Marxist scholars were to be found in other areas and although collectively they were to work towards a total interpretation of English economic and social development, the seventeenth-century revolution was for the next thirty years to be 'the gravitational centre' of English Marxist studies.[4] Alternative chronological fields seemed less enticing: the ancient and medieval worlds too remote and esoteric; the nineteenth century too recent and problematic; the eighteenth, an unwelcoming terra incognita. And the seventeenth century did seem crucial: for the overthrow of feudalism, the scotching of an incipient absolutism, the development of capitalism in Britain and the West, and the beginnings of the process which transformed a small island into a great colonial and industrial power. Above all, it was central to the task of historical demystification and political renewal: to the struggle against constitutionalism and gradualism. 'For Communists fighting to naturalize Marxism in a country which had brought the art of political compromise to a high degree of perfection,' comments Raphael Samuel, 'the example of a time when England "like Russia after 1917" had executed her king provided an encouraging proof that revolution was no alien, continental phenomenon, but could, on the contrary, be regarded as a sturdy native growth'.[5]

The reclamation of England's revolutionary past was to be effected after the war by the Communist Party 'Historians' Group' or collective, which flourished between 1946 and 1956. Their Marxism, however, was 'chronologically preceded by' and always co-existed with 'a more broadly based if less theoretically demanding "people's history", radical and democratic rather than socialist in its leading concepts'. And, as a number of commentators have noted, British radicalism, in turn, drew more inspiration from the native tradition of religious dissent than from any body of political theory; and radical history was steeped in the idioms of late nineteenth-century Nonconformity.[6]

In the genealogy of dissent – the 'majestically narrow' denominational histories which uncovered the 'tracks' of their 'hidden church', recorded the sufferings of their martyrs and the eventual triumph of their cause: engaged histories which invariably fostered the illusion of an unbroken line of descent – the Reformation was an inevitable point of departure, a focus sharpened by patriotic nationalism of the sort popularized by Motley, Froude or Bancroft.[7] The periodization came readily to early socialists also: to Engels and Kautsky, Hyndman and Max Beer, William Morris and his collaborator, Belfort Bax, in many ways it loomed larger than did the French Revolution.[8] The buffetings of the early sects, the persecutions of medieval heretical movements and of the primitive Church itself were deeply imprinted in socialist writing and experience. The rhetoric – indeed the very linguistic texture of English socialist thought – was likewise swathed in the idioms of the chapel. When the Communist Party General Secretary, Harry Pollitt, spoke of 'the gleam of socialism', or when its leading ideologue, Palme Dutt, recorded 'martyrdoms and sufferings' for the cause, they drew, unconsciously perhaps, on the language of dissent. In the case of the historian E. P. Thompson, as Raphael Samuel explains in his incomparable study of English Marxist lineages, the strain was unmistakable: the message was fundamentally ethical and the medium a form of pulpit oratory.[9]

For Christian exponents of the new social gospel, encapsulated in the teaching of Edward Carpenter and William Temple – men whose socialism was not so much an extension as the central expression of their faith – the parallels were obvious too. For Charles Raven, residential Canon of Liverpool Cathedral and Cambridge Regius Professor of Divinity, writing during the Depression, they revolved around the 'exaltation', the 'generosity of spirit' and the personal 'self sacrifice' which he associated equally with the early days of Christianity and with the communist movement.[10] For Archbishop Temple's great exemplar, R. H. Tawney, a High Church Anglican whose writing, none the less, pulsated with the metaphors of the English Bible, they centred on the battle against the acquisitive instinct which had dried up social charity and delegitimized the communal principle over the previous four centuries. Christians like Tawney, indeed, were filled with the same burning desire as were Marxists to uproot a social system which condemned millions to immiseration. Yet, as Christians, they were bound to reject the materialism of the Marxist ethic: Marxism, according to Tawney, was complicit with the impoverishment of the human spirit that it deplored, guilty of reducing human beings to mechanical units, moral relationships to collective class struggles, and issues of individual responsibility to the victory of the cause.[11]

For Communists, indeed, the borrowing of the idioms of Dissent went hand in hand with a rejection of its content. Religion was fundamental, yet it was a form of false consciousness; religious movements were central to the story of human emancipation, yet they invariably deflected radical energies. In his extended parallel of Christianity and socialism, Engels was at pains to point out the advantages of this-worldly salvation over the Kingdom of God; and the subject matter of his major historical study was not 'Justification by Faith' but 'The Peasant War in Germany', a story in which Luther's role was anything but socially 'emancipatory'.[12] A generation later, the pattern of borrowing and renunciation was repeated with John Lewis, the Nonconformist minister who eventually became the mouthpiece of Communist Party orthodoxy, and who progressed from the code of 'Jesus the rebel', formed in the likeness of Mahatma Gandhi, which he expounded as editor of *Christianity and the Social Revolution*, to the transcendant but Godless 'Holy Spirit' of 'the righteous social order', which he later preached as editor of the *Modern Quarterly*.[13] The same tense and ambiguous relationship was to run through the work of Hill and Thompson, historians peculiarly exposed by upbringing, residence and study to the Dissenting ambience of the Yorkshire West Riding. It can be seen in Thompson's disturbed if also perceptive dissection of popular Methodism as 'spiritual masturbation'; or in the various guises of Christopher Hill's studies of seventeenth-century religion: be it the overwhelming concern with the social byproducts rather than with the religious core of Puritan thought and practice; the oft-repeated differentiation between 'the biblical idiom' in which people expressed themselves and the secular content of their actions; and the curious but consequential interpretation of the century as the most and the least religious of eras.[14]

In the tradition of English Nonconformity, the seventeenth century was, of course, pivotal. For Gardiner, a lapsed member of the millenarian Catholic Apostolic Church, Puritanism fulfilled the Reformation's elevation of individual conscience over priestly dogma and was ultimately responsible for the formation of the sturdy independent English character.[15] For T. H. Green, who brought to his Balliol *Lectures on the English Revolution* a mind steeped in evangelical piety and fraternal social values, it was a spiritual eruption which saved England from Catholic reaction and sacerdotalism, and gave birth to Dissent, 'the great spring of political life in England'.[16]

The traditional view of Puritanism, as an ever-advancing movement of radical Dissent, was, if anything, further exaggerated in the 1930s and 1940s by the heroic overtones and 'almost cosmic significance' attached to it in the work of Weber, Tawney, and from across the Atlantic, of William Haller and Perry Miller. Since none of them were church historians, and since they approached religious teaching and practice through literature or through sociology, Puritanism was liberated from the tunnel vision of so much purely denominational history. But the vertical approach was not so much abandoned as displaced: the overwhelming concern with the end-products of the Puritan ethic diverted attention away from the study of religion itself to something else – in Weber and Tawney's case, an explanation of capitalist 'rationalization' with Puritans as mediators of nothing less than the transition from traditional to modern society; in the case of Haller and Miller, 'a geneticism' of English prose writing and American culture, which stemmed from the interior dialogues of the Puritan 'spiritual brotherhood', or from the 'majestic coherence' of the New England way.[17]

But it was the social and political message of Puritanism which exercised most power. Here, in some measure the priorities of Gardiner were inverted: Puritanism was depicted not so much as the product of constitutional reform, as the driving force of new democratic and egalitarian ideas. Within an agenda concerned with the continued inequalities of modern British life, the Puritan Revolution was now thought to contain an alternative vision of what England might have been. For once again, it was radicals who put Lilburne and Winstanley on the map. To the radical journalist Morrison Davidson, Lilburne was the first in a great line of master pamphleteers, an exemplary trouble-maker, 'a true champion of the people'; and Winstanley, 'the most penetrating of all the Commonwealth worthies', 'without peer' for 'the completeness and intelligibility' of his spiritual and economic message'.[18]

The Putney Debates – reproduced verbatim in A. S. P. Woodhouse's characteristically entitled *Puritanism and Liberty* of 1938 – rapidly assumed the proportions of a seminal text on democracy, and at Balliol College, Oxford, a course in social ethics and civic responsibility: a sort of Toynbee Hall training programme.[19] To A. D. Lindsay, Master from 1924 to 1948 – a true son of the manse who, in the view of his pupil and eventual successor, Christopher Hill, shared many of Oliver Cromwell's characteristics – the debates explored as did no formal work of political philosophy the moral vision and the practical limits of the democratic faith: the dialogue of those who had undergone the heady experience of participatory democracy in their self-governing congregations and wished to translate the priesthood of believers into a non-theological language of consent to each and every law, and those who were also aware of the ties of existing structures, conventions and engagements, and who viewed consent as 'the result and not the condition' of democratic rule.[20]

During the 1930s and 1940s, the Levellers and Diggers assumed a higher profile than ever before: the enhanced level of participatory politics during the war and 'the huge upsurge of concern about citizenship and democracy' seemed to match 'the spirit which had animated the rank and file army agitators of 1647. 'I got the impression,' wrote Lindsay of the Eighth Army 'parliament' of 1944, 'that there had not been an army in England which discussed like this one, since the famous Puritan army which produced the Putney debates and laid the foundations of modern democracy.' The Leveller and Digger 'programmes' – first published in Haller's *Tracts on Liberty* of 1933 and widely disseminated during the war through further editions of their manifestos and pamphlets from the British Museum collections, and through discussion in the army education units – were thought to contain a native version of liberty, equality and fraternity: a precocious if somewhat quaintly expressed indigenous socialism.[21]

But there was a darker side to the age of religious reform. Cutting across the liberation of the human spirit was the collapse of the old village agrarian community and the catastrophic deterioration in the material conditions of the common people. This was the leading theme of Thorold Rogers, the great radical economic historian, whose '*Six Centuries of Work and Wages*' – a shortened version of his monumental history of agriculture and prices, which ran to eleven editions and was extensively used in worker educational study groups – provided another point of departure for socialist thinking. Rogers was accused of writing 'class history', but he claimed to be simply recording the impact of agricultural prices and wages on the lives of ordinary English people. What this demonstrated, he believed, was a spectacular growth of economic dependence and pauperism during the course of the sixteenth century – the outcome of short-sighted profit-making and 'deliberate government policy'. Rogers' history was not without its contemporary implications: the sixteenth century saw a new rural order, 'from which the present conditions in England may be gathered' – conditions which had to be reversed were 'the agricultural labourer' to be 'recall[ed] . . . to effective and hopeful industry'[22]

The loss of fifteenth-century peasant ease and independence was likewise traced in J. R. Green's even more popular and influential *Short History of the English People* and in such well-known studies as Hyndman's *Historical Basis of English Socialism*. In this reading of English history, as Raphael Samuel points out, 'land [w]as the fundamental idiom of class division . . . enclosure . . . the archetypal act of capitalist appropriation, and the long process by which the majority of the people were ejected from the soil . . . the great national tragedy'. The sixteenth- and seventeenth-century 'agrarian problem' fitted into the story of industrialization, urbanization, deprivation and brutalization, which formed the major theme of Victorian social commentary.[23] In this decline and fall of English freedom, peasant revolts constituted the paradigmatic instances of class protest, the high points, according to Green, in the 'unwearied battle of the common people' against oppression; to Tawney, 'the cry of a spirit that is departing and which in its agony utters words which are a shining light for all periods of change'. The historical imagination of English socialists was stirred far more by tales of Robin Hood and Wat Tyler than by any of the heroes of modern labour. As Samuel points out, the idiom was overwhelmingly preindustrial: Morris and Bax devoted more attention to fifteenth-century guilds than to nineteenth-century trade unions; Hyndman quoted Tudor complaints about enclosure only slightly less than he did Karl Marx; and as late as the 1930s 'Bows against Barons' could compete with 'Our Lenin' as popular communist party reading.[24]

The theme of lost rural rights also meshed into an even more ancient piece of myth-history, the story of ancient English liberty and the Norman Yoke. Green's 'captivating picture' of an Anglo-Saxon farmer commonwealth and Freeman's patriotic oratorio to the departed glories of Godric the Sheriff, Aelfric of Gelling and the fallen of Senlac, found their way into socialist history also.[25] The last days of Anglo-Saxon England joined hands with the age of Chaucer and Caxton, in the evocation of a democratic English nationalism which was challenged by the barriers of primogeniture, blood and language set up by the Normans and by the divisions born out of agrarian change. The theme of racial deprivation and degeneration – of an English character once self-reliant and independent, but now physically and spiritually stunted – had a particular resonance in the late nineteenth-century milieu of Social Darwinism; and it could equally be detected in the 'poignant chapters' of the Hammonds' threnody to the lost manhood of the English countryside, or in Froude's search amongst the sturdy farmers of 'Oceana' for a free and uncontaminated Anglo-Celtic racial stock.[26] It drew on a long tradition of folk-nationalism most eloquently articulated in the radical polemic of the late eighteenth century – which, in turn, drew heavily on the myth-making of the seventeenth-century Levellers and Diggers. In this respect, radical history could be said to have described a magic circle of invention which began and ended in the English Revolution.[27]

Revolutionary Puritanism took its place, therefore, in an imagined popular lineage stretching back through John Ball and Wat Tyler to even earlier anonymous defenders of Anglo-Saxon rights against their Norman overlords. 'The real history of England ha[d] yet to be written', but when it was, it would be constructed from the history of peasant revolts, the struggle for communal rights, and a long popular revolution from Langland's 'great poem in praise of social labour' to the campaign for a participatory working class culture in the 1930s.[28] Just as the composers of the period turned to the madrigal, the plain chant, the metrical psalm, and, above all, the folk-song of Tudor and Stuart England, rather than to the bombastic strains of 'Rule Britannia' and 'Crown Imperial' for the authentic voice of the nation,[29] so could historians conjure up a radical pedigree as truly English as the manor houses and country lanes invoked by their opponents. As Joseph Needham put it:

is it not of some value to English socialists tired of hearing communism identified with foreign sounding names and doctrines, to know that the Communists of the seventeenth century had names that run like English villages – John Lilburne, William Walwyn, Gerard Winstanley, Robert Lockyer, Giles Calvert, Anthony Sedley?[30]

The 'People's History' of England, which derived from these radical and democratic concerns and which fed into the Communist movement in the period of the Popular Front and World War II, was indeed a reply to the 'popular authoritarian memory' invoked by the Right, a reclamation of historical 'birthrights' by the party:

We became the inheritors of the Peasants' Revolt, of the Left of the English Revolution, of the pre-Chartist movement, of the women's suffrage movement from the 1790s to today. It set us in the right framework, it linked us with the past and gave us a more correct course for the future.[31]

But there was a certain irony in this, for the continuities condemned in the form of constitutional adaptation and the broadening of the ruling elite were reinstated at the level of a national–popular tradition, stretching all the way from the 'Norman Yoke' to the Welfare State. And for thoughtful Marxists, there was a further catch: by constructing an ideal 'Englishness' out of a single stream of social protest and a continuous radical consciousness, the 'people's history' exuded a certain classlessness – or worse: it tended to give a legitimation to an equally time-honoured political and social structure which it confronted.[32] The story of the 'common people' was 'a record of glorious struggle', but also of repeated and continuous defeats: of peasant risings repressed and mutinies put down. Even in the seventeenth century, Giant Privilege was never slain. Such a radicalism, one might conclude, was only an inverted Whiggism; it could celebrate the course of the 'revolution', but it could not give it an alternative meaning.

Democratic socialism, however, had more to offer than an episodic people's celebration or unwitting whiggish–hegemonic tale. The reclamation of the period from 1540 to 1640 owed most, perhaps, to the impact of 'that very good man', R. H. Tawney on a generation of Oxonians: not for nothing was it known as 'Tawney's century'.[33] Before World War I, he had lent his considerable authority to the radical version of lost rural rights propounded by Thorold Rogers: his *Agrarian Problem in the Sixteenth Century*, a scholarly yet impassioned analysis of the impact of enclosure and engrossing on the small peasant farmer – in retrospect a monument of special pleading based on suspect or tainted evidence – charted the catastrophic effects of what he depicted as the massive economic and moral displacements of the period.[34] During the 1920s, his *Religion and the Rise of Capitalism* – the seminal democratic socialist historical study of the interwar period – took up the theme of the divorce of economic and moral thinking in a broader and subtler way. It appeared to combine a critical analysis of the interplay of religious and social thought and practice in the bourgeois 'construction' of modern England, and an appreciation of the democratic, collectivist aspects of Puritanism which constituted its first radical challenge.[35] Thus far, his writing had largely focused on the roots of the 'Acquisitive Society':[36] though he traced its pedigree back to the sixteenth century – to the evils of commercial landlordism and to the new religion of trade – he grappled with the same 'spiritual malady' and worked from the same seam of moral diagnosis – and indignation – as did Arnold Toynbee and the Hammonds. But, in the 1940s, he turned from men-devouring sheep and charity-devouring religion, from the social theory of the new practices and ideas which made the sixteenth and early seventeenth century 'the cockpit of modern history', to structural explanations of this 'revolution'; from the secret or psychic history of commercial relations, to the study of its economic character: from modified Weber to qualified Marx.

Two interlocking interests became paramount: the role of burgeoning trade and price inflation in transforming Tudor society, and the consequent redistribution of landed property and its political consequences: in brief, the creation of a world market and 'the rise of the gentry'. Tawney always held a commercially directed view of capitalism rather than a productionist one: 'trade was the dynamic that set everything in motion'.[37] For the imperatives of that 'prodigy of trade', the export of woollen cloth, not only 'brought England conspicuously into world commerce', but also caused the development of pasture farming and the commercialization of agriculture. He had already studied the erosion of copyhold tenures and the transfer of profits to landlords at the expense of customary tenants. Now, he related this process to the emergence of a 'rising' gentry, 'rural entrepreneurs recruited from among the local landholders, the lawyers and the merchants . . . with whom indeed they formed but a single social class', aggressive rack-renters, hard-headed estate managers, the beneficiaries of 'the Price Revolution'.

'The wave of rising prices', the more shocking as it 'broke on a world' of 'currency famine', and a society 'crossed by lines of petrifaction which make modern rigidities seem elastic', struck at 'the dyke of customary obligations, static burdens, customary dues' and threw up 'a precocious species' of businesslike landlords: a Sir Thomas Thesham 'selling everything from rabbits . . . to wool', a Robert Loder, 'all piety and profits' – 'nauseous' figures in a new capitalist rural landscape.

To speak of the transition from a feudal to a bourgeois society is to decline upon a cliché. But a process difficult to epitomize in less hackneyed terms, has left deep marks on the social systems of most parts of Europe. What a contemporary described in 1600 as the conversion of 'a gentry addicted to war' into 'good husbands' who 'know how to improve their lands to the uttermost as the farmer or the countryman', may reasonably be regarded as an insular species of the same genus.[38]

Some adapted; others did not. And for every Giles Overreach, there was a Lord Henry the Harmless, his wealth locked up in frozen assets, majestic but unremunerative franchises, fixed freeholds created in an age of falling prices, prickly copyholds 'whose occupants pocketed an unearned increment while the real income of their landlord fell': feudal lords, hit by the overheads of their regal establishments, 'endless hospitality to neighbours', 'visits to court at once ruinous and unavoidable', and a whole range of traditional liabilities compounded by 'the demands of a new world of luxury and fashion'. The correspondence of Burleigh in the last days of Elizabeth 'reads like a report of a receiver in bankruptcy'; and in 1642, when 'all went into the melting pot', the debts of these aristocratic anachronisms were found to be astronomical. 'Of the commercial magnates who, a few years later, scrambled for confiscated estates, not a few . . . were creditors entering on properties long mortgaged to them'; not for the last time, it was discovered, 'that as a method of foreclosure, war was cheaper than litigation'.[39] 'Forms must be adapted to social facts, not facts to forms'. This was the judgement of James Harrington: 'the revolution of his day had been determined by changes . . . which passed unnoticed until too late; . . . the old regime had been destroyed neither by the errors of its rulers nor by the intransigence of parliament, but by impersonal forces too strong for both': namely, a radical shift in the 'Balance of Dominion' and a 'three-fold process of decay, growth and stabilization which profoundly modified the contours of the social landscape'.[40]

Tawney's work on these 'portentous landslides' in the distribution of property was to provide respectable academic substance to the more overtly Marxist explanation of the causes and significance of the English Revolution. But it also drew on the familiar Scottish model of social transformation, with burgeoning trade under the 'New Monarchies' as the motor of economic change, and the emergence of a new class of commercial landlords as its substance. By focusing on the market as against 'social relations' as the defining characteristic of capitalism, he appeared to invoke an already existing bourgeoisie struggling to create the conditions for its existence: precisely the opposite approach from what was to become Marxist orthodoxy in the 'transition' debate. Equally, there was little sense of a struggle between contending social forces, little focus on the parallel development of a plebeian class – elements which were to feature prominently in the work of the Historians' Group. Indeed, he remained wary of 'bourgeois revolution', not just because he recognized that the bourgeoisie fought on both sides during the Civil War, but because he distrusted any sort of one-track determinism. For Tawney, history was a maze and a lottery, not a straightforward 'record of development in one direction'. He was not so much pro- or anti- as pre-Marxist, one whose socialism was formed before the split between Social Democrat and Marxist parties; if there was a Marx in his philosophy, it was the champion of the underdog in history, not the celebrant of its inevitable victors. He could never associate himself with what he saw as the triumphalism of Marxist historians – the 'doxology' of what he was in the habit of referring to as 'uneducated Calvinism'.[41] His own socialism was not without nostalgia for the tradition of those 'who saw in the economic enterprise of an age which enclosed land and speculated on the exchanges, not the crudities of a young and brilliant civilization, but the collapse of public morality in a welter of disorderly appetites'. Locked up in the new Tawney of the 'gentry' and 'Harrington's interpretation of his age', was the old High Anglican moralist, who yearned for a synthesis of Christian and socialist thought; who hated parasitism and acquisitiveness in equal measure – the 'pigeon-headed' royal favourites and the unscrupulous speculators in monastic real estate alike and who was reluctant to condemn even authoritarian paternalism, when exercised in a good cause.[42] Tawney, maintains his biographer, was a 'socialist for all seasons'. His moral passion disguised but by no means expunged a considerable slipperiness of argument and exposition – an ambivalence which perhaps explained his posthumous role as the simultaneously resurrected patron saint of the 'hard left' of the Labour Party and the soft centre of the SDP.[43]

2.2   THE MARXIST–LENINIST MODEL

The revived English Revolution initially sported a less parochial parentage, manufactured in Moscow rather than at the LSE.[44] The Marxism of Hill and his colleagues was intended to be of the hard-headed rather than the soft-hearted variety, to draw on notions of class warfare and power seizure rather than on the Sermon on the Mount, to appeal to 'science' and 'facts we can test' rather than to sentiment. Because they had no access to the critical revision of Marxist theory on the Continent, or to any native tradition of Marxist exegetics, their Marxism drew on a selection of sacred texts heavily biased towards 'scientism' and positivism, and on current Soviet reinterpretations made with an eye to Russian conditions or Communist Party strategy. In the long run, perhaps, once the Stalinist accretions had been purged, the orthodox grounding was to prove a strength – to provide a theoretical backbone, sometimes lacking in more heavily but flabbily populated areas of continental Marxist writing.[45]

It was characteristic of British Marxism that political economy, rather than the neo-Hegelian philosophy or contemporary political arguments pivotal in France, should have provided the framework for historical studies. The reworking of Marx's genealogy of modernism in the field of English history in the 1930s and 1940s was pioneered by the Cambridge economist Maurice Dobb. A dedicated Communist party member since the early 1920s, one of the first and most steadfast Soviet 'pilgrims', Dobb was remembered by his pupils as a persuasive proselytizer and a 'remarkable expounder' of Marxist theory, who consistently argued that economic analysis only made sense when 'joined to the study of historical development'.[46] His *Studies in the Development of Capitalism*, long gestated and only published in 1946, joyously hailed by the party as a demonstration of 'the superiority of the Marxist approach over the bourgeois eclecticism,[47] according to Hobsbawm, 'formulated our . . . central problem'. In a sense, it grew out of and in opposition both to the vein of neo-classical theory dominant in the Economics Faculty of his native Cambridge, and to the equally hegemonic and somewhat narrowly directed empiricism associated with the historical work of Sir John Clapham and his followers. For Dobb, capitalism was defined after the manner of Marx as a historically specific mode of production and a set of productive relations rather than a mechanism of exchange, a type of commercial activity or a 'culture'. And its genesis was to be discovered – again after the manner traced in Marx's chapters on primitive accumulation – in the breakdown of the previously existing mode of feudal production, and the subsequent emergence of a capitalist class from amongst the class of agricultural producers. Thus, argued Dobb, Marx's 'truly revolutionary' route from feudalism to capitalism, was traced in England during the sixteenth and early seventeenth centuries through the reciprocal movement of yeomen into trade and industry and of mercantile capital into the countryside – a development of capitalist relations in agriculture and manufacturing which led to the upheavals of the Civil War and the replacement of one social order by another. 'The portentous significance of the Puritan victory' could be gauged by the 'dramatic acceleration in the accumulation of capital and its investment in industrial enterprise during the ensuing half century' – changes which in turn provided the necessary foundation for the Industrial Revolution.[48]

Dobb's work traced the development of English capitalism with a theoretical sophistication and consistency of exposition which was altogether new; it provided Marx's sketch of primitive accumulation with a wealth of historical detail it hitherto had lacked; and it placed the English Revolution in the broader perspective of capitalist formation on a European scale. At the same time, it was problematic in a number of respects, for it appeared to explain the transition from feudalism to capitalism in terms which younger Communist historians were to find misleadingly abstract and schematic. Although it attempted to steer a course between ahistorical schematization and the 'nihilism' of historical specificity, its emphasis was on the internal dynamics of base and superstructure and on modes of production which were superseded or which triumphed through their own inefficiencies and contradictions or 'the inner logic of [their] own progressive nature'. But by focusing on these somewhat anonymous internal mechanisms – on the gradual disintegration of feudalism, as small rural proprietors sought to loosen the bonds of feudal exploitation, and on the subsequent development of capitalism as a system of production encompassing wage labour and surplus profit – Dobb veered towards a 'single-track presentation of English history', which seemed to neglect the specifics of political and cultural change and to minimize the 'discontinuities' and revolutionary 'ruptures' in the making of modern industrial society.

The narrowly directed analysis of feudalism as an economic bond between lord and peasant, the attenuated treatment of the state in the determination of social relations, and the underdeveloped understanding of class agency and ideology, also made for a number of difficulties in explaining the process by which one productive mode was replaced by another: difficulties which were to invite a whole set of evolutionary heresies. For he appeared to proffer three decisive periods in the long-term development of capitalism, stretching from the crisis of the feudal order in the fourteenth century through to the Industrial Revolution of the late eighteenth and early nineteenth, rather than one decisive moment in which 'two systems directly confronted each other and fought it out for supremacy'. True, he rejected Sweezy's heterodox 'solution' to this elongated transition in the shape of an intermediate mode of 'pre-capitalist commodity production'. Indeed, he loyally insisted on the continuation of the feudal order as an 'integument' or fetter to further growth, until swept aside by 'a new class with a new mode of production' in the seventeenth century, in a struggle 'which bears all the marks of a classic bourgeois revolution'. But he was largely unable to articulate the actual dynamics of what he dutifully referred to as the crucial episode in the whole history of European capitalism.[49]

Current Soviet writing, in a sense, offered something of an antidote to Dobb's formulaic trajectories.[50] Soviet historians, said Hill, started with one great advantage over their English counterparts: they had a first-hand acquaintance a social order 'a great deal more like seventeenth century England than anything we know'. Most of them had experienced Tsarist 'tyranny', war, political breakdown and, of course, revolution. Through the example of Lenin and Stalin, they had learnt the precise relationship between bourgeois and socialist modes of political and social change, between the more or less rapid bourgeois conquest of political power and the long haul of socialist transformation: the economic, administrative and cultural problems of building socialism in an isolated and backward peasant society.[51]

Clearly, Hill experienced his year of study in Moscow from 1935 to 1936 as a training in political and social realism.[52] After a distinguished undergraduate career at Balliol and a fellowship at All Souls, it must have been a crash course in the privations of ordinary life. But it was an emancipation also: after the exclusions of the Oxford syllabus, the breadth and verve of Russian historians

seems to have been a revelation. At the same time, their work
was lacking in empirical rigour – something which Hill saw it as
his task to remedy. His earliest work summarized recent *Soviet
Interpretations of the Interregnum* and writings on *The Agrarian Legislation of the Revolution*[53] – interpretations which 'from an English
point of view' appeared to be built on inadequate evidence, but
which opened up ground 'where Anglo-Saxons fear to tread'. He
was always to take his role as Soviet evangel seriously;[54] and in
a sense, these early 'utilitarian' articles established the agenda of
his own academic 'curriculum vitae' over the next twenty years:
the study of the Civil War as a conflict of classes, or as a more
complex division between the economically backward and progressive elements in town and country; the attack on episcopacy
as part of a bourgeois onslaught on the feudal hierarchical order;
the subsequent split between Presbyterians and Independents as
'a struggle between commercial and industrial capital'; and the
Leveller movement as a half-fulfilled rising of independent artisan masters and peasants against social inequality and scarcity –
'Jacobins manqués' who experienced 'their Thermidor before they
had won power because they had never been determined enough
in seizing it'.

His stay in Moscow coincided with a period of intense debate
in the Soviet academy. The struggle to reform the teaching of
history had gone to the very highest levels of the party, with the
Seventeenth Congress denouncing the hitherto authoritative work
of the 'Old Bolshevik' historical 'Commissar', N. M. Pokrovsky,
for its economic determinism and sociological schematization.[55]
During the 1930s, Pokrovsky became the whipping boy of an ideologically cleansed academic establishment: a historical heresiarch,
accused of just about every error in the party lexicon ranging
from 'rotten liberalism' to 'infantile Left Wing Communism'. The
real gravamen of the charges against him was that his Bolshevism and his Marxism never cohered: that, for all his professed
militancy, his acceptance of economics as 'a self-sufficient historical force acting without any intervening links', led to a Marxism
without dialectics, class war or revolutionary struggle – something which could be accepted by any bourgeois. This was particularly evident in his delineation of the period from the sixteenth
to the nineteenth centuries as a transitional era marked by the
existence of a rich and influential mercantile class and by an
Absolute Monarchy, which corresponded to the 'dictatorship of

Merchant Capital'. 'Obsessed' with changes in the sphere of exchange and finance, and unable to appreciate the difference between a society in which merchants found themselves a niche and one in which they had become the directors of production, he had produced a piece of 'reformist' historical 'illiteracy', which seriously underestimated the autonomy of the state, minimized the smashing of feudal fetters by new productive forces, and left no room for the actions of the masses, their leaders and political organizations.[56]

In ways other than those historical, and for an impressionable young Marxist, Hill's Moscow apprenticeship was happily timed, coming after the massive upsurge in industrial production had turned Russia into the economic miracle of the age, and after Stalin had enunciated the consolidation of the revolution and the stabilization of the new Soviet system.[57] Above all, it took place against the backdrop of disintegration in the West. The capitalist era was seemingly grinding to a halt: its factories idle, its workers thrown on to the streets. Fascism, virulent mutation of a dying capitalism, was on the march, its every advance connived at by Europe's traditional elites. Fearful of the egalitarian uses to which democracy might be put and forced to choose between their democratic professions and their class interests, men like Baldwin and Chamberlain opted for privilege and authority every time; while on the Left, parliamentary socialism and gradualism stood condemned in the pathetic self-deluding twilight of Ramsey MacDonald, captive Prime Minister of an increasingly Tory, National government.[58]

Betrayed by 'reformist' leaders who had achieved nothing but open collaboration with the enemy, appalled at the inequalities and injustices of their bourgeois society, and with a premonition of catastrophe around the corner, intellectuals on the Left were almost irresistibly drawn to the Communist Party.[59] And in the 1930s, membership of the Communist Party meant commitment to the USSR. The entire world was 'in the grip of chaos'; the Soviet Union alone was 'the lifeline of salvation, the beacon from which the light of Marxism still shines', the promised land.[60] Here, after all, was something to believe in; 'here', as one notable literary convert was to put it, 'is the hope of the world'. Trade unionists could look to it as the workers' state of full employment, no bosses and a seven hour day; socialist planners, a 'New Civilization' where the masses were organized by a dedicated and capable elite; radical humanists, a society 'capable of realizing cultural potentialities only glimpsed at in the West'; international socialists, the focus of anti-fascist solidarity; frustrated revolutionaries, the home of a revolution in action: for each a mirror image of their most personal socialist aspirations – a spirit country lost or concealed in their native land. Communism, as Orwell put it in a famous phrase, was 'the patriotism of the deracinated'.[61]

In Hill's case, the experiences of Soviet Russia were crucial to his understanding of the historical process. Looking ahead – as Marxists were wont to do – and with a global perspective, the Russian experiment in 'bringing civilization' and 'agrarian self-government' to backward people was bound to have an enormous influence on precapitalist societies in Eastern Europe, Asia and Africa. For the contemporary industrialized world, wallowing in the contradictions of bourgeois liberalism and a market economy, 'socialism and the Soviet single party system offered a solution to the conflict between economic planning and political liberty'. Most of all, to the historian of England's seventeenth century, the Russia of the 1920s and 1930s had a special resonance: Lenin and Stalin had revitalized and extended the dreams of an earlier revolutionary era, of giving the land to the peasants and workers, releasing 'the untapped forces of resistance to capitalism . . . latent in the people' and restoring 'their right to live in the possibility that they too might be served by the whole force of the modern centralized state'.[62]

'We are closely linked to the land of socialism with every fibre of our being': the commitment to Russia gave anchorage and empirical content to socialist beliefs. It made sense of the Marxist unity of theory and practice, invested a reading of the past with a sense of the present, and provided the laws of history with an end point: a society moving into a post-historical age where unalienated human beings and rationally organized human agencies would take charge.[63] But it also extracted a heavy price – the renunciation of intellectual freedom, the sacrifice of deeply rooted humanitarian principles, the surrender of theoretical consistency to the vagaries of Soviet policy. Eventually the strain would become too great and there would be a parting of the ways, a severance of Marxist theory and Russian practice, dated variously according to the degree of sensibility and commitment, 1939, 1948, 1956, 1968. Until that happened, so great was the investment, emotional and intellectual, that the convert had to explain away the stories of police terror, executions and slave labour, or to parade the extenuating circumstances: the dead weight of Russian history, the need to judge the reality as 'an experiment', carried out without any blueprints or precedents, 'in conditions of exceptional difficulty with desperately inadequate resources ... and in the face of the avowed hostility of practically every other government in the civilized world'.[64] As the 'link' frayed, there was the comforting illusion that no compromises had been made; or there was a sense of the compensations – the shared comradeship, the mental stimulus and the heightened sharpness of vision that had come with the faith. And when 'the tight-rope snapped', there was the safety net of Marxism: a theory so fine meshed and elastic that it could be worked into many a shape by the half-fallen but still dialectically supple veteran acrobats. The narrative of Marxist historical writing in England, as elsewhere, charts their subsequent contortions.[65]

The Marxist rereading of English history did not, of course, spring fully armed from student years in Moscow,[66] from the projected Marx House History Faculty syllabus of 1939, or even from the conferences and discussions which culminated in the formation of 'The Historians' Group of the Communist Party' in 1946.[67] It was always qualified and underpinned by a more ecumenical native Socialism. But, initially at least, the orthodox party flavour was unmistakable. And whether because of his slight seniority and early academic eminence, because of the cast of his mind or his crucial role as the instigator of 'The Historians' Group', and its continuing link with the world of Soviet scholarship, Hill's work in particular was to retain many of the features of its parentage.[68] 'Le style, c'est l'homme meme', and Hill's writing was always to be distinguished by a simplicity of expression and argument, a lack of nuance and a certain innocence or impatience of theory which marked it off from the rarefied subtleties of Marxist exegetic on the Continent. Although – as we shall see – the plain 'russet-coated' manner which he cultivated, corresponded to the idioms of seventeenth-century dissent, it was also in the 1930s and 1940s the approved Party manner – one which paralleled the expository virtues of the much beloved 'Uncle Joe' Stalin: his ability to cut his way through Marx's theoretical conundrums and to reduce 'questions which puzzle intellectuals into plain good sense'.[69]

The simplified building block manner of presentation, the accumulation and detailed marshalling of facts and 'proof texts', the card-index mentality and belief in the ideological neutrality of knowledge, also corresponded to the overwhelming 'scientism' of the British Party at this time. The 'red' professors of science – J. B. S. Haldane, Hyman Levy, Lancelot Hogben, Joseph Needham and, above all, J. D. Bernal – had acquired a pre-eminent position in the Communist Party's intellectual life in the 1930s and 1940s.[70] Its leading highbrow journal, *The Modern Quarterly*, first published in 1938 – its editorial council dominated by natural scientists, and its credo spelled out in a statement of aims which affirmed the role of scientific thought and management as the prime mover of human history – was indicative of the thinking of the party then, just as *The New Left Review*, *The Socialist Register* and *Marxism Today* were to reflect the broader theoretical and humanist character of British Marxism in the 1960s and 1970s. Marxism, according to Bernal, was not so much a creed or a cosmogony 'which men willy nilly must follow', as a method of scientific analysis and a guide to action.[71]

The method of scientific Marxism, he argued, was essentially critical, and its 'ultimate criterion' one of 'practical verification' rather than the making of new discoveries.[72] Bernal's discriminations were to be reflected in Hill's working procedures. Although his erudition is monumental and his reading of seventeenth-century printed materials awe inspiring, it is noticeable and suggestive that he has never conducted extensive archival researches: he seems to have preferred his materials ready made for use. Equally, it is striking that he has never written a conventional biography: he has always favoured a kaleidoscopic ensemble of biographical fragments, arranged under appropriate subject-headings. Simple-minded Rankean 'discovery' of a discrete past or resurrection of an unfolding, integral life-story or personality could never be an end in itself. Nor could he be accused of the academic scholasticism which enveloped much of Western Marxism in the 1950s and 1960s. Rather his faults were those of a militant involvement in the present 'battle of ideas'; a conviction that seventeenth-century investigations served contemporary political purposes; at times, a 'fixism' or a utilitarian positivism, a heaping up of decontextualized data and pellet-like pieces of information to 'prove' a thesis or argument already known to be true and held in advance.[73]

The Communism of the 1930s combined scientific certainty and political assurance in equal measure. The approved doctrinal enclosure of its Marxism, code-named 'dialectical materialism' –

'diamet' for short – was set out in the *History of the Communist Party of the Soviet Union*, commonly known as the *Short Course*, written under Stalin's supervision and piously attributed to the 'great Marxist thinker' himself, 'a brilliant sketch' of 'the science of history', said Hill, which 'party members and lecturers knew virtually by heart'.[74] Stalin was not a theoretical Neanderthal, and the scholars and party members who read his work as Holy Writ were not unintelligent or unenlightened; but the *Short Course* propounded methodological procedures and inculcated habits of mind which were to leave a lasting imprint on the 1930s generation of communist historians. To begin with, history itself became the major source of the ideological education of militants. In Stalinist theory, there was, as it were, a direct line between the axioms set out in the famous fourth chapter 'on dialectical and historical materialism' and the raw data of the past, and between the operations of the dialectic in the physical and the social worlds and the apparently chaotic sequences of history. Thus:

> the connection and interdependence of all the phenomena of social life are laws of the development of society, and not something accidental. Hence, social life . . . ceases to be an agglomeration of accidents and becomes the history of the development of society according to regular laws, and the study of history becomes a science . . . as precise as . . . biology, capable of making use of the laws of development of society for practical purposes.[75]

These were large and confident claims, and they imposed certain obligations on historians. Individual investigation was not sufficient to produce real knowledge of the past or mastery of its laws and lessons: an official interpretation had to be given. This did not necessarily preclude intense debate and vigorous discussion: individual contributions might well be sought, various points of view canvassed, Marxist and Soviet texts 'reviewed', even 'the best modern bourgeois research' sifted, before 'formulations were agreed upon'. Even so, there was always the expectation of an authoritative closure; discussions were expected to produce 'consensus'. Erring brethren were sometimes called upon to perform cleansing rituals of 'self-criticism'; and, of course, once a particular interpretation was accepted, dissenters were expected to keep their mental reservations to themselves and to propound correct doctrine.[76]

The history of the Communist Party of the Soviet Union was

widely regarded as exemplary – the direct and necessary product of Marxist–Leninist doctrine. Russia's Revolution was the only true socialist revolution and the subsequent history of the Soviet Union the culmination of socialist history. For other histories, this naturalistic sequence had curious and conflicting implications. Almost inevitably it underlined the monist view of historical development: societies were measured according to the various stages reached along the road to socialism; revolutions according to their proximate relationship to Russia's 1917. At the same time, the identification of socialist theory with the policies of the Soviet state introduced a random element into the historical trajectory. Since whatever served Soviet interests was progressive and whatever did not was reactionary, and since the interests of the Soviet state were in constant flux, the identity of these forces could change with some rapidity.[77]

In these respects, the *Short Course* mirrored an ideology characterized by an extreme flexibility of content and a rigidity of argument and format. Thus, from time to time, during periods of alliance with other socialist parties, in the late 1930s and again in the 1950s, communist theory envisaged the possibility of multiple paths to socialism corresponding to the different traditions and circumstances of each society. At others, it insisted on the straight and narrow way of violent revolution, the smashing of state power – the High Road of Russia's 1917. As long as they were tied to the party and their history was tailored to the changing policies of the Kremlin, communist historians outside Russia also would produce work which was deeply sectarian or more broadly based and patriotic, according to the politics of the moment. But communist writing was also marked by the wooden repetition of formulas. The *Short Course* offered a simplification and standardization of party doctrine, a straightening out of Marxist theory in the interests of current reality. Histories written under its influence would be schematic, reductionist, accessible, presentist.[78]

The simplification of doctrine also had much to do with their broadly based educational purposes. Few of the early communist historians had any formal Marxist training; there were no university Marxist courses, virtually no Marxist historians in the universities. Right up until the 1950s, 'adult education was the medium through which [their] histories were organized'. Usually they were conceived as student manuals, guides for party lecturers around the country, outlines for further work and discussion, rather than specialized monographs for an academic elite.[79] Since history served didactic purposes and since it was crucial to what was termed the 'battle of ideas', it was invariably conceived in combative terms, often defining itself by opposition to what was then deemed the prevailing bourgeois orthodoxy. Just as Stalin had defined a correct line against Trotskyite heresies and the Soviet Academy had unearthed the multiple errors of Pokrovsky, so too would British communist historians bring to light the evident explanatory evasion, the shallow contingencies and the despairing 'providentialism' of Whig historians. 'The Marxist renewal of British history' ran parallel with a critique of 'non-Marxist history and its reactionary implications': Whig theory was false, argued Hill, because it 'emphasizes constitutional forms and ignores their social content'; and it 'breaks down as soon as it comes up against facts that we can test'.[80]

At the same time, the facts which Hill appealed to had a certain malleability. The distinction between truth in the generic and in the conventional sense has always been obscure in Marxist theory; and in the Leninist–Stalinist version prevalent in the 1930s and 1940s, something could be known to be true and selectively 'verified' as such, because it corresponded to the 'laws of historical development', whether or not it could be 'proved' by universally admitted scientific procedures. These, of course, were a characteristic 'bourgeois illusion'.[81] Rather, the doctrine of class consciousness, coupled with the privileged cognitive position of the party and its vision of the social totality, enabled it to discern the inner kernel of truth and the connectedness of historical phenomena, as opposed to their contingent and apparently incoherent form considered from a narrowly empirical and hence an 'unscientific' point of view.[82]

Classes were, of course, the major protagonists of history. 'In the heyday of world Communism', as Raphael Samuel explains, the primacy of class was 'unchallenged whether as an explanatory category or a rhetorical device'.[83] In the military metaphor, so central to Marxist thinking of the period, where men and (ever so occasionally) women made their own history through 'struggle', classes were positioned on a scale of combativity, characterized in terms of the historical mission they were charged with.[84] Class struggle was a dialectical drama in which the young and creative challenged the parasitic and decayed. Class consciousness in this context was used in 'a metaphorical rather than a literal sense', and was not concerned with social or cultural peculiarities – with the languages of class, as it were – but rather with historic actions and ultimate ends. 'Class in its Leninist appropriation was a moral rather than a social signifier', and could best be measured by political allegiance and engagement. 'Politics was not so much a reflection of social class as constitutive of it'; it was not social being that determined consciousness, but political consciousness and revolutionary practice that gave a direction to social being.[85]

Revolution marked the transfer of class power, with the degree of struggle, violence or civil war determined by the historical conditions and the methods of resistance chosen by the ruling class. Sometimes, as in 1917, revolutionaries would encounter only token resistance indicating that the progressive forces had sided with insurgents and that the old order was rotten to the core; at others as in 1848 or again in 1870, they would be driven back – victims of a more astute and more entrenched ruling class; at others again, as in the English Civil War, the contending forces would be more finely balanced, sufficient to carry off a bourgeois revolution but insufficient for popular liberation. The job of the historian was, therefore, to measure the degrees of resistance and militancy; in the words of the *Short Course*, to trace 'the tremendous organizing, mobilizing and transforming value of new ideas, new theories, new political views and new political institutions ... whose mission it is to abolish by force the old relations of production through an act of conscious revolution'; to replace the economism, the formalism and the gradualism of earlier Marxist historians with a more realistic 'Jacobin' account of seizing power and reshaping society from the top.[86]

2.3 THE FIRST BOURGEOIS REVOLUTION

These concerns set the tone for Hill's earliest work, *The English Revolution*, the orthodox party essay of 1940. The English Revolution was 'a great social movement like the French':

> An order that was essentially feudal was destroyed by violence, a new and capitalist social order created in its place. The Civil War was a class war, in which the despotism of Charles I was defended by the reactionary forces of the established church and feudal land-

lords. Parliament beat the King because it could appeal to the enthusiastic support of the trading and industrial classes.[87]

The changes in the balance of property, concurrently observed by Tawney, were sharpened into an even more fundamental polarization between two different types of social organization, the one a bastard feudal society of rentiers and parasites, the other a new world of capitalist farmers and merchant middlemen, 'two social systems and their ideologies' in collision. And the victory of the latter was given a triumphalist reading: 'of the then existing alternatives', the bourgeoisie's was a cause 'without which advance to a better society would have been impossible': 'The parliamentarians thought they were fighting God's battles. They were certainly fighting those of posterity, throwing off an intolerable incubus to further advance.'

Hill was utterly sceptical of the Tory reading of Stuart paternalism; rather, 'the interests of the new class of capitalist merchants and farmers were temporarily identical with those of the small peasantry and artisans and journeymen'. Conversely, the victory of Cromwell and the parliamentary leaders would not have occurred without 'the efforts and the sacrifices of the common soldiers'; and the revolution 'would never have achieved all it did without the "plebeian methods" of the Independents'.[88] The fact that the bourgeoisie turned on its allies, the Levellers and the Diggers, did not alter the fact of the alliance. Or, as Hill put it in a rebuke to a purely people's history – 'a record of glorious struggles' but also 'continuous defeats' – which omitted Milton and Cromwell, Hampden and Pym from its account: 'Let us not surrender them to Chamberlain (not that he is likely to want to remember them). . . All England's past is ours including the best part of the past of the bourgeoisie.'[89] Hill's work was celebratory: composed in 1940 as the first part of a collective volume for the tercentenary of the revolution, it resembled Georges Lefebvre's *Quatre-Vingt Neuf*, written for the 150th anniversary of the events of 1789 and celebrating the first year of the French Revolution as a cooperative labour of every section of French society and especially the middle class and artisan, a sort of 1939 Popular Front before its time.[90]

Yet, it had little of Lefebvre's appeal to national revolutionary consensus. To begin with, as Trevelyan's apotheosis of compromise, conciliation and the prudential policies of Stanley Baldwin

and Neville Chamberlain in the year of Munich, had amply demonstrated, there was no agreement as to the precise location of
England's 'Revolution'.[91] So that Hill's celebration of 1640 was
partly designed as a riposte to the constitutional myth of 1688, in
a manner that combined historical and contemporary polemic. The
real question of power, he argued, had been decided once and
for all in the struggles of the 1640s, with the smashing of the
feudal aristocratic state and society. To achieve that victory, however, the bourgeoisie had been forced to rely on popular forces
and had opened the Pandora's box of democratic revolution. The
following thirty-five years did nothing to change these fundamentals: Charles II, like Cromwell before him, was 'the defender'
of 'the essentials of the (bourgeois) revolution against attacks from
the Left', not the restorer of 'the old order'; and James's subsequent attempt to set the clock back and to 'seize absolute power'
was 'doomed to fail'. The year 1688, therefore, was not 'the English Revolution' but 'a frustrated counter-revolution', a renewed
rallying of bourgeoisie and landowners under a Williamite flag
of convenience against the crown's attempted alliance of feudal
remnants, peasants and radical petty bourgeoisie. For the victors,
it was only glorious, in so far as it was not revolutionary; for the
vanquished, especially in Ireland, it was certainly not bloodless.[92]

The essay of 1940, Hill later recalled, was a manifesto 'written
in great haste and anger', a 'last will and testament', composed
by a young communist off to fight in a war 'which good socialist
policies could have prevented'.[93] Its stridency of tone and argument probably owed something to the particular period of its
composition and publication. Lefebvre's book was written at the
height of and reflected the democratic agendas and the inter-class
cooperation of 'popular front politics'; Hill's was composed in
the winter and spring of 1940, after the signing of the Nazi–Soviet
pact, when the party line had been redefined as one of opposition to the imperialist war through the struggle against 'the most
reactionary force in the world', 'the main stranglers of popular
revolution in every country' – the British ruling class.[94] Fascism
might be the immediate threat; liberalism was the real enemy.
Hill had grown up under the shadow of World War I, persuaded,
as were so many of his generation, that it was the product of the
expanding imperialist conflicts of advanced capitalism. Like many
militant socialists, he was equally convinced that the causes of
World War II were essentially those of the World War I; and that

only international socialist policies could have saved Europe from catastrophe. But it was precisely these policies which the British ruling elite had sabotaged, preferring illusory agreement with Germany to the common cause. Stalin had forestalled the reactionary alliance aimed at the Soviet Union; and Hitler had turned against his erstwhile abettors. So that when war broke out in 1939, it was as much the result of British bad faith and miscalculation as of German aggression: Great Britain, as one Communist put it, was 'the fountainhead of disaster'. A history written under the influence of these contemporary assumptions could not but be provocative.[95]

Hill restated the theory of a class controlled political apparatus and its revolutionary 'smashing' in its simplest form. Indeed, there was a note of bitterness in his nailing of the beast of the feudal state. Fiscal rackets and impositions, the resuscitation of feudal dues, authoritarian 'conceptions of colonization in Ireland', the revival of prerogative courts, 'the rusty sword' of ecclesiastical oppression, a foreign policy geared to the interests of Catholic 'reconquest' – these were not just ill-judged expedients or mistaken policies, but integral features of a viciously refeudalized court and church bureaucracy. Under the Tudors, the bourgeoisie and the feudal gentry had been able 'to get along together'. But now, 'a hardening process' had occurred and the interests of the state coincided only with those of an obsolete 'rentier' class and a parasitic nobility:

> The issue was one of political power. The bourgeoisie rejected Charles I's Government because . . . it tried to perpetuate a feudal social order when the new conditions existed for free capitalist development . . . The opposition . . . were fighting a system. Before the social order they needed, could be secure, they had to smash the old bureaucratic machinery, defeat the cavaliers in battle. The heads of a king and many peers had to roll in the dust before it could be certain that future kings and the peerage would recognize the dominance of the new class.[96]

One could not but think of the events of 1917, with Charles in the role of Czar Nicholas and Laud an unreconstructed Orthodox Patriarch – or, as Hill himself has suggested, regard it as a commentary on post-Munich Britain, in which the king was 'conflated with Neville Chamberlain' and the Archbishop with the Tory party at prayer.[97]

The model, of course, was not so much Marxist, as Leninist or Stalinist. Although Marx had always emphasized the dependence of the state on civil society (especially when he was self-consciously putting Hegel back on his feet), he had also been aware of its partial autonomy and possible balancing role between the social classes. Indeed, in his comments on Absolute Monarchy, he had gone further, arguing that its administrative structures 'were a peculiarly bourgeois instrument', serving both as a monarchical 'counter-weight' against the nobility and a possible conduit for nascent middle-class society in its struggle against feudalism.[98] Its supposed destruction in seventeenth-century England or eighteenth century France, therefore, could never of itself 'stand in' for the transformation from feudalism to capitalism. According to Stalin's new doctrine of the 'active superstructure', however, the state was at once 'the locale of revolution and power', the chosen instrument of historical change, and the vehicle of a ruling class, defined solely according to the nature of its possessor, whether feudal, bourgeois or proletarian. And Absolutism – or its Tsarist variant – was no mercantile–capitalist hybrid, no incubator of new bourgeois class relations, but rather a variant and a peculiarly virulent form of feudal class rule.[99] This was Hill's position also: 'The absolute monarchy was a different form of feudal monarchy from the feudal-estates monarchy which preceded it; but the ruling class remained the same, just as a republic, a constitutional monarchy and a fascist dictatorship can all be forms of the rule of the bourgeoisie.'[100] Hill's first version of the English Revolution was of a dramatic rupture with the 'feudal state', culminating in the abolition of the Monarchy, the Church and the House of Lords. In this respect, at least, it faithfully paralleled the voluntarist tendencies implicit in Marxist histories of the French Revolution: there was the same emphasis on political confrontation, revolutionary action and ideology as the catalysts of class formation, and social change – elements privileged in current Soviet theory.[101]

It was ironic, therefore, that an essay, 'drafted . . . after very full discussion by a group of Marxist historians', 'based' on the latest 'Soviet work', 'approved by the Centre Propaganda Department', and intended to strike a blow for the party in the 'battle of ideas', should have sparked off one of those obscure but bitter doctrinal disputes for which the CPGB was justly famous.[102] A review written by Jurgen Kuczynski, under the pseudonym P. F., for Palme Dutt's *Labour Monthly*, while welcoming the resurrection of a 'young and vigorous past' which the 'bourgeois world dare not remember', disagreed fundamentally with the 'interpretation of the course of political events and of economic conditions and movements leading up to the Civil War'.[103] Citing Marx's comments on the agrarian transformation of sixteenth-century England, Kuczynski argued that the economic base and its concomitant social relations in Tudor and Stuart England were already capitalist, that the monarchy was both bourgeois and absolute, and that the Civil War was simply a political response to Charles's attempted 'counter-revolution' in church and state.[104]

Sixteenth-century England, he maintained, had ceased to be feudal in any meaningful sense: the mass suicide of the Wars of the Roses had transformed 'the ruling class of feudal landowners into a new class of bourgeois aristocrats': a peculiarly successful blend of old families 'enriched by the agricultural revolution following the Black Death'. . . 'purely upstart families endowed with royal or confiscated monastic property'. . . and new city families 'enabled by their success in industry and trade to acquire the land and often the titles of old feudal holders'. Middle-class Tudor England was alive and well, and 'over the bridge which sheep and cloth formed between the country and the city, landowners and city men walked arm in arm'.[105] The bourgeoisie dominated the political life of the country: a truth variously illustrated by the position in the Council, the Courts and the Houses of Parliament of the Walsinghams, the Cecils and the Cromwells, by the new literature and ideology associated with Shakespeare and the English Bible, and by Elizabeth herself: 'not a feudal monarch bowing to the demands of an oppressed capitalist class', but 'the most prominent capitalist in capitalist bourgeois society'. 'If we compare conditions in Britain under Elizabeth around 1600 and conditions in France around 1780 we notice a decisive difference. In Britain capitalism dominated decaying feudalism, in France feudalism still held capitalism in fetters.'[106] The year 1640, unlike 1789, therefore, marked no transfer of state power from one class to another, no decisive battle in the transition from feudalism to capitalism, no revolution 'both in the strictly scientific and in the practical political meaning of that term'; rather, the Civil War was a Great Rebellion, 'a struggle on the part of the bourgeoisie to hold state power against its usurpation by a monarchy that had formerly been their instrument'.[107]

Kuczynski's article caused something of a storm amongst the party faithful, with the correctness of Hill's original formulation stoutly defended in subsequent numbers of *Labour Monthly* by Douglas Garman, Dona Torr, and, in a more qualified manner, by Maurice Dobb.[108] To begin with, Kuczynski was criticized for misrepresentation: far from 'underrat[ing] the capitalist elements and exaggerat[ing] the feudal remnants' in Tudor and Stuart society, Hill had pointed to important agricultural changes and to dramatic commercial and industrial developments; indeed, he had gone out of his way to show 'how an industrial revolution took place in the century before 1640'. But he had asserted that the fundamental structure of society was unchanged: that 'there were still countless legal restrictions on unhampered capitalist utilization of landed property'; that there were feudal tenures and manorial courts, trade monopolies and traditional Crown revenues; above all, that 'the political structure of the state' – 'the strongest of the fetters' on new economic development and 'the last to be broken' – 'remained essentially feudal'. Almost inevitably in a Communist Party fracas of this sort, Kuczynski was attacked for misquotation and misinterpretation of Holy Writ. Marx and Engels had not denied the English Civil War a critical place in the genealogy of modernism; nor had they distinguished between the 'gradual' erosion of feudal fetters in England, and a 'smash[ing] at one blow in France', as Kuczynski claimed; rather, they viewed 1640 and 1789 as comparable episodes in the making of modern capitalist society, marking the forcible overthrow of feudal–absolutist state power and the political accession of the bourgeoisie.[109]

More importantly, Kuczynski stood accused of failing to understand the dialectical distinction between material forces of production and the existing property relations, and of 'ascribing to Marxism a grotesquely vulgar concept of direct transition from large-scale feudal economy to capitalist economy'. As a result, he had ignored the 'decisive qualitative transformation of the social system' brought about 'by co-ordinated class action demanding the supreme expression of unified will, action and leadership'. What he had done was to repeat the undialectical errors of Pokrovsky: plotting the trajectory of modern history 'as a succession of neatly labelled social orders', confusing the gradual onset of middle-class society with 'the revolutionary transference of political power', 'adopting an exceptionalist and evolutionary theory of English development', thereby 'ranging himself with

Trevelyan against Marx and obscuring the vital lessons of 1640 for today'.[110] 'The capitalist state, however much today it may be aging, is a lion that was certainly not whelped in peace; and, if in 1940 we are to use the revolutionary lessons of 1640, we must be clear on this point.'[111] Kuczynski implicitly denied the importance of class struggle as the engine of historical advance: a position which was 'reformist' rather than Marxist.

Clearly, Hill and his allies suspected the powerful hand of the Acting General Secretary behind Kuczynski's critique, an impression confirmed by Dutt's reluctance to bow to pressure for public editorial retraction.[112] Within the spectrum of British Communism, the infirm and ascetic Rajani Palme Dutt was the arch-internationalist: with his exotic Swedish–Indian background, and his extended visits to Belgian bureaus, Swiss sanitariums and Russian academies, for fifty years he was to be the mouthpiece of orthodox Leninist theory, something he invariably identified with the narrower interests of the Soviet leadership.[113] One of the architects of the Bolshevization of the party in the early 1920s, and an unsparing critic of the native idiom of the British socialism – its antiquarian learning a reflection, he believed, of the backwardness and lethargy of the Labour movement as a whole – he was never much of an enthusiast for 'the academic brigade' within the party: 'incurable professorial types', who were apt to 'contaminate' their Marxist exegetic with the language of 'bourgeois liberalism' or to confound 'intellectual agreement' with the Communist position and 'real revolutionary consciousness'.[114]

But Dutt, usually so abreast of the latest directives from Moscow and so unbending on the correct party line, was out of his depth on Tudor and Stuart history. A series of meetings were arranged in which party gamekeeper was proved poacher, the editorial board of *Labour Monthly* indicted for relying on discredited authorities, 'demonstrating its ignorance of an issue which had 'been exhaustively discussed in the Soviet Union', and exhibiting division and 'provincialism', just when a celebration of 1640 might have paid off with 'young historians beginning to be drawn to Marxism'.[115] There followed a reluctantly conducted editorial retreat, with Dutt protesting in the margin at the progressively regretful statements drafted in his name for inclusion in a subsequent number of the journal.[116] The retraction, however, never seems to have been printed. Perhaps, it was the war; perhaps, there was something a little absurd about these talmudic exercises in seventeenth-century history as the bombs fell about Central London. Yet, clearly for Hill and his colleagues, a 'scientific' history was part of the present 'battle of ideas', and a correct interpretation of such topics as the 'bourgeois democratic revolution' was of 'immediate political importance'. Even for Kuczynski, the Civil War was 'the great example of a people in arms for democratic rights' and a radical 'leadership, fight[ing] against opportunism in its own ranks'. 'For us who are planning and working for a revolution which will bring a new class . . . to power . . . 1640 . . . is . . . a light which will help us to find the right way, a beacon which joins its beam to that of the great French Revolution and the October Revolution in Russia.'[117] So much the more for Hill. Hill 'may be said to have built his life work' on the perceived parallels between the seventeenth century Puritan Revolution and twentieth century Marxism'. And in the 1940s, certainly, the temptation to superimpose a political and social discourse on Stalin's Russia, or a commentary on the relationship of patriotism and internationalism, on to the events of 1640 or 1648, was quite irresistible.[118]

2.4 PATRIOT GAMES

Patriotism had always posed problems for the political Left; and good international socialists, in a misreading of Dr Johnson's dictum, had often characterized it as the last refuge of the scoundrel ruling elite and the first instinct of the politically deviant. Communists, of course, were inclined to attribute the phenomenon to the manipulations of advanced capitalism and the false consciousness of the 'lumpen' or the petty bourgeoisie. But the widespread support for 'small colonial wars', and the mass enthusiasm for the call to arms in 1914, posed a number of uncomfortable questions about popular psychology, democratic politics, and the persuasive powers of the traditional rulers: doubts reinforced in the 1930s by the rise of fascism and the continued public obsession with the monarchy. In spite of the Comintern's specific directive in 1935 that patriotism was compatible with Marxist–Leninism, party officials like Page Arnott and Palme Dutt found it difficult not to regard it as an inchoate 'moron' fascism: Britain's continued imperial role made it fraudulent or delusory to enlist patriotic sentiment in support of democratic, anti-fascist or socialist ends.[119]

'Imperialism was the bane of English working class formation.' This was Hill's verdict in 1938. In the nineteenth and twentieth centuries, it was clear enough; so too in the eighteenth century, the age of 'Rule Britannia', the Slave Trade and the First British Empire. The seventeenth-century case was less obvious and more tragic. During the English Revolution, the aspirations of the radicals were blasted when the Ironsides allowed themselves to be duped by Cromwell's diversionary tactics and shipped off to Ireland: the Protestant petty-bourgeoisie deprived themselves of 'the possibility of liberating themselves by becoming tools of 'the destruction of the Irish peasantry'. What Cromwell began, William and the Whigs completed; and the Puritan Revolution burnt itself out in sterile anti-Catholicism and the sickening apparatus of 'the Protestant Ascendancy'. In truth, of course, 'a full and frank alliance between a national colonial revolution and a revolution in the exploiting country is only possible when the revolutionary class in the latter is a class that has no interest in exploitation'.[120] Perhaps the die was cast long before the 1650s or the 1690s; perhaps, as Palme Dutt claimed, the English had always been militaristic and predatory.[121]

That was not how it looked to many on the Left in 1939. The coming of World War II was for them the moment of truth, a time for renewal of allegiance to the British state and a commitment to its defence. Left intellectuals like Kingsley Martin, Michael Foot, J. B. Priestley, Harold Laski, Victor Gallancz, John Strachey, and, most notably, George Orwell, now began to celebrate humdrum national habits and ordinary virtues, unencumbered by notions of class morality or party loyalty.[122] Their semi-mystical reabsorption within the body politic, and wide-eyed rediscovery of faith in the common people, was variously expressed in paeans to national 'decency', 'endurance', 'private liberties', freedom of speech and insularity – to the very quirks and idiosyncrasies of English character. Common to all the languages of renewed patriotism was an appreciation of the small-scale, parochial features of English life: to the fabric of civil society, generally dismissed in the Leninist tradition as an appendage of the state or an illusion of bourgeois democracy. Indeed, the 'New Left' of 1940 was explicitly to place its recovery of timeless communal and individual values in opposition to the orchestrated allegiance of Nazi rule and to what were now diagnosed as the deformities of Communist thought and practice.[123]

The international character of Marxism and the diagnosis of the British state and culture as ineradicably imperialist impeded this process for orthodox Communists: 'in the general patriotism of the country, they form[ed] a sort of island of dissident thought'.[124] For in the age of Comintern, there were the overriding priorities of the Soviet state: since the Soviet Union embodied socialist rectitude, and was now allied to Nazi Germany, 'revolutionary defeatism' was in the interests of the socialist cause – a moral slippage eased by the prevailing scepticism over ethics, which transformed political principles into matters of tactical flexibility. 'Communism is English,' trumpeted Jack Lindsay in 1939; but to many, the authentic voice of the Party, the voice of Palme Dutt or of William Rust, seemed anything but English in the dark days of the Nazi–Soviet pact.[125] The nadir was reached in the spring of 1940, when Comintern officials in Moscow celebrated German successes as defeats for reactionary imperialism and the Executive Committee in London declared that the best help to international socialism lay in an extended version of 'revolutionary defeatism' and 'moral sabotage' – a position which came perilously close to aligning Soviet and hence Communist Party interests with Nazi victory in Norway, Holland and France.[126] As the party threatened to tear itself apart, Hill himself was drawn into the debate on what some within as well as without now denounced as a Moscow-directed revisionism. In a letter ill-timed to the point of genius, published some eight days after Churchill became Prime Minister and the allied defences crumbled before Hitler's Blitzkrieg, he defended the party line from renegade 'pinks' and wobbling Left Book Clubbers, and reaffirmed the predatory class character of the war on both sides: the effective choice was not between Britain and Nazi Germany but between 'the umbrella men' of the Anglo-French bourgeoisie and international socialism – this, as British working-class soldiers began the long retreat to Dunkirk.[127]

Little wonder that born-again patriots like George Orwell should have seized on the 'myopic disregard' of religion, morality, liberty or 'plain loyalty' – all 'the things that men will die for' – of Hill's 'New Model' Marxist essay on *The English Revolution*, in a review published at the height of the Battle of Britain some three months later: 'It is easy now to debunk the English Civil War, but it must be admitted that during the past twenty years the predictions of the Marxists have usually been not only wrong, but . . . more sensationally wrong than those of much simpler people.'[128] Yet, a careful reading of Hill's text would suggest that 'truth' and 'freedom' were not entirely lacking from his vision of English history: the essay ended with a brief celebration of Rainborough and Winstanley and 'the living struggle of comrades to build a society . . . which ordinary people would think worth defending with all their might because it was their society'. Reading between the lines, one can sense that a conflation of Marxism and a broader radical–national agenda was by no means impossible.[129]

'People's Front' thinking had made a mark on Communist historical writing, and the late 1930s had witnessed a revival of the radical patriotic mode: a reaction against the 'squeamish' sensibilities of a decaying society, and 'an academic obscurantism which had hidden from the last generation the very landmarks of the English revolutionary heritage'.[130] The agenda can best be studied in a series of popular writings, spanning history and literature, on 'the record of English Democracy' and 'the Trials of British Freedom', 'through twelve centuries': the 'real history' of 'what men did' and thought as opposed to 'what it suits some people to have us think was done'.[131] Sometimes, as in Joseph Needham's celebration of the Levellers, Jack Lindsay's resurrection of *1649 – a Novel of a Year*, or Hymie Fagan's pastiche of John Reid and Russia's 1917, on *Nine Days that Shook England*, and the Peasant's Revolt of 1381, these constituted public and dramatic episodes in the national past; at others, English risings were interleaved with those in other countries, as in Tom Wintringham's record of *Mutinies from Spartacus to Invergordon*.[132] But usually the 'real history' was to be found in quite unspectacular happenings: in parochial and regional conflicts over enclosures and common pastures, 'in the combinations of recalcitrant journeymen, the staunch bearing of farm labourers in the felon's dock', and in the thoughts and words of 'many great patriots, poets and philosophers', whose 'contributions' were likened to 'the cliffs of an iceberg that reveal the greater power beneath', and whose 'testimony live[d] on to stimulate and instruct the future'.[133]

Revolutionaries, wrote Wintringham, had understandably been antagonistic to those 'who talked freedom in opposition to the ideas of . . . self-disciplined, organized working class action'. But now they had to abandon their sectarian impulses, and to renew the vitality of 'the tradition of freedom . . . which [was] fundamental in the development of this country'. From the barons at Runnymede to the early Labour leaders, 'Roundhead, Whig, Radical – there have been many versions of the idea. Each of their transcriptions into fact and action has been limited . . . Each has been progressive, driving the world forward; then stagnant; then reactionary, a shackle on further advance.' The common struggle against fascism now gave socialists the opportunity to wean 'the great freedom-loving class[es]' away from the tired conservatism of people like Trevelyan, and to reassure creative intellectuals of the congruence of Communist 'liberty' and their own: 'We must follow the French example . . . win from the enemies of peace and the working class, those symbols and that heritage which are the British equivalents of "Liberty, Fraternity [and] Equality".'[134]

The invocation of a democratic culture was particularly important: for Rickword, Lindsay and the contributors to the *Left Review*, a flourishing culture was not a commodity or an independent activity divorced from society, the product of leisure and sophistication; nor was it simply a 'reflection' of material conditions, with writers defined by their 'objective class positions'. Literature, in particular, was a distillation of the predicaments of an age rather than a supplement or an epiphenomenon: in John Strachey's description, 'a great sea into which for centuries have been poured all those thoughts, dreams, fantasies, concepts, unascertained facts and emotions which did not fit into other categories of human thought'.[135] Charting this hidden sea was crucial to the recapture of England's real history. Because the modern British state had no popular 'Foundation Deed', no institutionalized revolutionary tradition in modern times – no Bastille Day, Tricolour or Marseillaise – historians had to engage its radical metahistory through the mediation of a national culture or a literature – 'books, which have, so to speak, been historical acts'.[136]

The appeal to a national culture as the incarnation of England's hidden history and as the repository of human and social values which had disappeared elsewhere 'with the coming of the State', coincided in certain respects with the moral crusade for English studies conducted in the pages of *Scrutiny*.[137] Indeed, the ambiguous *pas de deux* of Marxists and Leavisites in the 1930s (with Marxists holding out hands and Leavisites playing hard to get), would suggest that there was much common ground: a root and branch rejection of a culture defined by 'the cosy recesses of [a] . . . well-stocked library and wine-cellar'; and a similar set of beliefs about the true value of literature as 'the spiritual essence of social formation'.[138] Situated on the margins of an academic curriculum defined by Quiller-Couch and H. A. L. Fisher, they had a common social point of departure and a particular idiom or 'style – lower middle class, Nonconformist, provincial, strenuous, earnest, quintessentially English. Both were instinctive Roundheads and Puritans; somewhat embattled 'trouble-makers', disturbers of the status quo.

In their different and contrasting ways, the intellectuals in each grouping shared an overwhelming sense of capitalism's impending collapse and the disintegration of liberalism as a credible moral or intellectual system. Thus, the young Herbert Butterfield, fresh from disposing of 'the Whig interpretation', commented favourably in the pages of *Scrutiny* on 'History and the Marxian Method', comparing the solidity and sophistication of Marxist social analysis with the jejeune biographical individualism, compartmentalization and implausible progessivism of most English historians. It was no accident, thought Butterfield, that bourgeois history 'fails most of all in what we may call social or even general history', producing trivialities, surface descriptions: stage settings for a story that goes on elsewhere, in the supposedly decisive actions of great men or an even more mystical movement of ideas viewed as sole agencies of historical change. In terms that could have come from Rickword or Lindsay, he noted the exclusions of the bourgeois past:

> I am not certain that we realize . . . how little the history of England that we possess in our minds really corresponds with the genuine fullness of the concept . . . how we seem to imagine that we are telling the story of the people when we are only giving the history of parliament or . . . governmental institutions . . . or the people who politically counted.

And indulging, as was his wont, in precisely the Whig vices that he castigated, he ventured the opinion 'that Marxist history is the direction in which our bourgeois history is moving'.[139]

Central to the Leavisite vision was the unity of life and culture, mediated through language and quintessentially expressed in seventeenth-century English drama, prose and poetry, only to be dislocated by science and industrialization, splintered by the emergence of an effete upper class and a brutalized lower, and finally swallowed up in the philistinism of a mass consumer society.

Such a 'pessimistic historicism', however, revolved around questions of value which liberal history did not begin to address. Even G. M. Trevelyan, who was unusually sensitive to literature and who shared some of Leavis's gloomy views about the nature of contemporary mass society, seemed unable to transcend its positivist limitations. So that his *English Social History*, which should have raised questions as to 'the conditions of a vigorous and spiritually vital culture . . . and the criteria by which one might attempt to judge . . . a national civilization', was content merely to illustrate, promiscuously to celebrate: reducing the cultural life of the community to a catalogue of its products – one damned masterpiece after another.[140]

The philistinism of contemporary consumer society repelled many Marxists also. They, too, found in literature a moral vision and a creative social energy weakened elsewhere by the commodification of life and the impoverishment of language typified 'by the products of Hollywood, Fleet Street and Elstree'.[141] Their history, too, was morally loaded: like the Leavisites, they were drawn to the myth of the organic society, where people expressed 'their human nature' and 'satisfied their human needs in terms of the natural environment'. In their effort to locate a tradition which differed from the long continuities of bourgeois culture, they, too, went back to the distant past. For England had the oldest working-class tradition in the world. 'The ideas of socialism were first put forward on English soil':

> in England as nowhere else we can find a solidly persisting communist tradition. Nowhere else, have the peasants so strong a sense of communal rights and been so ready to fight for these rights. Nowhere else, can we trace the rich and coherent development of peasant communism into fuller forms of thought and action, as industrial methods of production grew more efficient.

> Socialism [was] as English as the downs over which Ball's agitators must have tramped [in 1381] . . . as deeply embedded in the hearts of Englishmen as . . . the roots of the great elms in the English soil under whose shelter many a rebel gathering took place.[142]

Socialism was heritage: too, part of the 'storied' landscape – 'the collective recovery 'of the greater part of this island from forest and fen' – which stamped itself on the origin and development of the national culture.[143] Celebrating and reclaiming this heritage was part of the struggle for a People's Front and a democratic working-class culture: historical pageants became an important side of the Communist Party's propaganda, not least 'because they . . . spoke to and stirred great audiences and actively involved literally thousands of party and non-party people as amateur actors, costume makers, crowds and singers'.[144]

It was because it attempted to remap all of English history and not just certain portions or episodes within it, in a manner which corresponded to these Popular Front priorities, that Leslie Morton's *People's History* was to prove so influential – the book on which a generation of Marxist historians was to cut its teeth. Rickword and Lindsay might have evoked the language of patriotism, Fagan and Wintringham have celebrated the struggles for democratic freedom more explicitly, but it was Morton who incorporated the radical tradition of Tawney and Thorold Rogers into the Marxist schema of history as a whole. A Communist since the 1920s, who was to divide his time between journalism, school mastering and – when he could afford it – full-time writing, Morton was something of 'an accidental historian', one who would far rather have been a poet or an essayist than an academic or an antiquarian. His approach to the past almost invariably was to be through the written word: texts which he was to decode with an unusual sensitivity and originality. Time and again during his career, he was to anticipate the cultural readings of historians and literary critics on the Left.[145]

A People's History of England was a less original piece of writing but performed a similar trail-blazing role. The outlines of the story were familiar enough. But underlying the conventional staging posts of political history were deep currents of social change: the gradual onset, forcible imposition and piecemeal decay of feudalism, viewed not as a contract between lord and vassal, still less a harmonious order of estates, but as a social structure and a mode of production marked by baronial exploitation and peasant resistance; the emergence, the struggles and the stabilization of the bourgeoisie; the 'violent and predatory seizure of the land'; the creation of a market economy; the mobilization of labour; the triumph of industrial capitalism; the challenge to it of working-class organization and aspiration; and – writing in 1937 and looking to the future – the permanent crisis of British capitalism and imperialism, the intensification of class struggle and the eventual recovery of their own lives and destinies and with it the fate of the world by the people through the exercise of 'right judgment followed by right action'.[146]

Though the interpretative framework was a conventional vulgar Marxism, there was much that was native-born about Morton's approach. As it was for an earlier generation of radical historians, his story of the English people was rooted in the countryside: 'plough and pasture rather than shuttle and cage,' writes Raphael Samuel, 'were the imaginative focus of his vision; the common people of his narratives were not an industrial proletariat nor yet town dwellers . . . but first and foremost a folk'. Two thousand years of history were held together by the guileless anachronism of a continuous national identity, unproblematically encapsulated in a unitary 'free-born' English people, locked in struggle with a series of alien rulers. The central drama and tragedy of their story was the clearing, domestication, exploitation and appropriation of the land. As with Thorold Rogers and Tawney, it was the impact of the Norman Conquest on traditional village life, the conflicts of feudal society, and, above all, the advent of sheep-farming, the Agrarian Revolution, Tudor Enclosure – the moment at which 'the quantitative character' of land transfer 'assumed the qualitative character of widespread dispossession of the peasantry' – rather than the Industrial Revolution which fired his outrage and his imagination. In this respect, Morton's Marxism preserved the priorities and ensured the continuity – not least the chronological conservatism and the unreflecting folk-nationalism – of an earlier and a simpler age of radical scholarship.[147]

In the long socialist tradition, as we have seen, the seventeenth century had always occupied a privileged position. But in the writings of Morton and the Left intellectuals of the 1930s, its pivotal status was underlined. For Morton, the English Revolution was 'the grand climacteric' of English history, marking not just the end of feudalism and the creation of the bourgeois state and society, but the high point of class struggle: 'the time when the two-camp division of English society was most perfectly and most movingly realized', the moment of 'possibilism' also, when the people might have been able to abbreviate the processes of subsequent social development. The Elizabethan era was provocatively interpreted as its first act – internationally, through the consolidation of the Reformation and the defeat of Catholic reaction; domestically, through the patriotic mobilization and religious tempering of those classes which were to bring England's feudal monarchy crashing down – the eighteenth century as its coda: the unheroic working out of its successes and failures.[148]

'The century of revolution' was to prove a magnet to socialist scholars; and in the next decade or so, Joseph Needham, Alick West, Jack Lindsay, Montagu Slater, Iris Morley, Ernst Meyer, Leslie Morton, Edgell Rickword, David Petegorsky – none of them experts in the field – were to produce major works of interpretation or celebratory 'resurrection'.[149] For the literary Left, especially, it offered a still resonant source of radical thought and expression. To Christopher Caudwell and Edward Upward, Shakespeare, Marlowe and Jonson transcended their bourgeois limitations, and intimated the 'forces of the future beneath the surface' of their time.[150] The Protestant Bible ('the revolutionists' handbook'), Milton and *The Pilgrim's Progress*, according to Ralph Fox, formed the literary inheritance of the common people 'to an extent the upper classes could never claim'.[151] To understand the 'traditions of struggle and acceptance so deeply rooted in the English masses even today', wrote Jack Lindsay, one had to grasp the historical residuum of dissent': 'the glow and fire of grace', the hope of an effective bond of human unity' which always burned within it:

> Now when the hills of fellowship . . . can at last be reached, we can profitably return to Bunyan; by carrying his vision to its last steps of implication, we reach the stage where the Birthright once more comes down to earth . . . and this time the earthly goal will not be lost, will not be doomed to recede into the summer distance, the horizon of bounteous light.[152]

To trace the transformation from communalism and the struggle for equal rights in a world of primitive toil to modern scientific communism, one had to turn to Winstanley's vision of a society liberated by free enquiry and complete mastery over nature. And to recapture the 'lost soul' of that 'formative' era, one needed, said Edgell Rickword in the companion essay to Hill's *English Revolution*, to reclaim Milton from middle-class 'canonization' and reinstate him as a 'revolutionary intellectual', iconoclastic, subversive – the encomiast of 'radical enlightenment'.[153]

In many ways, Hill was ideally placed to complete the task of marrying party exegetic and patriotic scripture: the fusion interrupted but not entirely dislocated by the tactical aberrations of 1939 and 1940. His lifelong devotion to seventeenth-century

English history was first stimulated by T. S. Eliot and the metaphysical poets; and his enthusiasm for the literature of the period preceded and sometimes appeared to run across the grain of his Marxism.[154] Like many Marxists of his generation, he was deeply imbued with a feeling for the cultural glories of the bourgeois past – for Marvell and Traherne, Pepys and Defoe, and a host of writers whose works could be read as manifestations of the tension between their intellectual and aesthetic sensibilities and the political and conceptual possibilities available in their societies. He was always to insist that an understanding of seventeenth-century literature was central to an understanding of its history, and throughout his career, was to retain an overwhelmingly English sense of place.[155]

Indeed, for all his strictures on Whig exceptionalism, Hill's revolution was a strangely insular affair. 'Little Englandism' has its plebeian as well as its patrician exponents; and not the least reason for the popularity of Hill's reading of English history was its convergence with the Foxeite story – or, at least, its ethnocentric Miltonic metamorphosis – of Protestant England and its historic mission. The Nonconformist strain in British socialism rubbed off against his Marxism; and he could couple Marian and Comintern martyrs as historic freedom fighters with no apparent sense of incongruity. For Hill, as for Morton, the medieval Papacy was 'a centralized international organization which succeeded in establishing a profitable monopoly in the grace of God'. Sixteenth-century Reformers formed an anti-clerical underground of ordinary people who wished to 'think for themselves', the forerunners of the libertarians of the English Revolution; and Catholics constituted an alien fifth column 'subservient' to a foreign power – a Protestant, 'sceptered isle' version of the national past which had a particular resonance in 1940, 'when the eyes of the world were again turned to the shores of England and the surrounding seas'.[156]

In June, as his *English Revolution* went to press, he had repudiated the party line and volunteered for military service – not to fight for the discredited ruling elite but to defend this vision. At all events, by the end of the year, the party line had veered once more, and the previously disgraced but now recalled Harry Pollitt was instructing comrades to support 'The War on Two Fronts': the fight against fascism abroad and the domestic struggle for a people's government.[157] By June 1941, Operation Barbarossa and Stalin's 'Great Patriotic War' had made the reintegration of the party into the body politic officially acceptable once more: Russia's danger was now everybody's danger; and Russia's resistance the resistance of an ally in a life and death struggle against evil. And once the Red Army began to roll back Hitler's advance in Eastern Europe, devotion to communist internationalism could be combined with intransigent leadership in the fight for national liberation from German occupation. Communism now operated under the banner of national unity; and party members throughout Europe were encouraged to join hands not just with fellow socialists, but with all patriots 'regardless of party or religious faith'.[158] The latter stages of the war, indeed, were to see the partial self-liquidation of Soviet Marxism for a Greater-Russian patriotism, and the formal elimination of Comintern in the name of a 'common onslaught of freedom-loving countries', fighting under their own local 'conditions', and in their own 'national language', 'to finish off the fascist beast'.[159]

In Britain, as elsewhere, patriotic renewal had been placed high on the party agenda. But the form that it took was primarily historical: Britain did not experience the horror of Nazi occupation or the euphoria of liberation; she emerged from the war, exhausted and bloodied, but with her elites and her empire intact. 'The national struggle with Germany consequently preserved far more traditional overtones': a conflict still linked in the prevailing rhetoric and the collective memory 'with earlier contests against Habsburg, Bourbon or Napoleonic enemies'. In Britain, wrote Dona Torr,

> we have not been tried in the fire like our comrades in occupied Europe; our state forms have not been overthrown; we are not, like the French, entering upon 'the national insurrection which is inseparable from national liberation'; we are disunited, weak and backward in our assertion of class power.[160]

In France, party spokesmen could drape the hammer and sickle in the Tricolour and turn to 1792 and 1793 to justify the anticipated power seizure or the purging of Vichy traitors. In Britain, no such iconic authority existed; no revolution was in the offing. But it was possible, at a lower level of intensity, to substitute the recapture of national radical traditions for the armed destruction of collaborationist elites.[161]

Rank and file members had complained about the sectarian flavour of the party – the alien nature of its language, its international[e] anthem, its ignorance of the national past – and a long-running discussion in *World News and Views* had been given authoritative closure by Torr:

> it was a great thing that we are determined to enter into the glorious long neglected heritage of our land, its history and culture, [but] strong as our old love of them may be, it returns infinitely enriched in illumination and power when through Marxism we re-integrate it with our own creative life.

Nation had to be measured off against class, common heritage against the story of 'shame and bondage', 'things that unite us as a nation against a social system unstable and profoundly divided against itself, a civilization double-faced and double-tongued'. There was much to be ashamed of in British history. But there were things to be proud of too: 'centuries of past scufflings and struggles – for religious toleration, juries, the vote for men and women' – cooperative movements and voluntary associations, the creative achievements of ordinary people. Class demands that succeeded became common traditions: the right to read the Bible in English – a long story with much revolutionary heroism behind it, 'the highest form of the class struggle for the freedom of thought' – had, for example, gradually seeped into the fabric of the national character. The English, according to her wartime panegyricists, didn't like being pushed around. But their rights had to be prized from the monarchy, the aristocracy, the bourgeoisie and the church. 'We are what history has made us', and a reclamation of that history from its ruling class guardians was crucial to the task ahead. The trick was to avail oneself of the self-deceptions of nationalist discourse: to convert contingent historical struggles into self-evident, immemorial features of the native landscape; to transmute patriotic prejudice into socialism.[162]

It was a tactic which was employed most successfully by writers like J. B. Priestley in populist evocations of the Englishness of the Home Guard, the munitions girls and the little boats of Dunkirk, and in their calls for a change from the old-fashioned propertied view of country 'as a collection of things all owned by certain people' to a truer and more natural concept of 'country ... as the home of a living society' in which the welfare of the whole community would be the first and only test.[163] But it was prominent, also, in the rhetoric of the British Communist Party in 1944 and

1945 – implicitly in the forum on 'Our National Traditions' run by *World News and Views* which depicted the party as the heir of 'Queen Elizabeth and her pirates', or in the 'heritage' series, run by its literary offshoot, *Our Time*, which regularly enlisted Shakespeare, Milton (many times), Burns, Sidney, Bunyan ('the great proletarian . . . prophet of the dispossessed'), Morris, Swift and even Pope ('the radical') as poets of the people on the side of patriotic social renewal; or – at a more official level – in attacks under the approved mantle of Stalin's essay on the Nationality Problem, on the old line that 'the principle of nationalism . . . had brought the world to the edge of the abyss'.[164]

'The People's War' of the social nationalists sought to link the new ideals of citizenship and fraternity with the older 'hard won liberties for which [their] fathers had fought'.[165] This was, after all, according to its admirers, what had happened in the Soviet Union. The traditions of immemorial peasant fortitude and attachment to the Russian soil, had been successfully wedded to a 'specifically Soviet patriotism', based on the economic and social achievements of the Soviet regime as 'a multi-national state of workers and peasants', and 'the great emancipating power within an international alliance'.[166] These were the years of 'Uncle Joeism': of widespread reassessment of the Soviet system in the light of its military triumphs – the empirical 'verification' of dialectical materialism for a new generation of neophytes. 'Each victory of the Red Army,' wrote Hill, was 'more inflammatory than a score of manifestoes issued by the Communist International'. For the Soviet Union, it was widely felt, was not just winning the war through immensities of geography and weight of numbers – these had made little difference between 1914 and 1917 – but because of its system of government and society: 'the socialist ideology alive in the hearts of the whole Soviet people'.[167]

This was certainly Hill's perception; and, briefly, he was able to combine his democratic British nationalism and his admiration for the Soviet experiment. The monument to this dual vision of the good society, one historic and partly frustrated, the other very much of the present, was *The Soviets and Ourselves: Two Commonwealths*, a comparison of the United Kingdom and the Soviet Union, published in 1945 under the pseudonym of K. E. Holme, which balanced its appreciation of the traditions of English liberty and individualism with a populist panegyric on the spirit of Russian collectivism and equality, juxtaposing Cromwell and Lenin, *The Pilgrim's Progress* and *What is to be done*, and setting State Openings of Parliament and London 'Bobbies', in Dixon of Dock Green mode, alongside May Day military parades and Uzbek children learning the (Russian) alphabet.[168]

In the latter stages of the war, he had served in the notoriously pro-Soviet Northern department of the Foreign Office, as one of its Russian experts.[169] And quite clearly, he subscribed to the view put forward by G. D. H. Cole and E. H. Carr that the Soviet system was a legitimate form of democracy: a Commonwealth, run 'like an Oxford college', on the basis that 'if two heads are better than one, several hundred are better than two, provided they are in agreement on fundamentals'. The Bolshevik party was 'the true embodiment of the popular will' and proof 'that the common people of the earth can take over power and run the state infinitely more effectively than their betters'. In his first book after the war, the eulogistic *Lenin and the Russian Revolution*, he emphasized the liberating effect of 1917:

> I come back continually to this feature of the Russian Revolution that it uplifted the poor and the downtrodden and improved their lot in the everyday things of life. This is what most impresses in contemporary records of the revolution and this is what is likely to be its most widespread and lasting effect.[170]

And what of its effect on post-war Britain? The overthrow of the entire landlord class of Eastern Europe had been paralleled at a somewhat lower but, nevertheless, unexpected level of militancy, by the massive rejection of the Tories at the ballot box. The election of an avowedly socialist government was widely seen as part of a worldwide leftward march, 'a new type of government for a new age'. Labour, it was anticipated, would inaugurate a 'new age of social justice' and support the 'democratic upsurge' throughout the world.[171] For the past two years, Harold Laski, the party chairman, had been preaching the inevitability of revolution, preferably 'with the consent of all', but failing that 'by violence', to eliminate 'the irrational inequalities and the vested privileges of the old order'. Convinced that 'the liberal phase of bourgeois civilization [was] over' but sceptical of the willingness of the ruling class not to challenge democratic institutions, he had urged his colleagues to reach 'a genuine understanding' with the Soviet Union – 'the central support upon which the future of working class interests depends'.[172]

Such a political climate was bound to seem propitious to the further advance of the British Communist Party. Though small in numbers compared with its continental counterparts, it could build on the demonstrable desire for socialist transformation within the Labour movement. Genuine belief in a harmony of interests coincided with the soon to be familiar tactic of the 'Democratic Front' – affiliation, infiltration, assimilation. During the election, the party had gone out of its way to emphasize its reformist characteristics, had formally recognized 'the democratic nature of British society', studiously spoken of the people rather than the proletariat, had even suggested the possibility of achieving a redistribution of resources under the profit system of capitalism.

> The fact is [said Dimitrov] – and we Marxists should be well aware of it – that every nation, every people will effect its own transition to socialism, not by a mapped out route based on the Soviet model, but by its own road in accordance with its historical, national, social, cultural and other conditions.

Or, in the idiom of the Historians' Group at its inauguration during the summer of 1946, people's history and Marxist theory, hand in hand, would revitalize the study of England's past.[173]

3
Marxist History in a Cold War Era

On the work of the Historians' Group of the Communist Party set against the background of the Cold War and its ideological cognates from 1946 till the mid 1950s.

3.1 THE HISTORIANS' GROUP OF THE COMMUNIST PARTY

'The Historians' Group of the Communist Party' was formed early in 1946. Its precise genesis seems to have been a number of resolutions at the party Congress the previous November calling for increased educational activity, including the study of British history, and a subsequent conference ostensibly concerned with preparing a new edition of Leslie Morton's book and with launching a documentary series by Lawrence and Wishart: an agenda which reflected the popular and patriotic ingredients which had acquired such weight in the party at the end of the war. Period sections were quickly established, and of these the Tudor and Stuart subcommittee seems to have been easily the most vigorous and productive: something which no doubt owed much to Hill's energy as first chairman and chief organizer of the group.[1]

Its leading members, Eric Hobsbawm, Rodney Hilton, Victor Kiernan, George Thomson, Maurice Dobb, Leslie Morton and Dona Torr were 'old friends and comrades', united in their 'passion for history' and their commitment to waging 'the battle of ideas'.[2] From the autumn of 1946, as Hobsbawm recalls, a small band of them would 'make their way, normally at weekends, through . . . the dank, cold and slightly foggy streets of Clerkenwall to Marx House, or to the upper room of the Garibaldi Restaurant, Laystall Street, armed with cyclostyled agendas, sheets of theses or summary arguments for the debates of the moment'. In addition to the regular meetings in London, there were talks around the country at various

79

affiliated branches, and special conferences and summer schools usually held at Netherwood, near Hastings: over the next ten years, membership was to become for many 'if not exactly a way of life, then a small cause . . . a way of structuring leisure'. What Hobsbawm and his colleagues remember best is the physical austerity, intellectual excitement, political passion, and the friendship – the sense of comradeship and an equality which came from their common feeling of exploration. For although some of its members spoke with authority on certain issues, they were 'equally explorers', attempting to map out and to claim new territory, to establish a Marxist interpretation for the whole of English history. The Historians' Group was never just a professional, academic organization; its meetings were open to any interested party members; and the contribution of other intellectuals – non-academic writers like Jack Lindsay and Leslie Morton, or those who did not write books but who contributed to the collective work of discussion and organization like Daphne May, Alf Jenkins, Edwin Payne and Diana St John – was to be considerable.[3]

Eric Hobsbawm has written of the openness and the absence of constraint within the group: there simply was no party line on most of British history, and discussions were blessedly free of the rigidity and dogmatism of the Stalin–Zhdanov–Lysenko era. 'Few . . . hesitated to speak . . . even fewer to criticize, none to accept criticism'. Yet there were probably greater limits to intellectual freedom than Hobsbawm cares to admit. The history of the party itself was off-limits and significant areas of modern history were too politically sensitive for extensive debate or publication.[4] Even when it came to more remote periods, the linkage with present politics was a deeply ingrained assumption, so that correct thinking on England's seventeenth-century revolution might well be part of a correct socialist strategy in post-war Britain. Meetings – every three or four months in these early years – usually involved the reading of papers, and much of Hill's published work in the 1950s and 1960s was first aired in this form. But discussion was also important: discussion, wrote Daphne May in her report to the party, was the 'first purpose of the groups', and discussion was meant 'to produce concrete results useful to the party as a whole . . . and improve[s] our practical political work'. Especially when it came to the more highly organized conferences, run by the group from 1948 onwards, effective discussion depended on the choice of suitable subjects and on 'proper preparation', meaning not just the prior circulation of duplicated materials but preliminary study of appropriate texts and references by everyone who attended. By and large, members accepted the distinction between 'honest and acceptable' argument which strengthened the party and 'hostile and destructive criticism'; debate could be vigorous, but legitimate dissent was not expected to run to fundamental Marxist axioms. Moreover, if the answers were in no way predetermined, the questions certainly were; 'contributions' from participants tended to be organized as pieces of an already assumed overall structure; and there was always the expectation of an authoritative summing up and eventual consensus – a process in which the forcefulness or otherwise of the chair was of some importance. Hobsbawm's recollections notwithstanding, what the minutes of these events suggest is something short of an academic free-for-all.[5]

The broader educational role of the group was probably also of significance here. The London meetings formed the hub of a small network of provincial gatherings, and high amongst the group's activities, collectively and individually, were visits and reports to branches around the country, information for lecturers and teachers, and, in some instances, mimeographed notes on approved positions for the notice boards of sympathetic but fallible university departments. At the other end of the chain, liaison with the party and with party functionaries was close and constant.[6] The days when intellectuals would ritually be humiliated as dishonourable proletarians were well and truly over: the work of party intellectuals was now widely recognized as crucial to the 'battle of ideas', a battle of 'exceptional importance' in Britain and the Western world, 'the battle of classes as it is fought out in men's consciousness'. According to George Thomson, ancient historian and a member of the party's Executive Committee, there was no practical distinction between professional and party activity: the interaction of Marxist principles and research would illuminate specialist work and enrich everyday party life.[7]

The Historians' Group was only one of a number of professional organizations, which led in 1947 to the creation of a National Cultural Committee with a full-time secretary, Sam Aaronovitch. Along with other intellectual workers, and more than any, historians reported regularly to the party; and they were provided with limited but readily available space for publication in the major party journals. For their part, functionaries like James Klugmann, head of the party's education department, Douglas Garman, national education organizer, and Aaronovitch helped in the creation and the running of local branches and special party schools, and sometimes contributed themselves to the debate on such issues as England's revolutionary past and unrevolutionary historiography.[8]

Most important of all was Dona Torr. Though she was not a formal member of the group, she soon acquired the role of muse, galvanizer and facilitator. A foundation member of the party and a dedicated Marxist scholar, something of a perfectionist, she had long agitated for a 'higher level' of historical awareness within the party: Marxist historians were not born, they had to be 'trained'; they had to study Marx, understand 'revolutionary dialectics', learn to combine an awareness of class conflict and progressive evolution, productive forces and the antagonistic social relations in which they operated. At the same time, their creativity and their passion had to be 'awoken'. This is what her 'pupils' remembered most:

> She . . . taught us historical passion. For her the understanding of the historical process [was] an intense emotional experience . . . All of us can recall fierce arguments with her, words sharpened by the fact that she made us know that something important was at stake. She made us feel history in our pulses.[9]

The chosen subject of her own lifetime's work was characteristic – the life, the triumphs and the sufferings of Tom Mann, most militant of British working-class heroes, one whose life-story 'told of many roads and one pursuit'. For Torr, history could never be 'a dead record of the past'; it was 'dynamite' or it was nothing.[10]

'Presentism' and a sense of one's own place as 'a maker of history' were always modulated by a sense of past traditions, and these in turn were illuminated by Marxist theory. The interplay was what mattered. The writer who was conscious of this would be conscious also of the true dialectic of history: of a process 'in which gain and loss were aspects of the one movement', which under the conditions of class division and 'a breach at the heart of human society', simultaneously 'united and divided, juxtaposed pain and progress', brought 'power and wealth to some, dispossession and degradation to others'. Unlike many Marxists, Torr never forgot the dying bird, never succumbed to abstract economism, triumphalism, or the principle of the worse the better. Marxism could never be reduced to applied sociology:

what mattered was the engagement, the 'human sympathy', the passion.[11]

As a director of Lawrence and Wishart, and as general editor, she was the moving spirit behind the series, *History in the Making*, the volumes which more than any individual work defined the collective idiom of the group in the 1940s. As its titles and its contents suggest, this was a documentary series, drawn from 'the very words and thoughts' of ordinary people as they made their own history; and their history was the history of society not of constitutions or elite institutions. For all the appearance of 'history speaking', the extracts infact were artfully edited and organized to illustrate orthodox Marxist themes; indeed, the series was a local example of the approved Soviet genre of documentary history. Torr's Marxism was never just a history from the bottom up; she was a stickler for what she regarded as party orthodoxy: she was to be the group's chief censor as well as its guide and inspirer.[12]

The politics of the period may well have influenced the group's rapidly acquired party orthodoxy. Its formation had come at 'a very delicate moment in human civilization', in the afterglow of a war that had permitted 'a unique fusion of international and national causes on the Left'.[13] By the time of its first publications, however, Britain's 'brief moment of socialist populism' was a thing of the past. By 1947, Dalton and Morrison had abandoned anything resembling 'a new economic order'; and it was clear that Labour was intent on creating a more humane form of welfare capitalism not a socialist commonwealth. The diminution of domestic socialism was mirrored by an overtly 'revisionist' foreign policy, which ranged Britain with capitalist America in bitter hostility to socialist Russia and the new 'People's Democracies' of Eastern Europe; by a renewed 'momentum of imperial inertia', or an even more blatant resuscitation of world empire, as the 'liberators' of India yielded to Bevin's blinkered chauvinism and the argument that the well-being of British workers depended more than ever on the toiling masses of Africa and Asia. Many at the time and since have explained the shift in Labour policy as a response to economic and geopolitical realities: to the country's exhaustion and to Soviet worldwide aggression. And even on the Left, some would attribute the lost opportunities of 1945 – and the failure of World War II in Europe, at least, to yield the level of revolutionary potential unleashed by the World War I – to the perversion of socialist internationalism to the needs of Soviet security and Soviet expansion.[14]

But to committed Communists at the time, the thought that Soviet interests could differ from those of worldwide Communism was still unthinkable. The blocking of revolution in the West, therefore, was to be explained by the illusions and the false strategy of native socialists, the resilience and superior cunning of undefeated conservative elites and by battleship America. In Britain, the surrender of socialist policies by the Labour government was partly a matter of deliberate choice: the price paid to American capital for sustaining Britain's imperial illusions; the 'manufacturing' of a Cold War consensus. But it was a failure of theory and of history also: a disastrously inadequate analysis of the capitalist system; a childishly naïve understanding of the operations of the state; ignorance of the realities of Britain's colonial rule and the dynamics of capitalist imperialism; the mythology of constitutionalism, compromise and continuity. No doubt, the ambitions of Mr Attlee and his ministers were far more modest than talk about a new social order had led people to believe; but, said Hill,

> it would be no consolation to future generations of Englishmen to believe that every member of the present government was subjectively a passionately convinced socialist, if, nevertheless, for lack of a scientific theory of socialism that government had *in fact* led England to economic catastrophe and loss of national independence.[15]

Like the liberal theoreticians whose ideologies and cultural assumptions they had absorbed, the Labour leaders abstracted the political from the social and thought that they could modify the market without touching the existing state superstructure. Radicalism was quickly sapped by the traditional trappings of office, 'tamed' by the operations of 'parliamentary democracy'. Bolstered up by belief in the neutrality of state power, confident that by some miraculous dispensation it could achieve socialist transformation without fighting for it, the government drifted from crisis to crisis. Socialist policies were reduced to piecemeal social engineering; reforms drained of meaning by 'the Fabian eternity of their conception'; paradise postponed or eked out in evolutionary instalments. It was perhaps only fitting that Labour should have decreed its own quietus in 1951 – in an election it did not have to call and which it 'really' won, but, through the vagaries of 'parliamentary democracy', gladly lost – and have thankfully handed over to 'the forces of reaction'.[16]

The network of illusions under which the Labour leaders operated were in an important sense historical illusions also. Grounded in the idea of a national culture and the 'depth', 'rootedness' and 'elasticity' of British traditions, they had become a well nigh universal self-congratulatory belief system during the war. Like a latter-day Burke, Butterfield droned on about 'the Englishman's alliance with his history':

> Because we have kept continuity . . . gathering up the past with us as we marched into the future . . . waiting at times so that we could all move forward together as a nation, we have not been ravaged and destroyed by a tragic irredeemable cleavage within the state – a Tradition confronted by a Counter-Tradition. . . . the inevitable legacy of revolutions . . . too impatient to persuade, yet not cruel enough . . . to exterminate their enemies.[17]

In 1945 the *New Statesman* had applauded the near solecism of 'a Socialist King's Speech' and 'the continuity of tradition', believing that there was much to be gained in 'gathering national sentiment around the new government' and celebrating the triumph of Labour with the paraphernalia of age-old 'royal, imperial and religious ceremonies'.[18]

Marxists themselves had not been immune from the illusions of the period. But the very continuities which they applauded in 1944 and 1945, now militated against the transformation which they craved.[19] 'Bad history' led 'to bad politics' and bad history was rooted in 'the legend that English development had always been peaceful, gradual and evolutionary'.[20] The opiate of gradualism, 'swallowed whole by Labour party theorists', by Fabians, who 'deliberately omitted the revolutionary elements in Marxism' – 'dialectics, the class struggle, close analysis of the whole life of the community': everything that 'gives Marxism life' – and 'fostered for consciously political purposes' by their opponents, had immeasurably weakened radical resolve and set the Labour Party 'firmly behind the economic and cultural rejuvenation of the British ruling class'.[21] 'Since 1689 we have had for all effective purposes, a single party in control of the state', wrote Harold Laski in the 1930s: 'it has been divided, no doubt into two wings . . . but its quarrels . . . have always been family quarrels in which there has always been ample room for compromise.' Nothing had happened since 1945 to alter his verdict. Labour had taken over where Liberal left off, and the old game of alternating government and opposition was renewed under new titles.[22]

To recall something different, one had to go back before 1689. English history was long, but it was not unbroken; there were ruptures and revolutions; there had been transfers of power from one class to another. This was the essence of what had happened between 1640 and 1660: 'England hath received many a sudden change, but never such a change as now. Heretofore, the poor people toiled themselves in shifting one tyrant . . . to set up another; but now they have driven out . . . tyranny itself; and cashiered not a single king, but all kings forever.'[23] There was struggle in English history; there was a counter-tradition which could be juxtaposed to the evolutionary continuum which Butterfield identified as solely national. It was, therefore, of considerable importance to remind people of a time when 'the English genius for compromise was forgotten, and God's Englishmen behaved like bloodthirsty continentals' – 'to see that the real story of the bourgeois revolution of the seventeenth century should be made widely known'.[24]

The rescue of English history from the Whigs and Fabians involved a reassessment of the state also. 'Democratic institutions', elections, party politics and parliamentary legislation – all the supposedly sacrosanct features of English public life – were not immemorial, but historically contingent, the creation of 'bourgeois revolutionary movements' in the sixteenth and seventeenth centuries. The very concept of a national sovereign state – Henry VIII's dramatic discovery of an 'Empire' of England and Cromwell's even more revolutionary creation of a British Commonwealth – was the work of a historic class. And it still bore the mark of its makers. For the bourgeois state to exist, the feudal state had to be smashed; a civil war had to be fought, a ruling elite expropriated: 'the bourgeois conception of the state was sealed with the blood of the royal martyr'. How confused, therefore, were the Labour leaders to succumb to the tug of administrative continuity and 'legalism', and to delude themselves into believing that the existing institutions of political democracy would readily implement the policies 'necessary to establish socialism'.[25]

Under these circumstances, the work of the Historians' Group could not be simply a continuation of the broad progressive agendas which its older members had experienced in the 1930s and during the war. The critique of non-Marxist history was now also a critique of 'currently existing socialism' in Britain, and of the network of illusions which had eroded its substance from within. The first task, therefore, for Marxist historians', maintained George Thomson, was 'to rescue our bourgeois heritage from the bourgeoisie, to take it over, reinterpret it, adapt it to our needs, and renew its vitality by making it thoroughly our own' – something which, he argued, could only be done by refashioning the concepts and categories of historical writing so that it 'expressed the new world that [was] coming into being and [was] part of its realization'.[26]

The Marxist method alone, they believed, was 'adequate in science and scholarship' to provide a successor to the radical–populist tradition. Marxism, they insisted, was not to be confused with economic determinism, but it was significantly more than 'people's history': rather Marxism was a totality, requiring 'close analysis of the whole life of the community': the dynamics of productive forces and social relations, and the interaction of political and ideological superstructures, but also encompassing 'poetic moments', 'great individual gestures' and 'the struggles of real men and women'.[27] It was not just a 'theory' that one could pick up and apply; indeed, nothing was better calculated to raise the collective temperature of Communist intellectuals than the 'eclecticism' of people like A. L. Rowse, the concession that 'to be a good historian in our time one needs to have been something of a Marxist – to have seen the point of it all, to have felt the influence – even if one comes out the other side'. As Douglas Garman noted, the past tense was indicative: like first sex or adolescent communion, it was something to experience and purge from one's system to savour the more cerebral or ecumenical pleasures of All Souls. But Marxism was not an exercise nor an emetic; it was a militant and revolutionary 'praxis', concerned, as Torr put it, 'not only with the understanding of past and present, but with the creation of the future; its aim is to know the world and to change it'.[28]

3.2 COLD WAR POLITICS

In 1947, Stalin created a new organization for the exchange of information and the coordination of policy between communist parties, the so-called 'Cominform'. Even more than its predecessor, Cominform was a vehicle for the transmission of Soviet public directives and propaganda slogans, and in 1947 these were almost entirely geared to the maintenance of Soviet power in Europe. The world was divided into two countervailing 'camps': an 'anti-democratic imperialist camp' – made up of the United States, its major satellites, and a host of colonial and reactionary regimes – and a 'democratic anti-imperialist camp' with the USSR as its base and 'the new democratic countries' of Eastern Europe as its 'pillars'. The task for Communist parties in Western Europe was to 'hold aloft the banner of . . . national independence' against the threat posed by American expansion, American dollars and American culture; to take up the cause of peace and to 'close ranks' behind the Soviet Union.[29]

Over and again during these years, the cultural leadership of the party cried out for effective polemic in 'the battle of ideas'. The British crisis was part of a crisis of world capitalism: a quarter of the world's population had already been withdrawn from its orbit; imperialists with their base in the United States of America knew that they could not destroy these forces unaided; they had to win over the people of Britain and Western Europe. Party historians were, therefore, expected to 'attack all the attempts to provide a theoretical justification for war' and 'to awaken the national consciousness of the people' in defence of 'national independence' against the threat of American power and American products.[30]

In one sense, the international dimension of communist polemic cut across the critique of liberalism conducted at a local level in the name of a more militant Marxist analysis of society and history. For the strategic objective of the new line was to re-establish national unity with the section of the bourgeoisie threatened by American expansion and to create a 'vast front' for peace and national independence, not to preach revolution and class war. In another, Cominform polemic rigidified party thought, by ruling out talk of different roads to socialism and equating democratic values solely with those located in the 'People's Democracies'.[31] The strict limits of 'national banners' were revealed, moreover, when the star pupil of 1947 became the 'imperialist spy' of 1948: Yugoslavia, hitherto 'the most advanced of the new democratic regimes', was now anathematized for 'breaching the united socialist front' and turning their country into 'an American warbase', a 'semi-colony of monopoly capitalism'.[32] There was no room for ideological deviation, and the frigid atmosphere of Soviet politics in Stalin's later years – the attack on cosmopolitanism and bourgeois decadence, the persecution of writers, composers and scientists, the enthronement of Pavlov and Lysenko – was faithfully mirrored in Western Europe by the hunt for Titoist, anti-Soviet, nationalist agents, the sycophantic worship of currently approved idols, and heavy handed treatment of party heterodox.[33]

The battening down of ideological hatches at a local level was revealed in a number of 'purgative exercises in the Zhdanov mode' against idealistic or bourgeois residues in party thinking.[34] Party members had to be on their guard against false friends: the danger posed by those whom Garman called 'the platitudinists' – writers who tried in a characteristically British intellectual manoeuvre simultaneously to incorporate Marxism into their work and to emasculate it – was particularly insidious. Lies could stimulate contradiction, but platitudes were the false currency of intellectual exchange; and the reduction of Marxism to 'the proposition that long distance trends in history have been determined not by individuals or ideals but by economic and social forces' – a Marxism without dialectical conflict, class struggle or revolutionary practice: the semi-demi Marxism of Kingsley Martin and G. D. H. Cole, which cluttered up the progressive journals – opened the way for 'the counterfeiter, whether deliberate or unconscious'. As the class struggle developed and 'reformist' policies lost credibility, so the Labour party would wheel out its social democratic 'quack doctors' – 'various brands of leftists', seeking 'to capture the workers and keep them in the capitalist net'.[35]

The tightening of party control over affiliated but hitherto loosely organized gatherings like the Historians' Group was further evidenced in reprimands issued by the Cultural Committee about 'dilettantism, eclecticsm and tendencies to compromise', complaints of poor attendance at approved educational functions, increasing pressure for 'contributions to polemic', and directives to 'university members' about required party duties.[36] The influx of new comrades during and after the war had swollen the number of 'soft' Marxists; and professional organizations had to be on their guard not just against 'disruptive activities' but against any expression of 'views which could be considered harmful' to the party. After 1948, there seems to have been a thinning of the ranks: those unwilling to accept the basic catechism or enact the approved public self-criticism, quietly dropped out or parted in acrimony.[37] Loyal members seem to have felt more obliged than ever to deploy party rhetoric and appeal to history to justify or condemn the present. How far the process went – how deeply the phrases and analogies penetrated, how far one could pay out opponents in the short change of Cominform polemic without surrendering one's more valuable intellectual currency – no doubt varied from case to case, and must be a matter for surmise.

One of the distinguishing marks of Hill's writing lay in the direct and ever-changing 'dialogue between the present and the past, on the one hand by providing his analysis of contemporary issues with meanings . . . drawn from his seventeenth century sources, on the other by rendering seventeenth century issues in definitely modern terms'. Thus by 1947, the radicals in the English Revolution were enlisted in a 'democratic army' which 'would give our Whitehall brasshats the creeps if anything like it existed today', and were calling for a 'reformed educational system' and 'a free national health service'. A year later, 'the fight for an independent foreign policy' was likened to the ideological struggle in seventeenth-century Europe.[38] Mr Bevin's foreign policy was read off against 1918 as well as 1618 and 1638: Lenin, the patriot, had freed Russia from foreign domination and exploitation by surrendering the Tsarist empire; Charles I coupled his reactionary religious and economic policies with subservience to Spain. Mr Attlee's reluctance to challenge existing political institutions was contrasted with the scope and the daring of the Bolshevik programme and 'the speed with which it was put into effect'. And the geopolitics of Europe at the time of Czechoslovakia's 'democratic revolution' in 1948 were those of the Thirty Years' War all over again.[39]

In 1945 and 1946, he had set the achievements of Lenin and Stalin alongside the collective egalitarian aspirations of the Levellers and the Diggers. But with Attlee in power and the Truman doctrine in place, few in the Labour movement could share his vision of socialist 'Commonwealths', reaching out to each other across time and space, let alone his equation of Stalin and Gustavus Adolphus, the 'Democratic' Republics of Eastern Europe and the bastions of Protestantism in the 1620s, or James's pro-Spanish policies and Ernest Bevin's pro-American ones. The hardening of ideologies after 1947 had inevitably produced a renewed cultural mobilization against Communism on the Left. Laski, the academic revolutionary of 1944, now denounced the insurrectionary Jacobin strain in communist thought, and reaffirmed the fundamental split between authoritarian and democratic brands of socialism. In language, echoed by Michael Foot and John Strachey, he described the Communist Party as the Trojan horse of British socialism, 'the secret battalion', which endeavoured to destroy from the inside the very groups with whom they sought alliance'.[40] For their part, Dutt and Garman denounced these 'Bourbons of the working class movement' and proclaimed the bankruptcy of middle ways, in terms which suggested a return to the 'social fascist' line of the early 1930s.[41]

The logic of these exchanges left little conceptual space for the broad-church socialist culture of 1945. Now that the 'People's War' had given way to the 'People's Peace', and the wartime ideals of democracy and equality were supposedly embodied in the parliamentary legislation of the Labour government, the invocation of radical subversives like Winstanley and John Ball seemed provocative or eccentric. The celebration of participatory small-scale citizenship became once more the stock-in-trade of the political Right. Divorced from its wartime context, Orwell's patriotism increasingly lent itself conservative ends: George the rebel, became Orwell, the cold war ideologue, the petty bourgeois 'traducer of socialism', enlisted – along with Koestler and other witnesses to 'the God that Failed' – as St George of *Encounter* magazine and the Congress for Cultural Freedom.[42]

Whatever the misconceptions of the literary Left in the 1930s, those other celebrants of the national culture, F. R. Leavis and the Scrutiny Movement, had always been anti-Marxist:

> there was never any hesitation or inexplicitness about our anti-Marxism [he recalled in 1940], this negative being a corollary of our positive position. And our positive position was that, though without doubt the human spirit was not to be thought as expressing itself in a void of 'freedom' unconditioned by economic and material circumstances, nevertheless, there was great need to insist on the element of autonomy, and work for the preservation of the humane tradition – a tradition representing the profit of a continuity of experience through centuries of economic and material change ...

'The element of autonomy' and the 'continuity of experience through the centuries' were precisely what had been at issue in the friendly but inclusive exchanges of the 1930s. And in retrospect, it seems obvious that there were insurmountable differences between Leavis's literary idealism and a Marxist aesthetic which viewed literature as 'clotted social history'.[43]

The widening gap was now highlighted in a further instalment of the debate on the pages of *Politics and Letters* in 1947. Intended by its editors to mediate the claims of cultural criticism and political engagement, and to appeal to a readership 'which extend[ed] from people still in the Communist Party to those who were in the orbit of Leavis', the new journal soon found itself presiding over something of a communications' breakdown. In the view of the Leavisite 'critic', R. O. C. Winkler, confronting the modern 'Leviathan', it was possible and necessary to 'reconcile progressive political positions with humane and cultured resistance to the mechanical society of the present', but the key to the recovery of 'significant and permanent human values' lay in the creation of conditions where 'political and social forms' could be harnessed to 'traditional values' – 'the efficient could be the expression of the moral'. To Hill, however, this was to put the cart before the horse: the ills which Winkler deplored were the product not of machines and modernity but of the historically contingent capitalist relations in which they were located. 'Literary values [we]re human values' and to recover human values, one had to associate oneself with a political movement 'which set human values first'. By refusing such commitment and by relegating politics and society to the realm of the instrumental, the Scrutineers condemned themselves to the role of a 'literary critics party' in defence of traditional values, lost beyond recall.[44]

For the Marxist, history was lived on an upward curve, a curve punctuated by losses and by moments of cultural decadence to be sure, but one which looked forward to a new era of collective control over production, an era which many of its practitioners believed was dawning in the Soviet Union. But it was precisely the invocation of the word 'progressive' as a term of moral approval that Scrutiny had found objectionable in Hill's *English Revolution*; it was Marxism that ceased to be 'an approach to history' but which became a triumphalist 'verdict on the whole of history' that it unequivocally rejected. Such 'futurism' far from embodying a qualitative break with bourgeois civilization was, in fact, a consummation of it. The differences between capitalism and socialism in respect of culture were minimal and inessential; and, for all its critical and revolutionary self-advertisement, Marxism

– certainly the Marxism of Dnieper Dams and the wonders of
Soviet Science – was 'complicit with the machine civilization',
responsible for the commodification of life and the impoverishment
of the spirit in the modern world.[45] To the Marxist, on the other
hand, the Leavisite rejection of modernity in the name of a
politically neutral and socially undefined order of traditional values,
was another version of the illusions of the age. The belief that
the 'Decline of the West' could somehow be averted by 'the
preservation of the humane tradition' – through certain literary
texts upheld, not naturally and unself-consciously but with supreme
effort and against great odds, by a tiny cultural elite – was simply
a despairing restatement of the liberal myth of continuity as
embattled ideology, something which no less than the complacency
of the Fabians, eroded the morale of the British Left.[46]

The truth was that the Leavisite programme was, in the strictest
sense of the words, regressive and elitist. Manifestly different in
its sympathies and its point of departure, from the nostalgias of
'spiritually disinherited' High Anglicans and Catholics, it led to
the same evocation of culture as a retreat and a refuge. T. S. Eliot's
celebration of the graceful ease of Great Tew and the meditative
communion of Little Gidding in the 1630s, similarly shut out the
complex and contested nature of the past and failed to provide
any location for its disembodied cultural ideals: in this instance
'the luxurious oases' of a society rent by deep dissensions, about
to spill over into bitter civil war. Scrutiny's 'organic society' and
a golden rural world of unexploited seventeenth-century cottagers
and husbandmen was even more obviously idealized: a petty
bourgeois idyll spun out of the discontents of a Cambridge
intellectual faction whose ignorance and distrust of the people
was profound and at times absurd. In Eliot's and Waugh's case,
the note of disdain – the 'lack of reverence' for ordinary lives –
was unmistakable. A truly civilized society depended on hierarchy, Christianity and the class system; poverty 'smelt' and the
proletariat, given half a chance, would struggle not for cultural
renewal or human decency, but for a philistine nirvana of cheaper
and more readily available consumer goods.[47]

The coincidence of the High Anglican and the Leavisite reading
of general history was pointed by a parallel verdict on the cultural
effects of the seventeenth-century 'revolution'. In Eliot's version
of the decline and fall of English poesy, the age of the Antonines
was located before the Civil War when absolute monarchy and

the Anglican church still flourished, and poets like Donne and Herbert displayed 'a unity of sensibility and an easy fusion of thought and feeling', which were to be shattered by philistine Puritanism and social revolution. 'The upshot was the literary disaster of John Milton': the blind, withdrawn, unappealing 'virgin of Christ's' – who used English like a dead language, and drained from the poetic imagination all spontaneity of thought, word and image – exercised a wholly baneful effect on English sensibility. Thereafter, literature became a thing apart, the product of antinomian heresies such as 'poetic language', 'genius', 'the inner light': doctrines of an iconoclastic society which had severed its traditional roots, 'lost collective belief and declined into an errant individualism'.[48]

Leavis also believed that something disastrous had happened to English sensibility in the seventeenth century. And, once again, Milton was the key: whatever the merits of the early verse, the later epic style was deadened by 'the routine gesture', 'the heavy fall', the 'pedantic artifice', the 'inescapable monotony of the ritual'. In 1940, *Scrutiny* had complained of Rickword's failure to relate the principles expressed in Milton's political writing to the issue of his poetic sensibility. And what mattered was the latter: in Leavis's evaluation, the author of *Areopagitica*, *Eikonoklastes*, and *The Tenure of Kings and Magistrates* never surfaced. From a Marxist perspective, however, political engagement was fundamental: Leavis's Milton, like Eliot's Milton – indeed the whole treatment of literature as a disembodied continuum of texts – was a symptom of exactly the 'dissociation' they deplored. A Milton shorn of his revolutionary politics and demoted from Parnassus on purely formalist grounds, no less than a Milton reclaimed for post-medieval theology, authority and 'the Christian tradition', was the product of a deeply conservative intellectual enterprise.[49]

The intellectual idiom of the period was, indeed, particularly inimical to the Marxist endeavour. There were, of course, numerous cross-currents in the writings of the late 1940s, some destined to become the prevailing 'components' of an 'end of ideology' culture a decade later; but, in the history of *mentalité* there is invariably something of a hiatus between concept and reception, and what stands out in the 'debates' of the time is the liberal establishment's defence of moral values and the sacredness of individual conscience against the claims of scientism, determinism and collectivism – it was the Marxist materialism that was complained of not the underlying metaphysic.[50] The major features of this 'cold war' culture, widely diffused through the BBC and the middle-brow intellectual weeklies, were an embattled 'mythology of Western Civilization', a pervasive 'cultural pessimism' extending all the way from Victor Gollancz's disquisition on 'our threatened values' to Toynbee's successive versions of 'Civilization on Trial', a critical questioning and sometimes outright rejection of scientific optimism in the name of higher spiritual or moral values, and a literary culture characterized by traditionalism, idealism and escapism.[51]

The continuities of British history were now subsumed under those of a broader, ideologically defined, 'Western Civilization': a heritage derived from Hellenic culture and a Roman framework of law and government, preserved during the Middle Ages by the special care of the Holy Catholic Church and the Holy Roman Empire, and passed on directly to the commonwealth of European nations without significant breaks or discontinuities.[52] This well-known construct, widely popularized during the period in the work of Toynbee, Gilbert Murray, Maurice Bowra, Christopher Dawson, Ernest Barker, Bertrand Russell and a host of lesser lights, and travelling under many labels – a 'common western tradition', 'Western values', 'Atlantic culture', the 'free world' – as it emerged in political discourse, detached from its putative historical moorings could well be seen as 'a smokescreen' behind which its militant champions were 'wheeling up the more compelling western artillery of the atom-bomb'.[53]

Not without cause, perhaps, for the hinge of Western history, it transpired, the key link between the modern and the ancient world was the Middle Ages; and the crucial component of the medieval transfusion of the Graeco-Roman heritage was Christianity: 'the western tradition itself', said Christopher Dawson, 'is nothing more or less than the culture of Christendom'. And Christendom, as Toynbee reiterated in a number of works in which he extended the 'Great Schism' of the eleventh century and re-enacted the Mongul conquests of the thirteenth, specifically excluded Byzantium and its Muscovite heir: the third Rome, guardian of 'orthodox doctrine' against Western schismatics and unbelievers. Admittedly, 'the Marxian church which had been orthodox in Russia since 1917', did not quite play it that way; but the Soviet adoption of Marxism, like Peter the Great's earlier borrowing of bourgeois ways, was only made to defend Holy Russia: 'hating and despising western ideology', she was forced to adopt Western techniques and heresies to defeat the West at its own game.[54]

The Western tradition was steeped in Christian thought and Christian institutions, and Christian thought and institutions of a particular kind: not the traditions of the rebel Protestant churches or the radical early Christian communities, but those of the High Middle Ages and its modern votaries. The ideology, one might say, was Roman in a double sense: geographically – with Spain, Portugal and other authoritarian Catholic regimes, drafted into the defence of the 'free world' – but in a chronological sense also. The dominant position within the historical profession of medievalists, the continued importance of Anglo-Saxon and Middle English language and literature, and the more widely diffused influence of 'the Oxford fantasists', C. S. Lewis, J. R. Tolkein and their friends: these features, also, pointed to a closing of the ranks behind common Western Christian values.[55] In the widely diffused pastiche of the period stretching from St Augustine to St Thomas Aquinas, what was emphasized was transmission, conflation, continuity. Even the sixteenth century brought nothing new: the Reformation, Butterfield, the Methodist lay preacher, told his Cambridge audience in 1948, was simply 'an internal displacement within the system of medieval Christendom'. So great had been the changes in the last 200 years, that Catholic and Protestant should be viewed, he said, 'almost as twins, two aspects of the same thing'.[56]

Christianity, said Butterfield, was 'historical religion': embedded in the story of a particular people, in the life and ministry of God Incarnate and the ecumenical mission of the apostles, it offered a unique insight into the whole pattern of historical development and into the drama of sin and redemption played out not only in the fortunes of peoples and communities but in the life-stories of each and every human being. The most formidable challenge to Christianity today, namely the Marxist creed, was likewise based on an interpretation of history; it, too, boasted a way of looking at collective humanity. Technical history – a 'bloodless pedestrian thing' unable to satisfy the burning 'desire of the young' for a satisfying interpretation of history and life – and the parochial brands of national history – the political tradition which Butterfield himself once had lauded as the English way – were quite unable to meet the challenge: 'if events give Marxist history a chance to establish a foothold in this country, there is so much intellect as well as plausibility in its use of the general recipe, that the English version would collapse like a House of cards'. Indeed, the Whig tradition, weakened by complacency and bad conscience, was particularly vulnerable to aggressive Marxist colonization: a combination of imperial guilt, liberal tolerance and shallow progessivism, he thought, had 'almost embarrassed' its 'case in advance'.[57]

Like the wartime Englishman, but at a general and ecumenical level, the Christian was in 'a right relation to history'. A Providential view of history and of the human predicament was alone capable of addressing the mysterious antinomies, complexities and disproportions of the human story and of meeting the Marxist dialectic head-on. A Christian perspective enabled historians to move beyond the moral simplicities of the Victorians without succumbing to 'the equal and opposite' Marxist error of materialism – 'the bleak study of society as a mechanism or an organism' – by measuring the human texture of events and confronting the issue of sin, responsibility and moral judgement, in a story 'where disaster might come from man's selfishness and yet be nobody's fault'.[58]

The challenge to this Christian world view, according to Butterfield, dated from the Scientific Revolution of the seventeenth century – a sudden slippage in the foundations of Western thought which transformed the whole diagram of the physical universe, altered the nature of human life itself, and 'reduced the Renaissance and the Reformation to . . . mere episodes'.[59] The seventeenth century witnessed the secularization of the European mind, the loss of tragedy and the sense of sin, the banishment of Satan 'even more decisively than God', 'the disenchantment of the world' – a movement traced in somewhat different but complementary ways by Butterfield, Whitehead, Basil Willey, Michael Oakeshott, E. M. Tillyard and C. S. Lewis. The positive reassessment of the 'medieval world view' as a world of purposeful harmony and creative ideals, and the negative evaluation of the 'new philosophy' as something 'hard, cold, colourless and dead', an interpretation hitherto restricted to a scattering of Catholic eccentrics, was now academically respectable for the first time in 300 years.[60] Shakespeare was transformed from Renaissance humanist to the last and most eloquent spokesman of a 'discarded' world picture. Why, even the struggle between the Catholic Church and the 'new science' could be reinterpreted, not as a struggle between free enquiry and obscurantism, but as a battle between two equally valid orders of truth, with the church as a moderate and even-handed arbiter caught in the crossfire.[61]

'The politics of rationalism' – the substitution of universal rules for local habits, a 'master science' or 'method' for practical knowledge, personal attachments or moral traditions – could be dated from Bacon and Descartes' seventeenth-century bonfire of received wisdom in the name of demonstrable truths. And in Oakeshott's view, 'the politics of rationalism' lay at the root of all the ills of modernity.[62] Marxism was only one among many rationalist 'ideologies', but to many it constituted the most direct challenge to the moral traditions to which Oakeshott appealed. In 1946, the BBC had run a series entitled *The Challenge of Our Time*, and its recurring theme was the danger perceived by churchmen, writers, philosophers and historians in the collective management and the cooperative planning outlined by the scientific contributers. Where Arthur Koestler, Canon Demant and Professor Woodward felt nothing but forboding – 'a doom on our civilization', a disintegration and a degeneration of life, a dissolution of the self and the infinite in a social or utilitarian pseudo-ethics – the scientists recruited by J. D. Bernal – this was only 1946 and Bernal and his rationalist 'fellow-travellers' could still command the airwaves – exuded the positive faith and self-confidence of 'scientific humanism'.[63]

In the view of Marxist commentators – and one could hardly find a better example of their total instrumentalization of ethics at the time – these Sunday evening talks were nothing less than 'ideological war':

> Philosophies are not merely systems of ideas worked out in academic seclusion ... They are either the organizing conceptions of a progressive class giving its interpretation of the world that it is mastering, and helping to understand the forces it wishes to control; or the philosophy of a declining class by which it seeks to buttress its power and by which it opposes the class which threatens it with destruction.[64]

Bernal and his colleagues spoke of 'the freedom of necessity' in full confidence that necessity was coincident with the forward march of humanity towards socialism. Their opponents – this was the Marxists' perception – were no longer the triumphant bourgeoisie of the First Industrial Revolution but a decadent generation of worried capitalists. The 'science mysticism' of Jeans and

Eddington – the view that scientific truths were simply a collection of mental fictions – or the attack on 'objectivism' mounted
by Polanyi and Koestler – the disintegration of matter into
perception and the rejection of regularity or certainty for the
debilitating principle of indeterminacy – were of a piece with the
providentialism of Butterfield and the pessimism of Toynbee. The
repudiation of rationality and scientific progress, like the selective
historical amnesia when it came to its heroic and revolutionary
past, was symptomatic of a dying bourgeois order: the bourgeoisie
could no longer find a pattern to its history or a meaning to its
physical and material world, because it did not like what it saw.[65]

Like many such disputes of the sort, the argument between
Marxist scientists and non-Marxist literary intellectuals was a battle
over authorized discourse, over who made the rules and dictated
the language of discussion. Koestler and Co's defence of ethical
first principles, and the inviolable distinction of means and ends,
was a call for the continued priority of liberal values and personal
freedoms over changing social needs; while Bernal's espousal of
social needs, which would 'always justify the means if the end is
good and the means . . . adapted to promote it', was intended to
relegate tender moral sensibilities to the more urgent collective
responsibilities.[66]

Bernal and his fellow contributors to *The Communist Answer to
the Challenge of Our Time* were, of course, at pains to point out
that running society in a sensible and conscious way did not involve
the sacrifice of individual freedoms; quite the reverse: the
individual's role in the new democratic society would be enhanced
and liberated by its social content. Concepts like 'liberty and human
rights were neither eternal nor socially neutral'; in the last two
centuries they had come to mean private property, free trade,
inequality. As another 'red' professor, J. B. S Haldane explained:
'we are all suffering from spiritual planning . . . so efficient that
most of us have not even noticed it'. Koestler's verdict that the
remedies of the Yogi and the Commissar were equally doomed;
the frequently expressed clerical sentiment 'that . . . somehow, by
hook or by crook, this world must be robbed of [its] importance';
the retreat into an inner citadel of self and a realm of moral
abstraction; the revival of the Burkean case against human nature
and for original sin: these were part of a ruling class campaign
against 'the belief that the people can run the show by themselves'.
They added up to the Panglossian conclusion delivered by

Oakeshott as he stepped into Laski's chair at the London School of Economics: 'the world is the best of all possible worlds, and everything in it is a necessary evil'. 'We cannot', argued Bernal, 'leave this challenge to be taken up by soured intellectuals, with their eyes fixed on the past. It must be taken up by those who have the hope, the knowledge, the ability and the drive to define the problems of our time and to solve them.' The antidote to such poisonous despair was for people to take control over their own lives; and the precondition for that was a world of peace and cooperation, 'fellowship' and closer understanding with the Soviet Union and the defeat of those who were 'dissemenating suspicion and laying the groundwork for a new war'.[67]

There was little doubt where Marxist historians stood in this battle of the lay sermons. Humanists they might be; but first and foremost they were Marxists. Cut off from a Labour movement which had once again betrayed socialism, from erstwhile cultural radicals turned moral champions of the West, the members of the Historians' Group inevitably followed in the slipstream of the scientists: the intellectual leaders of the party at large. The party required commitment; and it was the compatibility of political commitment, common decency, humane values and fineness of sensibility which Hill considered in his first strategic article for *The Modern Quarterly* in 1946. The choice of subject, on 'Society and Andrew Marvell', was apposite in a number of ways. In one sense, it was a response to the Leavisite complaint that Marxist studies of political and social writings somehow excluded the poetic sensibility. For it was Marvell's poems that Hill chose to consider. But the complex metaphors, the double meanings and the 'dialectical thought' behind the poems of the 1640s and 1650s were more than conceits – all of them 'in the last analysis' dealt with 'adjustment of individual conduct to external conditions and forces'. Marvell was well aware of the nature of the conflict through which he lived and could see merit in both sides. Yet he was able to make an unreserved choice; unlike the sensitive souls of Great Tew and Little Gidding, he did not evade his social responsibilities – indeed his later writings projected a mature and untroubled belief in the political principles he had adopted amidst the brutal realities of the Civil War. The wise and virtuous man 'makes destiny his choice': the progressive artist did not have to surrender decency or sensibility to the requirements of living in the world.[68]

It was precisely this sort of spiritually mature commitment that was so lacking in many historians. There could be no question as to Toynbee's scholarship or his sensibility. Indeed his work was a standing rebuke to the parochialism and the myopia of the profession; he asked the big questions, ranged over the whole terrain, and was able to find a pattern, a recurrent theme in rise and fall of civilizations. Nevertheless, said Hill, *A Study of History* could 'only be described as a very sad book'. Toynbee retreated in dismay from his own creation into mystification and irrationalism. Denying the material basis of civilization and the progressive nature of humanity's control of the environment, reducing the dynamic of history to the play of spiritual forces and ideas, he was condemned to record the endless cycles of challenge and response – the 'civilizing' work of creative minorities and the revolutions of 'internal proletariats' – from which the only escape was the hope of spiritual regeneration in 'the bosom of Mother Chuch'. Toynbee's special brand of social and spiritual elitism, his political passivity and squeamish sensibilities were ideally suited to the sophistries of cold war ideology, and it was little wonder that the Director of Studies of the Institute of International Affairs was signed up as Britain's 'cultural legate' to *Time* magazine, 'a champion of the remnant of Christian civilization against the forces that threaten it', a pessimistic Fukuyama for the Forties.[69]

3.3   HOLDING THE LINE

Communist intellectuals were long used to defining themselves by a logic of alterity – 'I'm a Methodist', said the young Christopher Hill to Rodney Hilton: 'what's your heresy' – and the Marxism of the Historians' Group was something of a self-conscious antipode to Cold War orthodoxies.[70] The politics of the 1940s did nothing to change views they had acquired during what had seemed the last days of the old bourgeois order. Quite the reverse: it did not require much polemical skill to highlight the 'falsity' and despair behind the slogans of the time, to counter the wisespread idealism and 'providentialism' with the 'realities' of material structure and a 'science of history', or the supposed continuities of British and Western civilization with the breaks and ruptures of historical development. The rise and fall of classes formed the nucleus of their Marxism, both in the sense that it explained the dynamic of history and defined their 'revolutionary objective': the end of class struggle and the classless society. Class struggle as 'a universal condition and an absolute moral good' was of course a male and a public pursuit, a business of streets and barricades, parliamentary conflicts and formal battles in a Civil War. There was little room in this historical drama for the private and domestic. Thus, in Hill's reading of Stuart England, religion was seen not as an inner light or a personal calling but as the 'State Ecclesiastical' and its Puritan opposition; similarly, for Lindsay, the struggle between iconoclasts and iconodules in Byzantine history had little to do with a loathing or a love of images, but was really about social insurgency and political repression. Political and religious struggle resulted in victories and surrenders, involving the destruction of an old and institution of a new social order; it was predicated on zero-sum notions of power, in which exploited or frustrated classes, lacking even a partial interest in existing arrangements or an attachment to traditional values, had a world to win and nothing to lose but their chains.[71]

The version presented by Hill and Dell in *The Good Old Cause* was representative: 'Very briefly summarized our subject here is the story of how one social class was driven from power by another, and how the form of state power appropriate to the needs of the first was replaced by one appropriate to the second.'[72] The organization of the book, the tendentious extract headings ('Merchants in a feudal state'; 'how to become a gentleman'; 'the new power of money'; 'class feeling'; 'the trade union of kings'; 'religion or class interests' and so on), the laborious running commentary, were intended to demonstrate the 'deeper class struggle' and the progressive meaning of the English Revolution: 'we hear the English Revolution speaking for itself with its multitude of voices', enthused one party reviewer, but Hill and Dell were strict choir-masters and the class harmonies came over loud and clear.[73] No revolution in history was made by one class acting alone; there were complex alliances and schisms as the struggle unfolded. Nevertheless, classes were viewed as solid cohesive blocks capable of carrying out preconceived military strategies. These organized, disciplined, self-conscious corporate armies, in turn, matched a 'two camp' vision of society split down the middle, with progressives lined up against reactionaries through the ages under a number of historical guises – the model sketched in the first sentences of *The Communist Manifesto* and likewise consonant with polarized Cominform rhetoric.[74]

Nowhere was the tendency to conceive of the world in terms of opposing 'camps' more marked than in the field of thought itself – a schema derived from Marx's obsessive sense of 'idealism' as socialism's only serious philosophical rival, and greatly strengthened in the late 1940s by the anti-communist ends to which idealism was put: whether it was dressed up in the language of Orwell or Sartre, the defence of Western values or the assertion of existential freedoms, idealism meant a retreat from scientific analysis and concrete action into the inner life of the mind or spirit. Idealism 'was always doomed . . . to end in the rehabilitation of camouflaged theology'; materialism was invariably 'challenging, critical and revolutionary'.[75] 'In the beginning was the deed'; and the editorials of *The Modern Quarterly* were filled with fulminations against doctrines that failed to measure up to the journal's exclusive definition of 'material' grace. Somewhat less stridently, Christopher Hill's thumbnail sketch of 'The Materialist Conception of History' explained the 'advantage of Marxism over materialism': 'human reason [as] "the product of history" can be explained in terms of the physical nature which preceded and coexisted with it. But if ideas are the 'prime mover', then the human intellect is an unexplained miracle and a science of history is impossible'.[76] Even the journal that was to act as a bridge to sympathetic bourgeois historiography took its stand on these principles: *Past and Present* was to be 'a journal of scientific history', conceived, as its opening editorial pointed out, as a critical response to the 'recrudescence of certain schools of thought . . . which den[ied] the very possibility of a rational and scientific approach' to the subject.[77]

In Britain, as in France, the materialist and rationalist strain in the Marxist corpus dovetailed naturally enough with the long tradition of radical freethought – with a rationalist anthropology stretching back through the work of Jane Harrison and Sir James Frazer to Tylor, Morgan and Engels, and an epic version of the history of ideas popularized by such classics as Draper's *History of the Conflict between Science and Religion*, Lecky's *Rise of Rationalism in Europe*, Bury's *Idea of Progress* or Lea's *History of the Inquisition*.[78] Rationalism also provided a dramatic series of landmarks and confrontations in the history of thought entirely consonant with the turning points and revolutionary struggles of Marxist theory: an Ionian renaissance which had 'liberated reason from the thraldom of myth', a European Reformation which had thrown off the shackles of Popery and scholasticism, an Enlightenment which had launched a fearless attack on religious and political dogma, and an evolutionary science which had banished the remnants of the theological world view.[79]

'The historians recruited into the Communist party in the 1930s were steeped in the spirit of freethought.'[80] The archeologist, Gordon Childe – whose contempt for religion was notorious – consistently juxtaposed creative thought processes with 'theological and magical' consciousness. No ideology could permanently endure unless it was 'in harmony with the productive forces and compatible with their development'; but 'the reckoning could be long delayed': 'history bristles with examples of the hindrances imposed by superstitions on science and its applications'. The leitmotif of Benjamin Farrington's trilogy on *Science and Politics in the Ancient World* was the conflict between movements of popular enlightenment and the oligarchic manipulation of popular beliefs, irrational cults, later on, of Christianity itself: 'Jehovah definitely discourages natural philosophy', and the coming of Christianity 'jettisoned the whole cargo of pagan science which we in modern times labour so assiduously to recover'.[81] Such a recovery, argued Hill, was the achievement of seventeenth-century radicals: for the first time 'God . . . was . . . subordinated to man-made laws . . . and the Bible . . . interpreted with reference to social needs'. As for the goodly company of Civil War revolutionaries, they were on the Devil's side without knowing it: 'the intellectual advance of Levellers, Diggers and Ranters to a rational materialism was picked up by the French Encyclopaedists and late eighteenth century English radicals'.[82]

Anti-clericalism – an old ingredient in native socialism, where Nonconformist fear of priestcraft overlapped with rationalist suspicion of all religion – was given a new lease of life during the Cold War when Catholic parties took a lead in anti-communist political and trade union activity, and Catholic spokesmen were prominent in the defence of Western Christian values. Iconoclasm joined with materialism as a popular lower class movement; and the revival of icons – in eighth-century Byzantium, seventeenth-century Bohemia, or at a somewhat more prosaic level in Archbishop Laud's restoration of incense and altar rails – was depicted as a ruling class narcotic prescribed and administered by the state to giddy and anaesthetize the masses.[83] In Britain, it was Anglo-Catholicism which formed 'the ideological spearhead of a reaction which has affected all the English churches'. It was Anglo-Catholics who led the the flight into medievalism and the cult of Christendom or King Charles the Martyr; according to Hill, Catholic propagandists were 'almost as busily at work' on the historical 'as on the trade union front':

> Neither in the seventeenth century nor today were Catholic apologists interested in ordinary people having a creative vision. If we believe in the dignity of man, we may realize that we can get along without priests. If we believe in man's creative capacity, we may imagine that we can build a socialist society. That would never do. So Catholic propagandists . . . want to play down our past, to rob the English people of their traditions of struggle, to misinterpret them.[84]

Standing over against the hierarchic order of Catholicism was the 'democratic world' of science. The communist historians grew up in the shadow of the writer–scientists of the 1930s; they cut their teeth on such Marxist classics as Boris Hessen's *Social Roots of Newton's Principia*, J. G. Crowther's *Social Relations of Science* and Bernal's *Social Function of Science*:

> For them as for the scientists, science was a metaphor of the human achievement, a measure of progress, a crucial lever for change. Its method of propagating itself was by an appeal to reason, and it was the product of a society 'looking to a future of well being'. Science, in short, was a great progressive force in its own right as well as being a reflection of those positive forces in society which encouraged it.[85]

In science, said Bernal, one could not separate means and ends, thought and practice. 'The achievement of any human purpose [was] a unitary thing'; and the history of science had to be treated as a social and economic activity, reflecting the productive forces and the division of labour of the time, the social and economic 'needs' and the technology available to satisfy them, an institutional framework involving different types of social oragnization and changing patterns of patronage, and an ever- evolving methodology once philosophical but increasingly mathematical or mechanical in orientation – an interpretation which was to produce such monuments of Marxist endeavour as Bernal's own *Science in History* and Needham's great project on *Science and Civilization in China*.[86]

The history of science was a political history, also, with epochal leaps and revolutionary struggles; it, too, had its barricades, its Bastilles and its Committees of Public Safety. Thus, the Scientific Revolution was not just a victory for the new physics and astronomy, but for a progressive social and political order also. The world of the Schoolmen was a world of hierarchy and social stability: a static world order with planets circling round a central earth, priests subordinate to the Pope, subjects obedient to their sovereign, mathematicians answerable to theologians; and 'the transition to the progressively more "democratic" universes of Copernicus, Gilbert, Kepler and Newton reflect[ed] the struggle for the abolition of feudalism and the creation of a bourgeois democratic society'.[87] Similarly, in Britain, 'the battle of ancients and moderns' – of progressive adult education institutes and scientific literati lined up against the academic establishment – 'reproduced and formed part of the revolutionary struggle of the progressive bourgeoisie'.[88] As Hill was to explain in his review of Farrington's aptly named book on *Bacon, Philosopher of Industrial Science*: Bacon and Lavoisier had inaugurated 'the bourgeois epoch in science' against traditional 'feudal values', and 'against the prejudices and dogmas of an effete civilization... just as Lysenko and his colleagues were 'inaugurating a new epoch today'.

In the Soviet Union, the obstructive dogmas of bourgeois science have to be brushed aside ... if socialist science is to devote itself wholeheartedly to the relief of man's estate. So Bacon was fighting against the prejudices and dogmas which a priestly academic caste continued to preach ... Bacon's conception of science, in striking contrast to that of the high priests of bourgeois science in its decadence, was materialistic, utilitarian and profoundly humane.[89]

For even here, the worm of idealism was eating away at a scientific history of scientific thought and with it at the possibility of sensible cooperative solutions to contemporary problems. According to Butterfield and his followers, the history of science was a history of creative, imaginative voyages on the part of lonely isolated geniuses. Butterfield's 'happy' metaphors – 'putting on a new thinking cap', 'picking up the other end of the stick', seeing through 'a new pair of glasses'; Rupert Hall's rigid demarcation of the work of scholars and craftsmen, with scientific 'breakthroughs' invariably the work of ivory towered thinkers, 'deep intellectual' enterprises, abstract, unpractical, 'in the last resort philosophical'; Koestler's dramatic depiction of the scientist as creative artist 'sleep-walking' a crazy and unpredictable path to the truth – these interpretations turned the scientific revolution into an intellectual miracle and mystified the dynamics of historical change.[90] And they carried a clearly coded Cold War message that 'great ideas could not be hatched by mechanized husbandry . . . science had not chugged forward following Five Year Plans, but had been transformed in stupendous unpredictable' mental leaps. The freer it was from state planning and outside interference, the better it would be: Solomon's Houses and Soviet agrobiological institutes were apt to produce – well, Bacons (something of a bad joke to professional scientists) and Lysenkos.[91]

Moreover, for some of its proponents, this 'mystical' history of science carried its burden of pride and punishment. Butterfield's misgivings about a universe deprived of sympathy and humane associations were pointed by Koestler's bleak vision of a new spiritual ice age. The age of the Schoolmen was an ice age also: a 'glacial period' characterized by a 'pedantically graded universe, wrapped in cellophane spheres', 'froze[n] . . . in scholastic rigidity', and only gradually 'thawed' by a 'devious Gulf-stream' of the mind, wending its way from Arabia and Asia Minor to the wastes of the Baltic and Copernicus' celestial tower. But the new knowledge had brought a new Fall. Bacon's vision splendid of infinite human progress and 'a restitution and reinvigoration of . . . the sovereignty and power' which humanity possessed in 'the first state of creation', looked forward instead to a world of 'spiritual desiccation' – with humanity cut off from Nature, 'fact from value, head from heart, mechanism from meaning . . . mind-formed manacles from which the West has never escaped'.[92]

For Marxists, the bourgeois renunciation of its scientific revolution, like the denial of its social and political past, was another symptom of a dying culture rapidly being overhauled by that of the socialist world.[93] As with science, so too with political ideas, their task was to expose the illusions and mystifications of bourgeois analysis. In his opening address to the party conference on 'Liberty and Communism' in 1949, Rodney Hilton noted how a disembodied concept of individual liberty formed the basis of bourgeois apologetics. But society conceived as an arena of competitive individuals was inseparable from the class inequality and social anarchy of capitalism: the self-deception of bourgeois thinkers had as its 'necessary corollary . . . the deliberate deception of the masses'. Once again, the English Revolution prefigured the socialist transformation which would unravel the polarities of the past. Liberty in feudal society referred to a conglomeration of privileges – 'numberless indefeasible chartered freedoms' – which had to be smashed for the bourgeoisie to 'extend and generalize the concept of liberty'. To carry out their revolution, however, it needed support from 'all the other classes which were oppressed by the feudal absolutist state':

> It was not only the bourgeoisie, but as John Milton put it, 'this iron flail, the people, which drove the bishops out of their chairs and gave us what we most desired' . . . This is the only way in which we in our day, too, can 'weld the people into an iron flail', to 'win what they most desire'.

And in a remarkable passage which encapsulated the triumphalism of the movement in 1950, he summed up the international prospects:

> We live today at one of the greatest turning points in human history. Tremendous movements of human beings the world over are abolishing established social orders, some of which have seen little change for centuries. Together with the colonies of modern imperialism, layer upon layer of the old feudal and pre-feudal orders of Asia are being swept away by movements of national and social liberation. In what were the most backward parts of Europe, workers and peasants, liberated from home-grown despotism and foreign intervention, are laying the foundations of socialism. In those parts of Europe and America where power is still in the hands of the imperialists, the workers are hammering on the doors of the privileged, strengthened by the success of their comrades in the Soviet Union, the new democracies, in China and elsewhere . . . It is not only the working class and its allies which understand the significance of this turning point in history. The old ruling class whether in Washington, London, Delhi or Tokyo understand it too . . . They are . . . doomed.[94]

The global perspectives came naturally to historians of the group. A number of them had spent their war in India and the Far East, and had witnessed the receiving end of Western values, European traditions and British institutions: fifty years later, John Saville could still write of his experience of colonial injustice 'burning like acid into the brain'. Imperialism, they believed, was 'alive and virulent, if terminally ill': more than most, they were aware of the Labour Party's substitution of pious aspiration and economic manipulation for genuine decolonization.[95] Moral outrage – always the major ingredient in socialist anti-colonialism – was coupled in the 1940s and 1950s with widespread acceptance of the Leninist doctrine of capitalist imperialism. Here was a theory which seemed to bring together class analysis, the laws of capitalist accumulation and the whole panorama of global politics in a way which they found intellectually and emotionally satisfying. The doctrine gave an added relevance to their studies of pre-industrial societies like seventeenth-century England: for perhaps, as E. P. Thompson put it, 'causes which were lost in England . . . might in Asia or Africa yet be won'. It probably, also, reinforced their anti-Americanism, and assuaged their doubts about Soviet Russia.[96] Whatever its faults, the Soviet Union – a multinational commonwealth on a par in its diversity with the British Empire – exhibited none of the racism or institutionalized exploitation of native peoples that still characterized British rule.[97] And now that British rule was collapsing, how else could one explain the continued miseries of the Indian subcontinent or the Indonesian archipelago, save by the new chains of American economic control. Untrammelled by the guilts and delusions of the English bourgeoisie, preferring power to imperial pretension, the United States was the 'receiver' for the disintegrating British Empire. The destruction of Empire, therefore, involved a dual struggle for national liberation on the part of British and colonial people from the domination of American capital and from the privileged illusions of the British ruling class – from an 'uneasy alliance-in-rivalry' which 'stifled and subjugated' them both.[98]

The most obvious application of 'two camp' thinking – its natural element as it were – was in the arena of international politics. Over and again in the past, and especially during eras of dramatic social and political change, the world had divided into ideological blocks – the revolutionary and counter-revolutionary camps of the 1790s, the confessional divides of sixteenth- and seventeenth-century Europe, the confrontation of Greek democracy and theocratic kingship in the ancient world: 'a choice of systems' which allowed no room for indeterminates or 'nice shades of political opinion', and where not choosing degenerated into appeasement or political 'collaboration'. Communists formed by the ideological fault-lines of the 1930s were naturally drawn into thinking of post-war politics in pre-war categories: viewing the Greek as another Spanish Civil War, German and Japanese economic resurrection and rearmament as the re-emergence of Fascism and British connivance in the American 'Plot against Peace' as another version of the tactics of the 'traitor class' of 1938.[99] In language which mirrored and reversed the geopolitical distortions of cold war historiography, Hill pictured the 'battle for an independent foreign policy' 300 years before:

> All Europe was dividing into two camps – the Protestant camp looking to the revolutionary Dutch republic for aid and protection, supported by democrats and progressives in all countries; and the reactionary pro-Spanish camp . . . Between the progressive and reactionary camps, then as now, stood England.[100]

Evidently, the two camps were not moral equivalents: one was reactionary, aggressive, and anti-democratic, the other progressive, peace-loving and anti-imperialist; one was 'doomed', the other bound eventually to triumph. So too in the 1940s: scarcely an issue of Cominform's *For a Lasting Peace, For a People's Democracy* went by, without news of another great socialist leap forward, and 10 or a 100 million fresh souls netted for the cause; conversely, there was little in the shattered world of Marshall Plans and Sterling Crises presage the long post-war boom of Western capitalism. The only thing that kept the dilapidated show on the road at all was American money and American arms. Independence, therefore, was defined solely as a liberation from Catholic reaction and its twentieth-century counterpart: the American threat to British life and culture.

In 1948, Cominform had launched its famous peace campaign; and in his report to the organization in 1949, Suslov warned that Washington and London were 'carrying on preparations for war at top speed': peace hung 'by a thread'.[101] The fact that the anti-democratic camp was in advanced decay had not diminished the danger; quite the reverse: 'The experience of history teaches that the more hopeless the position of imperialist reaction, the more frantic it becomes, and the greater is the danger of its launching into military ventures.' As the Counter-Reformation and the Thirty Years War amply demonstrated, dying empires had a nasty habit of striking back.[102]

In this battle of the blocks, according to Hill, England's role was pivotal:

> The outcome in Europe, then as now, was closely related to the struggle of Englishmen to understand the issues and take control of their own destinies.

Subservience to Spain was the last hope of the doomed monarchy and the feudal ruling clique in the seventeenth century, just as licking Mr Truman's boots is the only hope of reaction in England today. In opposing this policy the bourgeosie led a struggle of the whole nation just as the working class can today . . .

During the English Civil War, Catholic reaction had been smashed once and for all, and England was set on the path to national sovereignty, bourgeois civil society – and trade war.[103] For here the obsessive similarities of seventeenth- and twentieth-century worlds ended: the bourgeois order was based on market competition and colonial rivalry; the socialist was cooperative and peaceful. When the bourgeoisie seized power in England, 'almost the first act of its foreign policy was to attack the Netherlands'; but 'a successful socialist revolution' would 'produce a new ally for . . . world peace'. And in an extraordinary passage, which perfectly captures his conflation of 'diamet', Puritan 'Good Old Cause' and embattled Communist Party apologetic, Hill surveyed the battle for a free England from 1649 to 1948:

The bourgeois revolutionaries were led by an exalted dream of patriotism. They wanted a new free England. 'Methinks I see in my mind a noble and a puissant nation arousing herself like a strong man after sleep, and shaking her invincible locks': so wrote Milton in 1644. They obtained some but not all of what they hoped and fought for . . . Feudalism could be overthrown, national independence established; but it was independence for a bourgeois nation, and brought with it as necessary consequences: capitalist exploitation at home, subjection of other nations and war abroad. The battle for a free England had still to be won.

Today we are more fortunate. National independence can be won only by ending capitalist exploitation. Patriotism and internationalism are no longer opposites, for patriotism in Britain today demands the reversal of the policy of subservience to American imperialism and a break with the instigators of a new war. 'Under another name', this is what Milton fought for: today there is a chance that we may make England what Milton . . . dreamed she might be.[104]

The struggle for social justice and for emancipation and the socialist incline of English and of world history culminated, therefore, in the battle against 'the instigators of a war' that would wipe out humanity. Along with the red professors of science, members of the group were mobilized for the peace campaign which reached its apogee in 1950 and 1951. None of them, admittedly, could keep up with the indefatigable Bernal – the J. D. Bernal Peace Library in Marx House a fitting memorial to his ceaseless peregrinations and addresses to Soviet-inspired congresses around the globe. But at a lower level of intensity, they wrote their articles on famous 'partisans of peace', arranged their conferences on the people's long tradition of opposition to war, sought to demystify 'episodes of national grandeur', and to give back to the working-class movement another suppressed part of its heritage.[105] The propaganda purposes that informed these activities were probably most evident in the Cultural Committee's jamboree of 1951 on *The American Threat to British culture.* Speaker after speaker attacked the Korean war, the Marshall Plan, and a whole set of American iniquities which made the world less safe for the Soviet Union and its satellites. E. P. Thompson fulminated against the transatlantic appropriation of native socialist heroes and called for 'a moral offensive' against the 'crass, vulgarized, unfree' 'slaughter-house' culture that was being built in England's pleasant land. As he later admitted, the Communist Party in the early 1950s was no place for the academically squeamish.[106]

Yet, Thompson's verdict is probably justified: despite the Cold War polemics, the work of the Historians' Group was 'never deformed beyond recovery'. To begin with, the empirical idiom in British historiography was very strong, though not for the reasons that Thompson adduces: it was not so much 'the living line of Marx's analysis' which was 'continually present', as their non-Marxist training and the need to demonstrate their credentials to colleagues 'only too ready to dismiss [their] work as dogmatic oversimplification and propagandistic jargon'. To be effective in the 'battle of ideas' they had to communicate, and 'outside the party there was no intellectual public which took Marxism seriously' – in the late 1940s, it is salutary to remember, there was still 'no discussion of dialectical materialism in any official course in philosophy in any university in Britain'. An ill-judged publication, and the academic establishment was ready to pounce on 'Marxian historiography' as 'fundamentally opposed to the canons of Western scholarship'. It would, said the *Times Literary Supplement*, on one such occasion, 'be a dereliction of duty for university administrators to appoint or to keep Marxists in teaching posts'; and the purge of the WEAs, the dismissals – on 'purely academic grounds', of course – the barriers to promotion – Hobsbawm, Thompson, Kiernan, brilliant men with encyclopaedic minds, were only to be rewarded comparatively late in life – probably helped them to make at least a partial 'intellectual disengagement from Stalinism'.[107]

Moreover, the split between Marxist and advanced liberal readings of English history was often more rhetorical than substantive. However absurd it might be as a description of the actual complexities of a Europe where dynastic rivalries cut across confessional divides, and where regionalisms and centralizing governments were at loggerheads, Hill's black and white picture of international politics in the early seventeenth century was not so different from the traditional Protestant accents of English historiography, or from the assumptions and prejudices of contemporary English patriots: at the very least, it corresponded to the confessional hyperbole of the time. Ironically, the interpretation carried little conviction as an 'objective' or 'scientific' analysis of political forces and underlying class realities; but it did have some plausibility as a pathology of the fears and the aspirations of seventeenth-century English men and women.[108]

The 'two camp' vision applied to domestic politics also restated the old adversarial interpretation of Macaulay and Gardiner, with government and opposition lined up over taxation, subject liberties, foreign policy and the like: contending camps, 'composed on the basis of a single, consistent set of principles – an ideology'. For all his strictures on traditional historiography, Hill's work complemented the progressive parliamentary story of Neale and Notestein, with a House of Commons, united, hyperactive and purposeful, 'winning the initative' on a range of fiscal and constitutional issues. Indeed, the compulsive pedigree hunting, the 'linkages' and genealogical chains so evident in his writing were at times curiously undialectical: like Macaulay and Trevelyan, he too could be accused of diverting attention from the antinomies of the historical process – the triumph of progressives over reactionaries was ever so much easier. The carefully chosen words of the revised preface of *The English Revolution* did not so much answer as confirm and update the criticism:

> The word progressive as used in this essay does not necessarily imply moral approval. It means simply that the tendency or social group so described contributed to the expansion of the wealth of the community . . . In the long run the creation of a new wealth by the rise of capitalism in England opened up the possibility of a more equitable distribution at a new level, just as the horrors of the industrial revolution

in the nineteenth century created the economic basis for the transition to socialism.[109]

Running alongside the progressivism, however, was something very different. Like many Marxist intellectuals, Hill inhabited a universe governed by precapitalist values. His work was haunted by the 'ancestral voices' of British socialism: by the set speeches of Protestant martyrs and the ringing phrases of buff-coated 'agitators' during the Civil War. It was touched, also, by what has been called a 'Romantic anti-capitalism', derived from the traditions and aspirations of native radicalism and from 'culturalist' residues never entirely obliterated by scientific Marxism.[110] Indeed, much of the appeal of Marxism to writers like Hill lay in its vision of a world where the hegemony of the market-place would be abolished and 'the untapped forces of popular resistance to capitalism' liberated.[111] The mixture of nostalgia and cultural revolt – the yearning for lost folk-worlds and the expectation of a communitarian socialist culture – can be seen at its most extreme in George Thomson, who combined an almost total identification with the myths and memories of the Gaelic-speaking but, by the 1940s, largely uninhabited Blasket Islands, with unreconstructed 'revolutionary dialectics' and latterly a demented Maoism. But it can also be found in his namesake Edward's resurrection of preindustrial popular traditions, and his 'participating witness' to the 'euphoric aftermath of a revolutionary transition' in post-war Yugoslavia.[112]

In a moving passage from his classic study of *Marxism and Poetry*, George Thomson conjured up Prospero's magic island: a subconscious world of the poet's imagination far removed from 'the sparkling surfaces' of his 'bourgeois city life'. The forces of nature are tamed by art, a fantastic masque performed, a poor man's heaven of ease and plenty set out before the revellers; but Prospero has to burn his books and bury his magic before he can return – such is the fate of the imagination in the 'real' world of unrestricted competition and exchange value. 'All art,' said Synge, 'is a collaboration. In countries 'where the imagination of the people and the language they use, is rich and living, it is possible for the writer to be rich and copious in his words, and at the same time to give the reality, which is the root of all poetry, in a comprehesive and natural form'. Where the harvest of popular culture was but a memory, poetry withered at the root: the bourgeois artist 'retreated to his ivory tower' – cut off from the people, spurned by the ruling class, with 'nobody to sing to but himself'.[113] Hill's enthusiastic descriptions of Tudor and Stuart literature, his evocations of the upside down worlds of the Civil War and his cheerless verdict on the linguistic refinement and emotional coarsening of post-revolutionary writing also came from Prospero's cell, and belonged to the same genre as Thomson's bardic communities, and the mythopoeic literary landscapes of F. R. Leavis. Naturally enough, he disclaimed sentimentality: the 'relative equality and communal spirit' of the medieval village was 'accompanied by grinding poverty for the mass of the population'. Yet one did 'not need to idealize "merrie England" to realize that much was lost' by its 'disruption': dilaectical materialism might have told him that it marked a further stage in the forward march of humanity; native socialism spoke otherwise.[114]

The result of these conflicting tendencies was that Hill's history like that of the group as a whole, spoke with a multitude of voices. A number of commentators have remarked on the tension in his writing and inspiration between what is sometimes referred to as a 'structuralism' and 'culturalism'. More correctly, what can be found are various layers of meaning and hidden agendas corresponding to the changing strategies and circumstances of the party in the period from the 1930s to 1956, and to the differing shades of pink and the rhetorical requirements of the various journals to which he contributed. Even in the late 1940s there were some rather distinctive rhetorical personae. There was the protégé of Kosminsky, the euologist of Lenin, the colleague of Dona Torr, and the somewhat literal-minded interpreter of Stalin's laws of historical change. Then there was Hill the modernist, the heir of the Enlightenment, the apostle of Bernalism and science: an activity conditioned by social needs, conceived, none the less, as mediator between base and superstructure, and as a congeries of true socialism – 'the cause of progress' throughout history. But there was also Hill, the deviant Leavisite, the celebrant of Milton, Marvell, and Winstanley, the true-born Englishman, the imitator of 'the plain homespun style of the mechanic preachers and pamphleteers of the 1640s', the sympathetic expositor of seventeenth-century religious ideas and expressions, the historian 'from below', concerned with looking at ordinary people on their own terms, in their own words and within their own sets of relations.[115] Some of these tensions were implicit in

the dual inheritance of British Marxism and in the hopes and
disappointments of the war and the immediate post-war period;
others can be traced back to the work of Marx himself; and later
in the 1960s and 1970s they were to inform a crucial reworking
of Marxism and a new socialist reading of English history under-
taken by Edward Thompson, Raymond Williams, Eric Hobsbawm
and, of course, by Hill himself. But in the 1940s and early 1950s,
no such mediation was evident. Instead the humanist mode and
the broader perspectives traced in his studies of radical myth-
history and popular prose coexisted uncomfortably with the crude
mechanical categories outlined in *The English Revolution*, the listing of proof texts in *The Good Old Cause*, and the scientific rationalism of the early essays in *The Modern Quarterly*.

Even for Hill's fellow Marxists, meeting in 1947 and 1948 to
consider *State and Revolution in Tudor and Stuart England*, the orthodox explanation of epochal change in seventeenth-century
England was not without its problems.[116] Thanks to the publication of Dobb's 'Studies' and to recent work by Soviet historians,
it was now thought possible to resume the discussion initiated
by Hill's 'pioneer essay' of 1940, 'on a better foundation' and to
reach agreement on 'the story of English capitalism'. 'The two
main questions at issue' were described in *The Communist Review*, as 'the class relations determining the basic character of a
given society' and the nature and dynamics of social revolution:

> The first question arose in concrete form: what were the predomi-
> nant relations of men in production in England at the beginning of
> the seventeenth century? Was it a feudal or a bourgeois society? . . .
> the second . . . what class controlled the State between . . . 1485 . . . or
> 1461 and 1640? Did the State serve the bourgeoisie and combat
> feudalism or not?[117]

In the event, these careful distinctions proved artificial, and participants ranged over the whole terrain of English history from
the fourteenth to the seventeenth century, at times with breathtaking intrepidity. They were not, of course, entirely without route-
maps: Hill provided 'Nine Theses on Absolutism', a long resumé
of relevant discussions in the Soviet Academy of Science and a
somewhat slanted summary of the Pokrovsky controversy; others
contributed 'notes' on feudalism, merchant capital and the Tudor
state. The cyclostyled documents failed to do their work, how-

ever, and debate had to be adjourned in July 1947, with the disagreements which had surfaced seven years' previously as pronounced as ever.[118]

According to Hill, the Tudor and early Stuart state was still 'a feudal landowners' state'. The disappearance of serfdom, the substitution of money-rent for labour services or produce rent, the ostensible changes in the composition and personnel of the ruling class qualified but did not fundamentally change its traditional character; feudalism was not so much superseded as relocated in the shape of 'its residual legatee', the misnamed 'New Monarchy'. The Tudor and Stuart state still relied on feudal taxes and on policies which inhibited social mobility and economic development. This did not, of course, rule out considerable commercial and industrial growth: internal order, the suppression of private armies, the expropriation of the church, internal peace and foreign warfare all worked to the advantage of the bourgeoisie. But merchants and craftsmen still carried on their activities within the envelope of traditional class relations; and the new capitalist landowners were not yet powerful enough to challenge the existing order – 'gentry and burghers were still non-revolutionary feudal estates'. Meanwhile, medieval kingship had been refurbished as absolutist monarchy – the penultimate form of feudal organization which initially strengthened but eventually antagonized its bourgeois grave-diggers. Only then, when it attempted to 're-feudalize' the state and 're-Catholicize' the church, was it challenged by the progressive gentry, the yeomanry and the bourgeosie; only with the mid-seventeenth century revolution was there a change from 'quantity into quality': feudal–absolutist monarchy gave way to constitutional monarchy and the state was put at the service of the new landlord–capitalist alliance.

To the group's 'chief doubter', Hill's concessions undermined his whole rickety structure.[119] How, asked Victor Kiernan, could one describe as feudal a state and society so manifestly devoted to 'the liquidation of feudal elements'? The destruction – on the battlefield and the executioner's block – of the old nobility, 'the consolidation of a powerful group of rural middle class', the emergence of London and the concomitant breaking down of economic regionalism, 'the growth of a progressive and ambitious secular intelligentsia', suggested something very different. Feudal rents had all but disappeared; feudal tenures were no more than vestigial legal categories; feudal taxes were outweighed by new and progressive forms of revenue raising – how then could the term in any useful way be applied to the Tudor or Stuart monarchy? Absolutism was even less apropos: 'there [was] no stage of Absolutism in English history'. The English state never resembled that of Louis XIV or Peter the Great: a predatory state organized for war, its estates pulverized, its local administration withering away, its caste boundaries preserved and accentuated. The only way to characterize its complex transitional nature – no longer feudal unless one wished such a term to be promiscuously applied to all forms of social organization between primitive communism and developed industrial capitalism – and assuredly not absolutist either – with 'no police, no standing army, no bureaucracy' – was through a transitional and mixed terminology, a terminology which reflected the interplay of commerce and land, merchant capital and industrial capital: a 'fusion of interests' responsible for the miracle of Elizabethan culture – something' unique in world history'.

Kiernan's analysis was far more nuanced, and in some respects more cogent, than the model presented by Hill. But it was no longer Marxist. English history was unique – not distinctive as Hill allowed, with a number of features responsible for minor variants in the overall schema of capitalist development. Worse than that, the supposed disappearance of feudalism by 1485, the relatively unrestricted commercial development in the sixteenth century, the 'alliance' of classes and the social 'solidarity' which underpinned the Tudor state, rendered its collapse under the Stuarts a superfluous mystery – a 'rapid and complex reshuffling of forces', 'not a decisive turning point, but only an important incident', in the history of English capitalism. The Civil War, as Kiernan described it, was a consumers' revolt not a producers' revolution: there was no major social transformation – no 'peasant programme' – because 'this part of the bourgeois revolution had been accomplished long before'; conversely, there was no major overhaul of 'medieval' state institutions, since an antiquated legal system and an unreformed parliament already served and continued to serve mercantile and landowning interests.

From a party perspective this was revisionism run riot. When discussions resumed in January 1948, the heavy artillery was in place: debate was far more clearly controlled; Dobb and Torr, Hilton and Hill came in on cue, and the doubters were – literally – silenced.[120] Hilton effectively undermined the notion of a total as opposed to a partial and uneven disintegration of the feudal economy in the later Middle Ages. Torr insisted on the continued importance of 'non-economic forms of compulsion' in preserving feudal relations. And Hill delivered a lengthy summation which reaffirmed the orthodox line: a revolution was 'the adaptation of politics to economics not vice-versa', and it represented a movement of progressive classes against existing institutions. Thus the bourgeois revolution took place *after* there had been significant economic development and *after* the revolutionary class had fully matured. The authority of Lenin was invoked to point the difference between a socialist revolution which had to create its social framework and a bourgeois revolution which inherited 'readymade' capitalist relations: the first task of a bourgeois revolution was to overthrow the feudal state, and to use its control of the political apparatus to remove 'obstacles to capitalist development'. 'Bourgeois Revolution [was] not a ladder up which one advances step by step' – 'a revolution by stages'. Conversely, 'state power [was] either bourgeois or it [was] feudal'; and however much the Tudor state might have encouraged trade or sought the support of gentry and merchants, however much it stood for 'national defence against international reaction represented by Spain and the Pope', its 'essentially feudal character' was 'clearly shown' in the Statute of Uses, the Court of Wards and the attack on Puritan 'bourgeois ideology'.[121]

> The Tudor Monarchy is . . . complicated and difficult to analyze. But do the Marxist categories apply to it, or do they not? If they do, let us refine our analysis within their terms of reference, which is what the original theses tried to do. If they do not, let us say so frankly and abandon Marxism.[122]

Clearly, there was a lot of special pleading and some tiresome recourse to chop logic, which allowed Hill and Dobb to distinguish between 'money rent' or tonnage and poundage which were feudal exactions and 'capitalist rent' or customs which were not, or to attack as non-Marxist the view that politics adjusts to economics while asserting a position which stated much the same. Indeed, Eric Hobsbawm has admitted that there was a certain lack of honesty in defining the party line through arguments 'designed a posteriori to confirm what we already knew to be necessarily correct'. The ill-defined parameters of the debate, the elision of state and society, and the constant blurring of discussion on the English Civil War and the total trajectory of European capitalism, probably encouraged a degree of confusion and self-deception, which could only be resolved by enforced 'consensus'.[123] The most compelling reasons for consensus, however artificial, were to be found in the present. Marxist history was 'a continuation of politics by other means'; and the importance of the debates over 'State and Revolution in Stuart England' lay in their 'relevan[ce to] the question: what is a capitalist and what is a socialist society' – a question 'where clarity is . . . greatly needed today'. Kiernan's bustling and progressive Tudor England 'played into the hands' of those who 'pushed the origins of capitalism further and further back . . . in order to show that it is really an eternal category'; in effect, if not intention, it cast doubt on the whole socialist project. 'Force,' declared Marx, 'is the midwife of every old society pregnant with a new'; and there were compelling reasons for emphasising political and military convulsions and relegating social and economic evolution in the birth of modern liberal and market society. So strong had been the grip of a non-revolutionary interpretation of England's past, and so great was the danger of a revisionist parliamentary socialism, that Marxist historians somewhat stridently defined their position around the categories of discontinuity, conflict, class struggle – and bourgeois revolution. And to maintain that position in the teeth not only of opponents but of doubting party Thomases, they had resolved the travails of 'transition' by a Jacobin – and Stalinist – formula. Combating the Pokrovskyite heresy of transitional modes, peaceful adjustments, and 'sliding' social transformations, argued Hill, was vital in 1948,

> because the Bourgeois revolution is still a real political issue in Asia, South East Europe, Spain and other parts of the world. Pokrovsky[ism] by ante-dating the Bourgeois revolution . . . leads to . . . a denial of the role of the party and of leadership. Pokrovskyism is fundamentally reformist because it assumes that a transfer of power is possible without revolution.[124]

Revolution and reform were fundamentally different. And the gap opened up in economic development between a feudalism dead in 1500 and a capitalism barely on the road by 1750, was closed at the level of political institutions by a state–church apparatus which was basically feudal, and was violently overthrown.

As a loyal if puzzled party member, who properly drew the line between 'honest criticism' and 'hostile' or 'destructive' opposition, Kiernan formally withdrew his objections. But his dilemma was not solved; and his recantation was only the first of many exercises in 'saving appearances'.[125] A state at once feudal and absolutist, decentralized and centralized, parliamentary and conciliar, economically progressive and fiscally backward, a powerful reactionary obstacle to reform and a puny underdeveloped establishment, coexisting with more effective units of local self-goverment: these political antinomies were hardly a convincing ring-in for demonstrable contradictions within a feudal mode of production and their resolution. The Marxist model which the members of the group had self-conciously applied and the empirical idiom in which they conducted their work were beginning to come apart.

4

Saving Appearances

On the substantive texts of Christopher Hill and Lawrence Stone from
the 1950s to the 1970s and their various strategies at 'saving appearances' and updating Marxist or social change interpretation.

4.1 EXPOSED POSITIONS

Historians of medieval cosmology are familiar with the expression,
'saving appearances'. By it, is meant the capacity of a model to
do justice to all the observed phenomena in the manner first formulated by Occam, with the most economy of explanation and
fewest possible assumptions. But gradually, the notion came to
mean something rather different: the success of the model in throwing up additional hypotheses, which explained away scandalous
inconsistency, regardless of whether they were true or not. In
this respect, the Marxism of the late 1950s and 1960s sometimes
resembled the abstract sky geometry of the Aristotelians: appearances were saved with additional epicycles – there was an enormous gain in the subtlety and range of analysis, but there was
also a price to pay for some of the refinements.[1]

By the early 1950s, it was already evident that the position staked
out in The Historians' Group over the previous decade was perilously exposed. Even where Marxist-inspired investigation was
sustained and amplified by later research, the interpretative uses
to which it was put often had to be questioned or qualified. Thus,
the emphasis on sixteenth- and seventeenth-century commercial
and industrial expansion appeared to be confirmed by detailed
study: spurred on by the exponential growth of London as a market
and an entrepôt, there was a considerable growth in inland and
overseas trade and an impressive spurt in industrial activity. But
it was questionable whether it constituted a 'first industrial revolution' or was different in kind from the changes transforming
other North European societies.

Moreover, it was impossible to relate these economic activities to the divisions in early Stuart England: to demonstrate a causal connection between a burgeoning economy and the breakdown of the Stuart *ancien régime* or a correlation between entrepreneurial interests and anti-court sentiments. The notion of a 'Feudal–Absolutist' monarchy under Charles I, like its French counterpart under Louis XVI, acting as a drag on new economic processes, was too simply formulated and was progressively undermined by detailed studies of business and politics during the period; as even a sympathizer like Victor Kiernan put it: 'on any narrow scrutiny of its policies and of capitalist requirements whether in land or industry . . . it seems impossible to conclude that the former constituted shackles which the latter were compelled to snap'.[2] Indeed the patrician elites of London, Newcastle and York depended for much of their prosperity on royal charters and monopolies rather than on entrepreneurial initiatives thwarted by crown policies; hardly surprisingly when the war came, many of them proved to be Royalist. The conventional Marxist distinction between a manipulated merchant capital and a truly dynamic industrial capital proved almost entirely elusive: it was coal owners who found the Stuart government a convenient ally in establishing a price-ring and mercantile interlopers in London who formed the economic backbone of the parliamentary cause. Antiquated guild restrictions which supposedly clogged production proved to be in a state of advanced decay; and the long list of monopolies paraded by Hill were almost certainly more irritating or painful to ordinary consumers than to capitalist producers.

The explanation of the Civil War as a consumers' revolt rather than a producers' revolution, put forward by Kiernan in 1948 and by Hill in the late 1950s and 1960s – heretical enough in Marxist theory – was likewise bedevilled by special pleading, chronological foreshortening, and a desire to have it both ways. Thus, Hill's evident relish in compiling taxpayers' complaints and businessmen's grumbles over subsidies, forced loans and fines for enclosure should not for one moment blind one to the fact that such complaints are common to every era. Similarly, the chronological foreshortening which 'links' Elizabethan monopolies, Jacobean Books of Rates or talk in 1604 of 'swarms of needy Scots brought in like locusts to devour the plenty of the land', to the outbreak of the Civil War, should come with a reminder of generational change. So that, however much the latter might have established itself in folk-memory, it probably tells us more about persistent xenophobia – since exactly the same language was used of the Dutch in the 1690s and the Germans in the 1720s – than about the realities of 1640: about Charles's notorious neglect of his northern subjects or the apparent readiness of the Long Parliament to subsidize a real army of needy Scots. On Hill's own admission, and as a necessary ingredient of the orthodox reading of a House of Commons and a gentry on the rise, MPs bought up land and invested in overseas trade, and 'those [they] represented waxed rich', secure in the knowledge that they were assessed for the purposes of parliamentary taxation at far less than their worth: the early Stuart fiscal problem was one of under-taxation not its opposite. As for the non-parliamentary expedients of Charles's 'personal rule', there is little to show that they were considered sufficiently onerous or unconstitutional to cause or to justify revolt. They were, of course, as nothing to the brutal escalation of 'arbitrary' taxation in most of continental Europe during the 1620s and 1630s or to the scarcely less dramatic and legally questionable increases effected by parliaments during and after the Civil War. Even Ship Money, *cause célèbre* of Victorian constitutionalists, was collected with comparative ease and unusual efficiency until 1638; and some of the most recalcitrant communities thereafter were to prove staunchly loyal to the king in 1642. Whatever else it may have been, the English Revolution was not a middle-class taxpayer's revolt.[3]

'In the hundred years from 1540 to 1640, England was swept by a durable economic tidal wave – the Price Revolution.' But the impact of inflation on social structure and mobility is notoriously difficult to pin down: if one is to judge from its most recent manifestations in the overheated economies of the 1970s and 1980s, it was just as likely to benefit debtors and gamblers as the thrifty estate managers favoured by Hill and by Tawney – in such an economic climate, ostentatious 'feudal' extravagance might well have proved an economic virtue, and disciplined bourgeois accumulation a liability.[4] At all events, the correlation of these habits with the different classes or status groups of Stuart England and with the protagonists of the Civil War – turned out to be a frustrating and pointless exercise. Thus, the Marxist anatomy of the feudal habits and loyalties of the peerage, appeared to be at odds with the deep divisions running through the House of Lords in 1640, and the overwhelmingly aristocratic character of the parliamentary military and naval leadership in the Civil War, at

least until 1645; while the supposedly progressive nature of industrial production and commercial investment did not stop 55
per cent of merchant MPs from supporting the king. Merchants
fought on both sides; so did nobles, so did gentry: indeed there
seemed to be no evident correlation between Civil War sympathies
and anything bar religious affiliation, geography, and age; and
none of these connections proved entirely responsive to Marxist
massage.[5]

Youth seemed to provide no guarantee for progressive attitudes:
if anything the reverse, with the parliamentary cause appealing
most to an Armada generation of Puritan greybeards, and Royalism rather more to the 'bright young things' born around 1620.[6]
And although, on the face of it, geographical configuration did
seem to offer some sustenance to the Marxist reading, with an
'economically advanced' South and East supporting Parliament
and a 'half-feudal' North and West the Crown, on closer inspection it, too, proved to be a broken-backed debating point, since
practically every county was bitterly divided, and since the geographical location of parliamentary and royalist 'power bases' could
well be 'ascribed to relative distance from London, or to the degree of Puritan feeling in the area . . . or to mere chance which
determined which activist minority moved fastest to seize power
in the first few weeks of the war'.[7] Moreover, the real periphery
was ignored; and in a manner not unknown to English historians,
with a geographical economy of scale most kindly described as
singular, Hill's gazetteer stopped at the Scottish border and the
Irish Sea. Yet, the so-called English Civil War was arguably in
substance a Scottish and Irish Civil War also. In view of the extreme difficulty of claiming Scottish lairds for the bourgeoisie or
Irish share-croppers for feudalism, the role of Charles's 'multiple
kingdoms' in the 'Fall of the British Monarchy' would, however,
have entirely unravelled the social pathology of 'The English
Revolution'.[8]

The equation of Puritanism and parliamentary sympathies did
appear still to hold, but the neo-Gardinerian catechism of its revolutionary characteristics and the neo-Weberian or neo-Marxist
version of its social and economic correlatives came under sustained and persuasive attack from students of Elizabethan and
early Stuart religious history.[9] A detailed decoding of the Puritan proof-texts used to demonstrate the putative link between
'advanced' Protestantism and capitalism, or, come to that,

Protestantism and scientific practice, only exhibited 'an attractive hypothesis treading water': the words of Greenham and Perkins, Sibbes and Dell, if sufficiently loosened from their specific historical moorings could carry any interpretative freight whatever, but when read as a whole and in context, appeared to be about salvation and purity rather than about 'accumulation' of a more worldly kind.[10] Similarly, the adoption of Harrington as the English Revolution's resident proto-Marxist, seemed now to require his doubling up rather incongruously as spokesman for the rising and for the declining gentry.[11]

Most important of all, the crucial Tawneyesque underpinning to the bourgeois revolution, of a progressive and a parasitic class simultaneously evolving from the economic tidal wave of the sixteenth-century price revolution, and of a subsequent conflict between feudal and capitalist groups in the countryside, proved to be based on questionable statistics, hidden biases and 'arbitrary and largely false taxonomic assumptions'.[12] Perhaps this was not so surprising, since the separation of bourgeois grain and feudal chaff in society at large, appeared to be reversed when it came to matters political. For the easy-going traditional landlords who made up the immobile elements of the rural economy also emerged as a clique of aristocratic 'sharks and toadies', 'sucking the life blood' of the community 'by methods of economic exploitation'; while the power-hungry improvers and rack-renters were simultaneously the guileless victims of exorbitant taxation and of court malfeasance. Clarendon regretfully noted at the time that entrepreneurial depopulating enclosers were more likely to have been Royalists than Parliamentarians; and Lawrence Stone was forced to conclude from a survey of the relevant fines for 'depopulation', 'that this evidence not only does not support, but tends directly to contradict the theory that bourgeois attitudes towards land management led to support of Parliament'.[13]

Not for the first time, the inverted Marxism that went back through Stalin and Lenin to the Jacobins of revolutionary France, and the emphasis on a powerful political apparatus as the manipulator and perpetuator of feudal society, cut across the traditional Marxist reading of a society simultaneously undergoing autonomous bourgeois transformation. 'It is not they who have the money must have the power, but they who have the power will have the money,' wrote Defoe early in the eighteenth century. But 'The Theses on Absolutism in England' argued both of

Defoe's propositions, and was consequently quite unable to conceptualize in a coherent manner the supposed transition from
feudalism to capitalism:

> If England was essentially [still] a feudal society . . . why should there
> have emerged in the countryside a bourgeois landlord class, a rising
> gentry. On the other hand, if English feudalism was on its way to
> dissolution . . . why should an aristocracy that had subjected its peasants
> to economic rents [and proved itself adept at courtly racketeering]
> have been unable to adjust to commercial pressures and opportunities.[14]

In a sense this issue was crucial. From the late 1950s to the
1970s, Hill poured out books of high quality and monumental
learning on the peripheral supports to his initial thesis: on the
economic problems of the church, the social and political pathology of Puritanism, or the interpenetration of the new science, the
new religion and emergent capitalism; but the central position,
which these were supposed to sustain, had crumbled. By a nice
irony, indeed, the Marxist interpretation of the bourgeois revolution proved more and more to be a particular type of political or
religious history. But its major protagonist was missing. No amount
of speculation about its religious or ideological disguises, no amount
of ingenuity in tracing the interactions between different elements
of the superstructure and the economic base, could fill up the
theoretical space of a vanishing bourgeoisie; and none of the magpie
accumulations of erudition used to line the nest of its revolution
in the England of the 1640s could make up for what appeared to
be its fundamentally unsound location. No longer could the 'revolution' be ascribed to a collision between pre-existing feudal and
bourgeois classes. Rather, as with its French counterpart in 1789,
political and ideological division in 1641 reflected lines of tension within a single elite of wealth and status, a heterogeneous
'ruling class'. Economic classes, argued Hill, did not necessarily
correspond to social and legal categories and some members of
the bourgeoisie economically considered might have been regarded
as gentlemen or even, occasionally, aristocrats in another sense.
There were, he added in a rather unconvincing gloss, degrees of
'revolution-ariness' amongst the bourgeoisie and likewise degrees
of 'bourgeoisie-ness' amongst the revolutionaries.[15] Whether these
qualified retractions amounted to a real gain in historical sophistication or analytical flexibility may be doubted. But, at all events,
he no longer suggested that the English Revolution was consciously

willed or made by the bourgeoisie. In the third edition of his *English Revolution*, published in 1955, reissued in 1976, and still in print, he proposed instead a new role for the bourgeoisie in their bourgeois revolution, rather like that of the Dutch at the Treaty of Utrecht: where their allies and enemies would, in the words of a friendly French diplomat to his hosts, make peace, 'chez vous, pour vous et *sans* vous'.[16]

4.2   FROM CLASS STRUGGLE TO IDEOLOGICAL REVOLUTION

The declension of Hill's revolutionary catechism corresponded to a gradual loosening of the cohesion and orthodoxy of the Historians' Group in the early 1950s. To begin with, the party itself had ostensibly softened its line on class war, revolutionary action and the smashing of the capitalist state machine. *The British Road to Socialism*, issued early in 1951, and given Stalin's imprimatur the following year, once again highlighted the uniqueness of English working-class traditions and the positive role of Parliament in the transition to socialism. Gone was the talk of an authoritative Soviet model: Britain would reach socialism 'by its own road, by transforming parliament, the product of Britain's historic struggle for democracy, into the democratic instrument of the will of the vast majority of her people'; socialism could be achieved, not without prolonged and serious effort to be sure, but by peaceful means and without armed struggle. Gone, too, was the anathema on all sorts and conditions of 'Labourism': the Communist Party did not seek an exclusive position of working-class leadership, but would work for 'united action . . . to win a parliamentary majority and form a People's government'.[17]

The focus of party polemic during the Korean War on the threat to British culture had been accompanied by a revival of the repertoire of national traditions. The public's interest in its past, epitomized by the success of such ventures as *History Today*, was evidence of a growing national consciousness; but it was important that it was channelled in the right direction. For it was 'easier through history than through any other subject to enmesh people in . . . lies about human nature, the structure of society and the nature of social change'. It was, therefore, 'the responsibility of Communists . . . to lead the fight for true British history', against the insufficiently contested bastard patriotism of the Right which basked in the mystique of monarchy, glorified predatory wars and naturalized the culture of colonialism. But it was also their duty to redress the less blatant distortions, silences and excisions of the liberal syllabus, which marginalized the lives and experiences of ordinary people, and transformed their cultural heritage – 'treasure houses of creative, progressive revolutionary ideas' – into respectable 'shrines' for the bourgeoisie.[18]

Inevitably, perhaps, in its early stages, the Historians' Group had been dominated by academics and specialists; it had now to reach out to those whose knowledge of the past came through the school textbook, the lending library, or the local historical society. Over time, and thanks to Penguin Books, the English Marxists would loom large in the classroom and the public library. But in the early 1950s, it was local history which offered the best opportunities for growth. The party already appealed to neighbourhood instincts at election time. But the historical dimension would give a depth and a permanency to these interventions, through the study of local traditions of militancy or collective self-regulation and self-help, or through the recovery of 'the half hidden history' of local class struggles during the great periods of 'national uprising'. Such work, properly carried out, not as 'a local antiquarian hobby', but as a means of illuminating present political problems and stimulating independent working-class action, could be an important means of focusing the party's campaign 'to wean the Labour movement away from the policy of . . . complete subjection to the ruling class of America'. These were the assumptions behind the formation of a 'Local History Section' – soon to be the largest and most active of the group's offshoots – and to the launching of a journal in 1953, fittingly entitled *Our History*.[19]

The apparent liberalization of doctrine on national roads and local traditions did not, however, extend to internal party discipline. Quite the reverse: under revised party rules, ordinary branch members lost the right to take part in the formulation of policy. Perhaps, the leadership feared the response of rank and file militants; for, ironically, it was a protest at the 'revisionist' character of the new platform that robbed the Historians' Group of its closest links with the Executive, through the resignations of Douglas Garman and George Thomson.[20] On the face of it, the group was as active as ever. The chairmanship of Eric Hobsbawm between

1953 and 1956, in particular, was marked by new initiatives: a spate of conferences, formal and informal exchanges with French and Soviet historians, and frequent requests for 'polemic' to rebut the claims of professional anti-Marxists like Peter Laslett or the doctrinal inaccuracies of non-Marxist Soviet sympathizers like E. H. Carr. Nevertheless, the impression one gets from the minutes is one of greater institutionalization, less cohesion and a growing gap between the original band of academics and an enthusiastic but less committed general membership. In Hill's case, the loosening of old ties was compounded by academic success. The party had encouraged Marxist historians to regard their professional work as a first priority and to beat the bourgeois historians at their own game. By the 1950s, Hill had started doing just that, and was beginning to reap conventional academic rewards: an army of devoted non-Marxist students, a growing empire of influence within the academic community, a regular column in the high-brow weeklies, college preferment, first as Senior History Tutor and eventually as Master.[21]

Writing of the defection of so many scientists from the Communist Party in the 1950s, Garry Werskey suggests 'that the radicalism of middle class men and women generally lasts only so long as they remain marginal to their chosen vocation'. But that is too pat an explanation for the subtle and unconscious compromises made by Hill and his Marxist colleagues. Rather, as Arnold Kettle explained to the party in 1959, 'their principal trouble is a persistent desire to have the best of both worlds – to retain the privileges of their position in bourgeois society while at the same time attacking bourgeois society and associating themselves with the socialist movement'. If they were seduced by anything, it was by the freedom of inquiry that the party had encouraged. Over time, tensions were bound to develop between officials inclined to look upon intellectual products as 'weapons of culture' which served the interests of immediate policy, and the intellectuals themselves who regarded their 'battle of ideas' increasingly as a struggle for empirical truth. The party had required them to act as bourgeois intellectuals. Bourgeois, 'left-leaning' intellectuals – committed to Marxist theory but not necessarily to Communist Party practice – was what eventually they would become.[22]

The ambiguities and tensions of these 'openings to the bourgeoisie' were significantly enlarged by the launching of *Past and Present* in 1952. Although initially graced with a Marxist subtitle as a journal of 'scientific and rational inquiry', and provided with editorial guidelines which included an excursus on dialectical method and historical materialism for the uninitiated, it was clearly intended to build bridges between the Historians' Group and the wider academic community. In the view of its founding father, John Morris, it was 'essential' that its editorial board 'should not contain above 50% Marxists', and that its non-Marxists be given absolute rights of veto on contributions – 'otherwise, with the best will in the world, it will become primarily a Marxist organ and, therefore, appeal only to a limited readership'. Hill, for one, had protested that 'the idea was to have a Marxist historical journal not another *Economic History Review*', and that he knew 'of no non-Marxists who could be relied on not to be a nuisance'. In the end, something of a compromise was worked out and the names of various sympathetic 'token' non-Marxists were canvassed, before R. R. Betts and A. H. M. Jones were added to an otherwise Marxist Board.[23] Nevertheless, the launching of *Past and Present* did mark something of a break from the self-confirming activities of the group, more especially as it coincided with the folding up – on party orders – of *Modern Quarterly* and the *Communist Review* in 1953.[24]

Yet, the retreat from the Marxism of 1948 was only partial and strategic: a refinement of categories to accommodate fresh evidence, not a theoretical surrender.[25] There still was a bourgeois revolution; feudalism was still destroyed. Appearances could still be saved, provided one dropped some of the cruder terminology of the 1940s (bourgeois, petty-bourgeois, feudal, proletarian) for looser contemporary words or idioms like 'freeholder', 'middling' or 'industrious sort of people', and the 'many headed monster'; provided one retreated from the simple economic model of class and accepted qualifications based on status, but insisted, none the less, that the split within 'the ruling elite', was one between its progressive and reactionary elements; provided one enlarged the definition of progressive elements to include its rank and file supporters; provided one rejected monocausal economic explanations and drew out the multiple interactions of social activity and ideological fabrication; provided, above all, one concentrated not on the causes or course of the revolution but on its *outcome*: the bourgeoisie did not make the revolution but the revolution made the bourgeoisie.[26]

One of the most telling complaints of the Marxist analysis of pre-industrial economies was that it was usually conducted in linguistic and conceptual categories which the societies in question would not have owned or understood: that the terminology of the seventeenth century was that of status and household rather than class or political affiliation.[27] The objection had always been met by the Marxist theory of ideology: 'The mind of man,' wrote Bacon, 'is far from the nature of a clear and equal glass wherein the beams of things should reflect according to their true incidence; nay, it is rather like an enchanted glass, full of superstition and imposture, if it be not delivered and reduced.'[28] Appendicitis was, no doubt, a common cause of death in the seventeenth century though no one gave it that name; and to suppose that the terms in which people fought out their historical struggles constituted the essence of those struggles was to succumb to 'imposture' in two senses: to assume that the categories of thought were the real structures of social life, and to believe that events were the result of conscious intention and design.

Marx's elaboration of the theory of unintended consequences provided the means of explaining the disproportion of perception and effect:

> The tradition of the dead generations weighs like a nightmare on the minds of the living. And just when they appear to be engaged in the revolutionary transformation of themselves and their material surroundings, in the creation of something which does not yet exist, precisely in such epochs of revolutionary crisis they timidly summon up the spirits of the past to help them, they borrow their names, slogans and costumes so as to stage the new world-historical scene in this venerable disguise and borrowed language.

The Cromwells and the Robespierres were at one level fantasists playing out heroic roles from an admired past; at a deeper level, they were like sleepwalkers, guided by the deeper rhythms of history. Later on, when the social evolution that constituted the real history of the epoch, was completed, words and things came into closer alignment – 'Locke drove out Habakkuk'.[29] Even, at the time – since there were degrees of somnambulism, and since in Marxist theory, socialist thought bore an altogether different relationship to social reality – there might be some like Winstanley or Hobbes who penetrated the disguises of the era, and saw through the transcendent mask of religion to 'the truth of this world' behind. The interplay of illusion and reality, intention and outcome, agency and structural determination revealed by this theory of ideology – the fairground hall of mirrors in which some words and thoughts appeared to 'reflect' while others distorted or distended the reality – gave rise to an infinite range of complexities and ironies peculiarly fitted to the multiple circumstances and interactions of historical actors and events. They also, one might add, provided a historian as steeped in the literature of his chosen period as Christopher Hill, with what J. H. Hexter in a slightly different context has called 'the professional gambler's dream, the no-lose wager, like being able to place your bet after the results of the race are in': if what was written appeared to be at odds with the social processes one was elucidating, it could be seen as an instance of the contradiction, the 'double heart', central to all class divided societies, and hence as a piece of 'negative' evidence for the processes in question; if not, it could be deployed for exactly the same purpose.[30]

Few things made it more difficult to understand the English Revolution fully than the vocabulary and the religious forms in which political and social issues were framed. Because they seemed so crucial to contemporaries, it was easy to fall into the errors of Whigs, to succumb to the perceptions of the participants and fail to see the underlying social or political realities. But in a cynical and anti-heroic historical environment, it was also possible to fall into the opposite error and brush aside as absurd the words and the emotions of people making their own history. 'To avoid such errors,' wrote Morton, 'involves a double process':

> First we have to put ourselves in the minds of the men of the seventeenth century . . . We have to understand that to them, religion was a reality and religious convictions were among the mainsprings of their lives. And then we have, as it were, to make the return journey from their world of religious conviction to our world of Marxist thought and to see what were the objective political issues which their cultural and ideological circumstances led them to express in what seems to us an indirect and perverse way.[31]

The idea was not to scrap Marxist categories but to provide Marxist elucidations for the words and categories in common use at the time. To a Marxist historian fallen in among the linguistic narodniks of North Oxford, the relationship between 'words and things' was likely to be a sensitive issue. For the philosophy of ordinary language – conceived as 'a common stock of words', validated by actual usage, and arranged as a timeless 'heteroclite' collection of games with discrete rules and conventions – which dominated the universities in the 1950s, blotted out external referents.[32] Hill's work concentrated on the written and spoken word; he, too, was concerned with syntax and with usage. But as an engaged Marxist, he was at pains to read the linguistic idioms of the seventeenth century as specific social products which vibrated according to the circumstances of the author and changes in the socio-economic structure. Sometimes shifts in reality could take place without much verbal disruption; at others, the surfaces could immediately be stirred by changing or disputed social practices. The trick was to have at one's disposal as large a range of relevant contemporary materials as possible and simultaneously to deploy the finest-meshed Marxist grid to arrange the specimens.[33]

This was certainly the process which Hill's severest critic discerned in his work. In an article notorious for its asperity even in the annals of academic warfare, J. H. Hexter was to credit his adversary with an unusual combination of the accumulative proclivities of the fox and the single-mindedness of the hedgehog, or what he dubbed 'source mining' and 'lumping': 'the examination of a corpus of writing solely with a view to discovering what it says on a particular matter narrowly defined', coupled with the compulsion 'to put the past into boxes ... and then to tie all the boxes together into one nice shapely bundle'. And in a critical reply to the inevitable academic fence-sitter in the dispute, he was to focus on Hill's 'systematic habit of looking at evidence' as 'custom-packed' information which could be used to support his case, and attribute this questionable working procedure to a selective system of files which had not altered save in their oceanic detail and overwhelming bulk over the years. But what his critique failed to observe was that the method was the direct result of a gargantuan accumulative scholarship and an empirical idiom of discourse, wedded to a particular type of Marxist thought.[34]

Hill's Marxism was recognizably still the Marxism of his youth: something which had originally appealed to him as a method of 'decoding' the 'contradictions' of metaphysical poetry, and which led him to the study of class structure and economics, but which he now was inclined to view as an organizing 'totality', capable of elucidating the multiple interactions of society and culture.[35] What interested him was the complexity and heterogeneity of the empirical content rather than the 'self-conscious elucidation of his analytical framework and explanatory assumptions'.[36] Thus, his investigation of 'the many-headed monster', a veritable galaxy of abuse, some 145 instances drawn from the period stretching from the 1520s to the 1660s, circling around the concept of 'the irrational multitude' – the overloaded metaphors of bestiality and disorder, the underlying hysteria and contempt which afflicted even the 'detached' Shakespeare, the 'gentle' Sidney and the 'sweet' Spencer – attested to the ubiquitous fear of all who fell outside the conceptual confines of a hierarchical agrarian society. It also provided the historian with evidence of physical mobility, social dislocation, popular tumults, falling standards of living, a background of class conflict and an undercurrent of incipient rebellion bubbling away beneath the surface of Stuart political life. And it undercut the self-regarding language of a harmonious 'body politic', authority, degree and obedience: all the 'illusions of the epoch' by which a dominant minority sought to impose its class interests and conceptual categories on society as a whole.[37]

'It [was] the ways in which different elements interconnect[ed] that [gave] them their particular historical significance and efficacy.' But the interrelationships could easily become fixed and reified. In principle, Hill was aware of the element of artifice in all historical writing – that the interconnections which he teased out were artifacts of his 'retrospective standpoint of interest'. But his focus on discrete ideas and his relative lack of interest in the traditions or conventions of discourse tended to close the gap between signifier and signified. Language for Hill was invariably political: words functioned as weapons, offensive or defensive, in a class divided society. Before 1641, they operated under an economy of political repression: the severity and ubiquity of censorship drove 'subversive ideas' underground and 'caused the courageous few to encode and disguise their protest'. After that, they were still encrusted in religious or mystical phraseology which had to be stripped back or loosed from their contextual moorings to reveal their full significance. So that the seventeenth-century historian had to read between the lines, 'go beneath' or 'make allowances' for the language, penetrate the codes as much as any contemporary China watcher or Kremlinologist.[38] Historians are frequently enjoined to work against the grain of their materials, to pick up the unintended clues, to listen for the silences. Yet there is a danger in such an approach: an alchemy of extraction and elision, which converts the language of soul liberty and spiritual treasure into that of capitalist emancipation and acquisitiveness – a premature 'return journey' to the 'world of Marxist thought' rendered more attractive and unconscious by the slippery nature of seventeenth-century religious sensibility and expression.[39]

A classic instance of the technique was to be observed in his study of 'Puritanism': starting from a semantics of opprobrium – an 'imagined heresy' in matters of morality, religion, church policy and 'affairs of state' – he proceeded to execute a breathtakingly simple but courageous methodological leap which bundled some very diverse verbal constructions into an identifiable object: 'I agree with contemporaries in thinking that there was in England for two or three generations before the civil war a body of opinion that can usefully be labelled Puritan'. And he then went on to examine what really interested him: the correlation between 'an aggressive Protestantism centred on a highly rationalized and articulated body of doctrine' and a set of emerging social practices and attitudes. There is much to be said for not being tied hand and foot to 'a laboratory-bench taxonomy of religious types and tendencies', and for concentrating on the moral and social substance of a 'Puritanism at once polemical and nominalistic'. But the dangers of a corrupt or unexamined taxonomy are considerable. For what Hill had done – and he was by no means alone – was to define a doctrinal 'mainstream or core' in terms which were simultaneously broad and narrow. The result was a Puritanism which combined the attributes of a moral Protestant majority and an embattled separatist minority, conflated Gardiner's constitutional *idée force*, Haller's spiritual 'way of life' and Tawney's 'religion of trade', a Puritanism, political, cultural and inheritantly modern – an ideology of bourgeois revolution.[40]

What was unstated but drew the religious and political threads together was the conviction that the rise of capitalism still constituted the real history of seventeenth-century England.[41] For it was noticeable that the new terminological refinement of his writing had its limits; if he eschewed 'proletarian' and 'feudal' as descriptive categories, he was not entirely ready to surrender 'bourgeois'. Whatever his doubts about feudal and proletarian forms of consciousness and social reality in Stuart England, he had none about the creation of a bourgeois society and its accompanying 'Protestant ethic'. And as a socialist, he still wished to highlight the contingency of bourgeois values and arrangments: like 'patriarchal' in the hands of feminists, the epithet defined and deconstructed its universalistic language and assumptions.

Linguistic 'change and continuity' was matched by a greater methodological flexibility. The earlier base-superstructure model made way for one which stressed totality and interaction with thoughts and experiences igniting or 'taking on', in contact with receptive groups in appropriate social conditions: a suitable ethic or ideology was necessary for the material to become combustible.[42] Thus, the central Protestant doctrine of justification by faith encouraged the individual conscience; but it also operated in a social environment where capitalism was beginning to bite, and where new forms of social consciousness corresponded to the new opportunities of the market-place. A religion of the heart, therefore, came to facilitate the triumph of new values by aligning individual conscience and collective behaviour and 'spiritualizing what men were doing anyway', with 'God, as his manner is helping those who help themselves'. Of course, this did not happen everywhere: 'men didn't become capitalists because they were Protestants or Protestants because they were capitalists' – the hard-bitten Calvinist gentry of Scotland and Hungary spiritualized their activities in rather different ways.[43]

Marxists had always insisted that dialectical materialism was fundamentally different from crude economic determinism and the ascription of individual behaviour to material self-interest. But, by the early 1950s, it was precisely this sort of interpretation, derived from the techniques applied by Namier and his pupils to the study of parliamentary and senatorial oligarchies, which was beginning to impinge on the English Civil War. The findings and methods of the new scholarship – its biographical detail, emphasis on locality and personal connection, increasing recourse to contemporary family or business records in preference to the tired old documents of political debate, its pointillism and underlying scepticism – applied to the English Revolution, dissolved the rough and ready categories of class warfare, political struggle or religious divide. Marxist strategy, therefore, had to be changed: 'twenty years ago', Hill told his fellow historians at the Marxist summer school of 1954, 'we had to attack the conception of a Puritan Revolution as an abstract constitutional experiment'; now 'we have to emphasize that religion is important . . . that politics is [not] just a dirty game with no principles involved', that the Revolution was a broader, a more vibrant and popular affair than the narrow denotation, 'bourgeois', might suggest.[44]

To begin with, the Tawneyesque mechanism of a revolution brought about 'exclusively [by] a shift in the ownership of landed property' had to be abandoned; whatever the shortcomings of the rival thesis of a declining gentry and the Revolution as a regressive Fronde, Trevor-Roper's iconoclasm had destroyed the idea of the gentry as a united class.[45] The English Civil War had its origins in a split *within* the ruling class; but the split was not arbitrary, personal or purely factional – it corresponded to fundamentally different interests. What mattered was not ownership, but the particular type of economic behaviour – the land management, leasing arrangements, entrepreneurial activities and so on – that bisected the rural and urban elites. Thus, a comparative study of the movement of rents and the entry fines showed up significant differences between those who conducted their estates according to the principles of capitalist landownership and those who still valued them primarily for the social power that they conferred: 'a comparison of the relationship of Sir Bevil Grenville with his tenants and that of Sir Arthur Haselrig with economic developments in the midlands' would provide a better insight into the nature of the conflict than the mere counting of manors. Similarly, a differentiation of commercial and industrial activity, whether through monopoly or free enterprise, would be seen to correlate with a mercantile 'parasitism' and a royalism characteristic of less economically advanced areas, and a totally different spirit to be encountered among a new breed of city businessmen who formed the backbone of the parliamentary cause.[46]

The English Revolution might have started as a split within the ruling class, but its meaning was to be found in the social divisions which manifested themselves during its course. What mattered, therefore, more than any attitudinal differentiation between the county families who divided up the parliamentary loaves and fishes in 1640, was the character of their supporters: the rank and file citizens of Leicester who lined up behind Lord Grey of Groby, the Buckinghamshire freeholders who rode up to London to protect Hampden early in 1642, the voters of the Common Hall who elected the City's radical MPs. Marxists had to show the fallacy of treating revolutions as the work of minorities.[47] Laslett's talk of a 'one class society' was, of course, a surrender to elite ideology; little wonder that its corollary was a denial of the possibility of social change and revolution. Similarly, after the manner of Henry Fielding's famous description of 'nobody' as 'everybody except 1200', all that Brunton and Pennington had 'left out' in their Namierite anatomy of the *Members of the Long Parliament* was 'the people of England'. But the Long Parliament set in train a mass movement 'involving citizens of London, demonstrating in their thousands, humble members of sectarian congregations fighting for the right to run their own affairs and the troopers of the New Model Army'. The bourgeois revolution depended for its success on these openings on to the world of small producers and artisans: the clothiers and the weavers of Bradford, Halifax and Leeds, the exporters and the seamen of the great Outports, and, above all, the craftsmen, the inferior clergy and the citizens of London.[48]

It was the London apprentices who terrified the Bishops and the Lords into submission in 1641; it was the London trained bands that checked Charles's cavalry at Turnham Green in 1642; and, of course, it was London wealth that financed the parliamentary war effort. Over the previous half-century, London had witnessed the growth of a new Protestant commercial culture: its merchants poured their money into lectureships, schools, almshouses, apprenticeship schemes – a 'bourgeois revolution' through voluntary, charitable means. In 1641, these donors – small businessmen outside the great City Corporations – challenged and overthrew the traditional mercantile elites: the first act in a drama that was to be repeated in other towns up and down the country.[49]

It was the exponential growth of London as a consumption centre and the hub of a home market which revolutionized the rural economy also. And the rural sector was crucial to the bourgeois revolution: it was lessees fighting for legal security of tenure, freeholders and 'independent small producers' introducing agricultural improvements who constituted the real cutting edge of capitalism in the countryside. This was, after all, the locale of Marx's 'truly revolutionary road' from feudalism to capitalism: the concentration on landlords had tended to divert attention from the real 'transforming agents' of British agriculture, the crucial 'middlemen' in the tripartite division of rural society – the progressive farmers. And it was these same farmers – the yeomen, freeholders and 'middling men' – who formed the rank and file of Cromwell's army, the 'russet-coated captains' and voluntary 'yeomen troopers', just as it was 'gentlemen of ancient families and estates', their tenants and retainers, who rallied to the King. The very names, 'Cavalier' (swashbuckling officer) and 'Roundhead' (crop haired citizen) were, said Hill, social denominators and not just political markers. They attested to a conflict which stretched far beyond the ruling elite to a society coming apart at the seams.[50]

A Marxist interpretation of the English Revolution had to focus on 'the people' as a pro-active element for reasons theoretical and contingent. To begin with, as Perry Anderson was to point out:

> A feudal mode of production requires the existence of a large non-possessing class of peasants in the countryside . . . On the other hand, capitalism as a mode of production requires the existence of propertyless wage-earners . . . In consequence, no revolutionary crisis could ever be a simple duel between a nobility and a bourgeoisie . . . [but involved] the pervasive presence of popular classes.[51]

Just as the French Revolution was transformed from a political into a social struggle by the Storming of the Bastille and The Great Fear; so, too, in England, according to Hill's pupil and fellow radical, Brian Manning, 'the mere fact of the involvement of the people changed political conflicts and religious antagonisms into social conflicts and class antagonisms'.[52]

It was important, therefore, to replace the deferential model of society and a Civil War in which the common people simply served as cannon fodder, targets for plunder, dependent pawns who did what they were told, with one which emphasized popular commitment to the parliamentary cause. Hill and Manning appeared to subscribe to Baxter's view that the sober, godly 'middling sort' supported Parliament against 'a corrupt gentry and the godless mercenary poor', but also to accept Clarendon's view of the 'natural malignity' of the 'common people . . . against the nobility and gentry': to elide 'the middling sort' and the varying degrees of commonalty, and to depict parliamentary allegiance as simultaneously bourgeois and popular. The outbreak of the Civil War coincided with an economic crisis: a decay of trade, a scarcity of money, high unemployment and popular distress. The year 1641, like 1789 and 1917, was a time of tumult and insurrection, some of it only tenuously connected with the constitutional issues of the moment, but none of it wholly apolitical either. The English Revolution, like the French, was 'saved' by its popular *Journées*: by the intervention of the London 'crowds' during the 'December Days'. In the countryside, there was agitation over enclosures and fen drainage, widespread refusal to pay tithes and rents, seizure of crops, destruction of property, breakdown of law and order, 'panic fear' of 'papists', 'delinquents', 'enemies of the people's peace and freedom' – 'a large part of the fenlands was in a state of open rebellion'. And, as with France in the summer of 1789, these rural discontents served political purposes: in the West Country and the North, violence was directed primarily against Cavalier gentlemen and 'great lords'; and the royalists in the eastern counties were crushed, 'never to rise again'.

But if the evidence of mass political intervention was quite impressive, its actual mechanics were a little unclear. For if, as Hill invariably maintained, modernization in the English countryside was primarily the work of the progressive landlords and well-to-do tenant farmers, who supported Parliament, why should dispossessed peasants have rallied to their cause: why should the Marquis of Hertford have been 'the enemy of the people' and Sir Arthur Haselrig not. If, on the other hand, as Manning contended, it was, rather, the crown, the nobility and the bishops who were 'the foremost defenders of the enclosures of fens and other wastes and commons', then, surely, they should have reaped some of the economic reward as well as the popular odium of their 'improvements'. The mobilization of the people threatened to add a further refinement to bourgeois revolution – a revolution which was not only *'sans* vous' but could be *'contre* vous', also. For the English parliamentary leaders, unlike their French and Russian counterparts, never attempted to win over the common people for the revolution through land division, price fixing and a swathe of economic controls. The lower class radicalism which surfaced in 1641 and 1642, therefore, was to be 'crystallized' and articulated in the Leveller attack on the whole governing class; and the revolution achieved its ultimate class meaning and its natural terminus in the programmes of Lilburne and Winstanley. These programmes were of course, defeated by bourgeois 'grandees'. They were however not extraneous to the bourgeois revolution, but central to its dynamic – and very much a part of it.[53]

Hill's model of the revolution had always been a three-cornered one, of ruling, rising and oppressed classes. But his earlier formulations had encountered some difficulty in relating the role of the oppressed to the struggles of the other two. The partial elimination of the feudal apex and the abandonment of the bourgeoisie as a rising class consciously seeking to appropriate power by revolutionary action – the replacement of a clash between bourgeois and feudal forces by a division between progressive and reactionary elements of a single ruling class – made the role of the oppressed and its relationship with the progressive section of a divided ruling class far subtler and more important to the outcome of the revolution. The effect was rather reminiscent of Albert Soboul's four act ballet for monarchy, aristocracy, bourgeoisie and sans culottes between 1787 and 1794. And, as with Soboul's refashioned Marxist interpretation of the French Revolution which focused overwhelmingly on 1793 and 1794, it was to mark a gradual move away from 1640 to 1649, from 'the revolution that succeeded' to 'the revolt within the revolution'.[54]

The increasing emphasis on popular action marked a further evacuation of the bourgeoisie from their bourgeois revolution in another sense also. Not the least objection to Manning's picture of a class divided society so polarized as to swallow up any significant neutralism or apathy, was that it was almost entirely derived from contemporary polemic: that it described an item of political propaganda or mythology rather than a demonstrable social reality. In a manner which, again, perfectly corresponded to the pattern of French revolutionary historiography in the 1950s and 1960s, class no longer referred primarily to economic condition, but to political behaviour and predisposition: feudalists became 'the party of order'; and the revolutionary bourgeoisie were bourgeois because they were revolutionary and not vice versa. The bourgeoisie were made up of those who went along with the reform of municipal government in 1641, supported a wider parliamentary franchise, responded and 'accommodated themselves to mass political mobilization to put pressure on an obdurate king': those, who 'as the war went on . . . increasingly came to see the conflict not so much as a struggle against the king but as a struggle against the aristocracy'.[55] It comprised, above all, 'the godly people': militant Puritans whose religious beliefs 'taught the middle sort of people to think for themselves and to assert their independence against King, lords and bishops'.[56]

Puritanism was still the key to 'revolution': the driving force of new social and political values. Puritanism, insisted Hill, was not the introverted, quietist, life-denying husk, familiar under the later soubriquets of 'Nonconformity' and 'Dissent'; nor was it simply concerned with matters of theology or soul liberty. It could not be dissociated from the rapidly changing society in which it grew up nor from the Church–State nexus which environed and occasionally threatened to envelope it.[57] Hill's exploration of the latter in his first, major and, in many respects, best book, subsequently a strangely unfashionable masterpiece of Marxist scholarship, *Economic Problems of the Church from Archbishop Whitgift to the Long Parliament*, has never been seriously challenged. The Church of England no longer effectively functioned as the guardian of the social order: plundered by courtiers, white-anted by lay patrons, challenged by would-be reformers, the Puritan 'Feoffees for Impropriations', it attempted to rebuild its fortunes under Laud with policies which antagonized virtually all sections of the propertied classes – it was a classic instance of an economically inelastic and, in its penultimate form, retrogressive institution precipitating revolution. Hill's study was a particularly skilful unravelling of the interplay of organized religion, church politics, landownership and the rise of capitalism. But it was not an anatomy of Puritanism as such; 'the living faith of puritan revolutionaries' could never adequately be defined by its Laudian opposite.[58]

He, therefore, went on in *Society and Puritanism in Pre-Revolutionary England* to explore its positive social and political correlations. Puritanism, he argued, appealed to the 'industrious sort of people – yeomen, artisans, small and middling merchants' – who found in sabbatarianism and self-discipline, the secularization of the parish and the spiritualization of the household, a means of rationalizing and purifying their everyday conduct. These patterns of behaviour went far to elucidate the revolutionary activism of ordinary people; and after the ostensible defeat of Puritanism as a political and a religious movement, to explain its subsequent social survival. *Society and Puritanism* was a work of extraordinary range and density, especially compared with some of the impoverished Weberian progeny which passed for religious history at the time. But the analysis was open to serious objection. The thickening mosaic of apposite quotation and example – the bricolage of learning, recognizable, henceforth, as the 'Hill method' – often disguised a circularity of argument and a blurring of cause and consequence. Hill registered surprise that much of the social content of Puritanism survived; but as he wrote in terms of a single Puritan movement and as so much of his treatment of its early manifestations was conducted through the social categories and terminology of a later period, the surprise seemed somewhat disingenuous. Indeed, although he deliberately reversed the priorities of Weber and Tawney, and attempted to unravel the social being which shaped and directed Puritan consciousness, like them, he was guilty of telescoping and homogenizing a multitude of 'Puritanisms', or, at least, a long series of ideological and social metamorphoses, and of minimizing and eliding a set of undistributed middle terms which lay between a religious 'ethic' and the 'spirit of capitalism'. It was noticeable that the most convincing sections of the book were those which were clearly sited in the 1620s and 1630s and which recapitulated the perceived evils of the Laudian Church-State. But much of Puritanism escaped its treatment as an oppositional politics and a bourgeois social ethic: what about the inner experience; what about redemption; what about salvation? And what about those groups that failed to register on Hill's selective social grid: 'the spirit bloweth where it listeth', and not every nobleman's hall fell into the category of stony ground – what about the godly gentry, the godly lord, or, come to that – until 1642, at least – the Godly Prince?[59]

The shift from economics to politics and ideology was, as Hill explained, partly a response to the now overwhelmingly material 'components' of the national historical 'culture'. For what united the most influential 'bourgeois' historians of the 1950s – Namier, Trevor-Roper, A. J. P. Taylor, Elton and Ashton – was a deep-seated distrust of ideology and the sociology of ideas. Politics was about power and perquisites, personal calculation and administrative efficiency, perhaps, but seldom about professed principle: this was usually high minded 'cant' or 'ex post facto rationalization'. Namier's adulatory studies of political elites, Trevor-Roper's reduction of the 'vast battles in Europe over the Reformation to the reflex of some English gentry being hard up', Elton's elevation of Cromwell – not Oliver but Thomas – to the ranks of statesmanship were of a piece: they reflected a preference for efficiency over justice or equality, a demonology of popular ideas, and 'a dislike of revolution as the work of instigators and agitators and never as the outcome of any legitimate struggle'.[60]

'Outside the China of the Mandarins,' wrote Edward Shils in 1955, 'no great society' – the epithet is striking – 'has ever had a body of intellectuals, so integrated with, and so congenial to its ruling class'. An Oxbridge appointment, membership of a London club, a niche in the BBC or the British Council, had replaced the spiritual self-exile and a homeland sited somewhere between Moscow, Los Angeles and the imagination, common to the intel-

lectuals of the 1930s. Political stability, a comparatively painless
transition from Empire to Commonwealth, a blurring and a withering of ideologies under the Butskellite consensus and growing
middle-class affluence, all attested to the success of British ways.
Exiles from East-Central Europe were by no means the only ones
to glory in the incommunicable wisdom of British institutions,
the soft contours and the nuances of British society, the longevity
of British traditions, the pragmatism of British scholarship. However discordant their voices on matters of historical detail, the
bourgeois academic chorus was unanimous in its self-regarding
empiricism and denunciation of any meta-history which 'challenged their workaday specialization'.[61]

The apogee of this undoctrinaire but comfortably conservative
ethos was probably reached about 1953. The Tories were back in
power, Churchill was PM, World War II was sufficiently proximate and remote for well nigh universal iconolatry, the British
Commonwealth still straddled the globe, and the accession of a
new Queen spurred A. L. Rowse (amongst many others) to throw
another arch across English history in an absurd evocation of the
new Elizabethan age.[62] In rather more serious vein, that same
year saw Geoffrey Elton announce his break with the parliamentary
whiggish traditions associated with his masters, Pollard and J. E.
Neale, in the first and crucial instalment of a new and powerful
reading of early modern English history. Central to his interpretation was *The Tudor Revolution in Government*: a revolution which
had nothing to do with insurrectionary movements and popular
forces, but which was engineered and effected from the top with
remarkably little opposition by pragmatic politicians in the service of an authoritarian monarchy. English history was remarkable as much for the development of strong, efficient and centralized
administration as in the constitutional and parliamentary safe-
guards against despotism which had hitherto obsessed its historians; it was the interaction of the two that lay at the root of
England's exceptional stability, a stability never seen more clearly
than at the time of challenge – 'a moment's comparison of the
great revolutions of France and Russia [would] show what [wa]s
meant'. The key periods of English administrative history were
the 1530s, when bureaucratic organization and national management replaced a patrimonial and household monarchy, the period
after 1660 when a new generation of officials adapted the weapons
of the paternal Tudor state to the needs of a parliamentary

monarchy, and the 1830s when a recognizably modern apparatus of government was constructed. Subsequent work on other key areas of executive authority went far to confirm this model – a model which threatened to reduce the Civil War and its immediate aftermath to a minor episode in the long continuities and gradually thickening textures of state formation and internal control.[63]

Marxist historians had, therefore, not only to combat Trevor-Roper's politics of musical chairs, but to rescue the seventeenth-century revolution from the bypass operation being mounted by Elton and the Namierites. Both of these threats required them to emphasize once more the importance of ideas and religion and to reassert some of the old Whig verities of parliamentary growth, constitutional reform and the struggle for civil liberties and property rights. Thus, Hill plotted his textbook narrative of the early Stuarts in *The Century of Revolution* around inevitable and escalating conflict between Crown and Commons, culminating in the destruction of Tudor conciliar government in 1641. Of course, he went on to point out that freedom for the pike was oblivion for the carp; and he was at pains to highlight the struggle for truly democratic liberties between 1647 and 1650. But these amendments and additions were not so much anti-Whig as supra-Whig; the Whig story was not entirely wrong, but it was too narrow in its social sympathies, too confined in its historical understanding. Indeed, the significance of the Revolution could only be grasped as part of a total history of society, a history which only yielded its truly progressive import at the level of ideas and ideologies.[64]

Almost from the beginning, Hill had spoken to his colleagues in the Historians' Group of the importance of ideas and of the potential conservatism of a history which dealt simply in material determinants. Moreover, he did not only view ideology as a form of false consciousness or an instrument of ruling class oppression; he was also conscious of the progressive potential even of an 'idealist world-view': something which, he said, could provide a moral drive, supply a revolutionary resource or 'serve as a weapon in gaining increased control over man's environment'. This was the theme of his most contentious book, *Intellectual Origins of the English Revolution*. The burgeoning of scientific and medical activity in sixteenth- and seventeenth-century London, which turned England from 'a backwater country' into 'one of the most advanced'; the emergence and the popularization of a scientific method through the work and the prestige of Francis Bacon; the secularization and modernization of history, transforming it from a medieval morality play into the study of political and social change associated with the writings of Sir Walter Raleigh; Sir Edward Coke's adaptation of the common law to the needs of a commercial civilization and the legal antiquarianism which gave parliamentarians a myth of the constitution as potent as Foxe's myth of primitive English religion – all of them intellectual transformations which separated science from religion, rational analysis from providential causation, individual rights from traditional authority – 'provided new ideological growing points' and 'prepared men for revolution'. The common ancestry, 'common enemies' and common objectives of this political, social, intellectual and religious radicalism also helped to make it a total revolution which altered men's minds and transformed the world.[65]

Arguably, the title of the book was a misnomer in two senses: rather like Tocqueville's work on the *Ancien Regime and the French Revolution* – but without any of the ironies of Tocqueville's understanding of the revolutionary process – it was as much about the genealogy of modernity as about the causes of the revolution. Although it explicitly acknowledged its debt to Daniel Mornet's *Intellectual Origins of the French Revolution*, it lacked Mornet's careful – and statistical – analysis of the diffusion and penetration of ideas, or his fastidious observance of chronological proprieties, to the paradoxical extent that his study stopped in 1788 with the observation that the Revolution and its intellectual origins were two distinct histories. Indeed, as an essay in the sociology of ideas, Hill's work was extraordinarily primitive: with little apparent recognition of the complexities of cultural production, or the problems of charting the reception and transmutation of ideas; a chronology which could only be described as chaotic, roaming backwards and forwards across four or five generations; and an emphasis still on 'great thinkers', with Bacon, Raleigh and Coke as 'the Montesquieus, the Voltaires and the Diderots' of the English Revolution, forging 'weapons of culture', 'catching on' in some undefined way with 'the men who hitherto had existed only to be ruled, but who in the 1640s would help take over the government'.[66]

Above all, it suffered to an acute degree from the defects of the 'genealogical' method – the sorting out process 'which retains out of the innumerable realities which make up the history of an epoch only the matrix of the future event'. These common sins of the search for origins were compounded by the peculiar defects of Hill's working procedures: the ideational atomism or tendency to treat 'thoughts' as decontextualized pellets of information, the characteristic piling up of opposites (in the red corner, 'Puritanism, the new science, optimistic belief and Parliamentarianism'; in the blue, 'neo-Popery, traditional medieval theology, sceptical pessimism and royalism'), the relentless recruitment of ideological allies, (Gresham College professors, London physicians, Elizabethan navigators and common lawyers, the Ramists, 'the honorary Protestants of Venice' and a veritable Vallombrosa of Puritan intellectuals), the ingenious search for corroborative evidence, 'linkages', parallels and similitudes (so that the Protestant substitution of unmediated divine grace for the gradations of intercession corresponded to the collapse of the crystalline spheres in the new solar system, while Harvey's circulation of the blood and 'dethronement' of the heart mimicked the decapitation of the monarch) – all of which rendered the book something of a methodological disaster.[67] But it also suggested that the revolution was no longer a rupture – an event unique in itself – but the centrepiece of a vast intellectual transmutation – a movement reaching from sixteenth-century alchemists and lower middle-class medieval heretics to Royal Society scientists and the materialists of the French Enlightenment. As with many exercises of the sort, it was by no means clear to what extent the origins made the revolution or the 'revolutionaries' their origins: and to what extent Hill had merely extended a legitimating pedigree created during and after the event.

Disputes about every major revolution are only partly caused by the passions let loose by the destruction of established interests and their replacement by something new; what keeps the controversies going is 'the complexity of the phenomenon, its fantastic many-sidedness which usually escapes the contemporary mind'.[68] To see what a revolution is really about, one has to stand back from it – not perhaps as far as Zhou-en-Lai, who in the 1960s thought it still 'too early' to make a judgement on 1789 – but sufficiently for John Locke to replace Habakkuk. The bourgeoisie did not make the revolution, but the revolution made the bourgeoisie. This was the fall-back position. The Civil War, insisted Hill, in the face of some newly emergent scepticism, was still very definitely a revolution: 'and I don't think much of some recent attempts to argue the contrary, on the grounds, for in-

stance, that nobody planned it'.[69] He was not particularly impressed
by the demonstration that classes did not line up like Tweedledum
and Tweedledee. 'Things . . . happen without conscious planning',
and 'a bourgeois revolution is not a revolution in which the bourgeoisie did the fighting': revolutions are not wanted by the bourgeoisie; and *bourgeois* revolutions are not wanted by the
revolutionaries. Judged by its participants and its ostensible character, it might sometimes be difficult to discern the bourgeois
delineaments of the English Revolution. Judged by its consequences,
however, it was very much a 'bourgeois revolution in the Marxist
sense': 'a revolution whose outcome is the clearing of the decks
for capitalism'. 'Revolution' was now not so much a description
of intended or executed action, as a retrospective abridgment of
social and ideological significance. It resulted in a political, social
and psychological shift towards free enterprise, social mobility
and untrammelled acquisitiveness; its outcome was to be found
in the thought-worlds of John Locke, Isaac Newton and Daniel
Defoe.[70]

4.3   FROM SOCIAL REVOLUTION TO BEHAVIOURAL CRISIS

The move from causes to consequences exposed what Hill and
Hobsbawm had long lamented as the group's greatest lacuna:
the period after 1660. Maurice Dobb's hiatus between the first
maturation of capitalism and its transformation into a fully fledged
factory system had always disconcerted his colleagues; and his
own suggestion that such an interval was natural, and that primitive
accumulation was inevitably a long-drawn out process, had been
once considered a solution perilously close to the Pokrovskyite
heresy of transitional epochs.[71] But the retreat from a single revolutionary struggle in the 1640s to a 'century of revolution', and
from a once and for all structural transformation to a more generalized ideological alteration – a loosening up process paralleled
by the gradual rehabilitation of Pokrovsky in the Soviet academy
– meant that the examination of post-revolutionary thought and
society could no longer be avoided.[72]

The most effective short cut to detailed research in this alien
territory was the reading of social or political texts; and the most
persuasive analysis of those texts in the 1950s and 1960s was widely

thought to be that of the Canadian political theorist, C. B. Macpherson.[73] A student of Laski and Tawney, who had grown up in the Great Depression, was committed to radical social improvement and was sympathetic to Marxism if never quite a fully paid up Marxist, Macpherson was a passionate believer in 'a democratic society which provide[d] equally for the self-development of all [its] members'. What he had in mind was a polity which combined the political principle of one person one vote with the socio-economic one of one person one equal effective right to a fully human life. Macpherson's manner of expressing the principle was unusual; but the project of attaching 'species' self-development to liberal democracy, separating out the emancipatory side of liberalism from the competitive 'market' element, and then subjecting the latter to a Marxist or Marxisant critique, was common enough. What was unusual about Macpherson's enterprise was the intellectual consistency and textual sophistication of the analysis. Modern liberal-democratic society, according to Macpherson, suffered from the contamination of its central principles by the concept of possession: a contamination so systemic that communist and third world societies, for all their lack of freedom, were arguably democratic in a 'broader' sense than were their contemporary Western counterparts.[74]

The task of 'retrieving' full democracy in the West from its disabling 'possessive' carapace took Macpherson back to the classic political theorists of the seventeenth century. Classic liberal theory was tainted at source by what he called 'possessive individualism': 'The concept of man as . . . an infinite desirer and appropriator, whose overriding motivation is to maximize the flow of satisfactions to himself from society'. The 'pushpin' precepts so flagrant in the writings of Bentham or James Mill could, in turn, be traced back to the political principles of Hobbes, Harrington and Locke: to their conception of the individual 'neither as a moral whole nor as a part of a larger social whole, but as an owner . . . of his own person'; to their consequent view of society as a collection of proprietors exchanging goods; and to their evaluation of the state as a calculated device for protecting properties and maintaining orderly exchange relations. Macpherson found similarites and connections where previously none had been perceived – between Hobbes's 'Mortall God', Harrington's republican utopia, Locke's joint-stock civil society, and even Leveller blueprints for parliamentary reform – and for good reason: seventeenth-century political writers were all grappling with the same problem, that of justifying minority political rights in a society where old hierarchical obligations had collapsed and new capitalist 'market' forces were at work.[75]

Clearly, Macpherson's study was intended to be historical, and Hill, for one, applauded his repudiation of the linguistic turn in political philosophy: the writers of the past would only yield their meaning to those who understood their unstated asssumptions and these could only be grasped by those who studied their societies. In another sense, however, Macpherson's project was pathological: he was not concerned with the precise historical contexts which occasioned the writings in question, only with an abbreviated version of their socio-economic environment. And he did not think it neccesary to show that the writers actually held the beliefs ascribed to them, only that their 'possessive market societies' required ideological justification and that the political theorists provided this, whether they knew it or not. Hobbes and Locke did not actually write about 'possessive individualism', 'consumers' or 'differential property rights': no matter. Through an elaboration of the Marxist theory of ideology, their silences could be written off as assumptions so obvious or common that they disappeared below the level of conscious articulation; their real message, as John Dunn wittily explained, was written in invisible ink which could only be deciphered by the light (or heat) of a socially engaged twentieth-century mind. Whether Hobbes or Locke or even Bentham (whose felicific calculus was, after all, not an abacus of middle-class pleasures but a device to ward off the dispositional despotism of officious moral experts) could survive this sort of conceptual transplantation was, to put it mildly, open to question.[76]

According to Hill, Macpherson's was one of those books 'which change the historical thinking of a whole generation'. Perhaps, for those to whom Hobbes was the theorist of absolute sovereignty and Locke the patron saint of constitutional politics, *The Political Theory of Possessive Individualism* was a blinding light. In Hill's own case, it largely confirmed what he already knew. Hobbes's natural man was not a historical description, nor simply the product of a compulsive behaviourism, but was 'constructed by successive degrees of abstraction from his own society' – or, as Hill had pithily put it way back in 1949, 'bourgeois man without the policeman'. Similarly, Hobbes's state of nature was 'a deduction from the socially acquired appetites' of seventeenth-century Englishmen, 'a statement of the behaviour to which such men would be led 'if all law and contract enforcement were removed'.[77] Macpherson teased out the congruence between the successive stages of Leviathan building and the freedoms and compulsions of a possessive market economy with considerable skill. But the assumed connection between the malevolent beings of Hobbes's natural jungle and the acquisitive animals who supposedly prowled around the English market economy was arbitrary in the extreme; and the 'description' could as well have been derived from travellers' tales of primitive society or from his own observations of the vainglorious compulsions of feudal–aristocratic households: to stretch the paradox further, it could even be argued – as, indeed, it was by 'bourgeois' Scottish philosophers a hundred years later – that commercial behaviour was a means of channelling and dissipating anti-social pride and civil strife rather than exacerbating it. Or again, it could well be that the older explanation of Hobbes's work was not so silly, and that a life that straddled the Armada, the English Civil War and a score of political assassinations did not need possessive market mechanisms to teach it 'the restless desire for power after power', the ubiquity of sudden death, or the necessity of a 'Mortall God' who would curb these ills.[78]

Even Macpherson had to admit that Hobbes showed a considerable 'dislike of bourgeois morality'; and that on the best Marxist construction, he was, as Hill put it, 'suspended' between bourgeois and feudal 'worlds'. Scoffing realists make uncomfortable icons, and its tone alone made his work unacceptable to middle class opinion. Hobbes held up a mirror to 'the anarchy of capitalist society', and then proposed a prudential mechanism of control; Locke presented its acceptable, self-regulatory liberal face: Hobbes was a 'ravening wolf who looked like one', Locke 'a capitalist wolf in . . . sheep's clothing'.[79] Locke's 'astonishing achievement', according to Macpherson, 'was to base property right on natural right . . . and then to remove all the natural law limits from property right'. By locating labour power in the state of nature, and conceptualizing a prepolitical monied economy as the mechanism of unlimited accumulation, by valorizing property ownership in the narrow sense as the index of rationality, and limiting political consent to the men of property, Locke provided the moral basis for a new order of inequality, economic oppression and minority political rights, and became, whether he realized it or not, the spokesman of 'the dictatorship of the bourgeoisie'. Once again, Macpherson recognized that there was much in Locke's writing that explicitly resisted 'capitalist' appropriation – the almost invariable equation of property with 'life' and 'liberty' as well as 'estate'; the consistent anti-paternalism which repudiated attempts to treat men as sub-rational children; the profound religiosity which read 'the law of reason' as a moral law, and 'rationality' as a 'gift' that God had implanted in every human – but these could be explained away as the confusions of a 'transitional mind', or Locke's 'two facedness'.[80]

The 'contradictions' were also what made Locke's work so acceptable to the dominant elements in his society. The post-revolutionary pike could afford to go hunting the 'Leviathan', when they got all the carp they wanted in the 'Second Treatise'. Again, there was much to admire in Macpherson's reading: it neatly resolved tired old academic wars between collectivist and individualistic readings of Locke's political theory and provided an elegant textual demonstration of the coexistant acceptance of unregulated economic and domestic inequalities, and the defence of political rights against the encroachments of arbitrary government. But it ignored nine-tenths of the 'Two Treatises' – which suggested a performance of some authorial inadvertence or ineptitude. The text might appear to be about biblical precepts, political trust, the security of subjects, the rights of resistance and the rule of law; what it was really about was differential ownership. There was little to suggest that Locke, for one moment, thought that this was his subject rather than the challenge to lives, liberties and estates contained in the policies of Charles II and James II and the attempted legitimation of them through the posthumous resuscitation of Filmer's 'Patriarcha'.[81]

Macpherson, of course was under no obligation to acknowledge these precise political contexts: the twentieth-century socialist might reasonably tiptoe through the familiar political acreage of the 'Second Treatise' to get down on his hands and knees to examine its most difficult tuft. But he also claimed to have discovered the key to the whole enterprise; and it was reasonable to respond that there was much that it did not explain; and that the proprietory cut was less materially fashioned or novel than he proposed. The proprietory metaphor had been deployed by generations of moralists to assert God's or the king's ownership; the Levellers had argued the radical case for 'self-propriety': the right of every man to his own person. Locke's argument for the connection between right and rationality was built on conventional belief in God's 'gift' of life: on the doctrine of an 'afterlife' and an egalitarian Calvinist notion of the calling – not a casuistry of endless accumulation but a directive to the strenuous discharge of one's duties, whatever one's station. Such a doctrine could and possibly did eventually help to produce work discipline, a docile labour force, condemnation of begging – and more unedifying things besides. But there was nothing to suggest that it presupposed virtue and prosperity to be natural bedfellows, that it denied rationality to the labouring poor or considered the state 'a joint stock company of owners' whose majority decision bound 'not only themselves but also their employees', rather than a temporary lodging which all men shared and in which all could unite against the danger of 'invasion' or 'usurpation'.[82]

Macpherson's polarized two class model of seventeenth-century society – with every political theorist catalogued a little possessive liberal or a little conservative – omitted most of the ambiguity and distinctiveness of his texts, and the complexity of the society they supposedly 'illuminated'. Squeezing Hobbes, Harrington, Locke and the Levellers into the straitjacket of bourgeois liberalism obliterated many of the issues that actually shaped political debate. Ironically, for a Marxist, it also swept away the 'revolution'. The Putney Debates became something of a minor border dispute within the bourgeois–liberal tradition: the 'overdetermined' triumph of possessive individualism shut out those moments when 'history' did not march to the big drum of market-oriented modernity. Even as a long-term classification, 'possessive individualism' was unhelpful. Released from the textual proprieties which informed Macpherson's analysis, taken for a general description of social practice and not just an important but narrow filament of political theorizing in early modern Britain, it had a particularly malign influence on radical historians. Confirming chonological preference, and reinforcing an already pronounced romantic anti-capitalism, what was an analytically superfluous and genetically improbable preface to a well-intentioned Left critique of modern 'democratic' practice, was often read as a shorthand for post-revolutionary *laissez-faire* society.[83]

Long before the 'rediscovery' of the seventeenth-century bourgeois revolution, radical historians had been familiar with the supposed bourgeois delineaments of early eighteenth-century England. Starting with Louis XIV's ambassadors and running through a gamut of Swiss travellers, German princes and French *philosophes*, scores of foreign observers were to remark on the absence or mutilation of the conventional hierarchical signposts in this strange country, 'where lords played bowls with trades-men and peasants rode on horseback'. On top of the traditional uncertainties of gentleman status were a new set of ambiguities brought about by static or falling rents, and the simultaneous development of new outlets for investment in banking and in company or government finance. The man who prospered in the City, and bought a park and a fine house in Surrey or Middle-sex, might indeed still call himself a gentleman, but it was his holdings in the Bank of England, investments in government debt, and loans on mortgage to needy landowners which provided him with the safe and easily managed income and with the life of leisure which was its basic requirement. For a while, indeed, during King William's and Queen Anne's wars, according to a steady stream of complaint on the part of the impoverished 'men of es-tates' against the supposed wealth and influence of the City, it appeared that, 'a new interest has been erected out of their for-tunes and a sort of property which was not known twenty years ago is now increased to be almost equal to the terra firma of our island'.[84] 'Poet laureate' of this brave new world of middle-class England was Daniel Defoe; and the comments of visitors and embattled contemporaries were capped in the descriptions of his-torians by Defoe's rapt panegyrics to the bustle, modernity and mobility of English society: his *Tour* was selectively deployed as a description of England on the eve of the Industrial Revolution; his *Plan for English Commerce* depicted as a manual of new econ-omic activity; his *Robinson Crusoe* as 'the great allegory of the Capitalist system'; and his *Complete English Tradesman*, 'the idyll of the English bourgeoisie'.[85]

Yet, the collected works of Daniel Defoe were curiously am-biguous social documents. Nothing could have been further from the truth than Morton's Marxist character reference: 'honest, straightforward, independent, industrious . . . a typical bourgeois of the best type'. As befitted a journalist employed by Harley and Walpole, Defoe was notoriously equivocal in his social com-ment, and for every *Essay on Projects* there was another on the *Villany of Stock Jobbing*; alongside *The Complete English Tradesman* stood *The Complete English Gentleman*. Selective 'source mining', of course, could throw up many a proof text in which he boasted the 'new race of tradesmen', spoke of 'ancient gentry' selling their estates to mere 'mechanicks as they call them', or rhapsodized about the charms of lower middle-class resorts like Epsom; these, however, were not simply balanced but outweighed by descriptions of 'the delicious seats of the nobility and gentry'. The *Tour* did not reflect a new middle-class society, but rather a society in which commercial wealth blended graciously into traditional contexts of status and gentility. Although his accounts of rising and falling families were often equated with a final shifting of the focus of wealth and power from landed nobility to capitalist middle classes, what he had in mind was an ebb and flow of family fortunes rather than a social transformation – a reciprocal process, which he exemplified with random examples from the early fifteenth century onwards.[86]

If the process had quickened in the early eighteenth century, that was to be explained by a number of short-term conjunctural factors, dating from the commercial boom of the late 1670s and 1680s, the wartime fiscal displacements of the 1690s and 1700s, and the speculative fever culminating in the South Sea Bubble of 1720.[87] And once the dust of war and speculation had settled and Walpole's solstice of peace, prosperity and low taxes lengthened out the years, England was still governed locally and nationally by its traditional landowning elites. And Defoe's mature writings reflected it. *The Complete English Tradesman* is not so much an arriviste's handbook or a tribute to the 'new economic order' as a manual of caution, thrift, diligence, avoiding snares and knowing one's place.[88] Defoe's own cringing humility in his dealings with the great was an analogue of the tradesman's subordinate position still; even his intermittent bragging and complaint were symptomatic of anxious insecurity, rather than middle-class ease. If its eventual outcome was to be judged by the ambiguities of Defoe's social commentaries, the English Revolution did not make for a society dominated by the bourgeoisie; but, rather, 'paved the way' for one with bourgeois tastes and standards.[89]

Perhaps, then, it was not so much a structural, as an attitudinal and a behavioural revolution; and bourgeois defined not a class, but a set of assumptions. This seemed to be the conclusion of a number of literary studies from Alick West, Arnold Kettle, Donald Watt and Hill himself on the imagined communities and the in-

ner worlds of Mr Badman, Robinson Crusoe, Moll Flanders, Clarissa
Harlowe, Jonathan Wild, Fanny Hill and a score of other eighteenth-century witnesses to the commercialization of life and leisure.
Indeed, the novel proved particularly amenable to Marxist analysis;
for here the exceptions and the antinomies which proved such a
problem in the area of social history, were easily disposed of as
instances of 'the contradiction that lay at the heart of the bourgeois revolution'.[90] Thus, Bunyan's condemnation of Mr Badman
for upholding the capitalist ethic and for flouting it, faithfully
reflected the 'confusions' which existed even amongst plebeian
Baptists.[91] A generation later, when pilgrim had become a trader,
the contradiction was still there: the bourgeois sought to create a
politically stable society which would facilitate steady and unin-
terrupted accumulation of wealth and power, but was forced so
to revolutionize social relations that no such stability could ever
be achieved. At the heart of Robinson Crusoe is the conflict of
parental authority, a settled and ordered life, and the compulsions of the bourgeois psyche. Just when his productive and accumulative labours have secured his island property, Crusoe finds
a footprint in the sand: his idyll irreparably broken, 'lying in his
hutch, stricken helpless by illness', he has a terrible dream that a
man 'bright as a flame' lifts up his spear to kill him. He repents
his disobedience, incorporates Friday into his 'little family', becomes what he has rebelled against and settles for the life of a
gentleman patriarch.[92]

History was not so readily manipulated by these dialogues of
the dialectic; and the ambiguities of Defoe's England could only
be explained by a society at once 'polite' and 'commercial', aristocratic in structure and bourgeois in aspiration.[93] This was the
'paradoxical', if unintended, 'thrust' of what one historian referred
to as the 'most oddly ambiguous monument to the social pathology of the revolution', Lawrence Stone's *Crisis of the English Aristocracy*.[94] Stone was not a Marxist and had never been a member
of the Historians' Group, but he shared their interests and priorities: an Oxford *enfant terrible* translated into a Princeton *eminence rouge*, a radical and a modernist, ever sensitive to the changing
fashions of social theory, he nevertheless believed passionately
in the pivotal nature of seventeenth-century English history, a
theme he beat out in a variety of harmonies and with great verve
and learning. Over the next twenty years, indeed, he was to prove
the past-master of pouring new wine into old bottles and providing

seductively revised old answers to new questions.[95]

In a sense his work was to prove a major pay-off for the revised agendas associated, first with the foundation and then with the broadening of *Past and Present*. The problem had always been finding 'the right kind of people' to complement the Marxist core; by 1958, the preferred associates had died off or dropped out, and the journal, in the view of its editors, was in need of rejuvenation. By then, many of those associated with it had formally severed their ties with the Communist Party and were only too anxious for *Past and Present* to move in the same direction as the now fashionable *Annales*. The Marxist subtitle was discreetly dropped; the editorial board totally revamped; and *Past and Present* ceased to be, in any meaningful sense of the word, a Marxist publication. Indeed, Stone had made it quite clear that this was a non-negotiable condition of his joining the board. Although several of the old guard saw the whole operation as a bourgeois takeover, it was to breathe new life into the journal; and more than any, Stone himself was to be responsible for the subsequent vigour and flexibility of its editorial policy.[96]

Early in his career, he had acted as Tawney's understrapper in the gentry debate with a much maligned early anatomy lesson on the Elizabethan aristocracy. Now, he reached the conclusion that the rise of the gentry was 'to some extent an optical illusion' resulting from the apparent collapse of aristocratic fortunes and prestige in the years leading up to the Civil War. The war, however, was not a cheap form of bourgeois foreclosure on an obsolete and immobile elite. Rather, it marked a final stage in the transformation of the military magnate into the commercial landlord.[97] Stone went a long way to discredit the old stereotype: 'there was nothing particularly feudal about the peers in 1641':

> if they fought for the State, they were paid for their services; their seats in the House of Lords bore no relation to feudal tenure; their client gentry were bound to them by personal not feudal ties; the feudal aspect of their relationships with their tenants was confined to the intermittent enforcement of obsolete taxes like fines for wardship; their estate management was as modern as the times and as their paternalist notions of fair treatment of tenants would allow.[98]

So much for the 'sweet simplicities' of 1940 and 1948. But, perhaps, as Hexter surmises, because his end point was rather different from his initial assumptions, he was reluctant to admit to the full implications of some oddly revisionist findings. For the economic crisis, which seemed to grip the peerage at the turn of the century, appeared to stem from short-term fiscal pressures rather than 'from any long-term problems of adjustment to incipient capitalism', and to have been surmounted by the 1620s through a mixture of Stuart largesse and growing commercial *savoir-faire*; while the loss of prestige which afflicted the nobility in 1640 appeared to be at odds with 'three decades of steady financial recovery'. The conclusion was inescapable: the crisis of confidence which struck at the nobility in 1641 was political and psychological rather than economic. And if in part, it reflected a gradual but irreversible loss of military capability, as a more settled society and more powerful state grew less tolerant of traditional aristocratic disorder, it also was the outcome of some purely local conditions – the inflation of honours, the polarization of court and country, biological chance, divided religious loyalties.[99]

In this respect, the ambiguities of Stone's aristocratic crisis mirrored those of seventeenth-century Europe as a whole. By the late 1950s, the concept of a 'seventeenth-century crisis' was beginning to unravel rather than confirm the epochal status of England's bourgeois revolution. Originally launched by Eric Hobsbawm as a Marxist elaboration of the 'transition debate' – an explanation of the varying chronologies, uneven roads and apparent false trails between the rapid commercial expansion of the fifteenth and sixteenth century, and the emergence of a fully fledged industrial capitalism in Europe some 250 years later; and as a triggering device for revolution similar to that of World War I in the crisis of 'capitalist imperialism', with England, like Russia, as the system's 'weakest link' – the 'crisis' rapidly acquired a momentum which led in some very unMarxian directions.[100] Hobsbawm had long been critical of the insularity of English historians and his interventions in the discussions of the Historians' Group had frequently drawn attention to the need to relate the history of England to the whole development of Western capitalism. His contribution to the siting of England's bourgeois revolution took the form, therefore, of an exploration of the contradictions of the European economy – the failure to generate mass home markets, the concentration on luxury goods, the 'refeudalization' of much of Eastern Europe as landlords sought to cash in on the increasing demands of the West, the haemorrhaging of resources into rapidly exhausted colonial windfalls, the immobilization of wealth in unproductive assets – contradictions which inevitably brought about a crisis when the first cracks appeared in 'the whole unstable structure'.[101]

But the crisis, patchy and uneven in its symptoms, its location and its chronology, could as well be explained by purely conjunctural features – by demographic stagnation, famine, plague, warfare, deteriorating climate, changing sexual practices – or by purely political models – the reaction of the 'country' against an overgrown 'Renaissance' court apparatus, the revolts of provinces against metropolitan centres – or, indeed, by a whole range of local factors.[102] At all events, it was not Hobsbawm's rather muddy analysis of the contradictions of a dynamic mercantile capitalism and a static and inflexible semi-feudal framework, but Trevor-Roper's characteristically sparkling interpretation of what he depicted as the retroactive rebellions of civil societies against oppressive yet fragile state machines, which sparked off the greatest response and seemed, for a while, destined to become an ingenious non-Marxist orthodoxy.[103]

In Hobsbawm's view, the crisis marked a decisive stage in the progression from feudalism to capitalism: a cold shower from which the cleansed and invigorated economies of England and Holland, and to a lesser extent those of France and Sweden, were ready to move on.[104] But it was difficult to see that the 'contradictions' had been overcome: that there was less immobilization of wealth, not just in Versailles and Drotningholm, but in Whitehall and the countless monuments to the post-revolutionary English aristocracy's country house megalomania; that the 'old colonial system' had been transformed and that there was an immediate breakthrough from the limited luxury trades of seventeenth-century Europe to elastic markets and mass consumption.[105] Yet, it was not these ambivalent outcomes which most weakened the elaborate Marxist model. Most damaging of all was the whole concept of a 'crisis', experienced alike by 'regressive feudal' societies, remodelled 'feudal absolutisms' and societies which had either completed or were about to enter their bourgeois transformation. For their strikingly common features seemed more likely to turn the crisis into a substitute rather than a triggering mechanism for revolution. Even as a linguistic device, 'crisis' suggested an eventual resolution and recovery of 'the body politic', rather than the decisive transfer of political and economic power. It was the same patient that recuperated on the operating table, not with a new social transplant, but with a 'restored' constitution.[106]

Stone's 'aristocratic crisis' was, of course, just that: a crisis not a permanent displacement, the culminating point of an aristocratic malaise stretching back into the sixteenth century, but also the stage immediately antecedent to recovery – a hiccup along the road from a hierarchical Tudor order to a Hanoverian country-house federation.[107] Despite Harrington's diagnosis – he believed that the decay of feudal tenures had made a hereditary nobility well-nigh impossible – the House of Lords was restored in 1660. And for the next two centuries, it was apparently more powerful than ever before or since. Collectively, their Lordships were to exercise effective political power as a constitutional backstop to monarchy during the dangerous years of the Exclusion Crisis and again during the Convention Debates of 1689. Thereafter, during 'the high noon of the whig oligarchy', they were to occupy the critical point of balance in the almost universally accepted system of 'mixed government', between the monarchical and the popular elements, embodied in the king and the House of Commons. Individually, as ministers or borough-mongers, or as the leaders of political clans fighting for place and preferment, they dominated day to day political life, threatening at times, in the words of one contemporary, to turn the Lower House into 'a parcel of younger sons'. Aristocratic power, consolidated after 1660, and, in the view of many historians, maintained as the English version of a 'persistent old regime' right up until the eve of World War I, was an overwhelming feature of English public life for over two centuries. The aristocratic 'isthmus' was clearly repaired; and it prompted the thought – formal abolition of the House of Lords notwithstanding – was it ever really 'broken'?[108]

Structurally, there was nothing very 'fluid' about the late seventeenth- and eighteenth-century aristocracy. After a brief flurry of creations in the early 1660s, a notable inflation of royal dukedoms in the 1670s and 1680s, and occasional bursts of political manipulation which swelled its ranks, the peerage settled down to a century of comparative immobility. Ploughboy to duke was fine in theory but extremely rare in practice: the cliché of an 'open elite' constantly reinvigorated by trade and the professions is simply not borne out by the eighteenth-century figures: if the incidence of upward mobility was to be the sole index of modernity, then, arguably, venality of office and military favour provided more effective accelerators of social change in eighteenth-century France and Prussia than anything available in post-revolutionary England. Equally, the Tocquevillean variant of an aristocracy by degrees, whose barriers were so ill-defined that entrance into its ranks was not so much easy as unperceived and imperceptible, is not really confirmed by the high incidence of aristocratic endogamy or by the evident 'pride of blood' that characterized so many of its members.[109] Economically, too, the peerage still comprised England's greatest landlords: 'in a society in which land remained the surest route to political consequence, the peers' . . . share of landed income appears to have been greater in 1688 than in 1601' – higher again, in all likelihood, in 1738 and 1788.[110]

But the English aristocracy was supposedly different. Unlike the absentee court nobility of France or the feudal castes of Eastern Europe, it was now bourgeois in instinct and aspiration. This was the nub of the new social change model of seventeenth-century England. The key to the transformation lay in the landed estate and in the process of subjecting customary tenants to market-determined rents traced by Tawney in the sixteenth century, and continued in the land-hungry seventeenth, when aristocrats increasingly 'set their minds to the problem of more efficient management'.[111] The landed elite had surrendered their coercive extra-economic dues and, therefore, had to derive their income from economic rents sensitive to the market value of property. Aristocrats or their tenant farmers were consequently alert to the new agricultural methods normally associated with the eighteenth century but now traced back to before the Civil War: the floating of water meadows, the substitution of mixed husbandry for permanent tillage or grass, the new techniques of stock breeding, the introduction of new fallow crops and grasses, marsh drainage, manuring and, of course, enclosure – the improvements which were to provide England with an agricultural surplus and a springboard for 'industry and empire'. The Civil War property transfers, in the metaphor borrowed from Eric Hobsbawm, acted as a broom sweeping away old rural practices and legal restraints, transforming lordship into absolute ownership.[112]

The Restoration land settlement confirmed a process which had started with the distribution of monastic property and culminated in the crisis of the 1640s: the weeding out of the backward and the inefficient and their replacement by the more successful adapters to the new capitalist agrarian order.[113] The consolidation of estates, the widespread adoption of legal entail and other devices designed to protect family property from wastrel heirs, the professionalization of estate management, sponsorship of private enclosure bills, large-scale investment – in agricultural improvements, Bank of England stock and other securities, in urban real estate, docklands, canal building, turnpike trusts and the rest: these and countless other entrepreneurial activities – attested to an elite metamorphosis. The aristocracy was still there; its structure was unaltered, but its constituent membership and its ethos was not: the label on the bottle was the same; what was inside it was remarkably different. The Revolution, so the argument now went, spawned a society dominated by a 'Venetian' aristocracy, bourgeois in attitude and aspiration.

Yet this updated Marxist reading – in which capitalist accumulation occurred within the existing envelope of landlordism and the rural community was transformed from within through the replacement of communities of peasant cultivators and feudal lords by the famous tripartite structure of capitalist agriculture constituted by landlord, capitalist tenant farmer and wage labourer [114] – was not without its problems either. The increasingly early dating of the agricultural revolution, pushing it back from the eighteenth to the sixteenth and early seventeenth centuries rendered the pivotal role of a mid-seventeenth-century revolution increasingly tenuous. As for the supposed bourgeois instincts of a reformed aristocracy revealed by patterns of commercial and industrial investment: for all Defoe's paeans, there was probably less interlocking of land and trade under Anne than under Elizabeth. And even later in the century, the Dukes of Bridgewater with their canals and the Dukes of Rutland, whose gardeners picked coal out of the garden beds, hardly measured up statistically to the 22 per cent of Tudor nobles who owned and exploited ironworks. There may be excellent reasons not to generalize from such statistical anomalies; and it would have been surprising if there were not more aristocratic involvement in urban real estate, bank holdings, turnpike trusts and, yes, canals and coal mines by the end of the eighteenth century; but again, there is little to suggest exponential growth in these areas – or to indicate that it was different in kind from the economic activities of the pre-revolutionary French nobility. There was considerably more investment in spas and seaside resorts than in industry, and in landscape gardening than in the more utilitarian forms of estate improvement.[115]

And the centrepiece of aristocratic expenditure, as of aristocratic life, was the modest little mausoleum of vanity which stamped the elite on the 'neighbourhood' and preserved its social power up until the last quarter of the nineteenth century. The architectural heroics of the second and greatest period of aristocratic gigantism stretching from the late seventeenth and through the eighteenth century – the millions of pounds poured into bricks and mortar, to provide the Buccleuchs with ten palaces, the Marquis of Exeter with four billiard rooms, or the Marquis of Rockingham with a 'frontage' of 606 feet – bespeaks a sense of competition amongst the great; but to refer to these rival displays of power and profusion as bourgeois is an abuse of language.[116] The ethos revealed by their public entertainments, their collecting enthusiasms, rural pursuits, even their sensitivity to 'improvements', bespeaks a domestication, a 'civilizing process' perhaps, common to much of eighteenth-century Europe, not a uniquely national configuration. What distinguished the English aristocracy was not its openness ('a well-rehearsed myth'), nor its entrepreneurial activities, nor its lifestyle, nor indeed any unique set of capitalist characteristics acquired through a process of Darwinian selection and adaptation, which parallelled a revolutionary crisis and its solution, but what had always marked it off from its continental counterpart: its absence of legally defined tests and privileges, its lack of rivals either in the form of a landless service nobility or an urban patriciate, its uniformity of wealth and power, its remarkable stability and perseverance. The English aristocracy was not an order, not a nobility; but it assuredly was never a super-wealthy middle class, an *haute bourgeoisie*.[117]

These eighteenth-century ambiguities and continuities made the social pathology of the events of the mid-seventeenth century, either as a gentry driven social revolution or as a convergent aristocratic crisis, even more of a problem. And once again, it was Stone who signalled a further retreat from the simple revolutionary model, as well as an up-to-date sociological disposition, by explaining the Civil War as the outcome of long-term and short-term political, religious and social 'desynchronization', rather than the compulsive resolution of socio-economic dynamics. Indeed, on one reading of his book on *The Causes of the English Revolution*,[118] it seemed not unreasonable to assume that this most ecumenical of scholars might eventually abandon his long-term 'preconditions' and 'precipitants' and concentrate on short-term 'multi-dysfunction', and the 'triggers' of 'power deflation', 'elite intransigence', duplicity and incompetence that rendered the Civil War an avoidable traffic accident, not the end of a Stuart 'High Road'.[119]

But Stone saw the war as symptom rather than mishap, the outcome of 100 years of change. Convinced, à la Harrington, that 'the collapse of the central institutions of State and Church' and 'the fissuring of the traditional elites' between 1640 and 1642 'caused the War, not the War the dissolution' of society and government, and – on the basis of a somewhat perverse misreading of the chiliastic rhetoric of the Puritan preachers and a conflation of the categories of spiritual rebirth and secular or cultural revolution; and likewise on a catalogue of the undoubtedly radical changes effected between 1646 and 1649, considered simply as a logical extension of the earlier 'challenge' to the 'established regime' – that the revolutionary nature of the English Revolution could be demonstrated by its words and deeds, he was determined to prove that so dramatic and important an event as this 'the first "Great Revolution" in the history of the world' must proceed from profound and long gestated processes. Cleopatra's nose was encased by 'multiple helix chains of causation more complicated than those of DNA itself', flattened by what irreverantly was called a 'rolling stone' interpretation, with the events of 1642 as the necessary culmination of virtually everything that had or had not happened in England since 1529: the 'High Road to Civil War' had become an Autobahn.[120]

As even unconvinced reviewers admitted, Stone's book was an intellectual *tour de force*, with a compelling if somewhat mad logic to it. It incorporated much of the revisionist critique of the traditional social change theory. The great contribution of Marxist or Marxist influenced historians, wrote Stone,

> ha[d] been to stress the extent and significance of early capitalist growth in trade, industry and agriculture in the century before the revolution ... Their weakness, however, ha[d] been their persistent efforts to link these developments to the revolution by means of a theory of class warfare that may work reasonably well for England in the early nineteenth century but which seriously distorts the social reality of earlier periods.[121]

Population increase and the expansion of agricultural output, the spectacular growth of London and burgeoning of internal trade, still constituted a crucial complex of 'endogenous environmental changes', and it certainly was 'no accident that the first of the Great Revolutions in the history of the West should have occurred in one of the two societies in which proto-capitalism was most highly developed'. But the role of these economic and demographic forces was not to delineate dynamic or immobile, revolutionary or reactionary classes, but in a more diffuse manner to provide the pre-requisites for a 'disequilibriated social system'. The crisis of the aristocracy had become the temporary reduction of peerage prestige; and the rise of the gentry, 'the proliferation of . . . middling estates', the log-jam of families fighting for profit and preferment – 'something a good deal more profound and complicated than . . . a redistribution of economic resources'. Much the same happened in the towns: growing splits between groups on the inside trying to hang on and non-elites trying to enlarge the area of privilege to let themselves in. Elite society was growing bigger, richer, more complex, better educated; and this created wide discrepancies between 'the three sectors of wealth, status and power', generating 'jealousy envy and despair among the failures and status anxiety among the successful'. Agrarian sheep and goats, Tawney's landlord entrepreneurs, Trevor-Roper's rural 'frondeurs', upwardly mobile but insecure merchants and lawyers, 'over educated and under-endowed' younger sons . . . condemned by the laws of primogeniture to slide down the social scale, were neatly comprehended in a theory of 'status inconsistency', produced by 'high social mobility' and 'at all levels . . . insecurity . . . unease, anxiety, anomie'.[122]

Indeed, the social science model was ever so flexible and up to date, allowing for multiple interconnections, and providing for groups rising, falling, expanding, shrinking, undulating. It was, none the less, a straitjacket. For, as Elton observed, it was only 'by directing all developments towards the distant end of 1640 that the debates and dissatisfactions which are the experience of any live society assume the guise of necessary causes'.[123] Nowhere was this more evident than when it moved from structure to conjuncture, from the analysis of forces and trends, to 'the options open to individuals' in the crucial decade before the Civil War. For what mattered here were the imponderables of psychological perception. As Stone explained:

the three theoretical propositions upon which the argument is based are that deprivation is relative not absolute, and has to be measured against some identified reference group; that deprivation leads to frustration, which can find relief only in aggression; and that this aggression is frequently directed not against the true source of the trouble but against a scapegoat . . . primarily identified not by its economic but by its cultural distinctiveness.[124]

For the sociologically inclined historian, setting out to reduce intractable individuals and resistant events to foreordained revolutionary 'precipitants', they were no-lose categories. At the same time, since social change interpretation and relative deprivation theory spoke only of possibilities and probabilities; and since the model required a so-called 'X Factor' – a series of 'short-term, even fortuitous' happenings – to convert its preconditions and precipitants into an actual political breakdown; since it was structured around a consecutive arrangement of hypotheticals, it lacked all sociological rigour: for all the talk of helix chains and DNA, the model was largely a sequence of events dressed up in the language of cause and effect – 'C'était magnifique, mais ce n'était pas la sociologie'.[125]

Moreover, the 'lockstep' of structure and event appeared more arbitrary and artificial than ever. For, in many ways, the strongest part of Stone's argument was that which focused on the fundamental deficiency of the Elizabethan and Stuart State 'in . . . the essential components of power': money, an army, an adequate bureaucracy, an effective state-ideology – features which rendered the long-term social pathology and the medium-term psychological precipitants of the revolution largely superfluous. The most damning criticism of the model was that it was unnecessary and rather trivial: for if there is something wrong with a society and if the state lacks an adequate means of coercion, a rising of some sort – a 'Great Rebellion' even – will occur. And if what was required to transform rebellion into revolution – to convert a poorly engineered motorway and a faulty vehicle into an actual accident – was 'the folly and intransigence of the government . . . and its obstinate departure on a collision course', one did not need to go back any further than Clarendon or C. V. Wedgwood – to Charles's Scottish Wars and to 1637.[126]

Moreover, it was impossible to relate subsequent social and political arrangements to the Parsonian syntax of dysfunction and disequilibrium. Stone was entirely unimpressed by Hill's redefinition of bourgeois revolution as a revolution which cleared the decks for capitalism. Arguing from results in history was always a questionable procedure; and on the face of it, 1660 was almost as far removed from a bourgeois triumph as it was from the Puritans' rebuilding of Zion.[127]

> What was important about the English Revolution was not its success in permanently changing the face of England . . . Monarchy, Lords and Anglican Church were restored . . . Reforms of the electoral system, the law, the administration, the Church, the educational system were completely blocked for nearly two hundred years . . . The social structure became a good deal more immobile after the Revolution than it was before.

But, 'something survived'. What survived were 'the creative ideas' and 'experiences' of the revolutionaries. The Toynbee Hall social ethics course was reinstated, and the result of the Revolution was something called a 'legacy' – an 'immensely rich' but largely subterranean 'reservoir' ready to be tapped 'in other times and places'.[128]

5

Levelling out the Revolution

On the 'world turned upside down' texts of the 1970s, and the attempt to redefine the Revolution through its radical 'legacy'.

5.1 RADICAL EXPERIENCES

In a personal reminiscence of the original Communist Party Historians' Group, one of its few surviving members was to comment on Hill's particular contribution to its legacy: '[an] advantage of our Marxism – we owe it largely to Hill... was never to reduce history to simple economic or "class" determinism or to devalue... plebeian ideology – the theory underlying the actions of social movements... "history from below" or the "history of the common people"'.[1] After the collapse of the group in 1956 and 1957, Hill's writing had initially focused on the relationship of religious ideas and social practices in the making of the English middle class during the revolutionary decades. During the late 1960s and 1970s, he was increasingly to turn to the parallel history of the 'common people' – to the cultural challenges to the bourgeois ethic, and 'the attempts of various groups of the common people to impose their own solutions to the problems of their own time'.[2]

In May 1957, after a year-long struggle to reform it from within, Hill left the Communist Party.[3] Of his close colleagues, only Hobsbawm, Dobb and Morton were to remain within the fold. Initially, the re-emergence of a collective leadership after Stalin's death and 'the great thaw' initiated by the new Soviet regime seemed likely to favour outside communist intellectuals: it suggested that Stalinism was a temporary deviation not a structural defect, that even monolithic socialism could be modified in a humane direction and that the admission of fallibility at the very top would restore freedom of discussion to the rank and file. This was certainly the theme of most of the first responses to Khrushchev's speech to the XXth Congress of the CPSU in the pages of the *Daily Worker*: diversity would be encouraged, the party could at last flesh out the rhetoric of the 'British Road to Socialism' and free itself from the straitjacket of Stalinist dogma. 'Peaceful coexistence' and *détente* had been signalled by the new leaders in the Kremlin; multiple paths to socialism had been pointedly endorsed with the rehabilitation of Tito; G. D. H. Cole and the other intellectual leaders of the socialist Left spoke encouragingly of a new Popular Front – it was all very promising.[4]

As the full import of Khrushchev's secret speech leaked out from the capitalist press and the crimes and abuses of the previous twenty years became widely known, however, more disturbing signs emerged. For a start, the party hierarchy was visibly reluctant to admit fault: Stalin's crimes were only minor blemishes, 'sunspots', said Dutt, which had to be placed 'within the framework of profound socialist advance and transformation'. Only intellectuals thought one could make a socialist omelette without breaking eggs: 'to imagine that a great revolution can develop without a million cross-currents, hardships, injustices and excesses would be delusion fit only for ivory-tower dwellers in fairy land'.[5] The crimes were then 'historically necessary'? In their anxiety to defend the Soviet Union despite its blemishes, Pollitt and Dutt came near to defending the blemishes themselves. The crimes were all the work of one man? Marxists knew better than to read history as 'the biography of great men'; why should they make an exception in the case of Stalin, and attribute everything to the superhuman power of a leader, who had single-handedly hijacked the Revolution and distorted socialism. But this was the 'line' assiduously propounded by Stalin's heirs in Moscow, and grudgingly but faithfully transmitted by party officials in England. To many rank and file members, however, the real issue was 'not that one man was a tyrant, but that hundreds and thousands of party members let go their individual consciences' and allowed him to become one: why had the party leadership not spoken out; what sort of a party fostered such a dictatorship; and what did it all mean for the forward march of history to socialism?[6]

But, significantly, the major focus of complaint was the local hierarchy's total lack of independent judgement and refusal to allow genuine inner party debate. For sympathetic socialists, this was the litmus test: whether the Communist Party could become 'a party free and unrestrained', capable of 'evolving its own ideas' and of tolerating 'open and reasoned criticism'. And it was the inability of the leadership to recognize the crisis that confronted the party, or to contemplate a relaxation of the constrictions of 'democratic centralism', which led even well-wishers like Konni Zilliacus to accuse it of halitosis: 'a stage army of stooges and political acrobats ... with no place in British ... life.[7]

The widespread misgivings of rank and file intellectuals were brought to a head with the publication of Thompson's and Saville's critique of party thought and practices in their unofficial discussion journal, *The Reasoner*, and with their subsequent suspension by the leadership for a breach of party rules. Along with most of his fellow historians, Hill initially distanced himself from what he registered as Thompson's extravagant polemics; but he was deeply uneasy at the party's authoritarianism and inertia: the habit of handing out 'the line' from on top and 'waiting for a line' below. Why did criticism of the leadership have to be accompanied by an official reply; why did it always have to be interpreted as an attack on the party; why the invariable denunciations, the thinly veiled threats about party unity? And – the 'point' on which 'our Labour friends are most critical of us' – 'was a system of organization worked out for the Russian party working underground under Tsarism' best adapted to British political traditions and conditions?[8]

For the moment, however, he did not despair of genuine 're-form'; slowly and reluctantly, the leadership was giving ground: he applauded the belated opening up of the columns of *World News* to rank and file 'discussion', looked forward to the special congress promised on party organization and policy, and agreed to serve on the 'Commission on Inner-Party Democracy' established in July.[9] But it was soon clear that the Executive was determined to see that the Commission would not reach any conclusion disturbing to the well-tried mechanisms of central control. Its composition and procedures, not least the chairmanship of John Mahon, a died-in-the-wool party functionary, indicated an exercise in damage control, 'a little oiling and tinkering' perhaps, but no real attempt 'to recreate a democratic spirit' or a different 'method of working'. For Hill and those who wished to reform and renew the party, it was a dispiriting experience, confirming their 'growing belief that ... change [was] virtually impossible at any level'.[10]

These domestic discontents were given a more tragic dimension by the events in Hungary. For a large number of party intellectuals, Hungary dramatically highlighted the deformities inherent in 'democratic centralism' and the chasm between 'Socialist Humanism' and Stalinism, which their leaders would not or could not comprehend.[11] Thompson, Saville, and a lengthening column of Hill's fellow historians resigned, and Hill himself initiated a more modest challenge to the leadership in the form of a letter from members of the group to the *New Statesman* and *Tribune*, attacking the Executive Committee for its uncritical support of Soviet action – 'the undesirable culmination of years of distortion of facts and the failure by British Communists to think out political problems for themselves'; the party, he said, had to repudiate past errors if it wished to win support for the 'Left wing and Marxist trend within the Labour movement'.[12]

Although it hardly seemed an insurrectionary affair, the letter was treated as a major act of indiscipline by the party hierarchy; indeed, the embattled reaction of the Executive Committee seemed quite disproportionate to the offense. The joint signatures – collected 'outside the democratic machinery of the Party' – the 'negative' and 'defeatist' tone, most of all, the publication of 'a political platform in conflict' with party policy in the 'bourgeois' press, were singled out for stiff criticism. The official line was put in an article of 'monumental complacency' by the Assistant General Secretary, George Matthews: Hill's letter, he said, talked about failures and mistakes when it should have spoken of 'incomplete successes' and 'partially' correct policies. The comrades who signed the letter were 'members of long standing'.

> The party regards the work of these comrades as an important contribution to its efforts on behalf of the British working class. But just as it needs the intellectuals, so they need the party. They need the sense of discipline that it can give them. They need its help in combating petty-bourgeois ideas. They need the understanding which it can give them that the party is bigger than any individual or group of individuals, however distinguished.

It was Palme Dutt's 'sunspots' again. Clearly, said Hyman Levy, the intention was to read the dissidents a lesson in orthodox party theory.[13]

These considerations were clearly evident in the Majority resolution on Inner Party Democracy, carried overwhelmingly at the

Special Party Congress in April 1957: 'democratic centralism' was not a foreign import but was consonant with the experiences and the circumstances of British socialism; the Communist Party was not a broad church 'affiliation' like the Labour Party, but 'a body of like-minded Marxists', exposed to the wiles of the capitalist state, united in their commitment to the class struggle, dependent on 'a strong disciplined and centralized party': it was all very reminiscent of Stalin's 'monolithic organization hewed from a single block, possessing a single will, uniting all shades of thought into a single current of practical activities' – exactly the conception that Khrushchev's secret speech was thought to have swept away. The trauma of 1956 had produced a hardening of official arteries; and the troubled debates over policy and organization were viewed by the leadership almost entirely as a struggle against what King Street jargon dubbed a 'Right opportunist and liquidationist outlook'. Underpinning these arguments was the old Leninist critique in the name of an authoritarian 'realism', of 'wavering intellectuals', as 'purveyors of petty bourgeois ideas which corrupt[ed] the class consciousness of the proletariat'.[14] Predictably, there were still plenty of intellectuals eager to indulge in 'self-criticism'; indeed, the attacks on academic 'factionalism' – 'the divine right of individuals to their own discretion' – were most openly articulated by some of Hill's fellow historians: by Joan Simon in a number of tart letters castigating 'puffed up' 'amateurs of revolution', who invariably 'lost their heads' at times of crisis, or by Andrew Rothstein in a peculiarly vituperative speech, in which he reminded fellow delegates of the early history of Bolshevism, when 'tens of thousands of workers left the Party because . . . they were bewildered and confused by . . . backboneless and spineless intellectuals.'[15]

Outmanoeuvred and isolated on the Commission, ill at ease in his critique of the party platform, outvoted in the Special Congress, Hill resigned from the party immediately after. His sense of pain and bitterness must have been considerable. More than most intellectuals, he was a natural loyalist and a 'sticker'. Always the rational, responsible academic politician who was also a totally committed Marxist, to be excoriated by the likes of Joan Simon, or to be gently but patronizingly lectured by Arnold Kettle for the 'immoderate parading of conscience' must have been gall and wormwood. It was twenty years before his name was to appear again under the communist masthead, and then only after an official olive branch in the form of a cautious exercise in revisionism by the General Secretary in the pages of James Klugmann's *Marxism Today*.[16]

A little history is a dangerous thing, and of the cultural groups associated with the party, the Historians' Group was especially hard hit by the inner party crisis of 1956 and 1957: over half of its members resigned, including most of its leading academics. Surveying the lists in 1960, John Gollan, the new General Secretary, had to admit that 'they made melancholy reading'.[17] Perhaps, as Palme Dutt surmised, the explanation for what he inimitably characterized as 'the considerable weakness' of 'its most distinguished' members 'during the time of testing', lay in their elevation of professional research over 'revolutionary political understanding'. But, as Betty Grant pointed out, none of them would have regarded their party duties and their historical work as mutually exclusive concerns. Perhaps, as Eric Hobsbawm subsequently suggested, it had something to do with their professional interest in the past and their determination to subject their own politics to the rigours of historical evaluation; though, personal reminiscence and incidental polemic apart, none of them was to venture into print on the record of the Communist Party in Britain or the Soviet Union. Probably, it had more to do with the personal dynamics of the group, and the sort of history they had come to write. The group had always been a meeting of minds: fellow 'heretics' steeped in sectarian thought, working on a variety of projects in the 'battle of ideas'. The result was a considerable range of idiom and interest behind the common endeavour – there was a world of difference between Edward Thompson's commitment to rethinking Marxism from a humanist perspective, and Eric Hobsbawm's reduction of issues of socialist principle to those of political strategy, or between John Saville's responsiveness to the traditions of the British Labour movement and Andrew Rothstein's adulation of the Bolshevik model.

Long before 1956, temperamental disparities and the tensions between people's history and socialist theory had begun to unravel the unity of the group; indeed, in retrospect, the Netherwood discussions of 1954, which were to launch the cooperative history of capitalist formation in Britain, proved to be its collective swansong. The grand study of British capitalism never eventuated – Hobsbawm was enthusiastic, but the other likely contributors were increasingly taken up with their own academic or personal concerns. And when they went on to produce their own individual histories in the years ahead, the parts never cohered: 'between them' – the verdict is damning but not unfair – 'they . . . created chaos with the basic chronology of the modern world'.[18]

Most of them, as Thompson explains, had yearned for an end of the 'siege mentality' of the late 1940s and early 1950s; some had anticipated the substitution of a national or a moral idiom for 'diamet'. The recovery of an indigenous tradition of political and social protest – the celebration of those whom A. J. P. Taylor had recently promoted as England's 'Trouble Makers' – probably exaggerated their suspicion of bureaucratic control. So much the greater their disappointment at the party's inability to renew itself democratically and their outrage at the heavy-handed executive intervention in their own domestic affairs.[19] While Thompson and Saville were airing their discontents, Hobsbawm had attempted to draw some sustenance from the crisis, by urging his colleagues to consider the new 'tasks for historians'. Pointing to the historical revision going on in the Soviet Union and to the opportunities of 'establishing the record of Party activity . . . [and doing] what the Webbs had once done for . . . Labour', he spoke of surveying it 'without prejudice or preconception, solely in the light of Marxist analysis' and of 'provid[ing] the historical background necessary for working out future policy'.[20] But the executive was suspicious of Hobsbawm's agenda: party history, if it was to be written at all, was to be written under the auspices of a tightly controlled 'commission', independently established for that purpose under the chairmanship of Harry Pollitt. The group was not consulted; and when it subsequently submitted three names for inclusion on the commission, these were turned down in favour of more orthodox additions.

Even more damaging was the Political Committee's interference in the group's own historical research and writing: for the first time, its published material was the subject of investigation and complaint by party headquarters. Work in progress on sensitive twentieth-century projects had now to be submitted before publication and was subjected to what Betty Grant referred to as 'constant . . . prevarication and opposition'.[21] Little wonder that its professional members refused to be lured from 'the recesses of the seventeenth century, the Peasant's Revolt or Chartism': an 'escapism' which was to earn them rebukes for neglect of party duty.[22] Little wonder either, that 'when the shooting up of youngsters on the streets of Budapest was being pronounced a great victory for socialism', Hill and Hilton should have formally moved the group's disaffiliation from the party. The group, they argued, was too vital a force in the battle for a truer past and a better future, to be pulled apart by rank and file dissent and executive constraint: better to preserve a loose Marxist organization, than to insist on its orthodox credentials. Weakened by earlier defections, by sniping at the 'cliquishness and snobbery' of university members, and by the reluctance of some colleagues to choose between party and group loyalties, narrowly defeated on a show of hands, they resigned shortly after. Though the period sections stopped functioning, the group, however, did not collapse. Eric Hobsbawm and Betty Grant managed to hold the rump together, encouraging contact with ex-members, fighting for a degree of intellectual independence, half expecting its formal disbandment or their own expulsion by the more obedient party faithful. But it was a very different organization that survived – only a shadow of the organization that had shaped the thinking of its founder members. For them, no doubt, the death of Dona Torr in January 1957 symbolized the end of an era.[23]

Yet, their intellectual allegiance to Marxism was undiminished: none of them 'entered the well-worn paths of apostasy' or added another generation of witnesses to 'the God that failed'. For the past twelve years, they had learnt to define their political values in opposition to what they saw as the phobic inversions of ex-Communists. As students of English history and literature, they reminded each other of the fate of the English ex-Jacobins, early enthusiasts for the French Revolution like Wordsworth and Coleridge, who rallied to the cause of Counter-Revolution and the Holy Alliance; better, they believed, to keep faith and integrity with Goethe or Shelley, or, in a different era with Milton and Marvell, than to repeat the isolation, the hysteria and the half-imaginary memories of the renegade. Hill's own position was publicly conveyed in the letter to the *New Statesman* and *Tribune*:

The exposure of crimes and abuses in the USSR and the recent revolts of workers and intellectuals against the pseudo-Communist bureaucracies and police systems of Poland and Hungary, have shown that for the past twelve years, we have based our political analyses on a false presentation of facts, not on an out of date theory, for we still consider the Marxist method to be correct.[24]

And in his speech to the Special Congress, he freely admitted that the suppression of facts had not just been limited to party functionaries: that he, too, as a Russian 'expert' who had visited the Soviet Union in the years after Stalin's death, had chosen to remain silent. The party, he said, had been 'living in a snug cosy little world' of 'illusions' which had to be exposed to 'fresh air': to 'analysis not slogan-shouting, facts not fancies, truths even if unpleasant'. Such truths might sweep away King Street's banalities; they would not undermine Marxist theory.

In 1956, 'the best' Hungarian Communist writers decided – 'after many troubles, grave errors, and bitter spiritual struggles – that never again under any conditions, whatever, [would] they write lies in the future'. 'These indomitable words', commented Michael Polanyi,

> reflect a bitter struggle of conscience which in turn arises from the internal contradiction between the ... two dominant passions ... of the age ... We are swayed by a moral dynamism which is without example in history; we demand justice, freedom and brotherhood beyond all precedent. At the same time we are determined to think scientifically; we have a passion for strict objectivity which is also without precedent in history.[25]

To its critics, Stalinism revealed the pathological propensities of Marxism; but to Hill and his colleagues, the 'magic of Marxism' was to unite the conflicting passions in a single system. They had their own 'experiential political reasons for being opposed to capitalist society, independent of any evolution in Eastern Europe', their 'intellectual reasons for associating with the Marxist tradition, independent of any follies or self-delusions of Stalinism': the moral credentials of a British state defined by Malaya, Mau Mau, Cyprus and that preposterous essay in 'gangster' imperialism, the Suez adventure, could still be juxtaposed to the educational, cultural and scientific potential of socialist societies in a sputnik era.[26] They were still possessed by a moral passion for socialism; and they continued to convert their aspirations into scientific affirmations of an alternative egalitarian world. They were driven by a corresponding hatred of capitalism; and continued, in the inversion characteristic of Marxists, invariably to discover selfish interests lurking behind its moral ideals.[27]

The moral repudiation of capitalism coupled with the rejection of actually existing socialism, however, placed socialist intellectuals in something of a dilemma: on the one hand, their professional activities, as critics of bourgeois society, were viewed as exemplary; on the other, these same activities might provide them with a favoured niche in capitalist society – they might live, however indirectly, off the profits of others' labour, the beneficiaries of a system that emotionally and intellectually they deplored. Such a condition could easily be construed as chronic 'bad faith': the demythologizers of bourgeois society could themselves be un-masked; their intellectual projects shown up as petty bourgeois posturing – accusations the more difficult to answer, since rebut-tal might deprive them of the anti-bourgeois credentials on which their self-respect was founded. At the height of the party's 'time of troubles', and with some acerbity, Joan Simon had pointed out the occupational hazards of armchair socialism: 'Most of us come from, and work, in bourgeois or petty bourgeois surroundings, and have been intellectually convinced by Marxism rather than convinced by the realities of class struggle . . . Most intellectuals don't really know what class solidarity is.'[28] How could they? Their struggle could not be a struggle for self-liberation – from the op-pressions of Balliol College or even Birmingham University – it had to be a struggle to change society – not their own situation – on behalf of others – not themselves. 'No one,' writes Garry Werskey, 'conveyed the position more succinctly than J. B. S. Haldane: "I am a socialist because I want to see my fellow men and women enjoying the advantages which I enjoy myself".' Such a socialism was bound to be altruistic and compassionate rather than self-transforming. In attempting to square an emotional and intellectual circle which could no longer be solved by simple self-effacement and party loyalty, the Marxist might cultivate 'a sec-ond identity' – an identity which for Hill, at least, increasingly revolved around the radical subversives of the English Revolu-tion, 'the struggles of men and women trying to make *their* world a better place'.[29]

In the 1940s and 1950s, it was possible to put one's name to a triumphalist reading of the bourgeois revolution, secure in the knowledge of historical laws leading to socialism, and one's own 'scientific neutrality' as a Communist Party member standing outside the world of capitalist illusion. These simplicities were no longer credible: socialism was a potentiality not an inevitable end-point, a hope not a reality, an alternative dispensation which had to be pieced together from the aspirations and the visions of those who had endeavoured to turn the bourgeois world upside down in the past. For the crumbling of socialist teleology coincided with a renewed questioning of bourgeois values: the 1960s saw a counter-cultural revolt, spearheaded by a new generation of students and intellectuals. They, also, witnessed global winds of change, blowing away the last filaments of Britain's imperial splendour and tearing at the centuries-old fabric of her industrial and commercial prosperity – the beginnings of the process, which Hill was to sum up with apparent satisfaction in 1984, as the 'whimpered' ending of 'England's historical destiny'.[30]

One of the most attractive and compelling features of Hill's historical work – the characteristic which more than any other explained the dominance which he achieved in the field of seventeenth-century English studies – was his extraordinary responsiveness to changes in historical fashion and in society at large. New evidence, new ideas, new sensitivities, new perspectives – these were some of the reasons, he concluded in his *Change and Continuity in Seventeenth Century England*,

> why history has to be rewritten in each generation: each new act in the historical drama necessarily shifts our attitude towards the earlier acts. So that there is a dialectic of continuity and change not only in the seventeenth century itself, but also in our awareness of the seventeenth century. We ourselves are shaped by the past; but from our vantage point in the present we are constantly reshaping the past which shapes us.

What was unusual about Hill was not his productivity or his erudition – though they were remarkable enough – but that he rewrote his own history so many times. The result was a Marxism which was constantly renewing itself; inevitably there was some repetition, much recycling of old examples; but there was also a freshness of perspective, an openness to new approaches and new materials, a readiness to accept criticism from others which kept his Marxism 'empirically responsible and . . . capable of engaging in debate with the broad community of English historians'.[31]

The writing of history, in Hill's opinion, had always been 'a battle against the self-styled expert'; the history of religion was painfully rescued from the theologians, constitutional history from the lawyers, economic history from the statisticians: total history always had to struggle against 'partial historians'. The 1960s and 1970s, however, witnessed a dramatic broadening of the discipline:

a neglected world of social and emotional life exploded the traditional boundaries of the subject; simultaneously, the work of social philosophers, anthropologists, literary theorists, and feminists was beginning to undermine its professional autonomy. Winds of change were blowing across the flat expanse of the English historical landscape, shaking the foundations of the traditional curricula, ruffling even the staid pages of the *Times Literary Supplement*. Hill's magpie mentality and responsiveness to academic novelty, his commitment to 'total history' and his position as a 'generalist' and a radical at the heart of the English academic establishment, made him particularly susceptible to these 'new directions'. Even his blind spots – his lack of concern for theoretical consistency or for the abstract debates and polemics which exercised the talents of many of his colleagues in the 1960s – may have made him more willing to accommodate them within a comparatively unsophisticated but expansive Marxist framework.[32]

At the height of the inner party crisis of 1956, Hyman Levy had commented on the irony of a 'heretic' party which left no room for 'heresy' in its own ranks. All organization leads to oligarchic control; and it is difficult to believe that Hill's increased responsiveness to the heretical and democratic elements in the English Revolution – sects some of them so fleeting and evanescent that their very existence was to be called in question – did not have something to do with his experience of a suffocating communist orthodoxy which had snuffed out the creativity and integrity of ordinary party members.[33] By the late 1960s, his vision of history from below had, of course, been enriched by the example of E. P. Thompson; but it was extended by Hill's academic and political experiences also. There was the student revolution of the late 1960s – the inevitable product of a growing number 'of alert and culturally equipped individuals' gathered together in medieval institutions; the 'contradiction' between capitalism's increased appetite for intellectual labour and the threat of egalitarian enlightenment to the capitalist system; the accentuation of the generational gap – 'an intense multidimensional cultural explosion' which meant 'that each new generation travels through a different mental universe en route to adulthood'.[34] There was discovery of 'repressive tolerance' by the radical gurus of California and other captive cultures – that 'pluralist democracy' exercised a form of constraint far more sophisticated, extensive and complete than the cruder and more overt forms of political dictatorship.[35] Some of this clearly rubbed off on a Marxist and a heretic: one whose 'deep-seated views, feelings and loyalties must have drawn him strongly towards the radical side' in the university and society at large, but who as Master of Balliol and icon of the establishment was an inevitable upholder of much that the radicals wished to destroy. Is it too much to suggest that his growing interest and sympathy for 'a world turned upside down' in the seventeenth century may not have been unconnected with the intellectual and emotional discomforts of maintaining an upside up world in the twentieth?[36]

The interest was not, of course, entirely new: he had written of the Levellers' campaign for the redistribution and extension of the parliamentary franchise, security of ownership and law reform, and the Diggers' programme of 'direct action' through occupation and tillage of the 'common land', as progressive statements of economic democracy and social revolution, which 'had much to say to twentieth century socialists'.[37] And he was working in a rich vein of twentieth-century socialist thought, stretching back through the writings of Margaret James and H. N. Brailsford to the work of L. H. Berens and Edward Bernstein.[38] What was different in his treatment during the 1970s was the richness and variety of the radical milieu which he uncovered, the comparative neglect of class determinations or meanings, and the evident sympathy for a world without power and institutional structures:

> The idea that the bottom might come to the top, that the first might be last and the last first, that 'community ... called Christ or universal love might cast out property called the devil or covetousness' and that the inward bondages of the mind ... might be 'all occasioned by the outward bondages that one sort of people lay upon another' – such ideas are not necessarily opposed to order: they merely envisage a different order ... Upside down is after all a relative concept ... [and] we may be too conditioned by the way the world has been for the last three hundred years to be fair to those in the seventeenth century who saw other possibilities. But, we should try.[39]

Hill's study of *The World Turned Upside Down: Radical Ideas During the English Revolution* was to establish itself as a classic radical text of the 1970s: for many, and especially the young, 'a liberating experience', a demonstration that history need not be boring and remote, a book of 'marvellous erudition', 'compassion[ate]', 'stirring' and 'memorable' – a bestseller, adapted even for the stage by the actors' and producers' cooperative of the Cottesloe Theatre.[40]

Why this should have been so may bear some examination. For at twenty years remove, the book does not seem quite as exciting as its reputation suggests. It was, however, perfectly attuned to the agendas and assumptions of the early 1970s; it drew the threads of new history, new theory and current radical politics together in a particularly potent and persuasive manner. In 'The Norman Yoke', he had explored the radical uses of secular mythology by different groups and classes during the Revolution.[41] And in his study of Puritanism, he had suggested the co-existence of two cultures in early Stuart England – an unreformed, semi-pagan, 'Margaret Murray' culture of wakes, ales, maypoles and parish revels, and a proselytizing Puritan culture of discipline, frugality, sabbatarianism and the reformation of manners, reaching out from the manufacturing towns and rural industrial areas into 'the dark corners of the land'. These insights had been given a depth and solidity by Keith Thomas in his magisterial study of *Religion and the Decline of Magic*: but whereas Hill had been primarily interested in the programme of Protestant reform, Thomas came at the cultural crisis from the other end, and focused on the gradual breakdown of traditional beliefs and practices and on the guilts and tensions released by a harsher and more individualized religious ethic.[42]

Hill's Puritanism had always been a fragmented and unorthodox affair: rooted in late medieval heresy and the anti-clericalism of the Reformation, it was always conceived in individualistic, oppositional, potentially radical terms. A pamphlet rather than a pulpit Puritanism, it carried the seeds of its own subversion. He had explored the ubiquity of prophesy, millenarian expectation, obsession with the Antichrist, and anti-Catholic paranoia during the period: an unsettling and combustible dynamic of belief and 'superstition' with clear revolutionary implications. And a number of his pupils had begun to tease out these combinations in detailed and sympathetic studies of the various sects that proliferated in England during the 1640s and 1650s.[43]

In the early 1950s, Leslie Morton – once again a harbinger of new developments in Marxist scholarship – had studied the interconnected story of the two islands of Britain and Utopia. The rise of utopian literature, he argued, coincided with that of the bourgeoisie within and in opposition to a static hierarchical feudal order, where such ideal commonwealths were almost unthinkable: nurtured on the hopes and despairs of a civic humanism, they took on the 'hard bright certainty' of practical social and political engineering in an age of revolution, when utopia seemed 'no longer a distant island or an enchanted dream, but a possibility that might take shape . . . at a moment's notice'. But alongside the scientific, capitalist and republican blueprints of Bacon, Hartlib and Harrington were the 'extravagant shapes' of religious fantasy at a time when the Kingdom of God on earth also seemed a distinct possibility.[44] About the same time, Norman Cohn, a historian of a very different ideological predisposition, had resuscitated the counter-cultural underground of England in the 1650s, as a link in the long chain of mystical or quasi-mystical anarchism stretching from the thirteenth-century Brethren of Free Spirit to the hippie amoralists of contemporary California. Cohn's interest was in a genealogy of religious aberration, somewhat in the manner of J. R. Talmon's famous demonology of 'totalitarian' lineages; and he found in the 'anarchic eroticism' and 'self-deification' of the 'Ranters' exactly the combination of 'blind devotion to their living God' and utter repudiation of conventional moral laws made notorious by Charles Manson and his 'family': 'the idiom belonged to seventeeenth century England and nowhere else'; the 'ideas and ideals [had] a far wider relevance . . . stripped of their original supernatural sanction, revolutionary millenarianism and mystical anarchism are with us still'.[45] Morton, too, viewed the underground of popular belief in the English Revolution as genealogy: part of the long history of English utopias or of the mystical tradition in English literature – which survived in 'odd corners of plebian society' to reappear in the prophetical writings of William Blake. In 1970, however, he went on to explore the milieu of the 1640s and 1650s itself, *The World of the Ranters*: a work which focused on the attempted 'reclothing' of political and social ideas in millenarian forms and antinomian practices – an 'immensely readable book', said Hill, which threw light 'on whole areas of our past which were previously obscure'.[46]

Morton put the Ranters on the map. They were not, he argued, a church or even a sect; there was no evidence of any formal organization or generally received body of doctrine; there was much incoherence in their theology and a 'contradiction' between the values of the leading ideologues and the rank and file; much of the evidence of their beliefs and activities was 'a vast confusion of charges, rebuttals and counter-charges' from which it was impossible to establish the truth 'with any certainty'. For all that, they constituted a 'militant tendency', an extreme moment in the English Revolution. Briefly, after the defeat of 'Levelling by sword and by spade', their heady mixture of 'pantheistic mysticism and crudely plebian materialism' attracted a mass following in the poorer quarters of London and in the Army, and was thought by the authorities to represent a genuine threat to the social and political order. Morton's work conveyed something of the passion, the poetry and the vision of the Ranters which gave them 'a firm but peculiar place in the English Revolution and in the list of English heresies'. He was less successful, however, in relating the idiom of their writings to their political and social significance. Their theology was located within Cohn's antinomian genealogy; their political and social ideas and practices were viewed through the prism of a reasonably orthodox Marxism, as the despairing ideology of the 'defeated and declassed': 'what the Levellers had failed to do with considerable mass support, organizing ability and an attractive programme based on a well considered political theory in a time of exceptional political fluidity was far beyond the powers of confused anarchists, at a time of political retreat'.[47]

Hill was more susceptible to the ambience of counter-cultural expectation. Once upon a time, he might have dismissed the enthusiasts and libertarians of the English Revolution as 'a lunatic fringe of self-appointed Messiahs'.[48] No longer: times change and fashions change, and an age of long hair, pop music, sexual freedom and student revolt could hardly be expected to find its heroes in the high-minded sophists of the Putney Debates, let alone more strenuous figures like Cromwell or Pym. C. B. Macpherson had already pruned Lilburne's socialist credentials and recaste the mainstream Levellers as radical liberals rather than full democrats: at best, the Leveller movement was concerned 'to slew the world round a little', not to turn it upside down or destroy its foundations. Soviet historians had uncovered a crucial fault-line within the radical movement between Levellers and 'true Levellers': the former, petty bourgeois believers in the immutability of existing property relations, predestined opportunists tugged into accommodations with the existing order; the latter, true republicans and socialists, shading off into near identity with the Diggers and other enemies of a repressive religious and social regime.[49]

'Upside down' was the test of Hill's 'revolt within the Revolution'. It was also the idiom of student revolt and of the philosophical apologists of 'Paradise Now'. Both cast doubt on traditional revolutionary tactics; both spoke the language of total transformation from a world of undifferentiated repression to one of complete self-realization. Little wonder that Hill's milieu of 'teeming freedom' seemed to have 'an uncanny relevance to the contemporary world'. Revolutionary youth conjured up the 'metaphysics of Doomsday': 'the days of the old order are numbered . . . For the first time in history, mankind is capable of living free without the chains of repression or alienation . . . The revolution that is coming will transform all life and culture as we have hitherto known it.' This was not Abiezer Coppe or Lawrence Clarkson, but the student representative of the LSE in June 1968.[50] Herbert Marcuse, who had once argued for the long Hegelian road to liberation, advocated a storming of the repressive heavens here and now; Hill's friend, Norman Brown, put the case for a 'life against death' alignment of sensual enjoyment, mysticism and liberation; Foucault explored the exclusions and the silences of a world of rationality and order, and an alternative 'episteme' where madness was a higher form of wisdom or saintliness.[51] According to Hill:

> Protestant preachers in the late sixteenth and early seventeenth centuries undertook . . . an exercise in indoctrination and brain-washing on a hitherto unprecedented scale. We only fail to recognize this because we live in a brain-washed society: our own indoctrination takes place so early, and from so many directions at once, that we are unaware of the process.

The World Turned Upside Down examined some of the early challenges to this process of internalized 'repression' from a still unsubdued 'natural man'; it was, indeed, another essay on the contingency of bourgeois arrangements and the possibility of overturning them.[52]

For many radicals in the 1960s, the key to Marx's thought lay in the concept of 'alienation', adumbrated in his early philosophical writings and fleshed out by the gurus of the new Marxist humanism.[53] Alienation was not simply the product of capitalist organization, commodity fetishism, and the extraction of surplus labour power, but was the outcome of a whole 'logic of domination' exerted over the human body and the human spirit, as old as civilization itself. Liberation, therefore, had to be sought in consciousness rather than material arrangements: in a war of the instinct against repression and self-hatred, rather than class struggle against oppression. Indeed, the conventional strategy of political and social revolution, unaccompanied by libidinal liberation, simply led to the substitution of a one repressive elite for another – to the corruption and 'self-defeat' of even the most well intentioned insurgents. For Norman Brown, in particular, the creation of 'a Dionysian ego' was central to the recovery of a non-repressive culture. And Brown found his inspiration in the tradition of apocalyptic illumination and transcendent body mysticism stretching back through the great antinomian seers and heretics of the higher religions. Only a resurrection of 'Love's Body' through the visionary imagination could rescue humanity from a culture, diseased and divided, product of the disintegrated metaphors, born of spiritual and sensual denial. Marcuse, closer to Feuerbach than to Freud, for whom repression was a historical construction rather than an ontological dilemma, rejected what he saw as a retreat from politics into a never-never land of mystical 'pentecostal tongues'. Repression could never be wholly transcended; only the 'surplus repression', imposed by particular groups and ideologies, could be defeated through setting aside the technological regimentation and artificially imposed psychic scarcity of Soviet and Western societies, for a society of affluence, erotic fulfillment and 'libidinal rationality'.[54]

To focus exclusively on these counter-cultural subtexts, however appropriate in an essay on the fabrication of the past, is of course, to mistake the idiom for the substance. Hill's study was not simply a tract for the times; it was an ambitious attempt to recover a complex social and mental 'milieu'. It opened conventionally enough with a brief sketch of the demographic and socio-economic conditions – the dissolution of the old agrarian order; a new economy of social mobility; a Civil War chronology of upheaval and unrest, with the New Model Army, a magnet for 'masterless men' and 'a short-lived school of political democracy'; a geography of isolation and freedom, with the woodlands and wastes providing 'longer lasting though less intensive schools of economic democracy'; the culminating dislocation of the Second Civil War – which set the scene for the radical experiments and upside down visions of 1649 and 1650.[55] They were not, however, determinants: cultural manifestations and religious ideas had to be studied 'in their own reality and autonomy', not as expressions of class cir-

cumstances or material interests. Indeed, the theoretical underpinning of Hill's work – though he was only partly aware of
borrowings, filtered through the writings of historians like Keith
Thomas or cultural theorists like Norman Brown – was derived
as much from Malinowski, Freud and Gramsci as from Marx. And
they, in turn, offered hypotheses to be explored and tested, rather
than models to be applied.[56]

They certainly enabled him to flesh out a more immediate and
plausible genealogy than anything to be found in the loose lineages of Norman Cohn or Leslie Morton. A tradition of popular
heresy, plebeian anti-clericalism and lower class materialism; a
mental universe saturated by magic, astrology and prophesy; a
dynamic 'signifier' of the Antichrist which inexorably enlarged
its 'signified' – from Pope, to Bishop, to any established church
order, to any form of external power; the tensions in Puritan thought
and practice between predetermination and the priesthood of all
believers, the doctrine of the elect and a preaching designed to
reach all, the singularity of God's Word and individual interpretation of the Bible: these were just some of the 'icebergs' of subversive thought that surfaced and coalesced in the relative freedom
of the English Revolution.[57]

But the crux of his argument, the issue on which the Revolution split and Protestant thought divided into a mainstream of
repression and a briefly articulated alternative of liberation, was
the little matter of sin and Hell. The destruction of the old order
of coercive 'domination' necessitated the creation of new controls.
For Protestants continued to insist on the absolute depravity of
humankind; salvation came through God alone and not through
merit. The doctrine of 'first disobedience', inherited sin and damnation not only supported the Protestant ethic – punctuality, frugality, self-control, the postponement of instinctual gratification
– but shored up the social and political order also. It was natural
depravity – 'an inherited characteristic, transmitted by the sexual
act' – which justified punitive magistracy; it was the Fall that transformed 'freehold' into 'villeinage'; it was 'the brutal ignorance and
palpable darkness possessing the greatest part of the people' which
made political and social 'levelling' unthinkable. The task of Protestant reformers, and the long-term effect of the Puritan Revolution, therefore, was to translate domination into hegemony: to
replace the rusty old mechanism of ecclesiastical and political control
with a far more effective internal economy of self-discipline and

self-repression. Briefly, however, and for reasons which were to be found in the contradictions of English Protestant thought as well as in the social circumstances of the 1640s, the new machinery of subordination was contested by 'an antinomian rejection of the bondage of the moral law' – a desperate struggle not simply over theology or religious freedom, but about social, political and personal repression and self-determination also.[58]

There was more of Gramsci than of Marx in this reading of the challenges to and eventual triumph of the Protestant ethic. Gramscian theory was perfectly fitted to the enlarged horizons of Marxist historians seeking to understand how ideas might reinforce or undermine existing social structures. Here was an explanation of the apparent exhaustion of the socialist ethic and a 'hegemonic' culture of affluence based on the active consent of the people; here, too, was a gratifying assessment of the role of intellectuals – not in the humble contemplation of proletarian backsides but in the formation and maintenance of cultural systems. Without the mobilization of these 'specialized standard bearers' of the masses, revolutionary movements ossified and decayed: it was the desertion of humanist intellectuals which doomed Luther's Reformation to political and social sterility; and it was only the formation of a new generation of Calvinist and Puritan intellectuals which made possibile the advances of the seventeenth century.

Gramsci identified a structure of thought as well as a power structure and a set of determining social relations: ruling groups did not simply impose their authority through institutional mechanisms; they also sought to win the consent of subordinate groups through the diffusion of their concept of reality. This 'cultural hegemony' was not, however, a closed or static system of class domination, but a process of continuous creation, uneven in the degree of legitimacy it could command and open to antagonistic cultural expressions amongst subordinate groups. In the version adopted by the New Left in the 1960s and 1970s, there were complex patterns of accommodation and resistance to the values imposed by the dominant public culture; and there was always the potentiality of a genuinely common culture based on reintegrating 'the life of the spirit' with that of the people. This was the message which Hill believed was to be found in the English Revolution.[59]

A society in upheaval like seventeenth-century England was characterized by the absence of an effective hegemonic 'block':

there was questioning of the doctrine of universal human depravity within the elite – from the Arminian doctrine of free will and the Baconian programme of rational improvement. But neither were interested in the emancipation of the masses: the Arminians looked back to a hierarchical mechanism of sacramental control; the Baconians looked forward to a utilitarian technocracy which polluted the planet and mechanized human nature. The English Revolution, however, threw up others who rejected eternal damnation and opted for human perfectability in a 'truly liberating' manner: in the words of Herbert Marcuse, during the Revolution 'the imagination was for a short period released and free to enter into the projects of a new social morality and new institutions of freedom'.[60]

The plebeian radicals of the English Revolution combined liberation from 'the superstition of imaginary . . . scarecrow sins' with social democracy, 'antinomian perfectabilism' with sensuous enjoyment of the body, belief in universal salvation with schemes of unlimited secular progress. The key to these beliefs lay in a natural extension of the Calvinist doctrine of the elect: if a man or a woman were predestined to be saved how could they sin; and if Christ died for all, why should not all be elect? 'To the pure all things are pure': and to some of the Ranters there was 'no such act as drunkenness, adultery and theft'; no distinction between sacred and profane, no immortality of the soul, no heaven; no need for clergy, Protestant ethic, property, family, monogamy. They preached – and some of them practised – polygamy, divorce, ritual nudism, love-ins, the taking of tobacco and alchohol to heighten visionary experience, the rights of the young against the old, children against parents, women against men. Of course, their writings were 'utopian', 'surrealist'; their behaviour eccentric and outrageous. Yet, in another sense, because they alone of the sects 'abolished sin', they alone were able to articulate 'a real subversion of existing society and its values'. 'Be a realist', read the student placard of 1968: 'demand the impossible'; 'utopia', said Marcuse, was 'the most real of all real possibilities'. So, too, the Ranter programme 'was a heroic effort to proclaim . . . the freedom of the human body and of sexual relations against the mind-forged manacles which were being imposed'.[61]

There was quite a lot of Norman Brown in Hill's evaluation of the liberating potential of body mysticism. But Hill was too much of a believer in the tangible world of privilege, injustice and oppression to follow Professor Dionysus into his visionary kingdom of poetic and sensual freedom beyond politics and necessity. Repression was a historical not a biological condition; its construction had much to do with the creation of bourgeois society and the concomitant internalization of its social divisions in a Puritan economy of spiritual scarcity and control. Hill's version of liberation, indeed, represented a narrowing of Marcuse's this-worldly realism in the direction of a more traditional appeal to supposed communal practice and *mentalité* before the seventeenth-century Fall.[62] Besides, as Keith Thomas wryly noted, there was something faintly comic at the Stakhanovite Master of Balliol – whose unrelenting application to historical scholarship had churned out a major historical work every other year since 1956 – applauding the repudiation of the Protestant ethic. And sure enough, there were sensible limits to his counter-cultural *schwarmerei*: the orgiastic aspects of Ranterism also brought disorder, idleness, the break-up of families and venereal disease; 'sexual liberty was a hit and run affair' which left others to carry the costs; and the concentration on personal self-fulfilment ultimately distracted and diverted revolutionary energies. This was, of course, the orthodox Marxist critique of 'Student Power'.[63]

The most powerful expression of the revolt within the Revolution was to be found rather in Winstanley's philosophy of social action: 'the one possible democratic solution which was not merely backward looking' or escapist. Like the radical sectarians, Winstanley believed in universal salvation and perfectibility on earth; he too attempted to demythologize God and Satan as 'inventions' – projections of the 'the serpent of selfishness' and 'the sun of righteousness' within. Unlike the other sectarians, however, he went on to translate his theology into a philosophy of political and economic praxis. He came to believe that 'all the inward bondages of the mind' were occasioned by 'the outward bondages that one sort of people lay upon another'. For Winstanley, the establishment of private property was not a painful and divisive consequence of the Fall, but *was* the Fall itself – 'a drama reenacted in every individual . . . subjected to the pressures of a corrupt propertied society'; correspondingly, the Day of Judgment was a series of events taking place in the hearts and actions of the saints on earth: in the abolition of private property and in the creation of a class-less society. Hill's Winstanley was recognizably 'a modern': despite the theological language, the apocalyptic visions and 'the mystical connotations' of his actions, he 'look[ed] forward' to eighteenth-century secularism and materialism, and to 'nineteenth and twentieth century socialism and communism'; and 'his insights [we]re important to those in the Third World today who face the transition from an agrarian to an industrial society'. Whether this was really the author of *Fire in the Bush* and *The New Law of Righteousness*, and whether Hill had really understood apocalyptic and visionary experience on its own terms, was open to question.[64]

The World Turned Upside Down and its companion pieces enormously broadened the scope of the English Revolution. They provided real substance to a 'history from below', mapped out a new territory of social protest, broke down the orthodox Marxist distinction between scientific and utopian ideas, and did much to make sense of 'what had hitherto appeared as a more or less promiscuously seething mass of heterodoxies'. Here was a map of the past experience which enlarged and 'humanized', entered imaginatively into 'the struggles of men and women trying to make their world a better place' and translated them into the idioms of the present. Even what some perceived as historical faults – the tendency to make it too rational and accessible, too much of a single 'brotherhood of social protest' – could be viewed as virtues. The sociology of religion had, arguably, suffered from an overdose of Weberian 'charisma': the emphasis on inspiration and the personal magnetism of the religious leader directed attention away from the ideas and activities of the movement and the aspirations of the rank and file. Hill did not play psychohistory with his characters; he did not suggest dark and compelling forces at work. Rather it was the rationality and practicality of the 'underground' programme that he underlined. Seventeenth-century radicals had conceived an alternative ethic and 'a different order' from that of bourgeois society – an order 'we are better placed to appreciate':

> As we contemplate our landscape made hideous by neon signs, advertisements, pylons, wreckage of automobiles; our seas poisoned by atomic waste, our shores littered with plastic and oil; our atmosphere polluted with carbon dioxide and nuclear fall out, our peace shattered by supersonic planes; as we think of nuclear bombs which can 'waste and destroy' to an extent that Winstanley never dreamed of . . .[65]

Scientific thought and development were no longer simply viewed from the Bernalian perspective of planned technological abundance, but from that of an ecologically sustainable or befouled planet also.[66]

Macpherson's project of retrieving liberalism's ethical core from its market assumptions – a project once dismissed by hard Marxists as an attempt to divide the indivisible – made better sense now that socialism was being defined in libertarian or participatory terms and now that the costs of unrestrained economic growth were part of every radical agenda. In Hill's text, the fabrication of a possessively individualistic bourgeois society was depicted in almost totally negative terms: from the worm's eye experiences of the defeated, as an ethic of repression and greed which led to 'a world in which poets went mad . . . Locke was afraid of music and poetry and Newton had secret irrational thoughts which he dared not publish'. The sublimated irrationality of the world of geometry and sensationalist psychology was the corollary of the rationality of a world turned upside down. The formulation, however, left much to be desired as a description of the England of Dryden, Purcell, Congreve, Wren, and – yes – Locke and Newton. Even a reading of Restoration society as a closing of ruling class ranks behind an ethos which 'fatally combined' liberalism and repression, could be criticized for a conceptual crudity that disqualifies it as a piece of serious analysis.[67]

'The irrationality of the Puritan Revolution,' wrote Isaac Deutscher, 'arose largely out of the clash between the high hopes of the insurgent peoples and the bourgeois limitations of those revolutions.' But the juxtaposition of a world based on sin, property, and the acceptance of inequality and one which, momentarily, tried to sweep it away, was partial and mechanical: the case against Hill was not that he had a revolutionary vision but that, in the last analysis he expressed it only in the form of an opposition between subjective aspiration and objective historical process. For his explorations of what might have been but wasn't – largely recovered through the words and aspirations of a small number of articulate radicals – marked a further retreat from what had actually happened. Despite the radicals, the world was not, in fact, turned upside down: 'in spite of the Levellers, there were still privileged and unprivileged; in spite of the Diggers, still rich and poor; in spite of the Ranters, still marriages and families; in spite of the Quakers, still parish clergy and tithes'. Recovering the 'blind alleys' and 'lost causes' of those forgotten or condescended to in conventional historiography was central to the enlargement and humanizing of the discipline by the New Left in the 1960s and 1970s; but losers' history could come perilously close to 'optative history', history as it might have been or should have been; and the task of rescuing everyone, turning the historical world upside down and upsetting the received criteria of importance and unimportance, could render the total historical picture less intelligible.[68]

> A map of the world which does not include Utopia is not worth glancing at for it leaves out the one country at which Humanity is always landing . . . When Humanity lands there, it looks out and seeing a better country, sets sail. Progress is the realization of Utopias.

But Hill no longer believed in progress; he no longer aligned himself with the 'futurist' ethic of an earlier, simpler Marxism. From the vantage point of the 1970s, the best one could hope for was the alternative vision which had to be 'painfully recovered' to escape the nightmare of a bourgeois 'Apocalypse Now'.[69]

5.2 REVOLUTIONARY LEGACIES

By the time Hill wrote his book, the bubble of revolutionary rhetoric had burst. The student revolt was over; Nixon was in the White House; the Tories were back in power; Wilson had betrayed the Left and had not even saved the Labour Party. So, too, in the seventeenth century: the radicals were smashed, monarchy reinstated and the revolution went out, not with a bang but a whimper. So 'where did it all go to' – or, as Hill put it in a telling semantic slide: 'what went wrong'? One answer, quickly dismissed, was 'that the radicals were always a tiny minority' who only 'appeared significant for a very short time' when a series of accidents played into their hands. The very idea was unthinkable: there were just too many revolutionary changes, too 'fantastic' an 'outburst of radical ideas and actions'. Indeed, the 'unheard of speculations' that surfaced during the breakdown of censorship in the 1640s and 1950s were, in his opinion, something of 'an optical illusion' for the opposite reason: 'we should not exclude the possibility that a class-dominated society, may contain an egalitarian society trying to get out; nor assume that the hegemony of one set of values excludes the possibility that other values exist, at a lower social level or in the interstices . . . of an apparently homogeneous society' – at all events, 'we should listen more carefully to the silences of the periods before and after'.[70]

A more plausible answer was that the revolution was betrayed from within, that Cromwell and the Puritans had deserted the cause in its hour of victory. A Thermidorian Cromwell had always loomed large in the imagination of the Left, but in the more or- thodox communist appropriation, this version had invariably been balanced by a more positive celebration of 'Britain's First Repub- lic' and by the recognition that revolutions could not be secured without the breaking of radical heads: that bourgeois revolution- ary regimes, in particular, the work not of a single class but of an alliance of bourgeois and democratic forces, were bound to knock away their plebeian supports.[71] Hill was still aware of what he might once have called the contradiction – and the tragedy – at the heart of Cromwell's quest for a settlement after 1649, but he was less appreciative than he once had been of the progress- ive elements of revolutionary consolidation either under the Stalinist or the Cromwellian dispensation.

In many respects, his portrait of *God's Englishman*, the biographical sketch of 1970 – a minor work, he insisted, but an immensely readable and imaginative reconstruction of the man and his milieu: still the best starting point for students – was scrupulously fair and balanced. Hill's Cromwell was no bull-headed iconoclast, no 'Puritan killjoy of vulgar convention', no blinkered back-bencher who rose to eminence simply through military prowess and who lacked the nous to make a fractured political system work; he went out of his way to make allowances, and to lay to rest ancient and more recent examples of conservative folklore. But he openly admitted that the 'boisterous and confident leader' of the 1640s appealed to him far more than 'the aging disillusioned man who struggled under the burden of the Protectorate, knowing that without him worse would befall'.[72] The journey not the destina- tion matters; and the interpretation of the 1650s – years in which Cromwell perhaps exercised more raw power than any English- man before or since – and the overall evaluation of Cromwell's actual place in the English Revolution, were strangely inconclu- sive and negative. Of course, it was true that the history of the Commonwealth and Protectorate was littered with apparent U- Turns, failures and compromises. It was probably also the case that the actual format of Hill's book – not so much a detailed narrative as a chronological summary followed by a kaleidoscope of interpretative essays – was ill-suited to a man as elusive and sometimes inarticulate in his beliefs and practices, or to a career as turbulent as was Cromwell's: something was bound to vanish through the cracks. But it was more than that. In the last analysis, Hill's evaluation of Cromwell as the radical leader of 1644 and 1645, who shot down the Levellers and suppressed democratic rights in 1649, was the product of his changed understanding of the revolutionaries and the Revolution.

The revolutionaries had always been placed along a spectrum from the True Levellers through the Independents to the Presbyterian Right. As the groups of the Left assumed more prominence, and the expression of their democratic ideas was given a more explicitly anti-capitalist and anti-Puritan perspective, so their targets were pushed further to the Right: the Cromwell of the 1650s emerged as the 'all-too-human class conscious conservative', the religious enthusiast whose imperturbable sense of Providence and Necessity dissimulated and served the ends of an Oliverian 'Divine Right', the 'wily politician using all his arts to preserve a hated military regime'.[73] There was little room in this picture, after 1649 – still less, after 1653 – for *both* the pragmatist and the revolutionary, the providentialist distrustful of human agency and the slippery rhetorician who always seemed to agree with his last interlocutor, the troubled seeker after civil and religious consensus and the anti-formalist man of action, apparently confident that 'grace once known could never be lost'; little explanation, either, of the continued faith reposed in him by radicals of practically every hue.[74]

Hill had always regarded 1648 and 1649 as the hinge of two revolutions, the revolution that succeeded and the revolt within the revolution. The growing focus of his work on the latter and the increasingly critical evaluation of the former, through a more and more negative balance sheet of its eventual consequences, left the actual achievements of the Commonwealth in limbo. To be sure 'Oliver Cromwell presided over the great decisions which determined the future course of English and world history'. But his legacy turned out to be not a godly community, nor even a very complete liberty of conscience, but an England 'made safe for its natural rulers', and 'set on the path of empire, economic aggression and naval war': 'whereas the trinities of later revolutions – liberty, equality, fraternity; bread, peace and land –

demanded something new, something to be fought for and achieved in the future, the trinity of the English revolutionaries – religion, liberty and property – was intended to defend what already existed or was believed to exist'. Even this traditional trinity, according to Hill, was too radical a brew for the victorious grandees in 1647 and 1649; and he appeared to subscribe to Filmer's view that 'liberty and property are as contrary as fire to water' and that only the divine right of property was really procured.[75]

But, if indeed this traditional but also newly acquisitive and aggressive society was the unintended outcome of Cromwell's career – and it embodied values and priorities which he would not have owned – the unwanted progeny takes us far away from earlier stages in the life cycle. Marginalized by the tidying up process which reduced the experiences of the 1640s and 1650s to just two revolutionary undertakings – the celebration of a partially submerged oppositional 'third' culture, and the pessimistic inventory of the eventually triumphant ruling class ethos – the actual attempt to realize a particular type of godly society during the Commonwealth and Protectorate was given only cursory and grudging treatment. That vision was flawed and impermanent, to be sure; at its worst – in Ireland – it spawned a repressive Old Testament culture of punishment and reward; unwanted offspring apart, it contributed little to the future. But it deserved to be treated not just as a retreat from the radical opportunities of the late 1640s, nor as a staging post en route to 1660 and 1688, but as an experiment in its own right, which encouraged talent and efficiency, was fiscally fairer, less corrupt and more competent than was any administration before the nineteenth century, established religious freedom on a scale hitherto unknown, and promoted, even if it did not always deliver, religious, economic, educational, medical, scientific, linguistic and legal reform: a decade of government-inspired improvement 'unmatched' before the 1830s or 1940s. It was difficult, however, for Hill to evaluate the Commonwealth and Protectorate on its own terms and for its own time: whatever his sympathies for the person of Cromwell, his heart lay with the radicals he defeated and disempowered; whatever his respect for the achievements of the Interregnum, his Marxist head told him that after 1649, all roads led to 1660.[76]

Nevertheless, as historical fact and moral signifier, the Restoration was still a problem: not because it happened – though Hill found that difficult enough to come to terms with – nor because the radicals were defeated – that had already occurred by 1650 – but because it was supposedly desired; that 'it happened because the vast majority of Englishmen wanted it to happen'. This was a problem not only for the true revolutionaries – a minority that needed more than three years to 'break the centuries old crust of custom' – but for mainstream Puritanism also. For the Restoration cast a shadow over the whole dynamic of early Stuart history: how was it that the tidal wave of Puritanism was so rapidly spent?[77] Partly through his reliance on printed sources, partly through predisposition, Hill had focused overwhelmingly on an articulate revolutionary minority; for all his talk of silences, he invariably concentrated on the noisy: the truly silent, less-than-radical conforming majority were left somewhat in the shadows. As David Underdown pointed out, plebeian neutralists during the Civil War, lower class royalists, those who simply wanted to be left alone – and who by 1659 longed for a return of 'normalcy' – were ignored or dismissed as 'people trapped in the bonds of deference and dependence'. But deference was an important feature of English agrarian society before, during and after the Civil War.[78] So too was Monarchy: 'we tend to forget', Hill told his American audience in 1976, 'the still surviving magical aura of kingship'; as one reviewer tartly commented: Hill might have forgotten it, but he was surely alone in doing so. He found it appalling to think that the 'fraudulent' *Eikon Basilike* could have outsold Winstanley, Milton, Hobbes, Harrington and the Levellers put together – 'all of whom discuss politics in rational intellectual terms'. One can almost hear the note of protest: it just should not have been so.[79]

One way to deal with the problem was to deny it: to dispose of the 'Great Myth' of the Restoration, 'that Charles was recalled from exile by universal acclamation of his loving subjects, now at last freed from a gloomy Puritan dictatorship'. This was, of course, to overstate the case, the better to overturn it. And Hill made much of reports of widespread dissatisfaction: there were anonymous Yorkshiremen who thought 'Cromwell and Ireton as good as the king', London ladies who 'did not give a turd for never a king in England, for she never did lie with any', glaziers from Wapping who would gladly 'run their knives into him to kill him' – a cast of thousands, or so it seemed in Hill's endlessly recycled illustrations of popular Republicanism.[80] Now, the restored regime was terrified of the Puritans; there were, indeed, plots and conspiracies during the 1660s; there were plenty of double-agents and agents-provocateurs ready to enlarge and capitalize upon the government's fears. Moreover, in the 1980s a number of historians were to uncover a rich vein of underground politics in the early Restoration period; others were to highlight the significance of aristocratic Republicanism during the 1670s and 1680s – an important and potentially powerful counterpoint to the Cavalier politics of Clarendon and Danby, or the shifting opportunism of the Cabal and the post-Exclusion authoritarian technocrats.[81] But as Hill himself admitted, they were minority movements: 'the Good Old Cause', as the name implied, was largely an exercise in the politics of nostalgia; it spluttered fitfully during the Exclusion Crisis, briefly flared in the Rye House Plot, before finally being extinguished in the forlorn episode of Monmouth's revolt. The Glorious Revolution belonged to a quite different drama: in 1689, 'when Edmund Ludlow returned from his twenty nine years of exile, thinking the day of the Good Old Cause had dawned at last, he was promptly whisked out of the country at the request of the House of Commons'.[82]

What happened to revolutionary Puritanism? The Presbyterians who had invited Charles back in the first place continued to occupy an ambiguous but increasingly marginal place within the political spectrum. The sects fragmented and turned away from politics altogether. Purblind James II might believe that they were still a threat or a counter-revolutionary resource, that he could play the two religious ends off against the middle; but, apart from the organization brought it by the monarchy itself, the Catholic–Puritan front of 1687 was a puny and an ephemeral affair. 'By the time dissent won toleration in 1689 it had ceased to be politically dangerous. Those who benefited by the Toleration Act were sober, respectable, industrious citizens, narrow, sectarian and unpolitical in their outlook'. In his distress at the decline of revolutionary Puritanism, Hill may even have overstated the case.[83]

So, 'what went wrong'? Perhaps, the answer lay in 'the savage legislation of the Clarendon Code', or in the Act of Settlement of 1662 which according to Hill, 'anticipated an Italian Fascist decree ... authoriz[ing] the police [in Restoration England?] to drive back into his native parish any person who lacked visible means of support'. Yet, this repression, 'as effective' perhaps 'as the Inquisition in suppressing Protestantism in Spain', on inspection dwindles into some fairly modest fines and occasionally enforced parliamentary statutes: a 'code' dependent on the ardour and efficiency of notoriously lax or unenthusiastic local authorities, and constantly undermined by ministers and by the king himself for their own political purposes.[84] Then, there was indoctrination: the powerful barrage of King Charles the Martyr, Non-Resistance, and 'The Whole Duty of Man' drumming in the message of 'subordination and submission'. But why should these things have been so effective in the 1660s and 1670s when they were not in the 1630s: why should Sancroft have succeeded where Laud failed? And why should the parish have successfully capped social mobility after 1661 when Elizabethan statutes were quite unable to cope with 'masterless men' before the Civil War – especially at a time when Hill's 'agricultural revolution' was releasing more and more surplus labour? The sad truth was that there was no adequate explanation for the collapse of revolutionary Puritanism – unless its apparent strength in the 1640s was something of 'an optical illusion' or a historiographical corruption. As a hostile reviewer noted, 'the basic trouble is that Hill sees the events of 1648–9 as natural and in some sense "right", and everything before and after them as unnatural or "wrong"'.[85] But for most contemporaries, upside down was not 'a relative concept'. It was the Revolution that was unnatural, the Restoration normal.

In his heart of hearts, Hill probably knew this. Except for a few heady years, when they occupied centre stage, the radicals of the English Revolution lived on the fringes of society. After the Restoration they disappeared into the shadows once more. Perhaps, then, they were 'just too far ahead of the technical possibilities of their time'. But this was simply another way of putting the case for optative history, suggesting a lack of realism while not acknowledging it. It could, indeed, be argued that the shift of focus away from 1647 and 1648 when the political and military elites were still nominally united with the militants, to the years after 1649 when the 'honest party' fragmented – the move from the Old Left's concern with the revolutionary transformation of political and social structures to the New Left's exploration of 'alternative' strategies and ideologies – marked an evacuation of the 'real' world in favour of a world of visionaries and cranks. Yet 'realism' is a notoriously slippery denotation; and Hill, for one, had consistently emphasized the radicals' realism – and their modernity. An alternative tactic, therefore, was to hook them on to some form of higher realism or some 'long term success story': 'confronted by failures to whom we feel sympathetic', it is tempting to seek their vindication in 'the uses of posterity'. But the lines of descent imposed by this neo-whiggery were long and very tenuous.[86]

In the meantime, the historian was still left with the question of their seventeenth-century failure. So how did the 'losers' come to terms with 'the desolation of defeat when they realized the world was not, after all, going to be turned upside down'? What did they leave behind apart from lost causes and broken if edifying lives; what were their immediate legacies? These were themes to which Hill was increasingly drawn in the 1980s, and which were central to his most elegiac book, *The Experience of Defeat* of 1984.[87] The cast of *The World Turned Upside Down* was lined up again in the 1660s and asked to reflect on the dissipation of the revolutionary ethos and the return of normalcy – the result reminded one reviewer of a group of famous pub-drinkers being asked to sing 'Time Gentlemen Please'.[88] Most of the 'losers' were silent: some were executed or died in prison; others like William Walwyn, Gerard Winstanley and Abiezer Coppe, once so vividly articulate, disappeared into the shadows of apparent conformity; others again – but Hill had little time for renegades – broke faith and denied their radical pasts. His was a study of the righteous remnant: anguished, dedicated souls, driven by the dispensations of Providence or the good of mankind, who now tried to make sense of God's purposes or 'as we might say, the historical process'. Some, like the Quakers, responded by adopting the Peace principle; others like Milton or the Behmenists, John and Samuel Pordage, transmuted their experiences into epic poetry. Some blamed Cromwell for the disaster, just as some had blamed Stalin – but Cromwell, like Stalin perhaps, was a loser also, a 'good constable' who lived to see the shipwreck of the Cause. Others again, like the once militant preacher, William Sedgwick, came to wonder whether it was not distorted from the beginning by violence, 'lordliness' and self-righteousness. Perhaps, he suggested in a remarkable passage, which seemed to run counter to Hill's own reading of the Revolution, the violence was inevitable and endemic: the necessary ingredient, as in 1917, of a minority coup:

> The whole magistry and ministry of the nation, the King, nobles and gentry, with many thousands of oppressed people has risen up against

you in all the power and strength of the nation . . . You are but a small part of the nation, it may be a tenth, even if a more active, vigilant, more spirited part . . . You can never hold power except by force.[89]

Hill teased out their Jeremiads with great understanding and sensitivity. But he did little to explore their legacies. He could not: his commitment to the upside down vision of their glory days, made it difficult for him to cast his net on to the waters of adversity, save in the role of a martyrologist, recording the sufferings of his saints in Babylon. How could they 'sing the Lord's song in a strange land'?[90]

Of course, the radicals were better at delegitimizing custom or 'divine right', through explorations of the Norman Yoke or the successive embodiments of the Antichrist, than they were at showing how the transfer from social usurpation to social usage or from the Satanic to the Godly, might be effected. For, if the legitimating principle of society lay in the rights of each individual, here and now, how could any social lineage or continuity be defended? And if, as Hill had brilliantly demonstrated, everything was potentially 'antiChristian in some or others' mouths', how could Christ's kingdom ever be objectified? Millenarian beliefs were not adapted to the theory or practice of human outcomes.[91]

But there was a further reason for Hill's difficulty with the modulations of radical descent. He had always sorted out his revolutionaries into proto-bourgeois and proto-socialists – profiteers and prophets. True, he no longer suggested that the radicals belonged wholly to the righteous; rather – repeating a pattern which ran through his elucidation of 'ruling class' divisions – the antithesis was internalized in the confrontation between Milton and Harrington, the prophet of social righteousness and the prophet of economic power. The defeat of the saints in 1660 ensured that England followed the unrighteous prophet and the 'realist' road that led to trade and empire, and eventually to the self-delusions and powerlessness of post-imperial decay. Milton was left 'eyeless in Gaza' to see more profoundly and to prophesy the prospective collapse of Dagon's temple. But the opposition of prophecy and profit – children of light and children of darkness – prevented Hill from exploring the intermediate lines of descent or from actually grounding his study of the post-radical radicals in the 'realities' of the Restoration period. It was too much second nature to remember Zion and weep by the waters of Babylon.[92]

Did not the 'experience of defeat', then, cast retrospective doubt on the earlier revolutionary 'victories'? Not at all, argued Hill, turning his back on William Sedgwick's eloquent self-criticism. The ostensible defeat was really a victory already won: the 'Providences' of 1640, 1649 and 1660 were dialectically related; and 'the answer to . . . how the God of 1649 could have willed 1660', turns out to be 'because he had already willed 1640–1' and foreordained 'the school solution' of 1688.[93] Thus were socialists apt to console themselves for their reverses, by arguing that socialism had already been achieved. The paradox of defeat in victory and victory in defeat could be resolved, also, through indirection and a further exercise in surreptitious whiggery. Loyalty to God occupied a median position between personal fealty to the king and obedience to the abstract state; and Puritan Zion was a halfway stage from sceptred isle to British Empire. Of course, there was a loss of zeal, a routinization: the disillusionment was real enough – and justified. But, eventually in 1688, millenarian and Harringtonian solutions coalesced and a 'historic compromise' was reached.[94]

Even so – despite the dizzying dialectics and a heroically sustained view of Restoration England, almost exclusively peopled by radicals, or by even more spectral groupings known as Harringtonians and Newtonians – the changes of 1640–1 no longer seemed up to the job. Of those that endured, the destruction of Star Chamber and the High Commission, the abolition of feudal tenures (never as important as Soviet historians suggested), and the Court of Wards, fen drainage and the Navigation Acts, were not such an impressive tally. And in crucial areas they were outweighed by post-Restoration reverses.[95] If the destruction of a feudal–absolutist 'state machine' was the turning point in English history, then the conditions of the traditional establishment's recall were a matter of some importance. Here, late Stuart scholarship increasingly cast doubt on the finality of 1641. The Monarchy restored in 1660 was not the conditional, apologetic affair that Hill and Co. had once surmised: it was not so much a 'king with a joint in his neck' as 'a king surrounded by majestic beams', the beneficiary of royal martyrdom and the rule of the Major Generals.[96] The Anglican Church was not yet – if it ever was to become – a Latitudinarian convenience; the Church of Sancroft, Ken and Turner with its Court of Ecclesiastical Commission and its Non-Resistance Test was no half-hearted affair.[97] And if there was an effective absolutism in England, arguably it was to be found in 1687 rather than in 1637: in the busy, bureaucratic apparatus of James II, with his servile Commons and loyalist Lords, his monarchist Anglican establishment, his army, his navy, and his more than adequate revenues. Indeed, in many respects, it could be argued, the Restoration did its work only too well. For along with the updated structures of early Stuart government and society went its 'fears, divisions and crises as well': the 'Popish Plot' of 1678, which made Charles II's England ungoverable for nearly five years, was in essence a repeat of the politics of 1640–1, and a demonstration that nothing had been decided for good or ill.[98]

None of this dovetailed very well with Hill's revised account: for, according to Hill, 'if the Revolution of 1640' was 'unwilled, the coup d'état of 1688–9 and the peaceful Hanoverian succession were very much willed. The self-confident landed class had now consciously taken its destiny into its own hands.' The Restoration of 1660 appeared to create an uneasy balance between new forces and traditional forms, but this was a ruling class ploy designed to sanctify the new social order. There was little doubt where real power lay: 1688–9 and 1714–15 were palace-revolutionary codas to a transformation already resolved – a spelling out of the facts of life for obtuse and, therefore, exiled Stuarts.[99] The events of 1688 however, were more contingent than this would suggest. Certainly, James's collapse was rapid and definitive, but that was a case of bad luck, miscalculation and religion rather than any deep-seated socio-economic split between him and 'the ruling classes', or any incompatibility between landed property or trade and James's 'new model' monarchy. James lost his throne because he was a Catholic in a hurry, not because he was a would-be feudal-absolutist.[100] Since its immediate socio-economic causes and now its political consequences were so problematical, Hill seemed to rest his case for the pivotal nature of the 'real' revolution on a somewhat uncomfortable explanation of how Britain became 'top nation': from the triumph of the bourgeoisie, to Cromwell's 'legacy', Dutch Wars and the Navigation Acts – it was something of a ceremonial hauling down of colours.[101]

No, at a political level, appearances could best be saved by stretching revolution to include a whole range of adjustments made between 1529 and 1725. According to one version of this revolution by instalments, 1641 was provisional, 1688 definitive: if 1641 had not witnessed the English Revolution, then it must have occurred in 1688.[102] But, by the 1980s, this too looked pretty rickety. The event itself would not bear too much pressure; not many bourgeois angels could be balanced on that aristocratic palace-revolutionary pin. Nor could a fundamental shift in political culture really be sheeted down to the wheeling and dealing of the Convention Parliament of 1689. The Revolution of 1688 had itself, therefore, to be extended to include a series of further adjustments in the 1690s and 1700s: something which had more to do with William's wars and Anne's failing progeny, than with any constitutional principles adumbrated at the time of James's flight.[103]

Socially, too, since a strong case could be mounted for the counter-revolutionary characteristics of 1688 – as a revolt of the traditional elites against James's half-baked alliance of city dissent and rural Catholic gentry – the Glorious Revolution had to be broadened to incorporate the foundation of the Bank of England and the creation of a machinery of public credit over the next twenty-five years. Ideologically, under the heading of 'Revolution Principles', it had to be selectively supplemented to cover the posthumous career of John Locke and the afterlife of a number of supposedly seminal seventeenth-century texts. For the most important thing about this Revolution, too, was its 'legacy': it, too, 'opened the road from privilege to pluralism and provided the commercial base for an industrial empire'. Thus redefined, the 'aristocratic coup' of 1688 could perhaps be considered as 'a shift in the process whereby England became recognized not as an ancien régime but as a nation of shopkeepers'.[104]

But the element of stretching of subsequent social and political thought and activity to force it on to the procrustean bed of a revolution made nonsense of the term as a useful historical category. And it conveyed an entirely false idea of the circumstances of the 1680s, the events of 1688–9, and 'the grievances and aspirations of those who chased James II off his throne'. James's bureaucratic apparatus survived and prospered under new management: a change of masters, and the Sunderlands, Rochesters and Godolphins were quickly back at the helm, assisting in 'the growth of the executive' and in the burgeoning of an aristocratic-court oligarchy which was to dominate political life for the next century.[105] Here Hill was surely right: 1688 was not an appropriate substitute for 1649. Judged by the usual criteria of revolutionary word and deed, the Glorious Revolution was a pretty half-hearted affair.[106]

The relationship of 1688 to 1649, moreover, was ambiguous in the extreme: not so much a deliberately engineered coda to an epic revolution some forty years before, as a conservative reaction to the revolutionary actions of James II, qualified by the earlier experiences.[107] Once bitten, twice shy, and the memory of the 1640s and 1650s, when gentlemen were 'made slaves to draymen and fanatics', dictated the content and the speed of events in 1688. James II was not the only person weighed down by the ghosts of the past; the local magnates were singularly determined not to be stampeded into any more change than was strictly necessary. As the phrase went, 1688 was a 'maintaining' revolution, a reaffirmation of prescriptive rights and transmitted law which Burke was to juxtapose to the bourgeois principles of the French Revolution a century later.[108] So that, if 1688 marked 'the decisive settlement' in the consolidation of bourgeois rule – admittedly in 'the most conservative form possible, consistent with the establishment of a stable bourgeois administration' – then it was the failure of the 'real' revolution of the 1640s, which made the English bourgeoisie – a bourgeoisie which, in turn, was not a bourgeoisie but an aristocracy of power and property.[109]

The most plausible version, therefore, was that of a single era of 'transformation', encompassing a number of different revolutions, which embraced 'the whole of life'.[110] The seventeenth century was still crucially discontinuous, but now the whole century rather than any one episode within it formed the break.[111] It still marked a political, social and psychological shift towards free enterprise, social mobility and untrammelled acquisitiveness. But these features were now viewed as symptoms of epochal transformation rather than the products of one single episode. With the England of Defoe, wrote Hill, 'we are already in the modern world – the world of banks and cheques, budgets, the stock-exchange, the periodical press, coffee houses, clubs, coffins, microscopes, shorthand, actresses and umbrellas'. And by 1780, 'we have moved from a backward economy to one on the threshold of industrial revolution'.[112] Harrington linked hands with Adam Smith, John Hampden with John Stuart Mill; Hill passed the baton on to Hobsbawm and Thompson, and the bourgeois transformation of English society was still in place.

According to one version of this theme:

Two conceptions of civilization were in conflict. One took French absolutism as its model, the other the Dutch Republic . . . [The Century of Revolution] set England on the path of parliamentary government, economic advance and imperialist foreign policy, of religious toleration and scientific progress.[113]

By 1689 England had chosen once and for all the triple blessings of Dutch finance, French wars and bourgeois hegemony. Not that Hill was an uncritical encomiast of the chosen path; it was sensible, but it was also soulless: 'economics made law, so that capitalist relations came to pervade all sectors of society'; the job of government was 'to increase the wealth of the country, and to furnish lucrative employment for the ruling families and their adherents'. 'Divine right was dead, and all roads led away from authority to rationalism, an appropriate state of mind for a society of atomized individuals' and an age

> of spiritual desolation as men contemplated the barren mechanical world of Newton and the new dismal science of economics ... [an age of] hypocrisy and humbug, great wealth based on starvation wages and the slave trade ... where religion was identical with self-interest ... [and] charity [with] joint stock principles.[114]

Another version of the same sequence was given a character-istically Californian treatment by Lawrence Stone in his essay on *The Results of the English Revolutions of the Seventeenth Century*: geology had replaced sociology and the mid-century Revolution was part of a series of 'seismic disturbances' which rocked society and modified its political culture between 1621 and 1721.[115] In a sense, this was the obvious answer to the conundrum left by his earlier work: for if the revolution was a 'crisis' and if its outcome was an invisible and long delayed 'legacy', could one really locate the crisis in 1640, 1642 or 1649? This time round, multiple seventeenth-century crises were retrospectively defined by the social and religious divisions revealed in the close-knit ideological parties of the early eighteenth century; and these, in turn, registered 'fissures' running through the political nation which dated back to the middle of the sixteenth century. By itself, the Civil War and Interregnum settled nothing: the attack on almost all aspects of the social and political order' was 'unsuccessful and premature', lacking 'solid material or ideological support in what was basically an agrarian and strongly hierarchical society' – before the decade was out the 'trees of liberty' planted in 1649 'had withered away'. In Stone's historical thesaurus, it was still, however, the 'major earthquake', England's only capitalized 'Great Revolution' which 'crystallized ideas and projected patterns of things to come'; but it only 'bore fruit' after further 'tremblers' later in the century. The Civil War joined hands with 'the rage of party' under Queen Anne and the simultaneous burgeoning of new economic and social interests associated with war finance and war profits. Stone passed his baton on to J. H. Plumb and the 'new eighteenth century': the Revolutions of 1640 and 1688, the parliamentary crisis of 1628–9, the Exclusion Crisis, and Hanoverian Succession crisis, were simply 'dramatic surface eruptions bubbling out of a century-long pool of turbulence and instability', which was only closed with the 'Growth of Political Stability' and the settling down of a 'Venetian Oligarchy' in the 1720s.

The picture of 'a choice of systems', with seventeenth-century England as a battleground between native versions of Louis XIV's Court Society and Amsterdam's burgher culture, is, however, open to serious objection. Stable and self-evident power blocs, backed up against each other along clearly delineated ideological, cultural and societal fault-lines, policed by armies, defence organizations, secret agents and religious commissars, seemed natural to historians during the Cold War and were sometimes reflected in the rhetoric of late seventeenth-century politics and religion; they bore little relation to the fluidity of international relations from 1648 to 1789.[116] As for the models themselves, entitled 'bourgeois' Holland and 'absolutist France': they, too, were arguably based on serious misreading. Dutch society was irreducibly burgher and civic not bourgeois – reaching back to fourteenth- and fifteenth-century Flanders rather than forward to nineteenth-century industrial England; and the more we know of the power structures and social presumptions of Louis XIV's France, the less its 'absolutism' equates with the arbitrary epithets of some contemporary English politicians and many subsequent historians – as for its supposed 'feudal' connotations, did not St Simon describe it as the reign of the 'vile bourgeoisie'![117]

Whatever mid-seventeenth-century English politics were about, they were not about France or Holland: three Dutch Wars, two of them conducted or inspired by Commonwealth parliamentarians, an alliance with France however uncongenial, and war against Spain as a means of maintaining righteous rule in England and filling godly pockets in the Caribbean, suggested a rather more complex or traditional set of priorities. After 1688, the juxtaposition was admittedly more obvious. But 'Dutch victory' came in the form of William III and the House of Orange; and William, the 'petit Sieur de Breda', with his fifty odd quarterings, his hereditary revenues and 'Domain's Council', his scattered territories and jurisdictions in France and the Empire was hardly a creature of bourgeois civil society.[118] Conflict with Louis XIV in defence of the so-called 'liberties of Europe' was largely a Williamite import and an item of party political warfare in the twenty-five years after 1688, but it was not a battle of opposed 'civilizations'. As for the eighteenth-century wars against France, though occasionally garnished with Roast Beef, Liberty, Popery and wooden shoes, they were, of course, overwhelmingly struggles for trade and empire, complicated from time to time by the defence of the Hanoverian monarchs' absolutist electorate; they were assuredly not about different systems of government and society.[119]

Stone's geological metaphor of earthquake and subsidence appeared likewise to compound rather than to salvage the problems of a mid-seventeenth-century crisis. Arguing from results in history, as he himself had observed, was a questionable procedure. If the truly significant long-term consequences of 'the seismic disturbances' which rocked English society between 1621 and 1721 were those of trade and dominion, bourgeois hegemony and an England on the threshold of industrialization, then it was the new 'sinews of power' forged after 1688 rather than the rusty old mechanisms of political turmoil in the 1640s which really mattered: Louis XIV not Charles I was the unwitting creator of the modern English state and society. And if, as Stone belatedly discovered, the emergence of the modern 'military-fiscal state' during the second Hundred Years War was, indeed, crucial to England's economic and imperial success, then how was it the outcome of seventeenth-century revolution? For certainly at the time, it seemed to many country gentlemen to represent everything they had fought against since the 1620s – high taxation, placemen, excise officers, a standing army, national debt – not part of the 'legacy' of 1641 or 1649.[120] If, further, to change the idiom, the period up to the 1720s was redefined as one of endemic desynchronization, then the fat years of the 'Revolution Families' had to be explained as the overnight creation of Walpole and the Pelhams – which was curious to say the least: a crisis, it appears, requires 'multiple helix chains of causation more complicated than those of DNA itself'; stability is the work of a single decade and a politician of genius.[121]

The truth was that Stone's 'crisis' was a noun that lacked a singular: drained of content, inhabiting a heterogeneous range of contexts from the parliamentary crisis of 1628–9 to the Jacobite Rebellion of 1715, it had lost all credibility as a useful explanatory device. The retrospective use of categories, coupled with a very general developmental sequence derived from a phenomenon, the identity of which was unexamined and unspecified, produced a genealogy which was neither falsifiable nor verifiable, took no explanatory risks and remained entirely within the realms of faith. The wider the chronological scope, the more the events of the mid-seventeenth century were retrospectively assigned the supposed 'choices' or geological characteristics of the eighteenth, the easier it was to demonstrate their long-term significance: it was merely a question of colouring in the yellow brick road.

According to Hill, 'England was the country of the first political revolution; this led to England becoming the country of the first industrial revolution, and, this in turn, led to her becoming the first world empire. The three processes are, I think, indissolubly connected.'[122] But why start with 'the Revolution', why stop with 'world empire', for it, presumably, also led to the end of Empire, the collapse of the British economy, 'the forward march of Labour halted', Mr Scargill, and Mrs Thatcher. Or more precisely, a 'serial' explanation in which we do not possess adequate analysis of how the successive stages generate each other, but in which it is simply assumed that the same kind of force is responsible for the upward propulsion at each stage in the series, is not an explanation at all. 'Only connect' and 'the Great Map of Mankind is unroll'd at once'; everything leads to everything else, and history remains where Hegel, the grandmaster of the idiom, always believed it should be: firmly anchored to the present.[123]

6

Retreating from the Revolution

On the debate between E. P. Thompson and Perry Anderson on England's past and the place of a seventeenth-century Revolution within it; likewise, on the genre of 'unrevolutionary', 'revisionist' studies popular in the late 1970s and 1980s.

6.1 'LONG REVOLUTIONS', 'GREAT ARCHES' AND OTHER 'FIGURES OF DESCENT'[1]

A history of the present was, of course, always intended; and the manifest convergence of seventeenth- and twentieth-century issues was the inevitable consequence of the sort of significance Hill and his peers had built into the English Revolution. Their strategic retreats on the narrow historical front of seventeenth-century change, therefore, ran parallel with a broader reassessment of the whole trajectory of England's past and its relationship with what was called 'the present crisis', conducted on the Left from the late 1950s onwards. And the debate on what became known as 'the peculiarities of the English', and the concomitant re-evaluation of Marxist theory and the writing of history, conducted by Edward Thompson, Perry Anderson and others was, in turn, to feed back into the rethinking of the seventeenth-century.

The Marxist reading of England's past had been forged in the period from the 1930s to the 1950s by Communist Party members, whose formative experiences had been the struggle against Fascism and solidarity with liberation movements in the occupied countries during the war.[2] For Edward Thompson, the moral and democratic dimension which he experienced in his post-war reconstruction work in Yugoslavia, and which he believed to be encapsulated in the 'great affirmative moment' of 1945, was to remain enormously important; so too, the criticism of British ruling-class values, which he had inculcated in a radical, philanthropic Anglo-

Indian household where he grew up expecting British governments to be 'mendacious and imperialist'.[3] It was this that informed his endeavour to redefine a Marxism which was truly humanist and transformative, after his dramatic break with the Communist Party in 1956.

'Through the smoke of Budapest', he discerned the true shape of Stalinism: its military vocabulary, its mechanized dogmas, its stone axioms, its confinement of the human spirit:

> Stalinism is socialist theory and practice which has lost the ingredient of humanity. The Stalinist mode of thought is not that of dialectical materialism, but mechanical idealism . . . Instead of starting with the . . . social reality . . . people must be brought to conform to the idea . . . Stalinist analysis . . . becomes a scholastic exercise: the search for 'formulations', 'correct' in relation to text but not to life.[4]

The attack on Stalinism which he conducted in the pages of *The Reasoner* and *The New Reasoner* in 1956 and 1957 was rapidly broadened to include features of Marxism itself, 'ambiguities', which became 'fallacies in Lenin' and deformities with Stalin: the 'constricting' metaphor of base and superstructure – an 'image' not of human beings changing society but of cogs 'operating semiautomatically and independently of human agency'; the suppression of cultural traditions and 'the transmission of experience from generation to generation'; 'the repeated lumping together of ideas, consciousness, thought and sensations as "reflections" of material reality'; the imperceptible slippage from Marx's observation that 'social being determines social consciousness' to the grotesque sophism that consciousness was a clumsy process of 'adaptation'; the short-circuiting of human motivation and social complexity by a class relativism or Pavlovian behaviourism which obliterated 'the creative spark' in men and women making their own history. To regain its soul, to reanimate a revolutionary potential 'made up of countless acts of heroism, voluntary sacrifice, innumerable liberating impulses', socialism had to revive the language of moral choice and rediscover the importance of conscious human agency in the making of history.[5]

Drawn from the Communist Party defectors of 1956, the early 'New Left' understandably found self-definition in its separation from Stalinism and rejection of dry scholastic Marxism. But it also had to define its goals in the context of the changed conditions of British politics. From 1951 to 1964, British politics was dominated by the Conservatives. The parliamentary Left was in disarray, torn by conflicts over the rival merits of the mixed economy and public ownership, and over membership of the Nuclear Club and Unilateral Disarmament, unable even to derive advantage from the Suez débâcle. At a more profound level, the corrosive embourgeoisement of the 'Opportunity State' and the straitjacket of 'Nato-politan' culture had produced a society disabused and apathetic, 'over-ripe' for socialism, dominated by consumerism and the 'philosophy of greed'.[6] This was Thompson's gloomy diagnosis. And there was no disguising the moral revulsion from 'consumer capitalism' – 'that old bitch gone in the teeth', responsible in her time for 'world-wide wars, aggressive and racial imperial-isms' and now 'co-partner in the unhappy history of socialist degeneration'. Old habits of thought had been banished far less decisively than the rhetoric of his anti-Stalinism suggested: so sharp had been the severance from official communist dogma that he could only sustain continued allegiance to 'the communist movement in its humanist potential' by an equally exaggerated rejection of bourgeois society.[7]

The anathema laid on 'Philistinism' on both sides of the Iron Curtain – as much an ingredient of social democratic 'pragmatism' and 'expediency' as of Stalinist 'fatalism' and necessity' – was crucial to the identity of the New Left. For Thompson it involved a new style of politics, exemplified by the Campaign for Nuclear Disarmament: a popular mobilization which was going to lead the masses 'out of apathy', break down the structures of Western Capitalism and revolutionize the world. The revolutionary transformation which he envisaged was to be found in neither of the inherited models of socialist change: neither in 'one more shuffle along the evolutionary path ... of gradual piecemeal reform in an institutional continuum' where 'the main participation demanded of the people [wa]s to cross the ballot paper thirteen or fourteen million times', nor in a leap on to the highroad of cataclysmic revolution, the model derived from the Marxist–Jacobin tradition of storming Bastilles and Winter Palaces, ossified into the law of a violent proletarian seizure of power. Rather it was to be sought in the 'elaboration of a democratic revolutionary strategy', which drew on the moral choices and the personal experiences of 'real men and women' in every area of life.[8]

Clearly the greatest problem for the early New Left was that of maintaining its distinctiveness and coherence. Its concern with

questions of morality and human agency, its oppositional stance
– 'revisionist with respect both to Labourism and to Marxism' –
its focus on real people and concrete experiences, its empiricism
and suspicion of abstract theory, inevitably threw it back on to
the long native tradition of radical dissent. Such intellectual cohesion
as it possessed, came from the far-reaching critique of contemporary
British society and the attempt to map out an alternative culture,
identified with the names of Richard Hoggart and Raymond
Williams.[9] The work of Raymond Williams, in particular, was
grounded in the literary and social criticism of the 'English
moralists': *Culture and Society* attempted to elucidate the changing
relationship between artistic and social development in the period
since the Industrial Revolution – a history of 'the idea of culture',
which would provide 'a major contribution to our common
understanding and a major incentive to its necessary extension'.[10]

In an unheroic decade, which had banished political revolution
and class solidarity from the lexicon, the idea of culture constituted
'the most generous and resourceful socialist model available' and
the most immediate and radical challenge to Nato-politan society.
For in Williams' view, culture defined 'the basic collective idea
and the institutions, manners, habits of thought and intentions'
which proceeded from it; and to the extent that capitalism was
rooted in the 'individualist idea', to that extent 'the development
of the idea of culture has throughout been a criticism of what
has been called the bourgeois idea of society'.[11] A market-place
was not a community; nor was 'how we are governed' an
explanation of democracy. True community – and with it a common
culture – could only be achieved through shared values and
solidarity, a common identity and 'an equality of being' achieved
under the conditions of a 'participating democracy'. Historically,
the ideal was located in the common bonds of the working-class
community and in 'the loving relations between men actually
working and producing what is ultimately shared'. Somewhere
it had been lost.[12]

The qualitative juxtaposition of *Gemeinschaft* and *Gesellschaft*,
and the conviction that human relationships had been destroyed
by the worship of the market-place or the state, was indispensable
to the New Left's vision of the good society. The solvent of that
society, and of the common culture which it embodied, was the
industrialization and democratization traced in *Culture and Society*.
Yet, those same forces were the preconditions of its recovery:

alongside the Industrial Revolution and the democratic revolution, which had so dramatically transformed individuals and pulverized their communities, was a third revolution of public information and communications, a 'long revolution' which would establish the conditions of an open, creative, cooperative society. But how this was to happen, how the instruments of communal dissolution were to be transformed into the vehicles of an 'expanding culture' was a little unclear. For the commentators whose yearnings for *Gemeinschaft* Williams had recovered seemed too thoroughly imbricated in the fabric of British bourgeois life to provide a coherent alternative to it; and the tradition which he charted, appeared, at best, to offer 'a purely immanent ideological critique' of British capitalism' – imagined aspirations and nostalgias extruded from reality or from actual history.[13]

Thompson shared much of Williams' faith in the good society and in the values of sharing and cooperation opposed to 'the innate moral baseness of capitalism'; he, too, was inclined to romanticize traditional working-class communities. But he was critical of the academicism and abstraction of Williams' tone and argument: the reader was offered a description of cultural production and reproduction which appeared to marginalize other determinants, a 'tradition' rather than the history of real men and women, a 'revolution' delineated as a textual commentary on the given or as a vague utopian expectation, rather than as a struggle against actual evils, 'a revolution against something'.[14] In seeking to steer socialism away from its Stalinist sponsors, Williams had substituted Leavis for Marx and come to define social being solely in terms of consciousness. Marxism had to remain an essential ingredient of socialist humanism. What sort of Marxism was the issue.[15]

When Christopher Hill was asked whether he was a Marxist historian, he replied by asking the interviewer for a definition. This attitude – symptomatic of the approach of British Marxist historians after 1956 – was most clearly elucidated by Thompson. The Marxism that informed his writing was no longer 'a self contained body of doctrine'; nor was it a clearly delineated 'method'. But a commitment to Marxism involved more than 'opportunistic' acceptance of its place in the cultural 'heritage', as a 'strain' of thought which had 'melted into the very tissue' of social analysis. The version to which he was committed was 'Marxism as Tradition', something practised when Marxists were willing to submit every part of Marxist thought to scrutiny, and to employ 'any instrument of criticism which seem[ed] legitimate', but which, nevertheless, emphasized 'those primary social divisions which are most fundamental in determining historical development', and was based on 'the conviction that human nature [was] the product of man's social history'.[16]

Almost alone amongst Marxist historians, Thompson produced a traditional narrative of political and social history: a 'long, sprawling, picaresque, Dickensian' story which captured the crosscurrents and contingencies of real historical processes. *The Making of the English Working Class* was never disfigured by the overt constructional engineering or reductive tidying up which sometimes deformed the writing of Christopher Hill.[17] But it was not quite so detached from conventional Marxism as its form and its polemic suggested. The idea of 'class' as a historical phenomenon, formed by the interaction of material circumstances, shared experiences, traditions, values, religious preconceptions and social customs which he spelt out in the book's famous preface, certainly embraced a far broader and more nuanced repertoire of responses, feelings and personal activities than the traditional Marxist notion of class struggle. But he was utterly committed to the conflict model of social change: class society was characterized by continual struggles between the rulers and the ruled. And he wholly identified with one of the adversaries: more consistently than any of his fellow Marxist historians, he produced a history not of the bottom but 'from the bottom up' – he did not only rescue hitherto submerged working-class experiences, but reconceptualized the whole society through them.[18] He was also firmly convinced of the importance of a 'secret revolutionary tradition' reaching back to the 1640s: a tradition which surfaced once more in the Jacobin movement of the 1790s and the agitations and conspiracies of the period from 1816 to 1820. The prejudices and panic fears of the English governing classes were central to the formation and the developing consciousness of the English workers; and the working-class struggle against economic exploitation was inseparable from the battle against counter-revolutionary political repression. He deployed an elaborate range of evidence to suggest the possibilities and dimensions of a lower class uprising in these years; and he appeared to endorse the rhetoric of his incendiaries – the book exploded with talk of 'Old Corruption', 'the Beast', 'the Whore' and 'the Enemies of the Human Race'. Not entirely without cause, reviewers less committed to the cause, blanched at the 'inextinguishable thirst for bourgeois blood' and the 'fixation on revolution'.[19]

Revolution he conceived, not as the necessary and automatic pivot of unfolding historical laws – the transition from one social structure to another – but as a happening whose 'very nature was derived from heightened political consciousness and popular participation' – 'a process not only of making but of choosing'. In the course of English history, the revolutionary idiom had ebbed and flowed many times, with the changing experiences of the people and the behaviour of their rulers: in the seventeenth century, one creative crystallization had occurred; again – in the early nineteenth-century when a modern working-class consciousness came into being at a time of great political tension – another such configuration seemed to be immanent. But there were always cross-currents in the historical process, fissiparous as well as unifying forces. Even in the ebb-tide of revolution, however, the potentiality did not disappear; it was preserved in new patterns of resistance, in tenacious community values, and in 'the slumbering energies' and the 'creative ability' of ordinary people. All but buried at the level of actual history, 'revolution' re-emerged as a categorical imperative – 'a kind of photographic negative of Stalinism' – in the assertion of values and moral choices made against the grain of historical processes, which orthodox Marxism presented as automatic and morally sovereign.[20]

Moral regeneration had to be the key to socialist transformation. It was precisely because the Leninist model had failed to embody the personal and ethical dimension of being, and evaded the truly 'species' project of creating a fundamentally new identity for the revolutionary class, that it had fathered the monstrosities of the Stalinist state.[21] And it was equally because of her democratic socialist tradition, with its moral and cultural preoccupations, its long and tenacious commitment to personal freedoms and communal ideals, its independence and libertarian spirit, its 'utopian realism' and humane class-consciousness, that Britain was 'the best placed' of all Western countries to effect the revolutionary transition to genuine socialism.[22] Although fiercely critical of the injustices and the pretensions of imperial power, Thompson's vision was corrupted still by the scope of the British imperial imagination, by a 'maundering populism' and by a form of salvationary nationalism: the Levellers, Chartists, John Bunyan, William Blake and William Morris conveyed a message of universal significance;

their morality was a force in global progress; and by following their example, England could 'put the coping stone on the New Society' and 'leaven the socialist world'.[23]

It was precisely against this sort of 'vapid meta-historical myth' that Perry Anderson and Tom Nairn reacted. Only in their mid-twenties, they had not experienced the popular élan of the period during and after the war; nor had they been seriously influenced by Stalinism. By contrast, the single overwhelming fact that they saw as demanding immediate confrontation was the deeply ingrained conservatism of British society and the lack of any critical opposition within it.[24] The starting point for their work, therefore, was the pathology of contemporary Britain: Britain was in the throes of 'a profound, pervasive but cryptic crisis, undramatic in appearance but ubiquitous in its reverberations', something which could not be localized or specifically defined, but was diffuse and all-inclusive, embracing the entire social structure. Its most visible symptom was 'the malady of the capitalist order', clear already in the mid-1960s and drastically manifest a decade later when the 'general malfunctioning of advanced capitalism was superimposed on the decrepitude of Britain within it'.[25] Because of its prolonged economic success and international dominance, because of its avoidance of the traumatic experiences of revolution and invasion in modern times, British society had failed to develop an awareness of its own contingency. Because they had never been fundamentally threatened, its distinctive arrangements appeared simply as fixed essences, given 'figures' of a benign 'descent', rather than social constructions, possible only under certain historical conditions. What was handed down as tradition, was confirmed as natural objects of thought or study by the well-nigh universal hegemony of British empiricism:

> we must be unique among advanced industrial nations in having not one single structural study of our society today; but this stupefying absence follows logically from the complete lack of any serious global history of British society in the twentieth century. The limits of our sociology reflect the nervelessness of our historiography'.[26]

Even those who supposedly still worked within a broadly Marxist framework were quite unable to conceptualize the nature of the 'crisis' or to provide the necessary pathology of British society as a whole. Since the rupture with Stalinism, English Marxist historians had come to regard grand historical schemas as intellectually crude

and politically suspect; and a small industry had arisen in reworking Marxist categories to allow for historical agency and
indeterminacy. With their new-found respect for empirical history
and their necessary abstinence as specialists, theirs was a fragmentary vision, 'confined in the main to the heroic periods' of
the seventeenth and early nineteenth centuries: at times, a 'might
have been' romanticism, at others, an exercise in 'pious reverence' for socialist forebears, rather than a consideration of 'the
total trajectory of Britain's past'. 'Trapped in a humanitarian niche
– chipping away at the easily sacrificed protuberances of the received historical interpretation' – their work was in danger of
becoming 'an ancillary part of the liberal orthodoxy'.[27]

What Anderson and Nairn were proposing was in a sense a
return to the priorities of Hill and his colleagues in the immediate
post-war years. But instead of seeking to recover the revolutionary
context of England's bourgeois construction as an exemplary
counterweight to Fabian gradualism, they sought to highlight the
contingency of contemporary thought and practice as a whole
through the study of Britain's pathway to the present; instead of
recalling and celebrating a heroic period, and then going on to
ask what went wrong, they asked whether the whole course of
modern British history was not in some sense faulty. They
attempted to broaden the focus of the Communist Historians'
project so as to consider not just the special case of British political
and social evolution from a 'global' perspective, but so as also to
include the manner in which history was considered – the empirical idiom which was both cause and consequence of England's
particular turn.

In the most general terms, Britain had avoided the conflicts
and ruptures that in other countries had been responsible for
bringing about social progress. Instead of conforming to the classic
epochal pattern derived from Marx's *Preface*, British history was
the story of partial or arrested transitions, of new classes who
proved unable to generate hegemonic ideologies, of archaic residues
and powerful surviving political elites. According to Nairn:

> The final destruction of English feudalism in the period 1640–60 took
> place long before the full flowering of bourgeois ideology. Initiating
> the cycle of bourgeois expansion in this way, the English middle classes
> could not hope to benefit from a new conception of the world that
> was itself produced in the course of the cycle and reached maturity
> at a later date.[28]

The destruction of the old society was partial and premature: set in the mould of a pre-Enlightenment, pre-industrial ideology, the Revolution petered out in a 'patchwork of compromise and makeshift', 'an organic coalescence' of the bourgeoisie with 'the English ancien regime': 'The Revolution . . . was buried in a morass of euphemism and misrepresentation, like some infantile trauma driven deep into the national subconscious.' In place of the truly epochal ideology of 1789 stood 'the shamanism of the British constitution', 'an assorted repertoire of (largely fake) antiquities', and 'the poisonous remains of a once revolutionary . . . Puritanism' – so much for 'the great spring' of English liberty. An underdeveloped and unselfconscious bourgeoisie duly spawned an atheoretical working class and a Labour movement anchored to the anachronistic tradition of radical Nonconformity and to the illusion of an 'insular and national road to socialism' – the 'conviction that British realities offered a peculiar and privileged environment for socialist development'.[29]

According to Anderson, 'England had the first, the most mediated and least pure bourgeois revolution'.[30] It 'shattered the juridical and constitutional obstacles to rationalized capitalist development in town and country' and quickened the whole economy; but it left the 'basic property statute' and the existing social structure intact. As a result, the 'rationalizing charge' of the Revolution was – in an inversion of Lenin's formula – only 'detonated overseas in the economic legacy of Commonwealth imperialism'. The Revolution – bourgeois 'only by proxy', fought within rather than between classes – 'profoundly transformed the roles but not the personnel of the ruling class'. No social group was evicted or displaced; rather the existing landowning class as a whole was won over to 'the ruthless and richly rewarding system' of capitalist agriculture practised by a few – the system which pulverized the English peasantry and made Britain 'the most agriculturally efficient country in the world'. But there was 'no weakening of the principles of heredity and hierarchy': aristocrats continued to rule the country, to participate in colonial and trading ventures or to dabble in 'the City'. Conversely, mercantile capital, the Revolution's major 'economic inheritor', remained 'a subaltern' element 'within the ruling system', an interest and not a class' – with its best talent and resources constantly 'haemorrhaging' into gentrification and landed estate. The ideological legacy of the Revolution was almost nil: individual 'soul liberty' could not mutate into a universal philosophy of civil rights; Cromwell could not beget Rousseau; and the English Revolution was cut off by its Biblical myths and its theological language from any direct contact with the modern world.[31]

These peculiarities of England's bourgeois construction produced an unusual accommodation of interests and an absence of major ideological conflict in the first stage of capitalist development:

> the eighteenth century sailed forward into an era of unparalleled stability. The landed aristocracy had, after a bitter internecine struggle, become its own capitalist class. The mercantile bourgeoisie was contained and decanted into an honourable ancillary status. By a classic process of psychological suppression, the Civil War was forgotten and its decorous epilogue, the Glorious Revolution of 1688, became the official, radiant myth of creation in the collective memory of the propertied class.[32]

The pattern was reinforced by subsequent developments. A hundred years later, just when the Industrial Revolution seemed likely to lead to an epochal clash between manufacturing and agrarian elites, the spectre of Jacobinism rallied the nascent industrial bourgeoisie to the aristocracy. The subsequent success of Britain in acquiring 'the largest empire in history' and in minimizing the shocks and dislocations of two World Wars 'welded aristocracy and bourgeoisie together in a simple social block' and 'set British society in a mould it has retained to this day'.[33] The English bourgeoisie had never needed to assert its own distinctive identity, but had been able to achieve all it wanted through mimesis: by adopting aristocratic speech and manner, supporting such institutions as the Monarchy, the Church, the Public School system and Oxbridge, and by thinking and behaving 'empirically'. Bourgeois indecisiveness, in turn, created the conditions for working-class weakness: 'a supine bourgeoisie produced a subordinate proletariat'. Born into a 'dearth of revolutionary ideas'; cut off from the rest of society, denied the support of an emancipatory bourgeois ideology, the English working class lacked the will and the resources to transform the society.[34]

English history was the history of failures: of successive turning points when history failed to turn; of revolutions – mediated or aborted – which failed to mark the epochal displacement of one social formation by another; of historic classes which failed to develop appropriate ideologies. By turns, premature and overripe, innovative and anachronistic, Britain became the first modern economy in the course of the seventeenth and eighteenth centuries; but it did not become a modern society: rather, the continued dominance of a rentier landowning elite meant the preservation of traditional pre-industrial values and with it the foundation of Britain's eventual economic retardation and social entropy. So that when Marx came to London during the 1850s, he could both marvel at the economic rationality of the most advanced capitalism of the time, and be utterly baffled by the 'conservative sheath in which the process had been compressed'. The major symptoms of this 'immensely elastic and all embracing hegemonic order' were a complex hierarchy of nuance and convention; a distinctively patrician style of leadership and an imperial iconography of power, based on a gulf between born rulers and 'natives'; and an indistinct but 'blanketing' ideological 'miasma of commonplace prejudices and taboos' – 'its two great chemical elements . . . traditionalism and empiricism'.[35] Bourgeois historians had, of course, made much of the benefits of England's political and social stability. But there was a cost: 'a culture of containment', which hemmed the whole society into historically predestined pathways: 'a universe . . . locked fast as in a family settlement; grasped as in a kind of mortmain, for ever'.[36]

For Thompson, whose world had remained sharply divided by the events of 1956, the analysis offered by Anderson and Nairn was fundamentally a reversion to Stalinist schematization. Here again was the old economic reductionism which sought to do away with the autonomy of the political and cultural fields; the treatment of class, conceived not as a relationship between people or as a historically specific 'happening', but as a 'thing', 'marshalled, sent on manoeuvres and marched up and down whole centuries'; the suppression of cultural traditions and of the complex and varied pattern in which these inheritances were transmuted; the 'obsession' with questions of power and hegemony which consigned most historical actors to the margins of history; the strident teleology which was so insensitive to 'the sufferings and satisfactions of those who live and die in unredeemed time'; worst of all, the bullying tone – 'that tone of bolts being shot against experience and enquiry' – which had sent so many native Marxists to their duplicators in 1956.[37]

Anderson and Nairn had located the first deviation of the native phenomenon from the approved model, in the premature unfulfilled character of its seventeenth-century Revolution – a revolution in which 'the industrial bourgeoisie had failed to attain to an undisputed hegemony and to remake the ruling institutions of society in their own image'. Setting aside the very real changes that did occur – the sweeping away of prerogative, the removal of the unregulated exactions of the crown, a change in the role and personnel of the monarchy itself – what Anderson and Nairn appeared to be unable to accept was 'the notion of an agrarian class, whether of rentiers or entrepreneurs, as a true bourgeoisie':

> It is a strain on one's semantic patience to imagine a class of bourgeoisie scattered across a countryside and dwelling on their estates, and it is easier to see in mercantile capital 'the only truly bourgeois kernel of the revolution'. But if we forget the association with the French model which the term introduces, and think rather of the capitalist mode of production, then clearly we must follow Marx in seeing the landowners and farmers as a very powerful and authentic capitalist nexus.[38]

Thompson, in effect, denied the whole distinction between a bourgeoisie proper and a capitalist landowning class: so close was the interplay of town and country, of commercial wealth and real estate in English history, that the search for a pure continental genus was bound to be impracticable; and any attempt to make sense of the concept in preindustrial England was obliged to argue that the gentry – risen, rising, and about to rise – were themselves a bourgeoisie or in the process of becoming one. The bourgeois construction of modern England, accordingly, was not a partial and aborted affair, located in the failed revolutions of 1640 or 1688, but a long-drawn out process, reaching back

> to the monastic wool farmers of Domesday Book, and passing through the enfeeblement of the barons in the wars, the growth of 'free labour', the enclosure of the sheep walks, the seizure and redistribution of church lands, the pillaging of the New World, the drainage of fens and thence through revolution, to the eventual acceleration of enclosure and the reclamation of wastes.

Within this process, one could discern an 'organic tendency' – an ebb and flow of wealth and talent from the land and back to the land again, something impossible to discern through continental eyes used to peering out at *tiefste Provinz*, but writ large in the Cotswold wool hamlets, the Suffolk clothiers' churches and the rural rebuilding of the sixteenth century. There was, of course, something very familiar about this description: Thompson's response to Anderson's model of failed transition and a persistent aristocratic *ancien régime*, was a rhetorically updated version of the rising middle class – a great arch of bourgeois fabrication curving over seven centuries from William de la Pole to Edward Heath.[39]

Such an inexorable middle-class ascent reduced the pivotal quality of a seventeenth-century revolution – even as 'one bourgeois revolution of many' – to negligible proportions: the revolution was a rung in the ladder or a conduit for pre-existing social forces, rather than a fundamental divide. Kiernan's heresies of the late 1940s had become the 'peculiarly English' orthodoxies of the 1970s and 1980s: a process of state formation and agrarian commercialization reaching back to the Middle Ages, the creation under the Tudors of a political culture and a 'national economic space within which capitalism could develop', the consolidation and thickening of social forces under Elizabeth, and the 'embourgeoisement of both gentry and aristocracy' in the early seventeenth century.[40] The origins of the Civil War were no longer sought in the confrontation between a capitalist gentry and a supposedly feudal peerage, or between a bourgeois society and a feudal–absolutist state, but in 'the formation of "Court" and "Country" as historic blocs': 'The Revolution confirmed a title not to new property, but to property which already existed – a title which was menaced by the unregulated exactions of the monarchy, and which had no secure sanction in the authoritarian and magical ideology which had outlived its feudal host'.[41] Briefly the Revolution threw up 'a quite different threat to property' from the Leveller Left; but the conservative repression of 1649 prefigured the settlement of 1688: a settlement which registered 'not some half-way house between "feudalism" and "capitalism", nor some adjustment of interests between a tenacious feudal superstructure and an embryonic capitalist base, but an arrangement exquisitely adjusted to the equilibrium of social forces at the time'.[42]

The major challenge to the absolute property ownership established in 1688 and the rationalization of new economic practices during the eighteenth century came from the customary community and 'the moral economy of the poor'.[43] Such beliefs, insisted Thompson, did not belong to an order of universal, transhistorical moral values, but were to be found in particular traditions – in the principles most dramatically practised by the Levellers and the Diggers during the English Civil War. The deer hunters and turf cutters of the 1720s defending their rights against a predatory market-oriented Whig oligarchy, became the unconscious heirs of seventeenth-century radicals, and the vectors of a partly submerged but significant vein of English culture reaching back to the Peasants' Revolt and forward to the making of the English working class.[44]

Thompson' s history juxtaposed a 'great arch' of bourgeois evolution, curving over seven centuries, consolidating itself from time to time in a number of different power formations – Stuart court culture, 'Old Corruption', Manchester liberalism, the 'establishment' complex of the 1950s, each of them requiring a different strategy of socialist opposition – and a selective libertarian tradition, the graffiti under the arch, which always seemed about to emerge from the shadows yet never did.[45] Whiggish in respect of the bourgeoisie, libertarian and morally engaged in respect of the workers, it was perfectly congruent with traditional explanations of Britain's role as the first modern society: the material success of British capitalism and the dominant place of Britain in the world were still regarded as 'givens'. For all the poetic loathing of capitalist society, and the deep antipathy for the English ruling class, Thompson's 'socialist humanism' was bound in the end to blur with democratic liberalism and encompass a positive valuation of the philosophy of individual rights, limited government and the rule of law. It dovetailed, easily enough, with such flattering Social Democratic texts as Barrington Moore's *Social Origins of Dictatorship and Democracy*, in which Britain was allotted the role of first-leg baton carrier in the bourgeois revolutionary passage to the modern world – a race in which the pioneers won all the democratic prizes and late-starters were doomed to experience either 'conservative revolutions from above ending in fascism or peasant revolutions leading to communism'.[46] It could even come to coincide with older liberal scenarios of English history – and a seventeenth century, not as the epoch of revolutionary social transformation but as the birthplace of modern liberty.[47]

Such a history had little to offer as an explanation of the 'present crisis'; little to offer either by way of cure, save at the level of evocation and exhortation. The trouble was that Thompson really considered the whole project of a 'totalizing history' or a genealogy of the present to be illegitimate. And his essay on *The Peculiarities of the English* was largely an exercise in empirical damage control: in keeping history pure from the illicit incursions of high theory. Historians were required by the fierceness of the polemic to choose a side; and most of them opted for the empirical idiom. Thompson's philippic severed communication between the new Marxist theory and socialist history, and marked a further move away from the sort of grand historical project that had once informed the debates of the Communist Group in the immediate post-war era.[48]

What he clearly rejected was the whole idea of a predestined pathway, in which history was directed towards some ideal endpoint or goal: 'History cannot be compared to a tunnel through which an express races until it brings its freight of passengers out into the sunlit plains. Or if it can, then generation upon generation of passengers are born, live and die while the train is still within the tunnel.'[49] The notion of an ideal historical process was essential to the political conclusion that Anderson attempted to derive from his work. If Britain had fallen behind the rest of Europe because of its blocked history, now was the time for it to comprehend its own contingency: 'history ha[d] tied th[e] knot; only history would ultimately undo it':[50]

> The crisis . . . is a logical outcome of the long pilgrimage of British capitalism from its origins to its present precarious position within the world of the second half of the twentieth century . . . Re-enacting the past has not restored it . . . The unfinished work of 1640 and 1832 must be taken up where it was left off.[51]

Britain must go back to her history and do it again – properly this time!

It was no accident that one of Thompson's major substantive disagreements with Anderson was over the nature of the English Revolution. For Anderson, the Civil War had to be seen as a substitute or 'proxy' for the bourgeois revolution England had to have; for Thompson the whole search for a bourgeois revolution was misconceived. For Anderson, the distortions and displacements of English history were the product of a few grand determining moments; for Thompson, the whole idea of strategic 'fixing' moments – turning points where history failed to turn – enormously oversimplified the continuities and discontinuities of the past, and discounted those episodes, like 1648 or 1797, where history might quite easily have taken a different path. For Anderson, these arrested transitions created an aristocratic 'hegemony', interpreted as nothing more or less than a form of total cultural and political dominance, an ideology which reinforced pre-existing power relations; for Thompson, the concept of hegemony would not bear this deterministic weight, but referred to 'a terrain of conflict, negotiation and consent, requiring much political and cultural labour for its reproduction and renewal'.[52]

If Thompson's diagnosis was correct, then the only reason why Anderson and Nairn were able to avoid overt schematization was that they were treating an aberrant case. If their method were to be applied to the normative abstraction entitled 'Other Countries', it would reveal a perfect progression from feudalism through an unequivocal bourgeois revolution to capitalism, and onwards to socialism. The application of new Marxist theory to the particular workings of English history – and the exemption of 'other' histories from the complexities revealed by that analysis – suggested, indeed, that Anderson and Nairn were not prepared to question the ideal against which England's past was measured, but, by a sort of surreptitious platonism, only to relocate it. Nor was the displacement simply the geographical one identified by Thompson;[53] it also could be detected at some ideal level beneath the surface, although its appearance in actuality was 'mediated' by the specificities of historical context. Thus, the English Revolution was a 'mediated bourgeois revolution', despite the fact that it was not brought about by the bourgeoisie and did not create a bourgeois society. The slippery concept of 'mediation' was tailor-made for Anderson's purpose: on the one hand, it appeared to take into account the exceptional nature of particular historical situations and could be used to answer Thompson's charge of reductionism and schematization; on the other, it suggested that true reality existed as some pure and unmediated ideal, and that mediation was a distortion or a failure to realize the ideal.[54]

Some twenty years after this passage of arms, Anderson returned to the themes of the mid 1960s. The intervening years had done much to dampen his enthusiasm for continental theory and to deepen his appreciation of Marxist writing in Britain. Whatever its faults, its affirmation of 'the independent reality of historical evidence' left open the possibility of genuine dialogue: something quite impossible with those who denied the central place of historical thinking and investigation in any socialist project.[55] At the same time, his substantive disagreements with

Thompson on the matter of the English past had not diminished with the years. Indeed, he argued in 1987, the intervening period had done much to confirm the intuitions of his early essays: the conventional verdict in favour of E. P. Thompson's version had been 'overturned in the court of appeal'. To begin with, the 'crisis', which had largely been denied or ignored on the Left, was now universally recognized. Its historical basis had been confirmed in many of its salient features: an early breakdown of feudalism, a decapitation of Absolutism at the centre, and a premature social synthesis marked by the formation of a 'hegemonic block': by 'agrarian paramountcy' and subordination of the financial, commercial and industrial bourgeoisie.[56]

The categories of the original analysis were, in Anderson's opinion, still valid. Revolution, for example, was a term 'with a precise meaning: the political overthrow from below of one state order and its replacement by another. Nothing was to be gained by diluting it across time, or extending it over every department of social space'. Revolutionary 'arches' were 'indistinguishable from mere reform'; and intellectual, religious or cultural revolutions could be reduced to 'psychological or moral conversions': experiences which – as the 'sombre parabola' of Maoist China indicated – invariably were quite at odds with their advertised character or declared goals.[57] By extension, too, the whole idea of 'a revolution within a revolution' was something which should be expunged from the historical lexicon:

> Against these slack devaluations . . . it is necessary to insist that revolution is a punctual and not a permanent process. That is: an episode compressed in time and concentrated in target, that has a determinate beginning – when the old state apparatus is still intact – and a finite end, when that apparatus is decisively broken and a new one erected in its stead.[58]

In a number of respects, however, the abnormalities of British history had been misstated: 'other countries' appeared to be not so different from England after all, both in the 'structural forms and historical record' of their initial bourgeois revolutions, and in the continued 'political power and cultural prestige' of their agrarian and titled elites: a 'persistence' of 'Old Regimes' which lasted into the twentieth century. All of the 'original' bourgeois revolutions were characterized by 'organic compromise' between the nobility and the bourgeoisie; all of them were thrown off course

by 'the pervasive presence of popular classes' in town and country; all complicated by the heterogeneity and internal divisions
of the bourgeoisie; all diverted by their containment within a
national state, situated within a competitive state system. Every
bourgeois revolution was 'denatured', 'every one . . . a bastard
birth'.[59] English history was not peculiar; it was not even fundamentally distorted. How then could one explain the English crisis?
The answer had to be sought 'at a lower level of individuation
than where we had located it . . . not in the general phenomenon
of landowner persistence, or mercantile association with it, but
in the particular patterns taken by these – or other forces and
factors'. English history was peculiar after all: only the peculiarities were very particular – and contingent.[60]

To begin, with the original bourgeois revolution was not so
much premature and mediated, as plain early: part of a cycle
that opened with the Dutch Revolt and closed in 1789. All of
these pre-industrial revolutions were fought under the banner of
liberation; all of them were marked by 'spontaneous social
turbulence, as successive layers of menu peuple erupted into
political life from below'; all were, first and foremost, political
events. The second wave of nineteenth-century capitalist revolutions
– in Germany, Italy and Japan – was marked by corresponding
strategic absences: no new political ideas, minimum popular
turmoil, no insurgent alliance between propertied and popular
classes. But these revolutions exhibited one great presence: 'the
world economic strength of the capitalist mode of production'
which largely explained their 'limited political thrust': 'the artillery
of commodities' was more than 'a substitute for the promises of
the Tennis Court'. Prior to the Industrial Revolution, 'a frontal
political assault against the old order was necessary precisely
because there was still no irresistible economic dynamic'.[61]

This would not have mattered so much, but for 'the rapidity
and finality of the sequel': the problem was not the prematurity
of 1640, but the permanency of 1688. Modern societies were not
formed overnight in one decisive episode: 'Rather the historical
genesis of the modern bourgeois state has normally taken the
pattern of a series of successive ruptures . . . concentrated in their
rhythm and coercive in their impact, [each] remedying the
omissions and reversing the defeats of their predecessors.' It was
in these second stage aftershocks that England was most defective:
the 'ossified magistrate oligarchy' of the United Provinces was

swept away by the Batavian Republic; the hybrid social hierarchy of 'notables' which had dominated France since 1799, destroyed in 1871. Only in the British case was the early half-hearted dismantling of the Restored Stuart regime and the subsequent political stasis crucial; only the British state remained 'magically pickled' by its very success in its early modern identity. When the victorious powers met at Potsdam in 1945, 'no gale of creative destruction had blown through [its] creaking political timbers . . . for nearly three centuries'.[62]

Figures of Descent and its companion pieces constituted a highly intelligent analysis of the British 'crisis' – in some respects, an improvement on the 1960s model: they were far more detailed; they tackled the continuum of modern British history and not just a few fixing moments; they substituted a more 'materialist' examination of British capitalism and the British state for the disproportionate 'culturalism' of the earlier account. But to their Left critics, they still confused style with substance, ethos with essence; and they ruled out the contingencies and creative potentialities of British history.[63] Most disturbing of all, their account of continuous decline – of the early containment and defeat of British capital and the long origins of the anti-industrial spirit – now coincided rather shockingly with the selective historical propaganda of the New Right: with Martin Wiener's illustrations of anti-business sentiment, and even with Corelli Barnett's jeremiad on the New Jerusalem mentality of 1945, the 'dream' which 'turned into the dank reality of a segregated, subliterate, unskilled, unhealthy and institutionalized proletariat hanging on the nipple of state maternalism'.[64]

The writings of Thompson and Anderson, in their very different ways, did much to extend the range and quality of Marxist writing in England. The originality and eloquence of Thompson's work inspired a younger generation of socialist historians to restore the exploited and oppressed to their 'rightful' place as historical and moral agents. Anderson presided over a vast expansion of theoretical Marxist literature: when he reviewed the major components of British intellectual life some two decades after his first survey, he was able to contemplate with undisguised satisfaction the marked disjuncture between Britain's reactionary politics and a radicalized academic 'culture in counterflow'.[65] When it came to preserving and updating a coherent Marxist inter-pretation of British history, however, their work had much more mixed results. Thompson's powerful but fragmentary studies of 'hard Whig gentlemen' defending their estates and politically self-conscious early industrial labourers forging a working class identity, appeared seriously at odds with the more traditional parts of the Marxist enterprise – with Hill's epochal seventeenth-century revolution and Hobsbawm's underdeveloped working class struggling into existence in the 1890s. And the polemically engaged version of bourgeois arches and libertarian struggles, which he developed in his recoil from the stone axioms of Stalinism and structuralism, seemed to have led to a Marxism which was not so different, save in its revolutionary temper and selectively differential empathy, from old-style radicalism or even uplifting Whiggism: Britain as the home of liberty, the rule of law and a humane working-class tradition.[66] It extended the national and empirical idiom of the Historians' Group in a manner that could easily be read as gratuitously chauvinistic and trenchantly anti-theoretical, polemically cut off from the new modes of discourse sweeping the other social sciences: the caricature version which Thompson himself sometimes projected of the self-styled squire of 'Empirica Parva', beating back French locusts and Dutch elm disease; his history, 'a pattern book of moral examples', which had to be defended at all costs against the Tebbitt-like sneers of professional revisionists, and which somehow, in a way that was 'quite illogical' and 'unacceptable to any grand theorist', were going to bring about 'the transition to democratic socialism'.[67]

Anderson's great arch of decline, on the other hand, looked like an upside down teleology: a not so benign 'descent' in which every attempted remedy produced a further loss of 'altitude', further confirmation of decay. Although the terminology and the analytical framework was relentlessly Marxist, the motor might almost have been borrowed from Alexis de Tocqueville's diagnosis of another *ançien régime* and its baneful legacy. If Thompson's vision was all about creativity, will, utopian transcendence, Anderson's was all about the burden of the past and inevitable entropy. And if Thompson seemed condemned to share his libertarian history with the Whigs and the non-Marxist radicals, Anderson and Nairn appeared to have established their theoretical vantage-point perilously close to the purlieus of the New Right. A change of vocabulary and the most theoretically self-conscious and sophisticated Marxist writers in the country could be enlisted as historical polemicists for the 'Enterprise Culture', which was going to give Britain a proper dose of the capitalism it never had. For, as Anderson himself noted, there was one exception to the radicalization of high culture in the 1980s, one subject area which seemed to be moving with the conservative political flow: that of history, or, at any rate, the history of England. And in a curious way, high Marxist theory and low revisionist practice seemed to have compiled a similar case against England's supposedly revolutionary past.[68]

6.2 REVISIONIST CHALLENGES

By the 1980s, in history departments up and down the country, the revolutionary version of England's past was in full retreat. For nearly half a century, the seventeenth-century transformation had been central to that interpretation; and the understanding of seventeenth-century English history had been dominated by a vision of deep and abiding social change. Despite the clamour of their disputations, the commitment to social change explanation had united Marxists, their progressive sympathizers and their critics: it was common to Hill whose 'revolution' was all about the confrontation of new and dynamic bourgeois forces and conservative or immobile 'structures'; to Stone whose 'breakdown' registered the 'dysfunctional' responses to economic and psychological change; and to Trevor-Roper whose Civil War was a successful revolt of regressive society against the modernizing state.[69] 'Each scenario,' as Jonathan Clark explains, 'shared the implausible assumption that one major element in the nation stood still in the midst of flux';[70] each, the conviction, the more compelling coming as it did from an anti-Marxist, that the 'seventeenth century [was] broken in the middle, irreparably broken, and at the end of it, after the revolutions, men [were] hardly able to recognize the beginning'.[71]

The 1960s had witnessed an increased emphasis on the 'social', associated with the broader sympathies, enlarged agendas and growing theoretical sophistication of historical writing: a focus sharpened on the Left by the recoil from Stalinism and from belief in political shortcuts; and by the example of E. P. Thompson's work on class formation and consciousness – its political dimension largely ignored or subsumed under the banner of a 'history from below', concerned with people's ordinary lives and experiences.[72]

Underpinning the commitment to social explanation was a rejection of the superficialities and evasions of political story telling. Hill's critique of C. V. Wedgwood's attempt to describe the events of the Civil War 'as far as possible in the order in which they happened', and to form a chronology which would 'make the immediate pressures and confusions which acted on contemporaries clear to the modern reader', could well stand for the general voice of the profession at the time: 'Miss Wedgwood's book . . . is a narrative not an explanation. It tells us all about the war except what they fought each other for . . . Two hundred facts do not make an interpretation . . . and Miss Wedgwood's refusal to analyze makes it impossible to see below the surface of mere events.'[73]

Nowhere, indeed, were the analytical priorities of the new social history more pronounced than in England's century of revolution. The stretching of revolutionary chronology and increased concentration on the long haul of attitudinal change distanced historians from the detailed study of events and personalities: revolution, they argued, was the coming together of many things, not the step by step unfolding of single and self-evident story line. Contemporaries could hardly have been expected to have grasped the full import of what was going on around them, and a sense of historical perspective – what historians thought was significant from the point of view of their enquiry rather than how the 'historical actors' saw things at the time – was a strategically necessary first step to any understanding of the era. No doubt, the psychology and research habits of historians had something to do with the sociological predisposition also. Political story telling focused on the thoughts and actions of a few individuals. But revolutions affect millions: portentous outcomes require profound causes. Just as it was unthinkable that the events of October 1917 could have been engineered by a small band of conspirators over a two-week time span, but must somehow have been a spontaneous explosion of worker and peasant masses, whose worlds could be explored through detailed research – a myth happily confirmed for anti-cold-warriors by the release of sanitized (if largely irrelevant) social documentation by the Soviet authorities – so, too, nothing appeared more certain than that the complex revolutionary challenge of the 1640s – which seemed unwilled, unwanted and reluctantly led – must have been the product of deep social tensions, fundamental economic changes, effervescent popular forces and profound religious passions.[74] And these could only be given proper weight by painstaking multi-causal analysis ranging over a long period of time – 'an approach' which, it was argued, provided 'a much closer approximation to the infinite complexity of real life than either an apparently straight-forward narrative or an explanation . . . around a single determining cause'.[75]

In this environment of detailed and monumental social research, Marxism was lauded by its exponents for its synthetic qualities: its ability to draw together the threads of partial analysis into a coherent overarching picture of the whole. Marxist explanations of the interconnectedness and interpenetration of social, economic, ideological and political phenomena and of the heterogeneity of means and ends, seemed peculiarly well suited to the questions that historians now considered important: in the land of myopia, the one-eyed but long-sighted Marxist was king. Nor was it the case that the Marxist ignored chronology altogether. Marxism enabled the historian to concentrate on the structure in the knowledge that theory had already taken care of the story-line: that it had already secured the English Revolution within the schema of the unfolding of bourgeois society in the Western world.

By the late 1970s, however, much of the substance of the socio-economic explanation had unravelled. The story of agrarian change, commercial enclosure, rural expropriation and popular rebellion, handed down from Tawney and Thorold Rogers to Barrington Moore and Perry Anderson, no longer corresponded to the work of agrarian or economic historians, demographers and geographers. For what this showed was enclosure, more often for arable than for pasture, rarely the work of manorial lords, but initiated by yeomen and copyholders usually with the agreement of the community, and emulated for its own fiscal purposes by the crown; and a trajectory of popular rebellion reaching its climax in the mid sixteenth century, but gradually subsiding thereafter into endemic riot or domesticated crime – the protest not of dispossessed cultivators in the agrarian heartlands, but of the squatters and landless artisans who occupied the forests, fens and common lands on the fringes of older settled areas. In the major outports, the trading elites were revealed as long-standing allies and not enemies of the crown; while the pattern of overseas exports – a boom followed by protracted decline after 1560 and levelling off thereafter – seemed out of step with explanations either of commercial expansion or commercial crisis as the catalysts of political upheaval.

Just about every element of the traditional scenario was now out of place: a chronology of declining popular unrest, demographic levelling off, gradually stabilizing prices, and economic stagnation; a complex geography of conservatism and radicalism which appeared to invert rather than to mirror the regional loyalties of 1642; and a distribution of personnel which seemed to have most of the wrong people doing the right things and vice versa.[76]

But it was also becoming evident that the real problem was not one of content, but of approach: that there was a fundamental disproportion between the explosive events of the 1640s and 1650s and the supposed social and ideological pathology of them.[77] The work of Brunton and Pennington exposed the fallacy of a one to one analysis based on the social divisions of elite politics; the gentry controversy, the difficulty of an agreed taxonomy of the social elite or a convincing picture of supposed sectional movements within it; Stone's research on the aristocracy, the artificiality of isolating one section of the elite from the elite as a whole. Initially, it seemed that the objections could be met by a further refinement of categories and of terminology, or by more sophisticated theoretical models of social change; but qualifications of language and elasticity of taxonomy turned the patterns into platitudes, and the addition of theoretical epicycles removed the analysis further and further from the realities of human existence: a moment of almost complete fantasy was reached when it was suggested that perhaps the Revolution owed something to the replacement of an Egyptian pyramid by San Gimignano skyscrapers. But even if it had been possible to prove the rise of one group and the crisis of another, it was no longer clear that the 'dissolution' of society caused the Civil War and not the war the dissolution of society.[78]

In the last analysis, the Marxist inability to come to terms with the normative features of most societies critically weakened its credibility when it came to explain genuine if occasional instances of political and social collapse.[79] The model of homeostatic integration and moral consensus derived from Durkheim appeared even less capable of explaining the singularity of 1640 or 1649. For, according to writers of this persuasion, there was really nothing to explain: the English Revolution was just another meteor streaking across the skies of early modern Europe, striking enough to contemporaries but in the *longue durée*, a delusive and insignificant surface occurrence in 'the history that stands still'.[80] Peter Laslett's domestication and vulgarization of Braudel's deep structures (and prejudices) in *The World we have Lost*, seemed, for example, to 'submerge' the English Revolution 'in a great sea of acts of political violence where it sank and disappeared from sight'; and even Perez Zagorin's more impressive comparative typology of early modern disorder, appeared to line up revolutionary civil war alongside the other categories of agrarian, urban and provincial rebellion, as yet another periodic eruption which tested but never entirely broke through the crust of early modern conservatism.[81]

The model of court and country division, popular for a while in the 1950s and 1960s, and also associated with Zagorin, had long since lost much of its credibility. Cut across by personal loyalties, factional infighting, the blending of patronage networks, common ideological and cultural assumptions, and by the sheer cussedness of individual conviction and behaviour, the categories proved to be even more porous and fissile than the much derided classes of the Marxists. As an explanation of the events of 1642, the model was open to all of the objections levelled at class struggle – invalidity, too general validity, and a scenario of the actual events as the simultaneous triumph, decomposition and collapse of the country, which seemed to be improbable and somehow irrelevant.[82] As for Stone's heroic attempt to combine all the social science models in a brilliant but perverse demonstration that the English Revolution was the product of everything that had or had not happened over the previous hundred years: there is little doubt that it was this more than any other endeavour, which provoked the backlash from a new generation of scholars who had not grown up under the influence of Tawney or been so intoxicated by sociological theory.[83]

On the face of it, the genre of local and provincial studies which attempted to cut grand theory down to size, and to reconceptualize English society as a federation of shires, controlled by a restricted number of families – introverted local networks, by turns, conservative and 'neutralist', reacting with suspicion to outside pressures from both sides of the political spectrum, endeavouring to preserve their counties as tax-exempt havens or military free zones – appeared at first sight to bury synoptic explanations of conflict in a morass of particularism and exception, to explain, as one exponent put it in a fit of remorse, why there was no Civil War.[84] Perhaps these studies marked the somewhat belated appearance of 'Namierism' in a field hitherto considered inviolate on account of its ostensible constitutional, ideological and social divisions; perhaps, as Clark wickedly suggested, their priorities were the historiographical analogue of the then fashionable SDP virtues of small government and environmental friendliness. In either guise, it seemed likely that localism would beat a counterpoint to more powerful or triumphalist messages concocted elsewhere.[85]

For the view from the provinces was arguably distorted also. There were questionable inferences drawn from negative or absent materials: the lack of constitutional challenge to government measures in the localities did not necessarily mean the absence of principled opposition. There was the suspect model of challenge and response, in which all the activism was concentrated at the centre, all the resistance at the periphery: perhaps the Privy Council was also lax from time to time; perhaps the local community was sometimes proactive, the instigator as well as the victim of incompetence and inconsistency. The unit of study itself was porous; there was not one provincial community but many: gentry activity usually occurred at a more localized level than the county; and the county community was 'a point of contact' with the wider world and not a self-sustaining isolate. Community activity appeared just as likely to divide as to unite the county elite; and when the war came, the regional variations of royalism and parliamentary support seemed 'to be related not to the complexion of the country community' but to broader national loyalties and configurations.[86] Christopher Hill was soon able to write off the provincial threat to overarching social and ideological explanations as a nine day wonder: 'what threatened to become an orthodoxy', he noted with evident satisfaction, 'disintegrated before it congealed'.[87]

Yet, in a number of respects, these new perspectives did contribute to the assumptions of what came to be known in the 1980s to its opponents and sometimes to its protagonists as a 'revisionist' reading of the English Civil War.[88] Though sometimes caricatured as little more than 'a mode of historical narrat[ion] which reject[ed] all long term structural causes and concentrat[ed] exclusively on personal and factional accidents in high politics', the so-called revisionism of the 1980s did, in fact, proceed from a number of structural assumptions about the nature of political and institutional life, derived from provincial studies, from work on the administration and the electorate and from the examination of Jacobean and Caroline 'culture'.[89] Conrad Russell's seminal work on *Parliaments and English Politics 1621–1629*, for example, was not just about the importance of warfare, factional infighting and the personality of the Duke of Buckingham in what had hitherto been perceived as a series of constitutional conflicts over matters of high principle, but about a new perspective for examining Stuart political life: one which sought to reconceptualize a parliament (the indefinite article is crucial) not as the arena of escalating struggle but as one of a number of occasional 'points of contact' between the crown and the political nation; but which also attempted to explain why it became a point of friction also.[90]

In similar vein, Patrick Collinson's studies of the Elizabethan and Jacobean Church depicted a broad-shouldered ecumenical 'Religion of Protestants', Calvinist in its theology, Erastian in its politics, far removed from the picture of an institution fundamentally divided, white-anted by separatism and laxism, tottering towards the breakdown of 1641.[91] Kevin Sharpe's exploration of the conventions of early Stuart literature and politics – and, more recently, his monumental work on the personal rule of Charles I – sought to a establish a new code for understanding an ordered, aristocratic style of *ancien régime*, not in any significant sense absolutist but based on 'the traditional symbiosis of prerogative and law'.[92] Even Russell's emphasis on the British problem and on the Scots and Irish Rebellions as necessary if not quite sufficient catalysts of political breakdown and the resort to arms – a 'peripheral' perspective which could be viewed as a massive extension of the view from the provinces – was not just about the importance of an external *deus ex machina*, and the role of accident and miscalculation in the coming of the English Civil War. It also proposed a new framework for what was now conceptualized as the collapse of a multi-kingdomed monarchy and what could hardly be the coincidence of three national crises.[93]

What was revealed by these studies was a relatively stable and by no means inelastic early Stuart polity, not without its weaknesses and areas of dissent to be sure, especially when it encountered the unpredictable strains of war, but one far removed from the picture of a chronically disequilibrated state and society. When it came to the Civil War itself, localism had uncovered not a vast struggle of popular forces but something cut down to more prosaic proportions – a war which was always raging somewhere else, impinging from the outside on the county in question. For many

English gentry, it seemed, the major aim was to steer the war away from their locality, and to preserve their community from disruption; for the vast majority of country folk, neutralism was the rule and not the exception. Even the supposed militants were less committed or monolithic than had been suggested: Mark Kishlansky's motley collection of officers and conscripts, primarily concerned with pay and conditions, was barely recognizable as the New Model Army of earlier accounts. David Underdown's parliamentarians of the crisis years of 1647 and 1648 – when ideological polarization might have been expected to be intense – seemed to comprise 'parties at best ephemeral and transitory', factional groupings of professional politicians, independent country gentlemen, office holders and noble clients, uncannily familiar to students of eighteenth-century English politics.[94] Even the regicides, 'cream of the revolutionary cream', proved, in the hands of Blair Worden, to be mostly skimmed milk: half-hearted revolutionists, who would if they could, have combined the execution of Charles Stuart with the preservation of the king.[95]

The impact of these studies was certainly often negative; they were better at showing what the Civil War was not than at indicating what it was. But they did narrow down the relevant questions; and, as revisionists never ceased to maintain, asking the right questions was crucial. The men of 1640 – men with limited aims and modest ambitions – came to Westminister for a settlement. How was it that they finished up with a war none of them wanted? How did these 'conservatives' come to fall out amongst themselves? Revisionism was concerned with what Russell referred to as a contingent form of causation: not the causes of the Civil War, and certainly not the causes of the 'English Revolution' – a historians' construct which reified an unpredictable sequence – but 'the causes of events and non events which led to the English Civil War'. To its critics this involved an illegitimate narrowing of the terrain to something more manageable but less important: not why was there such a tidal wave of hostility to the crown in 1640, nor why the instruments and institutions of the 'monarchical state' were so easily destroyed, but why fighting broke out over its ruins a year or so later.[96]

But that was only the beginning. So much attention has been paid to the revisionists' supposed preference for immediate short-term causes, that the importance of their endings has been largely unremarked. But the end-points were crucial also. The events of the 1640s were not a 'block'; they were a haphazard series of contingencies which could quite easily have led the country down one of a number of roads; or, to simplify a little, they witnessed the partial convergence of two ill-assorted and loosely connected happenings: a political crisis in 1641 and 1642, quite inaccurately referred to as a revolution, and a revolution proper – partially and temporarily accomplished but more generally contained – with a different cast of actors, different problems and different ambitions, thrown up by the radically changed circumstances of 1647 and 1648.[97] The explanations offered by the Marxists and Whigs – both wedded to an inevitabilist teleology – confounded the two; and were, therefore, quite unable to focus on the limited nature of the initial events and the adventitious quality of the later. Social change theory, in particular, was guilty of perpetrating a category mistake, seeking to explain the activity of a small group of political leaders at a specific moment, through vague and generalized causes which explained other events and non-events as well.[98]

According to Russell, 'to let the search for causes or explanations take priority over the establishment of the correct story [was] to put the cart before the horse'; and it was the essence of 'the revisionist creed . . . that we must establish the course of events by treating it as a subject worthy of study in its own right, and then and only then attempt to analyze its causes'.[99] There was a sense in which revisionist history did involve the reassessment of politics as an activity with its own irreducible characteristics. Political narrative, correctly pursued, involved a reconstruction of the conventions which governed or influenced political behaviour; a recognition of politics as an activity examined in particular, in detail, on a short time-scale; and a submission to the contingency and the partial blindness of events: to the inadvertence with which situations might arise, change and unforseeably develop into new situations.[100] And political narrative had to provide the cutting edge of any explanation of the breakdown of 1641 and 42: no analysis could demonstrate its realism and relevance, when it reduced politics to something else – the artificially choreographed clash of supposed constitutional principles, the elaboration of supposedly deep-seated socio-economic divisions or the even more dubious expression of some retrospectively conceived popular or public opinion. Perhaps, the primacy of political activity was easier to perceive at a time when

Mrs Thatcher's government was changing the rules and the conventions of social democratic consensus, when a command politics was tearing down a managed economy, and when the
improbability of a war with Argentina appeared to derail all the
calculations of sociologists and political scientists.

The focus on politics meant a return to detailed story telling of
a kind that had been out of favour for forty years. In 1979, Lawrence
Stone, sensitive as ever to historiographical weather-change,
signalled 'the revival of narrative'; it was, he argued, catching
the wind in his sails, a useful corrective to the structuralist mystique
of the previous decade. At the same time – tacking a little – he
defined narrative in a manner that rendered it innocuous: narrative,
it seemed, referred to small-scale stories of groups or situations,
which illustrated the non-narrative analytical categories of the
historians of social structure or of *mentalité*. High political narrative
as an end in itself – here he battened down the hatches – was the
'antiquarian' empiricism of a 'new British school of chroniclers',
who were 'busy trying to remove any sense of ideology or idealism
from the two English revolutions of the seventeenth century'. Stories
of this sort, as one practitioner conceded, 'tended to be long',
irreducibly 'complex . . . and relatively inaccessible'; they could
not easily be repackaged or, indeed, translated into a synoptic
version of the past. Besides, said Stone – here the voice of relativism
interposed – they were, surely, no truer to the irrecoverable reality
of the past than were the more honestly artificial constructions
of the analytical historians.[101]

According to many theorists, all narratives are artifacts: well-
made stories do not exist outside the pages of history books or
novels. In the 1980s, however, a strong case was mounted for 'a
temporal configuration bred in the bone of human events', and
for the congruence of narrative form and human perception –
the ways that individuals and communities remembered their lives
and experiences.[102] The life of high politics, in particular, it was
argued, could only be charted in this way: through a detailed
chronology of events which corresponded as closely as possible
to the order in which they happened and to the temporal sequence experienced by the actors themselves. Such narratives were
bound to be highly detailed; they were also bound in some measure
to be 'internalist': to register not just the event but 'the thought
in the mind of the person by whose agency the event came about'.[103]
Thus, Anthony Fletcher's *The Outbreak of the English Civil War*

concerned itself almost entirely with an eighteen months political time-span and with a psychodrama: an account of the ways
in which the suspicions, fears and manoeuvres of two men polarized the political nation.[104]

This sort of narrative involved a revision of the old Whig story-
line: for Whiggism, as Butterfield explained long ago, relied on
teleological strategies and assumptions ostensibly at odds with
the day to day inadvertencies and improvisations of 'high politics'.[105] Not the least reason for the eschewal of narrative by progressive historians of the seventeenth century, was the belief that
a secure and unassailable narrative already existed in the pages
of Gardiner's great history. Gardiner's was pre-eminently the story
of the growth of liberty and representative government:

> what gave form to the story was the succession of Parliaments from
> the first of James I to the last of Charles I. They were a set of nodes
> or junction boxes along the route, in which separate lines of develop-
> ment – foreign policy, domestic government, taxation and finance –
> converged momentously for a time and then spread out again. It was
> in the succession of Parliaments that the meaning of the flow of events,
> as Gardiner saw it, became clear.[106]

And parliamentary history meant the history of the House of
Commons.[107] Marxist historians did not deny this history; they
gave it a seat in the House of Lords. Its substance was elevated
to the epiphenomenal heights: the abundant actuality of parliamentary politics was an expression of some hidden reality – class
conflict, economic change, cultural or ideological division.

Although initially conceived as a riposte to the Whig parliamentary story, the Marxist reading had rapidly coalesced with it.
Indeed, one might argue that Hill and his colleagues in the Historians' Group succeeded in doing for the study of the English
Revolution what Jean Jaurès had achieved a generation earlier
for the French: the grafting of a model of social change and class
struggle on to the progressive story of political reform – combining
Marx and Gardiner, just as Jaurès had married Marx and Michelet.
The task had always been one of appropriation: of taking over
the bourgeois heritage and making it their own. The rejection of
Jacobin models of power seizure and change from the top down,
and the retreat from dramatic versions of class struggle, had, if
anything, strengthened the reliance on the Whig story-line. So
that Hill's textbook account of *The Century of Revolution* in the

1960s was crafted as a running commentary of social analysis and criticism on the potted Whig narrative which introduced each section. A decade later, when Marxists concerned themselves increasingly with the recovery of popular experiences, the dependence was undiminished. Sometimes, as in Thompson's case, the Whiggish implications were avowed; more characteristically perhaps, Hill's writings chronicled a 'continuous series of . . . liberal triumphs, highlighted by the intermittent presence of a radical underground or invisible church'.[108] Once he had complained of 'the tyranny of Gardiner'; now he embraced it: 'Whig interpretation' was 'the only possible historical attitude'.[109] .

'Revisionism', therefore, was bound by the logic of its own concerns and by the nature of the Marxist–Liberal alliance, to ignore what it saw as the irrelevancies of social change explanations and concentrate on the more formidable and widely shared whig assumptions. The major ingredients of its *nouvelle vague* parliamentary history are too well known to merit extended treatment here: instead of a powerful and purposeful body, a feeble, occasional assemblage, summoned and dismissed at the monarch's will, its debates disorganized, its supposed initiatives invariably the work of others, unwilling or unable even to withhold supply to force redress of grievances; instead of an adversarial politics focused on the clashes of 'government' and 'opposition' over a lengthening catalogue of 'issues', a common language of political propriety based on harmony and consensus, which parliament – the more and more uncomfortable and ill-equipped go-between of the court and the localities – was increasingly unable to embody; instead of the tale of great constitutional endeavours, a more prosaic story of incompetence and inefficiency, intrigues at court, the scramble for office, the pressure of local interests and private concerns; instead of a Commons increasingly aware of its legislative authority and its independence from the House of Lords, a Lower House deeply factionalized by aristocratic infighting, and tied to noble 'networks of patronage, kinship and friendship'; instead of a parliamentary continuum reaching from the early flexing of muscle in or before 1604, through the 'crystallization' of the 1620s, to the political revolution effected in 1641 and 1642, a number of discontinuous and episodic histories, occupying a mere three of the thirty-seven years of Stuart rule prior to the Long Parliament.[110]

There was a sense in which some of the tilting was expended on windmills: by the 1950s, few historians believed in the long-term 'struggle for sovereignty'; not many spoke of 'the government' and 'the opposition'; most were aware of the ostensible conservatism of parliamentary thought and behaviour. Students of the period were aware of the complexities of early Stuart political debate: that there could be agreement about the locus and nature of political authority, and considerable disagreement about its uses and its limits; and that conflict over these boundaries could occur within a common nexus of values, languages and ideologies. We knew, even if we did not put it that way, that leaders like Wentworth and Pym shared a common vocabulary of political discourse; we had even heard about Coke's Institutes and the importance of the Ancient Constitution.[111]

All the same, the scale and verve of the assault was a little intoxicating; and when the dust settled in the late 1980s, and the exaggerations and limitations of 'first wave' revisionism began to be exposed or explored, it was clear that it was no longer possible to reinvent the parliamentary route march to revolution. The early parliaments of the considerably rehabilitated James I were, by common consent, largely excluded from the canon; those of the 1620s were – with some disagreement over the significance of the long-term effects of consensual breakdown – held to operate under peculiar and unrepeatable circumstances, culminating not in royal but in parliamentary self-destruction.[112] The personal rule of Charles I was generally depicted in terms considerably closer to versions of the 'King's Peace' than to a polity and society trembling 'on the eve'. Most of the supposed revolutionary 'precipitants' of the 1630s dwindled or disintegrated at close quarters: financial expedients, remarkably successful for a while, rapidly surrendered in 1640 and 1641, and replaced by much more onerous parliamentary levies; a conciliar style of government considerably less repressive than its subsequent reputation would suggest; its critics far less alienated or sullenly opposed; a Puritan diaspora cut down to very modest proportions; court and country 'cultures' by no means as relentlessly polarized.[113] Which left the short-term crises of 1637 to 1642: 'the events and non-events which led to the English Civil War'.

Here, too, as we have seen, Occam's razor was at work, and omnibus explanations of the series were likely to run up against the historiographical salami tactics which were deployed. Those which were tentatively offered in place of social determination or the parliamentary struggle for liberty, duly fell victim to the very precision of the questions which had been formulated. According to one scenario, the events of the 1640s could best be understood as a traditional baronial revolt against what was perceived as royal misgovernment: a medieval throwback befitting a country so obsessed with gothic precedent. But, although the role of the peerage individually and collectively was significantly reassessed, aristocratic discontents hardly seemed to explain why the various 'sides' formed as they did, and why accommodation between them proved impossible. According to another, the major determinant was the British problem, with the Scots as the manipulators of English politics and support for the Scots alliance rather than social condition, political creed or even religious belief, the litmus test of Civil War loyalties. But the English effects seemed disproportionate to the Scottish and – later on – the Irish causes; and the Scots and Irish rebellions were not just symptoms of structural multinational deformations, but the outcome of particular policies, widely resented by many of Charles's subjects – in Westminster, as well as in Edinburgh and Ulster. A third wished to recast the English Revolution as the last of the European 'wars of religion', with the scale and the bitterness of divisions over church doctrine and organization a marked contrast to the yearning for settlement and compromise on constitutional issues. But, although religious belief still seemed the most likely cause of division and intransigence in 1642 and the most effective generator of further differences – the strongest thread which led from 1642 to 1648 – it appeared a less efficient explanation of the events of 1640. Yet another panned in on the person of the king: without the belief that Charles had somehow been turned against his people and that he had to be reprogrammed, if necessary by force, it was difficult to see how there could have been a civil war. But the events of the next twenty years were to indicate the massive residues as well as the limits of traditional allegiance; and even its proponents dismissed the idea that Charles's bottomless duplicity was a sufficient rather than a necessary explanation of them.

Now, the striking thing about these suggestions was not that they were lacking in originality and insight, but that they were all incomplete. Compared with the holistic explanations of the social determinists and the Whigs, they offered something considerably more modest in their range or synthetic power. And that may have been their point.[114] We are all revisionists now; perhaps, 'we' always are. By the late 1980s the term itself, always of questionable value, had become virtually meaningless. For polemical reasons, those who had challenged the traditional parliamentary story and focused on short-term political breakdown were dubbed revisionists; others not so entirely convinced were sometimes cast as unreconstructed whigs.[115] Yet, the revisionists and their ostensible critics shared a lot of common ground; and revisionism is best characterized not as the credo of a school of high and dry political historians – and certainly not a pride of Peterhouse Tories – but as a broad trend in historical studies evident since the 1970s. It was marked by a distrust of grand theory either in the form familiarly known as 'Whig interpretation' or in the various types of social, economic and ideological determinism popular over the previous thirty years, and by a desire to replace these omnibus theories with explanations better proportioned to a range of specific questions about the combination of crises erroniously called the English Revolution.[116] Inevitably, there was much dispute about the amount of demolition required and about the relative importance of the new pieces brought on to the site: the historical journals throbbed with academic controversy, and there seemed to be less agreement about the nature and significance of it all than at any time for nearly 200 years. Rather like the late twentieth-century itself, the breakdown of ideological systems had thrown up a new world order lacking form or coherence: here and there, new tribalisms appeared; here and there, triumphalists were heard arguing the victory of this or that brand of 'revisionism'; here and there, too – but this was unusual – spiritual cold warriors who yearned for a return to the certainties of the past.

Perhaps that is a convenient resting point for registering the demise of an over-arching revolutionary genealogy. There were, however, a number of oddities which suggested that 'revisionism' might not represent such a new world order after all, or that its life span might be limited. The first, as Hexter remarked, was the ghost of Samuel Ralston Gardiner. One of the ironies of the historiography of the period was the way that all the parties paid homage to the nineteenth-century master: not just whig historians who found in his narrative the crucial nodal points of parliamentary growth and constitutional evolution, but Marxists also, who eroded his priorities but treasured his 'facts', and considered him 'as nearly infallible as it is possible for a historian to be'. Most peculiar of all was the way that the new historians of political narrative invoked his spirit: for what they found in his work was an attention to the detail and a chronological rigour almost as complete as their own. Why was it, then, that where Gardiner perceived a chronological sequence moving forward deliberately and majestically year by year, his latter-day acolytes could only see a history moving by 'fits and starts . . . little tools and indirect ways'?[117]

The answer that is normally given is 'teleology': Gardiner, it is said, for all his chronological austerity, read his history backwards as well as forwards and conveyed an impression of inevitability: the step by step unfolding of a single process leading inexorably to civil war. Yet, even if one disregards other features of his work at odds with this supposed 'inevitabilism' – the acute sense of context, the Victorian emphasis on the importance of character and the role of heroic moral personalities in the shaping of great events – the accusation raises almost as many questions as it solves.[118] Ever since Butterfield published his insubstantial essay on the subject in 1931, whig hunting has been a favourite sport of the English academic classes. Yet, the notion of a 'Whig interpretation' appeared to confuse under the generic error of 'present-centredness', a number of avoidable evils with what might well be considered the unavoidable constraints imposed on all historical writing by its reconstructive and rhetorical functions.[119]

Anachronism of concept, terminology and evaluation by general consent might be thought of as real and unnecessary vices; and the whigs and Marxists might both have been guilty of egregious error in that regard. Gardiner, for example, might be held to have modelled John Pym and Oliver Cromwell in the likeness of Mr Gladstone, or – a more serious but a less immediately evident fault – to have envisaged a seventeenth-century parliament as behaving rather like a nineteenth-century one. Even here there might be room for legitimate dissent against a squeamish reverse discrimination which would permit people to read a terminology forward into an undefined future but not to project it backwards into a determinate past: language often limps after reality, and the absence of an authentic contemporary vocabulary should not necessarily inhibit historians from describing the phenomenon.[120]

But 'present-centredness' might also refer to still less certain vices: to a principle of selection and organization made with an eye to areas of present significance or concern – a criterion and a point of departure which by no means always entails anachronistic history. It could also refer to a necessary condition of all historical reconstruction or story telling: the shaping of the past from the point of view of the historian's own enquiry, the elucidation of a meaning or a set of meanings by selecting 'from the vast and uncontrollable mass of actual events a particular subset directed towards the historian's chosen end'. So that in telling the story of 'the origin of great events' which culminated in the Civil War and Protectorate, Gardiner could legitimately focus on the major highroad rather than on the pitfalls along the way.

If story telling was the most truthful and efficient way of conveying the complexity of the past, was it really possible to tell a political story without an end-point in mind? Admittedly, the 1970s did produce a few examples of high political narrative which came quite close to achieving the required condition of contextual immersion and chronological levitation, but the detail required seemed immense, the time-span minute, and the meaning of it all, rather inconsequential. Revisionist polemic at times threatened both to promote a return to narrative and to undermine the conditions which made it intelligible. John Pocock has described the seventeenth-century variety as a retreat from Harrington to Clarendon – a move from sociological necessity to political fortune. But the substance of Clarendon's history was exemplary rather than empirical: a confirmation – by example or default – of approved political and personal behaviour and an affirmation of power and the inscrutable purposes of God. To subscribe to the method without the metaphysic, therefore, was to subscribe to a world before the Creation – and whatever the current 'scientific' status of 'chaos theory', to date there is no acceptable historical equivalent of the butterfly's wings in Beijing producing a snowstorm in Berlin.[121]

The revisionist performance was usually quite different from the philosophy. Even Russell's examination of the causes of the English Civil War did much to belie the methodological scepticism expressed at the outset of his study. Historical reconstruction was like detective work and Russell started with the *corpus delicti* – a listing of seven high political variables, the particular combination of which led the country to civil war, and the absence of any one of which could have prevented it. Yet, when he moved from 'effect' to antecedent, he produced an analysis of 'multiple dysfunction' which was remarkably similar in outline, if different in its constituent elements, to the schema of that supposedly most determinist of historians, Lawrence Stone.[122] One of the causes – the financial and administrative deficiency of the crown – was, indeed, virtually the same; a second, a restatement or inversion of the traditional story of revolutionary Puritanism: the breakdown of Protestant consensus and the crumbling of 'a church designed by ... committee' during the 1620s in the face of an aggressive Arminian Counter-Reformation – an explanation which went back to 1559 and seemed, to its critics, to place an overheavy interpretative burden on the anti-Calvinism of a gaggle of Caroline bishops.[123] As for the third and most arresting of his structural fault-lines: the British problem and the difficulty of managing three societies, with mutually incomprehensible identities, and incompatible patterns of church organization and religious persuasion, in an age where effective regionalism was unthinkable – wasn't this present-centred with a vengeance? Wasn't this a fresh perspective, indeed a new subject-definition, proposed at a time when European integration and British devolution was at the centre of political debate, and when English as opposed to truly British history was ceasing to be a self-evident unit of study? In the case of Jonathan Clark, the most combative of revisionists, who relentlessly divided the historiographical world into a militant tendency of 'Old Guardians', 'Old Hatters' and 'the Class of '68', and a small band of the righteous, the contemporary agenda was even more polemically enunciated: seeking to alter the whole shape of modern British history in terms he thought appropriate to the post-industrial, post-imperial, post-liberal, post-socialist world of the 1980s.

The second oddity was the much less ghostly presence of Margaret Thatcher. Revisionism, under the sign of high political narrative, emphasized the ways in which the play of circumstance derailed long-term plans and eroded deeply held beliefs – to its critics, it sometimes appeared to marginalize conviction and principle altogether, and to be blind to continuities of thought and behaviour. In the 1970s, British politics reduced itself rather more severely than usual to the arts of survival. Past-master of this style of politics, personification of the virtues and vices of the time, was the supple and genial but also contemptible figure of Harold Wilson: a leader who 'subordinated all considerations not only of principle but of administrative effectiveness to balance of power manoeuvering'.[124] Yet, looking back on the period from the vantage point of the early 1990s, it is possible to discern a thread of consistency which was not grasped at the time. Politics still operated under the sign of the Welfare State; the economy was run along neo-Keynesian lines; parliamentary parties were broad-church coalitions to be managed, not units to be welded together by a single will; government was about deals and trade-offs: endeavouring to satisfy different interest groups and rival social philosophies by discussion and compromise.

It was the ostensible failure of this style of corporatist politics which produced Margaret Thatcher. For Margaret Thatcher was different: a conviction politician, obstinate, unbending, overwhelmingly certain in her views. Government by consensus and committee was anathema to her: there were enemies who were not to appeased; policies to be pursued whatever the cost. She aroused hatred and vilification like no other leader of her time; among her own, she also aroused intense loyalty. In a few years, she was to claim, she turned the country round: that was questionable; what she indubitably did, however, was to change the rules of political discussion and polarize the community.

The two politicians who really mattered in 1640 were much closer to Margaret Thatcher than to Harold Wilson. John Pym's managerial skills were far greater than Mrs Thatcher's, but he was also a man of strong convictions and a long political memory, convinced that, ever since 1626, there had been 'a design to alter the kingdom both in religion and government', and that it was his duty, as the dominating presence in the Long Parliament, to alert his fellow members to the dangers of such a design. This conviction overrode all other considerations – his genuine interest in strong and efficient government, his hopes for a settlement of outstanding financial and constitutional differences, his desire for mutually acceptable 'bridge appointments' – and led him to espouse the Scottish alliance and to employ the escalating tactic of pressure politics to root out 'popish' conspiracy. Clearly, the conspiracy became 'a self-fulfilling prophesy', the logic of threat and counter-threat, a mechanism for increasing the stakes not for re-establishing trust. But the particular tactics which were chosen, and the unintended consequences of their use, cannot be grasped without an understanding of the conventions and convictions that informed them: without what Lawrence Stone has called the 'continuity of memories and grievances', stretching back over thirty years.[125]

And what of the other actor of 1640: why did Charles not bend with the wind; why did he not do what his elder son and great-aunt would have done; why did he, too, engage in threat and counter-threat to get his way? Was it not, that he, too – for all the alleged duplicity – was not a conventional politician? In the words of the most recent study – by a leading 'revisionist' – was it not that he 'believed some principles worth adhering to whatever the political repercussions' – and, indeed, that 'he may even have been right'.[126] Was it then possible to banish principles so thoroughly and to disengage the politics of 1641 from those of 1628 or 1629: were not deep-seated values and traditions of behaviour an essential element in the reading of the short-term situation also?

The most disturbing question raised by revisionism, however, was whether any of it mattered. Asked to contribute an essay on the theme of 'choice and chance in history', Russell contemplated writing a piece on Charles I's victory in the English Civil War: 'to my surprise, he recalled, '[I] decided that I could not be certain any long term development would have been different if he had won it'.[127] Revisionist history by its philosophy and method questioned the centrality of the seventeenth century in the story of the British and American past. In a famous aside, Ranke enjoined historians to accept the relativity of their enterprise: there were no privileged ages, no chosen races, not even special classes – every epoch was 'immediate to God'. For the first time, perhaps, a generation of seventeenth-century scholars arose who took him at his word and who were not out to demonstrate that their period was of overwhelming and demonstrable importance in the creation of the modern world.

It was precisely this diminishment which historians of an older generation found most threatening – the liberal Hexter who (forgetting his 'splitting' proclivities and going in for a bit of 'lumping' also) thought that it made a mockery of the historical foundations of modern freedom; the radical Stone, for whom it made the modernity of manners and mentalities virtually incomprehensible; the Tory Trevor-Roper for whom it trivialized the attempt to create a civilized, ecumenical Anglo-Catholic world-order; and the Marxist Hill, for whom it involved a deadening conservatism and an end to the vision of a better and more equitable society.[128] Each had found a badge of identity in the century of revolution; and it was that identity which was now called in question.

Yet, there were indications that the new relativism was a heuristic device or a strategic corrective rather than a substantive principle. With some exceptions, revisionists lowered their sights and modified their language over the years: by the late 1980s, few called out for 'a return to the drawing board' or a root and branch recasting of British history any more.[129] Some reaffirmed their belief in a 'modulated' and defensive but, none the less, real parliamentary progress towards liberty; others, however doubtful about changes before 1640, believed that the next twenty years saw a fundamental shift from selective to elective politics.[130] Others, again, found in the whole period the birth-pangs of a single market economy, a Protestant nationalism, a modern British state. Many still attributed the breakdown of religious consensus, and the subsequent division of the religious nation into Anglican and Nonconformist communities, to the provocations of Laudianism and the subsequent Puritan backlash; or associated the mid-century turmoil with the emergence of new values: a 'cultural' transformation which lined up the English Civil War with a similarly reconstituted French Revolution.[131] By 1993, Hill was able to write off the revisionists also: they had made 'some useful contributions', he wrote, but 'we can now write off their more fanciful theories and get back to social interpretations'.[132]

7

Revolution as Text and Discourse

On the survival of the revolutionary paradigm as a cultural or literary phenomenon, and on the attractions and challenges of 'discourse analysis' to this updated radical reading.

7.1   CULTURAL REVOLUTION

By the 1980s, Marxist and Marxisant history had long ceased to be primarily about the social underpinning of high political events, but had become the history of ideological and cultural determinations in their own right. The English Revolution was no longer viewed as a socio-economic laboratory of modernity, but as a radical gymnasium – a cauldron of novel and unconventional ideas. The shift from Old Left to New Left, from 'the industrious middling sort' who were eventually to control the world, to the 'roving masterless men' who wished, but failed, to turn it upside down, was marked by an enlarged definition of the political also.[1] For the public domain could no longer be limited to high political action and argument from the world of Westminster or the Putney Debates, but must also refer to words and deeds which occurred at a communal, domestic or what might once have been considered, a personal level. The whole idea of a private or domestic sphere was, of course, under challenge in the 1970s and 1980s; and it was widely argued that the label was a construct of precisely the male bourgeois ideology which the seventeenth century brought into being – the haven of possessive individualism's heartless world. 'The personal is political' was a motto on which feminists and Sir Robert Filmer might be said to agree; so that collapsing the categories served respectable historical ends as well as 'politically correct' agendas.[2]

Investigation of these matters, for the most part carried out by 'historians from below', appeared to suggest that the communi-

252

ties of sixteenth- and seventeenth-century England were changing rather rapidly and were experiencing many of the pressures
and anxieties associated with the impact of the unfamiliar and
unpredictable. By and large, the historians of the 1980s had abandoned the model of a society trapped in its ecological envelope,
subsistence economy and deferential value system, and had opted
for something much more dynamic and disturbing. The demographic explosion – a population which almost doubled between
1500 and 1640 – and the problems which stemmed from it: land
hunger, inflation, agrarian change, increased mobility, vagrancy,
urban growth and decay, unemployment, declining living standards, the swelling numbers of the poor, placed enormous strains
on tightly knit traditional communities. For these changes, unsettling in themselves, produced a great economic divide: there
were winners and losers, 'unprecedented opportunities for profit
for those who supplied the market, and, at the same time, the
gradual impoverishment of those who depended for their living
upon wages or fixed incomes'. There was, indeed, as Stone had
argued, a swelling of the ranks and an increase in the prosperity
of the gentry (just as there was a similar burgeoning of the bourgeoisie in pre-revolutionary France), greater opportunities for
profitable landownership, more competition, altered relationships
with tenants and neighbours. The transformation of the landowning
classes was paralleled by complex development amongst the 'middling sort' – the upper yeomanry, tradesmen and artificers – as
some expanded their holdings and became commercial farmers
or successful merchants, whilst others, without the resources to
cope with rising costs, subdivided their tenements, sold off their
businesses and drifted into marginality and poverty. At the bottom of the social ladder, the impact of social change was more
clear cut: a widening of the gap between the comfortably off and
the poor, the emergence of a landless underclass dependent on
parish-based poor relief or forced into vagrancy – the masterless
men who struck such fear into Elizabethan and Jacobean moralists.[3]

The most interesting and plausible links between these patterns
of social change and the events known as the English Revolution
– viewed not as a self-contained arena of 'high politics' but as a
theatre of popular action – were now, however, widely assumed
to be 'cultural' ones. As we have seen, Hill had moved his work
progressively from the cellar to the attic, and had explored – in
increasingly flexible and unorthodox ways – the cultural

components of new religious beliefs and practices; in a number of especially suggestive Weberian essays, he had described the 'spiritualization' of the Protestant 'household' and the creation of new tightly controlled units of religious reproduction.[4] In his trailblazing but schematic and much criticized account of *The Family, Sex and Marriage in England*, Stone had traced the emergence in the sixteenth and seventeenth centuries of the 'restrictive patriarchal nuclear family', a counterpart, he believed, to the decline of clientage, the extension of the state and the missionary success of English Protestantism: a vale of connubial sorrows between the rather 'bleak and impersonal' plateaus of the 'open lineage family' and the smiling uplands of the companionate marriage.[5]

A number of younger historians – Keith Thomas, William Hunt, Keith Wrightson, Paul Seaver and especially David Underdown – had begun to unravel what was increasingly regarded as the clash of cultures in prerevolutionary England:

> the emergence of two quite different . . . responses to the problems of the time. On the one hand . . . those who put their trust in the traditional conception of the harmonious, vertically integrated society – a society in which the old bonds of paternalism, deference and good neighbourliness were expressed in familiar religious and communal rituals . . . On the other hand . . . those – mostly among the gentry and middling sort of the new parish elites – who wished to emphasize the moral and cultural distinctions which marked them off from their poorer, less disciplined neighbours and to use their power to reform society according to their own principles of order and godliness.[6]

Within 'the ruling class', court and country, so unsatisfactory as political labels, had always retained some plausibility as cultural denominators; and in the 1970s and 1980s, a number of historians of seventeenth-century art and literature explored the interplay of these overlapping but also distinctive and often divisive cultural 'styles'. What emerged was not the simple polarity propounded by Zagorin and Stone, but a subtler and more unsettling relationship. Under Charles, the court no longer resembled the cesspool of Jacobean moralists; nor was its culture the 'escapist self-regarding fantasy' of conventional accounts – art mirrored life and the masque, for example, was a political statement, not a frivolity. But Charles's court no longer reached out to the community as had the less well-regulated regimens of Elizabeth and even James I. Characterized by 'formality, distance and privacy', it bore the stamp of a monarch, frigid, decorous, authoritarian by instinct – who wished to regulate and reform society from the top downwards and who only knew how to do it in a tone of 'repeated hectoring enquiry'. Similarly, country values were often ambiguous. There was the court's 'country', the apolitical pastoral retreat where gentlemen were supposed to fulfil their traditional responsibilities of hospitality and good management. But there was, also, a very different country ideal derived from the Renaissance perception of public man as citizen and counsellor rather than subject, an Elizabethan imperative towards Protestant vigilance, and an even more pronouncedly Calvinist commitment to active cooperation in God's purposes: a civic consciousness which Charles and his advisers regarded as socially disruptive and politically threatening.[7]

What was now suggested was a second and much more bitter cultural split further down the social scale between the emerging parish elites, traditional local families and an unreformed and frightening underclass. The keys to this process were probably 'in the last analysis' demographic and economic – the fissures produced by the proliferation of middling estates and the exponential growth of 'the poor' – but they were more immediately educational and religious.[8] 'The educational revolution', adumbrated by Stone way back in 1964, and given detailed substance in the work of David Cressy, Margaret Spufford, Thomas Laqueur, Wilfred Prest and others, opened up a new divide between those who were able to avail themselves of the new opportunities and those who were not: 'educational expansion produced, not a literate society but a hierarchy of illiteracy which faithfully mirrored the hierarchy of wealth and status'.[9] In the higher reaches, the intelligentsia had ceased to be a subset of the clergy and the aristocracy, but had come to include a significant proportion of the propertied laity also. According to one conspiratorial scenario, it now constituted a pariah stratum: disaffected, 'alienated' intellectuals looking for work and finding trouble – the 1000 odd university graduates, lawyers and 'seditious ministers' whom Thomas Hobbes (anticipating Edmund Burke and Hermann Goering) would happily have had 'massacred' in 1640.[10] Among the newly literate, print culture, it was argued, ushered in the first age of the autodidact: intensive and imaginative readers, whose relation to the traditional or the official culture was supposedly oblique and sometimes subversive. And at the bottom of the social ladder, illiteracy, once a characteristic of the vast majority of the common people, now became 'a special characteristic of the poor'.[11]

But it was Puritan 'godliness' which really polarized communities: the attempt on the part of a new moral elite of parish notables and county magistrates to stamp out immorality, disorder and superstition, impose a hierarchy of merit, respectability, hard-work and property on hitherto more casually run neighbourhoods, and at the same time provide relief for the rapidly growing numbers of deserving poor: the process unforgettably conveyed by David Underdown's story of the 'cultural revolution' in seventeenth-century Dorchester.[12] Here – aided by 'Fire from heaven', the premonitory conflagration that destroyed much of the town in 1613 – the Puritan rector, John White, was able to galvanize a hitherto unregenerate community into an extraordinary outburst of collective piety. The next thirty years saw the collapse of the illegitimacy rates, an almost equally striking decline in the numbers of pregnant brides, an extensive but selective system of public relief, a planned programme of godly migration to New England, and an unprecedented outpouring of Protestant philanthropy. But piety was the fruit of discipline and control; and the assault on vice and sin bitterly divided the community: there were many upholders of the old permissive culture of neighbourliness and good fellowship, who thought it a dark day when John White first mounted the pulpit of Holy Trinity. Plain dislike of the relentless prying and snooping, accusations of double standards or 'class' purposes – the suspicion that moral reformation filled godly pockets – anonymous 'libels', public brawls, 'schisms' and 'ill-humours', the resentment of the young and high-spirited at middle-aged interference, of the rebellious lower orders at new oligarchic controls, of the traditional county elite at being lectured by upstart town magistrates, and of factious elements within the Corporation who found the new ways uncomfortable and uncharitable or who disliked being elbowed aside by upwardly mobile newcomers: these, too, were symptoms of the cultural revolution. For there is no doubt that the John Whites of this world were a sword to divide not to unite communities. And even if – as in the case at Dorchester – the enemies of godly reformation were quickly routed, the embattled psychology, predestinarian theology and flagrantly interventionist philosophy of the righteous made the ideal of an all-inclusive harmonious parish utterly unrealizable.[13]

By 1640, these moral and cultural divisions had bitten deep

into the fabric of English communal life; and in the decades before the Civil War they assumed political significance also. The court's undisguised anti-Puritanism, its patronage of traditional festivals and ceremonies, its Book of Sports, which encouraged recreational activities on the Sabbath, the deliberate effort in certain areas to revive popular pastimes – an 'invention of tradition', frequently the work of politically and culturally self-conscious outsiders which paralleled the activities of Puritan reformers – projected these battles over church ales and maypoles on to the stage of 'high politics'.[14] And it was these divisions which, according to Underdown, fatally undermined the search for consensus in 1640 and 1641. Through oaths of loyalty, petitions and counter-petitions, rival systems of values were skilfully translated into a language of political affiliation during the pre-war crisis of the Long Parliament. And when the war came, its most resonant stereotypes were the cultural ones which had grown up over the previous generation – the flashy, drunken 'Cavalier rogue' and the hypocritical, sermon crazy 'Roundhead dog' – as people on both sides 'engaged in symbolic behaviour to assert their identities'. The trail of burnt altar rails, broken stained glass and vandalized statuary provided the most visible and notorious inventory of parliamentary success; and the return of Charles II resembled 'a protracted May-Day celebration', the fountains running with wine, Morris dances on the village green, a 'Cakes and Ale' Restoration.[15]

Civil war is always hell, but the peculiar bitterness and destructiveness of the conflict owed much, in the opinion of Underdown, to the cultural 'street fights' of the previous decades. Localism did not necessarily mean neutralism; and if the English Civil War was not the tidy military exercise derived from a socially determinist gazetteer – a version 'time and again discredited by detailed local studies' – it was also not a confused welter of county struggles in which the common people either followed their superiors or tried to protect themselves and their communities from the armies on both sides. Many below the level of gentry did play an active role; they did choose sides. But they did not necessarily or overwhelmingly choose Parliament's. Underdown did not fall back on 'the people did it' scenario, enunciated by Hill and enlarged in Manning's account of the 'progressive' militancy of the middling sort. Indeed, not the least of his achievements was the recovery of 'popular Royalism' in the rich veins of a common festive culture, which rendered the Puritans' cultural revolution something of a forlorn crusade, and the Restoration a genuinely popular and restorative enterprise – an account which was entirely consistent with Thomas's compelling elucidation of a persistent old regime of folk belief and practice and with the emerging revisionist orthodoxy of a later and shallower Protestant Reformation.[16]

In the last analysis the English Revolution was brought about by a profound division which had emerged amongst the English people over the previous half-century about the moral basis of their community; and the Revolution marked an 'unsuccessful attempt to resolve the conflict by imposing a particular view of the moral order articulated in the culture of the Puritan middling sort'.[17] Underdown's model appeared to reinstate at the local level the aggressive evangelizing Puritanism which had been seriously undercut at the level of ecclesiastical politics and official theology by a consensus 'religion of Protestants': the Puritan Revolution still had life, it seemed, in places like Dorchester and Banbury. In other ways, as well, the detailed textures of his work appeared to provide a bridge between the hitherto introverted and intractable lowlands of provincial history and the commanding heights of national politics, and between the largely static anthropology of popular culture and the peculiar dynamics of a seventeenth-century English Revolution.[18]

There was much about the model which was, however, reassuringly familiar. Although the analysis was far subtler than a conflict between traditionalism and modernity would indicate – some of the best pages of his somewhat unfortunately entitled study of *Revel, Riot and Rebellion* were devoted to Laudianism and Caroline Puritanism as 'rival and conflicting evangelisms' seeking to assimilate or suppress the old festive culture – it coincided sufficiently well with the general theory of social transformation adumbrated by Marx, Weber, Hill and Stone not to cause serious dismay. Underdown did not really doubt that Puritanism had a particular appeal to the upwardly mobile: that it was distinctively a religion of the middling sort. Nor, despite the manifest authoritarianism of such as John White's attempt to create a new collective ethos in Dorchester, did he really question the equation of Puritanism and individualism: a theme engagingly illustrated in the physical and moral geography of football (a more or less ritualized conflict between communities dominant in the more stable and harmonious nucleated villages) and stoolball (a more individualized confrontation better suited to more fragmented wood-pasture villages where cultural and religious change was most marked).[19] Puritanism represented a transitional effort to give the new order a particular moral form: not so much a 'false' as a redirected and temporary 'social consciousness'. In its way, he suggested in a revealing autobiographical aside, it resembled the welfare state experiment of the 1940s, 'when to many people it seemed possible that we might be able to build a better world and that there was something else to life beyond the mere pursuit of our own self interest'. Like the heavenly city of the twentieth-century social reformers, it was, of course, unsuccessful, and self-interest triumphed. No wonder Hill was enthusiastic: his only complaint was its reverse-anachronism and abstinence over the semantics of class – but he added, if avoidance of the word helped to get the book 'read by the ideologically squeamish so much the better'.[20]

The study of cultural conflict in seventeenth-century England appeared, therefore, to add weight to the well-rehearsed trajectory from communal sharing to self-help and individual accumulation, and from a vertically or generationally integrated to a nucleated or *laisser-faire* society. But the gap between these paradigmatic displacements and what conventionally passed for social analysis was rather extreme: Underdown's attempt to provide an environmental explanation for the different patterns of moral or cultural behaviour struck most of his readers as ingenious but unconvincing.[21] Similarly, the attempt to align Puritanism with the middling sort – with progressive outsiders: insecure newcomers 'threatened by the soaring numbers of the poor' – still looked like an attractive thesis treading water. A religion of sheep and goats ought to have appealed to the upwardly mobile; a religion of the word ought to have been a religion of the literate. Whether this was really so, remained in doubt: was Puritanism socially specific; did it percolate downwards from the godly middle to the ungodly multitude; did communities divide along coincident cultural and socially horizontal lines? Very possibly; possibly not. There were just too many imponderables: too many maverick individuals like John White; local worthies, some of them wealthy capitalists, who rallied to the defence of conviviality; Puritans who were also poor.

The relentless reduction of religious belief to its non-religious cultural correlates also ran the danger of collapsing Puritanism into social respectability and of reinventing the killjoy stereotype that a generation of scholars thought they had banished for ever.[22] Perhaps, in some respects, the model was better suited to the physical and moral geography of America: a laboratory environment where migration had completed the task of cultural revolution, where 'Albion's Seed' was less promiscuously scattered, and where constricting communities of the righteous could be more easily located. Hill's version of Puritanism had always lacked this transatlantic dimension: not for him the little hothouses of righteous intellectuation that exercised the talents of so many American historians – the anguished struggles of Perry Miller's New England Minds grappling with the mysteries of the universe; or the eschatological visions of Sacvan Bercovitch's Puritan Jeremiahs fashioning the 'myth' of America's mission. In this, of course, he was not alone: not the least curiosity in the vast Puritan industry on both sides of the Atlantic was the comparative absence of 'Changing Places'.[23]

Be that as it may, the relationship between the Puritan orthodoxy described by cultural historians and the effervescent countercultural radicalism of the sects was a bleak and unrewarding one; the sanctimonious tramlines of White's world provided no easy *entrée* to the underground of heterodoxy and subversion which was central to the radical vision of the English Revolution. Perhaps the conventional Puritan virtues of hard work, self-discipline and personal responsibility had even less appeal now that Mrs Thatcher was kneading them into the compulsive moralism of a new conservatism. The crumbling of the political centre and the rise of the New Right was widely thought 'to obviate the need for a critical analysis of liberal humanism': since von Hayek, John Stuart Mill and John Pym offered different versions of the same ideal, the heroes of 'parliamentary democracy' were no longer worth celebrating.[24] It was the *déclassé* radical milieu that threw up the ideas and agendas which were most likely to engage the politically committed in the 1980s – issues of sexual equality and the politics of gender, generational continuity and rupture, libertarian rights and the struggle against repressive values, recalcitrant modes of thought and personal behaviour which resisted conventional social analysis: 'when history is making a daring leap forward, it does not find its agents among the solid men in the ruck of any class but among the [male and female] skirmishers on the flanks'.[25]

7.2 CULTURAL MATERIALISM

There were, therefore, reasons on the Left as well as on the Right for the retreat from social determination. Socio-economic categories were the notations of the capitalist order not those of socialism as an emancipatory project: as Leavis had always maintained, and as New Left critics now admitted, the theoretical reductionism of dialectical materialism mirrored the real reductions of bourgeois society.[26] 'Culture' had always been celebrated by the New Left as the most effective prophylactic against such devaluations: the term which, in Raymond Williams' words, 'more conveniently ... than society as it had come to be used ... indicates a total human order' – a 'structure of feeling' which places greater emphasis on the 'lived texture of the society' and was 'closer by its associations of inwardness, to subjective experience'.[27]

In the 1970s, Williams had discovered a theory of the specifics of 'cultural production within historical materialism', which explained how a system of shared values and a common language could, none the less, represent the interests of a particular class, and how a cultural product could be limited by and transcend the moment of its production.[28] His major complaint about traditional Marxism was now not so much that it mechanized historical processes, as that it etherialized superstructure: that it was not materialist enough. The country house poems, pastoral romances and aristocratic epithalamiums of early Stuart England could not be detached from their rural or historical setting. But they did not merely 'reflect' country life; they served as a 'social compliment' – 'to ratify and bless the landowner or, by a characteristic reification, his house'. They also existed as 'myths', which 'culturally reproduced' complex social relationships, transforming historical peculiarities into 'heritage'.[29]

Just as it had to be recognized that a Jacobean house was not just 'a nice place to visit' but a contested historical site, so, too, it had to be registered that one of the contestants – the 'rural idiots', 'barbarians and semi-barbarians' who bore the weight of these supposedly 'classless' and 'timeless' constructions – has 'for the last forty years [been] the main revolutionary force in the world'.[30] Williams was increasingly critical of his earlier gradualist assumptions: 'our interpretation of revolution as a slow and peaceful growth ... is at best a local experience ... at worst a sustained false consciousness'.[31] As so often in his career, his political path was idiosyncratic: while his peers progressively distanced themselves from the Marxism of their youth, he swam steadily against the current, an evolution marked, politically, by commitment to a variety of radical libertarian and socialist groups; intellectually, by the publication – less than a year after Thompson's anathema on continental theory – of *Marxism and Literature* in 1977.[32]

In the introduction, he wrote of his excitement on first 'contact' with the rich and varied tradition of Western Marxism, and his belief that it offered a more promising solution to the intellectual deadlock that afflicted socialist thought in Britain, than the native 'culturalism' he had articulated in the late 1950s and 1960s. Western Marxism, as Perry Anderson explained, was primarily concerned with the study of superstructures: initially, it had celebrated the emancipatory potential of culture as human 'self-fashioning'; subsequently, as the revolutionary lights went out over Europe, it had come to recognize its debilitating characteristics as 'ideology'. Cultural production was commensurate in its materiality with other forms of material production, through which societies sustained and reproduced themselves.[33]

But if literature and language were material, what was the relationship between culture and society? Clearly the old metaphor of determination and reflection was quite inadequate; and Williams canvassed a number of replacements before discovering in the writings of Antonio Gramsci a dynamic which resolved the culturalist and Marxist tensions in his work, and appeared to explain how cultural practices could be basic but not disembodied.[34] The 'keyword' was 'hegemony', which was more comprehensive than 'ideology' in recognizing the wholeness of the 'lived social process' and more 'realistically' attuned than 'culture' to 'specific distributions and power and influence'. This hegemony could be articulated in a number of different ways: through 'traditions' – not the inert hangover of some Marxist analysis, but constructions, sometimes tied to practical continuities, sometimes 'invented', always selective – and through a myriad of discrete and identifiable 'institutions'. But the complexity could also be registered in a diachronic manner by studying the interplay of 'dominant', 'residual' and 'emergent' modes within cultures: variables more finely tuned to the complexities of the historical process than the crude epochal notations of conventional Marxist history.[35]

For Williams, as for Thompson, a dominant, effective or hegemonic culture was 'materially produced by the practices of self-conscious agents': something 'created' not 'given', involving 'an active process' of exclusion, incorporation and contestation of other modes or elements of cultural stratification. By residual, he referred to features within the dominant culture formed in the past but still deployed as active ingredients of the present. By emergent, on the other hand – and it was this sphere which, naturally enough, engaged his sympathies – he thought of the creation of new meanings, values and relationships 'substantially alternative or oppositional to the dominant culture'. Sometimes, they 'actively anticipated subsequent mutations'; sometimes, however, they denoted 'spheres of practice or of meaning which, from its own limited character or its profound deformation, the dominant culture [was] unable . . . to recognize' – the stubbornly 'subaltern', the excluded 'other'. And these genuinely counter-hegemonic modes had, in turn, to be distinguished from strategies of incorporation or adaptation within the dominant culture – from the cult of the 'novel' as opposed to 'the shock of the new'. The triadic formulation did not exhaust the complexity of cultural fashioning or Williams' searching, rhetorically tortuous, analysis of it, but for 'cultural materialists' it was to provide a particularly useful code for registering 'the complex interrelations between movements . . . within and beyond an effective dominance'.[36] It also enabled them – and this was undoubtedly part of its appeal in the 1970s and 1980s – to tease out 'contradictions' in the contemporary scene, which resisted traditional Marxist analysis.

The mid 1970s witnessed what Gramsci would have called an organic crisis of British political culture: a 'profound restructuring of ideological discourses'. It was usually dubbed 'Thatcherism', but Thatcherism predated Mrs Thatcher's electoral victory by some years; indeed, Stuart Hall was to situate it very precisely in 1975, 'right in the middle of Mr. Callaghan's solar plexus'.[37] All the same, Mrs Thatcher's project was different: not government but 'a long historical occupancy of power', not business as usual but changing the political agenda, not manipulating the state apparatus but dismantling it, not managing the economy but 'privatizing' it. And her reconstituted conservatism was not the old paternalism of the shires, but a new hard-faced, utilitarian conservatism of the dormitory suburbs: what Hall later defined as a form of 'regressive modernization'.[38] In the aftermath of 1919 – a socialist turning point where Europe failed to turn – Gramsci had confronted just such another historic reversal of the revolutionary project; and he had written under the shadow of an even more virulent 'authoritarian populism'. Little wonder that his reflections on the crisis of his time seemed so apposite to the Left in the late 1970s. For what appeared to be occurring in Britain was what Gramsci had referred to as the formation of a new 'organic ideology'. Such an ideology was not necessarily entirely coherent – effective or 'organic' ideologies rarely were – but it united the residual themes of 'One Nation' Toryism with the aggressively emergent repertoire of a revived neo-liberalism; and it successfully appealed to different identities and different aspirations.[39]

Up to this point, Stuart Hall's diagnosis of 'The Great Moving Right Show' was unproblematic. But Hall's analysis of Thatcherism as a structurally defined ideology was too pessimistic not to be controversial. Even more of an outsider than Raymond Williams: a Jamaican Rhodes scholar and an early editor of *New Left Review*, he had become the Director of the Centre for Contemporary Cultural Studies at Birmingham University in 1968. Under his leadership, the centre became the institutional centre of the new 'discipline'. It also developed a distinctive position, sympathetic to the 'structural' tendencies within 'continental' Marxist theory and critical of what it detected as Williams' residual 'humanism'. According to Hall – and Terry Eagleton put the point more forcefully – for all the up-to-date Gramscian neologisms, Williams' approach was still characterized by an emphasis on creative agency and the 'authenticating test of experience'.[40] Hall shared none of Williams' idealization of working-class culture. What Williams viewed as a communal tradition and a reservoir of socialist potential, he saw as a repertoire of attitudes and prejudices, with no intrinsic class meaning – a discourse 'owned' by none, which could easily be reconstituted, so as 'to construct the people into a populist political subject: with and not against the power block': Thatcherism was able to constitute itself as a perfectly genuine version of working class culture and enjoy the support of those whose interests it could not be said to serve.[41]

Williams found the 'block diagnosis' of Thatcherism totally unacceptable, and not just on political grounds because it 'taught despair and political disarmament in a social situation which was always more diverse, more volatile and more temporary', and because it underestimated the continued resistance of the miners, the unemployed and the new popular forces – 'resources of hope'

– which, he was sure, were mustering in the wings; but, more fundamentally, because it relegated all but the dominant elements within culture and belittled creative human agency.[42] The Althusserian mode, which turned whole peoples into 'mere carriers of the structures of a corrupt ideology', was bound in the end to marginalize history, also: to turn it into just another 'discursive regime . . . through which the maintenance or transformation of the past as a set of currently existing realities is regulated'. These differences over culturalist and structuralist appropriations of Gramsci, variant readings of Thatcherism and resistance to it, the role of history as the 'ultimate ground' of understanding or simply an optional code among many, and over the control of language through authorial experience or what one commentator was to anathematize as a 'Descent into Discourse' – updated expressions of the familiar tension between those who emphasized human autonomy and those who concentrated on the unchosen conditions which constrained and fashioned it – were to be of some importance in the continued debate over England's past and the place of cultural production within it.[43]

An intense engagement with literature and language had always characterized the English Marxist historians. Some of the enthusiasm, no doubt, proceeded from a pure and simple love of English prose and poetry, which united Thompson, Hill, Kiernan, Morton and Jack Lindsay – in 1988, Hill was to speak of this as the strongest of all their professional ties. Some of it went back to the formative influence of the popular Left criticism of the 1930s; some, to the theme of 'national traditions' embedded in a radical literary heritage which had been placed so high on the agendas of the Communist Party and the First New Left. Some of it also stemmed from their desire to communicate with a wider public, and their belief that the combined study of literature and history would protect both subjects from the isolation and scholasticism of the university discipline. On his retirement from Balliol, Hill was to work with the Open University, where 'multimedia', interdisciplinary courses were being developed: it is surely no accident that his deepening interest in Milton, Bunyan and the Bible coincided with his involvement in the Open University Course on *Seventeenth Century England: A Changing Culture*.[44]

The focus of Hill's work lay at the junction of social and intellectual history; and his understanding of the terrain was almost entirely based on printed materials. His knowledge of these texts, however, was encyclopaedic and also very intimate. He was as adept at making a little go a long way – drawing out of a sentence or a stanza a whole range of meanings and connections – as he was in deploying an oceanic range of sources on a particular issue. But the growing sophistication of his textual investigations was not matched by a corresponding deepening of social analysis. The result was that his writing came to resemble a type of literary history: like Monsieur Jourdain speaking prose, what he practised without ever giving it so grand a name, was, in fact, 'cultural materialism'. Naturally enough, and with what Margot Heinemann referred to as 'alarming modesty', he disclaimed any literary expertise; and it was true that his approach was disarmingly – sometimes deceptively – straightforward and biographical, concerned with content rather than with verbal texture, style or genre: that he lacked the insight into the creative process or the poetic imagination which, alone of the Marxist historians, E. P. Thompson possessed.[45]

'Cultural materialism', as the study of intellectual production within determinate social contexts, endeavoured to break down the gap between conventional literary and non-literary materials, and between writing and other cultural practices. To the extent that it was moored to Marxism, it proceeded from a conception of the social totality; to the extent that it viewed society as a contested domain, it dismissed the notion of a social homogeneity. Its starting point was a critique of formalism and the idea of an autonomous and a unitary literary tradition: a 'Well Wrought Urn' politely in the foreground, an 'Elizabethan Word Picture', the secure background. Literary work as a form of intellectual production was in some sense political work also. It was not, of course, as in 'vulgar Marxism' simply a political blueprint or a 'weapon of culture'; nor was it 'determined' in the bad old mechanical manner by economic forces or social classes. Rather, it was 'mediated' by intellectual and religious traditions and by the changing world of 'lived experience' – 'a concrete, sensory and psychological world, [which] in some respects and to some degree we can still share'.[46]

Since 'lived experience' was the measure of the text, the much proclaimed death of 'authors' was somewhat 'exaggerated'. Authors, however, were not just people who wrote and read books; they lived in society, ate, drank, went to church or to the pub, talked to friends and neighbours about the burning issues of the day. And since people are seldom consistent or coherent about their ideas and beliefs – especially during periods of intense social and political division – most texts revealed muddle, inner conflict, contradictory positions, choices made or evaded, 'sedimented layers of past attitudes, some still held, some held no longer, some problematic and in process of transformation'. They also pointed to personal and institutional pressures, ambiguities unconscious or deliberate in an environment of political repression, censorship and ready reprisal.[47] Language as an intrinsic part of the material of history was never a socially innocent 'common possession'. Nor was it 'a system of arbitrary signs' operating within 'structures', but of 'signs which . . . take on the changeable . . . social relations of a given society, so that what enters into them is the contradictory and conflict-ridden social history of the people who speak the language'.[48] There was no 'prison-house of language', which precluded the agency of men and women making their own discourse. Marxists needed to listen for the silences, and to watch for the ruptures in the written and spoken word – tell-tale indications of cultural alternatives: visions 'muted' or 'repressed', but none the less 'manifest in the world of the text' – if they were to recover the historical process in all its richness and subtlety.[49]

No one was to do more than Hill to retrieve the 'repressed context' of seventeenth-century literature, or to break down the barriers of partial historians and myopic literary critics. He had always maintained that the academic divisions of the twentieth century were an impediment to the understanding of cultures which knew such divides. The separation of history and literature had produced historians guilty of the idolatry of the manuscript document – the belief that a laundry list buried in some private archive constituted the real stuff of their subject in a way that a pamphlet, play or poem never could – and literary critics, who divorced textual artifacts from the society that produced them, and elevated disregard for authorial intention, or, indeed, existence, into an evaluative virtue.[50] In seventeenth-century studies, the separation helped to foster revisionism and 'formalism'. For it was the coincidence of pre-revolutionary tensions – in the church, in politics, in urban and village communities, and in the drama and poetry of the age – which constituted the strongest argument for a deep-seated mid-century crisis. And nowhere was the crisis more evident than in the pages of pre-revolutionary literature.[51]

Now, there was a sense in which cultural conflict, subversive questioning and interrogative scepticism were to be found, because that is what literary critics were now looking for. When 'critical theory' burst onto the placid waters of Anglo-American literary criticism in the late 1960s and early 1970s, wrenching English departments – far more completely than their history counterparts – out of their theoretical innocence, and transforming them into combat zones of 'structuralists', 'post-structuralists', 'feminists', 'new historicists', and, occasionally, 'cultural materialists', the overall effect was a radical destabilizing of texts and decentering of literature itself. For the exposure of the contestations operating through all cultural, linguistic and knowledge systems by writers like de Man, Derrida, Foucault and Greenblatt, appeared to offer a way of disarticulating texts and deconstructing histories 'in the interests of change'. Even when it fell short of a politically engaged 'cultural materialism', the new 'theory' provided plenty of grist for the Marxist mill: analysis of the representations of state power and the resistances to it, evidence of the purported fissures and conflicts of class bound societies: here a *Political Shakespeare*, pullulating with instability, subversion, radical challenge and ruling class fear; there, a feminist Milton, placed 'at the turning point of modernity', encapsulating 'the contradictory pressures' of bourgeois family structures and new 'male and female stereotypes'.[52]

Nowhere, indeed, was the fracturing and politicization of texts more evident than in sixteenth- and seventeenth-century English literary studies. The idea of the modern 'self', soliloquizing as Hamlet or Edmund the Bastard, was long familiar from the classics of English literary criticism; and the notion of the self-conscious 'authenticating' individual set over against society, as a specific bourgeois illusion – a reading derived from Marx's critique of nineteenth-century philosophical romanticism – had been taken over by writers like Caudwell and Alick West for their analysis of Elizabethan and Jacobean literature. Given these pedigrees and its deconstructive hermeneutic, it was hardly surprising that the new critical theory should have developed something of a minor industry on the making of the 'bourgeois humanist subject' in the early modern era.[53] The scenarios varied from writer to writer: in some the move was from the discontinuous selfhood of the Middle Ages to the 'unified subject of liberal humanism'; in others, it was reversed, with the coherent 'feudalist' subject replaced by the 'deadly' interiority of the 'modern'. Sometimes, a three-stage sequence was envisaged, in which the metaphysically derivative medieval identity made way for the contradictory but potentially free 'self-fashioning' subject of the Renaissance, only for this, in turn, to be replaced by the socially constricted but spiritually autonomous self of the Enlightenment; elsewhere, inevitably, the process was 'gendered', involving the humanist creator, 'potent, phallic and male – God in relation to his world'. Selectively illustrated – to put it kindly – these literary 'fictions' were often characterized by what one critic called 'Edenism' – an idealized hierarchical Middle Ages, long abandoned in medieval scholarship – and by a demonology of the bourgeois subject – a being which, according to one writer, longed for the self-immolation of suicide or for a nuclear Götterdämerung as 'the crowning affirmation of the supremacy of self'. Burckhardt, T. S. Eliot and C. S. Lewis rubbed shoulders with Foucault, Kristeva and Irrigeray; and, somehow, Mr Reagan and Mrs Thatcher usually put in an appearance too.[54]

For much of the new literary theory was overtly political. The 'liberal' notion of literature was ideologically tainted: the conventional canon, a construct which perpetuated the assumptions of unjust and repressive societies; the erasure of history and politics, an attempt to conceal its class origins and promote itself as the disinterested repository of universal values; the 'genial ecumenicalism' of humanist academe, a hegemonic device for neutering genuine opposition; the very idea of 'English' as a discipline, a substitute religion of the personal and the national, with a Leavisite professoriate standing in for the decline of an effective clerisy. The 'violence, disorder and fragmentation' revealed by de-constructive criticism opened up new possibilities. Such characterizations were not necessarily more 'accurate', but they were more open and more radical: as one stalwart put it, 'A truly historical sense of the text means recognizing its historically variable meanings; and a truly materialist criticism will, therefore, recognize that it can put *its* readings to use in the social process' – that it can 'fiction a history in the interests of change'.[55] Even if one ignored the Orwellian overtones of the more extreme pronouncements, the undisguised 'presentism' was striking. It was also quite logical. Since all knowledge systems were power systems, and since the idea of the detached observer was another ideological sham, the only appropriate tactic was open political engagement: 'I am,' said Louis Montrose – by no means a radical in this company – 'not only engaged in our necessary and continuous re-invention of Elizabethan culture, but I am also endeavouring to make that engagement participate in the reformation of our own.'[56] The textual contestations traced by critics like Catherine Belsey, Jonathan Dollimore and Terry Eagleton in large measure coincided with the social and ideological conflicts perceived by Christopher Hill. Most literary critics like to think that the study of literature has some social value: here was a historian who told them that plays and poetry were critical elements of the political and social process. Many of them – especially on the Left – wanted a version of the 'big' historical 'picture' that they could relate to their own textual analysis and their present concerns: History with a large H rather than a small contextual c. Their belief in the social embeddedness of texts, however, also made them welcome – and rely on – the detail that a historian like Hill could supply in abundance. From the perspective of the new 'cultural studies', even his defects could be considered virtues: his tendency to tidy up intellectual muddle and to elucidate the processes of continuity and change in comparatively uncomplicated ways, preserved a sense of the general layout of the landscape, attractive to literary critics who wanted their history neat. And here, we come to another irony in the study of England's revolutionary past: that the version marginalized in many conventional history departments during the 1980s achieved a sort of foundational authority within 'cultural studies' at precisely the same time. Whatever the view from the tearoom of the Institute of Historical Research, from the perspective of the new Polytechnics and West Coast campuses, where the new knowledges and taxonomies of the 1980s were being fashioned – and where 'cultural studies' was set fair to claim the role of universal subject, once proposed for the classics, history, literary criticism and sociology – Marxist Old Guard looked rather like culturalist New Guard, and revisionist New Guard like very Old Hat.[57]

7.3   CULTURAL WITNESS

In the late 1970s this was not immediately clear. Indeed, at the time of his seminal study of *Milton and the English Revolution*, Hill's reputation had suffered something of a nose-dive – a loss of standing clearly registered in the criticisms and the silences of the major 'reviews'.[58] His book was certainly to come in for an unusual amount of criticism from revisionist historians and political theorists, sophisticated New Leftists, Socialist Internationalists and unreconstructed Leavisites alike. Its starting point was the interrupted but long-standing dialogue with Leavis and the Leavisites. Indeed, one of the striking features of the literary critical wars of the seventeenth century was the persistence of old battles; Tillyard's 'World Picture' and Cleanth Brooke's 'Urn' occupied a surprisingly important niche in the demonology of cultural materialists, despite the fact that the artifacts in question had been published in 1944 and 1947 respectively – surely in 1977 or 1988, no one still believed *that*. In their time, moreover, Tillyard's nostalgic commentary on the 'residual' ideology of Tudor and Stuart society, and Brooke's hermetic study of poems as objects with 'a life of their own', came from opposite ends of the critical spectrum; and the latter's preference for formal textual investigation was a reaction against the relentless historicizing of the previous generation. Like most literary fashions, the apolitical Milton was partly a matter of dates; and there was a sense of cyclical return, as Hill, 'the aging knight of the new', sallied forth in 1977 against the literary dragons guarding the cave of history.[59]

Nor was it the case that Scrutiny had ever sought to dispense with social context – an old canard that the most cursory reading of *Drama and Society in the Age of Jonson* or of Leavis's prospectus for a seventeenth-century English School curriculum should have laid to rest.[60] Milton, however, had always been something of a special case: not for nothing was the enormously influential Leavisite guide to the period entitled *From Donne to Marvell*, with Milton reduced to a 'poor' half-mystical 'relation' of the Metaphysicals. The trouble with the Leavisite programme lay not in the absence of a social framework, but in one that marginalized conflict and contradiction: the integrated organic community could accommodate a Shakespeare, a Donne, a Marvell, even a Bunyan, but not a Milton, save as its destroyer. Equally, the Leavisite concept of a common language and a continuous literary culture as the mediating agency between writer and society, could not cope with the linguistic artifice and the self-conscious ideological design of Milton's writing. As an embattled critic of Anglo-Catholic apologetics, Leavis had refused to relocate Milton within a benign Christian tradition, as 'a repository of timeless values' in a collapsing post-war world; but he could not come to terms with Milton's partisan commitment and emotional simplification either:

the preference for the openness and complexity of the Metaphysicals was of a piece with his baffled neutralism also.[61]

Hill placed Milton right at the centre of the cultural conflict of seventeenth-century England. The early writings were full of the smoke and stir of wassail, Morris dancing, corrupt clergy, and 'two handed engines': 'passages of heavy menace' which looked forward to the explosive pamphlets of the revolutionary era. But the conventional picture of Milton, the Puritan – the Whig Milton of Macaulay and the parliamentary cause – had him fighting the wrong Civil War, participating in the wrong revolution.[62] Even in the 1630s, beyond the venerable images of 'country' Puritanism, duly decoded in the 'pastorals' of the period, Hill detected another less well-known source of Milton's ideas: an underground radicalism, embedded deep in popular culture, which could be found in lower class heresy from the fifteenth century onwards and which fully surfaced during the years of free discussion after 1640.

The triadic formula derived from his reading of the socio-economic dynamics of the Revolution, and already sketched in religious and ideological terms in his treatment of 'the revolt within the revolution', was now given a fully fledged cultural status also. Alongside the dominant and emergent cultures of 'court' and 'country' was a third body of ideas growing up within the latter. Like mainstream Puritanism, it was anti-clerical, biblical and oppositionist; but it was also unorthodox, speculative and socially subversive. Or, as Hill was to put it in a novel reformulation of the Trinity in 1984, there were three Gods at work in the English Revolution: there was the God of Romans xiii who sanctified the existing order; there was the Old Testament God, invoked by Puritan preachers and parliamentarians in their struggles against the unrighteous. But there was a third God also, 'a God who . . . was to be found in every believer', a God who spoke in the apocalyptic voice of Daniel and the Revelation: God, the 'mighty Leveller', the revolutionary God of Abiezer Coppe, George Foster and Lawrence Clarkson, who would come 'as a thief in the night' to seize 'the purse' of the 'Appropriator', chop off 'the neck of horrid pride' and 'make the low and the poor equal with the rich'.[63]

Milton's position lay at the junction between these second and third cultures. He was never a Leveller, a Ranter or a Muggletonian – often, indeed, his opinions 'developed in conscious disagreement' with them – but he lived 'in a state of permanent dialogue with radical views which he could not wholly accept, yet some of which greatly attracted him: 'If we think of two eccentric circles, one representing the ideas of traditional Puritanism, the other those of the radical milieu, Milton's ideas form a third circle concentric to neither of these but overlapping both.'[64] Thus, the assault on 'prelatical duncery' in the early 1640s and the defence of the regicide Republic in 1651 coincided with the emergent public culture of the time, though, even here, the iconoclastic fury of his writing went far beyond his sponsors' limited ambitions. But the pamphlets on divorce, education and freedom of the press reached far beyond the holy circle of Puritan orthodoxy. And 'his dearest and best possession', and the 'taking-off point' for the great poems – the amalgam of biblical proof texts, Ramist logic, and rationalizing theology, *Of Christian Doctrine*, which he wrote and rewrote during the last decades of his life – was shot through with the most militant heresies of the age: views which, under the Blasphemy Ordinance of 1648 and on a conservative estimate, would have earned him two and a half death sentences and four life imprisonments.[65]

He was a Mortalist, denying the separation of the body and soul; an anti-Trinitarian, denying Christ's divinity; a radical Arminian or Pelagian, repudiating the doctrine of predestined damnation. He shared the apocalyptic millenarian expectations of many of his contemporaries; he was a materialist of sorts; he defended casual adultery; he teetered on the edge of Antinomianism. Hill suggested a whole range of 'elective affinities' between Milton and the Sectaries; indeed, the group that shared more of his beliefs than any comprised the followers of John Reeve and Lodowick Muggleton, the 'two last witnesses' of the Book of Revelation, whom even the Master of Balliol had hitherto assigned to the 'lunatic fringe'.[66] According to Hill, these 'links' were established early, in Milton's convivial undergraduate years at Cambridge, and were enormously strengthened during the 1640s and 1650s when radical ideas circulated freely. Though he associated with this world, however, he was never fully of it: his materialism never became a pantheism; he never renounced the doctrine of the elect; he accepted judicial oaths; he clung on to the formulations of the Bible. A radical fellow traveller, a perplexed 'middle of the road' revolutionary, 'a two-and-a-half culture man with a foot in both camps', he was constantly drawn to ideas that another part of him strongly disapproved. And it was this uncertainty at the heart of Milton's personality – the unresolved dialectic of discipline and liberty, predestination and freewill, reason and passion, godly élitism and radicalism, bourgeois rights and social responsibility, self-government and good government – that explained the tensions and also the greatness of his poetry.[67]

'Paradise Lost is a poem not a historical document.' Yet, Hill's Milton was 'always a politician', and the epic poems in large measure a continuation of revolutionary prose by other means. His political writings during the revolutionary era had to be seen as 'a series of attempts to unite the nation, or rather the second and third cultures' – against the forces of evil. For Milton – and it was a measure of his revolutionary commitment – there were no enemies to the 'Left': he never attacked the Levellers; never reneged on the Protectorate either. Despite his disappointments – and Hill suggested that by the early 1650s he realized that things had gone badly wrong – he still clung to the belief that God was leading the nation to the promised land. As late as 1660, he was to defend the republican cause in print in a last 'improvised attempt to reunite the radical coalition'. The return to Egyptian bondage was, therefore, a terrible blow, 'almost an act of divine betrayal'. For he never fully accepted the Restoration; and to some degree, the great poems were an act of defiance against the new Pharaohs. He could not write revolutionary prose any more – the censorship laws would not allow that. And so he redirected his political passions and his heretical beliefs into epic verse: expressed in the language of myth and veiled allusion – a veritable labyrinth of political and religious subversion – his reflections on the causes of present revolutionary discontents.[68]

The Cause was justified and God had let it fail: 'what had happened was arbitrary, unjust and unfair'. Wasn't God, then, also on trial? But Milton would not go all the way with the radicals and indict the God of 1660 as a wicked God; and Hill was not prepared to follow the logic of William Empson's famous deconstruction of 'Milton's God' as the corrupter of Satan and the tempter of Eve. For Milton to believe that would have made his life and work quite meaningless: his declared task was, after all, 'to justify the ways of God to Men', even if that meant most of all, 'to Milton'. His way out was partly heretical – a function of his Pelagian and anti-Trinitarian beliefs – an increased emphasis on free will, human agency and responsibility in terrestrial affairs; and a splitting of the Godhead: the one, a distant, abstract, unappealing Father whose will is Fate; the other, a human rather than fully divine Son, who 'salvages something of man's dignity, freedom and responsibility from the wreckage'. But it was historically revisionist also. Adam and Eve were tempted and they fell; and with them fell their 'little state'. The English, too, rejected the role of chosen people. The avarice and ambition of their leaders, the irreligious speculations of the radicals, the passivity and conservatism of the rank and file, the old idolatry of kingship, sensuality, 'short cuts', 'cowardly compromises', all played their part; so that 1660 was a judgement on revolutionary misdeeds, the culmination of a process of corruption, not a sudden act of undeserved divine retribution.[69]

'Paradise Lost', then, was not simply a meditation on the Fall of Man, but on the collapse of the Good Old Cause as well; and its argument was an index of Milton's attempts to come to terms with the failure of God's servants and the ostensible judgement of God, in the guise of fate or historical necessity, against them. The poetry was, of course, invariably oblique and often deliberately deceptive – Milton was 'a marked man' and his friends were relieved at the skill with which he covered his tracks. But the enormously rich content, the very intellectual strategies of the text, only made sense when one returned them to the historical context of the Revolution and its aftermath, and read them off against the complexity of Milton's radical and revolutionary politics. The inconsistencies and equivocations which had puzzled so many readers were largely to be explained by the uneasy position that Milton occupied within the radical spectrum: half accepting, half rejecting Fate; resigned to the Restoration as an historical event, repudiating it utterly as a providential fiat; half contrite, half defiant; overwhelmed by a sense of collective guilt, but kicking against the pricks of collective punishment; straddled still between the second and the third cultures. So that he was not, as Blake surmised, 'of the devil's party without knowing it: part of him knew that part of him was'.[70]

In 'Paradise Lost', Milton seemed to envisage a 'new dark age' in which God's servants could only 'keep the truth pure and hand it on'. But 1660 was not finality: the Fall is not the end; Paradise will be Regained through 'the perfect man'; the shearing, captivity and humiliation of Samson is but the prelude to the destruction of his enemies. The good would prevail; national failure could be redeemed through the righteous remnant. If only they would learn. Without the Fall, there could be no education through history and experience; without humiliation, no self-knowledge, no regeneration and – it was well to remember this – no revenge. Samson Agonistes was, after all, a poem in praise of political deceit and mass murder. 'As for a French patriot in 1943 or a black South African today, the question was not whether to resist but when and how to resist most effectively.'[71] 'Paradise Lost', belonging to the very moment of defeat, sent out sulphurous, confused signals; 'Paradise Regained', written when the revolutionaries had been forced to rethink and redate Christ's kingdom, was a rejection of premature political solutions; Samson Agonistes, his last published and, in Hill's view, last composed poem also, was about smiting the enemies of God – overturning the lordly Philistine oppressors – when the time was ripe.[72]

Milton and the English Revolution was possibly Hill's most ambitious book. In some ways, it was a great book. But it was much criticized. And one can see why. To begin with, much of the evidence was oblique and elusive to say the least; and many of the echoes, parallels and linkages which found their way into Hill's text were probably more of a tribute to their author's creative card index than to Milton's actual borrowings. Milton, as Hill ruefully admitted, kept his secrets to himself, but he might well have been surprised at some of the names pressed into service on his behalf.[73] Equally some of the intellectual giants, whom he did acknowledge, might have been surprised at their radical credentials. The problem, however, was not just one of selective headhunting. It was the way that Hill read texts. His common procedure was to break them down into their component parts or into 'unit ideas' and then to compare these items with a range of similar materials elsewhere – in the case of the great poems, with discrete historical events. But such a detotalizing technique – the thirty-four chapters and seventy separate sections of the book an index of its fragmentary nature – produced a tessellated mosaic of attitudes and incidents, a chaos of clear ideas. As a literary method, in particular, the technique was open to serious objection, for it undermined the actual structure and integrity of the text. In Milton's case, the weakness was doubly disabling, for what was factored out was precisely what many critics considered most important about his writing – its architecture, its internal coherence, its grand design.[74]

Historicizing commentators had long since picked up a number of contemporary allusions and hidden meanings in Milton's texts; Hill poured out a cornucopia: page after page of parallels with the actors, events and issues of the time. The character of Satan, in particular, was a veritable 'heteroglossia' of revolutionary history, 'a battleground for Milton's quarrel with himself' – and the 'most creative of all historical source miners', came up with a stunning array of contemporary 'echoes' and allusions. But Hill went further: he read the poems as historical documents. In a few unguarded moments, he even suggested that they were 'about' contemporary politics: that the story of the Fall told of the failure of the revolution – producing his own radical version of the metaphoric inversion that modelled Christ's sufferings on those of Charles I.[75]

His critics were quick to pounce on the impoverishment which followed from such a precise focusing of the poetic imagination: 'poets create poetry not reflections of reality'; and Hill's analogies and parallels weighed down the poems with superfluous ballast. Worse: they distracted attention from the nature of the creative process itself. If the litmus test was history, then Milton's province was the whole of history, human and divine: to parochialize it, was to destroy its universality – it was like reading Gibbon's 'Decline and Fall' as a commentary on the Hampshire Grenadiers and the First British Empire. If it was the poet's 'experience', then that experience was literary and scholarly as well as political, and it could be argued that the Bible and the Aeneid fired the narratives of 'Paradise Lost' more than the English Civil War. There was a world of the mind and the imagination, as well as a world of contemporary events; and Hill's allegorical reading of Milton's poetry – 'only appropriate to the analysis of literary works' where such parallels were intentionally constructed: a 'Gulliver's Travels' or an 'Animal Farm' – failed to address 'the process by which art came to transcend experience'.[76]

The key to Milton's life and work, according to Hill, was to be found in his revolutionary politics and radical religious ideas. Now, the most obvious sources for this reading were the political writings of the 1640s and 1650s and the hybrid heretical compendium, *Of Christian Doctrine*, published only in 1825. The writings before and after the Revolution – meaning all of his poetry – were composed under an economy of linguistic repression, and had to be read in the light of these free expressions of political and religious belief. Hill had always insisted on 'the severity and ubiquity of censorship' before 1641 and again after 1660. Designed 'to prevent the circulation of ideas among the masses', and 'to maintain ruling consensus in a deeply divided society', it drove subversive opinions underground and caused courageous writers 'to encode and disguise their protest'.[77] So that historians 'looking only at the words on the page' ran the risk of entering into 'an unwritten conspiracy with seventeenth century censors'.[78] But, as John Morrill pointed out, the mass of illustration which he collected of writings unpublished, plays withdrawn and authors punished or harassed before the Civil War, was no substitute for an analysis of the censorship laws themselves. And those who had looked at censorship not through the words not on the page, but through the study of court records and state regulations, came to a rather different conclusion: that the authorities were too inefficient and irresolute to do more than intermittently punish a minority of unlicensed printers or obstreperous critics.[79]

Listening for silences is not without its temptations, especially when the ear is attuned to a specific range of noises, audible elsewhere. In his essay on 'Censorship and English Literature', Hill suggested that the prerevolutionary situation corresponded 'more to eastern Europe today than to . . . England'. The analogy was intended to be provocative, but it undermined the whole analysis: for, if 'persecution' (as in eastern Europe) was 'only an extreme example of intentional and unintentional social pressure' (as in England), then 'camouflage and concealment' might only be an exaggeration of 'the normal situation'.[80] Censorship, in other words, operates on a continuum, and not under a simple economy of freedom and unfreedom; and to treat the texts of any period as transparencies of the author's mind, without taking account of the pressures of their particular moment of composition and publication – propaganda purposes, ties of friendship, obligations real or imagined – and then to treat these writings as a 'control', 'to throw light on what came before and after', is arguably more misleading than registering silence. Hardly surprisingly, the Milton who emerged from this selective hermeneutics of the audible, was formed in the likeness of the 1640s and 1650s – a forward looking revolutionary in the 1630s and a backward yearning radical in the 1670s. The theological compilation, *Of Christian Doctrine*, added problems of its own: built up on a card-index system, written over and revised many times, it bore all the traces of Milton's theological speculations over a period of twenty years;

and it would have been surprising if these had not included many heresies along the way. Whether they constituted Milton's 'settled' opinions – and to what extent – was another matter.[81]

But 'lived experiences' counted for more than books, and Hill's Milton got nearly all his ideas from talking to his contemporaries, and most of all from the plebeian radical thinkers whose cultural milieu he partly shared. Unfortunately, as there was virtually no evidence of contact between Milton and the radical underground, Hill was reduced to the slippery formula of a 'permanent dialogue' – 'dialogue' had a lovely dialectical ring to it; it suggested, without ever having to demonstrate, mutual influence and interaction.[82] Hill's critics had great fun with his wonderfully contorted attempts to get the notoriously fastidious 'lady of Christ's' into a pub, or down the road from his not so 'rural retreat' at Horton to the radical fun and games going on a mile away at Colnbrook – where mayors 'died of a surfeit of drink', local women got into trouble for abusing the Archbishop, and Digger emissaries were preparing their visiting cards![83] Even in the 1640s, there was little, save for some ambiguous self-promotion and highly suspect muck-raking to show for Milton's radical and heretical socializing. Presbyterian propagandists scandalized by the 'Doctrine and Discipline of Divorce' could reasonably have been expected to have included Milton in their list of subversives under the Westminster Assembly's bed; and not for the first or last time, readers of Hill were confronted by the 'strange paradox' of the country's leading radical historian relying on 'right-wing, authoritarian polemicists to construct his seventeenth-century radicals, misrepresenting polemic in the process as objective description'.[84]

As Quentin Skinner pointed out, the whole exercise was also largely unnecessary, for Milton's heresies were not the exclusive property of the radical underground; some of them were shared by Charles I's bishops; others by that scourge of the radicals, Thomas Hobbes. And they were to be encountered in many of the books which Milton owned, read and annotated. 'How many of those whom we call "Arminian" in seventeenth century England,' asked Hill, 'had read Arminius?' Milton had; and, whether Hill liked it or not, Milton was a prodigiously learned man, deeply committed to classical scholarship as well as to the Bible. His Commonplace Book attested to the intellectual preoccupations which, he said, were 'his portion in life'; and what it recorded was an immersion in humanist literature – some of it profoundly heretical – and no mention at all of Hill's radical underground. The same was true of his political ideas: the major sources were surely the classical and Renaissance republicans he quoted, rather than Levellers or Diggers he never acknowledged. If as Hill suggested, Milton was a 'great eclectic' – and there was reason to believe that some of the eclecticism came from Hill's own critical method – then it surely had more to do with the range and diversity of his intellectual borrowings than with a position half-in and half-out of the radical milieu.[85]

Hill's book was a statement about the primacy of 'lived experience' in all forms of cultural production. It was the recovery of these experiences which truly embedded texts and authors in their milieu; and it was this, in turn, which enabled twentieth-century readers to recover the meanings and intentions behind the words on the page. Milton, especially, had suffered from the academic assumption that texts should be read in the light of other texts: Hill was clearly a little tired of the intellectual daisy-chains with Plato, Origen and Lactantius at one end and Milton at the other: 'It is a prevalent donnish assumption that ideas are transmitted principally by books. But "Marxist" and Freudian ideas are held today by people who never opened a book by Marx or Freud.'[86] Just as Marx had been turned into an item of abstruse continental philosophy, so, too, Milton had been taken from the people and given to the professors. It was time to return him to his fellow seventeenth-century revolutionaries and to those who were still inspired by their words in the twentieth century.[87] Milton had always been something of an icon for the Left: a radical patriot in the 1940s, a class warrior wielding his 'iron flail' at the height of the Cold War, a humanist fighting the congealment of the human spirit in 1956, he was now a New Leftist, straddled between mainline socialism and radical splinter-groups, caught between his realism and his sympathies. But Milton's meanings were unclear: 'it is a little disconcerting,' commented Hill, 'to try to depict a man who has strong moral principles for which he would die, without being able to state clearly what those principles are and so being unable to submit them to precise rational analysis'. The admission – and it was a stunning commentary on Hill's own literary method – could well serve as an epitaph on the fragmentation of the Left in the late 1970s.[88]

Over the next decade – and he was now well into his seventies – Hill was to publish some seven more books, largely on the literary and intellectual record of the revolutionary period and its aftermath: an astonishing achievement. More than any other Marxist, he demonstrated an extraordinary capacity to move with the times, to incorporate into his work the most recent researches, even – and this was a tribute to his synthesizing skills – when they appeared to run quite counter to his own historical beliefs. There were essays on Defoe (a far more radical writer than he had once assumed), on Marvell (his sense of historic destiny now given political and religious rather than socio-economic significance), on more of Milton's radical contemporaries; there were even a few uncomfortable pieces on 'political discourse'.[89] Above all, there were the studies which culminated in the book on *John Bunyan and his Church*. The aim here, once more, was to take Bunyan out of the library and restore him to his revolutionary world: a restoration not without twentieth-century concerns and resonances. Was it just publishers' whim that gave to the English edition, in 1988 – year of the poll tax – the resoundingly populist title, *A Turbulent, Seditious and Factious People*, and to the American the rather less militant, *A Tinker and a Poor Man*?[90]

In some respects, the homely figure of Bunyan survived deep contextual immersion better than the aloof Milton. The social concerns were much more evident. No other great writer, said Hill, was 'as passionately, fiercely and theologically on the side of the poor': and he was largely successful in evoking Bunyan's humble background and calling, in highlighting his animus against the rich and powerful and his sympathy for the needy and impotent – his class consciousness or, as he was now more inclined to say, his 'class awareness' – and in elucidating the themes of dispossession (a piece of family history as well as a social concern) or vagrancy (likewise the personal baggage of a tinker and a mechanic preacher) in the great prose epics. There was real gain in being able to view *The Pilgrim's Progress* as the story, not just of the Christian's spiritual journey, but of the vagrant classes humping around their few possessions; and in being able to visualize the encounters on the way not just as representations of psychological or spiritual states, but as word-pictures of the actual terrors of the open road. Bunyan was also more easily situated in the community than was Milton; more easily located within the traditions of popular culture – and Hill's third culture now seemed closer to Underdown's folk world of ale houses, charivari, popular sports, itinerants, and vagabonds than to radical politics – 'lived experiences', which clearly worked themselves into the textures of his writing. Certainly, its deliberately allegorical character – the heavy stage machinery of castles, prisons, narrow gates, picket fences and the rest – was much better suited to the pursuit of material parallels and contemporary meanings than was Milton's more cerebral, 'high poetic' project.[91]

And yet the doubts soon crowded in. Bunyan was supposed to be part of the revolutionary world and of its radical internal diaspora; and his writings a response to social, economic, religious and political crisis. Unfortunately, even less was known of Bunyan's revolutionary experiences than of Milton's. As a young man, he appears to have served briefly in the parliamentary army; in the 1650s, he began preaching as a lay Baptist; in and out of prison during the 1660s, he was the beneficiary of 'Indulgence' in the early 1670s and again after 1678; he probably supported James II late in life. Into this biographical black hole, Hill poured copious substitute materials from the world of revolutionary politics: vibrant discussions in the army units at Newport Pagnell, possible acquaintances, hypothetical influences, other known Bedfordshire radicals, information about 'the Good Old Cause' after 1660. The world of 'may have', 'presumably was', and – by slow degrees – 'must have been', was never more in evidence. The red letter names of Harrington, Winstanley, Milton, Clarkson, Coppe and Co. flitted in and out of the narrative with a few wisps of Bunyan's biography floating between: 'for a country boy', wrote Hill of the young Bunyan's exposure to radical political debate in the New Model Army, 'to be plunged into the middle of discussions . . . on subjects which could never before have been openly talked about by ordinary people must have been an overwhelming experience' – or might have been, were there a shred of evidence that Bunyan knew or cared about these things.[92]

Bunyan's silences on matters political may have been the product of censorship and persecution; it is more likely that they sprang from quietist political beliefs. A passive millenialist, who counselled non-resistance to the instruments of the Second Coming; 'a popular preacher of the least popular of doctrines, double predestination', there was little to sustain the assertion that 'the radical discussions of the Interregnum [we]re essential' for the understanding of his writings. As far as the upside down libertarian world which rejected 'scarecrow sins' and 'inward bondages', there was evidence to the contrary. Pilgrim carried a spiritual burden on his shoulders as well as a vagrant's humpy; and Bunyan's work reverberated, not with the throb of counter-cultural debate from the 1640s and 1650s, but with the monotonous rattling of social and psychic repression: original sin and damnation, the never ending struggle for assurance of salvation, the condemnation of all but the doubly predestined elect.[93] Maybe, the traditional theme of giants and giant-killers did carry the weight of Hill's socially explicit subtexts; maybe, the evident satisfaction of Christian and Faithful, as the unregenerate were shunted off to eternal torment, was a glorification of delayed terrestrial justice; maybe, the pilgrims' pie in the sky was really as subversive as the Ranters' pie on earth – by a counter-Feuerbachian argument, 'almost a definition of sedition' – maybe, Bunyan was as socially engaged and politically shaped as Hill believed. The case remained strictly within the realms of faith – in the desire of a radical and a Marxist, who loved his *Pilgrim's Progress*, to reclaim one of the creative artists of English dissent as a child of 'the most turbulent, seditious and factious years of recorded English history' also.[94]

Hill's 'endings' invariably attempted to relate the historical terrain to twentieth-century concerns, and the message in the 1980s was 'keeping faith'. In 1972, he had still called his readers to radical political action:

> The radicals had assumed that acting was more important than speaking. 'Talking and writing books', Winstanley insisted, 'is all nothing and must die; for action is the life of all, and if thou dost not act, thou dost nothing'. It is a thought worth pondering by those who read books about the seventeenth century radicals, no less than those who write them. Were you doers or talkers only? Bunyan asked his generation. What canst thou say?[95]

A decade later, the radical doers were in full retreat. The danger was now one of apostasy, as the class of 1968 – lacking the staying power of those who had lived through the 1930s and 1940s – lapsed into cynicism or theoretical narcissism. 'In 1644,' Hill concluded his book on *The Experience of Defeat* – his symphony of sorrowful songs – 'Milton saw England as "a nation of prophets".' Where are they now'? The answer, replied Pocock in a devastating review, 'is distressingly obvious. They are where they have been before; trying to institute a rule of the saints under circumstances even less propitious than those of 1654 and 1659.' In 1984

– two years after the Falklands War, a year into Mrs Thatcher's second term – they certainly were not much in evidence on the Left. All but deserted by the Labour Movement, by repentant socialists who deplored the divisive rhetoric of class politics, Arthur Scargill's 'Rump' Union of Mineworkers was not about to dissolve the Parliament and 'summon Barebone's saints to Westminster'.[96]

7.4 REVISIONIST DISCOURSE

The picture of revolutionary experience, tempered through adversity to become the cultural witness of the survivors in unpropitious times, was attractive to the Left during the long retreat of the 1970s and 1980s, but it was also historically suspect. Arguably, all of the testifying voices were out of tune. Despite Hill's good offices, Milton was a rather cold Puritan intellectual who believed in the rule of a self-appointed spiritual elite; Marvell, an elusive and pragmatic figure – by turns a critical royalist, an exponent of *de facto* obedience to the Republic, an admirer of the Lord Protector and an outspoken critic of 'Popery and Arbitrary Power' – who could only with some violence to the irony, balance and diversity of his writings be accorded a fixed political identity.[97] Even Winstanley seemed less of the lovable socialist and a more inaccessible figure: a stranger not a village brother – his social gospel, religious and symbolic in intent, or (it was even suggested) the passing projection of personal mishap and resentment – a seeker after godly magistracy as well as natural rights, who quickly settled back into property ownership, religion and respectability, to become – of all things – a parish official and a litigant. He was not to be condemned for looking after himself and his family; and biographical revisionism did nothing to diminish the validity or significance of his work. But it did suggest that selective hagiography was not the best way of evaluating seventeenth-century radical ideas.[98]

The rogues' gallery of 'possessive individualists' or 'bourgeois humanists' – assembled by Macpherson and the cultural materialists – was arguably even more misconstrued. Harrington was increasingly seen as an 'ancient' rather than a 'modern', a civic humanist concerned with citizenship, virtue and corruption, not with trade, 'empire', or property rule – his thought entrenched within a pattern of cyclical, agrarian republicanism.[99] Contrariwise, Locke

– the contextualized Locke of Peter Laslett and Richard Ashcraft
– was depicted as a radical political activist seeking to legitimize
rebellion and electoral reform, not as a liberal apologist attempting to justify social and political inequality: all but ignored by
the revolution families after 1688, he belonged to the long seventeenth-century crisis concerned with prerogative and its abuse,
not to any categorical or predictive liberal tradition.[100]

As the proto-socialists and proto-bourgeois of the Marxist model
were reconstituted as millenarians, humanists, and classical republicans, it seemed that the whole picture of cultural division
in seventeenth-century England might have to be refashioned also.
Certainly, the notion of a secular progressive ideology of individualism and 'increase' as the uncomplicated legatee of the English
Revolution was emphatically repudiated by most of the younger
historians of 'political discourse' in early modern Britain. Quite
apart from biographical and textual criticisms – and it was widely
argued that none of the writings supported the interpretations
derived from them – it was the absence of precise linguistic and
political contexts which was most frequently urged against it by
the 'Cambridge School' associated with Quentin Skinner and John
Pocock. The history of political thought had conventionally occupied an uncomfortable niche in the Cambridge curriculum; and
its status was further reduced in the 1950s by the 'common sense'
reductions of historians and linguistic philosophers.[101] So much
so, that Peter Laslett, an unusually wide ranging student of ideas,
working on the boundaries of philosophy, politics and sociology,
was driven to announce that 'for the moment anyway political
philosophy is dead'. A few years later, however, he began to chart
its recuperation – a revival in which his own 'recovery' of Filmer
from oblivion and Locke from canonical misplacement was to
play an important part.[102]

While preparing his landmark edition of Locke's 'Two Treatises',
he had successfully attracted a gifted group of postgraduates –
amongst them Skinner, Dunn, Runciman and Pocock – who were
to build on 'the assumptions of his scholarship' long after he himself
had moved on to the study of population and household structures. Like Laslett, they focused attention on the precise contexts
of textual production; but they were also sensitive to the analytical concerns of linguistic philosophers and unusually welcoming
of new social theory. They may well have also inherited from
Laslett an extreme scepticism as to validity or appropriateness of

the Marxian method. A severe critic of the inadequacies of traditional social history – 'social description with the statics and dynamics left out' – and a champion of sociological model building, Laslett was, none the less, a vigorous and outspoken anti-Marxist – singled out by the Historians' Group as an inveterate opponent. Marxism, he was convinced, was inimical to the whole enterprise of an empirically based and philosophically sound history of political ideas. Besides, it was the wrong model for early modern England: a 'face to face' society organized around hierarchy, status, county community, household – here the future founder of the 'Cambridge Group for the History of Population and Social Structure' was visible – simply 'would not permit' the class conflicts, ideologies and revolutions of Marxist theory.[103]

In Skinner's view, textual 'performances' could never be fully explained by some general description of what society was like and how they might or might not have mirrored or legitimized it; they could only be understood through a 'closing' of the contexts of past thought in historically reliable ways. Any statement was 'the embodiment of a particular intention, on a particular occasion addressed to the solution of a particular problem'. To understand the 'illocutionary force' of a statement and the 'perlocutionary effect' it might have had on its audience, it was necessary, therefore, to study the linguistic and ideological conventions surrounding similar statements, the ways in which the author might have manipulated these conventions, and the extent to which the performance in fact challenged or reinforced them. 'Political life itself sets the main problems for political theorists', not just in the limited sense of providing the occasion and subject matter of political writing, but also by constraining its language, arguments and 'solutions'. Authorial intention not social assumption; the specific and local circumstances of textual fashioning not the metanarrative of the age; the audience or audiences addressed; the linguistic codes, political arguments and rhetorical devices deployed and avoided from the conventions available; the parallel history of contemporaneous communicative acts pertinent to the themes discussed or the languages utilized – these were the keys to meaning and significance in the history of political ideas.[104]

The work of John Pocock cut into the traditional divides of seventeenth-century intellectual history even more drastically. He, too, was concerned with performative acts in the history of political thought, but his 'Machiavellian moment' at its narrowest compass occupied three centuries of European history and stretched from the death of the Florentine to the birth of the American Republic. Where Skinner and his disciples moved from individual 'speech acts' to political contexts and linguistic conventions, Pocock was concerned with the discursive regimes and conceptual 'paradigms' which constrained political thinking in early modern times. He was also more broadly interested in the interplay of transmissive and creative processes in political thinking; more given to self-conscious reflection on the rhetorical functions of his own historical practice and of its impact on Marxist or Whig models of political and social change in early modern Britain.[105]

English political thinking had conventionally straddled 'custom' and 'grace' – a language of rights associated with an 'ascending' range of properties, jurisdictions and liberties; and an interlocking structure of authority which descended from God through kings and magistrates. Conventionally, these two political discourses had been viewed by historians as competing and opposed ideologies, but they were better described in the language of balance as the components of a *dominium politicum et regale*: a consensus which did not, of course, preclude discord and complexity. For Tudor and Stuart England also saw the emergence and extension of the languages of civic consciousness: whether as humanist counsellor, self-regulating country gentleman, Protestant patriot, Puritan saint, parliamentary representative or eventually radical soldier, Englishmen were inclined to regard politics as a theatre of purposeful political activity and not just a custom or God-given command structure. The breakdown of the framework which held these conventions together during the Civil War – the collapse of Tudor Monarchy in 1642, followed by the fragmentation of 'the Ancient Constitution' – the consequent dissolution of government and the spectre of millenarian radicalism in 1649, occasioned a number of attempts to reconstruct political authority and obedience from the ground up.[106]

Of the responses to the crisis – and one could distinguish those of Filmer, Hobbes and Harrington – it was the Harrington's *Oceana* which appeared to transcend its performative context most interestingly. Responding to a 'Machiavellian moment', which seemed to leave English society as it had the Florentine state 150 years before, at the mercy of 'fortune' or of conquest, Harrington attempted to reconstruct in an agrarian and Christian environment, and on the basis of the pre-existing codes of civic consciousness, a stable republican order which would combine legitimate authority with citizenship, political participation and civic virtue. This potent combination enabled his work to survive the collapse of the army rule it sought to legitimize, and the unexpected restoration of both monarchy and nobility. For over a hundred years, Whig political theorists were to swim in the waters of 'Oceana', not because it enclosed the radical vision of an alternative society – a millenarian enthusiasm soon snuffed out – or because it defined a nascent 'opportunity state', but because its major themes seemed to impinge on the issues which continued to dominate political life in England and America: a dialectic of virtue and corruption, civic duty and private interest, republic and empire, freehold independence and patronage, land and commerce.[107]

Pocock's great discursive arch of republicanism and civic humanism was on his own admission a peculiarly rich variety of 'tunnel history'; and he did not need to be reminded of alternative hierarchic or paternalist visions of politics and society.[108] Nor was the author of *The Ancient Constitution and Feudal Law* unaware of more familiar descriptions of liberty as a collection of historic and largely 'negative' freedoms attached to persons or to things. Indeed, both 'languages' were to survive the upheavals of the seventeenth-century to provide Burke with the core of his case against the French Revolution.[109] What was excluded from the repertoire, however, was the concept of possessive individualism. The trouble with Marxist or liberal models of political discourse in early modern Britain was not just one of false emphasis – that there was too much Winstanley or Locke and not enough Filmer – but one of linguistic and conceptual misapprehension. The terminology of class, economic interest and social ideology bore little relation to the contemporary linguistic conventions deployed: those of custom, common law maxim, godly rule, providence, political participation, public interest and virtue. Even when the words were the same, the meanings were different: property, for example, was a juridical not an economic concept – a condition of independent citizenship rather than a unit of exchange or accumulation. And in so far as vocabulary defined the character of political practice, these meanings and conventions affected the priorities of political and social history also.[110] The paradigmatic 'moments' of political debate were not those which announced social revolution or radical liberation, but those triggered by untoward political breakdown. The 'point' of most Civil War and Commonwealth texts was the search for settlement, the reconstitution of authority and 'balance'; and 'the central polemic' of the revolutionary era was not the Putney Debates but the Engagement Controversy.[111] Half a century later, the pattern was repeated: it was the issues of dissolution of government, conquest, usurpation, the legitimacy of resistance or otherwise, which dominated discussion in 1688, not the principles of natural rights, limited government or propertied oligarchy.[112]

The conceptual materials deployed in these ideological set pieces came from 'a tiny range of intellectual resources: Roman history, Roman law, Augustinian theology, Greek moral philosophy, Roman literature'; the languages were those transmitted by a Christian and classical literary tradition.[113] The dead weight of linguistic and ideological convention did not necessarily preclude radical action. What they did rule out was the concept of modernity: the nature of political activity and political discourse was essentially 'pre-technological and pre-revolutionary'.[114] It was only in the 1690s, and with some abruptness, that a paradigmatic shift in the 'structure, the morality and even the psychology of politics' set in. To the accompaniment of French wars, Dutch finance and Venetian oligarchy, political theorists started to grapple with a new vocabulary of credit, national debt, speculation, government patronage and corruption. What followed was a century long crisis of political discourse: 'a gigantic *querelle* between the individual as Roman patriot, self-defined in his sphere of civic action, and the individual in the society of private investors and professional rulers', a bitter dialogue from which both 'classical economic man and classical socialist man' were, perhaps, eventually to emerge.[115]

Clearly, the notion of a radical 'underground', spanning Hill's 1640s and Thompson's 1790s, disappeared under Pocock's very unbourgeois arches. Apart, altogether, from the well-known difficulties of charting the subterranean, Hill's radicals were too caught up in particular millennial and antinomian experiences to beget any meaningful social or secular progeny. Their conceptual and linguistic universe was disturbing, but it was also very remote: quite unlike the friendly socialist messages deciphered by Tony Benn and Ken Livingstone every May at Burford.[116] But the chief casualty was the progressivist version of English history: C. B. Macpherson was banished on far harsher terms than Christopher Hill; and his search for seventeenth-century possessive individualist origins likened to an attempted history of the early modern motor car.[117] By a nice irony, not unconnected with their need for a 'liberal' adversary, Marxists were the last believers in bourgeois revolutions and market societies: 'in contemporary scholarship', concluded Pocock in one of his many epitaphs for Macpherson, 'it is the Marxists who are the Whigs, their critics who command a dialectic'.[118]

The remapping of early modern political 'discourse' by Skinner and Pocock did much to unravel serial models of cultural and ideological change. The picture that emerged from Pocock's discursive paradigms was of a society lacking 'any concept of an indefinite secular future' or of purposeful 'revolutionary action', whose whole point was not to change the world but to secure or to interpret it.[119] Skinner's pitted terrain of early modern political thought, peopled by 'minute philosophers' crawling in and out of their linguistic trenches, driven by immediate political contingencies, and accidentally constructing in 'the course of hundreds of local ideological manoeuvres and counter-manoeuvres', the juridical edifice of the 'modern state', was equally removed from the purposeful inclines of Marxist or liberal theory. In their different ways both models left little room for human 'agency' or 'creativity'. The thinning down of 'experience' made for meanings which were largely impersonal, operating behind the backs of language users, whose linguistic actions exemplified the rules and procedures of languages they inhabited but did not control.[120] Such a history, it was argued, confused form and substance, a common political language with shared assumptions and beliefs. Methodological prescription – this was another criticism – triumphed over 'what actually happened': Thomas Kuhn's scientific 'paradigms' were imposed on the instrumental field of political expression to give the illusion of a conceptual *longue durée*; Austin's philosophical 'language games' were yoked to the actual continuities and changes of political thought, to produce an episodic and revisionist story-line. For Marxists, it was an object lesson in the dangers of a history defined in conceptual, linguistic terms, divorced from 'empirically grounded' social controls.[121]

The deconstructive idiom had additional dangers. For 'cultural materialists', its appeal lay in the exposure of the hidden power structures of all discourse. But the force relations, revealed by 'Foucaultian' analysis, were a ubiquitous, decentred, 'multiplicity' operating everywhere and nowhere. The history of Western civilization was a history of oppression – oppression of women, slave and serf populations, minority cultures, colonial victims; even its emancipatory projects were self-deceptive exercises by the oppressive culture. More of a sceptical anarchist than revolutionary Marxist, an iconoclast incongruously coopted by 'grand theory', relentlessly relativist, dismissive of historical determination of any kind – indeed, of all but the heuristic games which one played in constructing histories of the present – Foucault was a theorist with whom radical but 'realist' historians ought to have supped at the end of very long spoons. So much the more with 'cognitive minimalists' like Derrida.[122] The revelation of the sustained incoherencies and contradictions within all texts *differred* the very possibility of determinate meaning: the use of language pointed only to further language – a condition that the mythology or 'metaphysics of presence' was quite unable to cure. History itself was just another a text – 'a device', said Foucault, 'for the reduction of anxiety', a 'cunning collection of strategies' designed to bolster belief in authorial objectivity and an independent reality contained in documents.[123] The attempt to combine Marxism and deconstruction usually foundered at this point: for all the common ground, Marxism, too, was part of the 'logocentric' regime of repression in all Western 'discourse'. Little wonder that Marxists were to be found ringing humanist alarm bells also; or that Lawrence Stone, who had ridden wave after wave of 'new theory', now considered that history itself was in danger and called his fellow scholars to the barricades.[124]

Even the historically friendlier Anglo-American version of French theory was only a little further up the slippery semiological slope. The history privileged by the 'New Historicists' was episodic and often quite arbitrary: trapeze-act history, which juxtaposed a Shakespearean 'performance' and a tract on Virginia, far removed from the subject that most historians studied. In the place of chronology and sequence, it cultivated the epistemic leap from past to present; instead of olympian authorial invisibility, constant authorial intervention, reminding readers of the historical relativity and rhetorical artifice of their texts. For all the gesturing towards historical contexts, the evidence they deployed was oddly anorexic and immaterial: language was still the medium through which the world was constructed and apprehended; and historicizing texts was largely an exercise in textualizing contexts. For all the supposed 'circulation of social energy' – 'partial, fragmentary, conflictual . . . elements . . . crossed out . . . torn apart, recombined, set against each other' – it was difficult to know what was driving the merry-go-round, and where it was all going. The texts inevitably revealed subversion, but also diffusion and containment: positions which fell significantly short of true resistance. In a striking afterword to *Renaissance Self-Fashioning*, the seminal 'new historicist' study, Greenblatt explained how his original project – and the title of the book – constantly subverted itself:

> in all my texts and documents there were, so far as I could tell, no moments of pure unfettered subjectivity; indeed, the human subject itself began to seem remarkably unfree, the ideological product of power relations in a particular society. Whenever I focussed sharply upon a moment of apparently autonomous self-fashioning, I found not an epiphany of identity freely chosen but a cultural artifact.

The project which was going to liberate literature from its linguistic prison through the contingency and heterogeneity of historical context, finished up by embedding both text and context in 'a totalizing Foucaultian dystopia of power and knowledge'.[125]

The attempt to combine Marxism and gender analysis was no more successful. Despite the manifest sympathy of many socialist historians and the programmatic commitment of journals like *History Workshop* to 'feminist' history, few of the older generation were able to theorize or even to engage emotionally with issues of gender or sexual politics. The limits of understanding were quickly reached with a coincident critique of the bourgeois household or with the largely unsuccessful enterprise of bracketing modes of production, reproduction and the sexual division of labour under capitalism. The conceptual apparatus of Marxists was too closely tied to the public world of class, male solidarity and purposeful political activity to come to terms with the very different vocabularies and agendas of women's history. Even the enlarged vision of historical agency, articulated by Hill and E. P. Thompson, stopped well short of the rethinking that was required: their revolution remained deep-rootedly masculine.[126]

For historians of revolution, indeed, 'the linguistic turn' had its own particular perils. Stedman Jones's 'rethinking' of Chartism through the languages of eighteenth-century radicalism was often quoted as an example of a good Marxist fallen amongst discursive enemies.[127] But the revisionist flavour of event as text was best caught in the semiological reconstitution of the French

Revolution in the 1980s. Work on the linguistic structures and sign systems of the Revolution stimulated important new ways of 'reading' a subject long in need of historiographical rejuvenation. But the ease with which these approaches were coopted by right-wing historians like Furet and Schama was cause for concern. For the privileging of discourse seemed to come at the expense of material interest, class conflict, ideological coherence and long-term social significance. Certainly, it was difficult for the traditional class actors to breathe in the gravity-free atmosphere of symbolic myth-making, where donning a cockade, participating in a Feast of the Supreme Being, or talking about 'virtue' at the local Jacobin Club defined collective identity in rhetorical rather than solidly apprehensible social terms.[128] The myths and languages of the Revolution were revealed to be part of a discursive continuum rather than something altogether new: the rationality of the Enlightenment was inscribed in the 'rationality' of revolutionary sign. And the collapse and long-term sterility of the Revolution seemed to follow from the nature of its discourse: 'the semiotic circle [was] the absolute master of politics' – Descartes, Rousseau, Derrida and Furet, between them, hatched Thermidor. By charging historians with invention, semiotics invited consideration of the historicity of all historical thought, including its most sacred categories. Was not the Revolution itself another historians' construction, an invented tradition or myth – a 'catechism' which only survived because it served political and personal purposes?[129]

The linguistic repertoire of the English Revolution was ostensibly less rich; it 'invented' fewer symbolic forms, created fewer lasting myths. It was, therefore, rather more difficult for historians to effect the symbolic and linguistic laundering that had smartened up the 1790s, and turn the 1640s and 1650s into another semiological episode. Yet, the dominance of 'the word' was no less obvious: the English Revolution, too, was drowned in print. The linguistic explosion of 1642 was almost as striking as the revolutionary circumstances the writers and speakers were trying to explain. Lacking the theoretical guidance of Rousseau and Marx and with no experience of previous revolutions to draw on – this was Hill's verdict – they turned to the Bible for guidance. God's Word was the ultimate source of authority in intellectual as well as moral life: 'it was in biblical language, in conscious recapitulation of biblical history, with the constant aid of biblical metaphors, figures and paradigms' that contemporaries 'both understood the turbulence of their times and shaped them'. So that to say, that the Revolution was a religious or a biblical affair, was to say no more than that fishes swim in the sea and that it happened in the seventeenth century. Long abandoned as a class war and social transformation and increasingly difficult to defend as a coherent ideological revolution, the events of the 1640s and 1650s could be semiotically decked out also – as a biblical revolution.[130]

At the end of his 1993 book on *The English Bible and the Seventeenth Century Revolution*, Hill reiterated his long-standing plea for the merging of text and context. He drew an analogy between imaginative historical writing and 'retrospective poetry': like the poet, the historian spun interpretative webs by 'amalgamating disparate experience'; like the true poet, the good historian did not 'stay on the surface of events, but listened to the 'whisperings of the people' – the hidden signs of their emotional and mental life.[131] He had always been interested in the languages and myths of seventeenth-century radicals; and his well-known interpretation of the Norman Yoke – an imagined history of the ancient constitution and of lost rights – could well be considered an 'example of discourse analysis avant la lettre'. His preferred technique had always been that of bricolage: the accumulation and amalgamation of minutiae – a 'hyper-realism' also favoured in the 'thick descriptions' of cultural anthropologists and the 'deep play' of deconstructive semioticians. By 'reading' the Revolution through its 'Ur-text', and by 'unpacking' the biblical messages expressed in revolutionary speech and writing, was he attempting to redefine it by its semiotic components? Were its modes of representation rather than collective ideas and social conflicts now the major object of investigation? Was a 'biblical revolution' the English counterpart to the Enlightenment Revolution; and were the events, the actions, the radical fish themselves, about to disappear into a sea of inherited discourse? And was the English Revolution – always more precarious than its French counterpart: a much more recently 'invented tradition' under sustained attack from revisionists and partly abandoned by its protagonists – about to be dissolved by its leading champion into its rhetorical tropes, imaginings and myths?[132]

There were some indications that this might be so. The voices were certainly more disembodied than ever before, the 'authenticating test of experience' had thinned down; and the men and women of the revolutionary era appeared largely as users or vectors of biblical histories and metaphors. Biblical stories and word pictures shaped their conceptual world: the Egyptian 'House of Bondage' and the Babylonian captivity structured their understanding of current political events; Jacob and Esau told them of the common people's disinheritance; the imagery of trees, mountains, wilderness, garden and hedge carried a range of radical messages. Their millenarian projects – and the high tide of the radical millenarianism coincided with 'the high point of biblical influence on English politics' – were re-enactments of 'scenarios of Last Times' from the 'Book of Revelation'. Biblical language expressed and legitimized revolutionary opposition to Charles I's government; and in one crucial respect, Old Testament history might be said to have 'programmed' its readers: would the English have cut off the head of Charles I if they had not read about idolatrous and tyrannical rulers being struck down by the righteous, or been driven by the compulsive theory of 'blood guilt' and the 'Man of Blood' from the Book of Numbers? Hill seemed to think not: 'the Bible was primarily responsible for the execution of Charles I; and regicide may be held responsible for the ultimate failure of the radical revolution' – the 'semiotic circle' seemed to have enclosed everything between 1649 and 1660. Focus on the radicals had collapsed 'class' as a social category; focus on their biblical politics now threatened to dismantle them as a cultural collective also: to turn their revolution into a Bible-led readers' liberation movement.[133]

From a 'descent into discourse', he was saved by old-fashioned Marxist and empirical assumptions. A realist by instinct and by formation, he did not for one moment believe that the structures and processes of the past were indistingishable from the signs or discourses that constructed them; a 'rationalist by inheritance', never entirely at home in the world of the mysterious, he was always on the look out for the rational core of seemingly alien forms of representation or belief.[134] He still distinguished between text and context, or, as he put it, between 'the biblical idiom in which men expressed themselves and their actions, which we should today express in secular terms'. The medium was not the message: the king's execution was defended in religious terms, 'but we should hardly regard it as a religious act today'; similarly, 'the legend of Cain and Abel, Esau and Joseph derived significance from the tensions in society . . . what men and women found in the Bible derived from the questions they asked and these questions derived from the society in which they lived'. The biblical idiom was not simply 'a cloak to cover real secular motives'; but it was a hegemonic 'false consciousness', none the less, which needed to be exposed and demystified.[135]

'False consciousness' it might be; but it was not entirely effective or uniform. The Bible was a particularly porous signifier: the 'mystery was more important than the history', and people read the verses in a multitude of ways. Hill's focus was on the revolutionary Bible, and radical interpretations were, notoriously, a Babel of voices. Almost as an afterthought, he also admitted that there were a range of alternative texts and conservative readings which he had largely ignored. The meaning of the Bible, in other words, was instrumental rather than expressive and formal; and Hill's radicals read Scripture in much the same way that Hill was said by his critics to read his sources, extensively rather than intensively, as an assemblage of proof texts to be deployed and manipulated to provide evidence or support for opinions and actions already determined on other grounds. There was a sense in which biblical politics was an optional politics: if the Bible had not existed, people would have discovered something else. And the Bible was not a master narrative or a sustained symbolic structure which enveloped and defined revolutionary thought and behaviour, but the biggest source-mine of all: 'a rag bag' of proverbs and quotations 'which could justify whatever a given individual or group wanted to do'.[136] Now twentieth-century scholarship was familiar with the Bible as a 'diaspora of documents produced in very different times and societies'. But seventeenth-century readers were aware of no such historical or exegetical indeterminacy. 'The Book of the Word' like the 'Book of Nature' hung together: what seemed obscure in one place was made clear in another; and what could not be apprehended in the text was explained in commentary, concordance, catechism and verbal repetition; in 'the widespread practice of reading "throughly" and in the proofs provided by preaching'. How people read, and under what circumstances; how they internalized texts – these questions Hill completely ignored. He simply assumed a 'desacralized' manner of reading Scripture, 'crumbled into verses' – a practice which gave full scope to conscious choice and preserved human agency.[137]

The fragmentation of the Bible in the hands of imaginative radical readers led naturally enough to the radicalization of its myths and metaphors. But the use and abuse of Scripture also served to discredit Scripture: 'once it had been demonstrated that you could prove anything from it', the Bible lost its universal power. Since they deployed it in such self-consciously subjective ways, some daring spirits even argued that it was not the word of God at all.

The seeds of all heresy are to be found in the Bible, and most of them were cultivated and flowered during the Revolution ... The glory of the Revolution ... was the discussion, the ferment ... Failure to prevent continuing discussion by the middling and lower classes ... was perhaps as important in preparing the intellectual climate for the Industrial Revolution as the political changes and liberation of the revolutionary decades.[138]

Even the learned who strove in their 'vast exegetical tomes' to unravel the enigmas of the Old Testament, so that they could more effectively point the way to correct moral and political behaviour, unwittingly 'cut off the branch on which they sat, letting in more light, to the great advantage of those who followed them'. By the 1680s, the short-lived sovereignty of Scripture was at an end. What looked like an epistemic archipelago – a discursive regime of biblical myths and metaphors – was in fact an isthmus, opening out on to the familiar territory of individualism, secularization and modernity. Grand theory was still in place; appearances notwithstanding, it had never really gone away.[139]

Conclusion: The End of the Line?

A historical retrospect on the Marxist historians of modern Britain from the vantage point of the late 1980s and early 1990s, which attempts to balance a critical analysis of their departed values with a more sympathetic appraisal of their lasting rhetorical worth.

THE PERSISTENCE OF GRAND THEORY

One of the most powerful criticisms of Hill's new reading of the English Revolution was to be found in the last chapter of Andrew Milner's study of Milton. Reviewing Hill's work from the stance of an up-to-date theoretical Marxism, Milner deplored the evacuation of traditional political, social and ideological divisions in favour of indeterminate cultural affinities. According to Milner, Milton was not an internally torn 'two-and-a-half culture' man, but a supremely self-confident ideologue: the major intellectual spokesman of 'Revolutionary Independency'. His meritocratic 'rationalism' set him against privilege and tradition, but it also led him to reject social levelling, religious egalitarianism and radical utopianism. What Milner identified in his picture of Milton as a full-blooded English Descartes was, in effect, a native Jacobinism – 'the rationalist world vision of the revolutionary section of the English bourgeoisie'. For a few short years, it legitimized the rule of Cromwell and the Army Council. But, with the defeat of Independency, Jacobinism disappeared from the intellectual landscape; the English bourgeoisie retreated into gradualism and empiricism, and Milton was left to lament the moral failure which had led to the collapse of the revolutionary world vision. In the 1980s, however, 'John Milton, the critical-rationalist thinker, the regicide revolutionary [was] of more genuine modern relevance than John Milton, the seventeenth-century hippie, or . . . the perplexed middle-of-the-road liberal'. The Left could no longer afford the luxury of inconclusive radical dialogues, now that it was fighting for its life.[1]

What Milner was advocating – with some sophistication and from the perspective of a Lucien Goldmann-inspired structuralism – was in effect a return to an older Marxist interpretation.[2] From a historical perspective, closer to Hill's own writings of the 1950s and 1960s, his old pupil, Brian Manning, made much the same case: the abandonment of the world of politics and *idée force* for utopian radical cultures had unwittingly enshrined defeatism and lost causes. Manning's focus was now on *The Crisis of the English Revolution* and the *coup d'état* of 1648–9. Despite its reservations at Putney and its subsequent role in crushing the radicals, the Army High Command constituted a genuinely revolutionary vanguard in these months, and provided the only continuity between the parliamentarians of 1642 and the sectarians of 1650. By moving Cromwell to the Right and reducing Independency to vanishing point, historians like Hill had destroyed the unity of the Revolution and played into the hands of revisionists. Manning's revolution, on the other hand, was still a 'block', still a social revolution carried out by political force. The military *coup d'état* carried out by the Council of Officers – a dramatic exception to the civilian character of English history – meant 'a displacement of the English governing class', a shift of power from the peers and greater or county gentry 'towards the area of status uncertainty where minor gentry, yeomen, business and professional men merged'.[3]

Its chief catalysts were the Levellers, the radicalized soldiers of the New Model Army, the London sectaries, the 'middle sort of people'. And Manning picked up the story of middle-class insurgency and mass mobilization, which he had already traced during the December Days of 1641, at the other end of the Civil War. Behind the militancy of these groups lay the threat of popular revolt, product of a prices–wages 'squeeze' familiar to students of revolution, a burden of taxation greater than ever before, and a run of bad harvests, dearth, and depression. For good measure, he also threw in the recently identified pressure points of gender and generational division: the fear of unruly women and of rebellious youth. Social and economic consolidation and differentiation had been greatly speeded up by the dislocations of civil war, and 'the outcome of the revolution was determined by a widening of the gap' between the 'middle sort' and 'the poor' and its narrowing between the 'middle sort' and the 'gentry'. What Manning was trying to unearth was a radicalized English petty bourgeoisie, formed out of the decomposition of traditional urban and rural hierarchies: it was in the 'borderland between "gentlemen" and "plebeians" where the status system [was] being challenged that . . . the social basis for the coup d'état of 1648–9 [was] to be found' – amongst yeomen farmers, shopkeepers and professionals, who rose by individual merit and achieved 'class consciousness' through political action. As with the French Jacobins, class interests determined and set limits to their revolutionary action: radical in respect of Monarchy, the Church and the Lords, interventionist when it came to poor relief, grain distribution and the provision of employment, deeply conservative when private property itself was under threat. Once more, however, the actual mechanics of status decomposition, class mobilization and political action were a little unclear. It was difficult to square Manning's relentlessly secular, self-consciously revolutionary paradigm with the political incoherence and religious militancy which other historians found during these years. Like Milner's Independent party, defined by the 'world vision' of John Milton, which crumbled on analysis to an organization of one member, the choreography seemed to have more to do with the requirements of the 'Jacobin' model than with 'actual history'.[4]

Even more given to fundamentalism and to the devotional bile which sometimes went with it, was the Trotskyite 'collective' associated with the 'Socialist Workers' Party'. The group's major theoretical outlet, *International Socialism*, probably devoted more space to historical issues and to the familiar genealogy of revolutionary socialism than any comparable journal on the Far Left. But its regular 'historical' contributors, Norah Carlin, Ian Birchill, John Rees and Alex Callinicos, were openly critical of the empirical turn of historians like Hill and Hobsbawm: for what they saw as an anaemic *History Workshop* version of ordinary lives and experiences, a quietist celebration of declassed sectarians and a disembodied focus on radical ideas, when they should have been 'rearming . . . the Marxist tradition with the good proletarian weapons of class struggle'.[5] The syllabus errorum defined by Carlin, especially, included the failure to identify a revolutionary bourgeoisie; the reluctance to associate social categories with the different types and denominations of Puritanism; the misguided rereading of the Levellers as radical liberals which robbed Marxists of some 'doughty' class warriors and left them clutching at eccentric utopians; and the defence of Cromwell, the English Revolution's Stalin, on the curious ground that if he had not shot down the radicals someone else would have done so. Worst of all was the liberal–democratic notion of an 'internally divided' gentry, and through an imperceptable slippage, acceptance of the idea of a permanent 'ruling class' – an enduring patrician structure which somehow was said to accommodate a bourgeois or even a plebeian culture: an interpretation which could only encourage revisionist denigration of revolutionary change. Yet – carping apart – it was difficult to see what Carlin and the Socialist Workers' collective wanted other than a return to the 'tidy platonism' of 1940 – something long abandoned by Hill, in the interests of historical credibility.

The Marxist reading of English history was not, however, entirely trapped within an archaic dialectic of Jacobinism and native empiricism. One of the weaknesses besetting the attempt to locate 'the pristine culture of capitalism' in England, according to Ellen Meiksins Wood, had been precisely the forcing of 'a bourgeois paradigm' on to a recalcitrant history. At its most extreme, it had led to the theory that English history was fundamentally distorted and that English society was locked in precapitalist social, political and cultural relations. On the contrary, she argued, the absence of those features normally associated with bourgeois revolution and modernity – features derived from French revolutionary philosophy locked in mortal combat with an *ancien régime* – 'signalled the presence of a well developed capitalism and a state that was evolving in tandem with a capitalist economy': England's was not a 'peculiar' but peculiarly thorough capitalist history – state formation and cultural composition had been 'inextricably bound up with development of capitalism'. England had largely avoided the continental conflict of centralization and parcellization of territory, absolutism and popular sovereignty, and had experienced an 'organic' type of nation building, based on the evolution of a ruling class which did not depend on coercive extra-economic powers or on substitute forms of venal extraction, but 'on purely "economic" modes of appropriation . . . and competitive utilization of land'.[6]

Unlike France, with its age-old tensions of a bureaucratic and autocratic culture and a countervailing ideology of revolution, England was stamped by a culture of constitutionalism built up around property ownership, an integrated economy and the symbiosis of town and country. Even what were seen as its regressive features – amateurism, individualism, traditionalism, the mythology of rural life – and its fundamental economic flaws – its underdeveloped mechanisms of state regulation, its lack of 'true democracy', its inefficiency – had 'more to do with the early establishment', 'the advance' and the basic 'contradictions' of capitalism, than with its 'inhibition'.[7] If Wood's 'Left Burkean' model of English capitalist development seemed to marginalize an English revolution, she was not letting on: she was, she assured her readers, 'far from maintaining that the emergence of capitalism in England did not entail a great – as well as a contested and often violent – social transformation, or that the English Civil War together with its revolutionary ferment was a contingent and, in the long term, inconsequential episode'. Nor did she wish to 'suggest that other social transformations have not been, or will not in the future be, effected by something that even [conservative critics] would recognize as revolutions'. It sounded like a statement of faith not a consequential proposition.[8]

Wood's outline of English development was based in large measure on a series of studies on the origins of agrarian capitalism – concurrently graced with a whole literature bearing his name – by the Marxist historian and political economist, Robert Brenner. Brenner's picture of the self-transformation of the English landed classes from semi-feudal lords to neo-capitalist landlords was part of a wider assault on the neo-Smithean model of commercial society transforming a largely inert agrarian sector: the picture of rising prices, gentry and yeoman advance and landlord crisis or collapse, adapted to the particular circumstances of seventeenth-century England. Over the previous twenty years, it had become increasingly clear that far from suffering economic crisis, the great landlords enjoyed striking economic success during this period; that, as a result of their successful socio-economic transformation, they constituted an extraordinarily homogeneous aristocracy, with none of the internal continental splits between a court elite and an introverted, impoverished and semi-feudal provincial nobility; and that they actually carried out the legislative revolution of 1640 and 1641 and led the parliamentary armies into the Civil War. Not only could the war in no meaningful sense be described as an anti-aristocratic revolution, but the leading burgher stratum, which should have formed the core of the revolutionary cause, was actually more royalist than its landowning counterpart. Yet, Brenner was not a revisionist: he was convinced

that the political crises of the period were fought out in consistent religious and constitutional terms, and that the best way to
make sense of this principled conflict was to 'reassociate constitutional and religious ideas with [their] sociopolitical and economic contexts'.[9]

His point of departure was the transition from feudalism to
capitalism and the self-transformation of the English ruling class
from one dependent on its juridical and coercive powers over 'a
peasantry that possessed its means of subsistence', to one defined by absolute property ownership and by 'contractual relations with free market dependent commercial tenants'. This peculiar
development – largely explained by the history of English politics, law and property relations rather than by a 'mode of production' which it shared with the rest of Europe – in turn, led to
a very different relationship between the dominant landed classes
and the monarchy. Unlike their continental counterparts, English
landowners no longer required 'a piece of the state . . . to maintain themselves economically', but wanted rather a state that would
protect and respect their 'absolute private property'. During the
early stages of state formation, this had facilitated close cooperation between the monarchy and the dominant classes, but the
disappearance of internal and external threats brought them into
conflict. A monarchy, no longer feudal or in any effective sense
absolutist, but in Brenner's taxonomy, 'patrimonial', which tried
'to secure its viability, autonomy and dynamism' through effective taxation, and to preserve its international prestige through
appropriate dynastic arrangements, increasingly clashed with the
dominant landowning elite over matters of fiscal policy, trade
and religion.[10]

Brenner's explanation of the rise of capitalism, effected solely
through landowner choice and initiative – with little sense of the
structural determinants which might have constrained ruling class
action – had been criticized by his fellow Marxists as a politically focused voluntarism: class analysis unrelated to a mode of
production. And on the face of it, his treatment of continuous
ruling class success and a capitalism which took off within the
envelope of landlordism, seemed to offer little beyond a whiggish
catalogue of religious and constitutional differences to explain
the causes of the Civil War – even less to explain the ostensible
split that it occasioned within the landed elite. There was no indication, either, of the 'ideological role of the monarchy as the

keystone of the aristocratic order': indeed, a 'patrimonial' monarchy appeared to assume what it was supposed to demonstrate – a royal estate structurally isolated from the rest of society.[11]

When it came to the social origins of the English Revolution, instead of a divided gentry, he substituted a divided mercantile class. There was something deeply ironic about this: the Marxist historian, who had rejected the role of commerce in explaining the rise of English and European capitalism, turned to the towns – and especially to London – for an explanation of what many saw as its pivotal episode, to *Merchants and Revolution*.[12] Brenner's treatment of the not unfamiliar division between the traditional, well-connected chartered elite of the Levant and East India Companies who favoured tight regulation, and merchant interlopers, notably in the new competitive trades of the Americas: groups connected with the 'colonizing aristocrats' of the Providence Bay Company, was impressive in its detail. So, too, his analysis of the 'municipal revolution' in 1641 when the merchant radicals took control of the City: the divisions that opened up in 1641 and 1642, related not to capitalism or to the divide of ancient and modern landownership, nor to the religious issue, but to the division between those who were prepared to support the mobilization of the small shopkeepers, domestic traders and apprentices – the citizenry and the 'people' – and those who were not. The new merchant elite's first initiative was to launch expeditions to plunder Ireland and the Caribbean; and after the ups and downs of the Civil War, it was to find in the oligarchic republicanism and the militant imperialism of the Commonwealth, the ideal framework for the realization of their ambitions. In the 1680s, the pattern was repeated: Charles II was faced by the same combination of capitalist landowners, City merchants and radical citizens. And 'the Revolution of 1688 and its sequels not only realized the project of 1640–1641 of the Parliamentary capitalist aristocracy; in so doing, it also realized, in a politically subordinated form, the project of 1649–1653 of its leading allies outside the landed classes: the American, colonial and East Indian interloping leadership'.[13]

Once again, however, the political and social geography of the period was less coherent than the suggested scenario: the mercantile elites elbowed aside in 1642 seemed to be back in the saddle by the end of 1643, when 'City Hall' became a stronghold of reaction rather than the driving force of political change; in the early 1680s, the City was radical once again, but its radicalism was snuffed out long before 1688. Could one really connect the tight oligarchies of the Old East India Company and the Bank of England in the 1690s with the Caribbean interlopers of the 1620s and the 1650s, or the Williamite war against France with the events of 1641 and 1642? And was it the uneven West Indian record of the Commonwealth and not that of the Restoration when court and City combined to carry out a coherent colonial policy, that was crucial to the story of overseas trade, plunder and Empire? Brenner's 'revolution' – defined as the decisive episode in the consolidation of a landowning–mercantile nexus and in the story of commercial change from the Merchant Adventurers of the 1550s to the South Sea Company projectors of the 1720s – was an impressive piece of Marxist scholarship, to be sure, but it did not prove the case for the pivotal status of the mid-century decades.[14]

What was true in this instance was even more the case with more stratospheric exercises in sociological parachutism. Immanuel Wallerstein's original amalgam of market driven technological determinism, colonial dependence theory and the notion of core and peripheral interaction in the making of 'Modern World Systems', for example, depended too much on discredited models of a split between 'new capitalists' and 'old aristocrats' to shed much light on events in seventeenth-century England.[15] Charles Tilly's studies of endemic conflict, protest and collective action – on his own admission an attempt to put paid to models of homeostatic equilibrium – appeared to drown any large-scale displacements in a sea of external wars and internal disturbances.[16] At the other extreme, Jack Goldstone's explicit attempt to isolate the statistical peculiarities of 'great revolutions' through the oscillations of a 'political stress indicator' – with the graph peaking majestically in 1640 and 1789 – looked like an exercise from the Grand Academy of Laputa. Keen to distance himself from the collapse of traditional social explanations and to feed into his computer more up-to-date material of population pressure, geographical mobility, increased job competition, plummeting wages, bulges in the 'age cohort' and the like, Goldstone came up with the formula PSI = Fiscal Stress × Elite Competition × Mass Mobilization (Mass Mobilization Potential/MMP = average real wages × urban growth × cohort structure), all of which supposedly explained what happened in the 1640s. As many of the key features of the model did not actually work in the French case, the formula for 1789 was presumably different.[17]

Even further removed from what Geoffrey Elton would call 'the essentials' were the wonderfully exhilarating grand narratives of 'episteme' – the shift from resemblance to representation, synecdoche to simile, holy fool to lunatic, public to private, a society of blood to one of sexuality, and other *jeux d'esprit* of Parisian discourse. Or there were the variants proposed by philosophers, feminists, ecologists and animal liberationists – the creative and destructive moment in the 'hidden agenda of modernity', the move from uncertainty to rational assurance and from religious culture to religious belief, featuring such things as the mechanization of the world picture, the death of the soul, the decay of nature and the making of the modern self – all of them located one way or another in the seventeenth century. None was exactly untrue, and all of them were, doubtless, tremendously important, but they did not readily translate into what happened in England in 1640 or 1649.[18] Most of them, indeed, illustrated the difficulty of doctrines organized around identity and difference to do anything other than register discontinuity – radical and arbitrary shifts from one intellectually coherent moment to another. Even the most impressive historical study of early modern England in this mode was notoriously unable to explain a part of its title: *Religion and the Decline of Magic*.[19]

In Hill's view, it was quite inconceivable that these massive displacements could have occurred without revolution. Yet arguably, the great secularization of European thought could be more dramatically exemplified in France or in Scotland than in England. Long after the Restoration, Cambridge Platonists, Oxford Non-Jurors and London Latitudinarians continued to debate matters of politics and philosophy in traditional theological terms, to deploy scholastic methods, to turn to the conventional materials of Roman or Christian thought, to argue from the almost universally accepted analogy of the Book of Nature and the Book of Scripture, and to conflate the providential and the natural, the alchemical and the mechanical, the metaphoric and the literal. A comparison of the early novel and the mid-seventeenth-century sermon doubtless registers a profound shift of sensibility, but an examination of theological writings over the period would show no such rigid divide.[20]

And what of society? Outside the pages of Marx and his followers, a genuinely *laissez-faire* society has probably never existed; and what has usually prevented it has not been central planning or socialism but arrangements which invariably considered private individuals as members of families, communities and corporations, not as freely associating atoms. In this sense, at least, Burke's description of eighteenth-century England as a network of 'little platoons' is a lot closer to the reality of a society where church attendance was still expected and where local government was most accurately described as a unit of obligation, than were the bourgeois fantasies of Karl Marx. Jonathan Clark may have overstated the case for divine right, patriarchalism, elite hegemony, and a confessional state, but he has not invented these things.[21]

Eighteenth-century England, in Clark's view, was characterized by a notoriously conservative and aristocratic elite, or at best a symbiotic, socially mobile relationship between a landed elite and professional classes and an ethos based more on aristocratic than on bourgeois values; by a monarchical apparatus periodically reinvented, providing legitimation to the state and its agencies; by a confessional and status-oriented rather than an open or secular definition of social membership; by erratic and uneven industrial growth rather than a Promethean Industrial Revolution, and an anti-industrial spirit first defined as a Victorian counter-revolution in values, but now reformulated as characteristic of eighteenth- and seventeenth-century attitudes also; and by a working class, whose formation was now so long delayed – to the 1870s in fact – that it looked less and less like a response to a pre-existing eighteenth-century bourgeoisie.[22]

But one did not have to be Jonathan Clark to see that there was a problem with 'the long eighteenth century', stretching all the way from 1688, or was it 1660, to 1832. Why was it so long and so apparently conservative? If, as Clark pointed out, historians of the period 1540–1640 had traced the final decline of royal and aristocratic prestige and the victory of the parliamentary 'middle class', why did those of the period from 1760 to 1832 have to do exactly the same? If, as Hobsbawm argued the seventeenth-century 'transformation was so rapid that by the 1690s England seemed actually on the verge of industrial revolution', why was it 'delayed until the 1780s'? Thompson's answer to Clark's conundrum – through radical reformulation of Old Whig rhetoric and a reading of Georgian England labouring under 'Old Corruption', a 'sophisticated system of brigandage' and the 'silting up of state and civil society' for a century – and Perkin's to Hobsbawm's – with an England poised on the end of the pre-industrial 'runway', precariously poised for 'take off' waiting for the effects of gin drinking and low fertility to wear off – seemed rather to redefine these questions than to solve them.[23]

The most intelligent answer to root and branch revisionism had been to drop the bourgeois paradigm and the attendant *laissez faire*, individualist, contractarian, and utilitarian outcrop, admit the conservative, aristocratic framework and concentrate on the great arch of agrarian capitalism over many centuries. But in this case, one sailed perilously close to the model of age-old modernity and an economy of private ownership, common law traditions, the nuclear family, social mobility and affective relationships going back to the thirteenth and fourteenth centuries. Between Clark's eternal ançien régime and Macfarlane's antique culture of capitalism, there was little space for epochal transformation in the seventeenth century. Wood, who dealt with revisionist claims better than most, sounded apologetic and partly revisionist herself, when it came to saying what the English Civil War actually was.[24]

Of course, there were features of English political and social arrangements which had altered, but the transformation was nothing like as dramatic as Hill and Stone had once suggested: assuredly not one from 'a universe and society' organized 'in terms of degree and hierarchy' to one consisting of 'competing atoms', from 'the end of the Middle Ages to the beginnings of the modern world'. On closer inspection, 'the century of revolution' looked like a long-drawn out slippage, not a seismic rift. According to Albert Soboul, 'reform and revolution are not distinguished by their duration but by their content. It is not a question of choosing a longer or shorter route, leading to the same result, but of specifying an end: to wit either the establishment of a new society or of superficial modifications to the old society'. But – even allowing for the dismissal of the means and speed of locomotion – if the old is fairly new and the new is pretty old, it is precisely the end which is in question. Chronology is part of the problem; and one may surmise that an analysis that has lost its traditional chronological location (with its revolution shifting backwards and forwards in the English case from 1529 or 1640 to 1688 or 1721) is in serious difficulties.

But the problem is a logical one as well: if the *after* is eventually after, if the 'establishment of the new society' is elongated at will, we are caught up again in the old 'one-to-one' fallacy, common to Whig and Marxist models alike. It was not, as Butterfield pointed out long ago, seventeenth- or eighteenth-century 'progressives' that made the modern world, but the interaction over many centuries of different groups none of them clearly 'progressive' or 'reactionary'. Nor was it, in the Marxist–Jacobin formulation, the one dramatic episode, a seventeenth- or an eighteenth-century revolution, which established once and for all the parameters of subsequent history, but a series of mediations so complex and indeterminate as to render a causal connection between the perceived 'end-product', 'mid-points' and 'origins', without full account of the contexts in which these linkages were formed and transformed, almost meaningless. If there was a trade-off, as Thompson suggested, between the feudal–aristocratic and trading elements of society; or, if as Hill admitted, the revolution ended in 'sordid compromise' and a return of the 'natural rulers'; if, indeed, as Marx had always argued, 'its conservative character' was to be 'explained by the lengthy alliance between the bourgeoisie and a considerable section of the great landowners', then why was it so epochal? Why, as E. P. Thompson had asked way back in 1965, all the attention on 'one dramatic episode to which all that goes before and after must be related'? Why the English Revolution?[25]

FIN DE PARTIE?

In 1988 a conference was organized by the Communist Party publishers, Lawrence and Wishart, to celebrate the fiftieth anniversary of their publication of Leslie Morton's *People's History of England*.[26] It was called – with no great originality – 'Back to the Future'. And in July 1988, nearly five hundred delegates turned up to hear about Morton, 'People's History', the Marxist Historical Tradition, the Crisis in Historical Materialism, Soviet History under Perestroika, Black History, the Nation and the Left, Hidden History, Utopias, History Futures, History after Post-Modernism, 'Retro-Chic' and other radical topics. Hill and Hobsbawm, who opened proceedings, could not help comparing the current event with the meeting some forty-two years before when some ten or twelve of them had gathered together in the upstairs room of Garibaldi's Restaurant to plan their new edition of Morton's history and to set up the Historians' Group of the Communist Party: a Marxist success story, it would seem.

But there were a few ironies in the exercise. Lawrence and Wishart had not, in fact, published Morton's history; that had been done by Victor Gollancz. But Gollancz had long since parted company with the Communist Party, and had not been contacted about the celebrations. And the conference itself was a little odd: invitations had been extended to Asa Briggs, Quentin Skinner, John Kenyon and, of all people, Jonathan Clark – none of whom by any stretch of the imagination could be called Marxists; contrariwise, as its chairman complained, the 'Communist Party History Group' had been ignored. The list of speakers was, he wrote, quite amazing: people he and his colleagues had never heard of, while many party and ex-party historians had been omitted; and, 'what in God's name', he asked, 'is retro-chic?'. In reply, the organizer, Sally Davidson, pointed out that the members of the History Group originally contacted had 'more or less dropped out' and a new team 'of mainly young people' had been recruited 'who had enthusiastically shouldered a large burden of the organizational and planning work': 'I would have thought', she added, 'that the . . . group would have welcomed this new input and be pleased that there were people speaking they hadn't heard of – an indication that there was a new interest in history even if it might not be in exactly the same mould as the past' – 'I am sure', she concluded, 'Leslie Morton would have welcomed the spirit of the event – not a simple commemoration of something that is past, but a . . . continuing commitment to using a study of the past to throw light on the understanding of the present'. Whether Morton would have approved of all the activities mounted in his name is, perhaps, questionable. For what these appeared to reflect was not just the popularity and extension but also the fragmentation and trivialization of what had once been a coherent, if never quite a unitary, Marxist historical vision.

That same July, the Revolution of 1688 was being memorialized in Westminster and Whitehall. But the commemoration was not altogether successful either: while the Dutch – for whom the Revolution was a world historical event manufactured in The Hague – and the Americans – who still found constitutional sustenance in the adjustments of 1689 – celebrated the event with the usual string of exhibitions and conferences, the English tercentenary was a rather sorry affair. Two days before the Morton gathering, the Commons had indeed debated what Margaret Thatcher referred to as 'an anniversary of peculiar meaning for this House', since it was uniquely a revolution carried through by the action of parliament itself': a revolution which had established tolerance, respect for the law, the protection of private property, and the safeguarding of institutions – qualities which, she said, had established Britain's nationhood, and, 'with it, the energy and resourcefulness responsible for building up [her] industrial and financial power and giving her a world role'. Neil Kinnock was happy enough to go along with the celebration of a demi-semi revolution, which he noted – referring to his 'favourite historian', Christopher Hill – was written up by the winners and was still incomplete, but which, he hoped, would prove an inspiration for the present House to enlarge political, social and economic liberties in a manner that 1688 had not.[27]

It was Tony Benn who spoilt this shadow boxing over political glosses: pointing out that this was the first time in his thirty-eight years in the Commons that there had been a debate on parliamentary democracy and that 'if one blew on the embers of any old controversy the flames came up quite quickly', he characterized the events of 300 years before as an oligarchic conspiracy – certainly not bloodless since it involved 'hideous repression in Ireland', not democratic since only 2 per cent of the population was consulted, not a milestone in the history of toleration or liberty since the Bill of Rights was subtitled as an 'act for disabling Papists and for preserving the King's person'; not even parliamentary, since the crown was vested with massive residual powers, now in the hands of a prerogative Prime Minister. And where Wedgie – as Tom Paine recidivus – led, the Hard Left followed: some argued that it was all about the corruption of the state by the power of landowners; others saw it as a milestone in the sordid history of imperialism and colonialism; others again seemed to think it marked the route to the Poll Tax. Even in the Lords, some of the peers were unhappy at a celebration that might offend the Catholics, the Irish and the unemployed. The result was a muted and embarrassed affair. Boycotted by the social historians, an offence to Old Guard stalwarts like Hill, derided by the New Right for whom it was an inconsequential item of whiggish mythology (in one of the more amusing episodes surrounding the celebration, Tony Benn and Jonathan Clark were to be found harmonizing their contempt on the BBC), unable to mention the word Ireland since Sweet Williams or Stinking Billies might have to be included in the revolutionary garland, unwilling to address even the issue of a modern Bill of Rights, it reduced itself to a 'poky' and poorly attended exhibition in the Banqueting Hall (some 25 000 visitors in three months) and a reading of pious Whig platitudes to parliament.[28]

The following summer saw the bicentenary of a real revolution. And certainly the celebrations of 1789 were neither modest nor parochial. But as one witnessed the confused farrago of Senegalese tom-toms and Texan saxophones unleashed by Jean-Paul Goude (the art director of *Esquire* magazine) on the Champs Elysées on 14 July, or viewed the ecumenical but decorously statuesque figure of Jessie Norman intoning the Marseillaise, one could not but wonder whether the Revolution was not being interred – transformed into another article of global consumerism. For whatever it was, the bicentenary was certainly not an exercise in contemporary revolutionary politics. President Mitterrand had made that quite clear: this, he said, was a commemoration not an exercise in socialist uplift. Bastille Day was paralleled by the Archbishop's obsequies for Louis XVI and Marie Antoinette, the following month. And as the commemorative pageant droned on, the chariot wheels of bicentennial conferences turned and the torrent of words poured out from university presses around the world, one began to realize that it was largely an exercise in revolutionary amnesia. Forgetfulness was all. The Revolution, said Furet, was over: de Gaulle's monarchical Republic had finally healed the 200-year interregnum in French history, put an end to the revolutionary myth, and reconciled 'L'Ancien Regime' and 'La France Moderne'. It was light years away from Georges Lefebvre's 1939 volume on the lessons for the Left in the forthcoming struggle, of events 150 years before.[29]

It is hard to imagine a political and cultural climate less well equipped to make sense of what actually happened later in 1989. For scarcely were the burial services completed, than contemporary politics wreaked its revenge on historiograhical hubris in the tidal wave of revolution which swept over Eastern and Central Europe. Writers on the Left noted with some amusement the sudden enthusiasm of Mr Bush and Mrs Thatcher for revolutionary street politics, people power and the exercise of collective agency.[30] But the Left's position was no less ironic: for this was a revolution against socialism, or at least against the version most of them had known and many had endorsed for over fifty years. East European regimes, once the measure of socialist advance elsewhere, and into the 1960s, at least, solid and substantial alternatives to the acquisitive societies of the bourgeois West, crumbled as though they had never been. As the Marxist gravediggers of bourgeois society were toppled into their own dirty ditches and their regimes consigned to collective memory holes, the ledge of socialist credibility seemed to have narrowed almost to vanishing point.

Already in the 1980s, Western Marxists had been forced to come to terms with the almost universal disbelief in socialism of any type at virtually all points east of the Brandenburg Gate: this, at a time when Marxist academic ware was proliferating as never before. But, even in the West, the rhetoric of academe was utterly at odds with the withering away of socialism on the streets and in the factories. In Britain, the malaise was especially acute. The Thatcher era presented native socialists with an acute example of the difficulty of squaring their faith with social and political realities: the suspicion – clearly articulated in the pages of *Marxism Today* – that capitalism was not engendering the conditions of its transformation; that despite – worse, because of – its crises, its supposed antithesis was nowhere to be seen. For fifty years, British Marxists had sought to sustain belief in the historical immanence of socialism in the teeth of the evidence, with a variety of local alibis. There was the deadweight of continuity and parliamentarism, the corruptions of empire and the illusions of 'Labourism'; then there was the anorexia of native theory, the lack of proper working-class militancy, the alleged ruling class hegemony, the long post-war boom which had mitigated the contradictions of capitalism; or there was the grandiose intellectual subterfuge that somehow the whole of British history was 'distorted', and the rather more engaging proposition that socialist transformation was unnecessary because it had already occurred. But, now, the contraction and collapse of the manufacturing economy, soaring unemployment, the deliberate winding back of the welfare state and Mrs Thatcher's version of what should have been a catalytic pre-revolutionary social reaction, had produced – what: further erosion of Labour's electoral base, fragmentation of effective trade unionism, the increasing drift of the working class to the Tories, and the intellectual 'privatization' of Marxism, spawning special languages and esoteric debates – the world of *International Socialism* and the *New Left Review*.[31]

All the same, the crisis of 1989–91, the implosion – there is no other word for the phenomenon – of the Soviet Union and of

314   *The Rise and Fall of Revolutionary England*

actually existing socialism, was a defeat of a different order of magnitude.[32] The Soviet experiment had turned out to be a colossal failure: after seventy years, the society forged by the most revolutionary regime in history had, as it were, reverted to its former self: communism, in the words of the Russian joke, had proved to be the longest route from capitalism to capitalism. The Russian Revolution and what followed from it had formed an immense part of the common heritage of the whole socialist movement. And its disappearance amidst almost universal denigration inevitably threw into question a socialist future beyond capitalism: world historical processes instead of being governed by slow moving ineluctable laws suddenly seemed alarmingly autonomous and unpredictable, without compass or anchorage. Either that or the Hegelian card trick could be played against the Marxists and the 'end of history' returned to the present and to the platitudinous triumphs of Western Liberal Democracy.[33] Eric Hobsbawm, who almost alone of the Historians' Group had retained his party membership, and as recently as 1987 had completed his great trilogy on the rise and fall of bourgeois Europe, with socialism dancing on the grave of liberal society, appeared to throw in the towel. He now decided that 1917 was not the beginning of a new era, but a vast detour in world history. And 1989 and 1991 marked its 'final liquidation', the end of the 'short twentieth century'.[34]

And what of Marxism? In the light of the ruin of societies which claimed to have applied Marxist principles of political and economic organization, wasn't it a failed explanatory system, also: its 'triumphal arches' and 'vaunting inscriptions', like those of an ancient empire, 'increasingly unintelligible to modern inhabitants'?[35] Outside those societies, where it achieved the status of an official ideology, Marxism was fundamentally a critical project – a tool of historical revision, an instrument of cultural criticism, a method of sociological analysis. But the critical posture had never entirely obliterated the felt need for some defence of 'actually existing socialism' or for a sort of 'operation phoenix' – belief in a socialism which would rise 'out of the ashes'. Eric Hobsbawm, for one, continued to derive ironic sustenance, at least, from the responsibility of the October Revolution for the salvation and modification, 'both in war and in peace', of its capitalist antagonist. Elsewhere the separation of 'real socialism' from some future immaculate conception was more pronounced: it was the theme of numerous conferences, in which the fifty-seven varieties of post-communist socialists fitted out the funeral baked meats for some prospective post-capitalist marriage table. In the upper reaches of socialist unreality, it was maintained that 1989 and 1991 signalled only the final demise of Stalinism; that Russian Communism was, at best, an ugly vulgarization of Marx's ideas; and that its collapse marked a colossal 'tidying up', the sweeping away of one set of fixed fast frozen relations – the illusion of a socialist third of the world – which would in the long run make the case for socialist transformation truly global.[36] From his cloud of socialist unknowing, E. P. Thompson informed the world that the collapse of Communism had been brought about by the activities of Leftists like himself: socialist nuclear disarmers, 'breaking through Cold War force fields' – a spiritual debt largely unacknowledged by Russians and East Germans, who, alas, gave much of the credit to Ronald Reagan and Margaret Thatcher.[37]

Apart from these exercises in 'clinging to the wreckage', there were four continuities of Marxist historical writing in Britain 'after the Fall'. The first was an unabated demonology of capitalism, *laissez-faire* society and the market economy, which extended from what one commentator referred to as the fashionable literary 'bashing' of 'the bourgeois humanist subject', to the deeply ingrained dogma of the irrationality and self-destructiveness of the capitalist system itself.[38] The most eloquent exponent of the theme was E. P. Thompson; and in 1990, he was still exploring the struggles associated with the consolidation of the market economy in eighteenth-century Britain. The moral urgency of his writing attested to a continued belief in the contestability of capitalism: implicit within custom, as it survived and transformed itself within class society, was the possibility of living other than by the hated laws of the market. In the eighteenth century, wife sales, transportation and the slave trade constituted the case for a fundamentally different moral economy; in the late twentieth, the widening gap between rich and poor, and between the developed world and the rest of suffering humanity defined the agenda anew.[39]

Humanity, argued Hobsbawm, had reached the point where it could destroy the biosphere or 'create a world in which free men and women emancipated from . . . material need live[d] the good life in the good society'. Socialist practice had, it was true, created massive pollution, but the connection was adventitious and circumstantial – the result of particular distortions – whereas capitalism was committed *'by its very nature'* – by the insatiable dynamic of unlimited growth – to global destruction, 'sawing off . . . the branches on which it sat': it was still a case of 'socialism or barbarism'.[40] Hobsbawm's analysis – the more striking coming from a Marxist 'realist' who had always fought shy of the excesses of romantic anti-capitalism – unfortunately bore little relation to a world where societies run on Marxist principles – namely the abolition of the consumer market economy – had proved utterly incapable of rational resource allocation, and where those based on private ownership had shown themselves to be enormously versatile, engendering a vast array of hybrid economic arrangements and self-correcting mechanisms: little to say, either, to the socialist third of the world that was actually choosing 'the path of capitalist counter-revolution'. When even the *New Left Review*, much to the disgust of its editorial board, resorted to a bit of old fashioned privatization, the time for Manichean incantations was well and truly past.[41]

A second continuity lay in the insistence on the collective historical agency of men and women making their own history. For some, self-determination was still primarily defined by class; and during the late 1980s, semi-demi fundamentalists had fulminated against structuralist and post-structuralist fashions which ignored the operations of class consciousness and agency: indeed, nothing was better calculated to drive Marxists to their word processors than this particular 'orrery of errors' – the theory that the working class was withering away, or that nationality, ethnicity, lineage, language and locality was more important than the old 'horizontal beast'.[42] For others, class agency was indirect: more of an 'awareness' or a tendency, refracted by religious idioms or ways of life which had to be defined in non-class terms. What mattered, however, was the active as opposed to the passive voice. This, according to Hobsbawm, was the true significance of the twentieth-century experience: 'after a long wait in the auditorium, it meant the opening of the curtain on a great and exciting historical drama in which the audience found itself to be the actors'. For Hill and Thompson, actors they always had been.[43]

The third area of continuity was to be found in the notion of historical development itself. Marxist historians had shed the vulgar inevitabilism of earlier and simpler days: E. P. Thompson's work, in particular, had been a long sustained protest against moralizing the actual course of history; and Hill's, too, had focused increasingly on the vanquished not the victors – on 'the poetry of the past' not the prose of the 'future'. What, then, was left of the revolutionary model of social change? Revolution had not entirely disappeared from their understanding of history, but it did not swell inevitably from the process of social evolution. It existed rather as a transformative potency – an eruption into a chain of everyday happenings, a matter of desire or redemption not of necessity.[44] In his last book, Thompson once again celebrated the traditions of revolt in the late eighteenth century. And he endeavoured to perpetuate the legacy of Tom Paine, John Thelwell, William Cobbett and, of course, William Blake, just as Hill had perpetuated that of Gerard Winstanley and John Milton, 150 years before.[45]

Like Old Testament stories of regicide in an age of 'divine right', these traditions enabled socialists to imagine a different society. One of the greatest threats to that vision was the threat to radical memory: in an age of revisionism and post-modernity, historical transmission was more vulnerable than ever before: 'Every image of the past that is not recognized in the present as one of its own concerns,' wrote Walter Benjamin, 'threaten[s] to disappear irretrievably'; and 'only that historian will have the gift of fanning the spark of hope in the past, who is firmly convinced that even the dead will not be safe from the enemy'.[46] This was why it was so important to preserve the revolutionary legacy; why Hobsbawm was driven to reassert the traditional verities of Lefebvre and Soboul and the liberating message of the French Revolution against a largely faceless tribe of revisionists. The French Revolution 'gave peoples the sense that history could be changed by their action': that was sufficient.[47] The same case was made by Hill about the 1640s and by Thompson about the 1790s. None of them, indeed, seemed able to resist the 'authenticity' and emancipatory potential of revolutionary action, whatever the suffering and however appalling the sequel. Apathy, acceptance, the daily grind of exploitation, fate: they were the enemies.[48]

These evocations of socialism were products of continued faith in the 'Enlightenment project': the belief that through the understanding of their social condition and their history, men and women could escape from the 'nightmare' of the past. The greatest exponent of that project was Karl Marx, and Marxist thought in all its varieties was characterized by an 'instrumental proclivity towards a transforming intentionality' – belief in the capacity of ordinary people, through the exercise of will, to 'make' themselves – and by a refusal to be reconciled to 'the notion of the human condition as a permanent condition of incommensurate goals and irresolvable dissonances': something which led, in turn, to the hegemony of a single imaginable and legitimate future.[49] Over the years, the English Marxist historians had lowered their sights a good deal: they were more aware of the distance which separated ideas and their realization; they had jettisoned most of the functionalist aspects of Marxist materialism. But they had not surrendered the underlying Promethean faith. Or belief in the unity of theory and practice that made its realization possible.[50]

But it was precisely this unity, which had made Marxism into a genuinely self-refuting project. Marxism was not just an interpretation of the world but a revolutionary praxis; and the Marxism of the Historians' Group had been the continuation of politics by other means – part of the battle of ideas for a better future. Hill's role in that project had been the study of the English Revolution: through the study of England's seventeenth century, he believed, native socialists could be better prepared for their tasks here and now. For much of his working career, he had qualified this position, but he had never wholly abandoned it. In 1991, he was a luminary of a BBC television series on the English Civil War. There, against a backdrop of scenes from the Romanian Revolution and images of marmoreal Lenins being toppled, was Hill telling the viewers that the eruption of street politics in 1641 and 1642, and the collapse of the Stuart monarchy, was an analogue of the overthrow of East European Communist regimes the year before. For one who had compared 1640 with 1917; had divided the world into progressive and reactionary camps, with the Protestants of Central and Eastern Europe lined up against the Spanish Catholic colossus as were Czechoslovakia, Romania, Bulgaria and the other freedom loving democracies against American Imperialism in the 1940s and 1950s; and had always insisted that the limitations of England's bourgeois revolution could best be measured by the advances in truly socialist societies, it was a breathtaking performance.[51]

Times change and beliefs change, too. So it was not the consistency or the precise contemporary reference points of his Marxism which were at issue. It was the whole business of lining up an emancipatory vision of the past with the present. In 1955, he had intervened in a war of words sparked off in the correspondence columns of the *New Statesman* by a characteristic piece of coat trailing by Hugh Trevor-Roper over the rival merits of Marx and Burckhardt: certainly, he admitted, Burckhardt had made some prescient comments. But

> Marx had forecast the lines along which he thought a socialist society would be built. And action taken by men calling themselves Marxists has led to the establishment of socialism over a large part of the globe. This, whether we like it or not, is an achievement of a quite different order from Burkhardt's and is not affected by the fact that not all of Marx's detailed predictions came off.[52]

Quite so: Marxism could not be adopted without being acted upon. But once it was acted upon, it had to take its chances in the rough and tumble of political and social practice and not of theory. Since 1917, the actual fulfilment of socialism had constituted the most powerful refutation of Marx's principles. And in 1989, the refutation was rendered definitive: any society formed on Marxist lines would have failed, whoever had the running of it and whatever the society. And the only reason why historians like Hill and Thompson were still able to celebrate socialist forebears, and to associate them with some imagined future, was that the earlier 'visions of Albion' had never been tested in the real world.[53]

Let us suppose, then, that the Enlightenment project had failed; and that the grand narratives of history had ceased to be believable, what then? Abandon socialism altogether? But that was unthinkable, when one looked at suffering humanity, when even in England – in London's 'cardboard city' – there was more homelessness, squalor, deprivation, and inequality than ever. One of the most poignant messages of the post-Marxist era was E. P. Thompson's. Of all the historians in this study, he was the most passionately wedded to the socialist ethic, the most engaged in present politics and the most critical of the imperfections of the actually existing socialist enterprise. Probably, he experienced the trauma of the 1990s more acutely than any: not for him the glib assurance that Marxism was unaffected by the events of the previous years.[54] Amidst the general dismay at the collapse of all sorts and conditions of socialism, he had his own particular reasons for distress. Of all the socialist experiments, the one on which he had set most store – through his own experiences, and, adventitiously, through his brother's role in the partisan struggle – was the Yugoslav Federal Republic: the only socialist state formed by genuine popular insurgency, the only one to embody an authentic grass roots communism, to have rid itself of the Stalinist incubus, and to have forged a national road to socialism between the Cold War blocs. But in 1991, the combination of native socialism and the one party system had led to Slobodan Milosevic's nasty brew of Greater Serbian nationalism and authoritarian ex-communism. And from Thompson, not a word![55]

But there was an oblique historical verdict. Given the autobiographical resonances of his work there was something emblematic about his last book, *Witness against the Beast: William Blake and the Moral Law*: about a latter-day English Marxist interviewing the last Muggletonian – a recondite sect whose 'impenetrable and esoteric' beliefs might, he wrote, have been 'the extreme recourse of the excluded against the compulsive restraints of the ruling discourse'. Blake himself was not a Muggletonian but, like Milton before him, he lived in dialogue with them: his symbolic universe and spiritual vocabulary certainly owed much to their peculiar world vision. Thompson lovingly teased out the strands linking Hill's 'upside down' milieu and his own revolutionary 'moment' in the 1790s. But he also sought to recover the political dimension of Blake's thought: the Painite rationalism and the militancy, which informed his writing. 'Blake did not achieve any full synthesis of the antinomian and the rationalist. How could he, since the antinomian premised a non-rational alternative?' When the revolutionary fires burnt low, he was forced to chose – and, said Thompson, in a final romantic paragraph that was clearly self-referential – he chose the antinomian retreat. 'The busy perfectionists and the benevolent rationalists . . . ended up as disenchanted men'; the Enlightenment project led to false gods, unrealistic expectations, blighted hopes. And Thompson's response to a Fukuyama 'end game' of capitalist 'post-history' was withdrawal to the ethical 'kingdom within, which moth and rust does not corrupt'. When other modes of understanding were precluded by the shock of the unintelligible, love, forgiveness, and, above all, testimony – bearing witness against the Beast – was all that remained. It was a good point to stop.[56]

* * *

Most of the cast of this book – Hill, and Hobsbawm, Hilton and Kiernan, Stone and Macpherson – were born before, during or immediately after the Great War, had grown up under the shadow of the Depression, and reached early manhood during the era which saw the emergence of Fascism and its eventual defeat – a time when to be young and socialist was to be alive. E. P. Thompson, somewhat younger than his Marxist peers, was, if anything, even more emotionally tied to the hopes and fears of 1944 and 1945. For most of them, conventional academic fame had come rather late in life. During the 1940s and 1950s, they had operated outside the main avenues of academe, in the 'Historians' Group of the Communist Party', in WEA institutes and on the pages of their party journals. Of these, the group was the most important. Founded in 1945, in retrospect 'the high point in left thinking in England' – for many of its members, it was 'the best academic and educational experience of their lives'.[57] Here, in an era of Cold War politics, they had hammered out their interpretation of England's and Europe's past. Inevitably, it was a reading which was reductionist, and presentist to a fault. But it was never dull nor was it entirely doctrinaire.

Paradoxically, it was only after 1956, when the group splintered and many of its members left the party – when they refined and qualified many features of the archaic Marxist paradigm in an impressive list of publications and in their new House Journal, *Past and Present* – that they started winning 'the battle of ideas'. Retrospectively, indeed, the demise of 'The Historians' Group of the Communist Party' was a turning point in the growth of its members' individual reputations. Yet, their subsequent works were offshoots of the discussions of the 1940s and 1950s – in Hill's case, this was especially true;[58] only with Thompson, a peripheral member of the group, and symptomatically, perhaps, the most original voice on the Left, was it not really so. The 1960s were, as Deutscher had predicted, something of an academic 'red decade', the decade of *The Making of the English Working Class*, the seminal work in English social history, of Hobsbawm's *Age of Revolution*, surely the most influential textbook on Modern Europe, and of the growing list of Hill's seventeenth-century studies, which seemed likely to flatten the opposition by sheer weight of pages and erudition.

Despite their breach with the party in 1956 and their critique of its failure to live up to humane socialist principles, they all remained true to the Marxism of their youth. They were haunted by the spectre of the renegade – indeed, the language of 'opportunism' and 'apostasy' was still invoked in the 1980s against the backsliding of a less resilient generation. The loyalism probably bred a certain incestuousness: they applauded each others' books, attacked each others' intellectual opponents, and reinforced each others' views. On the face of it, the late 1960s and early 1970s witnessed a further extension of their influence. Much of the Marxist tradition had become common historical currency; the 'English Revolution' had been almost standardized in the titles of learned books and articles. The celebration of 'upside down worlds' and hitherto condescended majorities was given a new lease of life by the anti-elitist assumptions and expectations of a vastly widened audience of undergraduates. At the height of the Cold War, Hill had contrasted the privileged and hierarchical precincts of higher learning in Britain with the mass educational opportunities, the new democratic values and the vitality and passionate desire for knowledge which were to be encountered in the colleges and universities of Eastern Europe.[59] But by 1970, even in academically conservative Britain, the situation had dramatically changed, as the new universities, polytechnics and open learning programmes began to tap 'the vast reserves of intelligence and ability in the working class'. And naturally enough, these groups were attracted to the agendas of the new social history and to the radical theory that often went with it: Marxism, as it had in post-war Czechoslovakia and Hungary, started to 'permeate old departments from below by the exercise of consumer choice', thus producing by the late 1970s one of the stranger 'peculiarities of the English': the sudden addiction of its academics to Marxist theory in direct disproportion to declining Marxist practice.[60] For even as the tributary of Marxist history widened, it lost something of its original coherence. Chronology fragmented. Utopian voluntarism stood in for impersonal economic forces; personal liberation for social transformation; history from below and people's experiences for class struggle; revolutionaries for revolution. Theory became more arcane and further removed from the increasingly empirical character of Left historical studies; and conflict between the two styles came to divide the Marxist world into self-enclosed warring factions.

Some time in the late 1970s, a sea change came over seventeenth-century studies also: Hexter's article deflated Hill's reputation; the reviews dropped their reverential tone; Stone's sociological packaging of the English Revolution triggered a wave of provincial protest. By the mid 1980s, it seemed that Marxist history might only survive as a form of residual Whiggism or as the 'cultural materialism' of those who did not want too much history. Conrad Russell's brand of revisionism – precise, mathematical, sceptical, archivally focused – had come to dominate professional English Civil War studies. And the one thing they were not about were class conflicts, long-term social, economic or ideological displacements: the making of the modern world. Concurrently, the political climate had changed. Western European governments no longer sought legitimation in the traditional genealogies of modernism, least of all in the political and social upheavals which supposedly marked their genesis, and which consequently offered critics promise of their supercession. Simultaneously, in the realms of 'high theory', post-modernism and the linguistic turn threatened to marginalize the familiar events, processes and structures of the 'bourgeois past'. And amongst its major victims were notions of 'the social totality' and of 'human agency' which had formed so much of the rationale of Marxisant history.[61] Who had heard of Pym or Lilburne, Robespierre or Hébert – who cared?

Conservatism begets revisionism – or is it the other way round – and the academic climate of the late 1980s was partly caught by Jonathan Clark's demonology of liberal progressivism and Marxism. Or, at a lower level of ideological literacy, by Norman Cantor's polemic on the Left takeover of American universities: 'the real crisis in the humanities today', which stemmed from the academic patronage of well-placed 'Marxists' like Lawrence Stone and from their 'ideological cognates' in feminist studies and literary criticism: an attack so replete with error and inuendo that even Jack Hexter who had been 'crawling to the Right' for twenty years thought that it might be time to start crawling back again.[62] But Hexter and Stone, Hobsbawm and Hill were old men now; and academic witch-hunts were rather beside the point. The extravagance of the attack was probably only indicative of the selective ignorance which often goes with a generational purge. Like the sweeping away of Old Marxists in the Sorbonne, what was happening in English history was the making of a new agenda, set by men and women thirty or forty years younger and by issues very different from those which had dominated the field for so long.

Generational change is rarely quite as simple as that; and the academic environment of the late 1980s and early 1990s was not without its ironies: on the one hand, a student population possibly more conservative than at any time since the 1950s; on the other, a group of tenured radicals from the late 1960s and the 1970s, increasingly isolated by the receding tide of radicalism in the world at large; and another group of embattled young conservatives, ill at ease with what they saw as the 'politically correct' cultural agendas of many of their colleagues. The conservatism and revisionism of the 1980s had not necessarily translated into academic positions: resources had shrunk; social science apparatchiks ran the universities; the brightest students headed for business schools or for law; and, in an era of rationalization, cost efficiency, teaching and research profiles, everyone could indulge their own 'culture of complaint'.[63] In the longer perspective, the intellectual resources of the New Right were probably too limited and too emotionally mean to impose themselves on social and historical thinking for very long. But for the various Lefts of the generation covered by this book, the 1990s probably did mark the end of the line.[64]

The worth of a historical enquiry is not, however, something to be judged from a complaisant present with an invocation of the 'reality' effect of the latest piece of revisionist scholarship or the iconoclastic import of the most recent deconstructive strategy. 'All flesh is grass, and historians, poor things, wither more quickly than most': that was Tawney's verdict – last year's discovery was next year's discard. This book would be a waste of time and effort were this entirely the case; so, too, would much of the study of historical writing and the history of ideas.[65] If, on the other hand, history aspires to the condition of historiography: if the historical vision is irreducably opaque and relational; if historical writing is as much a branch of 'rhetoric' as of 'philosophy', concerned as much with representation as with 'discovery'; if the 'objective' historian is an undesirable will-o'-the-wisp, and interpretation can never be brought to an end because there is nothing wholly outside interpretation, then the work of the English Marxist historians may continue to have an interest and an appeal. Not for the reasons which they themselves – products of an empirical and positivist world view – would have respected: because theirs was a more truthful or scientific version of the past, because Marxism alone enabled them to grasp the full complexity of history as structure and as process; even less, because it validated a revolutionary praxis in the present; but because it enabled them to open up new areas of enquiry and propose fruitful hypotheses.

In an affectionate review of Hill's most recent book, Keith Thomas wrote of the author's unusual capacity for absorbing and transmuting new material. 'Christopher Hill must have read more of the literature written in and about the English seventeenth century than anyone who has ever lived'; he missed nothing; he was as receptive to the most recent work as the most avant-garde cultural materialist. Yet his world view and the historical vision that went with it was remarkably constant. There was, wrote Thomas, something of the woman in the poem about him: 'it's a very odd thing, as odd as can be, that whatever Miss T eats turns into Miss T'.[66] It was this combination which inspired Hexter's notorious attack on source mining and lumping launched from a redoubt firmly within the 'reality' rule, which elsewhere he called in question;[67] but it was this which, from a rhetorical perspective, made Hill's work, even more than that of his Marxist colleagues, such a sensitive barometer to the changing agendas of English history, and such a splendid index of the hopes and aspirations of the English Left over a period of fifty years. Of course, his writing evolved: unlike E. P. Thompson, he never allowed himself to become trapped in the emotional or polemical grooves of the past. Yet, as Thomas observed, it was of a piece. From the sometimes literal minded Stalinist of the 1940s, and the supple Marxist of the 1950s, to the warm-hearted New Leftist of the 1970s and the radical cultural witness of the 1980s – from Sovieticus Triumphans to Radicalistus Agonistes – Hill's work presented a wonderful ensemble of Marxist preoccupations and interpretations.

It may, therefore, continue to be of interest long after the credibility of the substantive faith behind it has withered away – and not just as a residual orthodoxy sustained by Penguin Books or redundant radicals entrenched in academe. His writings may be consulted as 'documents' charting the concerns and aspirations of a peculiarly gifted group of politically committed twentieth-century historians. But they may also be read as 'texts': for the passion and the rhetorical qualities of the writing itself – for the ways in which it enlarged the understanding and extended the sympathies of other historians; read, for that unusual combination of detailed scholarship and overall coherence, which most students of the past will continue to seek.[68] In hindsight, the attempt to fashion an indigenous revolutionary past may be judged a failure or, at best, a very partial success; but it was not an ignoble quest, nor was it an unproductive one. For over fifty years it challenged, provoked, stimulated and even uplifted other labourers in the vineyard. Is it reasonable to ask for more?

Notes

Place of publication is London unless otherwise stated.

Introduction

1. Harvey J. Kaye, *The British Marxist Historians: An Introductory Analysis* (Cambridge, 1984). In this general survey and in a number of subsequent volumes devoted to the historians Kiernan, Rudé, Thompson, etc., Kaye has publicized the work of the English Marxists in an accessible manner. The criticism of Bill Schwarz (*Times Higher Education Supplement* (*THES*), 11 September 1987) is, however, I believe accurate – and damning: 'He engages in the exemplary job of excavating and promoting the scholarship of an extremely talented group of historians. In the process, their work becomes transmogrified into a tradition which then takes on a life of its own . . . Everything which touches this tradition is itself sanctified, indiscriminately elevated for worship and celebration.' And Schwarz adds, 'there doesn't seem much point in resurrecting historical texts in this way'.
2. The victor ludorum is J. C. D. Clark, *Revolution and Rebellion: State and Society in England in the Seventeenth and Eighteenth Centuries* (Cambridge, 1986). Though not without its insights and felicities, Clark's study is primarily a demonology which makes little attempt either to distinguish its various 'Left' leaning targets or to explore the contexts in which they were established.

Chapter 1   The Great Bourgeois Revolution: A False Genealogy?

1. E. P. Thompson, 'The Peculiarities of the English' in R. Miliband and J. Saville (eds), *The Socialist Register*, No. 2, 1965, p. 45, subsequently reprinted in *The Poverty of Theory and Other Essays* (1978) 4th edn, 1981 (henceforth *POT*), p. 257.
2. 'Forms which precede capitalist production' from Part IV of The 'Grundrisse', see E. J. Hobsbawm (ed.), *Karl Marx: Pre-capitalist Economic Formations* (1964).
3. A. Giddens, *A Contemporary Critique of Historical Materialism* (1981), pp. 82–3.
4. L. Stone, 'The Results of the English Revolutions of the Seventeenth Century' in J. G. A. Pocock (ed.), *Three British Revolutions: 1641, 1688, 1776* (Princeton, 1980), pp. 23ff. For a not entirely convincing attempt to justify the applicability of modern usage to the period before 1688, see C. Hill, 'The Word "Revolution" in Seventeenth Century England' in R. Ollard (ed.), *Essays Presented to C.*

V. Wedgwood (1983), pp. 134–51, subsequently in *A Nation of Change and Novelty: Radical Politics, Religion and Literature in Seventeenth Century England* (1990), pp. 82–101.

5. Stone's supposed semantic demonstration of the existence of revolution in the 1640s only in fact illustrates the perception of rebellion and/or godly reformation. L. Stone, *Causes of the English Revolution* (1972), pp. 49–52. Likewise, Melvyn Lasky, *Utopia and Revolution* (1976) has much to illustrate 'the metaphysics of Doomsday', but little to demonstrate a more secular usage.

6. Louis XVI: 'C'est un revolte.' Duc de Liancourt: 'Non, Sire, c'est la Revolution.'

7. A. Cobban, 'The Myth of the French Revolution' in Cobban, *Aspects of the French Revolution* (1968), p. 95.

8. J. G. A. Pocock, op. cit., p. 7. For 'bourgeosie of convenience', see J. H. Hexter, *Reappraisals in History* (1961), p. 95.

9. Barrington Moore Jr, *Social Origins of Dictatorship and Democracy* (Harmondsworth, 1967), pp. 14ff; C. Hill, *Reformation to Industrial Revolution* (1967), part III, i, passim.

10. Indeed, this has become a standard item of the revisionist critique: the attribution of *solely* political meaning to the terminology of 1789 (aristocrat, bourgeois, people, etc.).

11. A. Soboul, 'Classes and Class Struggles during the French Revolution' in *Science and Society*, 17, 1953, pp. 239, 241–5; *The French Revolution, 1787–99* (1974), introduction, passim.

12. R. S. Neale, 'The Bourgeoisie Historically Has Played a Most Revolutionary Part' in E. Kamenka and R. S. Neale, *Feudalism, Capitalism and Beyond* (1975), p. 84–03, subsequently reprinted in R. S. Neale, *Writing Marxist History* (Oxford, 1985); D. Cannadine, *New York Review of Books*, 2 February 1985; J. H. Hexter, 'The Myth of the Middle Class' in Hexter, op. cit., pp. 76–116.

13. A. Soboul, 'Classes and Class Struggles', p. 245; G. Lefebvre, *Études sur la Révolution Française* (Paris, 1962), p. 246. Cf *The Coming of the French Revolution* (Princeton, 1947), introduction, conclusion.

14. E. P. Thompson, *Whigs and Hunters: The origin of the Black Act* (1975), pp. 190ff; 'The Peculiarities of the English', loc. cit., pp. 252, 258–62, 296.

15. K. Marx, 'The Bourgeoisie and the Counter-Revolution' in D. Fernbach (ed.), *The Revolutions of 1848* (Harmondsworth, 1973), pp. 192–3.

16. F. Furet, *Marx and the French Revolution* (Chicago, 1988), p. 45.

17. E. P. Thompson, 'Peculiarities', loc. cit., p. 288; G. McLennan, *Marxism and the Methodologies of History* (1981), p. 175.

18. Thus Furet almost completely inverts Thompson's point: 'Marx['s] explanation elaborated and developed at great length in the case of England, takes as its key the development of capitalism and of a class that was at once dominant and ruling, master of capital, of Parliament, and of the state. Couched on this Procrustean bed, the France of the Revolution and of the nineteenth century is not easily understood or even recognizable.' Furet, op. cit., p. 93.

19. See below Chapter 7.
20. E. J. Hobsbawm, 'The Historians' Group of the Communist Party' in M. Cornforth (ed.), *Rebels and their Causes: Essays in Honour of A. L. Morton* (1979), p. 27. Cf Raphael Samuel, 'British Marxist Historians, 1880–1980; Part One', *New Left Review* (*NLR*), 120, 1980, pp. 26, 28; Daphne May, 'Work of the Historians' Groups', *Communist Review* (*CR*), May 1949, pp. 541ff.
21. Tony Judt, *Marxism and the French Left* (Oxford, 1986), pp. 177ff.
22. George C. Comninel, *Rethinking the French Revolution* (1987), esp. chapters 3, 5. See also E. J. Hobsbawm, *Echoes of the Marseillaise* (1990), chapters 1, 2.
23. G. Rudé, Introduction to G. C. Comninel, Comninel, op. cit., p. 4.
24. See Duncan Forbes, *Hume's Philosophical Politics* (Cambridge, 1975). Also Duncan Forbes's introduction to *Hume: The History of Great Britain (The reigns of James I and Charles I)* (Harmondsworth, 1970).
25. Hume, *History*, ed. Forbes, pp. 219ff, 231; D. Hume, *History of England*, vol. VIII (1776 ed.), appendix III.
26. Hume, *History*, ed. Forbes, pp. 41–2.
27. F. Guizot, 'Discours sur l'histoire de la Révolution d'Angleterre' quoted in G. Plekhanov, *The Development of the Monist View of History* (Moscow, 1956), p. 29.
28. Augustin Thierry, *Vue des révolutions d'Angleterre* (Paris, 1817), p. 51, quoted in Comninel, op. cit., pp. 60–1.
29. *Communist Manifesto* (ed., A. J. P. Taylor), p. 2ff.
30. J. G. A. Pocock, *The Ancient Constitution and Feudal Law* (Cambridge, 1957); J. Q. C. Mackrell, *The Attack on 'Feudalism' in Eighteenth Century France* (1973).
31. R. Meek, *Social Science and the Ignoble Savage* (Cambridge, 1976), p. 98, 101ff; S. N. Mukherjee, 'The Idea of Feudalism from the Philosophes to Karl Marx' in E. Leach, S. N. Mukherjee and J. O. Ward, *Feudalism: Comparative Studies*, Sydney Association for Studies in Society and Culture, 2, 1985, pp. 34–5; Istvan Hont, 'The Rich Country Poor Country Debate in Scottish Classical Political Economy' in I. Hont and M. Ignatieff (eds), *Wealth and Virtue* (Cambridge, 1983), pp. 271–316.
32. R. Brenner, 'Bourgeois Revolution and the Transition to Capitalism' in A. L. Beier *et al.*, *The First Modern Society: Essays in English History in Honour of Lawrence Stone* (Cambridge, 1989), pp. 281–5. Cf R. Brenner, 'The Origins of Capitalist Development, A Critique of Neo-Smithean Marxism', *NLR*, 104, 1977; 'Agrarian Class Structure and Economic Development', *Past and Present* (*P&P*), 70, 1976, pp. 30–75, 'The Agrarian Roots of European Capitalism', ibid., 97, 1982, pp. 16–113.
33. *Communist Manifesto*, p. 4.
34. Brenner, Loc. cit., p. 284; L. Kolakowski, *Main Currents of Marxism*, II (1978), pp. 34ff.
35. See esp. Claude Lefort, 'Marx: From One Vision of History to Another', *Social Research*, xlv, 1978.
36. Brenner, Loc. cit.; Giddens, op. cit. pp. 81–9.

37. For a discussion of this radical divergence from the familiar evolutionary model, see esp. Claude Lefort, loc. cit.
38. Giddens, op. cit., chapter 3.
39. For these problems, see especially the debate in *Science and Society* between 1950 and 1953, *The Transition from Feudalism to Capitalism: A Symposium* (New York, Science and Society, 1954); R. Hilton (ed.), *The Transition from Feudalism to Capitalism* (1976); M. Dobb, *Studies in the Development of Capitalism* (1946); see Scott Meikle, 'Marxist Theory and the History of the Communist Movement' *Critique*, 10/11, 1978/9, pp. 88–91.
40. See esp. P. Anderson, *Lineages of the Absolutist State* (1974) pp. 18–19; L. Althusser, *Montesquieu: Politics and History* (1972), pp. 101–3; B. Porshnev, *Les Soulevements populaires en France de 1623 à 1648* (Paris, 1963).
41. F. Guizot, Preface to 'History of the English Revolution' in S. Mellon (ed.), *Historical Essays and Lectures* (Chicago, 1972), pp. 132–3; S. Mellon, *The Political Uses of History* (Stanford, 1958), pp. 12–13, 21–9; D. Johnson, *Guizot: Aspects of French History* (1963), p. 320ff.
42. Guizot, op. cit., p. 55f; quoted in M. G. Finlayson, *Historians, Puritanism and the English Revolution: The Religious Factor in English Politics before and after the Interregnum* (Toronto, 1983), p. 36.
43. See, for example, Marx's essay of 1847, *Moralizing Criticism and Critical Morality*. Also the passages quoted in C. Hill, 'The English Civil War Interpreted by Marx and Engels', *Science and Society*, xii, i, 1949, pp. 142–3.
44. See Marx's review of Guizot, D. Fernbach (ed.), *Karl Marx, Surveys from Exile* (Harmondsworth, 1973), *Surveys*, pp. 254–5.
45. G. Blainey, *The Great See-Saw* (1989).
46. J. Stewart, *The Moral and Political Philosophy of David Hume* (1967); D. Forbes, *Hume's Philosophical Politics* (Cambridge, 1976); J. G. A. Pocock, 'Hume and the American Revolution: The Dying Thoughts of a North Briton' in his *Virtue, Commerce and History* (Cambridge, 1985), pp. 125–42.
47. Guizot, of all people, pointed this out: Mellon (ed.), *Historical Essays*, p. xxxvi.
48. K. Baker, 'Enlightenment and Revolution in France: Old Problems, Renewed Approaches', *Journal of Modern History*, 53, 1981, p. 282. See also E. J. Hobsbawm, *Echoes*, esp. pp. 70ff; also, 'Mass Producing Tradition' in E. J. Hobsbawm and T. Ranger, *The Invention of Tradition* (Cambridge, 1983).
49. K. Baker, loc. cit., pp. 283ff; L. Kolakowski, op. cit., II, pp. 125, 130, 135. The elision of Republican and Marxist interpretations is the major theme of Alice Gérard, *La Révolution francaise: Mythes et Interprétations 1789–1970* (Paris, 1971), pp. 61ff.
50. Furet, op. cit., p. 55ff.
51. See R. Herr, *Tocqueville and the Old Regime* (Princeton, 1958).
52. For the classic statement of this difference see Tocqueville's early (and Burke influenced) essay in the *Westminster Review*, 1836, 'On the Social and Political Affairs in France and in England'.

53. Furet, op. cit., p. 57; Marx's review in *Surveys*, p. 255; C. Hill, 'The English Civil War as Interpreted by Marx', loc. cit. For some early texts of Tocqueville's closer to Marx's verdict than to Guizot's or his own after 1848, S. Drescher (ed.), *Tocqueville in England* (Cambridge, Mass., 1964).
54. Furet, loc. cit.
55. D. Forbes, 'Scientific Whiggism: Adam Smith and John Millar', *Cambridge Historical Journal*, 7 (11), 1954, p. 252f. For the incorporation of Hume into Whig historiography, see J. Burrow, *A Liberal Descent* (Cambridge, 1981), chapters 1, 2.
56. T. B. Macaulay, 'History of England', *The Works of Lord Macaulay*, ed. Lady Trevelyan, vol. 1 (London, 1879), p. 119.
57. J. G. A. Pocock, 'The Varieties of Whiggism from Exclusion to Reform' in *Virtue, Commerce and History* (Cambridge, 1985), pp. 304–5; P. B. M. Blaas, *Continuity and Anachronism* (The Hague, 1978), pp. 111–22. Recent studies of Macaulay have underlined his preference for balancers, reconcilers and pragmatists who successfully married continuity and change; see John Burrow, op. cit.; J. Millgate, *Macaulay* (1973); J. Hamburger, *Macaulay and the Whig Tradition* (Chicago, 1976), esp. chapter 6; J. Clive, *Macaulay: The Shaping of the Historian* (New York, 1973).
58. For this and the following sections see Blair Worden, 'The Revolution of 1688 and the English Republican Tradition' in Jonathan I. Israel (ed.), *The Anglo-Dutch Moment: Essays on the Glorious Revolution and its World Impact* (Cambridge, 1991), p. 241–80; 'Lawful Resistance', *London Review of Books*, 24 November 1988, pp. 5–6; J. W. Burrow, op. cit., chapter 2.
59. Worden, 'The Revolution of 1688', loc. cit., pp. 270–1; H. Dickinson, 'The Eighteenth Century Debate on the Glorious Revolution', *History*, 61, 1976, pp. 28–45; J. G. A. Pocock, 'The Fourth English Civil War: Dissolution, Desertion, and Alternate Histories of the Glorious Revolution' in L. Schwoerer (ed.), *The Revolution of 1688–89: Changing Perspectives* (Cambridge, 1992), pp. 52–64.
60. Worden, 'Lawful Resistance', p. 5. For Hume's belief that his comparatively Whiggish treatment of the later Stuarts would answer criticism of the supposed Tory features of his work on the early Stuarts, see V. G. Wexler, *David Hume and the History of England* (Philadephia, 1979), pp. 26–44; see also N. Capaldi and D. W. Livingstone (eds), *Liberty in David Hume's History of England* (Dordrecht, 1990).
61. B. Hill, *The Republican Virago: The Life and Times of Catherine Macaulay, Historian* (Oxford, 1992), p. 31ff; Lynne E. Witty, 'Catherine Macaulay and the Uses of History: Ancient Rights, Perfectionism and Propaganda', *Journal of British Studies* (JBS), 16, 1976, p. 59–83; P. Kirsten, *Patriot Heroes in England and America* (Maddison, Wisc., 1978), pp. 119–20.
62. P. Kitson, ' "Sages and patriots that being dead do yet speak to us": Readings of the English Revolution in the Late Eighteenth Century' in J. Holstun (ed.), *Pamphlet Wars: Prose in the English*

Revolution (1992), pp. 205–30; J. Burrow, 'Coleridge and the English Revolution', *Political Science*, 40, 1988, pp. 128–41; N. Leask, *The Politics of Imagination in Coleridge's Political Thought* (1988).

63. Worden, 'Lawful Resistance', loc. cit.; B. Fontana, *Rethinking the Politics of Commercial Society: The Edinburgh Review 1802–32* (Cambridge, 1985), pp. 11ff., 17, 37–8, 47ff.

64. (J. W. Croker), 'The Revolutions of 1640 and 1830', *Quarterly Review*, xlvii, 1832, pp. 261–300, esp. pp. 295–6; ibid., pp. 559–89 ('Stages of Revolution' – a review by Southey – of Lord Nugent's 'Memorials of John Hampden').

65. J. Morris, 'Republicanism and Public Virtue: William Godwin's History of the Commonwealth of England', *Historical Journal* (HJ) 34/3, 1991, pp. 645–64; R. C. Richardson, *The Debate on the English Revolution* (1977) chapter 2, passim; Worden in Israel, op. cit., pp. 274ff.

66. Quoted in Worden, 'Lawful Resistance', p. 5; Kirsten, op. cit., p. 156ff; Thomas Carlyle, *Oliver Cromwell's Letters and Speeches, with elucidations*, 2 vols (1845).

67. Burrow, op. cit., chapter 2; Roy Pascal, 'Property and Society: The Scottish Historical School of the Eighteenth Century', *Modern Quarterly* (MQ), 1/ii, 1938, pp. 167–79, esp. pp. 178–9.

68. Macaulay, *Works*, vol. 2, p. 396–7; Blaas, op. cit., pp. 143–4; Burrow, op. cit., pp. 46–9.

69. For this whole development see Blaas, op. cit., pp. 140ff; R. C. Richardson, op. cit., p. 69ff; J. S. A. Adamson, 'Eminent Victorians: S. R. Gardiner and the Liberal as Hero', *HJ*, 33/3, 1990, pp. 641–57.

70. T. H. Green, 'Lectures on the English Revolution' (The English Commonwealth), 1860, in R. L. Nettleship (ed.), vol. III *Collected Works* vol. III (1889), pp. 277–364, esp. pp. 362–4; M. Richter, *The Politics of Conscience: T. H. Green and His Age* (1964).

71. G. M. Trevelyan, *England under the Stuarts* (1965 ed), pp. 186–7, 215. First published in 1904, and running to twenty-three editions with many reprints, it was and perhaps still is *the* history of the seventeenth century in the classroom and the lending library. For a modern version of the contrast between French 'needs' and Anglo-American constitutional idealism, see Hannah Arendt, *On Revolution* (Harmondsworth, 1973) passim.

72. G. M. Trevelyan, *The English Revolution* (1938), pp. 240–5, esp. pp. 245. Written at the height of appeasement – which he approved – it marked a further declension of the Whig polemicist of *The Age of Wycliffe* and the *Garibaldi Trilogy* into the 'national historian' of *England under Queen Anne* and *English Social History*. see D. Cannadine, *G. M. Trevelyan* (1992).

73. G. M. Trevelyan, *English Social History* (1942), pp. 233–4. In his demonology of Marxism and Liberalism, J. C. D. Clark attacks Trevelyan for having 'unthinkingly absorbed Marxism'. Whatever the case may have been with his earlier works (and one doubts whether he ever absorbed much Marx), nothing could be

less true of his writing after 1918; indeed, as both Trevelyan and his Marxist critics made clear, his was an increasingly conservative and pessimistic vision, obsessed with what he saw as the mortally endangered fabric of traditional English life. See J. C. D. Clark, *Revolution and Rebellion*, pp. 144–5; D. Cannadine, op. cit., pp. 167–70.

74. L. Colley, *Namier* (1989), pp. 49–50.

75. H. A. L. Fisher, *History of Europe* (1935), introduction; E. J. Hobsbawm, 'Where are British Historians Going?', *Marxist Quarterly (MxQ)*, 2, 1, 1955, pp. 15–16; C. Hill, 'A Whig Historian', *MQ*, 1/iii, 1939, pp. 275–84.

76. W. S. Churchill, *The History of the English Speaking Peoples*, vol. 2 (1956–8), p. 219. Published in the 1950s, this volume was written in the late 1930s. There are three revolutions in Churchill's history, two good, one bad, none of them 1641 or 1649: namely 1688, 1775, 1789. Similarly, Arthur Bryant's ghostly monument to Whig history, a 3-volume *History of Britain and the British People* (1985–9), conceived in the 1930s but not published until the mid 1980s, reduced the English Civil War to vanishing point: barely one page (in volume 2, the characteristically entitled *Freedom's Own Island*) out of the total of over fifteen hundred!

77. Godfrey Davies, *The Early Stuarts, 1603–1660* (Oxford, 1938), preface, pp. 260 ff. Davies' relegation of social, economic and cultural history was extreme even by the modest standards of the other volumes of the Oxford History. For Hill's critique in 1938, of a history written 'in the old empirical way', with 'no philosophy' and 'no scheme', which fell 'a victim to words' and to 'conventional assumptions', *M.Q.*, I i (1938) pp. 91–4; in subsequent warnings to his students of the limitations of narrow constitutional history, the name of Godfrey Davies loomed large (communication from Dr John Morrill). See also 'Historians on the Rise of British Capitalism', *Science and Society*, (SS) xiv, 1950 pp. 307–8.

78. Douglas Garman, 'In Praise of Revolution', *CR*, February 1950, p. 59.

79. The interwar period witnessed a revival in the fortunes of Charles I, Laud and Strafford. See M. Meredith, *Charles I, King and Martyr* (1922); C. Colt, *Charles I* (1924); E. John, *Charles I* (1933); J. Brookes, *A Vindication of Charles I* (1934). Three better known (and better) examples of the now fashionable Cavalier genre of the period are: C. V. Wedgwood's super-sympathetic portrait of *Strafford* (1935); Esme Wingfield-Stratford's, *Charles, King of England* (1948–50), based on his earlier *King Charles and the Conspirators* (1937), and Bishop David Matthew's *The Social structure of Caroline England* (Oxford, 1948). H. R. Trevor-Roper's *Archbishop Laud* (1940), though by no means hostile either to Laud or to Charles's court, is rather more difficult to categorize.

80. C. V. Wedgwood, *The King's Peace* (1955); T. S. Eliot, *Selected Essays* (1961); *On Poetry and Poets* (1955); Irene Coltman, *Private Men and Public Causes: Philosophy and Politics in the English Civil War*

(1962); B. G. Wormold, *Clarendon: Politics, History and Religion* (Cambridge, 1964).
81. See the chapter headings of E. Wingfield-Strafford *King Charles and King Pym* (1948): 'The Reign of Terror'; 'Revolution by Law'; 'Trial and no Trial'; 'Terror by Legislation', etc.
82. The reinstatement of Cromwell as a national hero started in 1934 with John Buchan's biography: J. Buchan, *Cromwell* (1934); M. Ashley, *Oliver Cromwell: Conservative Dictator* (1937); C. V. Wedgwood, *Cromwell* (1938); E. Wingfield-Stratford, *The Foundation of British Patriotism* (1939); H Ross Williamson, *Charles I and Cromwell* (1940).
83. M. Beloff, 'The Good Old Cause', review in *The Observer*, 26 March 1950. The reference is to K. Feiling, *England under the Tudors and Stuarts* (1950).
84. For the historiographical battles between the Académie Française and the Sorbonne, see P. Geyl, *Napoleon, For and Against* (1958). See also *Encounters in History* (1961): 'Historians for and against the French Revolution'.
85. The terminology is Pocock's. J. G. A. Pocock, *Virtue, Commerce and History*, p. 305. H. Butterfield, *The Englishman and his History* (Cambridge, 1944), pp. 104ff. Cf H. Butterfield, *The Whig Interpretation of History* (Cambridge, 1931).
86. H. Butterfield, *The Englishman*, part II, passim., esp. pp. 84, 96, 106–7, 112–13, 116–17.
87. G. M. Trevelyan, *English Social History*, p. 408. Trevelyan's was not an isolated comment. See also H. A. L. Fisher, op. cit., p. 887: 'The French legislator did not hunt the fox. No French Epsom or Newmarket sweetened the severity or abated the logic of his political mediations'! For a comment on this and other sporting reflections, see C. Hill, 'A Whig Historian', loc. cit.

Chapter 2 Reclaiming the Revolution

1. C. Hill, quoted in Harvey J. Kaye, op. cit., p. 102.
2. C. Hill, 'Marxism and History' in *MQ* (new series), 3, 2, 1948, pp. 56, 58; 'The English Revolution and the State', ibid., 4, 2, 1949, pp. 110; 'England's Democratic Army', *CR*, June 1947, p. 171–2; 'The Fight for an Independent Foreign Policy, ibid., February 1948, pp. 46, 51–2.
3. J. G. A. Pocock, *Virtue, Commerce and History*, pp. 258–9.
4. Samuel, 'British Marxist Historians', loc. cit., p. 84.
5. Ibid., p. 55.
6. Samuel, loc. cit., p. 37ff. This whole section relies heavily on Samuel's account.
7. P. Collinson, *Godly People* (1983), p. 529ff; C. Hill, 'Religious History and Denominational History' in *Collected Essays, 1: Writing and Revolution in 17th Century England* (Brighton, 1985). The references are to J. Waddington, *Track of the Hidden Church or The Springs of the Pilgrim Movement* (Boston, 1863); and his monumental 5-volumed *Congregational History* (New York, 1869–80); H. M.

Dexter, *The Congregational Movement of the Last 300 Years as Seen in its Literature* (New York, 1880).

8. E. P. Thompson, *William Morris: Romantic to Revolutionary* (1977), p. 7ff; E. Belfort Bax, *The Rise and Fall of the Anabaptists* (1903); *German Society at the end of the Middle Ages* (1894); *The Peasants' War in Germany* (1898); *The Story of the French Revolution* (1890); *J-P. Marat: A Historico-Biographical Sketch* (1882); *J-P. Marat, The People's Friend* (1901); *The Last Episode of the French Revolution: Being a History of Gracchus Babeuf* (1911).

9. Samuel, loc. cit., p. 53ff.

10. Charles Raven in J. Lewis (ed.), *Christianity and the Social Revolution* (1935), p. 22; F. W. Dillistone, *Charles Raven: Naturalist, Historian, Theologian* (1975).

11. R. H. Tawney, *Commonplace Book* (J. Winter, D. M. Joslin, eds) (Cambridge, 1972), pp. 17, 34; J. Winter, *Socialism and the Challenge of War* (1974), p. 83ff.

12. Engels, *Primitive Christianity*, quoted in Samuel, loc. cit., p. 45; R. H. Hyndman, *The Evolution of Revolution* (1920), pp. 9–18, 207; E. Belfort Bax, *Anabaptists*, pp. 390ff; 'Folklore of the Reformation', 'Early Christianity' in *Outspoken Essays* (1897); *The Religion of Socialism and the Ethics of Socialism* (1889); S. Pierson, 'E. Belfort Bax: the Encounter of Marxism and Late Victorian Culture', *JBS*, 12, 1972; *Marxism and the Origins of Bolshevism* (Cornell, 1973).

13. Lewis, 'The Jesus of History' and 'Communism, Heir to the Christian Tradition', in his *Christianity and the Social Revolution*; cf his editorials in *MQ* (2nd series); *Marxism and the Irrationalists* (1955)

14. E. P. Thompson, 'The Transforming Power of the Cross', in his *Making of the English Working Class* (MEWC). For Hill see the works analyzed in Chapters 4, 5, and – most recently and explicitly – his *The English Bible and the Seventeenth Century Revolution* (1993).

15. See above Chapter 1.

16. T. H. Green, 'Lectures on the English Revolution' (The English Commonwealth), 1860, in *Collected Works*, vol. III (R. L. Nettleship, ed.) (1889), pp. 277–8, 358–64; M. Richter, op. cit.

17. M. Weber, *The Protestant Ethic and the Spirit of Capitalism* (first published in German 1904–5, Eng. trans. by Talcott Parsons, London, 1930); R. H. Tawney, *Religion and the Rise of Capitalism* (1926); William Haller, *The Rise of Puritanism*, (1938); *Liberty and Reformation in the Puritan Revolution* (1955); *John Foxe and his Book of Martyrs* (1965); Perry Miller, *Orthodoxy in Massachusets: A Genetic Study* (Cambridge, Mass., 1933); *The New England Mind* (Cambridge, Mass., 1939); *Errand in the Wilderness* (Cambridge, Mass., 1955); P. Collinson, *Godly People*, pp. 529ff; L. S. Trinterud, 'William Haller, Historian of Puritanism', *JBS*, 5, ii, 1965, pp. 33–55. I owe the idea of 'vertical' as opposed to 'horizontal' religious history to conversations with Professor Patrick Collinson.

18. J. Morrison Davidson, *The Wisdom of Winstanley, the Digger* (1904) pp. 3ff; J. Clayton, *Leaders of the People: Studies in Democratic History* (1910); L. H. Berens, *The Digger Movement in the Days of the*

Commonwealth as Revealed in the Writings of Gerrard Winstanley (1906); *The Social Problem . . . or the Creed of the Levellers* (1898); E. Bernstein, *Cromwell and Communism* (trans. from the original German edition of 1895 by H. Stenning, London 1930).

19. The Putney Debates became something of the centrepiece of the Balliol tutorial programme under A. D. Lindsay as Master in the 1930s and continued to be so up until Hill's retirement in 1978. Both C. H. Firth and A. S. P. Woodhouse published the text of the debates in full.

20. Drusilla Scott, *A. D. Lindsay, a Biography* (Oxford, 1971), esp. pp. 5, 271, 280–2; A. D. Lindsay, *The Essentials of Democracy* (1929), pp. 10ff; 'Socialism and Liberty', *Lindsay Mss University of Keele*; *The Churches and Democracy* (1934); *The Modern Democratic State* (1943): the theme of democracy and its seventeenth-century English roots runs through many of Lindsay's Balliol Sermons; C. Hill, *Oxford Magazine*, 23 February 1961.

21. Lindsay, 'Socialism and Liberty', loc. cit., p. 5; W, Haller (ed.), *Tracts on Liberty* (1933); W. Haller and G. Davies (eds), *The Leveller Tracts 1647–54* (Columbia, 1944); D. Wolfe (ed.), *Leveller Manifestoes of the Puritan Revolution* (1944). For an example of their impact, see A. Bevan, *Why Not Trust the Tories* (1944).

22. J. E. Thorold Rogers, *History of Agriculture and Prices in England* (1866–85), vol. I introduction p. vi, vol. IV, p. xv; *Six Centuries of Work and Wages* (1884), p. 340. Samuel notes (fn. 69) that the latter went though eleven editions between 1884 and 1912.

23. J. R. Green, *A Short History of the English People* (1874). In the period up to World War I, twelve editions of this extremely popular work were published. For an appreciation of Green's democratic reading of the past, see J. Burrow, *A Liberal Descent* (Cambridge, 1981); G. H. Blore, *Victorian Worthies: Sixteen Biographies* (Oxford, 1920); R. H. Hyndman, *The Historical Basis of English Socialism* (1883), p. 22.

24. Samuel, loc. cit., pp. 38–9; J. R. Green, *Stray Studies* (1876); W. Morris, *The Dream of John Ball* (1888); Morris and Bax, *Socialism, its Growth and Outcome* (1893) devoted nearly 100 out of its 220 pages to the period before 1500; Hyndman, *Historical Basis*; J. Clayton, *Wat Tyler and the Great Uprising* (1909); *Robert Kett and the Norfolk Rising* (1912); *Bows against Barons* (1934).

25. Burrow, op. cit., chapter 5; E. Freeman, *The History of the Norman Conquest* (1867–79); J. R. Green, *The Making of England* (1882); *The Conquest of England* (1884).

26. Asa Briggs, *Saxons, Normans and Victorians* (1966), passim; Thorold Rogers, in Briggs, p. 8; Green, *Short History*, vol. p. I, p. xi. For the works of J. L. and B. Hammond, see esp. *The Village Labourer* (1911); *The Town Labourer* (1917); *The Skilled Labourer* (1919); P. Clarke, *Liberals and Social Democrats* (Cambridge, 1978), p. 155ff; J. Froude, *Oceana, or England and her Colonies* (1886).

27. G. Newman, *The Rise of English Nationalism: A Cultural History 1740–1830* (New York, 1987), esp. p. 185ff; L. Colley, *Britons: Forging*

the Nation 1707–1837 (Yale, 1992), pp. 25ff; Obediah Hulme, *Historical Essay on the English Constitution* (1771). See above, Chapter 1.

28. E. Rickword, 'Culture, Progress and English Tradition' (1937), reprinted in *Literature in Society: Essays and Opinions (II) 1931–78* (Manchester, 1978), pp. 93–104; H. Fagan, *Nine Days that shook England* (1938); J. Lindsay, *England, my England* (1939); J. Lindsay, E. Rickword (eds), *A Handbook of Freedom: A Record of English Democracy through Twelve Centuries* (1939). For a further consideration of these and other texts in the 1930s and 1940s, see below, 'Patriot Games'.

29. R. Vaughan Williams and A. L. Lloyd, *The English Folk Song* (1956); A. L. Lloyd, *The English Folk Song* (1975) was to refer to it as 'the musical and poetic expression of the fantasy of the lower classes', p. 22; 'The People's own Poetry', in 'The Past is Ours', *Daily Worked* (DW), 10 February 1937.

30. J. Needham, 'Laud, the Levellers and the Virtuosi' in J. Lewis, *Christianity and Social Revolution*, quoted in R. Samuel, op. cit., p. 50; J. Holerenshaw (pseudonym for J. Needham), *The Levellers and the English Revolution* (1939).

31. James Klugmann, in J. Clark et al. (ed.) *Culture and Crisis in Britain in the Thirties* (1980), p. 25, quoted in Schwarz, op. cit., p. 56.

32. This is brought out in P. Dodd and R. Colls, *Englishness: Politics and Culture, 1880–1920* (1987). It is also implicit in R. Samuel, *Patriotism: The Making and Unmaking of British Identity* (1988), introduction.

33. The term is Geoffrey Elton's, see J. P. Kenyon, *The History Men* (1983), p. 248; *Times Literary Supplement* (TLS), 11 February 1977; C. Hill: 'Tawney Fired the Imagination of My Generation', *P&P*, 100, 1983, p. 5.

34. R. H. Tawney, *The Agrarian Problem in the Sixteenth Century* (1912).

35. London, 1926: described by Elton, *TLS*, 11 February 1977, as 'one of the most harmful books written in the years between the wars'; David Ormrod, 'R. H. Tawney and the Origins of Capitalism', *History Workshop Journal*, 18, 1984, pp. 138–59.

36. R. H. Tawney, *The Acquisitive Society* (1921); *Equality* (1931).

37. 'The Rise of the Gentry: 1558–1640', first published in *Economic History Review*, xi, 1941, reprinted in (amongst others) J. M. Winter (ed.), *History and Society: Essays by R. H. Tawney* (1978). pp 85–129; *Business and Politics under James I* (Cambridge, 1958), quotation at p. 19.

38. 'The Rise of the Gentry', in Winter, op. cit., p. 89. This characteristically urbane formulation is a splendid example of Tawney's capacity to eat his Marxist cake and explain that he did not have it.

39. 'The Rise of the Gentry', passim.

40. 'Harrington's Interpretation of his Age', originally given as a British Academy lecture in 1944, *Proceedings of the British Academy*, 27, reprinted in Winter, op cit., pp. 71, 74, 78.

41. D. Ormrod, loc. cit., pp. 153ff; T's review of Dobb in Winter, op. cit., pp. 202–14; 'I don't mind Hill being a Marxist but I do wish

he wouldn't sing the doxology at the end of every piece he writes', quoted in R. C. Richardson op. cit., p. 97.
42. Tawney, *Religion and the Rise of Capitalism*, pp. 210, 212.
43. R. Terrill, *R. H. Tawney and his Times* (1974), pp. 224ff; A. Wright, *R. H. Tawney* (1987), esp. 'Tawney, Tawneyism and Today', pp.130–54; R. Samuel has argued passionately and on the whole convincingly that the latter is 'an exercise in generating fictitious moral capital rather than the acknowledgement of a spiritual debt', *The Guardian*, 29 March, 5 April 1982.
44. A. Howe, *Hill*, p. 49.
45. The texts which crop up most frequently in Hill's early writings apart from *The Communist Manifesto*, show a fairly heavy bias in the direction of Engels's later writings: e.g. *The Anti–Duhring*, *The Dialectics of Nature*, and *Socialism Utopian and Scientific*. For this whole issue, see especially Stuart MacIntyre, *A Proletarian Science: Marxism in Britain, 1917–33* (Cambridge, 1980), p. 66ff.
46. In the plethora of 'Spycatching' books in the 1980s, Dobb was to figure as a Comintern 'talent spotter' who might have 'recruited' some of 'the Cambridge traitors'. See J. Costello, *Mask of Treachery* (1989 edn), pp. 108–9, 150–6, 184–5; Philip Knightley, *Philby: The Life and Views of a K.G.B. Master Spy* (1988), pp.31–2, 35–6; 'V. G. Kiernan on Treason', *London Review of Books*, 25 June 1987.
47. R. H. Hilton 'Dobb as Historian', *Labour Monthly* (*LM*), January 1947, pp. 29–30. Quoted, along with similarly effusive comments from Hill in R. C. Richardson, *The Debate on the English Revolution* (1977), p. 100.
48. M. Dobb, *Studies in the Development of Capitalism* (1946); E. J. Hobsbawm, 'Maurice Dobb' in C. H. Feinstein (ed.), *Socialism, Capitalism and Economic Growth: Essays Presented to Maurice Dobb* (Cambridge, 1967), pp. 1–2, 6. Although the detailed analysis was strenuously Marxist, Dobb's work always carried the imprint of Alfred Marshall's Cambridge style of formal economics.
49. For the various criticisms, see Schwarz, op. cit., p. 52–3; Simon Clark, 'Socialist Humanism and the Critique of Economism', *History Workshop*, 8, 1979, esp. pp. 140–9; M. Dobb, 'The Transition from Feudalism to Capitalism', *Historians' Group of the Communist Party, Our History series* (*OH*), 29, 1963; R. H. Tawney, 'A History of Capitalism' in J. M. Winter (ed.), *History and Society*, pp. 202–14.
50. Dobb was in intellectual disgrace within the CPGB for much of the 1930s, for appearing 'to think that the study of Marxism is rather an intellectual exercise than a method for advancing the class struggle'. See the review of his book *On Marxism Today* in *CR*, July 1932, pp. 343–8 ('Marxism vulgarized'); *Daily Worker* (*DW*), 26 July 1932 ('Maurice Dobb's Distortions of Marxism'; 'Our answer: Dobb's false basis').
51. C. Hill, 'Soviet Interpretations of the English Interregnum', *Economic History Review* (*EcHR*), VIII, 1937–8. p. 159.
52. For bringing to my attention the whole issue of the Soviet

background (including the Pokrovsky debate, borrowings from
'The Short Course', etc.) usually ignored in treatments of Hill's
work, A. Howe, *Hill*, chapter 1.

53. *EcHR*, viii, 1938, pp. 159–67 (comment on Soviet historians, at
pp. 159–60); *English Historical Review*, (*EHR*) lv, 1940, pp. 222–50.
Hill later noted that he read 15 Russian books and 30 articles on
seventeenth-century history during his stay: amongst them would
have been S. I. Arkhangelsky, V. M. Lavrovsky, M. A. Barg, V. F.
Semeonov, E. A. Kosminsky, see 'The Teaching of British History
in the USSR', *Anglo-Soviet Journal*, xii/3, 1951 pp. 16–22.

54. Hobsbawm, HG, p. 24.

55. For Pokrovsky, see A. Howe, *Hill*, pp. 4–5; P. H. Aron, 'N. M.
Pokrovskii and the Impact of the 1st 5 Year Plan on Soviet
Historiography' in J. S. Curtiss, *Essays in Russian and Soviet History* (Leiden, 1963), pp. 283–302, esp. pp. 287–92; John Barber,
'The Establishment of Intellectual Orthodoxy in the USSR, 1928–
32', *P&P*, 83, 1979, pp. 141–64, esp. pp. 150–5; J. Barber, *Soviet
Historians in Crisis, 1928–32* (1981), pp. 2–5, 19–23, 137–9; K. Shteppa,
Russian Historians and the Soviet State (New Brunswick, 1962),
pp.123–5, 127, 132; G. Friedman, 'Revolt against Formalism', *Science and Society*, II, i, 1937, pp. 300–21; L. Kolakowski, *Main Currents of Marxism*, vol. III (Oxford, 1978), pp. 49,91; B. H. Sumner,
'Soviet History', *Slavonic and East European Review*, xvi/46. pp.
601–15; xvii/49, pp. 151–61 (1937–8); R. W. Davies, 'The Discussion
on the Periodization of Russian History', *Anglo-Soviet Review*, xii/
4, 1951–2, pp. 4–12; C. Enteen, *The Soviet Scholar and Bureaucrat:
M.N. Pokrovskii and the Society of Marxist Historians* (Pennsylva-
nia, 1978), pp. 165–86; K. Mehnert, *Stalin versus Marx: The Stalinist
Historical Doctrine* (New York, 1952), pp. 11ff: 'Pokrovsky Died
Twice'.

56. See esp. Moscow Academy of Science, *Against M. N. Pokrovsky's
Historical Conception* (Moscow, 1939).

57. Bill Jones, *The Russia Complex* (Manchester, 1977), pp. 11–30; E.
Kamenka, *Bureaucracy* (Oxford, 1989), pp. 144–54; T. H. Rigby,
'Birth of the Soviet Bureaucracy', *Politics*, vii, 1972 pp. 121–35.
For the particular moment (1935) 'a good time to be a Left–wing
idealist', E.P. Thompson, 'Caudwell', *Socialist Register* (*SR*), 1977,
p. 27.

58. Jones, op. cit., pp. 12, 13–14; C. Hill, quoted in Harvey Kaye, op.
cit., p. 102.

59. G. Orwell, 'Inside the Whale', *Collected Essays, Journalism and Letters of George Orwell* (CEJL), ed. Sonia Orwell and Ian Angus vol.
1 (1968), pp. 561–5, gives the most persuasive account of this
process.

60. P. Spriano, *Stalin and the European Communists* (1985), pp. 86–7
(quoting Georges Cogniot).

61. Jones, op. cit., p. 13; M. Dobb, *Soviet Russia and the World* (1932),
pp. 144ff; *Russia, Today and Tomorrow* (1932), pp. 15ff; J. Lindsay,
'*A World Ahead': Journal of a Soviet Journey* (1950), pp. 5, 6, 10–12;

D. Caute, *The Fellow-Travellers: A Postscript to the Enlightenment* (1973), pp. 60ff; S. and B. Webb, *Soviet Communism: A New Civilization?* (1936): the second edition took off the question mark; Orwell, quoted in Richardson, op. cit., p. 102.

62. C. Hill, *Lenin and the Russian Revolution* (1947), 1978 edn, p. 167ff; K. Holme (pseudonym for C. Hill), *Two Commonwealths* (1945) in the series *The Soviets and Ourselves*.

63. Spriano, op. cit., p 88; F. Claudin, *The Communist Movement from Comintern to Cominform* (1970) 1975 edn,. p. 307ff.

64. C. Hill, *Lenin*, p. 169–70. This refrain has been repeated as recently as 1993 in *The Bible and the English Revolution*, p. 175.

65. A. Koestler in R. H. S. Crossman (ed.), *The God that Failed* (1948), pp. 73–82, esp. pp. 81–2; for the illusion that no compromises were made, see Hobsbawm, H. G.; for the heightened vision, R. Wright in Crossman (ed.), op. cit., pp. 42–4.

66. Hill worked primarily with E. A. Kosminsky, best known as the historian of peasant stratification in late medieval England, but also a student of 'Absolutism' who stressed its 'feudal' characteristics. For an appreciation, see his review of E. A. Kosminsky (ed.), *The English Bourgeois Revolution of the 17th Century* (2 vols, Russian) EHR, lxxi, 1956, pp. 458–62.

67. For the issue of Marx House and its 'History Faculty' in the late 1930s, see A. Howe, draft PhD, chapter on 'Origins of the Historians' Group'.

68. Hobsbawm, H. G., p. 24. For a sample of Hill's regular summaries of the work of Soviet historians, *Anglo-Soviet Journal*, xii/3, 1951, pp. 16–22; *LM*, June 1955; *EHR*, lxxi, 1956; 'The Bourgeois Revolutions in Soviet Scholarship', *NLR*, 155, 1986, pp. 107–13. Hill's *English Revolution, 1640*, was translated into Russian in the early 1950s.

69. Samuel, loc. cit., p. 55. Stalin enjoyed a peculiar prestige in the British Party. Here, as nowhere else, he was domesticated as Old or Uncle Joe. See R. Samuel, 'The Lost World of British Communism', Part 2, *NLR*, 156, March–April 1986, pp. 106ff.

70. G. Werskey, *The Visible College* (1978), pp. 176–211, 249–58 esp. pp. 252–3; M. Goldsmith, *Sage: A Life of J. D. Bernal* (London 1980).

71. *MQ*, 1, 2, editorials, 1938–9; J. D. Bernal, *The Social Function of Science* (1939), quoted in Werskey, op. cit., pp. 185–86.

72. Ibid., p. 193.

73. J. H. Hexter, 'The Historical Method of Christopher Hill', *TLS*, 25 October 1975, reprinted in Hexter, *On Historians* (1979), pp. 227–51; G. Himmelfarb, 'The Group: British Marxist Historians', *The New History and the Old: Critical Essays and Reappraisals* (Cambridge, Mass., 1987), pp. 70–93. For a further discussion of these proclivities, see Chapter 4.

74. Stalin *et al.*, *History of the Communist Party of the Soviet Union (Bolsheviks): Short Course* (Moscow, 1938), chapter IV, section 2, 'Dialectical and Historical Materialism' (London, edn 1938), pp. 106–14. Published in huge quantities and distributed to party

members, it was 'a complete Marxist catechism for a whole generation': Kolakowski, op. cit., vol. III, p. 93. Hill quoted great slabs of it in his 'Stalin and the Science of History', *MQ*, 8 (4), Autumn 1953, pp. 200–3; Dutt's *Labour Monthly* ran a series in 1933 (later published as *Dialectical Materialism and Communism*, in 1934) on the new orthodoxy; E. F. Carritt and J. D. Bernal, *Aspects of Dialectical Materialism* (Oxford, 1934); S. Parsons, *Communism in the Professions: The Organization of the British Communist Party among Professional Workers, 1933–1956* (Warwick PhD, 1990), pp. 175ff. for this whole issue.

75. J. Stalin, *Leninism* (Eng. trans. London, 1940), pp. 109–10, 114: the passage is quoted verbatim by Hill in 'Stalin', loc. cit., p. 199.

76. For some examples of these distinctions, see below, the debates on Hill's 'English Revolution 1640', the debates on 'State and Revolution', 1947–8, and on 'Inner party Democracy' in 1956.

77. Kolakowski, op. cit., vol. 3, pp. 103–4, 121ff; Spriano, op. cit., pp. 79–87.

78. Ibid., pp. 87–8.

79. Hobsbawm, H. G., p. 23ff. Bernal commented on the absence of Marxist teaching in the English universities as late as 1952, see *Marx and Science* (1952), pp. 28ff.

80. 'The British Constitution', *MQ* 2/ii, 1939, pp. 198–205; C. Hill, 'Marxism and History', loc. cit., pp. 56, 58; 'The English Revolution and the State', loc. cit. p. 110; 'A Whig Historian' (H. A. L. Fisher), *MQ*, 1, 1938, pp. 275–84; 'A Liberal (Trevelyan) looks at History', *CR*, 1946, pp. 27ff; Hobsbawm, 'Where are English Historians Going', loc. cit., p. 16.

81. L. Kolakowski, 'The Marxist Roots of Stalinism' in R. Tucker (ed.), *Stalinism: Essays in Historical Interpretation* (1976), p. 283–98.

82. Stalin, *Short Course*, pp. 54–5, 68–72.

83. R. Samuel, 'The Lost World of British Communism', Part 3, *NLR*, 165, September–October 1987, p. 64. Samuel's account of 'The Lost World of British Communism' (Part 1, *NLR*, 154, November–December 1985 pp. 3–54; Part 2, 156, March–April 1986, pp. 63–113; Part 3, 165, September–October 1987, pp. 52–92.) has been criticized for exaggerating its sectarian quality. See J. Saville, *SR*, 1989.

84. A. Metcalfe, 'Myths of the Class Struggle' (typescript, pp. 9–17). I would like to thank Andrew Metcalfe for a copy of this important article prior to publication.

85. Samuel, 'Lost World', Part 3, loc. cit., pp. 60–1, 62–5.

86. Stalin, *Short Course*, pp. 129–30; Hill, 'Stalin and the Science of History', loc. cit., p. 202; Samuel, 'Lost World', Part 1, loc. cit., pp. 36–7. R. Palme Dutt, *The Social and Political Doctrine of Communism* (1938), pp. 23, 25, 28–9 gives a particularly forceful Jacobin reading.

87. C. Hill, *The English Revolution 1640* (1940), p. 7.

88. Ibid., pp. 9–10, 43, 51.

89. 'Our England': review of Jack Lindsay's 'England, my England', *LM*, February 1939, p. 127. In his *1649; A Novel of a Year* (1938),

Lindsay set up an opposition between commerce and revolution; something which implicitly undermined the bourgeois character of the revolution, see H. Gustav Klaus, 'Socialist Fiction in the 1930s: Some Preliminary Observations', *Renaissance and Modern Studies*, XX, 1976, pp. 30–1.

90. G. Lefebvre, *Quatre–Vingt Neuf* (Paris, 1939). English version, '*The Coming of the French Revolution* (trans. R. Palmer) (Princeton, 1947) which omits the famous last paragraph calling on Frenchmen of 1939 to follow in the footsteps of 'our ancestors . . . who fought at Valmy', etc.

91. G. M. Trevelyan, *The English Revolution*, passim. Trevelyan's text is perhaps more interesting for its omissions than for its constitutional pieties: the crucial international dimension is notably absent. Since perhaps the most important consequence of the Revolution was twenty-five years of warfare in defence of 'the liberties of Europe', this might be thought surprising – but in the year of Munich (which T supported) and the prudential abandonment of small European countries a long way away, perhaps not.

92. G. E. Gore (C. Hill pseudonym: Gore=Hill in Russian), 'The 250th Anniversary of the "Glorious Revolution"', *Communist International*, November 1938, pp. 22–9; Blair Worden, 'Lawful Resistance', loc. cit.

93. C. Hill, 'The English Revolution Revisited', paper delivered at the Humanities Research Centre, ANU Canberra. February 1981, typescript; Barry Reay, 'The World Turned Upside Down: A Retrospect' in G. Eley and W. Hunt, *Reviving the English Revolution: Reflections and Elaborations on the Work of Christopher Hill* (1988), p. 55; T. Harris and C. Husbands, 'Talking with Christopher Hill', Part 1, ibid., pp. 99–100.

94. P. Dutt, '*Why this War*' (1939), p. 31ff; *LM*, 21, November 1939, p. 607–8; 'Manifesto of the Central Committee of the CPGB'; 'Statement issued by the Executive Committee of Comintern', November 1939, quoted in J. Attfield and S. Williams (eds), *The Communist Party of Great Britain and the War: Proceedings of Conference Organized by C. P. Historians Group 21 April 1979* (1980), pp. 169–74; F. King and G. Matthews, *About Turn: The Communist Party and the Outbreak of the Second World War: The Verbatim Record of the Central Committee Meetings 1939* (1990). For a somewhat anodyne account see N. Branson, *A History of the Communist Party of Great Britain* (1985); more critical are, K. Morgan, *Against Fascism and War: Ruptures and Continuities in British Communist Politics* (Manchester, 1989), pp. 85–200; H. Pelling, *The British Communist Party: A Historical Profile* (1958), pp. 109–19; J. Jupp, *The Radical Left in Britain* (1982), pp. 163–72.

95. Sidney Hook, *Out of Step: An Unquiet Life in the 20th Century* (New York, 1987), pp. 175–6, 298ff (quoting the American Communist leader, Earl Browder); Palme Dutt, Notes of the Month, July, November 1939, *LM* 21, pp. 352ff, 608; ibid., November 1940, 22/11, pp. 563–72.; Pelling, op. cit., pp. 110–12. E, Varga, *The Imperialist*

Struggle for a New Redivision of the World (Moscow, 1940) for the approved Soviet interpretation. Hill, himself, later seems to have been convinced that even after the defeat of Poland, the British and French governments were 'cheerfully planning a war against the Soviet Union', see his review of Andrew Rothstein, *History of the USSR* (Harmondsworth, 1950), *New Central European Observer* (*NCEO*), III/19, p. 211, 30 September 1950.

96.   *The English Revolution*, pp. 42–3.
97.   'My virulence against Charles I was, I fear, caused by conflating him with Neville Chamberlain just as my hostility to Laud was directed against the Tory school of historians': B. Reay in G. Eley and W. Hunt, op. cit., p. 55. The parallel between the Anglican Church of 1640 and the Russian Orthodox Church on the eve of the Revolution was stated in the *Two Commonwealths* of 1945.
98.   F. Furet, op. cit., pp. 95–6; P. Anderson, op. cit., p. 16, quoting passages from 'The Eighteenth Brumaire of Louis Bonaparte' and from 'The Civil War in France'.
99.   K. Mehnert, *Stalin versus Marx*, pp. 65ff., 111–13; J. Stalin,'On the Basis and Superstructure', *Pravda*, 5 October 1950.
100. C. Hill, 'Comment', in *Science and Society*, XVII, 4, 1953, p. 351.
101. Furet, op. cit., pp. 26–7; *Interpreting the French Revolution* (Cambridge, 1981); T. Judt, op. cit., pp. 177ff.
102. For the whole debate, see A. Howe, Draft PhD, chapter on 'The English Revolution' (unpublished materials cited in the following footnotes are drawn from Howe's photocopies); (Hill, Garman, Torr, Burns), 'Some Comments on the Present Controversy', 15 April 1941, Dutt Mss, file '1640', CPA.
103. Dr Jurgen Kuczynski, German CP member, refugee in England during the 1930s and 1940s, historian of nineteenth-century European capitalism, subsequently Professor of Economic History at the Humboldt University, East Berlin, see Howe, Draft chapter, p. 16.
104. This and the following paragraph is largely based on PF Review *LM*, 22, November 1940, pp. 558–9, and his much longer unpublished draft, 'The Great Rebellion', Dutt Mss, loc. cit.; K. Tribe, *Genealogies of Capitalism* (1981), pp. 9ff.
105. P. F. Draft, pp. 4, 7–8.
106. Ibid., pp. 5–6, 21.
107. *LM* Review, p. 559; Draft, pp. 6, 21, quoting Lenin to the effect that revolution 'in the strictly scientific and practical political meaning of the term', always involved 'the transfer of state power from one class to another'.
108. *LM* 22, December 1940, pp. 652–3 (Garman), 23, February 1941, pp. 90–2, 92–3 (Torr, Dobb); Tribe, op. cit., pp. 10–11.
109. See esp, 'Remarks on R.P.D's (Dutt's) Draft' from C.H.; unsigned 26p., 'Discussion Statement', Dutt Mss. loc. cit.; P. F. *LM*, 22, December 1940 pp. 653–5.
110. C. H. 'Remarks; Joint Letter, 15 April 1941, loc. cit; Torr, loc. cit. p. 91.

111. Garman, loc. cit.
112. Howe has uncovered material which makes this quite clear. See Draft chapter, pp. 18ff.
113. John Callagham, *Rajani Palme Dutt, A Study in British Stalinism* (1993). Amongst others things, Callaghan's study makes clear just how qualified was Dutt's conversion to Popular Frontism, and how much his espousal of the 'imperialist war' line of 1939 was a reinstatement of deeply held Leninist beliefs. See also, J. Callaghan, 'The Heart of Darkness – Rajani Palme Dutt and the British Empire – a Profile', *Contemporary Record*, 5/2, 1991; and the hostile Trotskyite sketch, C. Harman and I. Birchall, 'R. P. Dutt, Stalin's British Mouthpiece', *International Socialism*, 75, February 1975.
114. 'The British School of Marxism', *LM* 2, 1922, pp 429–31; 'More British Marxism', ibid., 4, 1923, p 124–8; 'Intellectuals and Communism', *CR*, September 1932, pp. 421–30. For the continuation of this attitude, see his correspondence with Betty Grant on the Historians' Group in 1957. CPA HG 60 C (General Correspondence).
115. Howe, Draft chapter, pp. 19–20; Joint Letter, pp. 3–4, loc. cit.
116. This can be followed in the various drafts in Dutt Mss.
117. 'Some Comments', p. 4; P.F. Draft, p. 22.
118. Samuel, 'British Marxist Historians', p. 55. For further examples, see below, Chapter 3.
119. For the following see esp. Miles Taylor, 'Patriotism, History and the Left in Twentieth Century Britain', *HJ*, 33/4, 1990, pp. 971–87. J. A. Hobson, *The Psychology of Jingoism* (1901); K. Martin, *The Magic of Monarchy* (1937); R. P. Dutt, 'The British School of Marxism', 'More British Marxism', loc. cit.; R. Page Arnott, '1914 and 1934', *LM*, 16/8, August 1934, pp. 488–96; S. MacIntyre, 'The Marxist Theory of Imperialism and the British Labour Movement', 'Our History', *OH*, lxiv (1975); George Orwell, 'Not Counting Niggers' in *CEJL*, vol. 1.
120. Hill (G.E. Gore), '250th Aniversary of 1688', loc. cit., pp. 23, 27–8; Hill always acknowledged that even among the radicals, Cromwell's Irish policies commanded widespread support, see 'Seventeenth-century British radicals and Ireland', in P. J. Corish, *Radicals, Rebels and Establishments* (Belfast, 1985).
121. For endemic imperialism, see R. P. Dutt, *Imperialism* (1939); *Modern India* (1927); *India Today* (1940); T. A. Jackson, *The British Empire* (1922); S. Howe, *Anticolonialism in British Politics: The Left and the End of Empire, 1918–1964* (Oxford, 1993), pp. 6–7, 27ff., 47ff, 53ff; J. Callaghan, *Rajani Palme Dutt*, pp. 82–109, 121–24, 153–162, 201–7.
122. Taylor, loc. cit., pp. 982ff; K. Martin, *Editor: A Second Volume of Autobiography* (1968); C. H. Rolph, *Kingsley: The Life, Letters and Diaries of Kingsley Martin* (1973); M. Foot ('Cato' pseud.), *Guilty Men* (1940); J. B. Priestley, *Our Nation's Heritage* (1939); *Postscripts* (1940); *Out of the People* (1941); *The English Spirit* (1942), etc.; H. Laski, *The Rights of Man* (1940); H. Deane, *The Political Ideas of*

Harold Laski (New York, 1955), p. 235ff; M. Newman, *Harold Laski: A Political Biography* (1993), pp. 206ff; I Kramnick and B. Sheerman, *Harold Laski: A Life on the Left* (1993); K. Martin, *Harold Laski, 1893–1950: A Biographical Memoir* (1953); V. Gollancz, *The Betrayal of the Left* (1941); J. Strachey, *A Faith to Fight for* (1941); D. Burchall, *Radical Descent: John Strachey and the British Left,* (Sydney PhD, 1991), pp. 388ff, who charts Strachey's 'seachange' more fully and persuasively than does H. Thomas, *Strachey* (1971); G. Orwell, *The Lion and the Unicorn* (1940) (esp. 'England, your England' – the title a response, not to D. H. Lawrence, but to J. Lindsay's essay of 1939), CEJL, vol. 2 pp. 75–134, esp. pp. 95ff.

123.   *Betrayal of the Left,* pp. 279–86.
124.   *Lion and the Unicorn,* CEJL, 2, p. 95.
125.   J. Lindsay, *England, My England,* p. 64; R. P. Dutt *Why this War* (1939); Notes of the Month, May 1940, *LM,* 22/5, pp. 285ff; E. Winterton, 'Left Intellectuals and the War', ibid., June 1940, pp. 355–60; 'Is this a War for Democracy', ibid., September 1940, pp. 285–94; Ivor Montague, *The Traitor Class* (1940).
126.   Attfield and Williams, op. cit., King and Matthews, op. cit., both give extracts from the relevant discussions and declarations; N. Wood, *Communism and the British Intellectuals* (1959), p. 188ff; D. Childs, 'The British C.P and the War 1939–41: Old Slogans Revived', *Journal of Contemporary History,* 1977, pp. 237–53; M. Shaw, 'War, Peace and British Marxism', in M. Taylor, and J. Young, *Campaigns for Peace: British Peace Movements in the Twentieth Century* (Manchester, 1987), pp. 48–72. Cf Hobsbawm's verdict – in his '*Revolutionaries*' (1973), pp. 5–6 – that 'there is something heroic about the British and French Communist Parties in September 1939. Nationalism, political calculation, even common sense pulled in one direction, yet they unhesitatingly chose to put the interests of the international movement first.' The one thing which, of course, is missing from his interpretation is Moscow's directive (which can be precisely placed with the arrival of Comintern's emissary, Dave Springhall, on 24 September 1939). The Communist parties of France and Britain were not fighting for socialist internationalism, they were doing what they were told to do by Stalin. For a view less clouded by special pleading, see Spriano, op. cit., pp. 116–25. 1 May, *CP Party Directive:* 'Demonstrate on this Day against Imperialist War'); *DW,* April, May 1940 passim (see esp. reports from C. Cockburn in Holland).
127.   *New Statesman (NS)* Correspondence, 27 April (J. Stratchey, V. Gollancz), pp. 559–60; W. Rust, 4 May pp. 588–9; C. Hill, *NS,* 18 May (in all fairness the letter was probably written a week earlier), p. 644.
128.   Orwell, Review of The English Revolution. *NS,* 24 August 1940, p. 193.
129.   Op. cit. pp. 61–2. Hill appears to have distanced himself from the excesses of the party's anti-war stance as early as June 1940.
130.   'Ajax', 'A Revolutionist's Handbook', *Left Review,* 1937 (reprint,

London, 1968); Taylor, loc. cit., p. 979; Samuel, 'British Marxist Historians', pp. 37ff; Schwarz, loc. cit., p 55–6; J. Klugmann in J. Clark, op. cit., p. 13–36; M. Heinemann, 'The People's Front and the Intellectuals' in J. Fyrth, *Britain, Fascism and the Popular Front* (1985), pp. 157–86.

131. J. Lindsay and E. Rickword (eds.), *A Handbook of Freedom: A Record of English Democracy through Twelve Centuries* (1939); T. A. Jackson, *Trials of British Freedom, Being Some Studies in the History of the Fight for Democratic Freedom in Britain* (1940); E. Rickword 'Literature and the Social Order' in *Literature in Society: Essays and Opinions 1931–78*, pp. 56–60; 'Culture, Progress and the English Tradition', originally in C. Day Lewis (ed.), *The Mind in Chains* (1937), reprinted in *Literature in Society*, pp. 93–104.

132. Jack Lindsay, *1649 – a Novel of a Year* (1938); *England my England* (1939); *Lost Birthright* (1939); H. Fagan, *Nine Days that Shook England* (1938); J. Holorenshaw, *The Levellers and the English Revolution* (1939); T. Wintringham, *Mutiny, Being a Survey of Mutinies from Spartacus to Invergordon* (1936).

133. Lindsay Rickword, *Handbook of Freedom*, pp. xx–xxi.

134. This paragraph follows David Fernbach, 'Tom Wintringham and Socialist Defence Strategy', *History Workshop Journal*, 14, 1982, pp. 63–91, esp. pp. 67–9; T. Wintringham, 'Who is for Liberty', *Left Review*, September 1935, pp. 484–5.

135. Rickword, *The Decline of Culture under Capitalism* (1936); D. Margolies, 'Left Review and Left Literary Theory' in J. Clark, op. cit., p. 68ff; J. Strachey, *The Coming Struggle for Power* (1932), pp. 186ff.

136. M. Heinemann, 'The People's Front', loc. cit., pp. 178–80 ('Reclaiming the past'); J. Saville, 'May Day 1937' in A. Briggs and J. Saville (eds), *Essays in Labour History, 1918–1939* (1977), pp. 232–84; Ralph Wright, 'The Past is Ours', *D.W*, 30 September 1936: subsequent articles were devoted to Defoe, Pepys, George Moore, Swift, Fielding, Shelley, Milton, Wordsworth, Hogarth, Popular ballads etc.; R. Swingler *et al.*, (eds), *Poetry and the People*' (later '*Our Time*') 1937–49. My assessment of the importance of 'cultural heritage' differs from H. Gustav Klaus, 'Socialist Fiction in the 1930s', loc. cit.

137. For this relationship, see esp. F. Mulhern, *The Moment of Scrutiny* (1979), pp. 63–72; T. Eagleton, *Literary Theory* (Oxford, 1983), pp. 28–30, 35ff. Amongst those involved in the exchanges during the 1930s, Leslie Morton and Douglas Garman (see *Scrutiny*, I/iii, December 1932, II/ii, March 1933) were especially prominent.

138. Rickword. op. cit., pp. 98–9. Francis Klingender and Anthony Blunt articulated a Marxist aesthetic which at times was practically indistinguishable from Scrutiny's. See Klingender, *Marxism and Modern Art: An Approach to Social Realism* (1943); Blunt, Art Criticism in *The Spectator*, 1934–5.

139. Butterfield, *Scrutiny*, 1/4, March 1933, pp. 339–55 (quotation at p. 342).

140. Eagleton, op. cit., pp. 35, 37; Ian Wright, 'F. R. Leavis, the Scrutiny Movement and the Crisis' in J. Clark, op. cit., pp. 37–65; A. Milner, *Cultural Materialism* (Melbourne, 1993), pp. 15, 20; F. R. Leavis, 'Sociology and Literature' in *The Common Pursuit* (1962 edn), pp. 200–1.
141. Rickword, op. cit., p. 99.
142. Lindsay, *England*, pp. 33, 64; Fagan, op. cit., pp. 159–60; Ted Bramley, 'Communism Grows from ENGLAND'S SOIL', *DW*, 14 September 1936 (ref. A. Howe, Draft chapter, pp. 4, 7ff.). Tony Howe will be providing further detail on the *Daily Worker* series, *The Past is Ours*, in his PhD.
143. Rickword, op. cit., p. 56.
144. Heinemann in Fyrth, op. cit. p. 180; *DW*, 14, 18, 21 September 1936; J. Saville, 'May Day 1937', in Briggs and Saville, op. cit. Tony Howe will be investigating a number of the pageants of the period – notably the great 'Pageant of English History' held on 20 September 1936 ('the onward march of English history for Peace, freedom and a merrie England'!) and the 'Heirs to the Charter' spectacular of 22 July 1938 (with a cast of 1500 and an audience of 10 000) – in his PhD thesis.
145. In addition to the Festschrift, edited by Maurice Cornforth, see R. Samuel, obituary in *The Guardian*, 5 November 1987; H. J. Kaye, 'History from the Bottom Up',*THES*, 28 August 1987; C. Hill, 'The Legacy of A. L. Morton', *Morton Memorial Conference*, July 1988 (tape kindly supplied by Lawrence and Wishart).
146. *People's History*, chapter headings, pp. 159ff, 527.
147. Samuel, obituary, loc. cit.; B. Schwarz, *THES*, Correspondence, 11 September 1987.
148. *People's History*, pp. 196–7, 218–23, 246–9, 310ff; 'Remember, Remember, the Fifth of November', *DW*, 4 November 1938 ('The English Revolution was just moving into a new phase . . .'); Howe (to whom I owe the reference) Draft, pp. 9–10; Samuel, obituary, loc. cit.
149. For Needham, Lindsay, Rickword, see above fn 28, 30; for Morton, fn 144–146; for West, see below fn 149; Iris Morley, *A Thousand Lives* (1954); Montagu Slater, *Englishmen with Swords* (1946); Ernst Meyer, *English Chamber Music from the Middle Ages to Purcell* (1946); David Petergorsky, *Left Wing Democracy in the English Civil War* (1940)
150. C. Caudwell, *Illusion and Reality: A Study in the Sources of Poetry* (1937); *Studies in a Dying Culture* (1938); *Further Studies in a Dying Culture* (1940); Edward Upward, 'Sketch for a Marxist Interpretation of Literature', in C. Day Lewis, op. cit., pp. 46–8, 54.
151. Ralph Fox, *The Novel and the People* (1937), pp. 132, 134; A. West, *Crisis and Criticism* (1937); E. Rickword, 'Milton Posed Problems that Still Remain', *The Past is Ours* series, *DW*, 2 December 1936; *John Milton, the Revolutionary Intellectual* (1940) – which formed the second part of Hill's 1940 essay on *The English Revolution*; J.

Lindsay, *John Bunyan, Maker of Myths* (London 1937); A. L. Morton, *The Language of Men* (1945).
152. Lindsay, *Bunyan*, pp. 249, 251.
153. Lindsay and Rickword, Handbook, Part III; Lindsay, *England*, p. 35. Rickword, 'Milton, the Revolutionary Intellectual', reprinted in *Essays*, pp. 165–83; cf Macaulay's *Milton* (1825) for liberal canonization.
154. Kaye, British Marxist Historians, p. 11; C. Hill, 'Marx's Virtues', *Listener*, 10 August 1967, p. 172; Hill's output over the next five decades was in many ways as close in substance to Leavis's programmatic jottings of 1943 for a university English course, as it was to any Marxism. See F. R. Leavis, *Education and the University* (1943), chapter 3; Heinemann,' How the Words Got on the Page' in Eley and Hunt, op. cit., pp. 73–99, esp. pp. 94–5; B. Schwarz, loc. cit., p. 64; J. 'Morrill, 'Christopher Hill's Revolution', *History* (1989), p. 247.
155. See esp. vol. 1 of his *Collected Essays: Writing and Revolution in 17th century England* (Brighton, 1985).
156. Samuel, 'British Marxist Historians', p. 52ff; C. Hill, 'Marxism and History', *MQ*, 3/2, Spring 1948, p. 60; 'From Lollards to Levellers' in M. Cornforth (ed.), op. cit., pp. 49–64; A. L. Morton, *People's History*, p. 182ff. For the congruence of the Marxist and the Protestant version of England's national past, presented in such works as A. G. Dickens, *The English Reformation*, see C. Haigh, *The English Reformation Revisited* (Cambridge, 1987). For the version of Foxe then current, see J. F. Mozley, *John Foxe and his Book* (1940) and the later extremely influential study by William Haller, *Foxe's Book of Martyrs and the Elect Nation* (1963). G. Mattingley, *The Defeat of the Spanish Armada* (1958), pp. i–ii.
157. Jones, op. cit., p. 74–87; Branson, op. cit., p 291–3; Spriano op. cit., p. 142. For Dutt's new line, anticipated in his May Day Speech of 1941, see J. Callaghan, *Rajani Palme Dutt*, pp. 196ff; Dutt, *LM*, 23, July 1941, pp. 342–50; *Turning Point of the World*, (London 1942) p. 3 ff; *Britain, today and tomorrow* (London 1943) pp. 1–15. For the earlier drift of Communist rank and file towards 'patriotism' v. Taylor, loc. cit. p. 982.
158. P. Anderson, *Arguments within English Marxism* (1980), p. 141–3.
159. Claudin, op. cit., pp. 15–40; Spriano, op. cit., pp. 166–7, 173, 192–203; Kolakowski, *Main Currents*, 3, pp. 117–21.
160. Anderson, *Arguments*, p. 143; Dona Torr 'Our National Traditions', *World News and Views* (*WNV*), 24, 3 June p. 183.
161. For the French Communist Party (PCF)'s appeal to revolutionary history in 1944/5, see T. Judt, *Past Imperfect, French Intellectuals 1944–56* (Berkeley, 1992), pp. 45ff; S. Khilnani, *Arguing Revolution: The Intellectual Left in Postwar France* (Yale, 1993), pp. 19ff; R. Gildea, *The Past in French History* (Yale, 1994), pp. 53ff; D. Johnson, 'The Cult of the Past and its Uses', *Times Literary Supplement* (*TLS*) 11 March 1994, p. 6.
162. *WNV*, 24, correspondence, 8 April–3 June (esp. at pp. 119, 137,

168); Torr, loc. cit; H. Pollitt, 26 August, ibid., p. 275. Hill's version in the 1980s, 'History and Patriotism' in R. Samuel (ed.), *Patriotism, the Making and Unmaking of British National Identity* (1989), pp. 3–9, repeats Torr's arguments of forty years before.

163. J. B. Priestley, *Postscripts* (1940), 5 June, 21 July 1940 (these were delivered as BBC talks every Sunday night for the seven months after Dunkirk); *The Secret Dream* (1946); *Out of the People* (1941); *Letter to a Returning Serviceman* (1945). See also *Playbill for 'An Inspector Calls'*, Royal National Theatre, 1993.

164. *Our Time*, March (J. Lindsay, *Bunyan*, p 13ff. where the phrase appears), May (C. H. Hobday, 'Milton the Revolutionary Poet', p. 12ff.), June, July, October, November 1944; ('Elizabeth and her Pirates'), *WNV*, 24, 6 May 1944, quoted in I. Birchall, 'Left Alive or Left for Dead? The Terminal Crisis of the British Communist Party', *International Socialism* 2:30, Autumn 1985, p. 72; J. Winternitz, *Marxism and Nationality* (Marx House Lecture 1944); cf D. Torr, *Marxism, Nationality and War* (1940); R. Swingler, 'Who are the Liberators', *DW*, 24 May 1940, for 'the 'old line'.

165. *WNV*, 24, 6 May 1944; T. Wintringham, *English Captain* (1939); *New Ways of War* (1940); *The Politics of Victory* (1941); *People's War* (1942); Fernbach, loc. cit; J. B. Priestley, *The Secret Dream*, passim. For a very different perspective, Paul Fussell, *Wartime: Understanding War and Behaviour in the Second World War* (Oxford, 1989), pp. 129–43, 182–3.

166. Torr, 'Our National Traditions', loc. cit; Hill, *Lenin*, pp. 167–8.

167. Hill, *Lenin*, p. 168; (K. E. Holme), *Two Commonwealths*, pp. 12ff.

168. *Two Commonwealths*, passim. Cf Francis Klingender, *Russia, Britain's Ally, 1812–1942* (1944). The reference to 'Dixon of Dock Green' is not entirely gratuitous: its author, Ted Willis, was for a while in the late 1940s a member of the Cultural Committee of the British Communist Party.

169. For the work of historians such as Hill and E. H. Carr (once an appeaser, now an ardent exponent of allowing Stalin his pound of flesh in Eastern Europe) in the FO, see H. Thomas, *Armed Truce* (1989), pp. 304–5, 708–10; V. Rothwell, *Britain and the Cold War, 1941–47* (1982), pp. 239–40. A. Glees, *The Secrets of the Service: British Intelligence and Communist Subversion, 1939–1951* (1987), pp. 279–88 ('A Marxist in the Foreign Office') credits Hill with considerable influence, notably in the matter of 'the Committee on Russian Studies', in which he is supposed to have been instrumental in recommending 'what amounted to a school for Soviet sympathizers and Fellow-Travellers' (p. 284). John Saville, *The Politics of Continuity: British Foreign Policy and the Labour Government, 1945–46* (1993), appendix 3, pp. 212–17, shows the argument to be inaccurate and tendentious.

170. G. D. H. Cole, *The Intelligent Man's Guide to Post-war Britain* (1945), p. 802ff; L. Labedz, *The Use and Abuse of Sovietology* (Oxford, 1989), p. 173; Glees, op. cit., pp. 286–7; Hill, *Lenin*, p. 169.

171. E. P. Thompson, *POT*, pp. 353ff; Anderson, *Arguments*, p. 143; G.

Barnsby, '1945 – the Year of Victory', *OH,* 62; P. Dutt, *The Road to Labour Unity* (1946); H. Pollitt in *WNV,* 25, November 1945, p. 386–7; 26 January 1946, p. 34ff; Jones, op. cit., p. 103ff; P. Weiler, *British Labour and the Cold War* (Stanford, 1988), pp. 3, 189ff; K. Morgan, *Labour in Power* (Oxford, 1984, pp. 232ff; A. Bullock, *Ernest Bevin, Foreign Secretary* (1983).

172. I. Birchall, 'Left Alive or Left for Dead?', loc. cit., pp. 72–3; *WNV,* 23, 27 February 1943; ibid., 24, 25 March, 1 April 1944; ibid., 25, 24 March, 7 April, 5 May, 1945; *NS,* 4 August 1945, p. 61; H. Laski, *'Reflections on a Revolution of our Time* (1943); *The Need for European Revolution* (1941); *London, Washington, Moscow* (1943); *Faith, Reason and Civilization* (1944); Deane, op. cit., pp. 241–2, 267ff. For Thompson's version of this moment see below, chapter 7.

173. R. B. McCallum and A. Readman, *The British General Election of 1945* (Oxford, 1947), p. 65–6; Spriano, op. cit., pp. 249–50 (Dimitrov), 251–8, 270–9; Claudin, op. cit., pp. 32–3, 35; Khilnani, op. cit., pp. 26–30.

Chapter 3   Marxist History in a Cold War Era

1. Material drawn from A. Howe, draft PhD chapter on 'The Origins of the Historians' Group'; *WNV,* 25/47, 1945, p. 388f: Report of 18th Congress of CPGB, November 24–6; *Report of Executive Committee to 18th Congress,* p. 16; cf *WNV,* 26/44, 26 October 1946, pp. 343–4, 'plans for implementing resolution on the study of British History passed at last Congress'; *CR* March 1946, p. 4f; Himmelfarb, 'The Group', loc. cit., p. 71; CPA HG 60 D, 'Minutes of Historians' Conference', 29–30 June 1946.

2. C. Hill, R. H. Hilton and E. J. Hobsbawm, 'Past & Present: Origins and Early Years', *P&P,* 100, 1983, p. 4.

3. Hobsbawm, HG, pp. 25–6; Harvey Kaye, op. cit., pp. 10–12; Himmelfarb, op. cit., pp. 72f.

4. Hobsbawm, HG, pp. 30–1; Himmelfarb, op. cit., pp. 90ff. Hobsbawm's account not only conflicts with what we know of party life from other sources, but with his own performance. See his impeccably orthodox contributions to the *New Central European Observer* between 1948 and 1951, and his bland defence of the workings of the CPGB in *Political Quarterly,* 25/1, 1954. For this issue, see N. Carlin and I. Birchall, 'Kinnock's Favourite Marxist: Eric Hobsbawm and the Working Class', *International Socialism,* 2/21, 1985, pp. 88–115.

5. Daphne May, 'Work of the Historians Group, *CR,* May 1949, p. 541–3; *WNV,* 28/10, /15, 13 March, 24 April 1948, pp. 110f., 168: reports by C. Hill on 16/17th c. Section; ibid., 29/44, 5 November 1949, pp. 536 ff, (S. Aaronovitch and G. Thomson on the importance of preliminary organization); Samuel, 'Lost World', loc. cit., passim. J. Klugmann, *Some Hints for Party Tutors* (CP Education Department, 1957) outlined the 'Controlled Discussion Method', and the 'Question and Answer Method': quoted in S. Parsons, op. cit., p. 250.

6. Hobsbawm, HG, p. 29–30, 33–4.
7. G. Thomson, 'On the Work of Party Intellectuals', *CR*, July 1946, pp. 11–15; S. Aaronovitch, 'The Communist Party and the Battle of Ideas' (Report to the National Cultural Committee, 11 April 1948), *CR*, 1948, pp. 148–57; H. Pollitt, *Professional Workers* (CP pamphlet, London 1946), pp. 6–7: 'we have to be the best writers, actors, singers, doctors etc. . . . the first duty of a Communist mathematician is to be a good mathematician'; Parsons, op. cit., pp. 235ff.
8. *WNV*, 28, 5 January, 24 April 1948, pp. 35f, 168: *Report on the Establishment of National Cultural Committee* (in 1947).
9. J. Saville *et al*. (eds), *Democracy and the Labour Movement: Essays in Honour of D. Torr* (1954), p. 8; Kaye, British Marxist Historians pp. 13–14; J. Klugmann, 'A Tribute to Dona Torr': obituary in *W(orld) N(ews)* IV, 26 January 1957, pp. 55–6; Torr–Palme or Salme Dutt, 22 April 1936; Dutt–Torr, 18 June 1936, Dutt Mss, CPA (materials provided by A. Howe). A. Howe is currently writing of Torr's role in promoting historical work in his PhD.
10. D. Torr, *Tom Mann and his Times*, vol. 1 (1956); fragments of vol. 2 ed. E. P. Thompson, published in *Our History*, 26–27, 1962. Cf T. Suzuki, *Tom Mann, 1856–1941* (Oxford, 1991); C. Osborne, *Tom Mann, his Australasian experience* (Canberra, ANU, PhD, 1976).
11. Torr, *Mann*, pp. 13, 15 ff; Kaye, British Marxist Historians pp. 13–14, 252; Klugmann, obituary, loc. cit.
12. 'History in the Making', prefaces. For the Soviet model see John Keep (ed.), *Contemporary History in the Soviet Mirror* (1964), pp. 95–7, 133–8; Howe, *Hill*, pp. 7–11. For some idea of Torr's Marxism, see also 'Productive Forces, Social Relations', *CR*, May 1947, p. 11 ff; 'On relations of National and International', ibid., March 1948, pp. 67–73; her intervention in the Labour Monthly debate in 1940–41, and her own editions of *Selected Correspondence of Marx and Engels* (1934); *Supplement to English edition of Capital* (1938); *Marxism, Nationality and War* (1940); *Marx on China* (1943).
13. See Chapter 2; E. P. Thompson, POT, pp. 353ff; Anderson, *Arguments*, p. 143; G. Barnsby, '1945 – the Year of Victory', *OH*, 62; P. Dutt, *The Road to Labour Unity* (1946); H. Pollitt in *WNV*, 25, November 1945, pp. 386–7; 26, January 1946, pp. 34 ff; Jones, op. cit., p. 103ff; P. Weiler, op. cit., p. 189ff; K. Morgan, *Labour in Power* (Oxford, 1984), p. 232ff; A. Bullock, *Ernest Bevin, Foreign Secretary* (1983).
14. For these processes see Weiler, op. cit.; Morgan, op. cit., pp. 232–84; Jones, p. 110 ff (quoting Zilliacus on 'the momentum of imperial inertia'); P. Dutt, *Britain's Crisis of Empire* (1949); J. Saville, 'Labour Foreign Policy, 1945–7', *Our History Journal*, May 1991; B. Moore, 'Labour–Communist Relations, 1945–51', *OH*, 84/5, 1991; and, most recently and fully, J. Saville, *The Politics of Continuity*.
15. Hill, 'Marxism and History', *MQ*, 3/2, 1948, p. 55; 'Lenin, Theoretician of Revolution' *CR*, February 1947, p. 59–60; cf D. Torr, *CR*, March 1948, p. 73.

16. Hobsbawm, 'The Taming of Parliamentary Democracy', *MQ*, 6/4, 1951, pp. 319–38; R. Milliband, *Parliamentary Socialism* (1961), chapter 9; *The State in Capitalist Society* (1969), 1973 edn, pp. 96–102; R. McKibbon, 'Why was there no Marxism in Britain', *EHR*, XCIX, 1982, p. 297–331; Hobsbawm, 'Parliamenary Cretinism'? *NLR*, 4, 1961, pp. 64–6; *POT*, p. 354f.; J. Lindsay, *Arena* 2/5, September–October, 1950 p. 3ff.; John Mortimer, *Paradise Postponed* (Harmondsworth, 1986); P. Dutt, *LM*, 33/12, December 1951, pp. 546ff (Labour received nearly 1/2 million more votes than the Conservatives in the 1951 elections).

17. Butterfield, *Englishman*, pp. 114, 116–17; H. Massingham, *The Natural Order* (1945), p. 5; A. L. Rowse, *The Spirit of English History* (1943); Taylor, 'Patriotism', loc. cit., pp. 981–3.

18. *NS*, 18 August 1945, p. 101.

19. J. Lindsay, *CR*, February 1949, p. 93 (on the 'illusions' of 1945/6); F. Finch, 'Patriotism', *CR*, October 1948, pp. 314–17; H. Pollitt, *CR*, January 1947, pp. 3–5.

20. C. Hill, 'The English Bourgeois Revolution': Report of the 16/17th c Section. *WNV*, 28, 13 March 1948, p. 110; A. L. Morton, *The Story of the English Revolution* (foreword by H. Pollitt) (1948), pp. 6–7; S. Aaronovich, 'CP and Battle of Ideas', loc. cit., p. 149.

21. C. Hill, 'English Revolution and the State', *MQ*, 4/2, 1949, p. 110; 'Marxism and History', loc. cit., p. 56; 'The First Socialist Revolution', *WNV*, 27, 8 November 1947, pp. 509–11; G. Werskey, op. cit., p. 278; Bill Schwarz, loc. cit., p. 58; E. P. Thompson, *POT*, pp. 355ff.

22. H. Laski, *Parliamentary Government in England* (1938) p. 72; Deane, op. cit., pp. 149–50; J. Klugmann, 'From Social Democracy to Democratic Socialism', *CR*, February 1947, pp. 47–53; April 1948, pp. 138 ff; November 1948, pp. 357 ff; December 1949, pp. 406–14; Hobsbawm, 'The Taming . . ., loc. cit.

23. Passage taken from an anonymous pamphleteer 1651, quoted in D. Garman, 'In Praise of Revolution', *CR*, February 1950, p. 60.

24. Hill, 'The English Revolution and the State', loc. cit., p. 110; 'The English Bourgeois Revolution, *WNV* 28, 13 March 1948, p. 110. For efforts at making it widely known, see A. L. Morton, *The Story of the English Revolution* (1949) with a forward by Harry Pollitt; 'The Tercentenary of the English Revolution', series of articles in *MQ*, 4/2 1949; in *WNV*, 29, 1949, (articles by Hill, Morton, etc.); *CR*, March, May 1949 ('The Great English Revolution'; 'James Harrington, Revolutionary Theorist', etc.); and *LM*, January, March 1949 (Morton, 'The Sovereignty of the People', Kiernan, 'When England was a Republic'). On a conservative count, there were over twenty such celebratory pieces in party journals in the first six months of 1949. For the party's verdict on their importance, see *WNV*, 28, 13 March 1948, p. 110: 'the political committee considers the celebrations of 1649 of the highest political importance'; in 1982, Hill recalled: 'I think that the celebration of 1640 – and especially of 1649 – did something for the party in giving it

confidence in a non-gradualist tradition to an extent that it is difficult for the younger generation perhaps to imagine'. *P&P* 100, 1983, pp. 4–5.

25. *WNV* 28, 1948 pp. 110–111; Hill, 'E. R. and the State', loc. cit., pp. 111–2, 123–4; 'Marxism and History', loc. cit., pp. 56–7; P. Dutt, Lessons of the '30s, *CR* April 1946 pp. 3–11; D. Torr, 'How is Democratic Advance Possible if the State is the Instrument of the Capitalist Class'?, Spring 1946, Torr Papers, C. P. A. 233D.

26. G. Thomson, *Marxism and Poetry* (1946) p. 115ff., quoted in *CR*, August 1947 p. 234; '*The battle of Ideas*', *Six Speeches on the Centenary of the Communist Manifesto*, *20th National Congress of the Communist Party* (1948) pp. 5–6. George Thomson was a distinguished classical historian, literary theorist, folklorist and for many years token academic on the Communist Party Executive Committee.

27. Hill, 'Marxism and History', loc. cit., pp. 54, 62; 'Marx's Virtues', loc. cit., p. 173; 'The Materialist Conception of History', *University*, 1, 1951, pp. 110–14; D. Torr, *CR* May 1947, pp. 13–15; *Tom Mann*, preface, pp. 15–16. The notion of 'totality' runs through the work of Hill and most other members of the group, see Kaye, British Marxist Historians pp. 54–8, 67–9, 107–8, 116–17, and esp. p. 236ff.

28. A. L. Rowse, *The Use of History* (1946), p. 139 ff; D. Garman, 'Marxism and the Platitudinists', *MQ*, 3/3, 1948, pp. 5–18, esp. pp. 10–11, 13; 'All Souls and No Body' (Review of Rowse), *CR*, October 1946. p. 29–32; P. Jones, 'Historical Thinking', *MQ*, 3/2, 1947; J. R. Campbell, 'Prophets of the Middle Way', *MQ*, 4/3, 1949, pp. 270–81; Torr, *WNV*, 23, 1944, p. 183; J. Lewis, 'Battle of Ideas', *20th National Congress*, 1948, pp. 8–9.

29. Spriano, op. cit., pp. 297ff; Claudin, op. cit., pp. 307–16, 365–73. Congress of Intellectuals, Manifesto (Wroclaw Congress), *CR* October 1948, pp. 317 ff; reports from Wroclaw Congress: R. Pascal *et al.*, *MQ*, 3/4, 1948; Hill, *NCEO*, 1/10, 18 September 1948, p. 99.

30. S. Aaronovitch, loc cit, p. 151; G. Thomson, 'Party Intellectuals', loc. cit., pp. 12–13; *WNV*, 28, 11 April 1948, p. 94f; *CR* October 1950, pp. 314–20.

31. K. Cornforth, 'British Road to Socialism', *CR*, 1947, p. 113 ff.; Executive Committee 1948: '*A Socialist Road for Britain*' (1948); P. Dutt, *LM*, 30, Notes of the Month 1948 charts the gradual tightening of party thought; A. J. P. Taylor, 'The Revolt from Within', *Listener*, 20 January 1949, pp. 86–8; E. Crankshaw, 'Tito and the Cominform', *Research Institute of International Affairs (RIIA)*, April 1950, pp. 208–13.

32. J. Klugmann, *From Trotsky to Tito* (1951), pp. 57–80, 191–204; D. Kartun, *Tito's Plot against Europe* (1949); *New Central European Observer*, 1948–9, passim; Claudin, op. cit., chapter 7, Jones, op. cit. p. 103 ff.

33. Kolakowski, *Main Currents of Marxism*, vol. 3, pp. 121 ff.

34. The most famous posthumous victim of King Street's heresy hunting was Christopher Caudwell, hitherto widely regarded as the party's leading cultural theorist. see, amongst others, E. P.

Thompson, 'Caudwell', *SR*, 1977, pp. 228–76; registering the extensive debate in *MQ* during 1950–1. For a less well–known victim, see Jack Lindsay's attempt 'to bring Marxism up to date'. J. Lindsay, *Marxism and Contemporary Science* (1948); M. Cornforth 'An Attempt to Revise Marxism', *CR*, December 1948, pp. 719–28; J. Lindsay, 'A Note of Self-Criticism', ibid., February 1949, pp. 93–5; J. Lindsay, *Life Rarely Tells* (1980), pp. 761–73. Lindsay was forced to recant his 'bad Marxism, explaining it as a product of "the illusions" of 1945 and '46. This was the period when in France, Albert Soboul (of all people) was similarly accused of 'writing' in the spirit of idealism and nationalism'. See I. M. Wall, *French Communism in the Era of Stalin* (Westport, Conn., 1983), pp. 137–8.

35. Garman, 'Platitudinists', loc. cit.; 'On the Middle Way', *WNV*, 28/17, 1 May 1948, pp. 181–3; J. R. Campbell, 'Prophets', loc. cit.; James Gardner, *The Battle of Ideas and the Importance of Theory* (1949), pp. 9–13; Klugmann, *Trotsky to Tito*, pp. 62–3, 81ff, 91–8, 100–1, 191ff, 199–201; J. Lewis, 'Battle of Ideas', loc. cit.; 'Marxism and Ethics', MQ 5/3, 1950, pp. 195–224.

36. CPA 60 A, HG Minutes, 26 September 1947, 10 April, 12 June, 29 October 1948; CPA Minutes of National Cultural Committee, 15 May, 11 July 1947, 26 September 1948.

37. Edmund Dell, joint editor with Hill of *The Good Old Cause*, seems to have cast doubt on dialectics as a useful or illuminating method of analyzing historical change, Hobsbawm, HG pp. 26–7. Dell was required 'to perform some definite party work not connected with teaching or writing', something which he appears to have been unwilling to do. CPA HG Minutes 14 May 1949, 14 January 1950. Others who parted company included Edward Miller and Gordon Leff, see Leff, *The Tyranny of Concepts* (1961), introduction.

38. Samuel, *British Marxist Historians*, p. 55ff.; C. Hill, 'England's Democratic Army', *CR*, June 1947, pp. 171–8; cf Daphne May, 'The Putney Debates', ibid., February 1948, pp. 21–7; *WNV*, 25, 1945, p. 388f; N. Branson and B. Moore, 'Labour Communist Relations, 1939–46', *OH* 83, pp. 16–18.

39. Hill, 'Independent F. P.', loc. cit., pp. 46–52; *Lenin*, pp. 169ff: 'Lenin, Theoretician', loc. cit., pp. 59–60, 64; 'The First Socialist Revolution', *WNV*, 27, 8 November 1947, pp. 509–10; 'History Teaching in Charles University', *NCEO*, II/10, 14 May 1949, p. 113; CP pamphlet, *Czechoslovakia: The Facts*, February 1948, pp. 4–6.

40. H. Laski, *The Secret Battalion* (1946); Branson and Moore, *OH*, 83, p. 25ff; Jones, op. cit., p. 178ff; M. Foot, 'Murder in Prague', *Tribune*, 27 February 1948; *Daily Herald*, 27 February 1948; D. G. Burchill, *Strachey*, pp. 462ff; R. H. S. Crossman, 'Class Warfare and the Western Tradition', *Western Tradition*, pp. 78–82; cf Attlee, speech to the Scottish Labour Party, September 1947, quoted in D. Morgan and M. Evans, *The Battle for Britain: Citizenship and Ideology in World War II* (1993), p. 147: 'from the point of view of freedom Communists are . . . more reactionary than some of the old tyrants we fought against in the past'.

41. Garman, 'Theorist of the Middle Way' *WNV*, 18, May 1948, p. 181; Dutt, *Mr Bevin's Lies* (1948); *LM*, 30, Notes of the Month, March 1948; A. West, *CR*, June 1949, p. 566 ff.
42. M. Taylor, loc. cit., pp. 983–4; J. Rodden, *The Politics of a Literary Reputation: The Making and Claiming of St George Orwell* (Oxford, 1989), esp. pp. 188–200; J. Walsh, 'Orwell', *Marxist Quarterly*, 3/1 January 1956, pp. 25–39; C. Norris (ed.), *Inside the Myth: Orwell, Views from the Left* (1985), esp. pp. 242–61; J. Lindsay and R. Swingler (eds), *Arena*, II/7, 8; E. Shils, 'Remembering the Congress for Cultural Freedom', *Encounter*, 75, ii, 1990, pp. 53–65; P. Coleman, *The Liberal Conspiracy* (1989); C. Lasch, 'The Cultural Cold War: A Short History of the Congress for Cultural Freedom' in *The Agony of the American Left* (New York, 1969), pp. 61–114; S. Hook, *Out of Step* (New York, 1987), pp. 420–60.
43. 'Retrospect of a Decade', *Scrutiny*, ix, 1940, reprinted in *Scrutiny, a Selection* (Cambridge, 1978), I, pp. 175ff; C. Caudwell, *Illusion and Reality*, pp. 29–30, 46, 130, 201; A. Milner, *Cultural Materialism* pp. 8–9, 29–30. Some idea of the aesthetic divide is conveyed by Leavis's damning critique in 1938 of Lindsay's *John Bunyan: Maker of Myths* (and W. Tindall's earlier *John Bunyan: Mechanic Preacher* – a book much admired and utilized by Christopher Hill): see 'Bunyan Through Modern Eyes', reprinted in *The Common Pursuit*, pp. 204–10.
44. *Politics and Letters* (eds C. Collins, R. Williams, W. Mankowitz), I, i, Summer 1947, pp. 39ff; Hill, ibid., I, ii/iii, pp. 58–60; F. R. Leavis, reply, ibid., pp. 60–1; Mulhern, op. cit., pp. 230–33.
45. T. S. Knights, review of 'The English Revolution', *Scrutiny*, ix (2), 1940–1, pp. 167–8; Leavis, 'Retrospect', loc. cit.
46. Hill, *Politics and Letters*, I, ii, pp. 59–60; Iain Wright, loc. cit., pp. 48, 51–2; Eagleton, op. cit., p. 30.
47. T. S. Eliot, *Notes Towards a Definition of Culture* (1950); *Selected Essays*; E. Waugh, *Brideshead Revisited* (1943); H. Laski, *The Dilemma of our Times* (1952), pp. 119–35, esp p. 123; Leavis, *Nor Shall My Sword: Discourses on Pluralism, Compassion and Social Hope* (1973).
48. C. Hill, *Milton and the English Revolution* (1977), pp. 2–3; M. Wilding, *Dragon's Teeth: Literature in the English Revolution* (Oxford, 1987), pp. 1–6; Eagleton, *Literary Theory*, pp. 32ff; L. C. Knights, loc. cit., p. 168.
49. F. R. Leavis, *Revaluations* (1936); *The Common Pursuit* (1952); Mulhern, pp. 135–6; Wilding, op. cit., introduction.
50. P. Anderson, 'Components of the National Culture', *NLR*, 50, July–August, 1968, pp. 3–58.
51. BBC series *The Challenge of Our Time*, *Listener*, 1946 (published, 1948); A. Toynbee, *Civilization on Trial* (Oxford, 1948); *Prospects for Western Civilization* (1949); *The World and the West* (Reith Lectures, 1952); 'The Soviet Idea', BBC series, *Listener*, 1948: see esp. Toynbee, 17 June 1948, pp. 959–60; C. Dawson, ibid., 6 May 1948, pp. 742–3; V. Gollancz, *Our Threatened Values* (1947); B. Russell, *Authority and the Individual* (Reith Lectures, 1949); J. Lewis, 'Battle

of Ideas', p. 7; 'The Great Moral Muddle', *MQ*, 1/4, 1946, pp. 55ff; 'Bertrand Russell and the Illusion of Freedom', ibid., 4/4, 1949; R. W. Clark, *Bertrand Russell and his World* (1981), pp. 517–30: 'Towards a Short War with Russia'; P. Johnson, *Intellectuals* (1988), pp. 205–6. For an extended critique of the literary culture of the period, see *Arena*, 1–2, 1949–51: amongst those singled out were Charles Morgan, Terrence Rattigan, Christopher Fry, Graham Greene, Aldous Huxley, George Orwell, Arthur Koestler and T. S. Eliot.

52. *The Western Tradition: A Symposium* (ed. Lord Layton) (BBC series, 1951); E. Barker, G. N. Clark and P. Vaucher, *The European Inheritance* (1952); C. Dawson, *Religion and Culture* (Edinburgh, 1948); *Religion and the Rise of Western Culture* (Edinburgh, 1950); *Makers of Christendom* (1952). The Western Tradition symposium included contributions from E. Barker, V. A. Demant (see below), J. Bowle, H. Butterfield, E. L. Woodward, H. Seton-Watson, J. Plamenatz, A Toynbee; E. L. Woodward, 'The Heritage of Western Civilization', *RIIA*, April 1949, pp. 137–48; H. M. Waddams, 'Communism and the Churches', ibid., July 1949, pp. 295–306.

53. G. Barraclough, 'Is there a Western Tradition?' *Listener*, 14 June 1947, p. 249; R. Pascal, *MQ*, 4/3, p. 253: on the use of 'Western Civilization' as a code for the 'new Fascism' – report from Wroclaw Congress; G. Clark, 'The Myth of Western Civilization', ibid., 5/1, 1949–50, pp. 3–18; C. Hill, ibid., 5/2, 1950, pp. 172–4; *WNV*, 28, 1948, p. 536 ('we expect our historians to attack theoretical justifications for war in defence of Western Civilization'). The arguments advanced by the proponents of 'Western Values' bore an uncanny resemblance to those deployed by Burke in the 1790s – the idea of a single 'Commonwealth of Europe' threatened by an alien style of political culture. See Martyn P. Thompson, *The Commonwealth of Europe: Ambiguity and Anti-politics in the French Revolution*, paper to 'The European Moment' Conference, Canberra, 6–10 June 1992; or Metternich in 1815, *NCEO*, I/i, 15 May 1948; cf H. Kissinger, *A World Restored* (Cambridge, Mass., 1960) for a similarly coded historical argument in the late 1950s.

54. Dawson, *Religion and Culture*, p. 52; Toynbee, *Listener*, 17 June 1948, pp. 959ff; *The World and the West*, passim; B. G. Rosenthal, 'Toynbee's Interpretation of Russian History' in C. McIntyre, and M. Perry, *Toynbee: Critical Reappraisals* (Toronto, 1989), pp. 160–79; D. MacKinnon, *Christian Faith and Communist Faith* (1953)

55. N. Cantor, *Inventing the Middle Ages* (New York, 1991), esp. pp. 205–44, 381–95; H. Carpenter, *The Inklings* (1979). Up until the 1960s, Medieval History continued to dominate the undergraduate curricula in Oxford and Cambridge, compulsorily occupying two out of the three years of study.

56. Butterfield, *Origins of Modern Science* (1949), pp. 3–4.

57. Butterfield, *Christianity, Diplomacy and War* (1953), pp. 39 ff; *Christianity and History* (1949), conclusion; *Christianity in European History* (1951), pp. 43, 102–3; *History and Human Relations* (1951), pp.

66, 100 ff; 'Reflexions on the Predicament of our Time', *Cambridge Journal*, I, i, October 1947, pp. 5–13; 'The Scientific versus the Moralistic Approach to International Affairs', *RIIA*, July 1951, pp. 411–22.

58. *Christianity and History*, pp. 103ff, conclusion; for a Marxist critique, R. H. Hilton, 'Jehovah's Witness', *CR*, July 1949, pp. 283–90.

59. *Origins of Modern Science*, pp. 163–74.

60. B. Willey, *The Seventeenth Century Background* (1934), 1961 edn, pp. 9–10; Butterfield, *Christianity and History*, p. 10; M. Oakeshott, *Rationalism in Politics and Other Essays* (essay of that name originally published in *Cambridge Journal*, 1947, republished London 1961); E. M. Tillyard, *The Elizabethan World Picture* (1943); C. S. Lewis, *The Discarded Image* (Cambridge, 1964) based on lectures given in the 1940s and 1950s.

61. Tillyard, op. cit.; A. Koestler, *The Sleepwalkers* (1957); B. de Sanillana, *The Crime of Galileo* (1958).

62. Oakeshott, *Rationalism*, passim. For O's view of Labour party policies as an expression of this see 'Contemporary British Politics', *Cambridge Journal*, 1, viii, pp. 474–90.

63. *Challenge*, see esp. contributions from A. Koestler, V. Demant, E. M. Forster, E. L. Woodward; C. P. Snow, *The Two Cultures* (Richmond Lecture, 1958), pp. 5 ff; J. D Bernal, 'Belief and Action', *MQ*, 1/1 December 1945, pp. 44–59; *The Social Responsibility of Science*, pp. 25–30; Bernal in *Challenge*, pp. 21ff.

64. Bernal, *Challenge*, pp. 23–4; G. Werskey, op. cit., pp. 288ff; *The Communist Answer to the Challenge of Our Times* (1947).

65. Bernal, *The Freedom of Necessity* (1949); J. Lewis, *Marxism and Modern Idealism* (1944); editorial *MQ* 1/1, 1946, pp. 3ff; *Communist Answer*, passim. For Jeans and Eddington, see C. Cohen, *God and the Universe: Huxley, Eddington, Jeans and Einstein* (1946); and amongst other writings, A. S. Eddington, *Science and the Unseen World* (Cambridge, 1929); *The Philosophy of Physical Science* (Cambridge, 1938); *New Pathways in Science* (Cambridge, 1947); J. H. Jeans, *Physics and Philosophy* (1948); *The Mysterious Universe* (Cambridge, 1930, new edns, 1947, 1948); *Stars in their Courses* (Cambridge, 1948); *Through Space and Time* (Cambridge, 1948); M. Polyani, *Challenge*, pp. 41 ff; *The Rights and Duties of Science* (1945) ; *Science, Faith and Society* (1946); *The Logic of Liberty* (1951); H. Prosch, *Michael Polanyi* (New York, 1987), chapters 1, 2; R. Allen, *Polanyi* (1990).

66. Bernal, 'Belief and Action', loc. cit., p. 53.

67. *Challenge*: J. B. S. Haldane, pp. 48f; Koestler, pp. 14–15; Forster, pp. 30–1; Koestler, *The Yogi and the Commissar* (1947); J. Lewis, 'The Great Moral Muddle', loc. cit., p. 63f; Lewis editorial, ibid., 1/3, pp. 3–4, quoting Rev. D. R. Davies (BBC talk December 1945) and C. S. Lewis, *The Screwtape Letters* (1946); *Communist Answer*, pp. 12–13; V. Dimant (Canon of St Paul's), *Challenge*, p. 53; M. Oakeshott, 'Political Education' (1951) in *Rationalism*, p. 133.

68. 'Society and Andrew Marvell', *MQ*, 1/4, 1946, pp. 6–31, revised in *Puritanism and Revolution* (1958), pp. 337–66, esp. pp. 341–2,

363. For a similar argument in the case of Harrington, see A. L Morton and James Harrington, 'Revolutionary Theorist, *CR*, March 1949, pp. 457–62.
69. 'Time and Mr Toynbee', *MQ*, 2/4, 1947 pp. 290–307, esp. pp. 293–4, 300, 303; *Time* magazine, 12 May 1947; A. H. Hanson, *MQ* 4/4 (review of 'Civilization on Trial'); 'History and Mr Toynbee', *Science and Society*, XIII/2, 1949; R. Hilton, *MQ*, 8/3. For relations between Henry Luce (editor of *Time* magazine) and Toynbee, see William McNeill, *Arnold J. Toynbee* (Oxford, 1989), pp. 213ff.
70. R. Hilton in D. Pennington and K. Thomas, *Puritans and Revolutionaries: Essays in Honour of Christopher Hill* (Oxford, 1977) p. 7; Samuel, *British Marxist Historians*, p. 52. .
71. Metcalfe, *Myths*, pp. 8–30; Samuel, *Lost World*, p. 3; Bryan D. Palmer, 'The Eclipse of Materialism: Marxism and the Writing of Social History in the 1980s', *SR*, 1990, pp. 111–46, gives a good indication of the continued importance of class struggle to the identity of historians bred in this English version of Marxist orthodoxy. Hill, *Society and Puritanism in Pre-Revolutionary England* (1964); 'History and the Class Struggle', *CR*, March 1949, pp. 475–80; Torr, 'Productive Forces', loc. cit.; J. Lindsay, *Byzantium into Europe* (1952), pp. 84–92, 221–36, 281–6; *TLS*, review 12 December 1952, p. 816; Hill, *MQ*, 8/3, 1953 pp. 186 ff.
72. C. Hill and E. Dell (eds), *The Good Old Cause: The English Revolution, its Causes, Course, and Consequences* (1948), p. 20.
73. *Good Old Cause*, chapter and subject headings; A. L. Morton, *WNV*, 30, January 1950, p. 48; R. Hilton *MQ*, 5/4, 1950, pp. 364–71; cf H. R. Trevor-Roper, 'The Puritan Class War', *NS*, 4 March 1950; *TLS*, 3 March 1950.
74. Samuel, 'Lost World', 1, pp. 9, 36–7; 'British Marxist Historians', p. 60.
75. Samuel, 'British Marxist Historians', pp. 62ff; D. Guest, *A Textbook of Dialectical Materialism* (1939), p. 75; Tom Jackson, *Dialectics* (1938), p. 81–2; Bernal, 'Belief and Action', loc. cit.; A. West, *CR*, June 1949, pp. 566–71; Hilton, 'Jehovah's Witness', loc. cit.
76. J. Lewis, *Marxism and the Irrationalists*, pp. 3–8, 62; see also Lewis's editorials in *MQ*, 1–3. For other examples, see V. G. Childe, *What Happened in History* (Harmondsworth, 1944), pp. 32ff; *Man Makes Himself* (1936); *The Story of Tools* (1944); *History* (1947), p. 67 ff; *Prehistory and Marxism* (1949); 'The Sociology of Knowledge', *MQ*, 4/3, 1949, pp. 302–9; B. G. Trigger, *V. G. Childe: Revolutions in Archaeology* (1980); S. Green, *Prehistorian: A Biography of V. Gordon Childe* (Bradford on Avon, 1981); C. Hill, S. Lilley, G. Thomson, reviews of Childe in *MQ*, 4/3, 1949, pp. 259–69; G. Thomson, *Studies in Ancient Greek Society: 1. The Prehistoric Aegean* (1949); 2, *The First Philosophers* (1955), pp. 435 ff; *Aeschylus and Athens* (1941); *Essay on Religion* (1951), pp. 9 ff; 'Basis and Ideology', *CR*, August 1952, pp. 239–46; C. Hill, 'Materialist Conception', loc. cit., pp. 111–12.
77. *P&P*. I, 1952, editorial, pp. 3–4 (P&P carried the coded subtitle 'a

Journal of Scientific History' until 1958); Morris Mss Box 34: 'Draft on Marx's method to the editors of P&P'.

78. Jane Harrison, *Prolegomena to the study of Greek Religion* (1903) 1962 edn, p. vii; F. J. West, 'Myths about Myth', in F. West (ed.), *Myth and Mythology* (Canberra, 1989), p. 10; J. D. Bernal, 'How Men First Came to Reason', *MxQ*, 3/1, January 1956, pp. 3–13; Thomson, *The First Philosophers*. For this whole subject, see Samuel, 'British Marxist Historians', pp. 60ff, whose account I have followed.

79. Ibid., pp. 61–2.

80. Ibid., p. 64. Samuel remarks on the importance of the Rationalist Press Assocation and the publisher C. and A. Watts. Likewise, the annual *Conway Lecture* played host to a number of Marxist intellectuals.

81. V. G. Childe, *History*, p. 76; *What Happened*, pp. 70, 120–2, 149, 190, 218; B. Farrington, *Science in Antiquity* (1936); *The Civilization of Greece and Rome* (1938); *Science and Politics in Antiquity* (1939); *Greek Science: its Meaning for Us* (Harmondsworth 1944); 'What Can We Learn from History'?, *Communist Answer*, pp. 46–57; 'What Light from the Ancient World'?, *Challenge*, pp. 36–40; *Has History a Meaning* (Conway Lecture 1950); quotation from *Science in Antiquity*, in Samuel, op. cit. p. 72.

82. C. Hill, *Intellectual Origins of the English Revolution* (Oxford, 1965), p. 298; *English Revolution*, p. 69; 'History and Class Struggle', loc. cit., p. 478.

83. Samuel, British Marxist Historians, pp. 66 ff; L. Munby, 'Religious Reaction in an Epoch of Imperialism', *MQ*, 5/4, 1950, pp. 328–41; Hill, ibid., 5/2, pp. 172–4; G. Thomson, *Essay on Religion*, pp. 3–4; T. Jackson (ed.), *'The Fight'* (*against Superstition, Clericalism and Cultural Reaction*) (1934–5); Archibald Robertson, *Man his Own Master* (1948) pp. 120–2; *Jesus, Myth or History* (1946); *Morals in World History* (1945); *The Origins of Christianity* (1953); Marxism and Christianity, *MQ*, 2/1, 1946–7, pp. 65–73; W. Gallacher, *Catholicism and Communism* (1948); J. Lindsay, *Byzantium*, p. 221ff.

84. Hill, 'History and Class Struggle', loc. cit. pp. 474–5, 476; *Good Old Cause*, pp. 26, 171, 175.

85. Samuel, 'British Marxist Historians', p. 80; Werskey, op. cit., pp. 147ff; B. Hessen, *Social Roots on Newton's Principia* (1931); N. Bukharin et al., *Science at the Crossroads: Papers presented to the International Congress of the History of Science, June 29–July 3 1931*, 2nd edn (1971); J. G. Crowther, *The Social Relations of Science* (1941); Bernal, as cited above, fn 63, 64, 65.

86. Bernal, *Science in History* (1957); J. Needham, *Science and Civilization in China* (Cambridge, 1954–); S. F. Mason, *History of the Sciences* (1953); C. Cipolla, *European Culture and Overseas Expansion* (Harmondsworth, 1977); J. Ravetz and J. Westfall, 'Marxism and the History of Science', *Isis*, lxxii, 1981 pp. 393–405; I. Bernard Cohen, *Revolution in Science* (Cambridge, Mass., 1985).

87. S. Lilley, 'The Origins of Modern Science', *MQ*, 7/2, 1952 p. 109;

Men, Machines and History (1948); S. F. Mason, *A History of the Sciences* (1953)
88. Hill, *Intellectual Origins*, pp. 280ff; S. F. Mason, 'The Influence of the English Revolution upon the Development of Modern Science', *MQ*, 4/2, 1949; 'Historical Roots of the Scientific Revolution', *SS*, xiv/3, 1950; J. Bernal, 'Comenius' Visit to England and the Rise of Scientific Societies' in J. Needham (ed.), *The Teacher of Nations* (Cambridge, 1942); Hill, 'When Comenius Came to England', *NCEO*, V/17, 16 August 1952, p. 265.
89. Hill, *MQ*, 7/1, 1951–2, p. 58; B. Farrington, *Francis Bacon, Philosopher of Industrial Science* (1951); cf A. L. Morton, *The Language of Men* (1949), chapter 2; *The English Utopia* (1952), chapter 4; J. Bernal, *Science in History*, introduction.
90. H. Butterfield, *Origins*; R. Hall, 'The Scholar and the Craftsman' in H. Kearney, *Origins of the Scientific Revolution, 1500–1700* (1966); *From Galileo to Newton* (1963); C. G. Gillispie, *The Edge of Objectivity* (Princeton, 1960); J. Bronowski, *The Ascent of Man* (1974); A. Boorstin, *The Discoverers* (1984); A Koyré, *From Closed World to Infinite Universe* (Baltimore, 1957); *Etudes Galiléennes* (Paris, 1939); 'Galileo and Plato', *JHI*, 4, 1943, pp. 400–28; A. Koestler, *The Sleepwalkers* (1958); *The Act of Creation* (1955); for a critique, M. Fores, 'Constructed Science and the Seventeenth Century Revolution', *History of Science*, 22, 1984, pp. 217–44.
91. R. Porter, 'The Scientific Revolution, a Spoke in the Wheel' in R. Porter and M. Teich, *Revolution in History* (Cambridge, 1986), pp. 295–7; B. Farrington, *Bacon*, pp. 13ff; J. Bernal, *Social Function*, pp. 77–89.
92. Koestler, *Sleepwalkers*, pp. 75–6, 99–102, 104, 107, 537 ff; Porter, loc. cit., pp. 297–8.
93. Bernal, *Challenge*, p. 28; cf *The Freedom of Necessity*, passim; 'The Place and Task of Science', *SS*, xiii/3, 1949.
94. R. Hilton, 'The Idea of Liberty' (Opening Statement at Conference 25 September 1949), *CR*, November 1949, pp. 711–19 (quotes pp. 713, 719); *Communism and Liberty* (1950), p. 5; Samuel, 'British Marxist Historians', p. 90.
95. J. Saville, *SR*, 1991, p. 21; *The Politics of Continuity*, esp. chapter 5; S. Howe, *Anticolonialism in British Politics*, pp. 55ff., 159–67; R. P. Dutt, *Britain's Crisis of Empire* (1949) pp. 3–10, 62 ff.; *Mr Bevin's Record* (1949); *The Crisis of Britain and the British Empire* (1953); and numerous pieces in *LM*, from 1946–51; J. Callaghan, *Rajani Palme Dutt*, pp. 234–38; M. Heinemann, 'Labour Imperialism', *CR*, May 1949, pp. 518–33; V. G. Kiernan, 'India and the Labour Party', *NLR*, 42, March–April 1967 p. 44ff; S. MacIntyre, 'Imperialism and the Labour Movement', *OH*, 64; B. Moore, Labour-Communist Relations III, section ix: Labour Imperialism. *OH*, 84/5. Thanks especially to Dutt's writings, the C.P. critique of Labour Party colonial policy was and is especially compelling: 'imperialism is dead', proclaimed a Labour party manual in 1948, 'but the Empire has been given a new lease of life'! See, D. K. Fieldhouse,

'The Labour Governments and the Empire Commonwealth 1945–51, in R. Ovendale (ed.), *The Foreign Policy of the British Labour Government 1945–51* (Leicester, 1984) pp. 95ff; c.f. J. Strachey, *The End of Empire* (London 1959).

96. D. K. Fieldhouse, *The Theory of Capitalist Imperialism* (1967); A. Brewer, *Marxist Theories of Imperialism* (1980); E. P. Thompson, Open Letter to L. Kolakowski, in POT; V. Kiernan, *Marxism and Imperialism* (1974); *The Lords of Human Kind: European Attitudes to the Outside World in the Imperial Age* (1969); *European Empires from Conquest to Collapse* (1982); 'Imperialism and Revolution' in Porter and Teich, *Revolution in History*; *America, the New Imperialism* (1978); *History, Class and Nation States: Essays of V. G. Kiernan* (ed. H. Kaye) (Cambridge, 1988), pp. 1–28, 234–44; E. J. Hobsbawm, *The Age of Capital* (1971); *The Age of Empire* (1987); *Nations and Nationalism*, p. 148: 'Theories of Imperialism had long formed an organic part of socialist thinking.' Dutt was, of course, especially wedded to Leninist categories of analysis.

97. Dutt, *Britain's Crisis of Empire*, pp. 12–14; *We Speak for Freedom* (CPGB Conference Report, 1947), pp. 28–9; S. Howe, op. cit., pp. 166–7; Hill, *Two Commonwealths*; Hobsbawm, *Nations and Nationalism*, pp. 148, 150.

98. For the concept of American 'imperial receivership', C. Hitchens, *Blood, Class and Nostalgia* (1990), pp. 259 ff; J. Burnham, *The Struggle for the World* (New York 1947); Orwell, *CEJL*, IV, pp. 361–75; Heinemann, *CR*, 1947, pp. 508–9; V. G. Kiernan, *CR* February 1947, pp. 57–9; S. Howe, op. cit., p. 167: the argument of subordination to America 'became the most persistent theme of CPGB anticolonial propaganda'.

99. R. Samuel, 'Lost World' Part 1; 'British Marxist Historians', pp. 90–1; J. Lewis, *MQ*, 1/4, pp. 55ff; Garman, *WNV*, 28, 1 May 1948, pp. 181–3; Campbell, 'Prophets', loc. cit.; I. Montagu, *Plot against Peace* (1952), pp. 87–92; CPA Diana Sinnott, 'The Work of the Historians' Group', 1953 (mentioning a recent crop of Cold War writings on the Fall of Constantinople).

100. Hill, 'Independent FP', loc. cit., pp. 48ff.

101. Suslov, Speech to Wroclaw Conference, 1949, in Claudin, op. cit., chapter 7.

102. Spriano, pp. 191 ff; Claudin, pp. 580ff, 583–6, 596.

103. Hill, loc. cit., pp. 48, 51.

104. Ibid., pp. 51–2; 'The First Socialist Revolution', loc. cit., p. 511.

105. Marx House, *J. D. Bernal Peace Library* (Boxes on Cultural Congresses 1948–56); D. McLachlan, 'The Partisans of Peace', *RIIA*, January 1951, pp. 10–17; CPA HG Minutes, 1 April, 8 July 1950 (arranging for a series on 'the causes of war' for the *Daily Worker*, August–November 1950), 9 December 1951; R. Hilton, 'The Historians' Group and the British Tradition', June 1951; 'The History of the British People's Opposition to War Conference', 18 May 1952: CPA HG 60 D; Hill, 'Comenius, Partisan of Peace', *NCEO*, V/18, 30 August 1952, p. 289.

106. *Arena* (eds. J. Lindsay, R. Swingler) 1950–1. esp. II/8, 'The American Threat to British Culture', 1951. Contributors included E. P. Thompson, D. Sinnott, G. Thomson, A. L. Morton, R. Swingler, J. Lindsay; E. P. Thompson, 'On the Liberation of Seoul', *ibid.*, II/6, pp. 61–2; 'The Murder of William Morris', *ibid.*, II/7, pp 9–28; Anderson, *Arguments*, p. 144.
107. Thompson, *P.O.T.*, p. 333. Hobsbawm, HG, p. 33; Bernal, *Marxism and Science*, p. 95; CPA HG Minutes 16 September 1950, for 'purge of the WEAs'; *TLS* review of Lindsay's *Byzantium*, 12 December 1952; editorial, 2 January 1953; C. Hill, protest, ibid., 19 December; subsequent correspondence, 9, 16 January 1953; A Rothstein, 'Marxism and the TLS', *MQ*, 8/2, 1953, pp. 69ff; C. Hill, ibid., p. 187. Rothstein himself – an ultra-orthodox Stalinist – had lost his job at the School of Slavonic and East European Studies in 1949, *MQ*, 4/4, 1950, p. 258.
108. Samuel, 'British Marxist Historians', pp. 49–55.
109. Ibid p. 84; *English Revolution*, revised edn, 1955, pp. 4–5; H. Butterfield, *Whig Interpretation*; P. Christianson, 'The Causes of the English Revolution: A Reappraisal', *JBS*, xv, 2, 1976, pp. 40ff; J. E. Neale, *Elizabeth and her Parliaments* (1958); W. Notestein, *The Winning of the Initiative by the House of Commons* (1924). The coincidence is especially marked in Hill's textbook, *The Century of Revolution* (1961).
110. M. Lowy, *G. Lukacs, from Romanticism to Bolshevism* (1981); R. Scruton, *Thinkers of the New Left* (1986); M. Ignatieff, *The Needs of Strangers* (1984). See esp. Chapter 5 below for Hill's version of this in the 1970s.
111. Hill, *Lenin*, pp. 165–6.
112. T. Enright, *Island Home: The Blasket Heritage – a Memoir of George Thomson* (Co. Kerry, 1988), pp. 119–50; G. Thomson, *Aeschylus and Athens*; *Capitalism and After: The Rise and Fall of Commodity Production* (1973); *From Marx to Mao* (1971); E. P. Thompson, *William Morris* (1955); *MEWC*, Part I; *The Railway: An Adventure in Construction* (1948); *POT*, pp. 354–5. Cf Raymond Williams' 'Border Country' laments, and his attempts to chart the long revolution which would reinstate a democratic working class 'culture' in place of consumerism and an elitist 'civilization': R. Williams, *Border Country* (1968); *The Country and the City* (1977); *Culture and Society* (1958); *The Long Revolution* (1961), esp. Part 3; J. Gorak, *The Alien Mind of Raymond Williams* (Columbia, Missouri, 1988); Lin Chun, *The British New Left* (Edinburgh, 1993), pp. 38–43, 51–5.
113. G. Thomson, *Marxism and Poetry* (1945) pp. 52–3, 54 (quoted), 55–61. Cf Thomson's analysis of the social basis of the greatest classical music (with Beethoven as the supreme musical dialectician) *The Human Essence: The Sources of Science and Art* (1974); C. Caudwell, *Illusion and Reality*; J. Lindsay, *A Short History of Culture* (1939).
114. C. Hill, *Reformation to Industrial Revolution* (1967) 1969 edn, pp. 63, 89, 130, 143, 161, 173, 175, 200, 206–7, 213–12, 218–19, 275–6,

279–80, 283–4; 'Clarissa Harlowe and Her Times' in *Puritanism and Revolution*, pp. 367–92; *The World Turned Upside Down* (1972), pp. 261ff, 311; *Century of Revolution*, pp. 300–1; 303, 305–6.
115. Samuel, 'British Marxist Historians', p. 55.
116. For the following I have drawn on Tony Howe's photocopies of the Morris papers (University College London, file 66) 'Minutes of Debates July 1947, January 1948' (with numerous enclosures and appendices); 'State and Revolution in Tudor and Stuart England', *CR*, July 1948, pp. 207–14; K. Tribe, op. cit., chapter 1.
117. 'State and Rev', loc. cit., p. 208; Dobb, *Studies*, passim.
118. CH, 'Theses on Absolutism', July 1947; K. Andrews, 'The Role of the State in England, 1540–88'; 'Minutes of Discussions in Soviet Academy of Sciences, 1940–41': all Morris Mss; Tribe, op. cit., pp. 19ff.
119. VGK, 'Theses for discussion on Absolutism', pp. 1–5; 'A Note on the Origin of the Tudor State' (no. 9); 'On Merchant Capital' (no. 7); 'Postscript', Appendix J (22 February 1948): all Morris Mss.
120. Minutes 10/11 January 1948, Morris Mss.
121. Hilton (no. 6) Comments on VGK's 'Feudalism'; Torr in Minutes, pp. 2, 3; Dobb (no. 8) 'A Comment on Merchant Capital' (no. 7); CH, Summary, Minutes, pp. 3–4, 6: all Morris Mss; *CR*, p. 214; Tribe, p. 22.
122. CH, Summary, loc. cit.
123. Hobsbawm, HG, p. 31.
124. CH, Summary, loc. cit.; Tribe, pp. 23–4.
125. For Kiernan's subsequent efforts to square his 'revisionism' with the approved position, see *State and Society in Europe, 1550–1650* (Oxford, 1980), pp. 35–6; *History, Class and Nation States*, pp. 18–19, 103–4.

Chapter 4 Saving Appearances

1. See the discussions in C. S. Lewis, *The Discarded Image*, pp. 15–16; A Koestler, *The Sleepwalkers*, pp. 73–4.
2. Kaye/Kiernan, *History, Class, and Nation States*, p. 209; review of Hill, *The Century of Revolution*, NLR, 1, 1960, pp. 62–6.
3. Hill, *Century of Revolution*, 31ff, 37f, 42, 49–52, 55–6, 101–3, 107.
4. J. H. Hexter, 'Storm over the Gentry', *Encounter*, x, 5, May 1958, reprinted in *Reappraisals in History*, pp. 117–62 at pp. 117, 118.
5. L. Stone, 'The Anatomy of the Elizabethan Aristocracy', *Economic History Review*, 18, 1948. Cf *The Crisis of the English Aristocracy, 1558–1641* (Oxford, 1965); J. Adamson, 'Parliamentary Management, Men of Business and the House of Lords' in C. Jones, *A Pillar of the Constitution* (1989) pp. 21–50.
6. D. Brunton and D. H. Pennington, '*Members of the Long Parliament*' (1954), passim; M. Keeler, *The Long Parliament 1640–1641: a bibliographical study of its members* (Philadelphia, 1954)
7. L. Stone, 'The Bourgeois Revolution Revisited', *P&P*, 109, November 1985, p. 46, reprinted in Pocock, *Three British Revolutions*.

8. C. Russell, *The Fall of the British Monarchies, 1637–42* (Oxford, 1991); 'The British Problem and the English Civil War' in *Unrevolutionary England, 1603–42* (1990); *The Causes of the English Civil War* (Oxford, 1990); B. P. Levack, *The Formation of the British State: England, Scotland and the Union, 1603–1707* (Oxford, 1987); J. G. A. Pocock, 'British History: A Plea for a New Subject', *JMH*, 67. 1975, pp. 601–21; 'The Limits and Divisions of British History: In Search of the Unknown Subject', *American Historical Review*, LXXXVII, 1982, pp. 311–36; J. C. D. Clark, 'English History's Forgotten Context: Scotland, Ireland, Wales', *HJ*, 32/1, 1989, pp. 211–28.

9. P. Collinson, *The Religion of Protestants: The Church in English Society, 1559–1625* (Oxford, 1982); *The Elizabethan Puritan Movement* (1967); *Godly People* (Brighton, 1984); W. Lamont, *Godly Rule* (1969); C. H. and K. George, *The Protestant Mind of the English Reformation* (Princeton, 1961); P. Christianson, *Reformers and Babylon: English Apocalyptic Visions from the Reformation to the Eve of the English Civil War* (Toronto, 1978); N. Tyacke, *The Anti-Calvinists* (Oxford, 1987); 'Puritanism, Arminianism and Counter-Revolution' in C. Russell (ed.), *The Origins of the English Civil War* (1973), pp. 119–43; M. G. Finlayson, *Historians, Puritanism and the English Revolution: The Religious Factor in English Politics before and after the Interregnum* (Toronto, 1986). For a somewhat different version of fundamental and deep-seated religious division going back a generation and more, see P. Lake, *Anglicans and Puritans? Presbyterianism and English Conformist Thought from Whitgift to Hooker* (1988).

10. J. H. Hexter, 'The Historical Method of Christopher Hill', reprinted in *On Historians*, p. 248.

11. Hill, 'James Harrington and the People' in *Puritanism and Revolution* (1958), pp. 299–313 (with quotations from an annotated Moscow copy of the text); *Good Old Cause*, pp. 117, 141–2, 261–3, 266, 466, 473–5 ('where H speaks of the people, we should speak more precisely of the bourgeoisie'); A. L. Morton, 'James Harrington, Revolutionary Theorist', loc. cit. But cf J. G. A. Pocock (ed.), *The Political Works of James Harrington* (Cambridge, 1977); James Harrington and the Good Old Cause, *JBS*, 10, i, 1970, pp. 36–9; *The Ancient Constitution and Feudal Law* (Cambridge, 1957) chapter 6; *The Machiavellian Moment* (Princeton, 1975), pp. 383ff; W. D. Greenleaf, *Order, Empiricism and Politics: Two Traditions in English Political Thought, 1500–1700* (Oxford, 1964).

12. J. H. Hexter, 'Storm over the Gentry', first published in the anti-communist journal, *Encounter*, in 1958, effectively put paid to the gentry, rising, falling, undulating or whatever, as credible social catalysts of revolution in seventeenth-century England. See Hexter, *Reappraisals*, pp. 117–62; H. R. Trevor-Roper, 'The Gentry, 1540–1640', *EcHR*, Supplement 1, 1953; J. P. Cooper, 'The Counting of Manors', ibid., 2nd series, viii, 1956, pp. 377–89.

13. Stone, *The Bourgeois Revolution Revisited*, quoted in Eley and Hunt, op. cit. p. 296.

14. Brenner, 'Bourgeois Revolution', loc. cit., pp. 296–7; Tawney, 'The

Rise of the Gentry', loc. cit., passim; 'The Rise of the Gentry, a Postscript', *EcHR*, 2nd series, vii, 1954, pp. 91–7; Defoe, 'Faults on Both Sides' (1710), p. 3.

15. 'The Bourgeois Revolutions in Soviet Scholarship', *NLR*, 155, 1986, pp. 107–13; 'A Bourgeois Revolution' in Pocock (ed.), op. cit., p. 110.

16. Polignac to the Dutch Deputies, 1713 in A. MacLachlan, *The Great Peace* (Cambridge PhD, 1965), p. 98.

17. *The British Road to Socialism* (1951), pp. 8, 14–17; H. Pollitt, July 1950, October 1950, *WNV*, 30; 'A New Perspective for the British People', *CR*, February 1951, pp. 35–7; E. Burns, 'People's Democracy, Britain's Path to Socialism', ibid., March 1951, pp. 67–71; P. Dutt, *LM*, Notes of the Month, February, March 1951; P. Dutt, 'A Real People's Democracy', *DW*, 1–5 February; J. Stalin, Speech to XIX Congress of CPSU, 1952, pp. 3ff. For Stalin's personal role in the policy change, see G. Matthews, 'Stalin's British Road?', *Changes*, 14 September 1991.

18. CPA HG 60 A, Minutes 16 March, 8 June, 9 December 1951; 'The Historians' Group and British Tradition', statement on behalf of the group by R. H. Hilton (Chairman) June 1951; D. Sinnott, note to the 'Aggregate', October 1951; 'Britain's Cultural Heritage in the Service of Peace and National Independence': 'Cultural' conference, 24–5 May 1952, attended by 900 delegates and visitors, with the keynote opening speech by George Thomson, later published by *Arena*; *Daily Worker* series, G. Thomson, 'Britain's Cultural Heritage: A Treasure House of Creative Ideas', *DW* 27 May 1952; *WNV*, 32/24, 14 June 1952, D. Kartun, 'The Conference on Britain's Cultural Heritage'. For this and other conferences organized by the National Cultural Committee, see S. Parsons, *Communism in the Professions*, pp. 283–302. For the party's attack on the mystique of monarchy at this time, see esp. the *Daily Worker* series on the Coronation in 1953 ('The Coronation Plot against the British people'; 'The Truth about the Coronation'; 'They Locked up the King', by R. Hilton; 'Britain's First Republic', by A. L. Morton; 'Why *They* love *Their* Queen'; 'The Dangers of a Prince Consort', etc. – including a strip cartoon series, 'Commons against Kings', with 11/12 of the series devoted to the seventeenth century – culminating on 2 June in Harry Pollitt's, 'Long Live the People') and assorted articles in *CR* and *MQ*.

19. Hilton, 'British Tradition', passim; CPA HG General Corresp., 22 July 1955 from Hill and Edwin Payne on the need to tackle the school and circulating library situation; D. Sinnott, January 1952: complaints at inactivity of Teachers' section; Local History Bulletins 1–8, esp. 2: 'Class Struggles in the Countryside' (L. Munby), 7, June 1951, 'The American Threat to British Culture' (B. Grant); Minutes 19 July 1953 (on the launching of *OH*).

20. Many of the contributors to the debate on inner party democracy in 1956 commented on the restrictions imposed at this time: J. Saville, *SR*, 1976, pp. 1–22; C. Hill, *W(orld) N(ews)* 3/33, 18 August

1956; J. Saville 3/18, 5 May; J. Mahon, *CR*, February 1951, pp. 38ff. The closing down of *Modern Quarterly* in 1953 – according to Tribe, op. cit., p. 23, on Palme Dutt's orders – and its replacement by the (initially) much more tightly controlled *Marxist Quarterly* (see list of editorial staff) may be further evidence of this trend; G. Thomson, *From Marx to Mao*, introduction.

21. CPA HG Minutes Books 2 and 3: on contacts with French and Soviet historians, 30 September 1952; 26 September 1954; 2 January 1955; 23 January 1955; requests for 'polemic', 30 September 1952; 20 March 1955; 20 April 1955. Hill started to review regularly for *The Spectator* in 1955.

22. Werskey, op. cit., pp. 331–5; A. Kettle, 'Problems of Intellectuals: Socialism the Answer, *WN*, 6/14, 18 April 1959, pp. 193–4; 'Communism and the Intellectuals' in B. Simon, *The Challenge of Marxism* (1963), pp. 178–206; 'Politics and Culture', *WN*, 1/26, 26 June 1954, pp. 513–14, and subsequent correspondence.

23. J. Morris, UCL File 34: letter to Editorial Board, pp. i–iv, 15 January 1951; Hill to Morris, 22 May 1951, 15 August 1951. (Morris files kindly lent by A. Howe. Howe will be discussing the connection between *Past and Present* and the Historians' Group in his forthcoming PhD.)

24. It was noticeable that Hill's articles for these party journals trailed off after 1950 – apart from a particularly idolatrous obituary piece on 'Stalin and the Science of History' – and that he was not to contribute significantly to their successors, *Marxist Quarterly*, and *Marxism Today*. (*MQ* Stalin Obituaries: Hill, 'Stalin and the Science of History', 8/4, 1953, pp. 198–212 – cf J. Bernal, 'Stalin as Scientist'; R. L. Meek, 'Some Aspects of Stalin's "Economic" Problems'). *Modern Quarterly*, long criticised for its intellectual bent, may have also erred in allowing the Caudwell controversy to continue long after the party had given it an authoriative closure. Its replacement – *Marxist Quarterly* – was intended 'to be understood by all readers and not only by experts'; it certainly had a far more tightly controlled editorial board. See S. Parsons, *Communism in the Professions*, pp. 311–13, 315–16.

25. 'As evidence accumulates we shall need, not to scrap our Marxist categories, but to refine them until they can accommodate the facts.' A. L. Merson, 'Problems of the English Bourgeois Revolution: Some reflections on the recent work of Christopher Hill', *Marxism Today*, October 1963, p. 315.

26. Ibid., p. 312; Hill, Century of Revolution p. 105. 'A Bourgeois Revolution', in Pocock, *Three British Revolutions*, pp. 109–139; 'The Bourgeois Revolution in Soviet Scholarship', loc. cit. c.f. Colin Lucas's somewhat orthodox conclusion to a famous revisionist article, 'Nobles, Bourgeois and the Origins of the French Revolution', *P&P*, 60, 1973 pp. 84–126.

27. P. Collinson, letter to *Encounter*, October 1958 p. 69. C. V. Wedgwood, ibid., November 1958 p. 80.

28. F. Bacon, *Essays* (1968 ed.) p. 41.

29. K. Marx; *The Eighteenth Brumaire of Louis Bonaparte*, part 1, in D. Fernbach (ed.) *Surveys from Exile*, pp. 147–48.
30. K. Minogue, *Alien Powers: The Pure Theory of Ideology* (London, 1981) chapter 4, esp. pp. 90 ff.; 'Bacon and Locke: on Ideology as Mental Hygiene' in A. Povel (ed), *Ideology, Philosophy and Politics* (Waterloo, Ont. 1981); J. H. Hexter, *On Historians* p. 252.
31. A. L. Morton, 'Religion and Politics in the English Revolution', *Marxism Today*, 1960, pp. 367–72; *The World of the Ranters* (1970), chapter 1; *The English Utopia* (1952), introduction; cf Hill on the difficulty of 'opening our minds to revolutionaries and Puritans', *Puritanism and Revolution*, p. vii: this formulation, however, has in a certain sense already made the 'return journey' to a modern – post 1789 – conception of revolution which it then attributes to the seventeenth-century world which has to be recaptured.
32. E. Gellner, *Words and Things* (1959); – a book much admired by Hill (information kindly provided by Mr A. J. Cahill); P. Anderson, 'Components of the National Culture', loc cit.
33. For Hill's concern with language and words, see *Change and Continuity in Seventeenth Century England* (1974), pp. 103 ff; *Collected Essays*, vol 1; *A Nation of Change and Novelty*, esp. pp. 3, 5, 7, 10; M. Heinemann, 'How the Words got on the Page: Christopher Hill and 17th Century Literary Studies', in Eley and Hunt, op. cit., pp. 73–98.
34. Hexter, loc. cit.; William G. Palmer, 'The Burden of Proof: J. H. Hexter and Christopher Hill', *JBS*, 19/1, 1979, pp. 122–9. Palmer managed to reduce a real dispute about historical method to a historiographical commonplace about different styles of history and a dispute 'as natural as that between the meanest dog on the block and the most lordly house cat'; J. H. Hexter, 'Reply to Mr Palmer: A Vision of Files', ibid., pp. 130–6. In a characteristically 'empirical' move, Hexter chose to disregard Hill's 'substantive philosophy' on the ground that mention of Hill's Marxism was 'ungracious' and perhaps 'irrelevant'. But see Himmelfarb, op. cit., p. 88: 'the idea that it is invidious to consider the substantive philosophy of a Marxist historian is itself invidious, for it refuses to take seriously what a Marxist takes most seriously'.
35. Hill, 'Marx's Virtues', loc. cit.; H. Kaye, op. cit., pp. 112–14.
36. M. Fulbrook in Eley and Hunt, op. cit., pp. 48ff.
37. 'The Many-Headed Monster' in *Change and Continuity*, pp. 181–204.
38. Fulbrook, pp. 37 ff; Hill, 'Political Discourse in Early Seventeenth Century England' in *A Nation of Change*, pp. 24–5; 'Censorship and English Literature', *Collected Essays*, 1, pp. 32–71; also, *AntiChrist in Seventeenth Century England* (Newcastle, 1971); *Milton and the English Revolution* (1977); 'Irreligion in the Puritan Revolution' in J. H. McGregor and B. Reay, *Radical Religion in the English Revolution* (Oxford, 1984), pp. 191–211; cf A. Patterson, *Censorship and Interpretation: The Conditions of Writing and Reading in Early Modern England* (Maddison, Wis., 1984); M. Heinemann, *Puritanism and the Theatre: Thomas Middleton and Opposition Drama under the Early*

Stuarts (Cambridge, 1980); M. Butler, *Theatre and Crisis, 1632–42* (Cambridge, 1984); J. Limon, *Dangerous Matter: English Drama and Politics in 1623/4* (Cambridge, 1986).
39. Morton, *World of Ranters*, p. 3; Hexter, *On Historians*, pp. 245 ff; see Hill's explanation in Eley and Hunt, op. cit., p. 102 (Talking with Christopher Hill): 'it seems to me that it's only worth writing history if you've something new to say, then you collect evidence which doesn't mainly contradict what you're trying to say . . . I was trying to pick out new elements in Puritan thought . . . It seemed to me this was more interesting than drawing attention to elements in Puritan thought that are wholly conventional – which is of course 95 per cent of Puritan thought. The other 5 per cent seemed to me more interesting for what I was trying to do.'
40. *Society and Puritanism in Pre-Revolutionary England* (1964), chapter 1; C. H. George, 'Puritanism as History and Historiography', *P&P*, xli, 1968, pp. 77–104; W. Lamont, 'Some Further Thoughts', *P&P*, lv, 1969, pp. 68–90; P. Christianson, 'Reformers and the Church of England under Elizabeth and the Early Stuarts', *JEccH*, 31/4, 1980, pp. 463–82; P. Collinson, 'A Comment Concerning the Word Puritan', ibid., pp. 483–8; M. G. Finlayson, 'Puritanism and Puritans: Labels or Libels', *Canadian Journal of History*, viii, 1973.
41. This is still the subtext of most of Hill's surveys of the period; it also informs such Left anthologies as C. Hampton, *A Radical Reader* (1984), chapter 3, pp. 1603–88, entitled 'The Rise of Capitalism' (though none of the extracts seems to be about capitalism).
42. *Intellectual Origins of the English Revolution* (Oxford, 1965), introduction; 'Partial Historians and Total History', *TLS*, 24 November 1972, pp. 1431–2; Kaye, op. cit., pp. 113, 115–17.
43. 'Protestantism and the Rise of Capitalism' in *Change and Continuity*, pp. 81–102, see esp. 83–4, 95, 99–100, 102; M. Walzer, *The Revolution of the Saints* (Cambridge, Mass., 1965) for a version of Puritan modernity more responsive to these elements.
44. Historians' Group Summer Conference, Netherwood, July 1954, Morris Mss Box 66: iii: 'Problems of the Bourgeois Revolution' (C.H.), pp 1–6.
45. Ibid., p. 6.
46. *Century of Revolution*, pp. 120–3; B. Manning, 'The Long Parliament and the English Revolution', *P&P*, pp. 71–6; E. Kerridge, 'The Movement of Rent, 1540–1640', *EcHR*, new series 6/1, 1953, pp. 16–34. Hill appeared to think that Kerridge's work would 'bowl out' Trevor-Roper. See C. H. to John Morris, 25 August 1954?, Morris Mss File 32.
47. Problems (Netherwood), p. 5; *Century of Revolution*, pp. 118ff; B. Manning, *The People and the English Revolution* (1976).
48. Review of Laslett in *Change and Continuity*, pp. 205–18, esp. pp. 215–6; of Brunton and Pennington, *DW*, 25 February 1954: 'The People Did It'!
49. Hill, *Society and Puritanism*, pp. 59ff, 78–120; W. K. Jordan,

Philanthropy in England, 1480–1660 (1959); B. Manning, *The People*, passim; V. Pearl, *London and the Outbreak of the Puritan Revolution* (Oxford, 1961). Pearl's work was deployed by both Marxists and anti-Marxists to argue their case. On the one hand, Manning and Hill pointed to the importance of London, the effective mobilization of popular support for the radical cause, and the eventual alignment of the City behind the parliamentary cause; on the other, Trevor-Roper (*NS*, 9 July 1961, pp. 16–17) pointed to the Royalist affiliations of the City government before 1641 and the fact that it took a revolutionary seizure of power to dislodge the traditional oligarchies; Richardson, op. cit., p. 124; R. Howell, *Newcastle-upon-Tyne and the Puritan Revolution* (1967).

50. Dobb, *Studies*, pp. 123 ff; Brenner, 'Agrarian Class Structure and Economic Development in Pre-Industrial Europe', *P&P*, 70, 1976, pp. 30–75; Hill, *Century of Revolution*, pp. 121–5, 127–8; Manning, 'The Nobles, the People and the Constitution', *P&P*, 9.

51. P. Anderson, 'The Notion of Bourgeois Revolution' in *English Questions* (1992), p. 111. This was originally presented as a lecture in 1978.

52. For this and the following paragraphs see Manning, *People*, pp. 84–113, 142, 182, 197, 202, 203–4; Richardson, op. cit., pp. 144–5; D. Underdown, *Revel, Riot and Rebellion: Popular Politics and Culture in England, 1603–1660* (Oxford, 1984), pp. 1–4.

53. Hill, *Century of Revolution*, Part II; Manning, *The People*, pp. 202ff; Hill, 'Agrarian Legislation', loc. cit.; *English Revolution*, pp. 58 ff; 'The First Socialist Revolution', loc. cit.

54. Fulbrook, loc. cit., pp. 35–6; Hill, *Century of Revolution*, p. 105; A. Soboul, *The Parisian Sans-Culottes and the French Revolution* (English translation – and abridgement, Oxford, 1961).

55. This is the substance of J. S. Morrill's critique, *HJ*, 20, 1977, pp. 229ff; Manning, *The People*, chapter 3.

56. Manning, *The People* p. 162; Richardson, op. cit., p. 145.

57. Hill, *Society and Puritanism*, pp. 26ff, 490ff.

58. *Economic Problems of the Church from Archbishop Whitgift to the Long Parliament* (Oxford, 1956) – a work hailed by one reviewer as marking the breaking of the Marxist spell: A Simpson, quoted in Richardson, op. cit., p. 104.

59. Hill, *Society and Puritanism*, passim; c.f. M. Walzer, *The Revolution of the Saints*; W. Lamont, *Godly Rule*.

60. Netherwood Conference File III, pp. 1, 3; VII ('Ideas and the State'); Hill to Morris, 12, 19 May 1955, Morris Mss., File 32.

61. E. Shils, 'The Intellectual: Great Britain', *Encounter*, IV/4, November 1955, pp. 52, 57–8; Anderson, 'Components', loc. cit.; CPA HG 60 D: 'Tasks for the Historians Group', undated but *c*. June 1955.

62. A. L. Rowse, *A New Elizabethan Age?* (British Academy Lecture, 1953); *The England of Elizabeth* (1950); *The Expansion of Elizabethan England* (1959) charted the deepening conservatism of this 1930's radical.

63. G. R. Elton, *The Tudor Revolution in Government* (Cambridge, 1953),

pp. 1–8, 419–21, 424–7; *England under the Tudors* (1955); 'The Political Creed of Thomas Cromwell', *Transactions of the Royal Historical Society* (TRHS), VI, 1956.

64. Hill, *Century of Revolution* (Edinburgh, 1961).

65. *Intellectual Origins* (Oxford, 1965); The main features of the argument had appeared in six BBC talks in 1962 (31 May–5 July) *Listener*, 1962 vol. I pp. 943–6, 983–6, 1023–6, 1066–8, 1107–9, vol. 2, pp. 17–19.

66. *Intellectual Origins*, pp. 2–4; 280ff, 298; D. Mornet, *Les Origines Intellectuelles de la Revolution Française, 1715–1787* (Paris, 1933); Samuel, 'British Marxist Historians', loc. cit., p. 81; Kaye, pp. 115–17.

67. H. Trevor-Roper, *History and Theory*, V, 1966, pp. 61–82; R. Chartier, *Cultural Origins of the French Revolution* (Chicago, 1991), pp. 4ff. For subsequent debate, see H. Kearney, 'Puritanism, Capitalism and the Scientific Revolution', *P&P*, 28, 1964, and the replies (from Hill, *P&P*, 29, 1964; Kearney and T. K. Rabb, 31, 1965; Hill, 32, 1965); C. Webster (ed.), *The Intellectual Revolution of the Seventeenth Century* (1974); *The Great Instauration: Science, Medicine and Reform 1626–1660* (1975).

68. C. Hill, 'The Theory of Revolution' in D. Horowitz (ed.), *Isaac Deutscher, the Man and his Work* (1971), pp. 115–31. This is based on Deutscher's lectures at Harvard in 1950 and 1959 (which looked forward to Russia's 1688/1830 as the next stage in the revolutionary process). Cf Deutscher's 1945 essay on 'revolution' in T. Deutscher (ed.), *Marxism, Wars and Revolutions* (1984); I. Deutscher, *Ironies of History: Essays in Contemporary Communism* (1966), esp. pp. 3–145.

69. 'Christopher Hill and Lawrence Stone Discuss with Peter Burke the English Revolution of the Seventeenth Certury', *Listener*, 4 October 1973, p. 448; 'A Bourgeois Revolution' in Pocock, *Three British Revolutions*, pp. 109–39; 'The Bourgeois Revolution in Soviet Scholarship', loc. cit.

70. C. B. Macpherson, *The Political Theory of Possessive Individualism* (Oxford, 1964); L. Stone, *The Family, Sex and Marriage in England 1500–1800* (Oxford, 1977); Hill, 'The Place of the Seventeenth Century Revolution in English History' in *A Nation of Change*, pp. 6–23; *Century of Revolution*, conclusion; C. Condren, 'Christopher Hill on the English Revolution' in S. Mukherjee and J. O. Ward (eds), *Revolution as History* (Sydney, 1990), pp. 34–5.

71. CPA HG 60 A., Minutes, 16 March 1952 (Hill); Netherwood Notes, passim; Minutes 16 August 1954 (Hobsbawm); General Correspondence, 'Review of our Work', undated, c. 1953–4; Hobsbawm, HG loc. cit., passim.

72. G. Enteen, 'Soviet Historians Review their Own Past: The Rehabilitation of M. N. Pokrovskii', *Soviet Studies*, 20, 1969, pp. 306–20; S. Dubrovskii, 'M. N. Pokrovskii and his Role in the Development of Soviet Historical Studies', *Soviet Historical Studies* 1/i, 1962, pp. 21–51. Pokrovsky was successively restored from 1954 to 1964; after the fall of Krushchev, he fell into disfavour once more.

73. For the following section on Macpherson, see W. Lees, *C. B. Macpherson: Dilemmas of Liberalism and Socialism* (New York, 1988); A. Kontos (ed.), *Powers, Possessions and Freedom: Essays in Honour of C. B. Macpherson* (Toronto, 1978); *Canadian Journal of Political Science*, IX/3, 1976 pp. 377–430 (essays by K. Minogue: 'Humanist Democracy: The Political Thought of C.B.M'; V. Svacek, 'The elusive Marxism of C.B.M').

74. S. Lukes, 'The Real and Ideal Worlds of Democracy' in Kontos, op. cit., pp. 140–1; C. B. Macpherson, 'The False Roots of Western Democracy' in F. Dallmayr (ed.), *From Contract to Community* (New York, 1978) pp. 25–6; *The Real World of Democracy* (Oxford, 1966), pp. 22–3, 29, 31–2; *Democratic Theory: Essays in Retrieval* (Oxford, 1973), pp. 14–15.

75. *Democratic Theory*, p. 43; Lukes, loc. cit., p. 141.

76. C. Hill, 'Possessive Individualism', *P&P*, 24, 1963, pp. 86–9; G. Lichtheim, 'Leviathan' in *The Concept of Ideology and other Essays* (1967), pp. 151–8; J. Dunn, *The Political Thought of John Locke* (Cambridge, 1969), p. ix; 'Democracy Unretrieved or the Political theory of Professor Macpherson', *British Journal of Political Science*, 4, 1978, pp. 489–99; Q. Skinner, 'Motives, Intentions and the Intrepretation of Texts' in J. Tully, *Meaning and Context: Quentin Skinner and his Critics* (Cambridge, 1988), p. 78.

77. Hill, 'Possessive Individualism', loc. cit., p. 86; 'Thomas Hobbes and the Revolution in Political Thought', originally in R. W. Sellars *et al.* (eds), *Philosophy for the Future* (New York 1949), subsequently revised in *Puritanism and Revolution*, pp. 275–98 (see p. 279); Macpherson, 'Hobbes Today', first published 1945, reprinted in K. Brown (ed.), *Hobbes Studies* (Oxford, 1965), pp. 169–83 as 'Hobbes's Bourgeois Man' (see p. 243); see also, Macpherson (ed.), *Hobbes: The Leviathan* (Harmondsworth 1968), introduction, pp. 12ff.

78. I. Berlin, 'Hobbes, Locke and Professor Macpherson', *Political Quarterly*, xxxv, 1964, pp. 444–68 (see pp. 451ff); J. Viner, 'Possessive Individualism as Original Sin', *Canadian Journal of Economics and Political Science*, xxix/4, 1963, pp. 548–59 (see pp. 552–3); K. Thomas, 'The Social Origins of Hobbes's Political Thought' in K. Brown, op. cit., pp. 185–236 (esp. pp. 189–90, 202).

79. Macpherson, *Possessive Individualism*, passim; 'Hobbes's Bourgeois Man', loc. cit., pp. 239–40; Berlin, 'Hobbes, Locke', loc. cit., p. 461.

80. Macpherson, *Possessive Individualism*, pp. 221ff; J. Dunn, op. cit., passim esp. pp. 262–5; A. Ryan, 'Locke and the Dictatorship of the Bourgeoisie', *Political Studies*, xiii, 2, 1965, pp. 219–30.

81. Dunn, op. cit., pp. 206, 212ff; P. Laslett, 'Market Society and Political Theory', *HJ*, vii/i, 1964, pp. 150–4; ed. *Locke: Two Treatises of Government* (Cambridge, 1960); R. Ashcraft, *Revolutionary Politics and Locke's Two Treatises of Government* (Cambridge, 1986), which sums up many articles and essays of the 1970s and 1980s.

82. Dunn, op. cit., pp. 189, 222–9; *Rethinking Political Theory* (Cambridge, 1985), pp. 55–67; Ryan, loc. cit., pp. 223, 229.

83. A. Arblaster, 'Revolution, The Levellers and C. B. Macpherson' in F. Barker (ed.), *1642: Literature and Power in the 17th Century* (Essex, 1981), pp. 220–36; K. Thomas, 'The Levellers and the Franchise' in K. Aylmer (ed.), *The Interregnum* (1972), pp. 52, 57, 66–7; Macpherson, *Possessive Individualism*, pp. 23, 83, 114.

84. P. Earle, *The World of Defoe* (1976), pp. 15ff; D. Jarret, *The Begetters of Revolution: England's Involvement with France, 1759–89* (1973); St John-Orrery, July 1709 quoted in G. S. Holmes, *British Politics in the Age of Anne* (1967), pp. 176–7.

85. G. D. H. Cole, introduction to *A Tour through England and Wales* (1928), pp. v–xiv; D. George, *England in Transition: Life and Work in Eighteenth Century England* (1931), esp. chapter 2; I. Watt, *The Rise of the English Novel* (1963); I. Kramnick, *Bolingbroke and his Circle: The Politics of Nostalgia in the Age of Walpole* (Cambridge, Mass., 1968), esp. pp. 188–200; C. Hill, *Reformation to Industrial Revolution*, pp. 9–10; 'Daniel Defoe and Robinson Crusoe' in *Collected Essays* I, pp. 105–30; R. H. Tawney, *Religion and the Rise of Capitalism*, pp. 197–8; 210–11, 251, 253.

86. A. L. Morton, 'Mr Crusoe and Mr Gulliver', reprinted in M. Heinemann and W. Thompson (eds), *History and the Imagination: Selected Writings of A. L. Morton* (1990), p. 229; Defoe, *Complete English Tradesman* (ed. Tegg) (1727), I, pp. 227, 246–7, 236–8; *A Plan of English Commerce*, p. 9; *Tour* I, pp. 15, 18, 37–40; 76, 114, 193–6; G. Healey (ed.), *Letters of Daniel Defoe* (Oxford, 1955); Kramnick, op. cit., pp. 188ff.

87. G. Holmes and W. Speck, *The Divided Society* (1968); W. A. Speck, 'Conflict in Society' in G. S. Holmes, *Britain after the Glorious Revolution* (1969); P. Dickson, *The Financial Revolution in England: a Study in the Development of Public Credit, 1688–1756* (1967); J. H. Plumb, *The Growth of Political Stability in England, 1675–1725* (1967).

88. Defoe, *CET*, II, pp. 87, 90. The 'avarice of the overgrown tradesman' and the need for restraints are a constant theme of the work, as is the vulnerability of tradesman especially to the vagaries of overseas trade: *CET*, I, pp. x, 44–5, 71–3, 238–9; II, pp. 36–7, 69, 108–11.

89. J. Sutherland, *Defoe* (1937), pp. 26, 31, 32–42, 46: G. Holmes, *Britain*, pp. 26–34; R. Davis, 'English Foreign Trade', *Ec HR*, 2,vii, 1954, p. 161.

90. Alick West, *The Mountain in the Sunlight* (1958), p. 8; A. Kettle, *An Introduction to the English Novel* (1951, 1953); *Essays in Socialist Realism and the British Cultural Tradition*; 'The Progressive Tradition in Bourgeois Culture' in *Literature and Liberation* (Manchester, 1988); Watt, op. cit.; C. Hill, 'Clarissa Harlowe and her Times', *Essays in Criticism*, v, 1955, pp. 315–40, subsequently in *Puritanism and Revolution*; *Collected Essays* I, pp. 1–25, 318ff.

91. West, op. cit., pp. 12–57, esp. pp. 17, 21–2, 44–5; Hill, 'John Bunyan and his Public', *History Today*, October 1987, p. 16 ('*The Pilgrim's Progress* is as class conscious as the sermon on Dives and Lazarus'); 'John Bunyan and The English Revolution', *Marxist Perspectives*,

2, 1979; *A Turbulent . . . People*, pp. 212ff, 231–9; Lindsay, *Bunyan*, esp. conclusion, pp. 250ff; see Kettle's criticism of Lindsay: 'Bunyan believed in life after death – there is no point in insinuating that had he known better he would have believed in something else' (*Introduction to the English Novel I*, p. 44).

92.   West, op. cit., pp. 58–109, esp. pp. 73–85; A. L. Morton, review of West in *WN*, 5/46, 12 November 1958, p. 672; *The English Utopia*, pp. 86–96; Hill, 'Defoe', *Collected Essays I*, esp. pp. 112ff.

93.   P. Langford, *A Polite and Commercial People: England 1727–1783* (Oxford, 1989).

94.   Stone, *Crisis of the English Aristocracy, 1558–1640* (references are to abridged edition, Oxford 1965); J. H. Hexter, 'Lawrence Stone and the English Aristocracy', *On Historians*, pp. 149–227.

95.   Stone, *Festschrift*, ed. Beier and Canandine, *The First Modern Society*, C. S. L. Davis, 'The Enfant Terrible?', pp. 9–14; J. M. Murrin, 'The Eminence Rouge', pp. 21–31.

96.   *P&P*, Morris Mss. File 34, Stone–Morris, 13 February 1958; Morris–Stone 24 February 1958 (a three-page assurance that *P&P* was not tainted by Marxist fundamentalism).

97.   'The Anatomy of the Elizabethan Aristocracy', *Ec HR*, xviii, 1948, pp. 1–53; H. R. Trevor-Roper, 'The Elizabethan Aristocracy: An Anatomy Anatomized', ibid., 2nd series, iii, 1951, pp. 279–98; Stone, 'The Elizabethan Aristocracy – A Restatement', ibid., iv, 1952, pp. 302–21; Hexter, 'Storm', op. cit., pp. 120ff. Stone was to repudiate much of his original argument in *Social Change and Revolution in England, 1540–1640* (1965); Richardson, op. cit., pp. 96ff.

98.   Stone, *Crisis*, pp. 11ff; Hexter, op. cit., p. 158.

99.   Hexter, op. cit., pp. 192ff. The perception of crisis may have been reinforced by the aristocratic families Stone primarily studied, namely, the Cecils, Manners, Wriothesleys, Berkeleys, Howards, see *Family and Fortune: Studies in Aristocratic Finance in the 16th and 17th Centuries* (Oxford, 1973), esp. pp. 145–60, 200–41.

100.   Hobsbawm, 'The Overall Crisis of the European Economy in the 17th Century, *P&P*, 5, 1954, pp. 33–53, subsequently revised, in T. S. Aston, *Crisis in Europe* (1965), pp. 5–58.

101.   See Hobsbawm's contributions to the debates on 'State and Society' in 1948 and to the Netherwood conferences in 1954, loc. cit.

102.   Stone, 'Century of Crisis' in *New York Review of Books*, vi (3), 1966, pp. 13–16, subsequently in *The Past and the Present*; T. K. Rabb, *The Struggle for Stability in Early Modern Europe* (Oxford, 1975).

103.   H. R. Trevor-Roper, 'The General Crisis of the 17th Century' in Aston, pp. 59–94.

104.   Aston, op. cit., pp. 5–6.; Hobsbawm, 'The 17th Century and the Development of Capitalism', *SS*, xxiv, 1960, pp. 97–112.

105.   See Trevor-Roper's damaging critique in 'Marxism and the Study of History', *Problems of Communism*, V, v, 1956, pp. 36–42, esp. 40: in effect. Hobsbawm had attached an orthodox 'progressivist' Marxist conclusion to an inverted if nominally Marxist analysis

of decline. Cf *NS*, 20 August 1955 (and subsequent correspondence). It was notable that the one major Soviet contribution rejected the whole idea of 'Crisis' in the interests of Marxist hygiene: A. D. Lublinskaya, in Aston, op. cit; *French Absolutism: The Crucial Phase, 1620–9* (Cambridge, 1968); D. Parker, *Europe's 17th Century Crisis: A Marxist Review*, OH, 56, 1973.

106. Rabb, op. cit., pp. 32–4. The whole Crisis Debate is a good illustration of the tyranny of metaphor: see C. M. Turbayne, *The Myth of Metaphor* (S. Carolina, 1970), esp. pp. 46–50. For Hill's objection to an earlier version of the metaphor of 'fever' and 'recovery', see his critique of C. Brinton, *The Anatomy of Revolution* (NY., 1952), *Science and Society*, xvii, 1953 pp. 270–3.

107. Hexter, op. cit., pp. 184ff.

108. J. Cannon, 'The Isthmus Repaired: the Resurgence of the English Aristocracy, 1660–1760', *Proceedings of the British Academy*, 1982, pp. 431ff. (The reference is to Harrington's observation in 1656 that the House of Peers 'which alone had stood in this gap, now sinking down between the King and the Commons, showed that Crassus was dead and the Isthmus broken'); J. Cannon, *Aristocratic Century: The Peerage in 18th Century England* (Cambridge, 1984); C. Jones, *A Pillar of the Constitution*; D. Cannadine, *The Decline and Fall of the English Aristocracy* (Yale, 1990); J. V. Beckett, *The Aristocracy in England, 1660–1914* (1986).

109. Beckett, op. cit., pp. 92–3, 96; B. Behrens, *Society, Government and the Enlightenment: The Experiences of Eighteenth Century France and Prussia* (1985); J. H. Plumb, *Men and Places* (Harmondsworth, 1969) Part I; Tocqueville, *Ancien Regime*, pp. 88–90; 'Social and Political Conditions in England and France', *Westminster Review*, 1836; S. Dresher, *Tocqueville in England* (Cambridge, Mass., 1964) records a somewhat different – and less familiar – verdict.

110. H. J. Habakkuk, 'English Landownership', *EcHR*, x, 1940; 'Marriage Settlements in the 18th century', *TRHS*, 4th ser., xxxii, 1950; 'The Rise and Fall of English Landed Families', ibid., 5th ser., xxix–xxx, 1979–80. Habakkuk initially regarded his work on aristocratic consolidation as consistent with the seventeenth-century social revolutionary picture; his later writings reversed this judgement. As did L. and J. F. Stone, *An Open Elite? England 1540–1880* (Oxford, 1984); G. E. Mingay, *English Landed Society in the 18th Century* (1960). See, most recently, Sir John Habakkuk's monumental 786 page study, *Marriage, Debt and the Estates System: English Landownership 1650–1950* (Oxford 1994).

111. Stone, *Crisis*, pp. 135ff (quote at p. 159); Brenner, in Beier and Cannadine (eds), op. cit., pp. 299–300.

112. E. Kerridge, *The Agricultural Revolution* (1967), pp. 181–221, 251–67, 326–48; Brenner, *Merchants and Revolution: Commercial Change, Political Conflict and London's Overseas Traders, 1550–1653* (Princeton, 1993), pp. 647ff, which sums up his position; Hill, *Reformation to Industrial Revolution*, pp. 146–54; E. Hobsbawm, *Industry and Empire* (Harmondsworth, 1969), introduction.

113.   D. Ogg, *England under Charles II* (Oxford, 1934), pp 163ff; J. Thirsk, 'The Restoration Land Settlement', *Journal of Modern History* xxvi, 4, 1954; 'Sales of Royalist Land during the Interregnum', *EcHR*, II series v, 1952–3; *The Agrarian History of England and Wales*, vol. V (Cambridge, 1985), pp. 119–61.
114.   Brenner, loc. cit; Giddens, op. cit., pp. 81–9.
115.   Kerridge, *Agricultural Revolution*; Beckett, op. cit., chapters 6–8; L. and J. F. Stone, op. cit. For the surprisingly low incidence of rural pedigrees amongst the London elite of the early and mid eighteenth century, see P. Earle, *The Making of the English Middle Class* (1989). For aristocratic building investment, see J. Summerson, *Georgian London* (Harmondsworth, 1962); *Architecture in Britain, 1530–1830* (Harmondsworth, 1953); D. Cannadine, *Lords and Landlords: The Aristocracy and the Towns, 1774–1967* (Leicester, 1980); Neale, *Bath, 1680–1850* (1981).
116.   For some of these examples, see J. H. Plumb, *Sir Robert Walpole*, vol. 1 (1956), pp. 9–10; *Men and Places*, Part 1 passim; H. J. Habakkuk,'The 2nd Earl of Nottingham, his House and his Estate' in J. H. Plumb (ed.), *Studies in Social History Presented to G. M. Trevelyan* (1955); M. Girouard, *The English Country House* (1981); L. and J. F. Stone, op. cit.
117.   G Chaussinand-Nogaret, *The French Nobility in the 18th Century* (Cambridge, 1985), pp. 141ff; A. Goodwin (ed.), *The European Nobility in the 18th Century* (1953); C. B. A. Behrens, *The Ancien Regime* (London 1967); N. Elias, *The Civilizing Process* (Eng. trans., Oxford, 1982).
118.   Stone, *The Causes of the English Revolution* (1972).
119.   Stone's framework of analysis drew heavily on the Talcott–Parsons' derived work of Chalmers Johnson, *Revolution and the Social System* (Stanford, 1964); *Revolutionary Change* (1966); see *Causes*, pp. 3–25. G. Elton, 'A Highroad to Civil War?' in *Studies in Tudor and Stuart Politics and Government* II (Cambridge, 1974), pp. 164–76.
120.   Stone, *Causes*, pp. 48ff, 146; J. P. Kenyon, *Stuart England* (Harmondsworth, 1978).
121.   Stone, *Causes*, p. 54; cf pp. 36–9, 47.
122.   Ibid., pp. 112–13; J. C. D. Clark, *Revolution and Rebellion*, pp. 30–2.
123.   G. Elton, review of Stone in *HJ*, 16, i, 1973 pp. 205–8; 'The Unexplained Revolution' in *Studies*, II, pp. 177–89; 'Highroad', passim; C. Russell, review in *EHR*, 88, 1973, pp. 858–9.
124.   Stone, *Causes*, p. 134; cf pp. 126–35; P. Zagorin, *The Court and the Country*, passim.
125.   Stone, *Causes*, pp. 117–18, 135ff; C. Johnson, *Revolutionary Change*, chapter 5. For a critique of the model, see A. S. Cohan, *Theories of Revolution: An Introduction* (1975) chapter 6: the 'X Factor' like the famous 'J Curve' became something of a minor scandal in the sociology of revolution. (J. C. Davis, 'Towards a theory of revolution', *American Sociological Review* xxvii, 1962.) As a number of commentators have pointed out, there was a marked disjunction

between the functionalist analysis of social integration and the conjunctural analysis of voluntaristically conceived social action.
126. Stone, *Causes* pp. 58–67, 76–9, 118. As Robin Blackburn had already pointed out in a critique of Chalmers Johnson's work, Stone's analysis limited initiative to the action of elites (elite intransigence) and denied effective historical agency to the 'insurgents', see 'A Brief Guide to Bourgeois Ideology' in R. Blackburn and A. Cockburn (eds), *Student Power* (Harmondsworth, 1970), pp. 182–8.
127. Stone in Hill and Stone, *Listener*, 4 October 1973, p. 449.
128. Stone *Causes*, pp. 146–7; 'The Revolution over the Revolution' *New York Review of Books*, 11 June 1992, p. 47.

Chapter 5 Levelling out the Revolution

1. Hobsbawm, H.G. p. 38; Kaye, op. cit., p. 129.
2. Hill, *The World Turned Upside Down* (1972), p. 11.
3. For the following section, see *World News*, 3, 1956; *DW*, esp. March, correspondence from over thirty intellectual figures; *NS*, editorials, 3, 31 March; N. Wood, op. cit., pp. 188ff; J. Saville, 'The XXth Congress and the British Communist Party', *The Socialist Register*, 1976 (and further articles by N. MacEwen and M. Heinemann).
4. *DW*, correspondence includes, 6 March, M. Dobb; 12 March, R. L. Hilton; 21 March, M. Dobb and R. L. Meek; 23 March, M. Cornforth; 27 March, C. and Bridget Hill; 29 March, J. Lewis; G. D. H. Cole, 'Socialists and Communists', *NS*, 5 May, pp. 472–4; *DW*, May 14; R. H. S. Crossman, 'The C.P. in Poland', *NS*, 5 May, pp. 476–7; J. Klugmann, 'Communists and Socialists', *MxQ*, 3/3 July, 1956, pp. 147–57 (Klugmann's *Trotsky to Tito* had already been quietly 'withdrawn' in 1955, see Wood, op. cit., pp. 222–3).
5. P. Dutt, Notes of the Month, *Labour Monthly*, 36, May, June 1956, esp. pp. 250–5; J. Callaghan, *Rajani Palme Dutt*, pp. 265–73 (for Dutt's refusal during and after 1956 to accept the truth about Stalin); A. Kettle, 'Cultural and Ideological Work of the Party', *WN*, 3/16, 21 April, p. 256; H. Pollitt, Speech to 24th National Congress, WN, 3/14, 16, 18: 7, 21, April 5 May, esp. pp. 278–81, 285–6; Saville, *SR*, p. 23 has argued that passages of Pollitt's report show a knowledge of Khrushchev's secret speech (something that the CP hierarchy was always to deny); *NS*, 31 March, editorial, 'The Long Voyage Home'.
6. Saville, loc. cit.; D. Lessing, *The Reasoner*, 3, November 1956, and associated correspondence.
7. K. Zilliacus letters to *DW*, 12, 17 April; *DW* comment: 'Don't Talk Silly, Zilly'!
8. For Thompson's 'revolt', see below Chapter 6; C. and B. Hill, *WN*, 3/33, 18 August, pp. 524–5; see some much stronger letters on intellectual bullying, Stella Jackson, 3/31, 4 August; E. and M. Barratt Brown, 3/30, 28 July.

9. M. MacEwen, 'The Day the Party had to Stop', *SR*, 1976, pp. 24–42, esp. p. 27; Commission (first announced in May) *WN*, 3/36, 11 September, 3/40, 6 October.
10. *WN*, 3/36, 11 September; MacEwen, loc. cit., pp. 30–2.
11. Thompson, *Reasoner*, 2, September 1956; A. L. Morton, 'Socialist Humanism', *CR*, October 1953, p. 298–300; *Reasoner*, 3, 'Through the Smoke of Budapest'; P. Fryer, *Hungarian Tragedy* (1956); P. Fryer, *NS*, 24 November p. 668; F. Feher and A. Heller, *Hungary's 1956 Revisited* (1983), pp. 42–9; M. Molnar, *Budapest 1956* (1971); Saville, op. cit., pp. 18ff.
12. C. Hill, H. Levy, R. Browning, H. Collins, J. Lindsay, R. L. Meek, E. J. Hobsbawm, V. G. Kiernan, E. A. Thompson, *NS*, 1 December, pp. 700–1; *Tribune*, 30 November, p. 3; Wood, p. 209.
13. G. Matthews, 'Lessons of a Letter', *WN*, 4/2, 12 January 1957, pp. 24–6; J. Gollan, Political Committee to CH, *WN*, 4/3, 26 January, pp. 61–3; Wood, pp. 209–11; H. Levy, 'Lessons of an Article', *WN*, 4/8, 2 March, pp. 138–9; J. Gollan, ibid., 4/9, 9 March, pp. 154–6. My reading of the letter as a minor act of disobedience is at odds with Eric Hobsbawm's subsequent estimation of it as 'the most massive expression of dissidence' – a verdict which contrasts rather oddly with his less than generous evaluation of the significance of *The Reasoner*, see E. J. Hobsbawm, '1956', *Marxism Today*, November 1986, p. 19.
14. *Majority Report* (1957), pp. 10–11, 14–18; *The Organizational Principle of the C.P. – Democratic Centralism* (1957), pp. 6–7, 18, 26–8, 31–2; MacEwen, pp. 35–9. Cf Matthews, 'Lessons of a Letter' ('redolent of petty-bourgeois thinking . . . remote from the working class'), loc. cit.
15. Joan Simon, *WN*, 3/50, 15 December, p. 797–8; ibid., 4/8, 23 February pp. 125–6; A Rothstein, ibid., 15 December, p. 797; Wood, op. cit., p. 212.
16. (Cadogan, Hill, MacEwen), *Minority Report* (April 1957); A. Kettle, *WN*, 4/16, 22 April; J. Mahon, *DW* 22 April; *WN*, 4/20, 18 May, p. 318 (for Hill's speech at Special Conference); *The Times*, 23 April (Hill 'went out of his way to spare the platform's self-esteem'. He did, nevertheless, propose an investigation of the anti-Titoist line between 1948 and 1955 – an issue on which the party was especially vulnerable); MacEwen, pp. 40–1 (The voting was 472–25 in favour of the Majority Report with fifteen abstentions).
17. CPA HG, 60, General Correspondence: List of members 1955–60; Note by Joan Simon, September 1960; J. Gollan and J. Simon, September 1960.
18. CPA HG 60, General Correspondence, Palme Dutt and Betty Gant, 6, 13 November 1958; B. Grant and P. Dutt, 10, 12, 16 November 1958; Hobsbawm, HG, pp. 40–1; Saville, op. cit., pp. 7ff; Himmelfarb, op. cit., p. 92. For E.P.Ts attitude see below Chapter 6; and at much greater length my *Marxist Historians and the Pathology of British History* (forthcoming); for Hobsbawm see also *WN*, 3/28 16 June, 3/41, 6 October; ibid., 4/2, 12 January; Saville, p. 19 (letter

to unidentified correspondent, clearly E.J.H.); Himmelfarb, op. cit.,
p. 81; A. Rothstein see fn 15, and also his review of Deutscher,
MQ, 5/2, 1950 pp. 122ff; CPA HG, 60 General Correspondence
25 September 1953 (for project of a cooperative history of capitalism). F.M.L. Thompson, 'A Marxist Quintet', *TLS*, 23 May 1986,
p. 572.

19. E. P. Thompson, 'An Open Letter to Leszec Kolakowski' in *POT*,
p. 304; A. J. Taylor, *The Trouble Makers* (Ford Lectures Hilary Term
1956, London, 1956): as usual Taylor's timing was impeccable.
20. CPA HG 60, A, Minutes, 8 July 1956.
21. CPA, Political Committee, Minutes, September–October 1956; HG,
60, General Correspondence, B. Grant and J. Gollan, 8 May 1957.
The particular item of investigation was a Thompson-inspired
pamphlet on 'Luddism'.
22. R. Palme Dutt, *LM*, October 1958, p. 433; Protest Letters were
sent by Betty Grant to LM (November 1958); see also, B. Grant
and J. Gollan, 13 October; Grant–Dutt correspondence, November
1958: HG 60, General Correspondence.
23. CPA HG 60, Minutes 25 November 1956; for the fragile condition
of the group see HG, Joan Simon file 1957–8; for accusations of
Oxbridge snobbery (E.J.H. excepted) and for Hobsbawm's
vulnerable position, see Betty Grant correspondence with J. Gollan,
May–June 1957. Obituaries for Torr in *WN*, 4/3, 26 January 1957,
pp. 56ff.
24. Letter 30 November–1 December, *Tribune*, *NS*; Thompson, *POT*,
pp. 305–6.
25. M. Polanyi, 'The Magic of Marxism', *Encounter*, 7, vi, December
1956, pp. 5–17 (quotation p. 5).
26. Thompson, *POT*, p. 306; Crossman, *NS*, 5 May 1956, loc. cit.
27. David Horowitz, 'Socialism: Guilty as Charged', *Commentary*,
December 1990, pp. 17–24.
28. Minogue, op. cit., p. 221; Joan Simon, *WN*, 3/50, 15 December
1956, p. 798; A. Kettle, 'Communism and the Intellectuals' in B.
Simon, op. cit., pp. 192ff; D Widgery, *The Left in Britain, 1956–68*
(Harmondsworth, 1972), p. 58.
29. G. Werskey, p. 332; Wood, op. cit., p. 193; Hill, *The World Turned
Upside Down* (*WTUD*), p. 9; R. Cobb, *A Second Identity: Essays on
France and French History* (1969).
30. Thompson, *POT*, p. 306; C. Hill, *The Experience of Defeat: Milton
and Some Contemporaries* (1984), p. 328; *Some Intellectual Consequences
of the English Revolution* (Wisconsin, 1980), pp. 4–5.
31. C. Hill, *Change and Continuity*, p. 284; J. C. Davis, 'Puritanism
and Revolution: Themes, Categories, Methods, Conclusions', *HJ*,
33/3, 1990, pp. 693–4.
32. Hill, 'Partial History', loc. cit., p. 1421; *TLS* Series, ed. Keith Thomas,
'New Ways in History', 7 April 1966; L. Stone, 'History and the
Social Sciences' in *The Past and the Present* (1981), pp. 3–44.
33. H. Levy, 'The Place of Unorthodoxy in Marxism', *Reasoner*, II pp.
14–15; 'Lessons of an Article', loc. cit.; Wood, op. cit., p. 198.

34. C. Cockburn and R. Blackburn, *Student Power* (Harmondsworth, 1968), esp. G. Stedman Jones, *The Meaning of Student Revolt* (1968); A. Quattrocchi and T. Nairn, *The Beginning of the End* (1968); G. Stedman Jones, 'Student Power: What is to be Done', *NLR*, 43, May–June 1967; B. Brewster and A. Cockburn, 'Revolt at LSE, ibid.; A. Waring, *The British New Left: Historical Process and Socialist Strategy* (University of Sydney, B.A. Thesis 1991), pp. 63–82; Student Revolt, Symposium, *Encounter*, 31/1, July 1968.

35. H. Marcuse, *Essay on Liberation* (1969); 'Repressive Tolerance', in R. P. Wolff, *The Critique of Pure Tolerance* (1969); *One Dimensional Man* (1964); *Eros and Civilization* (New York, 1962); M. Cranston, 'Marcuse', *Encounter*, xxxii/3, March 1969, pp. 38–50; a longer version, *Marcuse* (1970).

36. Maurice Keene, 'Memoir of Hill' in K. Thomas, K. Pennington, *Puritans*, pp. 19–20.

37. 'The Norman Yoke' in Saville, *Democracy and the Labour Movement*, reprinted in *Puritanism and Revolution*, pp. 50–122; Kaye, op. cit., pp. 121–2; *English Revolution 1640*, pp. 52ff; *Lenin*, pp. 167ff.

38. M. James, *Social Problems and Policy during the Puritan Revolution* (1940) – published as Part 3 of Hill's *English Revolution*; D. Peterogorsky, *Left Wing Democracy in the English Civil War: A Study of the Social Philosophy of Gerrard Winstanley* (1940); J. Holorenshaw, op. cit.; E. Rickword, *John Milton*; H. N. Brailsford, *The Levellers and the English Revolution* (with an introduction by C. Hill) (1961); L. H. Berens, *The Social Problem in the Days of the English Revolution or the Creed of the Levellers* (1898); *The Digger Movement in the Days of the Commonwealth as Revealed in the Writings of Gerrard Winstanley* (1906); E. Bernstein, *Cromwell and Communism: Socialism and Democracy in the Great English Revolution* (1930); M. A. Gibb, *John Lilburne, the Leveller* (1947).

39. Hill, *The World Turned Upside Down*, pp. 12, 13, publisher's 'blurb'; p. 312 (I have reversed the order of the original).

40. Barry Reay, 'The World Turned Upside Down, a Retrospect', in Eley and Hunt, pp. 53–72; K. Thomas, 'The Ranters', *NYRB*, 30 November 1972, pp. 26–9; *TLS*, 'Revolt within a Revolution', 18 August 1972, p. 969; J. Kenyon, 'Christopher Hill's Radical Left', *Spectator*, 8 July, p. 55; J. Dunn, 'Tiggers and Diggers', *Listener*, 3 August, p. 152. For its impact on the 1970s, Reay, loc. cit., p. 56.

41. 'Norman Yoke', esp. pp. 57ff, 86–8, 94ff.; Kaye, p. 122; cf S. Kliger, *The Goths in England* (Cambridge, Mass., 1951) esp. Appendix III (which anticipated much of Hill's argument); A.L. Morton, *The English Utopia*, passim; V. Geoghegan, *Utopia and Marxism* (1987) chapter 4: Golden Ages and Myths.

42. *Society and Puritanism*, pp. 140–211 esp. pp. 181ff; 'Puritans and the Dark Corners of the Land' in *Change and Continuity*, pp. 3–47; K. Thomas, *Religion and the Decline of Magic*.

43. C. Hill, 'AntiChrist in 17th Century England'; W. Lamont, *Godly People*; B. Capp, *Astrology and the Popular Press: English Almanacks, 1500–1800* (1979); B. Capp, *The Fifth Monarchy Men* (1972); F.

McGregor, *The Ranters, 1649–1660* (Oxford B.Litt, 1968); B. Reay, *The Quakers and the English Revolution* (1985).

44. Morton, *The English Utopia*, pp. 60ff: 'Religion and Politics', *Marxism Today*, December 1960, pp. 367–71.

45. N. Cohn, *The Pursuit of the Millennium* (1957) Appendix: The Free Spirits in Cromwell's England: the Ranters and their Literature; 'The Ranters', *Encounter*, 34/4, 1970, pp. 15–25, esp. p. 25 (for Charles Manson's 'family'); J. C. Davis, *Fear, Myth and History: The Ranters and their Historians* (Cambridge, 1986), esp. chapters 1, 6; J. R. Talmon, *Origins of Totalitarian Democracy* (1952); *Political Messianism* (1962); E. J. Hobsbawm, 'Who is for Democracy?', *MQ*, 8/2, 1953, pp. 96–103.

46. A. L. Morton, *Utopia*, passim; *The Everlasting Gospel* (1958); *The World of the Ranters: Religious Radicalism in the English Revolution* (1970); Hill, 'Abolishing the Ranters' in *A Nation of Change*, p. 190.

47. *World of Ranters*, 1979 edn, pp. 17–18, 70–1, 85, 111–12, 197–219; M. Cornforth, 'Portrait of a Marxist Historian', loc. cit., pp. 16ff.

48. Hill, *The World Turned Upside Down*, pp. 13–14: the reference is to *Century of Revolution*, p. 167 (again illustrating one of Hill's most winning characteristics – a considerable capacity for self-criticism).

49. Thomas, 'Ranters', loc. cit., p. 26; MacPherson, *Possessive Individualism*, pp. 142–7, 154–9; 'Revolt within a Revolution', loc. cit., p. 969; Hill, *The World Turned Upside Down*, pp. 97ff, referring to the work of M. Barg (Popular Classes in the English Revolution), see C. Hill, review in *Agricultural History Review*, xvi, 1968, pp. 75–7; *P&P*, 126, 1990, pp. 215–16.

50. Student Representative to Conference of Revolutionary Youth, June 1968, quoted in Melvyn Lasky, 'The Metaphysics of Dooms-day', originally published in *Encounter*, 1971, subsequently in *Utopia and Revolution: On the Origins of a Metaphor* (Chicago, 1976), p. 260; E. Shils, 'Plenitude and Scarcity; the Anatomy of an International Cultural Crisis', *Encounter*, 32/5, May 1969, pp. 37–57; R. Lowenthal, 'Unreason and Revolution', ibid., 33/5, November 1969, pp. 22–34; Tariq Ali, *The Coming British Revolution* (1972).

51. Marcuse, see. fn 29, cf Marcuse's study of Hegel, *Reason and Revolution: Hegel and the Rise of Social Theory* (Oxford, 1941); N. O. Brown, *Life against Death: The Psychoanalytical Meaning of History* (Middletown, Conn., 1959); *Love's Body* (New York, 1966); 'Apocalypse: The Place of Mystery in the Life of the Mind', *Harpers*, May 1961; M. Foucault, *Madness and Civilization* (English trans of *Folie and Deraison*, 1967); R. Sheridan, *Foucault, the Will to Truth* (1982).

52. C. Hill, *The World Turned Upside Down*. p. 260 (the title of the chapter, 'Life against Death', is, of course, taken from Norman Brown, op. cit.; Hill was to dedicate his *Experience of Defeat* to Brown); Davis, op. cit., pp. 7ff; Thomas, 'Ranters', loc. cit., p. 27.

53. Marx, *The Economic and Philosophic Manuscripts of 1844* (Moscow, 1959). For the re-evaluation of Marx in the light of these early manuscripts, see R. Tucker, *Myth and Philosophy in Karl Marx* (Cambridge, 1959); E. Fromm, *Marx's Concept of Man* (New York, 1960); D. Bell, 'In Search of Marxist Humanism: The Debate on Alienation', *Soviet Survey*, 32, 1960.
54. This section is largely based on T. Roszak, *The Making of a Counter Culture: Reflections on a Technocratic Society and its Youthful Opposition* (1970), chapter 2, esp. pp. 109, 114, 116.
55. Hill, *World Turned Upside Down*, chapters 3, 4 passim. esp. pp. 68–9; cf Hill, 'England's Democratic Army', loc. cit.
56. Thompson, *POT*, p. 316; Hill, 'Gramsci, the Modern Prince', *New Reasoner*, 4, 1958, pp. 107–13.
57. *AntiChrist*, I–III passim; *TLS* review, 'An Enemy for all Seasons', 9 September 1971, p. 1049; *World Turned Upside Down*, chapter 8; Kaye, p. 123; Hill, 'Irreligion in the English Revolution' in J. McGregor and B. Reay, *Radical Religion in the English Revolution* (Oxford, 1984), pp. 191–211 (this first appeared as a lecture in 1974); W. Haller, *Liberty and Reformation in the Puritan Revolution* (New York, 1955); E.S. Morgan, *The Puritan Dilemma: The Story of John Winthrop* (Boston, 1958); A. Simpson, *Puritanism in Old and New England* (Yale, 1956); A.S.P. Woodhouse, op. cit.
58. Hill, 'God in the English Revolution', *History Workshop Journal*, 17, 1984, pp. 19–31; Davis, op. cit., pp. 7ff.
59. Hill, 'Gramsci', loc. cit.; G. Williams, 'The Concept of "Egomonia" in the Thought of Antonio Gramsci', *Journal of the History of Ideas*, 21/4, 1960, pp. 586–99; T. J. Jackson Leers, 'The Concept of Cultural Hegemony: Problems and Possibilities', *American Historical Review*, 90, 1985, pp. 567–93; P. Anderson, 'The Antinomies of Antonio Gramsci', *NLR*, 100, November 1976–January 1977; C. Mouffe (ed.), *Gramsci and Marxist Theory* (1979).
60. Quoted in Hill, *The World Turned Upside Down*, p. 336; cf ibid., pp. 236–7.
61. 'God in the English Revolution', *History Workshop Journal*, 17, 1984, pp. 19–31; Marcuse, quoted in Lasky, op. cit., p. 220; *World Turned Upside Down*, p. 273.
62. T. Roszak, op. cit., pp. 119–20.
63. Thomas, 'Ranters', pp. 17–18; *World Turned Upside Down*, p. 273.
64. *World Turned Upside Down*, pp. 91–120, 313–19, esp. pp, 104ff; Hill, 'The Religion of Gerrard Winstanley', *P&P*, Supplement 5, 1978, subsequently in *Collected Essays* II, pp. 185–252; Thomas, 'Ranters', p. 28 (on W as the real hero' of *WTUD*); Winstanley, *The Law of Freedom and Other Writings* (ed. C. Hill) (Harmondsworth, 1973), esp. pp. 9–10, 19; 'Winstanley and Freedom' in R. C. Richardson and G. M. Ridden (eds), *Freedom and the English Revolution* (Manchester, 1986), pp. 151–68. The celebration of Winstanley, of course, went back to Hill's earliest work, see *English Revolution, 1640*, pp. 61ff; *Lenin* pp. 167–8. For somewhat different readings (which criticize Hill's modernization and secularization of W), L.

Mulligan, J. K. Graham and J. Richards, 'Winstanley: A Case for the Man He Said He Was', *JEccH*, 28/1, January 1977, p. 57–75; C. H. George, 'Gerrard Winstanley: A Critical Retrospect' in C. Cole and M. Moody (eds), *The Dissenting Tradition* (Ohio, 1975); G. E. Aylmer, 'The Religion of Gerrard Winstanley' in J. McGregor and B. Reay, op. cit., pp. 91–120. J. G. Davis, 'Gerrard Winstanley and the Restoration of True Magistracy', *P&P*, 70, February 1976, pp. 75–93 gives another modern reading but one that is markedly different from Hill's ('a model for Joseph Stalin', cf Hill's 'gentle communist'); R. C. Richardson, *The Debate on the English Revolution Revisited* (revised and extended version of his earlier text) (1988) p. 186.

65. 'Revolt within a Revolution', loc. cit.; B. Reay in Eley and Hunt p. 64; H. Marcuse, 'Max Weber', *NLR*, 30; D. Caute, 'Three Dimensional men', *NS*, 23 June 1972, pp. 872–3; Hill, *World Turned Upside Down*, p. 236–7; Davis, *Fear*, chapter 6.

66. It was, however, not envisaged that socialist central planning could produce far worse environmental damage than uncontrolled capitalist economies.

67. J. Dunn, 'Democracy Unretrieved or the Political Theory of Professor Macpherson', *British Journal of Political Science*, 4, 1976, p. 489; S. Lukes, 'The Real and Ideal Worlds of Democracy', in A. Kontos, op. cit., pp. 139–152; *World Turned Upside Down*, p. 311; Netherwood notes, July 1954, 'Ideas and the State', p. 6; Morton, *Utopia*, chapter 5: 'Reason in Despair'. The response of Hill, Morton, Thompson, et al. to eighteenth-century culture was, of course, fundamentally jaundiced. E.g. C.H. Netherwood Notes: '4: The End of Integrated Sensibility; The Vacuum; Ideology of the New Class Limited and Hypocritical; The Intellectually Terrible Years, 1713–40'. Or, in a small but give-away phrase, A.L. Morton's review of *Mountain in Sunlight*, loc. cit. 'Defoe, writing a generation later [than Bunyan] and in a *worse* time . . .'. Why worse? For whom? Surely not for Defoe whose life – despite the pillory – was a bed of roses compared with Bunyan's. Worse in what sense? Material? Moral? The answer seems to be that it is worse because it is an age supposedly dominated by the market-place and by corrupt politicians, an age more distant than Bunyan's from the morally uplifting years of the Revolution. For the issue of the Historians' Group 'Romantic anti-capitalism', see above pp. 114ff, 193. For liberalism and repression, see Macpherson, op. cit., pp. 274–6; Davis, *Fear*, pp. 135ff; Hill, *World Turned Upside Down*, p. 281ff.

68. David Underdown, *Revel, Riot and Rebellion*, p. 210. For blind alleys, etc. E.P. Thompson's famous introduction to *MEWC*; 'Optative history' was the term first employed, I believe, by David Underdown.

69. I. Deutscher in Horowitz (ed.) op. cit. p. 128–9; Hill, 'The English Revolution and the Brotherhood of Man', originally published 1953, subsequently in *SS*, xviii, 1954 pp. 289–309, and revised in *Puritanism and Revolution*; J. G. A. Pocock, 'No room for the

Righteous', *TLS*, 28 December 1984, p. 1494; Oscar Wilde, quoted in Geoghegan, op. cit., p. 139; Hill, *Some Intellectual Consequences*, passim; *The Experience of Defeat*, passim; C. Cook and R. McKie, *The Decade of Disillusion: British Politics in the Sixties* (1972).

70. *Some Intellectual Consequences*, pp. 4, 7–8ff, 17; Hill *World Turned Upside Down*, chapter 6; Hill, 'Why Bother about the Muggletonians?' in C. Hill, B. Reay and W. Lamont, *The World of the Muggletonians* (1983) pp. 11–13; Reay in Eley and Hunt, pp. 61–2.

71. Hill, 'Was Cromwell Progressive?', *DW*, 22 March 1939, p. 7 (a review of Needham's book on the Levellers, brought to my attention by Tony Howe – see Draft chapter cited in chapter 3, p. 13): Hill criticized Needham's neglect of the liberating role of the bourgeoisie; *English Revolution*, pp. 52–7; V. Kiernan, 'When Britain was a Republic', *LM*, March 1949, pp. 87–90; A. L. Morton, 'Britain's First Republic', *DW*, 14 May 1953; 'Cromwell, Our Chief of Men', ibid., 3 September 1958; 'Cromwell and the English Revolution', *OH*, 3, 1958.

72. C. Hill, *God's Englishman: Oliver Cromwell and the English Revolution* (1970) 1972 edn, pp. 39ff, 73–4, 109–15, 190, 261, 266. He also gave short shrift to the Trotskyite reading of Cromwell. Indeed, it was the complaint of some commentators in *International Socialism* (IS), that he 'cheered' Cromwell on, when he should have been denouncing him. See N. Carlin, 'Marxism and the English Civil War', *IS*, 2/10, Winter 1980–1, p. 123.

73. Cromwell, pp. 224–6, 266; 'Oliver Cromwell' in Hill, *Collected Essays*, III (Brighton, 1986), pp. 72–3, 75; *TLS.*, 26 September 1970, p. 1070: 'Protector's Portrait'.

74. *TLS*, loc. cit.; J.C. Davis, 'Cromwell's Religion' in John Morrill (ed.), *Oliver Cromwell and the English Revolution* (1990), pp. 186–7, 206–7. For the complexities of Cromwell's mind and activities, see esp. the articles by Blair Worden referred to in this volume.

75. Hill, *God's Englishman*, pp. 202–3, 251, 253; 'A Bourgeois Revolution' in Pocock op. cit., p. 134; Collected Essays, III, pp. 113–17.

76. This paragraphs draws heavily on W. Lamont, 'The Left and its Past: Revisiting the 1650s', *HWkJ*, 23, 1987, pp. 141–53, esp. pp. 142–3, 151; 'Left Let Down by the Levellers', *The Guardian*, 14 November 1983: Lamont's criticism, in fact, matches Hill's own criticism of earlier radical writings on the Levellers which neglected 'the liberating role of the bourgeoisie' and turned the 1640s and 1650s into 'a source book of early democratic and Utopian-Socialism theory', see his review of the 'slightly out of focus' study of Joseph Needham (Holorenshaw), *DW*, 22 March 1939; J. Morrill, *Oliver Cromwell*, introduction, pp. 2 passim.

77. Hill, 'Some Intellectual Consequences', p. 10, quoting Godfrey Davies, *The Restoration* (Oxford, 1958); J.P. Kenyon, *Stuart England*, p. 182; Lasky, *Utopia* pp. 295ff. According to Finlayson (op. cit., pp. 7–8) the whole idea of a tidal wave was misplaced, and Hill's query a classic 'question mal posée'.

78. Peter Burke, 'People's History or Total History' in R. Samuel (ed.), *People's History and Socialist Theory* (1981), p. 7; D. Underdown, 'Puritanism, Revolution and Christopher Hill' in Eley and Hunt, pp. 337–8; Laslett, *World We have Lost*, pp. 81ff.
79. Hill, *Some Intellectual Consequences*, pp. 27ff; J. P. Kenyon, 'Roundheads for Ever',*TLS*, 28 November 1980, p. 1365.
80. Hill, 'The Start of a Great Myth: The Restoration of Charles II', *Manchester Guardian*, 25 May 1960, p. 8; 'Republicanism after the Restoration', *NLR*, 3, 1960, pp. 46–51; Hill, *Some Intellectual Consequences*, pp. 11–15. Cf R. Hutton, *The Restoration* (Oxford, 1985), p. 119: 'the unpopularity of the Republican regime must survive any revisionary study'.
81. R. L. Greaves, *Deliver Us from Evil: The Radical Underground in Britain, 1660–63* (Oxford, 1986); *Enemies under his Feet: Radicals and Nonconformists in Britain, 1664–1677* (Stanford, 1990); J. Scott, *Algernon Sidney and the English Republic* (Cambridge, 1988); *Algernon Sidney and the Restoration Crisis* (Cambridge, 1990); K. D. Haley, *The First Earl of Shaftesbury* (Oxford, 1968); J. R. Jones, *The First Whigs* (1961); R. Ashcraft, *Revolutionary Politics and Locke's Two Treatises of Government* (Cambridge, 1986); T. Harris, *The London Crowd in the Reign of Charles II* (Cambridge, 1987); J. Miller, *Popery and Politics, 1660–88* (Cambridge, 1973); M. Jacob, *Henry Stubbe: Radical Puritanism and the Early Enlightenment in England* (1983); A. Marshall, 'Colonel Thomas Blood and the Restoration Political Scene', *HJ*, 32/3, 1989, pp. 561–82; M. Watts, *The Dissenters from the Reformation to the French Revolution* (1978); J. R. Jones, 'A Representative of the Alernative Society of Restoration England', in M. M. and R. S. Dunn, *The World of William Penn* (Philadephia, 1986), pp. 55–69.
82. Hill, 'Republicanism', loc. cit., p. 49; *Some Intellectual Consequences*, pp. 24–5.
83. For indications that Hill may have overstated the defeat, G. F. T. Jones, *Saw Pit Wharton: The Political Career from 1640 to 1691 of Philip, fourth Lord Wharton* (Sydney, 1967); J. R. Jones, *The Revolution of 1688 in England* (1972); R. Clifton, *The Last Popular Rebellion: The Western Rising of 1685* (1984); P. Earle, *Monmouth's Rebels* (1977); Haley, op. cit; Ashcraft, op. cit. and other authorities noted in fn 81.
84. Hill, *Some Intellectual Consequences*, pp. 14, 24; 'Republicanism', loc. cit., p. 47; R. Bosher, *The Making of the Restoration Settlement, 1649–1662* (1957); J. R. Abernathy, *The English Presbyterians and the Stuart Restoration, 1648–1663* (Philadelphia, 1965); I.M. Green, *The Re-establishment of the Church of England* (Oxford, 1978); A. Whiteman, 'The Restoration of the Church of England' in G. F. Nuttall and O. Chadwick (eds), *From Uniformity to Unity* (1962); M. Lee Jr, *The Cabal* (Urbana, Ill., 1972); A. Fletcher, 'The Enforcement of the Conventicle Acts, 1664–1679' in W. Shils (ed.), *Persecution and Toleration*, Studies in Church History 21 (Oxford, 1984), pp. 225–46. According to Greaves, fines for the period 1660–7 netted the grand sum of £148 – hardly, one would have thought,

a fiscal 'white terror'; similarly, of the 230 conventiclers in London sentenced to transportation in 1664–5, less than 10 per cent were actually banished. For an older version closer to Hill's convenient mythology, see C. R. Cragg, *Puritanism in the Period of the Great Persecution* (Cambridge, 1957).

85. Hill, *Some Intellectual Consequences*, pp. 13, 27ff; Kenyon, 'Roundheads', loc. cit.
86. J. C. Davis, 'Radicalism in a Traditional Society: The Evaluation of Radical Thought in the English Commmonwealth, 1649–1660, *History of Political Thought*, III/2, 1982, pp. 193–4 (quoting Hill, *New Zealand Listener*, 11 April 1981); *Utopia and the Ideal Society* (Cambridge, 1985), pp. 16ff; C. Hill, 'Religion of Winstanley', loc. cit.; *Milton and The English Revolution* (1977), pp. 117ff.
87. C. Hill, *The Experience of Defeat: Milton and Some Contemporaries* (1984), pp. 17, 28.
88. J. Scott, 'Radicalism and Restoration: The Shape of the Stuart Experience', *HJ*, 31/2, 1988, p. 456.
89. Hill, *Experience of Defeat*, passim (quotation at p. 113).
90. T. Rabb, 'Levellers and Fellow Travellers', *The Guardian*, 17 March 1985; Psalms, 137 v. 4.
91. J. C. Davis, 'Radicalism', loc. cit., pp. 203ff, 208; M. Walzer, 'A Theory of Revolution', *Marxist Perspectives*, 5, 1979, pp. 30–44.
92. Hill, *Experience of Defeat*, pp. 319ff; J. G. A. Pocock, 'No Room for the Righteous', *TLS*, 29 December 1984, p. 1494.
93. Hill, *Experience of Defeat*, introduction, conclusion, p. 326.
94. C. Hill, 'The Protestant Nation', in *Collected Essays II: Religion and Politics in 17th Century England* (Brighton, 1986), pp. 28–9.
95. Hill, *Experience of Defeat*, esp. chapters 6 and 8; M. C. Jacob and Henry Stubbe; *The Newtonians and the English Revolution* (1976).
96. See esp. J. R. Western, *Monarchy and Revolution* (1972); J. R. Jones, *The Revolution of 1688 in England* (1972); J. R. Jones (ed.), *The Restored Monarchy* (1979); *Charles II: A Royal Politician* (1990); R. Hutton, *The Restoration; Charles II* (Oxford, 1989); J. Miller, *Popery and Politics; James II: A Study in Kingship* (Hove, 1977); *Charles II* (1991). All of these studies argue in somewhat different ways against viewing Charles II simply as a post-revolutionary ruler, tied down by changes made in the 1640s. A. Bryant, *Charles II* (1931), made a similar case half a century ago.
97. R. Beddard, 'The Commission for Ecclesiastical Promotions, 1681–4: An Instrument of Tory Reaction', *HJ*, 10, 1967, pp. 11–40; 'The Restored Church' in J. R. Jones (ed.), *The Restored Monarchy* (1979), pp. 155–75; C. Bounds, *Archbishop Sancroft and the Restoration Church* (Sydney, B. A. thesis, 1986) (Beddard's own thesis on *William Sancroft as Archbishop of Canterbury*, Oxford D.Phil 1965, is unavailable for consultation); N. Sykes, *From Sancroft to Secker: Aspects of Church History, 1660–1788* (Cambridge, 1958).
98. W. A. Speck, *Reluctant Revolutionaries: Englishmen and the Revolution of 1688* (Oxford, 1988), pp. 243ff.; J. Scott, *Sidney and the Restoration*

Crisis; 'Radicalism and Restoration', loc. cit., pp. 455–6; J. P. Kenyon, *The Popish Plot* (Harmondsworth, 1972).

99. C. Hill, 'A Bourgeois Revolution', in Pocock, op cit. pp. 128, 134–5.
100. Speck, op cit; Miller, *Popery and Politics; James II; Seeds of Liberty: 1688 and the Shaping of Modern Britain* (1988); 'The Potential for Absolutism in Later Stuart England', *History*, 69, 1984, pp. 187–207; J. R. Jones, *The Revolution of 1688*. 'Well, doctor, what do you think of Predestination now', William is supposed to have quipped to Gilbert Burnet on 5 November 1688. For the importance of luck, see Conrad Russell's pastiche on 'The Catholic Wind' in J. Merriman (ed.), *For Want of a Horse: Choice and Chance in History*, republished in C. Russell, *Unrevolutionary England* (1990), pp. 305–8. All modern work on 1688 emphasises the importance and unpredictability of international politics (and the crucial miscalculations of Louis XIV) in the making of the Revolution.
101. C. Hill, 'The Place of the English Revolution' in *A Nation of Change*, pp. 11,16–17, 20; *God's Englishman*, pp. 253–4. As the history of 'Mercantilism' and of Colbert's policies under Louis XIV make abundantly clear, there is no necessary connection between the encouragement of trade and 'liberal' regimes. And if the Navigation Acts are to be the litmus test of bourgeois transformation, then James II as Lord High Admiral and King would appear a better bourgeois epigone than Oliver Cromwell, and Arthur Bryant, the then High-Tony biographer of Samuel Pepys ('Saviour of the Navy', etc.) a better guide to the process than Christopher Hill.
102. This was the position of Angus McInnes, 'When was the English Revolution?' *History*, 67, 1982, pp. 377–92.
103. G. Holmes (ed.), *Britain after the Glorious Revolution*, esp J. Carter: 'The Revolution in the Constitution', pp. 39–58; J. H. Plumb, *The Growth of Political Stability* (1967); D. Ogg, *William III; England under James II and William III* (Oxford 1957); H. Horwitz, *Parliament, Policy and Politics in the Reign of William III* (Manchester, 1977); J. R. Jones, *Country and Court, 1658–1714* (1978); H. T. Dickinson, *Liberty and Property: Political Ideologies in Eighteenth Century Britain* (1977). For an attempt to retain the constitutional importance of the Declaration of Rights, see Lois G. Schwoerer, *The Declaration of Rights, 1689* (Baltimore, 1981).
104. G. Holmes, *Britain after the Glorious Revolution; British Politics in the Age of Anne*; Plumb, *Political Stability*; Dickson, *Financial Revolution*; J. P. Kenyon, *Revolution Principles: The Politics of Party, 1689–1720* (Cambridge, 1977); J. G. A. Pocock, 'The Varieties of Whiggism from Exclusion to Reform: A History of Ideology and Discourse' in *Virtue, Commerce and History*, pp. 215–310; Speck, *Reluctant Revolutionaries*, p. 251. Cf however, J. C. D. Clark, *English Society, 1688–1832: Ideology, Social Atructure and Political Practice during the Ancien Regime* (Cambridge, 1986).
105. Amongst many others, J. H. Plumb, *Growth of Political Stability*; J. P. Kenyon, *Sunderland* (1956); J. Brewer, *The Sinews of Power*.

106. Appropriately celebrated in a half-hearted way in 1988. For the celebrations, see below, conclusion: *The End of the Line?*
107. Speck, op. cit., pp. 213–14.
108. A. McInnes, 'The Revolution and the People' in Holmes, *Britain after the Glorious Revolution*; J. P. Kenyon, *The Nobility and the Revolution of 1688* (Hull, 1963).
109. Ashcraft, op. cit.; B. Worden (ed.), *Edmund Ludlow: A Voyce from the Watchtower* (1978). See, however, M. Goldie, 'The Revolution of 1688 and the Structure of Political Argument', *Bulletin of Research Humanism*, 83, 1980, pp. 473–564; 'The Political Thought of the Anglican Revolution' in R. Beddard (ed.), *The Revolutions of 1688* (Oxford, 1991), pp. 102–36; *Tory Political Thought, 1689–1714* (Cambridge, PhD 1977).
110. At various times, Hill has listed a political, a social, an agricultural, a commercial, a financial, a foreign policy, a scientific, a cultural, a literary, a historical, a 'cakes and ale', and, most recently, a biblical revolution.
111. The idea of a fundamental break is probably reinforced in the case of Europe as a whole by the habit of thinking in terms of reigns and by the exceptionally long reigns beginning mid century, of Louis XIV (1643–1715), Leopold I (1658–1705) and Carlos II (1665–1700: one whose sickly life and disastrous reign was locked into the Spanish Succession crisis which began in the 1650s and was only resolved in and after 1713). Likewise in the field of intellectual history, the late seventeenth century – the age of Paul Hazard's famous *Crise de la Conscience Européene* or of a 'Pre-Enlightenment' – has usually been depicted as 'looking forward' to the eighteenth century 'Siècle des Lumières' rather than backward to the age of religious warfare. For reinstating a 'long 17th century', see J. Scott, 'Radicalism and Restoration, the Shape of Stuart experience', *HJ*, 31/2, 1988, pp. 453–67.
112. C. Hill, *Century of Revolution*, pp. 1, 4–5, conclusion; *Reformation to Industrial Revolution*, Part III.
113. Hill, *Century of Revolution*, pp. 4–5.
114. *Reformation to Industrial Revolution*, pp. 63, 89, 130, 143, 173, 175, 200, 206ff, 213, 218–19, 275ff. Clearly, as the parentheses indicate, I have taken some liberties with the scattered phrases in the text. I do not, however, believe that I have misrepresented Hill's meaning. For J. C. D. Clark's powerful critique of this formulation, see *English Society*, pp. 3ff.
115. 'The Results' in Pocock, *Three British Revolutions*.
116. J. Adams, 'Spain or the Netherlands' in H. Tomlinson (ed.), *Before the English Civil War* (1983), pp. 79–102. For a more nuanced – but still overschematic – consideration of seventeenth-century foreign policy, J. R. Jones, *Britain and Europe in the 17th century* (1966). And for a very different and far more persuasive version of international relations after 1660 see Jeremy Black's numerous studies, esp. *British Foreign Policy under Walpole* (1986); *Britain in the Age of Walpole* (1984); *Natural and Necessary Enemies: Anglo-*

French Relations in the Eighteenth Century (1986); *The Rise of the European Powers, 1679–1793* (1990); *A System of Ambition: British Foreign Policy, 1660–1793* (1991).

117. Simon Schama, *The Embarrassment of Riches: An Interpretation of Dutch Culture in the Golden Age* (1987); P. Geyl, *The Netherlands in the 17th century* (1961); *Orange and Stuart, 1641–1672* (1969); *The Revolt of the Netherlands* (1954); R. C. Parker, *The Dutch Revolt* (1976). For some of the – by now considerable – body of literature which has significantly revised older verdicts on the 'absolutism' of Louis XIV, see R. Hatton (ed.), *Louis XIV and Absolutism* (1976); J. Rule, *Louis XIV and the Craft of Kingship* (Columbus, Ohio, 1969); D. Parker, *The Making of French Absolutism* (London 1983); N. Elias, *The Court Society* (Oxford, 1983); R. Mettam, *Power and Faction in Louis XIV's France* (Oxford, 1988). For a spirited statement of the case for doing away with 'Absolutism' entirely, see N. Henshall, *The Myth of Absolutism* (1992). Hume made the case 200 years ago.

118. S. Baxter, *William III* (1958); J. Carswell, *From Revolution to Revolution* (1973), p. 185; J. Bromley and A. Lossky (eds), *New Cambridge Modern History, vol VI*, 'International Relations in Europe, 1688–1725', pp. 154–92; R. Hatton and J. Bromley (eds), *William III and Louis XIV; Essays by and for Marc Thomson* (1967).

119. A. MacLachlan, 'The Road to Peace' in Holmes, *Britain after the Glorious Revolution*, pp. 196ff; J. Black, works listed in fn 116; S, Baxter, 'The Myth of the Grand Alliance in the 18th century' in *Anglo-Dutch Cross Currents in the 18th Century* (Los Angeles, 1976); *England's Rise to Greatness, 1660–1763* (Berkeley, 1983). For a recent consideration of the rhetoric, see Linda Colley, *Britons* (Yale, 1992). For the continuing rich veins of Hollandophobia from Swift to Gilray, see D. Coombs, *The Conduct of the Dutch* (The Hague, 1958); Schama, op. cit., chapter 4.

120. Stone, *The Listener*, 4 October 1973, p. 449; Plumb, *Growth of Political Stablity*; Dickson, *Financial Revolution*; D. W. Jones, *War and Economy in the Age of William III and Marlborough* (Oxford, 1988); Brewer, *Sinews of Power*, chapter 5. For the outcry in the Commons during the 1690s about these issues see K. Feiling, *A History of the Tory Party, 1660–1714* (Oxford, 1924); Horwitz, op. cit. For Stone's belated discovery of the state, see L. Stone (ed.), *An Imperial State at War: Britain from 1689 to 1815* (1992), pp. 1–12, 30; for his failure to take account of criticisms of its extensive powers, J. Clark, 'Success Stories', *TLS*, 10 June 1994.

121. L. Stone, 'Results', loc. cit; Plumb, *Political Stability*, chapter 6.

122. C. Hill, 'The Place of the Seventeenth Century Revolution in English History' in Mukherjee and Ward, op. cit., pp. 24–30; *A Nation of Change*, p. 23.

123. C. Condren, in Mukherjee and Ward, op. cit., pp. 33–4, 37; E. Burke, 'The Great Map', quoted in P. Marshall, *The Great Map of Mankind* (1980), p. 3.

Chapter 6 Retreating from the Revolution

1. This section is a much shortened – and schematized – version of my *Marxist Historians and the Pathology of English History*, forthcoming; see. also Bryan D. Palmer, *The Making of E. P. Thompson: Marxism, Humanism and History* (Toronto, 1981).
2. Anderson, *Arguments*, p. 142.
3. J. L. and E. P. Thompson, *There is a Spirit in Europe: A Memoir of Frank Thompson* (1947), pp. 169ff; E. P. Thompson, *The Railway: An Adventure in Construction* (1948), pp. 2–3; *POT*, p. 353; Bryan Palmer, op. cit., p. 34; M. Thompson, *A Paper House: The Ending of Yugoslavia* (1992), p. 119. For 1945, see Open Letter, op. cit., pp. 354–5; M. Merrill, Interview with E. P. Thompson, *Radical History Review*, 3, iv, Fall 1976, pp. 2, 9–11, 20–1; 'Recovering the Libertarian Tradition', *The Leveller*, 22, 1978, pp. 22–3; G. Barnsby, '1945 – The Year of Victory', *OH*, 62.
4. *Reasoner*, 3, 'Through the Smoke of Budapest', pp. 3ff, reprinted in Widgery, op. cit., pp. 66–72; Wood, op. cit., p. 200; 'Socialist Humanism: An Epistle to the Philistines', *New Reasoner: A Quarterly Journal of Socialist Humanism (NR)*, 1, Summer 1957 pp. 107ff.
5. Thompson, 'Socialist Humanism', loc. cit., pp. 111–12, 114, 116, 125–8; 'Agency and Choice', *NR*, 4, Summer 1958, pp. 95–6.
ɔ. Anderson, 'The Left in the 50s', *NLR* 29, January–February 1965, pp. 3–18; R. Williams, 'The British Left', ibid., 30, March–April 1965, pp. 18–26; 'Notes on British Marxism since the War', ibid., 100, November 1976–January 1977, pp. 81–94; E. P. Thompson, 'At the Point of Decay' and 'Outside the Whale', in *Out of Apathy* (1960), pp. 3–15, 141–94; 'Socialist Humanism', loc. cit., pp. 139–40.
7. Open Letter to Kolakowski, *POT*, p. 392f; 'The New Left', *NR*, 9, p. 8; A MacIntyre, 'Notes from the Moral Wilderness' I, *NR*, 7, pp. 91–2.
8. 'Revolution', in *Out of Apathy*, pp. 298ff.
9. S. Hall, 'The First New Left, Life and Times', in S. Hall (ed.), *Out of Apathy: Voices on the New Left Thirty Years on* (1989), pp. 15ff; R. Hoggart, *The Uses of Literacy* (1955). Williams had worked within the *Scrutiny* tradition as well as on the margins of English Marxism (idiosyncratically, he joined the CP at the time of the Hitler–Stalin Pact, and left it again at the end of the war): he had been one of the editors of the *Scrutiny*-inspired, 'Politics and Literature'. See above Chapter 3.
10. Raymond Williams, *Culture and Society* (1958) Penguin edn, pp. 16f, 305–24; cf R. Williams, *Marxism and Literature* (Oxford 1977) chapter I, R. Williams, *Keywords* (to 1976) see under 'culture'.
11. Ibid., pp. 16, 42, 47, 52–3, 59–60, 74–84, 95–8, 120–37, 145–9, 155–6, 166–7, 192–4, 218–21, 228–38, 247–8, 258–75, 285–7, 305–24; T. Eagleton and B. Wicker, *From Culture to Revolution* (1968), pp. 8ff; R. Williams, *Politics and Letters* (1979), pp. 112ff.
12. R. Williams, *The Long Revolution*, Part III (1961) Penguin edn, introduction, chapter 2 esp. pp 140ff; 'Democracy and Parliament',

Marxism Today, June 1982, pp. 14–21; Border Country (1961); R.
Scruton, Thinkers of the New Left (1985), pp. 56ff.
13. R. Williams, Culture and Society, passim; The Long Revolution, Part
III: Anderson, 'Origins of the Present Crisis', NLR, 23, January–
February, 1964, p. 43, subsequently reprinted in English Questions
(1992); V. G. Kiernan, 'Culture and Society', NR, 9, pp. 74–83
14. Thompson, 'The Long Revolution', I, NLR, 9, May–June 1961, pp.
24–33; II, ibid., 10, pp. 34–39, esp. p. 33.
15. Thompson, 'The Long Revolution, loc. cit., passim; R. Williams,
Politics and Letters, pp. 135ff; cf T. Eagleton, Criticism and Ideology
(1976), pp. 11–43; 'Criticism and Politics: The Work of Raymond
Williams', NLR, 99, January–February 1976, pp. 3–23; Marxism and
Literary Criticism (1976).
16. 'Talking with Christopher Hill', Eley and Hunt, pp. 101–2; also
in A. Marwick, The Nature of History (1970), p. 206; Thompson,
POT, pp. 320ff. For other attempts of British Marxist historians
to distance themselves from unacceptable forms of Marxism, see
J. Saville, Marxism and History (Chapel Hill, 1974), p. 4ff; E. J.
Hobsbawm, 'Karl Marx's Contribution to Historiography' in R.
Blackburn (ed.), Ideology in Social Science (1972), p. 270–1.
17. The Making of the English Working Class (MEWC) (1963). For this
reading of MEWC, see William Sewell Jr, 'How Classes are made:
E. P. Thompson's Theory of Working Class Formation' in Harvey
J. Kaye and K. McClelland, E. P. Thompson: Critical Perspectives
(Cambridge, 1989), pp. 50–2.
18. Kaye, The British Marxist Historians, pp. 222ff; Hill, 'Men as They
Live their Own History' in Change and Continuity, pp. 229–37;
Thompson, 'History from Below', TLS 7 April 1966, pp. 279–80.
19. MEWC, Part I; Kaye, pp. 176ff; J. D. Chalmers, review (on 'a thirst
for bourgeois blood'), History, June 1966, pp. 184–5; R. Currie and
R. M. Hartwell, EcHR, 2, XVIII/3, pp. 638–9; G. Best, HJ, 8, 1965,
pp. 273–4; Thompson, 'God, King and Law', NR, 3, Winter 1957.
The fact that Thompson answered his critics so passionately
(Postscript, pp. 916–39) and that they may have had an ideological
axe to grind (notably in the case of Chalmers, Hartwell, Smelser
and the reviewers in The Economist, 'Enter the cloth Cap'; NYRB,
'Hard Times'; and Commentary, 'Those Dark Satanic Mills') does
not remove the point. For a review of the reviewers, passionately
committed to Thompson's position, see Palmer, op. cit., pp. 65–6,
77–8.
20. E. P. Thompson, MEWC, Part I; 'Revolution Again, or Shut your
Ears and Run', NLR, 6, November–December 1960, pp. 18–31; A
MacIntyre, 'Notes from the Moral Wilderness' I, NR, 7, pp. 91–2;
II, ibid., 8, pp. 88–9.
21. Thompson, 'Revolution', loc. cit., pp. 300ff; Charles Taylor, NLR,
4, July–August 1960, pp. 3ff; 'Marxism and Socialist Humanism'
in S. Hall (ed.), Out of Apathy, pp. 61–78; NR, 2, pp. 92–8; Hegel
(Cambridge, 1978); P. Fryer, 'Lenin as Philosopher', Labour Review,
2, September–October 1957, pp. 136–47.

22. Thompson, 'Revolution', *Out of Apathy*, p. 308; MEWC, pp. 9ff; R. Boochin, *Post Scarcity Anarchism* (1974) quoted in Metcalfe, 'Myths', p. 36. Metcalfe, 'Myths', pp. 31ff; 'Class Struggle in an Intimate Relationship'; R. Sennett and J. Cobb, *The Hidden Injuries of Class* (Cambridge, 1984); *For Freedom and Dignity* (Sydney, 1988). For similar views, M. Ignatieff, *The Needs of Strangers: An Essay on Privacy, Solidarity and the Politics of Being Human* (1985), pp. 140ff.

23. Thompson, 'Revolution', op. cit., pp. 308–9. For the 'imperialist imagination' of the Left see Donald Horne, *God is an Englishman* (Harmondsworth, 1970); Anderson, 'Socialism and Pseudo-Empiricism', *NLR*, 35, January–February 1966, p. 37. For critiques of 'Revolution' (less a programme for changing the world than for moralizing it) *NLR*, 4, July–August 1960, pp. 3–10.

24. For the section on Perry Anderson, I have relied particularly on Mark Gibson, *Perry Anderson's Project: The Defence of Marxist Historicism in Britain* (Sydney, B. A. Theiss, 1987); Anderson, *Arguments*, p. 147; Gibson, op. cit., pp. 15ff.

25. Anderson, 'The Figures of Descent', *NLR*, 161, January–February 1987, pp. 20ff; 'Origins of the Present Crisis', loc. cit., p. 26; Gibson, op. cit., pp. 18–19.

26. Anderson, 'Components of the National Culture', *NLR*, 50, July–August 1968, pp. 3–58, esp. 7–8; 'Origins', p. 27.

27. Anderson, 'Components', passim; 'Socialism and Pseudo-Empiricism' ('The Myths of E. P. Thompson'), pp. 33, 39ff; G. Stedman Jones, 'The Pathology of English History, *NLR*, 44, July–August 1967, pp. 29–44; 'History: The Poverty of Empiricism' in R. Blackburn (ed.), *Ideology in Social Science*, pp. 96–115.

28. Nairn, 'The English Working Class', p. 44

29. Nairn, 'The British Political Elite', *NLR*, 23, January–February 1964, pp. 20, 23ff; 'Landed England', *ibid.*, 17, September–December. 1962, pp. 116–19; 'English Working Class', loc. cit., p. 47; 'Anatomy of the Labour Party' 1, *NLR*, 27, September–October. 1964, pp. 38–65; 2, *ibid.*, 28, November– December. 1964, pp. 33–62.

30. Anderson, Origins, p. 28.

31. Ibid., pp. 29–30; Nairn, 'English Working Class', pp. 44, 54ff; 'British Political Elite', pp. 23ff.

32. Anderson, Origins, pp. 30–1.

33. Ibid., pp. 31, 34.

34. Ibid., pp, 33, 40, 43; 'The Left in the '50s', loc. cit., pp. 15ff; 'Critique of Wilsonism', *NLR*, 27, September–October 1964, pp. 3–27.

35. R. Johnson, Peculiarities of the English Route: Barrington Moore, Perry Anderson and English Social Development', *Contemporary Cultural Studies*, Occasional Paper, 26 (Birmingham, 1976), pp. 21–2; K. Neild, 'A Symptomatic Dispute: Notes on the Relationship between Marxist Theory and Historical Practice in Britain', *Social Research*, 47, Autumn 1980, pp. 479–506, esp. pp. 486–7; Thompson, 'Origins', pp. 37ff; 'Socialism and Pseudo-Empiricism', pp. 3–4, 33ff; 'Components', passim.

36. Anderson, 'Origins', pp. 40, 43; T. Nairn, *The Break-up of Britain* (1977); M. J. Wiener, *English Culture and the Decline of the Industrial Spirit, 1850–1980* (Cambridge, 1981), p. 32.

37. Thompson, 'Peculiarities', loc. cit., pp. 247–8, 287ff, 298.

38. Ibid., pp. 249–50.

39. Ibid., p. 251; P. Corrigan and D. Sayer, *The Great Arch: English State Formation as Cultural Revolution* (Oxford, 1985), p. 11; P. Corrigan (ed.), *Capitalism, State Formation and Marxist Theory* (1979), pp. 30ff.

40. See above Chapters 2 and 3 for similar formulations by 'P.F.' and Kiernan; 'Socialism and Pseudo-Empiricism' (pp. 8–9) accused T of reinventing the oldest cliché in history and of treating capitalism as an eternal category, quoting J. H. Hexter, 'The Myth of the Middle Class in Elizabethan England', in *Reappraisals*, pp. 71–116.

41. Thompson, 'Peculiarities', loc. cit., pp. 251–2; Corrigan and Sayer, op. cit., p. 75. The privileging of court–country divisions (especially in Corrigan and Sayer) was, of course, also – from a Marxist perspective – unorthodox.

42. Thompson, 'Peculiarities', p. 252.

43. E. P. Thompson, *Whigs and Hunters: The Origin of the Black Act* (Harmondsworth, 1975); *Whigs and Hunters*, passim; D. Hay (ed.), *Albion's Fatal Tree* (Harmondsworth, 1977), esp. D. Hay, 'Property, Authority and Criminal Law', pp. 17–64; Thompson, 'Time, Work Discipline and Industrial Capitalism', *P&P*, 38 December 1967; 'The Moral Economy of the English Crowd in the Eighteenth Century', *P&P*, 50, February 1971, pp. 76–136; 'Rough Music: Le charivari anglais', *Annales ESC.*, 27, 1972; 'Patrician Society, Plebeian Culture', *Journal of Social History*, 7, 1974; 'Eighteenth Century English Society: Class Struggle without Class?', *Social History*, 3/2, May 1978, pp. 133–65; and most recently, *Customs in Common* (1992).

44. Thompson, *Whigs and Hunters* passim; D. Hay, op. cit., pp. 35 ff; L. Stone, 'Whigs, Marxists and Poachers', *NYRB*, 5 February 1976, p. 26, for a critique of T's depiction of eighteenth-century politics as 'sophisticated brigandage'; for a somewhat hysterical reaction to T's work, see J. C. D. Clark, 'Namierism of the Left', *Cambridge Journal*, 22, October 1976, pp. 25ff.

45. Thompson, 'Peculiarities', loc. cit., p. 266; 'Revolution Again', loc. cit., pp. 18–31.

46. J. Barrington Moore Jr, *Social Origins of Dictatorship and Democracy* (Harmondsworth, 1969), esp. p. 113ff, 418–21; Johnson, 'Peculiarities', loc. cit., pp. 3ff, 14–15; D. Smith, *Barrington Moore and the Uses of History* (1983); T. Nairn, 'English Working Class', loc. cit., p. 52.

47. Thompson, *Whigs and Hunters*, pp. 258ff; 'Law as a Part of Culture', *TLS*, 24 April 1969, pp. 425–7; Anderson, *Arguments*, p. 199; Stone, 'Whigs, Marxists and Poachers' (on Thompson as a 'Whig after all'), loc. cit.; J. H. Hexter, 'The Birth of Modern Freedom', *TLS*, 21 January 1983, pp. 51–4.

48. Nield, 'A Symptomatic Dispute', loc. cit., p. 492; Thompson, 'The Poverty of Theory, or an Orrery of Errors', originally in *SR*, 1978, subsequently *POT*; Kaye, op. cit., pp. 207ff, 220; M. Merrill, 'Interview with E.P. Thompson', *Radical History Review*, 3/iv, Fall 1976, pp. 16–17.

49. Johnson, 'Peculiarities', loc. cit., p. 296; 'Poverty of Theory', quoted in Bryan Palmer, op. cit., pp. 108ff.

50. Anderson, 'Components', loc. cit., p. 57.

51. Anderson, 'Origins', loc. cit., pp. 50, 53.

52. Thompson, 'Peculiarities', loc. cit., pp. 246–7; Johnson, 'English Route', loc. cit., pp. 24–5; D. Sassoon, 'The Silences of the New Left Review', *Politics and Power*, 3, 1981, pp. 237–8, 298–9.

53. For the platonic ideal of 'other countries (with 'mature' Bourgeois Revolutions, proper class struggles, etc.), Johnson, 'Peculiarities', *POT*, p. 246. The model, in fact, seemed limited to just one case: Germany had its *Sonderweg*, Italy its failed transition, Spain its peculiarly arrested development, and Russia – well, Russia was 'otherness' all right, but in a different sense altogether. Only in the case of France did history appear to measure up to its rendezvous with ideality – except, that is, for the disturbing thought (barely perceived in 1964 but well established by 1989) that perhaps even French history did not fit the model derived from the history of France.

54. For similarities with Voltaire's belief in the 'ends' of history, with most of the actual story getting in the way, see C. Frankel, *The Faith of Reason* (Cornell, 1952); for the concept of 'mediation' see Gibson, op. cit., p. 46.

55. Anderson, *Considerations on Western Marxism* (1976), pp. 21ff, 29, 45, 100ff; *Arguments*, pp. 2–4; *In the Tracks of Historical Materialism* (1983), pp. 32ff.

56. Anderson, 'Figures of Descent', loc. cit., pp. 21–7.

57. Anderson, 'Modernity and Revolution', *NLR*, 144, March–April 1984, pp. 111–13 (a critique of Marshall Berman's *'All that is Solid Melts into Air'* (New York, 1983); *In the Tracks*, pp. 72–6, esp. p. 74. Cf Palmer's comment, op. cit., p. 18 on Anderson's (earlier) 'exuberant enthusiasm for the Chinese Revolution'.

58. Anderson, 'Modernity and Revolution', loc. cit., p. 112.

59. Anderson, 'The Notion of Bourgeois Revolution' in *English Questions*, pp. 110–14, quotation at pp. 112–13.

60. Anderson, 'Figures of Descent', loc. cit., p. 27.

61. Anderson, 'The Notion of Bourgeois Revolution', loc. cit., pp. 116–18.

62. Anderson, 'Figures of Descent', loc. cit., pp. 23, 35ff, 47–8; T. Nairn, 'The Fateful Meridian', *NLR*, 60, March–April 1970, pp. 3–36; 'The Twilight of the British State', *NLR*, 101–2, February–April 1977, pp. 3–61, esp. pp. 14–15; *Breakup of Britain*, pp. 30ff; 'The House of Windsor', *NLR*, 127, May–June 1981 pp. 96–100; and, at much greater length, *The Enchanted Glass, Britain and her Monarchy* (1988), esp. pp. 142–250.

63. M. Barratt Brown, 'Away with all the Great Arches: Perry Anderson's History of British Capitalism', *NLR*, 167, January–February 1987, pp. 22–52, passim; A. Callinicos, 'Exception or Symptom: the British Crisis and the World System', *NLR*, 169, May–June 1988, pp. 97–107, esp. pp. 99ff; C. Baker and D. Nicholls (eds), *The Development of British Capitalist Society: A Marxist Debate* (Manchester, 1988); E. M. Wood, *The Pristine Culture of Capitalism* (1992), pp. 11–17 (for further consideration of this text, see below, Conclusion: The End of the Line?).

64. M. Wiener, *English Culture*, passim.; C. Barnett, *The Audit of War* (1986), esp. p. 304; *The Collapse of British Power* (1972); B. Hutber (ed.), *What's Wrong with Britain?* (1978). For a review of the extensive literature of 'decline' and its (largely Thatcherite) political subtexts, see J. Raven, 'British History and the Enterprise Culture', *P&P*, 123, May 1989, pp. 178–204, esp. pp. 181, 183ff.

65. 'A Culture in Counterflow', 1, *NLR*, 180, March–April 1990, pp. 41–80; 2, 182, July–August 1990, pp. 85–138; see also his reviews of various British sociologists (hitherto 'the absent centre' of British 'culture', but now rippling with theoretical muscle) in *A Zone of Engagement* (1992).

66. See above, Chapter 5; F. M. L. Thompson, 'A Marxist Quintet', *TLS*, 23 May 1986, p. 572. For attacks on Edward Thompson's neo-Whiggism, see A. Merritt, 'The Nature and Function of Law: A Criticism of E. P. Thompson', *Journal of Law and Society*, 7, 1980, pp. 194–214, esp. pp. 197–201, 210; M. J. Horwitz, 'The Rule of Law: An Unqualified Human Good?' *Yale Law Journal*, 86, 1977, pp. 566ff; Anderson, *Arguments*, pp. 198ff; Bob Fine, *Liberty and the Rule of Law* (1984) pp. 175ff; H. Collins, *Marxism and Law* (Oxford, 1986), pp. 144ff. Thompson's particular offence was in the last chapter of *Whigs and Hunters* which seemed rather similar to J.H. Hexter's 'The Birth of Modern Freedom', loc. cit.

67. 'Going into Europe', in *Writing by Candlelight*, pp. 85–8 (Dutch elm disease was listed as 'Europe's most viable export to England'); POT, p. 188; Anderson, *Arguments*, p. 198ff; P. D. Hirst, 'The Necessity of Theory' in *Marxism and Historical Writing* (1985), pp. 57–90, esp. 64ff.

68. J. Raven, 'British History and the Enterprise Culture', loc. cit.; 'A Culture in Counterflow', 2, *NLR*, 182, July–August 1990, pp. 121–30.

69. L. Stone, *Causes*, p. 39. Quoted in J. C. D. Clark, *Revolution and Rebellion*, p. 14. This section is heavily indebted to Clark's uneven and unfair, but also sometimes brilliant, critique; even more, to Glenn Burgess, 'Revisionism: An Analysis of Early Stuart Historiography in the 1970s and 1980s', *HJ*, 33/3, 1990, pp. 609–27; J. H. Hexter, *Reappraisals*, p. 141.

70. J. C. D. Clark, op. cit., pp. 166–7. In addition to Trevor-Roper's famous inversion of the rise of the gentry, one might mention some of the contributions to the 'Crisis in Europe' debate and – as does Clark – J. H. Elliot's elaboration of his essay on that

occasion, in 'England and Europe: A Common Malady' in Conrad
Russell, *Origins of the English Civil War* (1973).
71. Quoted in Finlayson, op. cit., p. 35.
72. E. H. Carr, *What is History*; Thomas, 'New Directions', loc. cit.;
and for a Marxist perspective, E. J. Hobsbawm, 'Where are British Historians going?' loc. cit.; G. Stedman-Jones, 'The Poverty of
Empiricism', loc. cit.
73. C. Hill, reviews of 'The King's Peace', *TLS* ('The Eve of the Civil
Wars'), 7 January 1955; and of 'The King's War', *The Spectator*, 12
December 1955. Just how general the attitude, may be judged
from Peter Laslett's almost identical complaint of an updated
version of Trevelyan, that 'whilst everything has been described
nothing has been accounted for . . . a social description with the
statics and the dynamics left out': review of W. Notestein, *The
English People on the Eve of Colonization* (1954), *The Listener*, 17
March 1955, pp. 474–5.
74. For the events of 1917 as a spontaneous explosion of the masses,
see R. Pipes,'The Great October Revolution as a Clandestine coup
d'état', *TLS*, 6 November 1992 p. 3; '1917 and the Revisionists', in
The National Interest, 31, 1993, pp, 68–79; *The Russian Revolution*
(1990). For England, Hill, 'A Bourgeois Revolution', loc cit. p. 135.
75. Stone, *Causes*, p. 57.
76. For a brief summary of these problems, J. A. Goldstone, *Revolution and Rebellion in the Early Modern World* (Berkeley, 1991), pp.
68–83.
77. Burgess. 'Revisionism', loc cit. pp. 610ff.
78. Brunton and Pennington, op. cit., pp. 176ff; Stone, *Crisis*, passim;
D. C. Coleman, 'The Gentry Controversy and the Aristocracy in
Crisis', *History*, 51, 1966, pp. 165–78; Stone, 'Social Mobility in
England', *P&P*, 33, 1966, pp. 16–55
79. D. Lockwood, *Solidarity and Schism: The Problem of Disorder in
Durkheimian and Marxist Sociology* (Oxford, 1992).
80. F. Braudel, 'History and the Social Sciences: The Longue Durée',
On History (1980), pp. 23–54; E. Le Roy Ladurie, 'The History
that Stands Still', in *The Mind and Method of the Historian* (Chicago,
1981).
81. Laslett, op. cit (see esp.7: 'Social Change and Revolution in the
Traditional World'); P. Zagorin, *Rebels and Rulers, 1500–1660* (Cambridge, 1982).
82. Zagorin, *Court and Country*; Stone, *Causes*, pp. 105–8; K. Sharpe,
*Criticism and Compliment: The Politics of Literature in the England of
Charles I* (Cambridge, 1987), pp. 1–53; Ann Hughes, *The Causes of
the English Civil War* (1992), pp. 84–8.
83. Burgess, 'Revisionism', loc. cit., p. 612.
84. Major County Studies include A. Everitt, *The Community of Kent
and the Great Rebellion* (Leicester, 1966); J. S. Morrill, *Cheshire, 1630–
60: County Government and Society during the 'English Revolution'*
(Oxford, 1974); D. Underdown, *Somerset in the Civil War and Interregnum* (Newton Abbot, 1973); A Fletcher, *A County Community*

in Peace and War: Sussex, 1600–60 (1975); B. G. Blackwood, *The Lancashire Gentry and the Great Rebellion, 1640–60* (Manchester, 1978); C. Holmes, *Seventeenth Century Lincolnshire* (Lincoln, 1980); Ann Hughes, *Politics, society and Civil War: Warwickshire, 1620–60* (Cambridge, 1987). A summary of some of the arguments can be found in J. S. Morrill, *The Revolt of the Provinces* (1976). For Morrill's 'remorse', see *The Revolt* (new edn 1980), p. x; Burgess, 'Revisionism', loc. cit., p. 617.

85. Clark, op. cit., p. 57. Since the same pattern could be observed in French revolutionary studies in the 1970s and 1980s, the explanation has its limitations. The expansion of local archives and of PhD topics is a more plausible reason.

86. For these criticisms, see C. Holmes, 'The County Community in Stuart Historiography', *JBS*, XVII, 1978 pp. 54–73; A. Hughes, 'Local History and the Origins of the Civil War' in R. Cust and A Hughes (eds), *Conflict in Early Stuart England: Studies in Religion and Politics 1603–42* (1989) pp. 224–53; D. Underdown, 'Community and Class: Theories of Local Politics in the English Revolution' in Malament, op. cit., pp. 148–69; Clark, op. cit., pp. 57ff.

87. P. Collinson, *The Birthpangs of Protestant England: Religious and Cultural Change in the Sixteenth and Seventeenth Centuries* (1991), pp. 8–9; C. Hill, 'Parliament and People in Seventeenth Century England', *P&P*, 92, 1981, p. 103.

88. For the term 'revisionist', see Burgess, loc. cit., p. 617.

89. Stone, 'The Revolution over the Revolution', *NYRB*, 11 June 1992, p. 48; Burgess, loc cit., p. 619.

90. C. Russell, *Parliaments and English Politics, 1621–1629* (Oxford, 1979); 'Parliamentary History in Perspective', *History*, 59, 1976, pp. 1–27; *The Crisis of Parliaments* (Oxford, 1977); 'The Nature of a Parliament in Stuart England' in H. Tomlinson, *Before the English Civil War* (1983), pp. 23–50. Many of Russell's articles are now collected in his *Unrevolutionary England, 1603–42* (1990); G. Elton, 'Tudor Government: The Points of Contact: I Parliament', *TRHS*, 5th ser., XXIV, 1974, pp. 183–200; 'Parliament in the Sixteenth Century', *HJ*, XII, 1979; D. Hirst, *The Representative of the People? Voters and Voting in England under the Early Stuarts* (Cambridge, 1975); 'Unanimity in the Commons: Aristocratic Intrigues and the Origins of the English Civil War', *JMH*, 50, pp. 51–71.

91. P. Collinson, *The Religion of Protestants: The Church in English Society, 1559–1625* (Oxford, 1982); *Godly People* (1983).

92. K. Sharpe, *Criticism and Compliment*; (ed.), *Faction and Parliament: Essays in Early Stuart History* (Oxford, 1978); *The Personal Rule of Charles I* (Yale, 1992).

93. C. Russell, *The Causes of the English Civil War* (Oxford, 1990); *The Fall of the British Monarchies, 1637–1642* (Oxford, 1991); *Unrevolutionary England*, Part IV.

94. M. Kishlansky, *The New Model Army* (Cambridge, 1979); D. Underdown, *Pride's Purge: Politics in the Puritan Revolution* (Oxford, 1971). However, cf I. Gentles, *The New Model Army in England,*

Scotland and Ireland, 1645–53 (Oxford, 1991); A. Woolrych, *Soldiers and Statesmen: The General Council of the Army and its Debates 1647–8* (Oxford, 1987).

95. B. Worden, *The Rump Parliament* (Cambridge, 1974).
96. Russell, *Causes*, chapter 1; 'Why Did Charles Call the Long Parliament' in *Unrevolutionary England*, pp. 253–63; 'Why did Charles Fight the Civil War', *History Today*, June 1984, pp. 31–4.
97. The parallel with the new plurality of French Revolutions is striking: cf Mona Ozouf, 'The French Revolution is not Like a Fixed-price Menu in a Restaurant', quoted in Gildea, op. cit., p. 15.
98. These distinctions were already formulated by Russell in *The Origins of the English Civil War*, introduction; *Unrevolutionary England*, introduction. See esp. his famous description (*Origins*, p. 7) of Stone's *Crisis of the Aristocracy* as an attempt 'to explain events that did not happen in terms of social change for which the evidence remains uncertain'.
99. Russell, *Unrevolutionary England*, introduction p. x.
100. For one formulation of this, Clark, op. cit. pp. 15ff; for another, J. R. Vincent and A. B. Cooke, *The Governing Passion: Cabinet Government and Party Politics in Britain, 1885–6* (1974).
101. Stone, 'The Revival of Narrative', originally *P&P*, 85, 1979, reprinted in *The Past and the Present*, pp. 74–96: as Clark remarks, 'a curious feature of this oft-cited article is its omission of any serious consideration of historical narratives' (op. cit., p.17). Exactly the same technique can be observed in his treatment of the revival of the state, a decade later: after admitting that 'the rush to social history' had led to 'a neglect – in some cases a positive denigration – of critically older areas of historical enquiry', he then went on to define these in structural terms: i.e. not military, diplomatic or political history, but the state of 'political scientists, historical sociologists' etc. See L. Stone (ed.), *An Imperial State at War*.
102. See esp. David Carr, *Time, Narrative and History* (Bloomington, 1986), pp. 100ff.
103. This formulation relies on Carr, op. cit., and harks back to Collingwood's famous distinction between 'inside' and 'outside' knowledge, *The Idea of History* (Oxford, 1946), pp. 217ff.
104. A. J. Fletcher, *The Outbreak of the English Civil War* (1981). This incidentally might be called an instance of Namierism – not the detailed chronology which Namier (an exponent of the cross-section rather than the story line) abominated, but the reduction of political bevaviour to psychological drama, see his *England in the Age of the American Revolution* (1930).
105. E.g. the simplification, foreshortening, and dramatization of events: H. Butterfield, *The Whig Interpretation of History* (1931), passim.
106. J. H. Hexter, 'The Early Stuarts and Parliament: Old Hat and the Nouvelle Vague', *Parliamentary History*, I, 1982, pp. 181–215: quotation at p. 182.
107. Ibid.

108. Hill, *Century*, passim; Thompson, 'Peculiarities', loc. cit., passim; Pocock, Virtue . . ., pp. 52–55; Clark, op. cit., pp. 98–9. Whig texts did not always lend themselves to Marxist appropriation: for a text deliberately resistant to this tactic, see, for example, G. E. Aylmer, *The Struggle for the Constitution* (1963).

109. *M.Q.*, I i (1938) p. 91; introduction to new edition of S. R. Gardiner, *History of the Great Civil War* (London, 1987) p. xxv; J. S. A. Adamson, 'Eminent Victorians . . .', loc. cit., p. 641.

110. For a resumé, T. K. Rabb, 'Revisionism Revised: The Role of the Commons', *P&P*, 92, 1981, pp. 55–78; D. Hirst, 'The Place of Principle', ibid., pp. 79–99. For some examples, the articles collected in *JMH*, 49, 1977; 50, 1978.

111. M. Judson, *The Crisis of the Constitution* (Rutgers, 1949). For a less sophisticated Whig account from an inveterate genealogist (in other fields also), see G. E. Mosse, *The Struggle for Sovereignty in England from the Reign of Queen Elizabeth to the Petition of Right* (Michigan, 1950).

112. Russell, *Parliaments*, passim.

113. Sharpe, *The Personal Rule*; D. Cressy, *Coming Over: Migration and Communication between England and New England in the Seventeenth Century* (Cambridge, 1987); Sharpe, *Criticism and Compliment*; R. Malcolm Smuts, *Court Culture and the Origins of a Royalist Tradition in Early Stuart England* (Philadelphia, 1987).

114. For these positions, J. S. A. Adamson, 'The Baronial Context of the English Civil War', *TRHS*, 5th ser., xl, pp. 95–120; *The Peerage in Politics 1645–9*, Cambridge PhD 1986; Russell, *The Fall*, etc.; J. S. Morrill, 'The Religious Context of the English Civil War', *TRHS*, 5th ser., xxxiv, 1984, pp. 155–78; and the essays now collected in Part 1 of *The Nature of the English Revolution* (1993); Fletcher, *Outbreak*; C. Daniels and J. Morrill, *Charles I* (1988); Russell, *Causes*, chapter 8.

115. For the abuse of the term, M. Kishlansky, *Parliamentary History*, vii, 1988, pp. 331–2; Burgess, loc. cit., p. 617. The term carried exactly the opposite meanings in, for example, Russian history.

116. For 'Peterhouse Tories', see M. Cowling, 'Sources of the New Right: Irony, Geniality and Malice', *Encounter*, November 1989, pp. 3–13; R. Brent, 'Butterfield's Tories: High Politics and the Writing of Modern British History', *HJ*, 30/4, 1987, pp. 943–54;

117. Hexter, 'The Early Stuarts and Parliament', pp. 182ff; Burgess, loc. cit. pp. 613ff. The quotation is taken from Bolingbroke's *Letter to Sir William Wyndham* (1718).

118. Adamson, 'Eminent Victorians', loc. cit.; J. W. Burrow, *Whigs and Liberals: Continuity and Change in English Political Thought* (Oxford, 1988), chapter 4; S. Collini, 'The Idea of character in Victorian Political Thought', *TRHS*, 5th ser., xxxv, 1985, pp. 29–50.

119. H. Butterfield, op. cit.: Butterfield's 'Whig Interpretation', one might argue, provided just enough theory for the atheoretical to justify their empiricism. A. Wilson and T.G. Ashplant, 'Whig History and Present-centred History, *HJ*, 31, 1988, pp. 1–16; 'Present-centred

History and the Problem of Historical Knowledge', ibid., pp. 253–74; R. W. Hinton, 'History Yesterday: Five Points about Whig History', *History Today*, 1959, pp. 720–8; W. Dray, 'J.H. Hexter, Neo-Whiggism and Early Stuart Historiography', *History & Theory*, xxvi, 1987, pp. 133– 49; Burgess, loc. cit., p. 614ff. For *Whig Hunting*, see Clark, op. cit., passim; J. G. A. Pocock, '1660 and All That; Whig Hunting, Ideology and Historiography in the Work of Jonathan Clark', *Cambridge Review*, 108, October 1987, pp. 125–8; G. Watson, 'The War against the Whigs: Butterfield Reconsidered', *Encounter*, January 1986, pp. 19–25.

120.   R. Zaller, 'The Continuity of British Radicalism in the Seventeenth and Eighteenth Centuries', *Eighteenth Century Life*, 6, 1981, pp. 4–7; cf Clark, op. cit., pp. 100–1; English Society, 1688–1832, pp. 65ff.

121.   Pocock, '1660 and All That', loc. cit.; *Three British Revolutions*, pp. 5–6; Russell, *Origins*, pp. 3–4. The equivalent in Butterfield's nomenclature was 'technical history' – a counting of the circumstantial pennies, while Providence attended to the rational pounds: see above Chapter 3, pp. 96–7.

122.   Russell, *Causes*, passim. For the similarities with Stone, see B. Worden, 'Conrad Russell's Civil War', *London Review of Books*, 29, August 1991, p. 13.

123.   N. Tyack, *Anti-Calvinists*; P. Lake, 'Calvinism and the English Church 1570–1635', *P&P*, 114, 1987; Collinson, *The Religion of Protestants*. For some criticisms, C. Hill, 'The Godly Community', *TLS*, 18 March 1983 p. 257; P. White, 'The Rise of Arminianism Reconsidered', *P&P*, 101, 1983; C. Haigh, review of Tyack, *EHR*, 103, 1988 pp. 425–7; S. Lambert, 'Committees, Religion and Parliamentary Encroachment on Royal Authority', *EHR*, 105, pp. 60–95.

124.   Noel Annan, *Our Age: The Generation that Made Post-War Britain* (1990) 1991 edn, pp. 558ff.

125.   Stone, 'Revolution over the Revolution', loc. cit.

126.   Sharpe, *The Personal Rule*, p. 954.

127.   Russell, 'The Catholic Wind', originally in J. Merriman, *For Want of a Horse: Choice and Chance in History*, reprinted in *Unrevolutionary England*, p. 305.

128.   For Hexter, 'The Birth of Modern Freedom', *TLS*, 21 January 1982; (ed.) *Parliament and Liberty from the Reign of Elizabeth to the English Civil War* (Stanford, 1992). (Hexter was editor of the series *The Making of Modern Freedom* and holder of a personal chair in The History of Freedom, at Stanford). For Trevor-Roper, 'The Continuity of the English Revolution' in *From Counter-Revolution to Glorious Revolution* (1991); L. Stone, 'The Undaunted Whig', *TLS*, 5 June 1992.

129.   Sharpe, *Faction and Parliament*, p. 3. Russell's retreat from revisionist 'excess' may be gauged by his review of Sharpe, *The Personal Rule*, 'Draining the Whig bathwater', *London Review of Books*, 10 June 1993.

130.   D. Hirst, 'Freedom, Revolution and Beyond' in Hexter, *Parliament and Liberty*, pp. 252–76; J. Somerville, *Politics and Ideology in En-*

gland, 1603–1640 (1986); R. Cust and A. Hughes, *Conflict in Early Stuart England*, see esp. introduction: 'After Revisionism'; M. Kishlansky, 'The Emergence of Adversary Politics', *JMH*, 49, 1977, pp. 617–40; *Parliamentary Selection: social and political choice in Early Modern England* (Cambridge, 1986); R. Cust, *The Forced Loan and English Politics, 1626–28* (Oxford, 1987); T. Cogswell, *The Blessed Revolution: English Politics and the Coming of War 1621–24* (Cambridge, 1989); L. J. Reeve, *Charles I and the Road to Personal Rule* (Cambridge, 1989); R. Cust, 'Revising the High Politics of Stuart England', *JBS*, 30, 1991.

131. Amongst many, Collinson, *Birthpangs*, passim; Morrill, *Nature of the English Revolution*; M. Watts, *The Dissenters* (Oxford, 1978); K. Wrightson, *English Society, 1580–1680* (1982); D. Underdown, *Fire from Heaven* (London, 1992); D. H. Sacks, *The Widening Gate: Bristol and the Atlantic Economy 1450–1700* (Berkeley 1991); D. Rollinson, *The Local Origins of Modern Society: Gloucestershire 1500–1800* (London 1992); J. F. McGregor & B. Reay (eds.), *Radical Religion in the English Revolution* (Oxford, 1984); Hill, *A Nation of Change and Novelty*; C. Jones et al. (eds), *Politics and People in Revolutionary England* (Oxford, 1985); Davis, 'Radicalism in a traditional society', loc. cit.; G. E. Aylmer, 'Collective Mentalities in mid Seventeenth Century England: III Varieties of Radicalism', *T.R.H.S.* 5th ser. xxxviii, 1988, pp. 1–25; Burgess, loc. cit., pp. 625ff.

132. 'Trading Places', *The Guardian*, 4 May 1993.

Chapter 7 Revolution as Text and Discourse

1. Pocock, *Virtue, Commerce and History*, p. 53.
2. A few of the more obvious texts are: G. Schochet, *Patriarchalism in Political Thought* (Oxford, 1975); S. D. Amussen, 'Gender, Family and the Social Order' in A Fletcher and J. Stevenson (eds), *Order and Disorder in Early Modern England* (Cambridge, 1985); *An Ordered Society: Gender and Class in Early Modern England* (Oxford, 1988); P. Laslett (ed.), *Patriarcha and Other Works of Sir Robert Filmer* (Oxford, 1949); C. Pateman, *The Sexual Contract*; E. Zaretsky, *Capitalism, the Family and Personal Life* (1976); E. Figes, *Patriarchal Attitudes* (1978); M. George, 'From Goodwife to Mistress: The Transformation of the Female in Bourgeois Culture', *SS*, xxxvii, 1973; M. Barrett, *Women's Oppression Today* (1980); C. Lasch, *Haven in a Heartless World* (New York, 1977); and, of course, F. Engels, *The Origin of the Family, Private Property and the State* (Harmondsworth, 1985)
3. For a brief outline of this 'new' social history, K. Wrightson, *English Society*; B. Coward, *Social Change and Continuity in Early Modern England, 1550–1750* (Oxford, 1988); P. Clark and P. Slack, *Crisis and Order in English Towns, 1500–1700* (1972); J. Thirsk, *The Agrarian History of England and Wales 4, 1500–1640* (Cambridge, 1967), 5, *1640–1750* (Cambridge 1984, 1985); J. Sharpe, *Early Modern England: A Social History, 1550–1760* (1987); Buchanan Sharp, *In Contempt*

of *All Authority: Rural Artisans and Riot in the West of England, 1586–1660* (Berkeley, 1980); A. L. Beier, *Masterless Men: The Vagrancy Problem in England, 1560–1640* (1985).

4. Hill, *Society and Puritanism*, chapter 13, 'The Spiritualization of the Household', drawing on Engels, and on L. Schücking, *The Puritan Family. A Social Study from Literary Sources* (1929, Eng. trans. London, 1969); E. Morgan, *The Puritan Family* (Boston, 1944); cf, however, A. Macfarlane, *Marriage and Love in England, 1300–1800* (Oxford, 1986).

5. L. Stone, *The Family, Sex and Marriage in England, 1500–1800* (Oxford, 1977), passim. E. Shorter, *The Making of the Modern Family* (1976); P. Aries, *Centuries of Childhood* (1962) offer variants of the Stone trajectory. Of the many critiques of this oft-cited text, see A. Macfarlane, review essay, *History and Theory*, XVII, 1977, pp. 103–26; E. P. Thompson, 'Happy Families', *New Society*, September 1977, pp. 499–501: K. Thomas, 'The Changing Family', *TLS*, 22 October 1977 p. 1226, and subsequent correspondence; and, especially, R. A. Houlbrooke, *The English family, 1450–1700* (1984), introduction; also, F. Mount, *The Subversive Family* (1982).

6. D. Underdown, *Revel, Riot and Rebellion*, p. 40; K. Thomas, *Religion and the Decline of Magic*; Wrightson, op. cit.; W. Hunt, *The Puritan Moment: The Coming of Revolution in an English County (Cambridge, Mass.*, 1983); P. S. Seaver, *Wallington's World: A Puritan Artisan in Seventeenth-Century London* (Stanford, 1984).

7. For a splendid summary, Ann Hughes, *The Causes*, pp. 84–7; Smuts, *Court Culture*, passim; M. Butler, *Theatre and Crisis, 1632–42*; K. Sharpe, 'The Image of Virtue: The Court and Household of Charles I, 1625–40,' in D. Starkey (ed.), *The English Court from the Wars of the Roses to the Civil War* (1987); J. Richards, ' "His Nowe Majestie" and the English Monarchy: The Kingship of Charles I before 1640', *P&P*, 113, 1986; J. G. A. Pocock, 'Modes of Action and their Pasts in Tudor and Stuart England' in O. Ranum (ed.), *National Consciousness, History and Political Culture in Early Modern Europe* (Baltimore, 1975), esp. pp. 103ff; D. Norbrook, *Poetry and Politics in the English Renaissance* (1984); K. Sharpe, *Personal Rule*, Part IV.

8. L. Stone, 'The Century of Revolution', *NYRB*, 26 February 1987, p. 40.

9. L. Stone, 'The Educational Revolution in England, 1540–1640, *P&P*, 28, 1964, pp. 70ff; 'Literacy and Education in England, 1640–1900', *P&P*, 42, 1969; (ed.) *The University in Society, vol 1: Oxford and Cambridge from the Fourteenth to the Early-Nineteenth Centuries* (Oxford, 1975). For an overtly Marxist reading, Joan Simon, *Education and Society in Tudor England* (Cambridge, 1966). Major works on this theme include, D. Cressy, *Literacy and the Social Order: Reading and Writing in Tudor and Stuart England* (Cambridge, 1980); M. Spufford, *Contrasting Communities: English Villagers in the Sixteenth and Seventeenth Centuries* (Cambridge, 1974); T. Laqueur, 'The Cultural Orgins of Popular Literacy in England, 1500–1850', *Oxford Review of Education*, 2, 1976; W. Prest, *The Inns of Court*

under Elizabeth and the Early Stuarts (1972); *The Rise of the Barristers, 1590–1640* (Oxford, 1986); *The Professions in Early Modern England* (1987).

10. M. Curtis, 'The Alienated Intellectuals in Early Stuart England', *P&P*, 23, 1962, pp. 25–43; *Oxford and Cambridge in Transition* (Oxford, 1959); M. Walzer, *The Revolution of the Saints*; T. Hobbes, *Behemoth or the Long Parliament* (F. Tönnies ed., London, 1969) quoted in Richardson, *Debate*, p. 23; for Burke, see *Reflections*, passim; for Goering, see Collinson, *Birthpangs*, p. 94.

11. Wrightson, *English Society*, p. 190, 192; C. Hill, 'Medieval to Modern', *The Literary Review*, May 1982, pp. 11–12; *The English Bible*, chapter 1, 'A Biblical Culture'; E. Eisenstein, *The Printing Press as an Agent of Change* (Cambridge, 1979); P. Burke, *Popular Culture in Early Modern Europe* (1978). Cf however, M. Spufford, *Small Books and Pleasant Histories* (1981); T. Watts, *Cheap Print and Popular Piety, 1550–1640* (Cambridge, 1990); P. Collinson, *From Iconoclasm to Iconophobia: The Cultural Impact of the Second English Reformation* (Reading, 1986) which deny the divide and the subversion.

12. D. Underdown, *Fire from Heaven: Life in an English Town in the Seventeenth Century* (1992). Other versions of the scenario, in K. Wrightson and D. Levine, *Poverty and Piety in an English Village: Terling 1525–1700* (1979); Hunt, *The Puritan Moment*; Underdown, *Riot, Revel and Rebellion*. Earlier versions of the theme, in C. Hill, *Society and Puritanism*, chapter 13: 'Puritans and the Dark Corners of the Land', 'Propagating the Gospel' in *Change and Continuity*; K. Thomas, *Religion and the Decline*, chapters 1, 3.

13. Underdown. op. cit., esp. chapters 2–4; S. Brigden, 'Up and Doing', *London Review of Books*, 6 August, 1992.

14. For the court's counter-cultural revolution, Underdown, *Riot*, pp. 63ff, 130ff; Sharpe, *Personal Rule*, pp. 351ff; T. Barnes, *Somerset, 1625–40 (Cambridge Mass.*, 1961); 'County Politics and a Stuart Cause Célèbre: Somerset Church-ales, 1633', *TRHS*, 5th ser., IX, pp. 103–32; Collinson, *Birthpangs*, pp. 141ff.

15. Underdown, *Riot*, chapters 6, 9, 10, passim; C. Hill, 'The Cakes and Ale Revolution', *The Guardian*, 12 December 1985; J. Morrill, 'The Ecology of Allegiance', *JBS*, 26, 1987, reprinted in *The Nature of the English Revolution*, pp. 229–30; Underdown, *Fire from Heaven*, chapter 6, passim.

16. Manning, *The English People*; Hill, *Century of Revolution*, pp. 111–13; Underdown, 'Community and Class', loc. cit.; Underdown, in Eley and Hunt, *Reviving the English Revolution*, p. 376; J. J. Scarisbrick, *The Reformation and the English People* (Oxford, 1982); C. Haigh (ed.), *The English Reformation Revised* (Cambridge, 1987) chapter 1; *English Reformations: Religion, Politics and Society under the Tudors* (Oxford, 1993); K. Thomas, *Religion*, passim.

17. Underdown, 'What was the English Revolution?', *History Today*, March 1984, pp. 22ff.

18. For Banbury, see Collinson, *Birthpangs*, pp. 137–9, 141.

19. Stone, 'The Century', p. 40; Underdown, *Riot*, pp. 67–9, 75–7, 94, 106, 111.
20. Underdown, *Fire from Heaven*, p. x; Hill, 'The Cakes and Ale Revolution', loc. cit.
21. For a critique, see Morrill, *The Ecology of Allegiance*, esp. Parts IV, V. *JBS* 26, 1987, pp. 458–67; D. Underdown, 'A Reply', ibid., pp. 469–70, quoting especially regional contrasts noted by J. Thirsk, 'Seventeenth Century Agriculture and Social Change' in Thirsk (ed.), *Land, Church and People* (Reading, 1970).
22. Collinson makes this point in *Birthpangs*, pp. 149, 153; P. Clark, *The English Alehouse: A Social History* (1983); Wrightson and Levine, *Poverty and Piety*; Hunt, *The Puritan Moment*. For attempts to banish the stereotype, see esp. C. Hill, *Society and Puritanism*, chapter 1, conclusion.
23. D. H. Fischer, *Albion's Seed: Four British Folkways in America* (New York, 1989); D. Boorstin, *The Americans: The Colonial Experience*; P. Miller, *The New England Mind; Orthodoxy in Massachusetts; Jonathan Edwards* (*Cambridge Mass.*, 1949); *Errand into the Wilderness* (*Cambridge Mass.*, 1956); S. Bercovitch, *The Puritan Origins of the American Self* (1975); *Rites of Assent: Transformations in the Symbolic Construction of America* (1993); D. Cressy, *Coming Over*, introduction (which notes and explains the absence of a mid-Atlantic idiom).
24. For a characteristic statement, C. Belsey, *The Subject of Tragedy: Identity and Difference in Renaissance Drama* (1985), introduction.
25. Noted by J. S. A. Adamson, 'Protesters at the Establishment', *TLS*, 7 June 1991.
26. See above, Chapter 4
27. Williams, *Politics and Letters*, p. 154; *Marxism and Literature* (Oxford, 1977), p. 16; 'Culture and Revolution' in T. Eagleton and B. Wicker, *From Culture to Revolution* (1968), pp. 27–8; *Keywords* (1976), pp. 80ff.
28. The following section on Williams is largely based on Milner, 'Cultural Materialism' in T. Eagleton (ed.), *Raymond Williams: Critical Perspectives* (Cambridge, 1989); C. Lin, *The British New Left, 1957–77* (Cambridge PhD, 1989) Part III; Lin Chun, op. cit., pp. 147–52; N. Tredell, 'Uncancelled Challenge: The Work of Raymond Williams', *PN Review*, 15:3, 15:5, 16:1, 16:3, 1989; I. Birchall, 'Raymond Williams, Centrist Tragedy?', *IS*, 2:39, 1988, pp. 139–62.
29. R. Williams, *The Country*, pp. 44–5, 348 ('we have to be able to explain, in related terms, both the persistence and the historicity of concepts'); *Politics and Letters*, pp. 324ff; *Long Revolution*, p. 68.
30. E. P. Thompson, 'A Nice Place to Visit', *NYRB*, 6 February 1975; Williams, *The Country*, p. 304.
31. R. Williams, *Politics and Letters*, pp. 421ff; Milner, op. cit., p. 51.
32. Ibid., p. 50
33. Milner, op. cit., pp. 48–9.
34. See above Chapters 6, 7; Gramsci, *Prison Notebooks*, pp. 258ff; S. Hall, 'Introduction' to R. Simon, *Gramsci's Political Thought* (1991), p. 8.
35. *Marxism and Literature* (Oxford, 1977), pp. 108–20.

36. Ibid., pp. 121–7.
37. For this and the following, see esp. S. Hall, *The Hard Road to Renewal: Thatcherism and the Crisis of the Left* (1988); S. Hall and M. Jacques (eds), *The Politics of Thatcherism* (1983); 'The Toad in the Garden; Thatcherism among the Theorists' in C. Nelson and L. Grossberg (eds), *Marxism and the Inter-relation of Culture* (1988). For Mr Callaghan, 'Gramsci and Us'; cf 'The Great Moving Right Show' in *The Hard Road*, pp. 40, 166.
38. Ibid., pp. 7–9, 45–51, 164ff.
39. 'Gramsci and Us', ibid., pp. 161–72, cf pp. 138ff.
40. Milner, op. cit., pp. 76–81; S. Hall, 'Cultural Studies and the Centre' in *Culture, Media, Language* (1980); 'Cultural Studies; Two Paradigms' in T. Bennett (ed.), *Culture, Ideology and Social Process: A Reader* (1981); 'Politics and Letters' in T. Eagleton, *Williams*, pp. 62–3; Eagleton, ibid., Introduction, 'Base and Superstructure in Raymond Williams'; T. Eagleton, *Marxism and Literary Criticism* (1976); *Criticism and Ideology* (1976).
41. Hall *et al.* (eds), *Policing the Crisis* (1978); *The Hard Road*, pp. 7–11, et passim.
42. 'The Uses of Cultural Theory', *NLR*, 158, July–August 1986, pp. 19–31 ; R. Williams, 'Class, Politics and Socialism', and 'Resources for a Journey of Hope', in *Towards 2000* (Harmondsworth, 1983), pp. 153–74, 244–68; *Resources of Hope* (1989), passim; Milner, op. cit., pp. 82– 3. The celebration of the miners strike in 1984–5 was a particularly marked feature of Williams's writing, see esp. *Loyalties* (1985); cf R. Samuel, 'Friends and Outsiders', *NS*, 11 January 1985; H. Benyon (ed.), *Digging Deeper; Issues in the Miners' Strike* (1985). It should, however, be noted that W was extremely vague about whether ecology, peace, feminism or Mr Scargill's class struggle would actually renew socialism.
43. Williams, *Marxism and Literature*, pp. 4–5; Anderson, *Considerations*, pp. 75ff; Milner, op cit., pp. 46–7.
44. Hill, in Morton conference (see below, 'The End of the Line'); Heinemann, 'How the Words', in Eley and Hunt, *Reviving the Revolution*, loc. cit.
45. Morrill, 'Christopher Hill's Revolution' in *The Nature of the English Revolution*, pp. 279–80; W. Lamont, *History*, 56, 1971, pp. 268– 9: 'his greatness as an historian may be related to his miserliness: he hates to waste material'; M. Roberts, 'A Nation of Prophets: England and Christopher Hill', *HWkJ*, 27, 1989, pp. 164–73.
46. Milner, op. cit., pp. 9–10, 46ff; Williams, *NLR*, 158, passim; *Problems in Materialism and Culture: Selected Essays* (1980); Hill, 'Total History', loc. cit.; *Collected Essays* 1, introduction; C. Brooks, *The Well Wrought Urn* (New York, 1947); 'A Note of the "Limits" of History and the "Limits" of Criticism', *Sewanee Review*, 61, 1953, pp. 129–35; E. M. W. Tillyard, *The Elizabethan World Picture*; Heinemann, 'How the Words', loc. cit., pp. 86–7.
47. Wilding, op. cit., pp. 2–3; Hill, 'The Pre-revolutionary Decades' in *Collected Essays 1*, pp. 3–31; Heinemann, loc. cit., p. 83.

48. Williams, *Politics and Letters*, pp. 176–7; *Marxism and Literature*, pp. 21ff, 165–7; *Keywords*, introduction; Asa Briggs, *Collected Essays: Words, Numbers, Places, People* (Urbana, 1985), pp. 3–54; P. Burke and R. Porter (eds), *The Social History of Language* (Cambridge, 1987): introduction by P. Burke.

49. Williams, *Keywords*, passim; F. Jameson, *The Prison House of Language* (Princeton, 1972); Bercovitch, *Rites of Assent*, p. 361. For E. P. Thompson's responsiveness to language, see Palmer, *Descent into Discourse*, pp. 67ff. For Hill's see below.

50. Hill, 'Total History', loc. cit.; *Collected Essays* 1, pp. 3–5; L. Martines, *Society and History in English Renaissance Verse* (Brighton, 1985); Sharpe, *Criticism and Compliment*, pp. ix–x; and S. Zwicker, *The Politics of Discourse: Literature and History in 17th Cenury England* (Los Angeles, 1987); J. Richards, 'Literary Criticism and the Historian: Towards Reconstructing Marvell's Meaning' in *Literature and History*, 7:1, 1981, pp. 28–9.

51. Hill, *Collected Essays* 1, passim; 'The Godly Community' (review of Collinson, *The Religion of Protestants*) loc. cit.; M. Heinemann, *Puritanism and Theatre*; M. Butler, *Theatre and Crisis*; D. Norbrook, *Poetry and Politics* (and many others).

52. For a few examples, J. Dollimore and A. Sinfield, *Political Shakespeare* (Manchester, 1985); J. Dollimore, *Radical Tragedy: Religion, Ideology and Power in the Drama of Shakespeare and his Contemporaries* (Brighton, 1984); A. Sinfield, *Literature in Protestant England* (1982); J. Holstun, *A Rational Millenium: Puritan Utopias in Seventeenth Century England and America* (New York, 1987); F. Barker, *The Tremulous Private Body: Essays on Subjection* (1984); C. Belsey, *Tragedy; John Milton: Language, Gender, Power* (Oxford, 1988); M. Nyquist and M. Ferguson, *Re-membering Milton* (New York, 1987).

53. E. Eisenstein, *The Printing Press as an Agent of Change* (Cambridge, 1979); for the ubiquity of the notion of 'print culture', S. Greenblatt, *Renaissance Self-Fashioning: From More to Shakespeare* (Chicago, 1980); B. Anderson, *Imagined Communities* (1983).

54. For a review of these trends, R. Levine, 'Bashing the Bourgeois Subject', *Textual Pratice*, 3/i, 1989, pp. 76–86; J. Goldberg, 'The Politics of Renaissance Literature: A Review Essay', *English Literary History*, 49, pp. 514–42; N. Tredall, 'The Politicization of English', *PN Review*, 10:5, 1984, pp. 12–14; C. Rawson, 'The Crisis and How not to Solve it', *TLS*, 10 December 1982; G. M. Spiegel, 'History, Historicism and the Social Logic of the Text in the Middle Ages', *Speculum*, 65, 1990, pp. 59–86; L. Patterson, 'On the Margin: Post-Modernism, Ironic History and Medieval Studies', ibid., pp. 87–106. For a defence, C. Belsey, 'Literature, History, Politics', *Literature and History*, 9, 1983; 'The Subject in Danger: A Reply to Richard Levin', *Textual Practice*, 3/i, pp. 87–91; *Critical Practice* (1980); P. Widdowson (ed.), *Rereading English* (1982); T. Moi, *Sexual/Textual Politics: Feminist Literary Theory* (1985).

55. Widdowson, op. cit., p. 13; Belsey, 'Re-reading the Great Tradi-

tion', ibid., pp. 121–35; A. Easthope, 'Poetry and the Politics of Reading', ibid., pp. 136–48.

56. L. Montrose, 'The Poetics and Politics of Drama', quoted in Wright, *Historicizing Texuality*, p. 24.

57. For characteristic appreciations of Hill, see J. Holstun, 'Ranting at the New Historicism', *English Literary Renaissance*, 19/ii, 1989, pp. 189–225; *Pamphlet Wars: prose in the English Revolution* (1992); Belsey, 'Towards Cultural History – in Theory and Practice', *Textual Practice*, 3/1, 1989, pp. 159–72; *Tragedy*, introduction; Milton, pp. 3–6. For some of these claims, K. Ruthven (ed.), *Beyond the Disciplines; The New Humanities* (Australian Academy of Humanities, 1992); S. Hall, 'The Emergence of Cultural Studies', *October*, 53, 1989–90, pp. 10–23; L. Grossberg (ed.), *Cultural Studies* (New York, 1991).

58. For the decline in Hill's reputation see Eley and Hunt, introduction (as many reviewers noted, the whole book adopted a somewhat embattled, apologetic tone); Roberts, 'A Nation of Prophets', loc. cit., notes that much of Hill's historical writing was not reviewed in the major historical journals in the mid 1980s.

59. For critiques of these dated positions, Hill, *Milton*, introduction; Wilding, *Dragon's Teeth*, pp. 1–6, 233ff; Heinemann, 'How the Words', pp. 87ff. For the sense of cyclical return, Goldberg, *The Politics*, pp. 514–15 (G was, in fact, referring to William Empson locking horns with Dame Helen Gardner).

60. L. C. Knights, *Drama and Society*; Leavis prospectus in *Education and the University: A Sketch for an English School* (1943; new edn, Cambridge, 1979);

61. B. Ford (ed.), *From Donne to Marvell* (Harmondsworth, 1956); Hill, review in *The Spectator*, 6 April 1956, pp. 454–5. For a retrospective critique of *Scrutiny's* position by one of its major lights, L. C. Knights, *Sewanee Review*, 89, 1981, pp. 560–85. For Anglo-Catholic apologetics, C. S. Lewis, *A Preface to Paradise Lost* (Oxford, 1942); D. Bush, *Paradise Lost in Our Time* (New York, 1945). For Eliot and Leavis after 1945, see S. Orgel and J. Goldberg, *Milton* (Oxford, 1991), pp. xxiii–iv; Eliot, Milton (II) in *Poetry and Poets* (1957).

62. Hill, *Milton*, passim; the point is more sharply formulated in his pilot essay, 'Milton the Radical', *TLS*, 29 November 1974, p. 1330; cf 'The Politics of John Milton', *The Listener*, 12 September 1963 (for a more 'modern and democratic' Milton); D. Wolfe, *Milton in the Puritan Revolution* (1941): Hill's book was dedicated to Don Wolfe.

63. Hill, *Milton*, Part II, chapters 6–8; 'God in the English Revolution', *HWkJ*, 17, 1984, pp. 19–31; Davis, *Fear, Myth and History*, pp. 7ff.

64. Hill, *Milton*, pp. 114–15.

65. Ibid., pp. 233ff; *TLS*, 29 November 1974, p. 1332.

66. Hill, *Milton*, pp. 111–13; cf *TLS*, pp. 1331–2.

67. Hill, *Milton*, pp. 463ff.

68. Ibid., pp. 354, 165ff., 205–12; *TLS*, p. 1332; *Experience of Defeat*, pp. 307ff.

69. Hill, *Milton*, p. 354; T. L. S. ibid; W. Empson, *Milton's God* (1961).
70. Hill, *Milton*, pp. 367ff, cf M. Radzinowicz, 'Samson Agonistes and Milton', PQ, 44, 1965; C. Ricks, *Milton's Grand Style* (Oxford, 1963). Hill relied on Ricks's reading in response to the denigration of Leavis, etc.
71. Hill, *Milton*, p. 442.
72. Ibid., pp. 412–48; *Experience*, pp. 310ff; B. Lewalski, *Milton's Brief Epic: The Genre, Meaning and Art of 'Paradise Regained'* (Providence, 1966).
73. *TLS*, 29 November 1974, p. 1332.
74. For a critique, A. Milner, *John Milton and the English Revolution* (1981), pp. 202–3.
75. Hill, *Milton*, esp. pp. 371ff; Z. S. Fink, 'The Political Implications of Paradise Lost', *JEGP*, 40, 1941; 'most creative', P. Collinson, *TLS*, 9 April 1993; Q. Skinner, 'Milton, Satan, Subversion', *NYRB*, 23 March 1978, p. 9.
76. For this criticism, see esp. B. Worden, 'Milton among the Radicals', *TLS*, 2 December 1977, p. 1394; Milner, op. cit., pp. 204–5; J. Broadbent, 'How Not to Write History?', *English*, Spring 1978, pp. 38–44; Heinemann's defence of Hill's method, loc. cit., p. 95 (to attack Hill for referring P.L. to the Civil War and Restoration was like denying that Wilfred Owen's poems were about The Great War, misstates the criticism: Owen's poems are *clearly* about his experiences on the Western Front, though they may also carry timeless and universal messages; Milton's are *ostensibly* about Genesis and not about the Civil War. My own parallel with Gibbon makes the point, I believe, correctly).
77. Hill, *Collected Essays* 1, 'Censorship and English Literature', pp. 32–71; see also, above, Chapter 6; J. Morrill, *The Nature of the English Revolution*, pp. 280ff.
78. *Collected Essays* 1, p. 50; Heinemann, *Puritanism and the Theatre*, pp. 38–9, 46ff; cf M. Butler, *Theatre*, pp. 26–35, 100–40, 181ff. The case remains 'not proven'.
79. A. Patterson, *Censorship and Interpretation: The Conditions of Writing and Reading in 17th Century England* (Madison, 1984); Hill, review, in *Literature and History*, 12, 1985, pp. 252–3; S. Lambert, 'The Printers and the Government 1604–40' in R. Myers and M. Harris, *Aspects of Printing since 1600* (Oxford, 1987); Blair Worden, 'Literature and Political Censorship in Early Modern England', in A. Duke and C. Tamse (eds), *Too Mighty to be Free: Censorship and the Press in Britain and the Netherlands* (1987).
80. Hill, 'Censorship', loc. cit., pp. 32–3; H-G. Gadamer, *Truth and Method* (New York, 1975), p. 488.
81. For his use of the works of the 1640s as a 'control', *Milton*, Part II; *TLS*, p. 1330; Wilding, 'Milton and the English Revolution' in Mukherjee and Ward, op. cit, pp. 38–46; *Dragon's Teeth*, pp. 233ff, 257–8. For 'Of Christian Doctrine', *Milton*, pp. 235ff.
82. Goldberg, 'Politics of Renaissance Literature', loc. cit., p. 523.

83. Worden, Skinner, reviews, loc. cit.; *Milton*, pp. 35ff (see p. 39 for the information about Digger emissaries in 1650).
84. Ibid., pp. 100ff, 130ff; J. Scott, 'Radicalism', loc. cit., p. 454; for Hill's reliance on, 'Irreligion', loc. cit. p. 206; Collinson on the 'strange paradox', *TLS*, 9 April 1993.
85. Skinner, Worden, loc. cit.; cf Z. S. Fink, *The Classical Republicans* (1962); for an account which does recognize these influences, H. R. Trevor-Roper, 'Milton in Politics', in *Catholics, Anglicans and Puritans* (1987), pp. 231–82. For an influential 'literary' reading, H. Gardner, *A Reading of 'Paradise Lost'* (Oxford, 1965).
86. *Milton*, introduction, p. 5.
87. Hill's reading was partly a riposte to the comfortable literary figure of W. R. Parker, *Milton, A Biography* (Oxford, 1968).
88. For the various Miltons, see Rickword, *Milton* (1940); *Our Times*, 1943, 1944, loc. cit.; Hill, 'Independent Foreign Policy', 1948, loc. cit.; Hilton, 'The Idea of Liberty', 1949, loc. cit.; Thompson, 'Winter Wheat in Omsk', *WN*, 3/26, 30 June 1956 (the article which announced T's break with the party); Milner, op. cit., pp. 208–9, for the 1970s New Left 'hippie'.
89. 'Danel Defoe and Robinson Crusoe', 'John Milton and Andrew Marvell', 'George Wither and John Milton', 'Francis Quarles and Edward Benlowes', all in *Collected Essays 1*; *Experience*, passim, for other contemporaries; 'Political Discourse in Early Seventeenth-Century England', in *A Nation of Change*, pp. 23–55.
90. 'John Bunyan and his Public', *History Today*, October 1988; English edn (Oxford, 1988), American edn (New York, 1989).
91. Hill, 'A Turbulent . . . People', pp. 16ff, 68ff, 213ff, 254ff, 348–57; 'Bunyan and his Public', pp. 15–16; J. Turner, 'Bunyan's Sense of Place' in V. Newey (ed.), *The Pilgrim's Progress* (Liverpool, 1980); W. Y. Tindall, *John Bunyan, Mechanick Preacher* (New York, 1934).
92. Hill, 'A Turbulent . . . People', pp. 45–60, 90–100, 311–12, 322, 334.; 'Milton and Bunyan: Dialogue with the Radicals', *WTUD*, pp. 395–414; R. Adams, 'Tolstoy in Embryo', *NYRB*, 2 March 1989, p. 2; T. Shipley, *London Review of Books*, 2 February 1989, p. 8.
93. For this reading see Davis, 'Puritanism and Revolution: Themes, Categories', loc. cit., pp. 696–7; Blair Worden's *London Review of Books*, 23 January 1986; W. Stachniewski, *The Persecutory Imagination: English Puritanism and the Literature of Religious Despair* (Oxford, 1991), introduction.
94. Hill, 'A Turbulent . . . People', pp. 4–15; 219, 223, 372–3.
95. *WTUD*, p. 386.
96. Hill, *Experience*, p. 328; Pocock, 'No Room for the Righteous', loc. cit.; M. Ignatieff, 'Strangers and Comrades', *NS*, 14 December 1984; *The Needs of Strangers* (1984), pp. 141ff; for the lack of 'staying power', Tariq Ali, *Street Fighting Days* (1983), pp. 197–203.
97. For Marvell, see C. Condren and A. D. Cousins, *The Political Identity of Andrew Marvell* (Aldershot, 1990), introduction (on Hill's necessary but premature rescue of writers like Marvell from the

Leavisites), pp. 2–8; J. M. Wallace, *Destiny his Choice; The Loyalism of Andrew Marvell* (Cambridge, 1968); A. Patterson, *Marvell and the Civil Crown* (Princeton, 1978); R. Hodge, *Foreshortened Time: A.M. and 17th Century Revolutions* (Cambridge 1978); R. Brett (ed.), *A.M: Essays on the Ter-centenary of his Death* (Oxford, 1979); Blair Worden, 'Andrew Marvell, Oliver Cromwell and the Horatian Oath' in Sharpe and Zwicker, *Politics of Discourse*. For a qualified protest against the 'inconclusive' Marvell, W. Lamont, 'The Religion of Andrew Marvell: Locating the "Bloody Horse"'' in Condren and Cousins, op. cit., pp. 135–48.

98. J. D. Alsop, 'Gerrard Winstanley: Religion and Respectability', *HJ*, 28/3, 1985, pp. 705–12; 'G.W's Later Life, *P&P*, 82, 1979, pp. 73–81; J. C. Davis, Winstanley, loc. cit.; Radical Biographies', *Political Science*, 37, 1985; 'Religion and the Struggle for Freedom in the English Revolution', *HJ*, 35/3, 1992, pp. 507–30; Pocock, *Virtue, Commerce and History*, p. 30; review of Hill, 'Winstanley', *Political Theory*, 13/3, 1985, pp. 461–5. For a secular radical view, close to Hill's, T. Wilson Hayes, *W, the Digger, a Literary Analysis of Radical Ideas in the English Revolution* (Cambridge Mass., 1979). For views which accept W's inconsistency, but do not attempt to write off his ideas as personal resentment, or his later conformity as victimization, G. E. Aylmer, 'The Religion of G.W.', in McGregor and Reay, *Radical Religion*; G. M. Shulman, *Radicalism and Reverence: The Political Thought of G.W.* (Berkeley, 1989).

99. Pocock, *The Political Works*; 'James Harrington and the Good Old Cause', *JBS*, 10, 1970; *The Machiavellian Moment* (Princeton, 1975), pp. 383–405.

100. R. Ashcraft, *Revolutionary Politics; Locke's Two Treatises of Government* (1987); and J. G. A. Pocock (eds), *John Locke* (Los Angles, 1980). For a recent review of the state of Locke studies in the light of Ashcraft's work, see *Political Studies*, XI, 1992, pp. 79–115 (D. Wootton and R. Ashcraft); 'The Radical Dimension of Locke's Political Thought: A Dialogic Essay', *History of Political Thought*, XIII/4, 1992, pp. 703–72 (cf Ellen M. Wood, 'Locke against Democracy: Consent, Representation and Suffrage', ibid., pp. 657–89, and N. Wood, *John Locke and Agrarian Capitalism* (Berkeley, 1984), reinstating the 'bourgeois' Locke); R. Ashcraft and M. Goldsmith, 'Locke, Revolution Principles and the Formation of Whig Ideology', *HJ*, 26, 1983, pp. 773–800. For a summary of views, R. Ashcraft (ed.), *John Locke: Critical Assessments*, 4 vols (1991). The debate continues.

101. For the Cambridge background, M. Richter, 'Reconstituting the History of Political languages: Pocock, Skinner and the Geschichliche Grundbegriffe', *History and Theory*, 29, 1990, pp. 38–70; *Political Theory and Political Education* (Princeton, 1980), pp. 6–15; Pocock, *The Ancient Constitution and the Feudal Law: A Reissue with a Retrospect* (Cambridge, 1987), pp. 3ff.

102. P. Laslett, *Philosophy, Politics and Society* (Oxford, 1956), introduction, p. vii; cf P. Laslett and G. Runciman, *2nd series* (Oxford, 1964)

including I. Berlin's celebrated, 'Does Political Philosophy Still Exist'; *subsequent series*, 1967, 1972, 1979; P. Laslett, *Filmer*; *Locke's Two Treatises*. Laslett might also be noted as one of the earliest exponents of 'the provincial model', the importance of county consciousness and local contexts in the study of political theory: 'The Gentry of Kent in 1640', *Cambridge Historical Journal*, 9, 1948, pp. 148–64; 'Sir Robert Filmer: The Man versus the Whig Myth', *William and Mary Quarterly*, 3 ser., 5, 1948, pp. 523–52.

103. For Laslett's anti-Marxism see above Chapter 4; for his sociological predisposition, see introductions to *Philosophy, Politics and Society*; also, *The Listener*, 17 March 1955; for subsequent work on the history of the family, *Family Life and Illicit Love in earlier generations* (Cambridge, 1977); *Household and Family in Past Time* (Cambridge, 1972) etc.

104. For Skinner, I have relied on J. Tully (ed.), *Meaning and Context: Quentin Skinner and his Critics* (Cambridge, 1988); see also, amongst the many reviews of S's work, L. Mulligan, J. Richards and J. Graham, 'Intentions and Conventions: A Critique of Quentin Skinner's Method for the Study of the History of Ideas', *Political Studies*, XXVII, 1, 1979, pp. 84–98; C. Tarlon, 'Historicity, Meaning and Revisionism in the Study of Political Thought', *History and Theory*, 12, 1973, pp. 307–28; B. Parekh and R. Berki, 'The History of Political Ideas: A Critique of Q. Skinners Methodology', *JHI*, 1973, pp. 168–84; J. Wiener and G. Schochet, 'Political Thought and Political Action: A Symposium on Q. Skinner', *Political Theory*, 2, 1974, pp. 251–76.

105. Pocock, *Politics, Language and Time* (1972); *Machiavellian Moment*, Part 1 et passim; 'The Machiavellian Moment revisited', *JMH*, 53, 1981, pp. 49–72, with a review of much of the secondary literature; 'Political Ideas as Historical Events: Political Philosophers as Historical Actors' in M. Richter (ed.), *Political theory and Political Education*; J.H. Hexter, 'Republic, Virtue, Liberty and the Political Universe of J.G.A Pocock', *On Historians*, pp. 255–303.

106. Pocock, *Ancient Constitution . . . a Reissue*, introduction; *Machiavellian Moment*, pp. 333–60; 'Transformations in British Political Thought', *Political Science*, 40/1, 1988, pp. 160ff; 'England' in Ranum (ed.), op. cit.; G. Burgess, 'Common Law and Political Theory in Early Stuart England', ibid., pp. 4–17; *The Politics of the Ancient Constitution; An Introduction to English Political Thought, 1603–1642* (1992), passim (see esp chapter 4), which supersedes previous accounts; M. Judson, *Crisis of the Constitution*; W. H. Greenleaf, *Order, Empiricism and Politics: Two Traditions of English Political Thought, 1500–1700* (Oxford, 1964). For a 'conflict' rather than a 'consensus' model, see J. P. Somerville, *Politics and Ideology*. The 'ascending and descending' idioms were coined by Walter Ullmann.

107. This summarizes *The Machiavellian Moment*, pp. 401–22; *Wealth, Commerce and History*, pp. 55–68, 106–9, 221–36.

108. Laslett, *Filmer*; Schochet, *Patriarchalism*; Greenleaf, *Order, Empiricism*; J. Daly, *Sir Robert Filmer and English Political Thought* (Toronto, 1979).

109.   Pocock started his Ancient Constitution as a continuation of the
       argument of Herbert Butterfield in *The Englishman and his History*
       (he was Butterfield's most gifted student in the early 1950s); for
       Pocock's 'Burke', see his essays in *Politics, Language and Time* and
       in *Virtue, Commerce and History* (cf C. B. Macpherson, *Burke* (Ox-
       ford, 1980) – which treats Burke as a 'bourgeois political economist').
110.   Pocock, 'Languages and their Implications' in *Politics, Language
       and Time*, pp. 3–41; *Virtue, Commerce and History*, 'Introduction:
       The State of the Art', esp. pp. 7–32; 'The Reconstruction of Dis-
       course: Towards a Historiography of Political Thought', *Modern
       Language Notes*, 96, 1982, pp. 959–80.
111.   Skinner, 'History and Ideology in the English Revolution', *HJ*, 8,
       1965, pp. 151–78; Aylmer, *Quest for a Settlement*; Pocock, *Virtue,
       Commerce and History*, pp. 54–8 (quotation p. 55).
112.   See the extensive literature on the settlement published in or about
       1988.
113.   This is especially clear in Skinner, *The Foundations of Modern Pol-
       itical Thought* (Cambridge, 1978); but see also *The Machiavellian
       Moment*.
114.   Pocock, 'On the Non-Revolutionary Character of Paradigms' in
       Politics, Language and Time, p. 273.
115.   Pocock, *Virtue, Commerce and History*, pp. 69ff, 233ff; *Machiavellian
       Moment*, pp. 423–61; 'Machiavellian Moment Revisited', loc. cit.,
       pp. 61–2, 66–7.
116.   J. C. Davis, 'Radicalism in a Traditional Society: The Evaluation
       of Radical Thought in the English Commonwealth, 1649–60', *His-
       tory of Political Thought*, 3/2, 1982, pp. 193–213; Pocock, *Virtue,
       Commerce and History*, pp. 30, 62; Clark, *Revolution and Rebellion*,
       pp. 98ff.; cf R. Zaller, 'The Continuity of British Radicalism', loc.
       cit., and other literature discussed by Clark.
117.   For Macpherson, see above Chapters 5, 6; Pocock, 'Authority and
       Property: The Question of Liberal Origins', 'The Mobility of Prop-
       erty and the Rise of 18th Century Sociology', both in *Virtue, Com-
       merce and History*, pp. 51–72, 103–24; 'To Market, to Market:
       Economic Thought in Early Modern England', *Journal of Inter-
       disciplinary History*, 10/2, 1979; 'Early Modern Capitalism: The
       Augustan perception' in E. Kamenka and R. S. Neale (eds), *Feu-
       dalism, Capitalism and Beyond* (Canberra, 1975); 'The Myth of John
       Locke and the Obsession with Liberalism', in Pocock and Ashcraft,
       John Locke.
118.   Pocock, 'Cambridge Paradigms and Scotch Philosophers' in I. Hont
       and M. Ignatieff, *Wealth and Virtue: The Shaping of Political Econ-
       omy in the Scottish Enlightenment* (Cambridge, 1983); D. Forbes,
       Hume's Philosophical Politics; D. Winch, *Adam Smith's Politics: An
       Essay in Historiographic Revision* (Cambridge, 1978); D. Miller, 'Hume
       and Possessive Individualism', *History of Political Thought*, 1/2,
       1980, pp. 261–78. For the older liberal scenario, A. Arblaster, *The
       Rise and Decline of Western Liberalism* (Oxford, 1984); S. Lukes,
       Individualism (Oxford, 1973).

119. Pocock, *Politics, Language and Time*, pp. 3–5, 273–6.
120. This description is based on Tully, *Meaning and Context*, introduction, esp. pp. 22–5; J. Dunn, 'The Cage of Politics', *The Listener*, 15 March 1979, pp. 389–90; see the critiques of Skinner collected in *Meaning and Context* and those listed above.
121. Hill, 'Politics of Discourse', loc. cit.; K. Thomas, 'Politics as Language', *NYRB*, 13 March 1986.
122. The term was coined by Fredick Crews, *NYRB*, 29 May 1986.
123. Foucault, *Discipline and Punish*, introduction; R. Samuel, 'Reading the Signs', *HWKJ*, 32, 1991, pp. 88–109, at p. 93; R. Barthes, 'The Discourse of History', in *Comparative Criticism*, III (Cambridge, 1981); P. Ricoeur, 'The Reality of the Past', in *Time and Narrative*, vol. 3 (Chicago, 1985), pp. 142–55; A. Kemp, *The Estrangement of the Past* (Oxford, 1991). For the 'Reality Rule' of most historians, J. H. Hexter, 'The Rhetoric of History', *History and Theory*, 6, 1967, pp. 3–13. Cf Foucault in *Time* Magazine, 16 November 1981: 'Among the reasons it is truly difficult to have a dialogue with Americans and English is that for them the critical question for the philosopher is, 'is it true?', whereas the French–German tradition consists basically of posing the question, 'why do we think as we do? what effect does it have?'. See M. Foucault, *Power/ Knowledge: Selected Interviews* (ed. C. Gordon) (Brighton, 1980).
124. For characteristic demonologies, B. Palmer, *Descent into Discourse*; P. Anderson, *In the Tracks*; L. Stone, 'History and PostModernism', *P&P*, 131, 1991.
125. H. Veeser (ed.), *The New Historicism* (1989); S. Greenblatt, *Renaissance Self-Fashioning; The Power of Forms in the English Renaissance* (Oklahoma, 1982); *Shakespearean Negotiations: Circulation of Social Energy in Renaissance England* (Oxford, 1988); J. Goldberg, *James I and the Politics of Literature* (Baltimore, 1983); for a critique, A. Liu, 'The Power of Formalism: The New Historicism', *English Literary History*, 56/4, 1989; Iain Wright, 'Historicizing Textuality or textualizing History?', *ANU Occasional paper* 1993. I follow A. Liu, loc. cit., passim; and Iain Wright, pp. 18ff.
126. See Joan Scott's critique of Thompson in Scott, op. cit., pp. 68–90; Jane Lewis, 'The Debate on Sex and Class', *NLR*, 149, 1985; D. Riley, *Feminism and the Category of Women in History* (New York, 1988); Joan Kelly-Gadol, 'The Social Implications of the Sexes', *Signs: Journal of Women in Culture and Society*, 4, 1976, pp. 809–23; Lin Chun, op. cit., pp. 167ff, 'Women: The longest revolution'. On Hobsbawm's 'macho' male history, *IS*, 2: 21, pp. 97–8. Hill's sympathy for seventeenth-century women did not really go beyond enthusiasm for such classics as Alice Clark, *Working Life of Women in the Seventeenth Century* (1919, 1992). Cf S. Amussen, op. cit.; P. Crawford, *Women and Religion in England, 1500–1720* (1993).
127. G. Stedman Jones's, *Languages of Class: Studies in English Working Class History, 1832–1982* (Cambridge, 1983) occasioned a wave of Marxist criticism: see *Descent into Discourse*, pp. 120–1, 141–4 and references on pp. 252, 256, 259.

128. *Descent into Discourse*, pp. 87ff. For some examples, F. Furet, *Interpreting the French Revolution*; L. Hunt, *Politics, Culture and Class in the French Revolution* (1986); M. Ozouf, *Festivals and the French Revolution* (Cambridge, Mass., 1988); S. Schama, *Citizens: A Chronicle of the French Revolution* (Cambridge Mass., 1989) see esp. introduction (for the designation of the 'bourgeoisie' as histographical 'zombies'); F. Furet and M. Ozouf (eds), *A Critical Dictionary of the French Revolution* (Cambridge, Mass., 1989); K. Baker (ed.), *The French Revolution and the Creation of Modern Political Culture* (New York, 1987–9).
129. I am summarizing my 'Myth of the French Revolution Revisited', in D. Garrioch (ed.), *A Hundred Years of the French Revolution* (Melbourne, 1990); also Mukherjee and Ward, op. cit., pp. 47–61; Furet, *Interpreting the French Revolution*, pp. 50–61. For the rationality of the Enlightenment and its inscription on the Revolution, J. Starobinski, *The Invention of Liberty* (Geneva, 1964); K. Barth, *From Rousseau to Ritschl* (1958), pp. 11–57; J. Derrida, *Of Grammatology* (Baltimore, 1976), pp. 297ff; and, most recently and fully, S. Khulnani, op. cit., chapter 6: 'The Revolution is Over: François Furet and the Historians' Challenge'.
130. Hill, 'A Biblical Culture' in *The English Bible*, pp. 1–44; comment on BBC Radio 4, 29 March 1993.
131. Hill, *The English Bible*, pp. 436–8.
132. Samuel, 'Reading the Signs', loc. cit., pp. 96, 106–7; N. Frye, *The Great Code: The Bible and Literature* (1981); E.J. Hobsbawm and T. Ranger, *The Invention of Tradition* (Cambridge, 1983). For similarities with the work of cultural anthropologists, see C. Geertz, *The Interpretation of Culture* (New York, 1975); *Local Knowledge: Further Essays in Interpretative Anthropology* (New York, 1983); R. Darnton, *The Great Cat Massacre* (Harmondsworth, 1988).
133. Hill, *The English Bible*, pp. 109–53, 324–31 (quotation at p. 329); P. Crawford, 'Charles Stuart: That Man of Blood', *JBS*, 1977.
134. R. Samuel, 'Reading the Signs II: Fact-grubbers and Mind-readers', *HWkJ*, 33, 1992, pp. 228ff (Samuel attributes these traits to Marxists in general; they are, I think, particularly appropropriate to Hill); A. Kemp, *The Estrangement of the Past* (Oxford, 1990), p. vii, (for the formulation of a 'void' filled by 'webs of narration').
135. For these distinctions, Hill, *The English Bible*, pp. 34–5, 39, chapter 8 and passim; B. Manning, 'God, Hill and Marx', *IS*, 59, 1993, pp. 86, 88–9.
136. Hill, *The English Bible*, pp. 31, 196–7, 397ff, 428; 'The Mystery . . .', Hill's comment on BBC programme cited above; Collinson, review, *TLS*, 9 April 1993.
137. B. A. Cummins, 'Words at War', *NS*, 26 February 1993, found the 'diaspora' (a commonplace of biblical scholarship for 150 years) a revelation, but failed to ask whether the revelation was available to seventeenth-century readers; cf Collinson, loc. cit. Curiously, therefore, a hermeneutics of reading appeared to add support to the privileging of discourse over agency.

138. Hill, *English Bible*, pp. 428, 432.
139. Ibid., p. 442.

Conclusion: The End of the Line?

1. Milner, *Milton*, pp. 50–9, 94ff, 138ff, 200–1, 208–9; J. Rees, 'Revolution Denied', *Socialist Worker Review*, 103, November 1987, pp. 20–4.
2. Milner drew on L. Goldmann, *The Hidden God*, trans. P. Thody (1964); *Towards a Sociology of the Novel*, trans. A Sheridan (1975); Milner, *Cultural Materialism*, pp. 52–3.
3. B. Manning, *1649: The Crisis of the English Revolution* (1992), pp. 14–17, 64–70 (quotation at pp. 68–9); N. Carlin, 'A New English Revolution', *IS*, 58, 1993 pp. 125–7; Manning, *God, Hill and Marx*, pp. 81, 85, 91.
4. Manning, *1649*, pp. 59–60, 69–71, 78, chapter 3 passim, 136ff, 153ff; Hill, 'Milton Again', *Literature and History*, 7, 1981, pp. 230–2, for a critique of Milner's *Independency*.
5. N. Carlin, 'Marxism and the English Civil War', *IS*, 2:10, 1980–1 pp. 106–27, esp. at pp. 107–9, 124–6; *The First English Revolution* (1981); B. Manning, 'Class and the English Revolution', IS, 2:38, 1988, pp. 41–52; A. Callinicos, 'Bourgeois Revolutions and Historical Materialism', *IS*, 2:43, 1989, pp. 136ff; Rees, 'Revolution Denied', loc. cit., p. 24.
6. E. M. Woods, *The Pristine Culture of Capitalism* (1991), pp. 3ff, 95ff, 161–77. Hill, rightly, hailed this book as one of the most original and clear-headed applications of grand theory to English history in decades.
7. Ibid., pp. 39–41, 59–62, 75ff, 87–90, 173–6.
8. Ibid., pp. 126, 160; Corrigan and Sayer, *Great Arch*, pp. 72ff. The epithet 'organic' runs through Wood's account.
9. For Brenner's work, see above Chapters 1, 5; T. Aston and C. H. Philpin (eds), *The Brenner Debate* (Cambridge, 1985); *Merchants and Revolution: Commercial Change, Political Conflict and London's Overseas Traders, 1550–1653* (Princeton, 1993), pp. 638ff (which gives an up-to-date synoptic account of his position); Goldstone, op. cit., p. 68ff; P. Anderson, 'Maurice Thomson's War', *London Review of Books*, 4 November 1993, pp. 15–17; Review Symposium by Ian Gentiles, John Morrill and Alex Callinicos in *N.L.R..*, 207, September/October 1994, pp. 103–33.
10. Summarizes, *Merchants and Revolution*, pp. 651–3, 661–6; Anderson, loc. cit.
11. C. Mooers, *The Making of Bourgeois Europe* (1991), pp. 33–7; Guy Bois, 'Against Neo-Malthusian Orthodoxy', in *The Brenner Debate*, pp. 107–18; Callinicos, 'Bourgeois Revolutions', loc. cit., pp. 130–3; Wood, op. cit., pp. 10–11.
12. *Merchants and Revolution*, pp. 681ff; Anderson, loc. cit., p. 16.
13. *Merchants and Revolution*, Part 2.
14. This is indicated by Brenner's uncertainty about terminal dates for his study: the connection of 1653, 1689 and the British Empire was,

of course, also formulated by Hill. Cf K. Andrews, *Trade, Plunder and Settlement* (Cambridge, 1984), pp. 338–9, 356 ff. Andrews – a one-time member of the Historians' Group who 'ceased to subscribe to any sort of Marxism nearly 20 years ago' – was much more circumspect about the Commonwealth achievement than was Brenner.

15. I summarize, I. Wallerstein, *The Modern World System I: Capitalist Agriculture and the Origins of the European World Economy, in the 16th Century* (New York, 1974); *II: Mercantilism and the Consolidation of the European World-Economy, 1600–1750* (New York, 1980); *Historical Capitalism* (1983). For a critique, T. Skocpol, 'Wallerstein's World Capitalist System', *American Journal of Sociology*, 82, 1977, pp. 1075–90; C. Ragin and D. Chirot, 'The World System of I. Wallerstein' in Skocpol (ed.), *Vision and Method*, pp. 276–312 (with a note of other reviews); J. A. Goldstone, *Revolution and Rebellion in the Early Modern World* (Berkeley, 1991), pp. 68ff; C. Mooers, op. cit., pp. 7ff.

16. C. Tilly, *European Revolutions, 1492–1992* (Oxford, 1993): a taxonomy which treats the events of 1642–7 and of 1608 (Sir Cahir O'Doherty's Revolt in Ireland) as comparable 'Revolutionary situations', and then collapses revolutions and external wars (including such blockbusters as the English war with Tripoli, 1675–6), has little explanatory force. Cf for a strict definition of Social Revolution, which specifically excludes the English experience, T. Skocpol, *States and Social Revolution* (Cambridge, 1979).

17. Goldstone, op. cit.; Stone's review, 'Revolution over the Revolution', loc. cit.

18. G. R. Elton, *Return to Essentials* (Cambridge, 1991) – an acerbic attack on Hill and Stone; Stone review, 'Dry Heat, Cool Reason', *TLS*, 31 January 1992. For some examples of these epistemic adventures, M. Foucault, *Madness and Civilization* (1967); *The Order of Things* (1970); *The History of Sexuality, I.* (1978); S. Toulmin, *Cosmopolis: The Hidden Agenda of Modernity* (New York, 1990); M. Polanyi, *The Great Transformation* (New York, 1944, etc.); C. Merchant, *The Death of Nature: Women, Ecology and the Scientific Revolution* (1982); *Ecological Revolutions* (Chapel Hill, 1989); W. Barrett, *The Death of the Soul* (Oxford, 1986); Charles Taylor, *Sources of the Self: The Making of the Modern Identity* (Cambridge, 1989). K. Weintraub, *The Value of the Individual: Self and Circumstance in Autobiography* (Chicago, 1978) And many others!

19. Jameson, *Prison House of Language*, pp. 170ff; K. Thomas, *Religion and the Decline of Magic*; for a critique Ashplant and Wilson, 'Present Centred History, loc. cit.

20. There is a growing literature on the persistence of the theological idiom in English thought after 1660: T. Harris, P. Seaward and M. Goldie (eds), *The Politics of Religion in Restoration England* (Oxford, 1990); J. Spurr, 'Latitudinarianism and the Restoration Church', *HJ*, 31, 1988, pp. 61–82; Clark, *English Society*, chapters 2, 3.

21. Oakeshott, 'Contemporary British Politics', *Cambridge Journal*, May

1948, pp. 474ff; E. Gellner, *Plough, Sword and Book* (1988) on Marx's 'bourgeois fantasies, pp. 34–5; D. Winch, *Adam Smith's Politics*; S. Letwin, *The Anatomy of Thatcherism* (1992), pp. 50ff. For the persistence of *laisser-faire* demonology, see below, 'Fin de Partie?'

22. J. Clark, *English Society*, passim; for a critique, Woods, *Pristine Society*, pp. 117–43; Innes, *P&P*, 115, 1987, pp. 165–200; Clark's reply, ibid., 117, 1987, pp. 195–207. For Hill on Monarchy, see above Chapter 6; cf Nairn, *Enchanted Glass*; L. Colley, 'The Apotheosis of George III', *P&P*, 102, 1984; *Britons*, chapter 5; Clark, *Revolution*, pp. 68ff.

23. Hobsbawm, 'The Seventeenth Century in the Development of Capitalism', *SS*, xxiv, 1960, pp. 97–112, and his contributions to 'Crisis Debate', see above, chapter 5; H. Perkin, 'The Social Causes of the Industrial Revolution', in *The Structured Crowd: Essays in English Social History* (Brighton, 1981), pp. 28–46; *The Origins of Modern English Society* (1970). For Thompson's 'Old Corruption', see above Chapter 6, and my 'Marxist Historian and the Pathology of English History' (forthcoming).

24. A. Macfarlane, *The Origins of English Individualism* (Oxford, 1978); *The Culture of Capitalism* (Oxford, 1987), chapters 7, 8, Postscript.

25. For the critique of Marxist one-to-one causation, I am indebted to the late Eugene Kamenka, who used to make the point as follows: if water leaks through the roof onto an iron bedstead, producing rust, the cause of the rust is said to be water; if on the other hand, the bedstead is thrown into a swimming pool, it is the bedstead that is said to cause the rust – in other words, 'the field' is of crucial importance in the attribution of cause, and it is precisely the different 'fields' that Marxist accounts often ignore. Cf Butterfield, *Whig Interpretation*, passim; E. P. Thompson, *POT*, p. 257.

26. For the Morton conference, see *Lawrence and Wishart Files and Tapes*, kindly lent by Sally Davidson: esp. Hill and Hobsbawm, 'The Legacy of A. L. Morton'; Morton, *History and the Imagination*, Introduction, Appreciations ('A People's Historian', by C. Hill); CPA HG 60 D, Correspondence, Bill Moore–Sally Davidson, May–June 1988; *OH Journal*, January 1988 with details of Conference.

27. *House of Commons, Parliamentary Debates (Hansard)*, 6th series, vol. 136: Address, 7/7/88 on 'Revolutions of 1688/9 Tercentenary', pp. 1233–66 (the celebrations were agreed to 139–18 against); Lords Debates may be studied in HL *Parliamenary Debates, Hansard*, vol. 450, pp. 129–31; 472, p. 796; 476, pp. 678ff; 500, pp. 8–9.

28. For Hill's comments on not celebrating in 1988, see *The Independent*, 10 February 1988; see also his comment on tape ('it's all so boring') in 'The Legacy of A. L. Morton'; Morton's last (unfinished) work was on *1688: How Glorious was the Revolution* (OH Pamphlet 1988): the answer was, of course, not very; J. C. D. Clark, '1688 and All That', *Encounter*, January 1989, pp. 14ff; 'The Glorious Revolution debunked', *Sunday Telegraph*, 24 July 1988; *Sunday Times* 14 July 1988; D. Szechi, 'Mythistory versus History: The Fading of the Revolution of 1688', *HJ*, 33/1, 1990, pp. 143–53; S. Taylor, 'Plus ça Change . . .? New Perspectives on the Revolution of 1688', *HJ*,

37/2, 1994, pp. 457ff; Just how anodyne an affair the Bicentennial was may be judged from the official publication, *Parliament and the Glorious Revolution, 1688–1988* (HMSO, 1988). For the celebrations see L. Schwoerer, 'Celebrating the Glorious Revolution, 1689–1989', *Albion*, 20, 1990, pp. 1–19. Schwoerer's enthusiasm for the celebrations cannot disguise the fact that it was a rather low key affair, inhibited by some uncertainty about what precisely was being celebrated and in what year, dwarfed in 1988 – as in 1888 – by the Armada celebrations, and in 1989 by the French revolutionary juggernaut. For the differences in scholarly reactions, compare J. Israel (ed.), *The Anglo-Dutch Moment: Essays on the Glorious Revolution and its World Impact* (Cambridge, 1991); L. Schwoerer (ed.), *The Revolution of 1688–89: Changing Perspectives* (Cambridge, 1992); E. Cruickshanks (ed.), *By Force or Default? The Revolution of 1688–89* (Edinburgh, 1988). The first volume is a grand – if somewhat uneven – publication, defined by its title; the second focuses on the constitutional and ideological significance of the settlement which in the main it finds to be considerable: both are explicitly anti-revisionist. The third (revisionist) is a curious affair, designed, it would seem, to illustrate the insignificance – or wrong-headedness – of the event with many more references to Jacobitism and the Old Pretender than to the Declaration or the Bill of Rights. It was, however, the only one of the three to be published on – or before – time!

29.   R. Gildea, *The Past in French History*, pp. 13ff (with references to the extensive literature on the celebrations). I have written about them in 'The Myth of the French Revolution Revisited', in Mukherjee and Ward, op. cit., pp. 57ff; 'Visiting and Revisiting the Myth(s) of the French Revolution' in *Novo Historian*, 1/1, August 1990, pp. 32–4.

30.   A. Callinicos, *The Revenge of History: Marxism and the East European Revolutions* (Cambridge, 1991), pp. 10ff.

31.   These themes can be followed in *Marxism Today*, and especially in the articles of Eric Hobsbawm from 1981 onwards; *Politics for a Rational Left* (1988). For criticisms, N. Carlin and I. Birchall, 'Kinnock's Favourite Marxist: Eric Hobsbawm and the Working Class', *IS*, 2: 21, 1985; A. Callinicos, 'The Politics of Marxism Today', ibid., 2: 29, 1986; *Against Post-Modernism* (London 1990); D. Selbourne, *Against Socialist Illusion* (1986), esp. pp. 3–30.

32.   For much of the following argument, I am indebted to Baruch Knei-Paz, 'Can Historical Consequences Falsify Ideas: Karl Marx after the Collapse of the Soviet Union', *Eugene Kamenka Valedictory Conference*, ANU, Canberra, July 1993.

33.   F. Fukuyama, *The End of History and the Last Man* (New York, 1992), orginally published in synopsis in *The National Interest*, 16, 1989 pp. 3–18. The response of the Left (with the notable exception of Perry Anderson's thoughtful essay: 'The Ends of History' in *A Zone of Engagement*, pp. 279–376, was uniformly hostile and obscurantist).

34.   E. Hobsbawm, 'Goodbye to All That', *Marxism Today*, October 1990, reprinted in R. Blackburn (ed.), *After the Fall* (1991), pp. 115–25;

The Age of Empire (1987) pp. 327ff; *Age of Extremes: The Short Twentieth Century* (1994), pp. 5–11.

35. Burrow, *A Liberal Descent*, p. 300; John Gray, 'Among the Ruins of Marxism' in F. Mount (ed.), *Communism* (1992), reprints from the *TLS*, p. 432.

36. Hobsbawm, *Age of Extremes*, pp. 7–8, 142ff; Callinicos, *The Revenge of History*, p. 14.

37. E. P. Thompson, 'Making History', *Sanity*, March–April 1991, pp. 26–8; 'Ends and Histories' in M. Kaldor (ed.), *Europe from Below: An East–West Dialogue* (1990); 'The Ends of Cold War: A Rejoinder' in R. Blackburn, *After the Fall*, pp. 100–9. Thompson's earlier END pieces can be studied in *Exterminism and the Cold War* (1982); *Zero Option* (1982); *The Heavy Dancers* (1985). For an effective critique M. Howard, 'Two Controversial Pieces', in *The Causes of War* (Hounslow, 1983), pp. 116ff.

38. See above Chapter 7; R. Levin, 'Bashing the Bourgeois Subject', loc. cit., pp. 76–86; Reply from C. Belsey, ibid., pp. 87–90.

39. E. P. Thompson, *Customs in Common* (1991), esp. 'Introduction: Custom and Culture'; E. M. Wood, 'Custom Against Capitalism' *NLR*, pp. 21ff; C. Barker, 'In Praise of Custom', *IS*, 2: 55, 1992, pp. 139ff; P. Linebaugh, *The London Hanged: Crime and Civil Society in the 18th Century* (Harmondsworth, 1991); D. Selbourne, 'The Light that Failed, Again, *TLS*, 10 May 1991, pp. 7–8; S. Lukes, 'What is Left'?, ibid., 27 March 1992.

40. Hobsbawm, 'Goodbye', loc. cit., pp. 123–5; 'Out of the Ashes', *Marxism Today*, April 1991, pp. 18–22; 'The Crisis of Today's Ideologies', *NLR*, 192, 1992, pp. 55–64.

41. D. Selbourne, loc. cit.; for the travails of the *New Left Review*, see letters to *NS*, (from most of the editorial board, outlining reasons for their resignation) and from Blackburn putting the case for financial survival, 5, 12 March 1993.

42. Thompson, *Customs*, p. 17ff; E. M. Wood, *The Retreat from Class: A New 'True' Socialism*; B. Palmer, *The Descent into Discourse*, passim;

43. Hobsbawm, *Age of Empire*, p. 326.

44. A. Callinicos, *Making History* (Cambridge, 1987), chapter 5: 'Tradition and Revolution'; W. Benjamin, *Illuminations* (1970), pp. 259–60, 263.

45. E. P. Thompson, *Witness against the Beast: William Blake and the Moral Law* (Cambridge, 1993).

46. Benjamin, op. cit. p. 257.

47. Hobsbawm, *Echoes of the Marseillaise* (New Jersey, 1990), p. 112; for a critique of this dated piece of 'tribal' piety see N. Hampson, 'All for the Better?' *TLS*, 15 June 1990, p. 637; cf G. Rudé, *The French Revolution* (1989).

48. One is reminded of Raymond Aron's famous riposte to Sartre's encomium on the healing properties of violence, 'the revolutionary myth bridges the gap between moral intransigence and terrorism'. see Judt, *Marxism and the French Left*, pp. 178–9. Cf also Judt, *Past Imperfect*, p. 40, on Sartre's belief that revolutionary action 'is what sustains the authenticity of the individual'.

49. B. Knei-Paz, loc. cit., pp. 20–1; R. Jahanbegloo, *Conversations with Isaiah Berlin* (1992), pp. 126ff.
50. Callinicos, *Making History*, p. 227 ('to be a living tradition requires its constant renewal . . . Marxist social theory can only be tested through attempts to apply it').
51. BBC Channel 4 Series: '*Civil War*', esp. Programme 1: Crisis (The written text by T. Downing and M. Millman excludes most of this material).
52. H. Trevor-Roper, 'The Faustian Historian', *NS*, 6 August 1955, pp. 164; C. Hill, Correspondence, 'Marx as Historian', 1 October, pp. 397–8. The correspondence over Trevor-Roper's denigration of Marx was initiated by Eric Hobsbawm and went on for over two months.
53. On Marxism as a self-refuting theory, Knei-Paz, loc. cit.; John Gray, loc. cit., p. 219; F. E. Manuel, 'A Requiem for Karl Marx', *Daedalus* 21/2, 1992: 'The Exit from Communism', pp. 1–20.
54. For Hill's assertion that Marxism was quite unaffected by events in Eastern Europe, 'Premature Obsequies', *History Today*, April 1991, pp. 44–47; similar versions in M. Barratt Brown, 'Lessons from the Wreckage', July–August 1990; Cf G. Stedman-Jones, 'Marx after Marxism', *Marxism Today*, February 1990.
55. Mark Thomson, *A Paper House: The Ending of Yugoslavia* (1992), p. 119; B. Magas, *The Destruction of Yugoslavia: Tracking the Break-up, 1980–92* (1993).
56. 'Witness against the Beast', esp. pp. 106ff, 114ff, 222–9; 'The Blake Tradition', *Guardian*, 4 September 1993; P. Anderson, Diary, *London Review of Books*, 21 October 1993; M. Foot, 'Visions of Albion', *TLS*, 19 November 1993. On the importance of Witness, S. Felman and D. Laub, *Testimony: Crises of Witnessing in Literature, Psychoanalyses and History* (New York, 1992).
57. 'The Good Old Cause – an Interview with Christopher Hill', *IS*, 2: 56, 1992, p. 128.
58. Thus his work on ideology, science and the English Revolution during the 1950s and 60s can be traced back to a series of Group conferences in 1949, 1950 and 1954. Hobsbawm, H.G. p. 36; C.P.A. H.G. 60 A.
59. 'History Teaching in Charles University'; 'Workers in New Universities', *NCEO*, II/10, 14 May 1949, p. 113; ibid., III/8, 15 April 1950, pp. 81–2.
60. Ibid., p. 82; Hobsbawm, *Age of Extremes*, pp. 295–301.
61. 'History and Post-Modernism', *P&P*, 133, 1992, pp. 205–9, esp. at p. 208; Gabrielle Speigel, 'History, Historicism and the Social Logic of the Text', *Speculum*, lxv, 1990, pp. 59–86; G. Eley, 'Is All the World a Text: From Social History to the History of Society Two Decades Later' in T. McDonald, *The Historical Turn in the Human Sciences* (Michigan, 1993).
62. J. C. D. Clark, *Rebellion and Revolution*, passim; N. Cantor, 'The Real Crisis in the Humanities Today', *The New Criterion*, June 1985, pp. 28–38; ibid., December 1985, pp. 85–8; March 1986, pp. 84–8. A more considered verdict can be found in *TLS*, 5 April 1991, p. 15.

Stone, of course, as this narrative makes clear, was not and never had been a Marxist.

63. R. Kimball, *Tenured Radicals: How Politics has Corrupted our Higher Education* (New York, 1990), with extensive illustration; J. Diggins, *The Rise and Fall of the American Left* (New York, 1992); Robert Hughes, *The Culture of Complaint* (New York, 1993).

64. For the retreat of revisionism, see H. Wainwright, *Arguments for a New Left* (Oxford, 1993); Taylor, 'Plus ça Change', loc. cit., p. 457.

65. R. H. Tawney, quoted in Richardson, op. cit., p. 153.

66. Keith Thomas, 'Pandora's Protestants', *The Guardian*, 9 March 1993.

67. For Hexter's doubts about 'the reality rule', see his article on 'The Rhetoric of History', *History and Theory*, 6, 1967, pp. 1–12.

68. The distinction between 'document' and 'text' is drawn from M. Foucault, *The Archeology of Knowledge* (London 1972) introduction.

Index

Aaronovitch, Sam 81–2
absolutism 123
  Absolute Monarchy 20, 27
  absolutist states 18
  French 205–8
  Hill 59, 116–17, 126–7
  James II 202–3
  Kiernan 117–18
Act of Settlement 1662 198
action 190, 283
administration 145–6
agency 211, 213, 221, 316
agrarian capitalists 10, 162–3, 222
agrarian problem 37–40
alienation 185–6
Anderson, Perry 210
  culture 262
  disagreement with
    Thompson 2, 217–31 *passim*
  popular classes 140
Andrews, Ken 414
Anglican Church 93–4, 143, 202
Anglo-Catholicism 105
Annales 158
aristocracy
  baronial revolt 244
  bourgeoisie welded to 220
  capitalism, state and 301–3
  crisis of 157–61, 372
  monarchy, church and 10, 18–19
  nature of English 161–5
  rise of the gentry 124–7;
    Tawney 41–3
  split within 138
Arminians 189
Army High Command 299
Arnott, Page 63
artisans/small producers 139–40
Ashton, T. S. 144
Attlee, Clement 84, 90

'Back to the Future'
  conference 309–10
Bacon, Francis 106, 107, 132
Baconians 189
Baldwin, Stanley 48, 56–7
Ball, John 39, 91
Bank of England 204
Barnett, Corelli 229
baronial revolt 244
Barrington Moore, J. 224
Baxter, Richard 140
behavioural crisis 149–68
Belloc, Hilaire 30
Beloff, Max 30
Belsey, Catherine 270
Benjamin, Walter 317
Benn, Tony 289, 311
Bercovitch, Sacvan 260
Berens, L. H. 181
Bernal, J. D. 51, 100, 112, 115, 340
  The Challenge of Our Time 98, 99
  history of science 105
Bernstein, Edward 181
Betts, R. R. 131
Bevin, Ernest 90
Bible 24, 34, 72, 293–7
  biblical idiom 35, 293–4
Birchill, Ian 300
Blake, William 24, 183, 216, 275, 317, 320
body 185–6, 189–90
'bourgeois' historians 144–5
bourgeois ideology 12, 14, 151–4
bourgeois revolution 1, 227–8
  Hill 55–9, 119, 127–8;
    Kuczynski's critique 59–63;
    national independence 111
  Marx 9–10, 12, 14–16, 18–19
  models of 7–11, 15–16

bourgeoisie 126–8, 148–9
  Communist Manifesto 9–10, 12, 14
  French and English
    Revolutions compared 8–10,
    11–12, 20–5, 27, 30–1, 56–7,
    59, 140–1, 292–3, 309–12
  growth of 155–6, 222–4
  mass mobilization 141–2
  Tawney 43
  welded to aristocracy 220
Brailsford, H. N. 181
Braudel, F. 235
Brenner, Robert 302–5
Briggs, Asa 310
Brodie, James 25
Brooke, Cleanth 271
Brown, Norman 185, 186
Bryant, Arthur 28, 332
Burckhardt, J. 319
Bunyan, John 281–3
Burgh, James 24
Burke, Edmund 205, 307
Bush, George 312
Butterfield, Herbert 85, 308–9
  Christianity 96–7
  history of science 106, 107
  Marxist history 68
  Whiggism 30–1, 241, 246

Callinicos, Alex 300
Cambridge School 285
Campaign for Nuclear
    Disarmament 212
Cantor, Norman 323
capitalism 11–12, 327
  agrarian capitalists 10, 162–3,
    222
  Brenner 302–4
  Britain compared with
    France 22, 66
  development and
    revolution 165–6
  Dobb 44–6, 149
  evolutionary model 16–18
  Hill 136–7
  Hobsbawm 159–60, 315–16
  state, aristocracy and 301–3
  Thompson 315
  World Wars and 57

Carlin, Norah 300–1
Carpenter, Edward 34
Carlyle, Thomas 26
Carr, E. H. 77, 130
Cartwright, Thomas 24
categories 131–4
Catholicism 104–5
Caudwell, Christopher 72, 268,
    352
censorship 278
Central/Eastern Europe 312–15,
    318
Centre for Contemporary
    Cultural Studies 264
Challenge of Our Time series 98
Chamberlain, Neville 48, 56–7
Charles I, King 29, 244, 249–50
  Bible and execution of 295
  court 254–5
  ruling style 243
Charles II, King 57, 304, 384
  Restoration 197, 198, 257
Childe, Gordon 104
Christianity
  dissent 33–7
  Western civilization 95–7
  see also Bible; Church of
    England; religion
church: aristocracy, monarchy
    and 10, 18–19
Church of England 93–4, 143,
    202
  see also Anglo-Catholicism
Churchill, Winston S. 28–9, 332
civic humanism 287–8
Clarendon, Earl of 126, 140,
    247
Clark, J. C. D. 231, 248, 310,
    323, 326, 331
  society 307
class 54–5
  see also aristocracy; bourgeoisie;
    mercantile
  class; working class
Cobbett, William 317
Cohn, Norman 183, 184
Cold War 83, 84, 104, 107
  politics 87–101
Cole, G. D. H. 77, 170

Coleridge, S. T. 24
collective historical agency 316
Collinson, Patrick 237
Cominform 87–8, 110
commercial wealth 139–40,
   155–7, 304–5
Commonwealth and
   Protectorate 195–6
Communism, collapse of 312–15,
   318
Communist Manifesto, The 14
Communist Party 1, 78, 91, 112
   Commission on Inner-Party
      Democracy 171
   commitment to Soviet
      Union 48–55, 344
   crisis in 1950s 169–75, 180
   defection of scientists
      from 130
   Historians' Group *see*
      Historians' Group
   Kuczynski article 61–3
   membership 89–90
   National Cultural
      Committee 81–2, 89, 112
   1945 party Congress 79
   Political Committee 175
   and tradition 69–70, 128–9
   and World War II 65, 73–5,
      75–6
Communist Review 131
conservatism 217–21, 323–4
consumers' revolt 123–4
contingent causation 238–9
Coppe, Abiezer 200
Council of Officers 299
counter-cultural revolt 2, 179,
   183–93
court 257
   and country 254–5; division
      model 235
critical theory 268–70
Cromwell, Oliver 24, 200, 300–1,
   333
   Gardiner 26–7, 246
   Hill 194–6, 382
cultural hegemony 187–9, 262–3
cultural materialism 2, 261–70
cultural revolution 252–60

cultural witness 270–84
culture
   Cold War 92–5
   counter-cultural revolt 2, 179,
      183–93
   good society 213–14
   national 66–73
   'culture of containment' 221

Dalton, Hugh 83
damnation 187–9
Davidson, Morrison 36
Davidson, Sally 310
Davies, Godfrey 29, 332
Dawson, Christopher 95
defeat, experience of 200–9
Defoe, Daniel 126, 149, 155–7,
   281
Dell, Edmund 102, 353
Demant, Canon 98
democracy 150
demographic explosion 253
Derrida, Jacques 291, 293
Descartes, René 293
Deutscher, Isaac 192
dialectical materialism 1, 51–5
Diggers 37, 56, 181, 192
discourse analysis 284–97
dissent, religious 33–7
Dobb, Maurice 61, 79, 116, 118,
   119, 169, 337
   capitalism 44–6, 149
Dollimore, Jonathan 270
domestic/private sphere 252–4
Dorchester 256
Dunn, John 151, 285
Durkheim, Emile 234
Dutt, Rajani Palme 34, 62–4, 65,
   91, 343
   Communist Party crisis in the
      1950s 174
   Labour Monthly 60, 62
   Soviet Union 170

Eagleton, Terry 270
East India Company 304
Eastern/Central Europe 90,
   312–15, 318
economic crisis 140–1

economic transformation 205–6
Eddington, A. S. 99
educational revolution 255–6
Eikon Basiliske 197
Eliot, T. S. 73, 93–4, 269
Elizabeth I, Queen 60, 76
Elton, G. R. 144, 166, 306, 416
empiricism 217–21
Engels, Friedrich 35, 61
Enlightenment project 317–19, 320
experience, lived 270–84

Fagan, Hymie 66, 70
family 252–4
Farrington, Benjamin 104
Feiling, K. 30
feudalism 123
  debate in Communist
    Party 117–19
  Dobb 45–6
  Hill and 58–9, 117, 119
  Kuczynski 60, 61
  liberal ideology 14–15
  Marxist theory 17–18
'figures of descent' 210–31
Filmer, Sir Robert 252, 285
Fisher, H. A. L. 28, 68, 333
Fletcher, Anthony 240–1
folk-nationalism 38–9, 71
Foster, John 25–6
Foucault, Michel 185, 291, 411
Fox, Ralph 72
France 392
  absolutism 205–8
  Communist Party 74, 344
  see also French Revolution
French Revolution 142, 317
  bicentenary 312
  comparison with English
    Revolution 7–31; Marxist/
    Liberal genealogy 11–19;
    models of bourgeois
    revolution 7–11; triumph of
    gradualism 19–31
  linguistic analysis 292–3
Freud, Sigmund 187
Froude, J. 39
Fukuyama, F. 101, 314, 416

Furet, F. 22, 293, 312, 327

Gardiner, Samuel Ralston 113, 241
  Puritanism 26–7, 35
  revisionism and ghost of
    245–7
Garman, Douglas 61, 82, 87, 91, 129
Gellner, Ernest 366
Gemeinschaft/Gesellschaft 213
gender analysis 292, 411
gentry *see* aristocracy
Giddens, Anthony 7, 17
Glorious Revolution 23, 27, 198, 203–5, 415–6
  tercentenary 310–12, 416
God, Milton and 272–3, 274–5
  see also Christianity; Church of
    England; religion
Godwin, William 25
Goldstone, Jack 305
Gollan, John 174
Gollancz, Victor 95, 310
'Good Old Cause' 23, 198
good society 213–14
Goude, Jean-Paul 312
gradualism 84–5, 261
  comparison of French and
    English Revolutions 19–31
Gramsci, Antonio 187, 188, 262, 263–4
grand theory, persistence
  of 298–309
Grant, Betty 174, 175, 176
'great arches' 210–31
'great thaw' 169–70
Green, J. R. 38
Green, T. H. 27, 35
Greenblatt, S. 292
Guizot, F. 14, 19, 20, 21, 22
  monarchy, aristocracy and
    church 18–19

Habbakuk, H. J. 373
Haldane, J. B. S. 51, 99, 178
Hall, Rupert 106
Hall, Stuart 263–4
Haller, William 36

Hammond, B. 39
Hammond, J. L. 39
Hampden, John 26, 29
Harrington, James 42, 126, 150, 154, 201, 373
  revisionism 284, 287–8
Hayek, Friedrich von 260
Hegel, G. W. F. 16, 209
hegemony, cultural 187–9, 262–3
Hexter, J. H. 133, 158, 245, 250, 323
Hill 134, 322, 325, 366
High Anglicanism 93–4
Hill, Christopher 32, 47–8, 133, 156, 180, 193–4, 280–1, 289, 292, 306, 320–1, 323
  academic success 130
  'Back to the Future' conference 309
  BBC series on Civil War 318
  bourgeoisie 127–8
  Century of Revolution 146, 205–6, 241
  Change and Continuity 179
  class war and World War II 65
  'Committee on Russian Studies' 348
  Communist Party 171; letter attacking 172; resignation 173–4
  conflicting tendencies in work of 115–16
  consumers' revolt 123–4
  dialogue between past and present 90, 209
  dispute with Kuczynski 59–63
  Economic Problems of the Church 143
  English Bible 35, 294–7
  The English Revolution 55–9, 65–6, 73
  Experience of Defeat 200–6
  family 253–4
  Gardiner, S. R. 241–2
  God's Englishman 194–6, 382
  Good Old Cause 102–3
  higher education 322
  Historians' Group of the Communist Party 79, 169, 176

historical development 316–17
human values 92
imperialism 64
Intellectual Origins of the English Revolution 146–9
Labour government 84
language 134–7, 265–6
literature 72–3, 267; Bible 293–7; Bunyan 281–3; censorship 278; Milton 270–80
Macpherson 151–2
Marxism 32, 44, 134–5, 137, 179–80, 214, 318–19
mass mobilization 140, 141–2
'Materialist Conception of History' 103
method of working 51
'Nine Theses on Absolutism' 116–17, 126–7; debate following 117–19
Open University course 265
Past and Present 130–1
patriotism 73, 111
progressivism 113–14
provinces 236
religion 35, 102, 104, 105; Puritanism 136–7, 142–4, 182, 259, 260, 367
Restoration 196–9
revisionism 250, 251
romantic anti-capitalism 114, 193, 381
and Russia 49; and Stalin obituary 365; Stalinism 176–7; stay in Russia 46–7, 48, 338, 339
science 106
Short Course 52
'Society and Andrew Marvell' 100
Some Intellectual Consequences 197–9
The Soviets and Ourselves 76–7
Thomas 324–5
Toynbee 101
A Turbulent, Seditious and Factious People 281–3
'two camps' 110–11

view of eighteenth century 149, 205–6, 381
volunteer for military service 73
Wedgwood 232
Whig theory 54, 241–2
Winstanley, Gerrard 190–1, 284, 380–1
The World Turned Upside Down 181–93
writing style 50
Hilton, Rodney 79, 107–8, 118–19, 176, 320–1
Historians' Group of the Communist Party 1, 33, 50, 78, 79–87, 100, 309, 321–2
American Threat to British Culture 112, 361
Britain's Culture Heritage 129, 364
Cold War 112
and Communist Party 129–30; crisis of 1950s 174–6
exposed position in 1950s 122
Hill 79, 169, 176
historical development 255–6, 316–17
Hobsbawm *see* Hobsbawm
Local History Section 129
Marxism 101–2, 318
Netherwood discussions 174–5
historical development 316–17
History of the Communist Party of the Soviet Union (Short Course) 52–3
History in the Making series 83
History Today 128
Hitler, Adolf 58
Hobbes, Thomas 132, 150, 151–2, 154, 255, 279
Hobsbawm, Eric 116, 119, 162, 230, 307, 320–1, 323, 349, 376
Age of Revolution 321
agency 316
capitalism 159–60, 315–16
French Revolution 317
Historians' Group of the Communist Party 79–80, 80,

81, 129–30, 159, 169; 'Back to the Future' conference 309; crisis of 1950s 174, 175, 176
seventeenth-century crisis 159
Soviet Union 314
Hogben, Lancelot 51
Hoggart, Richard 213
Holland 205–8
House of Lords 161
Hume, David 13, 19, 20, 23
Hungary 172
Hunt, William 254
Hyndman, R. H. 38

idealism 103
ideology
ideological revolution 128–49
organic restructuring 263–4
imperialism 64–5, 108–9, 159, 359–60
independence, national 88, 109–11
individualism, possessive 150–4, 289–90
intellectuals 146–9, 188, 255
International Socialism 300
Ireland 196, 244

Jacobinism 298–300
James I, King 243
James II, King 57, 198, 203, 205, 385
James, Margaret 181
Jaurès, Jean 21, 241
Jeans, J. H. 98–9
Jenkins, Alf 80
Jones, A. H. M. 131
Jonson, Ben 72

Kaye, H. J. 326
Kenyon, John 310
Kettle, Arnold 130, 156
Khrushchev, Nikita 170
Kiernan, Victor 79, 223, 265, 320–1, 337
feudalism 117–18, 120, 121, 123
Kinnock, Neil 311
Kishlansky, Mark 238

Klugmann, James 81–2
Koestler, Arthur 91, 98, 99, 106–7
Kosminsky, E. A. 115, 339
Kuczynski, Jurgen 59–63, 342
Kuhn, Thomas 290

Labour Monthly 60–3
Labour Party 89, 351, 359
post-war government 77, 83–6
see also New Left
laissez-faire 154, 306–8, 315
Lamont, W. 382
land 162–3
loss of rural rights 37–40
language 131–7, 265, 267
linguistic conventions 286–97
Laski, Harold 77, 85, 90–1, 99
Laslett, Peter 130, 138, 234–5, 394, 409
anti-Marxism 285–6
political philosophy 285
Laud, Archbishop 29, 104
Lavoisier, Antoine 106
Lawrence & Wishart 83, 309, 310
Leavis, F. R. 67–9, 91–2, 94, 100, 115, 261, 271–2
Lefebvre, Georges 56, 57, 312
Lenin, V. I. 38, 46, 49, 77, 90, 115, 119, 126
Leninist-Marxist model 44–55
Levant Company 304
Levellers 37, 56, 141, 181, 192, 300
Macpherson 153–4, 154, 184
Levy, Hyman 51, 172, 180
Lewis, C. S. 97, 362
Lewis, John 35
Liancourt, Duc de 8, 327
liberalism 1
French 11–19, 20, 21
Victorian 29–30
Whiggism 28–31, 54, 241–2, 246
liberation
libidinal 185–6, 189–90
national 88, 109–11
liberty 107–8

libidinal liberation 185–6, 189–90
Lilburne, John 36, 141, 184
Lindsay, A. D. 36, 37, 335
Lindsay, Jack 65, 66, 70, 80, 265, 353
literary tradition 72
religious struggle 102
linguistic conventions 286–97
see also language
literature
cultural materialism 265–70
cultural witness 270–84
patriotism 67–73
lived experience 270–84
Livingstone, Ken 289
local history 129
localism 235–8
Locke, John 23, 149, 192, 204, 284–5, 285, 288
Macpherson 150, 152–3, 154, 192
London 139
'long revolutions' 210–31
Louis XIV, King 207, 208, 386
Louis XVI, King 8, 327
Ludlow, Edmund 198
Lysenko, T. D. 106, 107

Macaulay, Catherine 24
Macaulay, T. B. 25, 26, 113, 330
MacDonald, Ramsay 48
Macpherson, C. B. 184, 192, 284, 320–1
possessive individualism 150–4, 289–90
Mahon, John 171
Malinowski, B. 187
Mann, Tom 82
Manning, Brian 140, 141, 142, 299–300, 368
Manson, Charles 183
Marcuse, Herbert 185, 186, 189
market 41–3, 315, 381
Marlowe, Christopher 72
Marvell, Andrew 100, 281, 284
Marx, Karl 7–8, 12, 21–2, 61, 120, 221

Absolute Monarchy 59
alienation 185
English and French
  Revolutions 10–11
Enlightenment project 317, 319
feudalism 17
theory of unintended
  consequences 132
Marx House History Faculty 50
Marxism Today 174, 313
Marxist-Leninist model 44–55
Marxist Quarterly 365
Marxist training 53–4, 82, 340
Marxists, purge of 112–13
mass mobilization 138–42, 299
materialism 103–4
  cultural 2, 261–70
  dialectical 1, 51–5
Matthews, George 172
May, Daphne 80
mediation 226
Members of Parliament 124, 125
mercantile class 139–40, 155–7,
  304–5
Middle Ages 95–7
military coup 299
Mill, John Stuart 260
Miller, Perry 36, 260
Milner, Andrew 298
Milosevic, Slobodan 320
Milton, John 24, 26, 72–3, 76,
  201, 284, 317
  Eliot 93–4
  Hill's study 270–80
  Leavis 93–4
  Milner's study 298
Mitterrand, François 312
Modern Quarterly 51, 103, 131,
  365
'modern society' 1, 7–11
monarchy
  absolutist *see* absolutism
  church, aristocracy and 10,
    18–19
  mystique of 63, 197, 364
  restored 202
Montrose, L. 269–70
morality 216–17
  Puritanism 256–60

Mornet, Daniel 147
Morrill, John 278
Morris, John 131
Morrison, Herbert 83
Morton, Leslie 133, 169, 265
  Historians' Group 79, 80
  People's History 70–1;
    celebration of fiftieth
    anniversary 309–10
  Ranters 183–4
  Utopia 182–3
Muggleton, Lodowick 273, 320,
  382
multiple dysfunction 247–8
'municipal revolution' 304

Nairn, Tom 217–19, 221–2, 226,
  230
Namier, Lewis Bernstein 137,
  144
Namierism 235–6, 396
narrative 239–41
national culture 66–73
national independence 88,
  109–11
nationalism, folk 38–9, 71
Neale, J. E. 113, 145
Needham, Joseph 39, 51, 66, 105
Netherwood discussions 174
'new historicism' 291–2
New Left 64, 177–80, 193,
  211–14, 252, 261
New Left Review 316
New Model Army 238
New Right 260
  see also Thatcherism
New Statesman 85
Newton, Isaac 149, 192
nobility *see* aristocracy
Notestein, Wallace 113

Oakeshott, M. 64–5, 97, 98,
  99–100
Open University 265
organic crisis 263–4
organic tendency 222–3
Orwell, George 49, 65, 91
Our History 129
Our Time 76

Paine, Thomas 23, 317
Palmer, W. G. 366
parliament 310–11
    revisionism 237, 238, 242–3
Past and Present 103, 130–1, 158
patriotism 63–78
Payne, Edwin 80
peace campaign 110–12
'peculiarities of the
    English' 210–31
pedigrees, revolutionary 23
Penguin Books 129
Pennington, D. H. 139, 234
'People's Front' 66, 70
'people's history' 33–40, 70–1,
    78
platitudinists 89
platonism 7, 392
Plumb, J. H. 207
Pocock, John 9, 247, 283, 285,
    409–10
    revisionist discourse 286–90
Pokrovsky, N. M. 47–8, 61, 116,
    120, 149, 338, 369
Polanyi, Michael 99, 177
political stress indicator
    (PSI) 305
politics
    of rationalism 98
    revisionism 239–40, 248–50
Politics and Letters 92
Pollitt, Harry 34, 73, 170, 175
'Popish Plot' 1678 203
possessive individualism 150–4,
    289–90
predestined pathway 225
'present-centredness' 246–7
Price Revolution 124
prices 41
Priestley, J. B. 75
private/domestic sphere 252–4
progress, social 19–20, 22–3
property ownership 223–4
Protestant ethic 187–90
Providence Bay Company 304
provincialism 235–6
'Puritan Revolution' 26, 28
Puritanism 35–6, 39, 125–6
    cultural revolution 256–60

Hill 136–7, 142–4, 182, 259,
    260, 367
Putney Debates 36–7, 154, 335
Pym, John 29, 30, 243, 246, 260
    political skills 249

Quarterly Review 25
Quiller-Couch, Sir Arthur 68

radicalism 283–4, 323–4
    Marxist renewal and 32–43
    revolutionary legacies 193–209
    'world turned upside
        down' 169–93
Ranke, L. von 250
Ranters 183–4, 189–90, 192
rationalism 103–4
    politics of 98
Raven, Charles 34
Reagan, Ronald 269, 315
realism 199–200
'reality' rule 4, 325
Rees, John 300
Reeve, John 273
Reform Bill 1832 25
regicides 238
religion 244
    cultural revolution 256–60
    dissent 33–7
    see also Anglican Church; Bible;
        Catholicism; Christianity;
        God; Protestant ethic;
        Puritanism
rents 162
repression 185–6, 187–90, 198–9
republicanism 20–1
    arch of 287–8
    'aristocratic' 23
resistance 55
Restoration 196–9, 202–3, 257,
    274, 275
revisionism 2, 308, 323–4
    challenges 231–51
    discourse analysis 284–97
Rickword, Edgell 67, 70, 72, 94
Rothstein, Andrew 173, 174, 361
Rousseau, Jean-Jacques 293
Rowse, A. L. 87, 145, 368
rural rights, loss of 37–40

Russell, Conrad 237, 238, 239,
    250, 323
  multiple dysfunction 247–8
Russia/Soviet Union
  collapse of Communism
    312–15
  Communist Party membership
    and 48–50
  'great thaw' 169–70
  World War II 65, 74, 76
Russian Revolution 58, 77, 314
Russian/Soviet historians 46–8
Rust, William 65
Rutt, John 25

St John, Diana 80
St Simon, Louis de Rouvroy, Due
    de 207
Samuel, Raphael 33, 34, 38, 54,
    71
Saville, John 108, 171, 172, 174,
    175
'saving appearances' 122
Schama, S. 293
Schwarz, Bill 326
science 105–7
  Cold War politics 97–100
  Communist Party 51–2
Scientific Revolution 97, 106–7
Scotland 244
Scottish social theory 12–16, 26
Scrutiny 67–8
Scrutiny Movement 91–3
Seaver, Paul 254
Sedgwick, William 200
self 268–9
Shakespeare, William 72, 97
Sharpe, Kevin 237
Shils, Edward 144
Sidney, Algernon 23
Simon, Joan 173, 178
sin 187–9, 190
Skinner, Quentin 279, 285, 286,
    290, 310
small producers/artisans 139–40
Smith, Adam 16
Soboul, Albert 9, 142, 308, 353
social action 190, 283
social change model 162–8, 231–4

social progress 19–20, 22–3
Socialist Workers
  'collective' 300–1
Southey, Robert 24
Soviet Union *see* Russia/Soviet
    Union
Stalin, Joseph 49, 58, 87, 170, 339
  'active superstructure'
    doctrine 59
  Short Course 52
Stalinism 169–71, 176–7, 211
Stedman Jones, G. 292
Stone, Lawrence 2, 8, 126, 231,
    234, 235, 247, 250, 291, 320–1,
    322, 323, 327, 418
  *Causes of the English
    Revolution* 164–8, 375
  *Crisis of the English
    Aristocracy* 157–61
  education revolution 255
  Family, Sex and Marriage 254
  military-fiscal state 208, 396
  *Results of the English
    Revolution* 206–9
  revival of narrative 240, 396
  rise of the gentry 253
Strachey, John 67
Strafford, Thomas
    Wentworth 29, 243
student revolution 179, 180,
    184–5, 190, 193
Suez adventure 177
Suslov, M. A. 110
Synge, John M. 114

Talmon, J. R. 183
Tawney, R. H. 34, 36, 40–3, 324
taxpayers' revolt 123–4
Taylor, A. J. P. 144
teleology 246
Temple, William 34
tercentenary 310–12, 416
Thatcher, Margaret 248–9, 263,
    269, 310–11, 312, 315
Thatcherism 263–5
Thelwell, John 24, 317
Thierry, A. 14
Thomas, Keith 182, 190, 254,
    258, 324–5

Thompson, Edward P.   2, 7,
    10–11, 116, 174, 180, 210–12,
    242, 265, 266, 307–8, 309, 321,
    325
  agency   292
  capitalism   315
  collapse of Communism   315
  Communist Party   112, 172,
    175; *The Reasoner*   171
  disagreement with
    Anderson   2, 217–31 *passim*
  Enlightenment project   319–20
  historical development   316–17
  history's preoccupation with
    the Revolution   7
  *Making of the English Working
    Class*   215–17
  Marxism   214–15
  modern society   10
  New Left   211–12
  pre-industrial societies   109,
    114
  religious dissent   34, 35
  Stalinism   211
  'stretching of historical
    textures'   11, 19
  Williams   214
Thomson, George   79, 81, 87,
    114, 129, 352
Thorold Rogers, J. E.   37–8
Tilly, Charles   305
Tillyard, E. M. W.   97, 271
Times Literary Supplement, The   112
Tocqueville, Alexis de   21, 22,
    147, 230
Toleration Act   198
Torr, Dona   61, 79, 87, 118–19,
    176
  Marxism   82–3
  patriotism   74, 75
Totalitarian Theory   183
Toynbee, Arnold   95, 101
trade   41–3
tradesmen   139–40, 155–7, 304–5
tradition   95–6, 214–21
  see also culture; literature
transformation, era of   205–6
Trevelyan, G. M.   28, 30, 56, 113,
    331–2, 341

English and French
  Revolutions compared   27–8,
    31
English Social History   69
Trevor-Roper, Hugh   138, 144,
    160, 231, 250, 368
  Marx and Burckhardt   319
  'two camps'   102–3, 109–14

Underdown, David   197, 238,
    281
  cultural revolution   254, 256–9
  unintended consequences, theory
    of   132
United States of America   88,
    109–10, 112, 260
Upward, Edward   72
utopia   182–3

Vane, Henry   26

Wallerstein, Immanuel   305
Walpole, Sir Robert   156
Walwyn, William   200
Watt, Donald   156
Waugh, Evelyn   93
Weber, Max   36
Wedgwood, C. V.   232
welfare state   259
Werskey, Garry   130, 178
West, Alick   156, 268
'Western Civilization'   95–6, 355
Whiggism   28–31, 54, 97, 241–2,
    246, 355
White, John   256
Wiener, Martin   229
William III, King   208
Williams, Raymond   116, 361,
    388, 403
  culture   213–14, 261–5
Willis, Ted   348
Wilson, Harold   193, 248
Wingfield-Stratford, Esmé   30,
    332–3
Winkler, R. O. C.   92
Winstanley, Gerrard   36, 72, 91,
    141, 200, 284, 317
  Hill's study   190–1
  social action   190, 283

Wintringham, Tom 66–7, 70
Wood, Ellen Meiksins 301–2, 308, 413
Woodhouse, A. S. P. 36
Woodward, E. L. 98
Worden, Blair 238
Wordsworth, William 24
working class 215–20
World News and Views 76
World War I 57

World War II 57–8, 64–5, 73–7
Wrightson, Keith 254

'X Factor' 167, 374

Yugoslavia 88–9, 319–20

Zagorin, Perez 235
Zhou-en-Lai 148
Zilliacus, Konni 171

DATE DUE

			Printed in USA

HIGHSMITH #45230